Commentary on the Writings of St. John of the Cross

A Cruciform Mysticism and Christocentric Anthropology

Dr. Richard E. Dumont

Commentary on the Writings of St. John of the Cross
Copyright © 2010 by Richard E. Dumont

ISBN-13: 978-1456497248

Dedication

This commentary is dedicated to Victor and Jean Lane and their children and in-laws.

I am indebted to them for their outstanding christian neighborliness.

Acknowledgment

I would like to express my deepest gratitude to all who with their prayers and encouragement have contributed to the process culminating to the publication of this project. In a particular way to Gabriel and Patricia Giralt for their assiduous preparation of my manuscript for publication.

Also, I would like to acknowledge Carmen Graves who so zealously encouraged me to have this work published; as well as the members of my Carmelite community to whom I presented the content of this manuscript in preparation to pronounce their Carmelite Promises.

I am indebted, to our late Holy Father John Paul II for providing me with the framework to reconcile the intellectual order with the experiential order which became, if you want, the key in resolving the disparity between the two.

Since I do not know the Spanish language, I am indebted, to Fr. Kieran Kavanaugh, OCD and Fr. Otilio Rodriguez, OCD English translation of St. John of the Cross collected works.

Note

The process of editing this manuscript has been more of organizing the material to present it in a more organic and clear manner, than editing the text itself. The latter was done minimally, as required, careful to preserve in its entirety the author's work as it stands in its original form.

The original manuscript carries many of the authors mannerisms expressed as "underlined" "bolded" and "upper case" words. Those were the author's spontaneous emphasis applied without consistency through the course of presenting his own ideas. In those cases, of textual punctuation, we limited ourselves to make use of "italics" for the sake of textual uniformity and continuity throughout the manuscript.

Also. throughout the text, the reader can notice easily what appears to be, a certain redundancy in the presentation of an idea. However, more than redundancy, it is the author's personal style; he revisits the idea to present it in a deeper light and provide a wider resonance in the overall text. (i. e., the author's frequent reference to the *cruciformal* structure, as the framework in St. John's writings.)

Another particular aspect of the manuscript is the author's personalization in the treatment of the words, (i. e., nouns transformed into adjectives, verbs, adverbs, etc. creating his own idiomatic expression: *superhuman, superhumane, superhumanized, superhumanistically, superhumanely.*) It is the result of an effort to use the word in the proper context, as the author ventures through such difficult material. In conclusion, all these textual idiosyncrasies reveal the author's passion, yet temperate admiration and profound gratitude for the mystical work of St. John of the Cross. – To this respect, we can also make mention of the rich vocabulary. There is an extensive use of uncommon words that the author uses to explicate with greater freedom (linguistic conventions) and fidelity St. John's text which is the source of this manuscript.

The reader should be advised that to make full profit of the commentary the reader must be familiar with the works St. John of the Cross. Such knowledge will make up for the areas this commentary does not touch or treat in full vigor.

Finally, in the design of the book cover, the image of the "flame" as a visual motif, was chosen because it encapsulates St, John's entire teaching. For him the "flame" exemplifies God's transforming power. Its action permeates the mystic's journey that begins as purgation, followed by illumination, and culminates its effect in union with God.

In chapter 10 of book II of the *Dark Night*, as well as in the first stanza of the *Living Flame*, the reader can find in words, first in poetry and later in prose, the synthesis of the action of the "flame" and the effect on the person.

... It should be known that the same fire of love which afterwards is united with the soul [the person], glorifying it, is that which previously assailed it by purging it, just as the same fire that penetrates a log of wood, first attacks it, wounding it with its flame, drying it out, and stripping it of its ugly qualities until it is so disposed, by the heat of the flame, that it can be penetrated and transformed into fire itself. (Living Flame, stanza 1:19)

December 26, 2010 feast of The Holy Family

Table of Contents

COMMENTARY ON THE DARK NIGHT OF THE SOUL.

COMMENTARY ON THE SPIRITUAL CANTICLE.

COMMENTARY ON THE LIVING FLAME OF LOVE.

Preface

The rudiments of St. John's cruciform mysticism and Christocentric anthropology.

This commentary focuses on the four major writings of our Holy Carmelite Father, St. John of the Cross. He rightfully enjoys throughout Holy Mother, the Church, not only the title of Doctor of Mystical Theology but also the reputation of being a most august and excellent mystagogue among all of the Church's mystics. The key to our Holy Father's mysticism is the cross of Christ with its triune cruciformity. The vertical beam embraces the eternal/temporal order of the universe's existence; the horizontal beam spans the historical order of the world's resistance beginning with the Book of Genesis and the world's future end culminating eschatologically in the Last Judgment. The third order is the cross's cruciformity consistently reconciling these two vertical and horizontal beams together in the Paschal Mystery of Jesus Christ's crucifixion, resurrection, ascension, and Parousia, final return in glory.

Consonant with this three-dimensional cruciformity there are two non-educible and irreducible orders, the objectively transcendent order of the universe of God's existence and creation and the subjectively immanent order of the world of the creature's own resistance and self-cultivation. These two orders are reconciled with each other in the Paschal Mystery of Jesus Christ, God/Superman. Jesus Christ crucified and risen is the Catholic Christian mystic's daily prayerful Gospel ascesis of embracing Him as the Way, Truth, & Life. Catholic Christian prayer is not so much the creature respectfully addressing his Creator as it is God's Triune Godhead incorporating His creature within the familiarity of His own Triune bosom through Christ's Incarnation & Paschal Mystery.

Catholic Christian prayer is more God graciously supernaturally alive in His creature than it is His creature prayerfully alive in God.

The mystic is one who not only theologically believes and objectively understands in faith and ponders this revealed Truth but, moreso, theologically hopes and ascetically experiences subjectively the Way of this Paschal Mystery as the Love of his own life and the Life of his own love: the Holy Spirit of Christ and His Father. The Sacramental Church as the Mystical Body of Christ prays, on the one hand, publicly objectively in the liturgy of its sacramental rites and sacred scripture and, on the other hand, privately subjectively in the mystic's mental and contemplative prayerful response to these sacramental encounters with God. These two orders of public and private prayer complement each other in a fundamental-supplemental ordering of prioritization.

The human person, male & female, was created preternaturally to know, experience, and rejoice in God's divine Triune friendship. Original sin lost this friendship which resulted in the body's suffering, death & corruption. God Himself in the Person of Jesus Christ freely and graciously entered the history of this death & corruption and suffered its degradation, humiliation, and dehumanizing abandonment in order to restore God's Triune friendship to mankind. He accomplished this in His crucifixion, resurrection, and ascension into heaven. His human creature is now invited, in turn, to personally enter into this supernatural restoration--salvation, sanctification, and glorification--by freely surrendering his own freedom to Christ's free sacrificial surrender of His own Divine/Superhuman freedom to liberate the creature from the futility, turpitude, and destitution of his own mortal desolation and isolation from God. The mystic is one who knows that this sacrificial surrender to Christ's own Selfless Self-surrender is impossible without the supernatural power of the Catholic Church's objective sacramental, liturgical prayer as well as his own subjective commitment to mental and contemplative prayer.

Prayer, then, is not merely a special activity reserved for either special occasions or a special technique to periodically gain some self-serving advantage from God. It is a Gospel lifestyle of dying to one's own selfish self-interests and self-attachments and rising beyond the slavery of this egocentric selfishness. It entails not merely an objective conduct that is voluntarily morally virtuous, orthodox, and upright--

honest, chaste, prudent, courageous, noble, trustworthy, worshipful, etc.--but a subjective mental attitude which is Christ's very own Be-attitudinal messianic mindset. It is not a me-myself-I need-more have-attitude; rather, it is a paradoxical have-not need-less attitude in order to be-more like Christ's Selfless Selfhood. It is paradoxical because one can only be-more in the vertical order of the grace of God's existence if one has-less resistance to Christ's superhumanized Selfless Selfhood in the horizontal order of one's own egocentric partisan self-serving selfish self-interests. Such detachment from one's own worldly and religious selfishness requires Christ's own totally Self-detached messianic Be-attitudinal mindset. "Being full of God" means placing less stock in one's own self-importance while placing more trust in God-the-Father's providential omnipotent paternal care. Hence, our subjective self can only paradoxically and transcendentally find its own complete self-fulfillment beyond the selfish subjectivity and servitude of its own egocentric selfhood.

This prayerful ascetic volunteer sacrificial dying to one's own subjective selfish self-interest is the key to St. John's mysticism and the horrendous darkness which characterizes the mystic's prayerful experience of living in religious darkness and even feeling and bearing the conviction of being abandoned by God. Of course, this dark religious ordeal of the mystic's prayerful experience of being ignored by God eventually yields and gives way to the mystic's full participation in Christ's very own experience of His bodily resurrection and ascension. This prolonged prayerful period of dark forbidding purgation, hence, eventually gives way to a prayerful period of illumination (viz., the resurrection) and perfect union (viz., the ascension). This perfect union itself as a foretaste of heaven may itself include spurts of ecstatic bliss even in this present life anticipating Christ's ascension into the paradise of heaven: the bosom of God's Triune Godhead and the Sacramental Church's New Jerusalem.

This prayerful process of dying and rising does not occur automatically, of course. It is a process that is totally contingent on God's very own Divine Will & pleasure as well as the mystic's prayerful persevering resolution and commitment to become charitably attached to God and completely detached from his own selfish self-interests.

Thus, the mystic prayerfully experiences in his own lifestyle Christ's very own Gospel lifestyle of dying and rising. These three distinctive phases of mystical prayerful experience--the purgative, illuminative, and unitive--are carefully, intimately, and poignantly described in the four major writings of our Carmelite Holy Father. They deserve our utmost prayerful attention and emulation. Certainly, only a fool would tackle an ascent up Mount Everest without availing himself of appropriate equipment as well as the help and experience of an experienced guide. The same holds true for the Carmelite mystic who is summoned by Christ to climb to the solitary summit of Mount Carmel, God's very own heavenly abode.

The four major writings of St. John of the Cross are the *Ascent*, the *Dark Night*, the *Spiritual Canticle*, and the *Living Flame*. In a broad sense they correspond to the three major phases of the mystical life paralleling Christ's Paschal Mystery. The *Ascent* deals with the mystic's active ascetic efforts to prayerfully detach his self-centered selfish selfhood from all that hinders its total selfless attachment to God. *The Dark Night* deals with the mystic's humiliating prayerful experiences of God's deliberate withdrawal and withholding from him all religious symptoms of His divine security and of His sublime joy and divine serenity. *The Spiritual Canticle* deals with the religious enlightenment, wisdom, peace, joy, etc., that the mystic prayerfully experiences in the aftermath of the prolonged turbulence and trials of *The Dark Night*. *The Living Flame* describes the perfect ecstatic union of the mystic with the Blessed Trinity through being nuptially bonded to the Father's Holy Will through the subtle encouraging sublime influence of Christ's indwelling Holy Spirit.

The Catholic Christian mystic's religious experience of the Blessed Trinity is expressed throughout in our Sanjuanistic writings in trilogies that parallel the cross's cruciform triunity with its vertical-horizontal crossbeam configuration. This parallel also evokes the trilogy of the Father, Son, and Holy Spirit. Of course, the prayerful life of the mystic is sublimated to the Divine Life itself of God's Triune Godhead. Hence, it is vertically supernatural, horizontally superhuman, and cruciformly superhumane.

It is supernatural inasmuch as the mystic partakes of the supernatural sacramental grace of the Father's infinite providential magnanimity and is fortified in his intellect with the theological virtue of faith to totally trust the Father's infallible providential trustworthiness. It is superhuman inasmuch as the mystic prayerfully confides his body's own hopeless mortality to the Son's bodily invincibility made manifest in His resurrection and ascension into heaven. This prayerful conviction vested in Christ's very own invincible superhuman confidence is, in turn, fortified by the theological virtue of hope which sustains the mystic's memory throughout his own span of historical vicissitudes from birth to death. Finally, it is superhumane inasmuch as the mystic partakes of the supernatural gratuitous selfless Giftedness proper to the Father and Son themselves: their Holy Spirit. The mystic's own willful selfhood is superhumanely sublimated with the theological virtue of charity to enable the mystic through the Holy Spirit's Giftedness to requite the Father's magnanimity with the Son's own ransoming love that is befitting the Father's own infinite Loveliness.

Given these trilogies, St. John pays close attention to the centrality of the faculties of the intellect, memory, and will and to the theological virtues of faith, hope, and charity. While it is very much the case that these three faculties are endowed with properties and activities peculiar to the human person's own nature, self-humanized personality, and humanitarian altruism, these very same faculties and activities are in the mystical life of the Catholic Christian supernaturally, superhumanistically, and superhumanely sublimated to the Trinity's very own divine Paternal providential gracious initiative, Filial sacrificial Selfless consummation, and Pneumatic gratuitous integrating amicable benevolence.

Further, we will pay close attention to the cross's threefold order of vertically virtuously (i.e., morally) being more holy by horizontally attitudinally (i.e., ascetically and spiritedly) having less command of one's own selfish self-control, and cruciformly by integrating together both separate orders of being and having in order to be-have more like Christ and less like Adam and Eve in their fall from grace. The vertical beam is that of the fundamental being of the created universe itself. The horizontal beam is the overriding supplemental historical order of mankind's self-cultivated fallen world and civilization very much in need of reformation and redemption. The cruciform intersection of these two beams is that of be-having well with an integrity and solidarity that is congruent with having-less and being-more assimilated to Christ's very own Gospel life-style. The disciple is not above the Master.

These three separate orders of the cross's cruciformity are crucial in coming to grips with our Carmelite mystagogue's writings. Each order entails transcendence peculiar to that order itself. In the objective vertical order of existence, the mystic must transcend the material body's finite sensory animal palpability and affectivity in order to intellectually and volitionally attend to recognizing and worshipfully honoring God's infinite intangible immutable Divine Nature as the Author of his own existence.

This order is one of orthodox intelligible positive (i.e., cataphatic) knowledge and worship of God. The subjective horizontal order of resistance is one of paradoxical religious experiential apophatic conative awareness of God in which the mystic remains virtually ignorant of God Himself transcendent to this religious experience. The mystic must transcend the body's egocentric self-serving sensational tactuality and sensuality (i.e., somaticity), on the one hand, and its nontactual impassivity (i.e. psychicity), on the other, in order to overcome its own resistance to the objective reality which transcends the subjectivity of its own selfish self-serving psychosomatic partisan willful self-interest. Again, this horizontal order is one of unintelligible paradox steeped in a conscious self-centered phenomenal experience of things and especially of the Catholic Christian mystic's religious sacramental encounter with God's Triune Personhood. It is paradoxically one of self-conscious (i.e., apophatic) religious ignorance of God's actual existence and transcendent divine nature even though the experience itself is conatively very attentive and attracted to the unusual sublimity of such mystical experiences. This conscious experience is religious inasmuch as it engages the selfhood's determinate persevering willful self-commitment and self-surrender to God's transcendence beyond this experience's personalized possessive subjectivity.

These two orders coalesce in the cross's cruciformity on which

Christ, God/Superman, is crucified and undergoes His volunteer passion and death. In this crucifixion these two non-educible and irreducible orders are reconciled with each other through the power of Christ and the Father's Holy Spirit residing within the innermost intimacy (and spirited morale) of the mystic's own selfhood. Mankind's liberation from the historical prison of the self-alienating hell of his own selfish selfhood and his corresponding peaceful reconciliation with God's very own transcendent eternal sublime Nature are purchased by the Blood of Christ's passion and crucifixion.

This cruciform coalescence is focused in the mystic's conscience which is a fusion between the intellect's objective intelligible cognizance of Truth's moral practicality and the mind's subjective willful self-conscious awareness of its own self-centered conscientious volitive surrender and submission to the integrity of this same transcendent conscionable Truth. In this conscionable-conscientious coalescence the mystic simultaneously understands and experiences the supernaturally revealed Word of God interiorly (i.e., intellectually by faith), intimately (i.e., mindfully by hope), and integrally (i.e., by charity) in the Person of Jesus Christ, God/Superman. This cruciform coalescence entails undergoing and sharing sacramentally in the sanctifying crucible of Christ's very own suffering and glory. This is nothing less than objectively dutifully voluntarily living Christ's very own Love of and for the Father's Wise Holy Will and subjectively experiencing his own willful selfhood yielding ascetically to the influential subtle influence of the Holy Spirit's amorous Wisdom of unfettered Love.

The extraordinary genius of our Sanjaunistic mystagogical writings is their cruciform integrality and theological triune integrity. They are first presented in poetic verses steeped in the religious resonance of the mystic's own subjective personalized religious experience of God's Trinitarian supernatural sacramental self-revelation. They are subsequently presented in a prose proper to the Catholic Christian's objective intellectual theological insight into this same self-revelation of God's Triune Godhead vis-à-vis the creature's creation, historical journey, and final eternal destiny. They are inspired, studded, and buttressed with citations from Sacred Scripture.

A word of explanation seems in place regarding St. John's heavy emphasis on the element of ascetic darkness and nullity throughout his writings. How can this be reconciled with the Gospel's revelation that Christ is the Light of the world? The key to this stems from the unremitting struggle that confronts the Catholic Christian sacramentally baptized and confirmed into the death and divine Life of Christ's Paschal Mystery. This struggle continuously countermands the instincts of mankind's very own nature precisely because it engages the mystic vertically in a supernaturally sublimated prayerful activity initiated and sustained by God-the-Father Himself. This prayerful activity introduces the mystic into a profound mystery of God's wedding to man and man's marital response to this wedding which exceeds the native light of the mystic's own intelligence and comprehension. Hence, the element of intellectual darkness peculiar to the supernatural gift of faith accompanies the mystic's intellectual prayerful contemplation of God's sacramental gracious presence in the human soul. So infinitely intelligible and trustworthy is this supernatural Self-revelation of Christ's incarnation and Paschal Mystery that the mystic's native intelligence is overcome in the sacramental presence of this awesome miraculous theophany.

This sacramental presence is further entirely horizontally counter-cultural because it cuts against the grain of the self's worldly willful selfish self-centeredness inasmuch as it entails the mystic's prayerful selfhood's willful self-surrender to and embrace of God-the-Son's consummate volunteer sacrificial redemptive self-oblation to the Father's Holy Will. Further, it cruciformly in the coalescence of these two orders demands a prayerful superhumane superheroic religious volunteer self-giving self-surrender to God empowered with God-the-Spirit's very own unbounded largesse and unfettered freedom of selfless benevolent Giftedness.

This negativity may be best explained in the light of the Supreme reality which is God's very own Triune Godhead. God is not only the preeminent Being among all beings, God is Beingness itself outside of which there is only non-being (i.e., not God). God's divine existence exhausts the totality of existence itself. No creature is Beingness; hence, no creature is identical with God's own divine existence. Accordingly, there are different intelligible renditions of "non-being."

One is entirely negative. This is the non-being as a mere point of reference from which every creature is created by God. We frequently employ this sense of non-being when we declare to speak "nothing but the Truth." The "nothing" in this expression refers to what is opposite to the Truth as a complete nullity.

Another sense is entirely positive. This is the creature itself created by God. The creature is a relative being inasmuch as no creature is God's very own absolute Beingness. Each creature is a relative being because its very own existence exists only in reference to God. Its being is simultaneously dependent on God for its own existence and since this existence is not that of God's own Beingness, it is a non-being. Hence, St. John of the Cross insists that no creature is to be whole-heartedly worshiped in the same manner that one worships God. Of course, this includes the Blessed Virgin Mary who is never an object of prayerful worship within the Catholic Church. She is prayerfully venerated for her holiness which comes entirely through her Son, Jesus Christ. In this sense, she is nothing without Christ and with Christ she is His Blessed Mother, a singular honor which places her above every other creature within the universe of creation, including the angels. Hence, we venerate her because her holiness is a mirror of God's own infinite holiness.

Finally, there is the privative sense of non-being. This is a lack and a need for an existing being in a selfhood that remains lacking until it finds its very own self-fulfillment in an existing reality beyond the subjectivity and emptiness of its own supplementarity. Accordingly every human self must die to its own subjective selfhood in order to participate through Christ in God's Triune divine Life beyond the deficiency of its own selfish self-centered needfulness. In other words, the mystic's willful selfhood and personality demand and need to have God to fully overcome their imponderable lack of self-fulfillment. Such a lacking needful subjectivity is exclusively peculiar to mankind's own personhood and personality. The brute animal has no egocentric self-consciousness and neither do the angels. This self-centered ego-subjectivity is the mark of the dignity and sovereignty of the human person's own personhood capable of autonomously cultivating and civilizing its own personhood by artificially and artfully

cultivating its own personality. This willful selfishly self-centered personalized selfhood with all its civilized worldly and religious possessive self-attachments constitutes a formidable impediment to the mystic's total dutiful, self-controlled, submissive, volunteer worshipful attachment to God's very own adorable divinity transcendent to and
independent of this willful selfhood itself. Total selfless self-detachment from the non-being (i.e., lack) of self-fulfillment beyond one's
own partisan selfish selfhood is the inescapable ascetic condition for
becoming unconditionally attached to God's very own Beingness.
Here, St. John of the Cross is uncompromising. There must be no
selfish --- none-whatsoever---nada---willful self-attachment (i.e., addiction) whether worldly or religious remaining in the mystic's willful selfhood. As long as there is the slightest selfish self-attachment,
the mystic is still fettered and addicted to his own selfishness and
barred from a total unconditional selfless attachment to God along
with the peace, serenity, and divine joy which that divine attachment
affords.

For St. John, the mystic must actively forego maximizing created
goods for their own sake. Such goods are serviceable but not adorable. This is the case even if such goods are used in a morally upright
manner consonant with God's very own blessing. God's very own divinity alone is worthy of an unconditional love of selfless worship
and adoration. God alone is Supreme Goodness. God's own glory is
the only purposeful intention worthy of the mystic's optimal purposeful free choices, motivations, and actions. Further, the mystic
must actively mortify his very own egocentric personalized selfishly
self-serving motivations. His motivations must be principally and exclusively selflessly at the service of God and not at the service of his
own partisan selfish self-interest. St. John's religious abstemious nada
ascesis is predicated on the lavishness of God's infinite love for mankind. The Catholic Christian mystic is called to respond to God's infinite love, measure for measure, treasure for treasure. This, of course,
is humanly impossible due to the effects of original sin. The mystic remains prone to cater to his own selfishness and self-aggrandizement
even in the case when he experiences the most sublime religious encounters with God.

The creature is finite; God is infinite. Hence, the mystic's task is to actively strip himself of every willful self-serving impediment to hospitably welcoming God's gracious gratuitous invitation to become enveloped with the familiarity of the consummate supernatural love and loveliness proper to God's very own Triune Godhead. The brunt of this ascetic stripping away for the mystic occurs in the horizontal order of the subjectivity of his own religious personalized consciousness and mystical life. Here he becomes deliberatively aware of his own incessant need for following the Gospel life-style of Christ's austere self-denial and adopting Christ's be-attitudinal mindset of supplementally having less in order fundamentally to be more God-like. Try as he may, the mystic can never strip himself utterly of his own selfish selfhood. To further facilitate this stripping, God denies to the mystic's religious experience every vestige of sensitized bodily selfgratification and intimate mental self-justification. For, these detract from the mystic's total service and selfless self-surrender to God's Holy Will. It is precisely this lack of religious bodily feeling of selfgratification and religious mental deportment and poise of self-justification that constitutes the soul's (i.e., the selfhood's) "dark night" of the senses, on the one hand, and the spirit, on the other.

Caught in the painful throes of this divine retreat and evanescence, the ensuing emptiness of the mystic's religious emotional feelings and turbulence of his religious mental bearings is devastating to his own morale. He experiences no special incentive to continue serving and praying to God in his customary engagement in activities beneficial to the Church and to his neighbors. The upshot of living through this prolonged excruciating religious ordeal of experiencing God's abandonment is that the mystic by persevering prayerfully in the service of God despite his religious forlornness, discovers himself to be truly a servant of God and no longer a prisoner of his own partisan pious self-serving self-aggrandizement and subjective mystical experiences. At this point in the mystic's maturity God can flood the mystic with ecstatic religious somatic emotional delights and mental oceans of serenity precisely because these previous possessive self-attachments (i.e., addictions) to his own subjective mystical experiences are no longer impediments to the mystic's selfless willful adoration and embrace of God over, above, and beyond these experiences themselves.

The three major stages of the mystical life, the purgative, the illuminative, and the unitive, have their roots in Sacred Scripture itself. The Old Testament is a testimonial to God the Father. It is the salvation history of the Jewish people and the covenant God made with them. They were bound to obediently keep this covenant in which the primacy of God was to be observed faithfully and religiously. This covenant entailed a rigorous ascesis and fulfilling prescribed religious rites which required that the Jewish people abide in a culture segregated from the behavior and influence of pagan cultures of their neighboring countries. They frequently failed in these practices and were subsequently punished by becoming exiled from their own homeland. These ascetic religious practices and total reverence for God the Father including their exile from their homeland sum up the purgative phase of the mystic's life. This purgative phase involves two dimensions.

The first consists of the mystic's active life-style of self-abnegation. This is nothing less than the prescriptions which the Church requires of her members to remain faithful to God's commandments and the Church's regulations. The second occurs when the mystic is deprived by the Holy Spirit of all sensuous religious experiences and mental consoling religious experiences of God usually accompanying meditative and contemplative (i.e., mental) prayer. This is frequently described as dryness typical of the Jewish people who remained in the desert for nearly two generations and anxiousness/desolation, when the same Jewish people were exiled from their temple where they worshiped God.

The second stage, called the illuminative stage, is redolent of the New Testament and the incarnation of God the Son into mankind's history. The New Testament is prefigured in the Old and, accordingly, is the illumination and fulfillment of the Old Testament. In the New Testament the symbolism of the Old Testament gives way to a sacramentality in which what is symbolized is actually what is and what is is precisely what is symbolized. The divine and the human are mystically joined with each other in the Person of Jesus Christ, God/Superman. Indeed, this incarnation of God into mankind invites a rejoicing and jubilation that overshadows the ritual (i.e., purgative) practices of the Old Covenant. Here, the mystic comes to recognize and appreciate the wisdom of having lived an ascetic life of purgation. He comes to appreciate with St. Paul that he himself is to experience personalistically within his own subjective selfhood and personality the very august and sublime "personality" and persona of Jesus Christ as an *alter Christus*. Thus, the ordeal of suffering and anguish which characterizes the purgative stage gives way to periods of illumination and joy in the illuminative stage.

The third stage has its root in the Acts of the Apostles and the founding of Christ's Sacramental Church with her special ministers and faithful. Here the Holy Spirit which is the soul of this Church becomes the indwelling of God within the mystic in whom the mystic is no longer merely addressing the Father who is remotely in heaven and the Son who is his adopted Brother as a member of the Father's divine family. The mystic is now mystically and religiously in very much the same way as Mary, our Blessed Mother, was overshadowed by the Holy Spirit and becomes alive with the very life of God the Son. This third stage is known as the unitive stage. For, here there is a perfect marriage between the mystic and the Holy Trinity consummated by the Holy Spirit's indwelling as the very "spirit" of the mystic's personality and persona.

Two further notes seem important enough to emphasize here. St. John refers all activities to the mystic's soul. Without in the least compromising the integrity of his mystagogical writings the use of the word, person, will be preferred in these commentaries to St. John's use of soul. The soul is the substantive natural spiritual animating dynamism of the human body's substantive corporeality. In addition to this animation, the soul itself is endowed with spiritual activities above and beyond the body's corporeal organicity (viz., intellectual pondering and the will's volitions). The person, on the other hand, while naturally endowed with a soul and entirely capable of acting objectively and transcendentally within the power of this soul's dynamism, is not limited to its animating activity, whether this be independent of the substantive corporeal body or in conjunction with it.

Within the personalism of Cardinal Karol Wojtyla, Pope John

Paul II, who is intimately familiar with St. John of the Cross's writings, the human person in virtue of his own personhood willfully cultivates within his own egocentric subjectivity a self-humanizing and self-civilizing personality mindful of his own autonomous ingenuity and social communication and collaboration with others. This subjective egocentric personalized selfhood (i.e., the human person's own personality) has a willful mind of its own quite distinct from the human soul's intellect and will. Furthermore, this self-conscious egocentric psychosomatic selfhood's mind and heart exhibit all of the traits peculiar to St. John of the Cross's memory and even to his descriptions of the Will. In other words the very pith and core of the personality of the human person's subjectively cultivated personhood is the psychosomatic mind and heart of the person's personalized egocentric selfhood. When St. John's mystagogy speaks of the memory and the will, it is most definitely not the soul's faculties which he is notably describing in accounting for their engagements. Rather, it is the selfhood's mindful facilitators and their functioning which he is delineating. He himself had no subjective personalized egological anthropology distinct from his Scholastic philosophical anthropology. Hence, he attributes every mystical activity and engagement directly to the soul. Of course, every mystical experience is radically rooted in the human soul's spirituality supernaturally engrafted into God through the Church's sacramentality.

We must appreciate to the full the tripartite dimension of the human person if we are to capture the plenitude of the mystical resonance inherent in the writings of St. John's elucidation of the mysteries of Christ and His revelation. The human person in the vertical order achieves and attains to the informative excellence of his personhood personally and responsibly through the vigor of the upright moral rectitude of his will dutifully obedient to honoring the conscionable truth which he intelligently learns and knows to be objectively the practical moral good of his own innate freedom of choice. Supernaturally this practical good known by faith to be the supreme excellence of his sovereign intelligent and free personhood is revealed and known as God's very own transcendent supreme Goodness and Holy Will revealed through the Tradition of the Church's liturgy, Sacred Scripture, and the Church Magisterium. The mystic's rotund dutiful moral conduct supernaturally buttressed by God's sacramental grace and infused theological virtue of faith characterizes the fiber of his moral character which should be nothing short of the holiness proper to God-the-Father when the mystic attains to the supreme excellence of his own sovereign personhood.

In the horizontal order the person achieves the plenitude and self-fulfillment of his own personalized personality transformatively through the process of ascetically cultivating a self-detachment from the possessions which he acquires and to which he is prone to cling as a guarantee of promoting and safeguarding his very own autonomous social security. This ascesis is rooted in Christ's revelation that the key to the New Testament is living the Gospel kenotic life-style spelled out in the Beatitudes. This life-style is entirely counter-cultural in terms of the secular world's self-centered selfish esteem for its own personalized partisan autonomous social welfare. In such a secular framework it is the self and not God that is autonomously in self-control. However, a total self-detachment pertinent to becoming transformed into living the Gospel life-style of the Beatitudes is impossible to the mystic's fallen nature. God Himself in the Person of Jesus Christ's own Selfless crucified oblation superhumanistically and redemptively detaches mankind completely from one's self-alienating partisan selfish self-interest impeding the mystic's personality from becoming utterly attached to God's own Godhead as his utmost everlasting eschatological security. Hence, it is through, with, and in virtue of Christ's own volunteer Self-immolation that the mystic becomes superhumanistically (i.e., heroically) enabled to advance in his own ascetic self-detachment. What is impossible to man is possible to God. When this ascetic self-detachment is sufficiently progressed, the mystic's very charm makes itself manifest in the charisma of his sanctified personality that lives in the holy theological hope of eschatologically transcending secular history's hopeless doom and ultimate extermination by being assumed into heaven through Christ's resurrectional victory over death.

The reconciliation of these two vertical-horizontal orders is achieved in the cross's cruciformity when the mystic's personhood through its own transformed personality achieves processively the plenitude of its own Gospel self-fulfillment. In this reconciliation the mystic not alone achieves through faith the moral excellence of his own personhood, the stout indomitable morale of the hopeful eschatological assured security of his own personality, he further arrives at the integrity and integrality of his own personage as a disciple of Christ. Of course, this performative reconciliation combines the elements of the mystic's moral conscionable duty with his unstinting conscientious morale to sacrificially serve God selflessly. Hence, this cruciform reconciliation integrates the vertical informative order of faith with the horizontal transformative order of hope into the cruciform performative order of charity in which the mystic acts not only supernaturally and superhumanistically but inclusively superhumanely in virtue of God's very own benevolent divine friendship in behalf of Holy Mother the Church and her members for their own redemption, sanctification, and glorification. Of course, this final cruciform performative integral stage is superhumanely effectuated only under the subtle and unctuous influence of the Holy Spirit inhabiting the innermost inner intimate recesses of the mystic's selfhood.

In this cruciform order of integral reconciliation the mystic's personhood and personality fuse into that of a Christian personage who is simultaneously supernaturally morally conscionably upright, in possession of a stout indomitable superhumanized conscientious morale, and solidly and integrally conscionably conscientious and conscientiously conscionable in all of his conduct. In other words, he is at once a personage of supernatural moral excellence, of a superhumanistic indomitable morale, and a superhumane religious solicitude for both God and mankind. He is, in brief, a saintly personage who is willingly dutifully obedient to God through the Church's magisterial ministration, willfully sacrificially submissive, and amicably and benevolently an ambassador of Christ's very own messianic mission in the world. In other words, the mystic in his superhumane personable self-fulfillment attained only when he reaches Christ's very own cruciform integrity, the mystic himself in this cruciform stage becomes integrated in the very Godhead of God's own family Personhood: the Father, the Son, and the Holy Spirit. Just as it is the Father's Holy Will which is the goal of Christ's messianic mission consummated in His crucifixion under the power of their Holy Spirit, so also it is the

Father, Son, and Holy Spirit who triunitively concur in bringing the mystic to attaining the cruciform culmination of his own Christian mission of becoming an *alter Christus*.

The triune cruciform and Christocentric anthropology inherent in this commentary incorporates the personalism of our late Holy Father, Pope John Paul II, nascent in his philosophical writing, The Acting Person, written when he was still known as Cardinal Karol Wojtyla. This personalism was further expounded by this same Pope in a long series of papal conferences he presented as a Scriptural exegesis on the subject of the intricacies of the marital compatibility and reciprocal self-fulfillment inherent in a man and a woman's bodily masculinity and femininity. This protracted exegesis has come to be known as "the theology of the body." It is a phenomenological rather than an ontological exploration of the human body as Scripturally recorded and subjectively experienced by Adam and Eve's own respective masculine and feminine self-awareness before and after their fall from grace. In this present commentary, it is the mystical marital union between God and mankind within the Church's sacramentality that necessitates having recourse to this same personalistic "theology of the body" in order to adequately and fully explicitate and expatiate the depth and amplitude of the spirituality inherent in the four major SanJuanistic mystagogical Carmelite writings.

Our Blessed Mother, Mary, holds a preeminent place in the prayerful life of the Catholic Christian Mystic. Not only is she the Mother of Christ, God/Superman, but also Mother of His Sacramental Church and every member baptized into this Church. She is the Mother of Christ's very own Divine Life sacramentally alive in this Mystical Body, the Church. It behooves the Carmelite to explicitly prayerfully have recourse to Mary in order to become more perfectly conformed to the Supernatural Life of her Divine Son, Jesus Christ. It behooved God-the-Father through the Holy Spirit to have recourse to Mary's maternal virginal mediation to confer on mankind His own Divine Son. Likewise, it behooves the mystic to have recourse to this same Marian maternity in responding to God-the-Father's Holy Will to become His adopted child as a brother of His Son, Jesus Christ, in the power of the Holy Spirit. Our Blessed Mother, Mary, is not consummately Christ's mother and the mother of Christ's Church until she is also consummately the perfection of Christ's own divine sacramental life in the Church's own members. Since it behooves God-the-Father choose to have recourse to Mary; the mystic can do no less than to honor the Father's Holy Will by having recourse, in turn, to Mary as the mother of Son's mystical Life in himself and as the spouse of the Holy Spirit.

Praised be Jesus Christ! now & forever!

Blessed be Mary! now & forever!

Honored be St. Joseph! now & forever!

COMMENTARY ON
THE ASCENT OF MOUNT CARMEL

THE ASCENT Book I Chapters 1-15: THERE ARE TWO SEPARATE NIGHTS

Chapter 1: There are two separate nights: one of the senses & one of the spirit.

The mystic's personhood is naturally and fundamentally hylemorphically constituted and endowed with a material substantive principle (viz., the corporeal body) and an immaterial animating substantive principle (viz., the incorporeal spiritual soul). The faculties of the soul are the intellect & the intellect's volitional drive, the will. These two faculties are entirely inorganically spiritual and not constrained by the spatio-temporal conditions peculiar to the corporeal substantive body's sentiency. The mystic as is the case with every human person is also endowed with special faculties proper to the human corporeal body dynamically animated by the human soul's spiritual animation. These corporeal organic faculties are the external and internal senses with their accompanying appetitive instinctive affective drives. This anthropological constitution of each human person is not empirically or rationally established. It is based on an essentially intellectual intelligible (i.e., transhistorical) metaphysical approach to the human person that traces its historical roots back to Aristotle and Greek antiquity.

The mystic's personhood like every other human being is additionally and incrementally psychosomatically self-cultivated and self-humanized. This psychosomatic selfhood is supplementally not a natural (i.e., innate) endowment of the human person's personhood. Rather, it is a person's self-cultivated personality in addition to his personhood's innate dynamic hylemorphic endowment. In view of this, there is no communal selfhood or personality proper to each human person as is the case with the human person's innate dynamic human hylemorphic substantive nature. Every human person is communally endowed with one and the same nature. There is no exception to this. This includes both male and female human nature. Of course, each individual human person exercises that communal human nature individually, sovereignly, and uniquely as his own individual nature.

The mystic's psychosomatic personality and selfhood, like that of every humanperson, is processively self-cultivated and personalized within the context of his own regional conventional self-civilized self-humanization. It follows, prima facie, that an individual of an American and an individual of a Chinese personality differ culturally in each's respective personalized traits and psychosomatic selfhood precisely because each is born into a different cultural region of the earth. There is no communal, universal selfhood, nor communal cultural world of self-cultivated persons. However, each individual human person is constituted in his/her subjective corpuscular body of two dichotomous nuclear psychosomatic cores. The human person's bodily somaticity (viz., sensational sensitivity) is constituted of a heartfelt core while his bodily psychicity (viz., inspirational intimacy) is constituted of a mental core.

It is very important to differentiate between the human person's innate soulful faculties (viz., the intellect and will) proper to his inalienable incorporeal nature and his self-cultivated facilitators (viz., the heartfelt willful somatic and the mindful willful psychic self) proper to his alienable corpuscular psychosomatic cultivated personality and selfhood. A faculty, whether organic or inorganic proper to the person's hylemorphic human nature operates spontaneously and dynamically in virtue of that nature's inherent dynamism. A psychosomatic nuclear facilitator, on the other hand, whether it be heartfelt or the mindful involves no such dynamic operative spontaneity. Its own dynamism is only that which is sponsored and instigated by the person's own personhood's egocentric self-serving willfulness. Indeed, such facilitators function only through the exerted effort of the person's personhood who forcibly exerts such facilitators to function skillfully or to malfunction unskillfully by reinforced training. In other words, the personhood's psychosomatic selfhood is composed of a somatic physiological willfulness and a psychic psychological willfulness which forcibly function only through the personalized exerted training of the human person's self-cultivated personhood.

These two very distinct and irreducible orders of the human person's personhood, namely his sovereign personal communal human nature together with his autonomous personalized self-humanized and self-cultivated conventional personality, become fully and solidly a personage when the two orders, the vertical and the horizontal, become integrally reconciled and integrated with each other safeguarding and promoting each's own proper logical consummation. It is the contention of this commentary on St. John of the Cross' mystagogy that this consummation and integral reconciliation is impossible without the superhuman, superhumanizing, superhumane, and supernatural-sacramental intervention of Jesus Christ's redemptive intervention into mankind's own history. Indeed, it is the very premise of these Sanjuanistic mystagogical treatises to be expatiated in these commentaries that it is Jesus Christ who fully reveals mankind's integral authentic anthropological identity, make-up, and ultimate immortal destiny. The integral reconciliation of these two distinctive and irreducible anthropological orders, the natural vertical and the conventional horizontal, are efficaciously integrated by the very cruciformity of Christ's own cross of crucifixion in which He within His own impaled body reconciles the vertical and horizontal beams with each other while still retaining each's respective configuration.

Chapter 2: The mystic's experience of the "dark night's" darkness is divisible into three different phases.

The initial phase of this mystical experience is its point of departure. What is characteristic of this phase is the mystic's complete lack of conscious sensual pleasure and satisfaction regarding everything religious and especially regarding God Himself who had been up to the onset of this phase of emotional aridity the special object of the mystic's intense prayerful enjoyment and exultation. The second phase is the mystic's prolonged journey and pilgrimage of persever-ingly scaling the heights of Mount Carmel, the Gospel figurative ref-erence to God's heavenly transterrestrial and transhistorical eternal abode. The characteristic of this phase is the mystic's steadfast de-termination to persistently continue to address and engage God pray-erfully in spite of his complete lack of experiential awareness of God's response to his prayers. This phase is marked by the mystic's resolve to live exclusively within the darkness of faith intellectually inde-pendent of and transcendent to his own subjective lack of any sup-porting mystical experience insuring the mystic that God is attentive to these prayers.

The third and final phase of this "dark night's darkness is the mystic's emergence from this darkness in the very way that the day's dawning holds the promise of the rising sun. This dawning and emer-ging reassuring experience of God's divine and delicate touch within the mystic's own experiential awareness is at first very gradual as is the daylight's own dawning announcing the sun's arrival on the hori-zon. Hence, the darkness of God's complete withdrawal from the mystic's own subjective religious experience is now giving way gradually to an enhanced experiential awareness of God's delicate and sublime influence on the mystic's own subjective religious psychosomatic affectivity and serenity. This marks the promise of the final unitive stage of the mystic's ascent toward a perfect communion with God in God's Trinitarian Personhood. Of course, in this third stage the previous night-time darkness of prolonged emotional reli-gious aridity and emotionless vexing religious anxiety do not entirely dissolve with the dawning of the mystic's renewed experiential brief periods of religious emotional delight and emotionless religious im-ponderable divine serenity. In other words, the mystic is here in this third stage emerging from his prolonged subjective doubt that he is still experientially alive in the very embrace of the Blessed Trinity. He finds himself in this third stage able as never before previously to theologically trust and hope that God's exquisitely divine benevolent redemptive merciful love is also his very own. For, he now is more fully aware that in his previous mystical stages that he was more fo-cused on himself and his own condition rather than on God and God's infinite Goodness and Loveliness.

In sum, St. John delineates the darkness which the mystic experiences in his spiritual pilgrimage toward perfect union with God as having three distinctive phases paralleling the sun's movement around the earth. The first is a twilight when the Son of God, Jesus Christ, seems to have ceased favoring the mystic with the gratifying benefit of His ingratiating delicate influential touches arousing in the mystic emotional feelings of religious righteous bodily self-satisfaction and mental self-contentment. With the complete disappearance of these delicate religious bodily feelings, the mystic enters into the first twilight phase of this religious emotional aridity. The second phase is even more rigorously dark and devoid of every mystical experience of God's influential delicate reassuring activity within the mystic's very own inner inmost intimate emotionless selfhood. Here, suffering through the brunt of the mystic's prolonged prayerful pilgrimage toward God, the mystic no longer hopes nor even expects to be impelled toward God by personalized subjective mystical deep-seated peaceful mental emotionless yearnings, sighings, and longings. The mystic presses on prayerfully without enjoying in the least any reassuring bodily gratification or mental vindication that God is both attentive to and responding to his prayerful ministrations.

His only guide in this prolonged, strenuous, and tedious climb up to the height of Mount Carmel is his own subjective tenuous hope in Christ's bodily resurrection, trustworthy sacramental presence, and ascension into heaven awaiting the mystic's own arrival following his physical death. The dawning third phase arrives when the mystic fleetingly experiences within his own subjective psychosomatic self-awareness (i.e., in his willful heart and mind) the gifts and fruits of the Holy Spirit. In stark contrast to the many months and even years in which he perseveringly pursued God in prayer bereft of all bodily religious feeling and mental yearning, the mystic is now momentarily flooded with bodily emotional religious feelings of exultation and mental religious yearnings of exquisite peace and profound serenity. The hallmark that these are gifts and fruits are from the Holy Spirit is that the mystic is neither in charge nor in control of them. The mystic is eager to entertain them but cannot control their arrival, their duration, or their departure.

It must be immediately pointed out to the reader of this commentary that this threefold unfolding of the mystic's experience of the "dark night" does not span the three major phases of the mystical life: the purgative, the illuminative, and the unitive. These three phases of darkness cover merely the first two major parts of the mystical life, the purgative and the illuminative. In the second major phase, the illuminative phase, the mystic becomes gradually aware that in his prolonged purgation and nights of darkness involving both his sensory bodily religious feelings and his mental bearings, he was engulfed and entirely enmeshed within his own self-centered selfish religious interest in God. While mired in the purgative phase of his nights of purification, he could not appreciate nor fathom the depth of his own selfish self-interest within which he was captively self-addicted. With the arrival of this illuminative phase in his approach to God the mystic is no longer a prisoner of his own addictive possessive attitudinal mindset. This liberation from the prison of his own attitudinal addictive mindset now enables him to appreciate to the full the blessing this prolonged ordeal of purgation had brought him. The horrendous religious afflictions which he has prayerfully and patiently endured have succeeded in finally ridding himself of his own selfishness, religious self-concern, and allowed him to be more bent and desirous of serving God's glory rather than aggrandizing his own selfhood. These three phases of darkness are covered initially in the *Ascent* and additionally in the *Dark Night* treatises.

Chapter 3: Examples of darkness.

Here St. John simply puts forward examples of "darkness" with which anyone would be quite familiar. These examples emphasize that "darkness" is the absence and lack of what customarily is required for the normal operation of the mystic's human faculties. Thus, in the darkness of night when the sun's light is hidden the faculty of sight is unable to operate normally. The eye's inoperative state does not mean that it is disabled. Really, its operative power is still as able to see as is the case in plain daylight. What darkness brings to the faculty of sight is the absence of its normal mode of illumination enabling its operative power to see. Of course, when one is in such pitch darkness as a night bereft of even the moon's light, one can only grope about rather tentatively if one is in an unfamiliar environment and finds it necessary to try to move from one place to another. In this very uncomfortable position a person's appetitive drive to affectively approach a desirable edible object is also nullified and rendered inoperative. For example, sparked by the eye's normal visualization of a desirable object (viz., a ripe apple or other fruit on a tree), a person's instinctive appetitive hunger drive for food would spur the person to approach and pluck the edible fruit. The eye's incidental blindness brought on by the absence of light also brings about a lack of appetitive stimulus which is the normal way of arousing a person's sentient appetency. What is the case for one's eyesight and sensory appetency is also the case for one's intellectual insight and its corresponding intellectual appetency, the will. When the soul's intellect is plunged into the darkness of faith, its natural activity of intellectual insight along with the soul's intellectual will and volition are naturally stunted.

Chapter 4: It is very necessary for the mystic's advancement in spiritual perfection to suffer the "dark night."

In comparison to God all creatures are nothing. God is the Beingness of existence. Outside of God there is only non-being and non-existence. Compared to God's divine comprehensive existence every creature is a non-being. For, every creature exists with its own creaturely finite existence which is not integral to God's infinite existence. Yes, each creature has its own existence distinct from God's absolute existence. This existence is a dependent created existence and not one with God's uncreated existence of Beingness. Apart from God's causation, every creature would cease to exist. Given this radical disparity between God and God's creature, any attachment on the part of the mystic to a creaturely being (including his own addictive have-attitudinal self-attachment) is an impediment to his perfect attachment to God over, above, and beyond any and every creature. Why so? Because it is the case that we are more possessed by our attachments than we are actually in possession of them. We are possessively prisoners of our own willful possessions. Accordingly, it is necessary that we become self-detached from our foolish self-serving selfish attachments in order to be wisely attached to God and completely free and rid of the prison of our selfhood's self-attachments. The religious harrowing ordeal of the dark nights of the senses and spirit brings about such a complete selfless self-detachment. Therefore, such dark nights are necessary for the mystic's advancement in the spiritual life of becoming perfectly united with God in God's Triune Godhead.

Chapter 5: Sacred Scripture provides ample evidence of the necessity of this religious "dark night" ordeal.

The mystic is self-possessed by an overriding have-attitude typical of everyone living in the world's secularity in which each individual seeks his own prejudicial advantage in pursuing the social security of his own autonomous freedom of self-control. Even the individual mystic who enters a religious community committed to practicing the evangelical counsel of absolute poverty brings his own secular have-attitude into this community. Because of the lingering effect of original sin we all have an overriding have-attitude bent to promote our own preferential advantage in contraposition to others who, in turn, are promoting their own opposite antipodal advantage. Individuals who actually are unaware of this cultural overriding have-attitudinal proclivity in themselves tenaciously strive in a have-attitude tenacity to have their own prejudicial advantage prevail over their opponents who prejudicially possess have-advantages opposing their own overriding outlook. This becomes acutely evident when individuals of different religious or political persuasion find themselves debating with each other over their overriding preferential differences.

The mystic who is committed to following Christ's Gospel lifestyle is also committed to put on the mind of Christ. This means that the mystic must cope and contend with his own prepossessive prejudicial have-attitudinal mindset. Of course, at the outset of his spiritual pilgrimage to scale Mount Carmel symbolizing the utter remoteness of God from His creature, the mystic is not fully aware of his own self-cultivated overriding self-esteem issuing from his self-possessed prevalent addictive overriding have-attitude even toward religious objects and religious activities. He must be purged of his own possessive selfish partisan have-attitude mindset and be converted to Christ's utterly Selfless be-attitudinal mindset which demands that Christ's disciple skillfully exercise a mortifying and ascetic have-not attitude of complete self-denial and self-abnegation. For, one with a have-attitude mindset is possessively self-attached and a virtual prisoner to his own self-esteem and selfish partisan attitudinal self-attached mindset. Becoming weaned away from this overriding proclivity is the crux of the "dark night's" harrowing and excruciatingly painful ordeal. Sacred Scripture is replete with examples of individuals chosen by God undergoing severe trials testing their own commitment and "spirit" of loyalty to God above and beyond their own possessive have-attitude selfish self-interest.

Chapter 6: St. John indicates the privative and positive harms that self-attachments bring about to the mystic.

The first harm is a privative one. That is, by continuing to harbor and to be motivated by his own selfish overriding have-attitude toward himself (i.e., his own selfish self-esteem) and toward God and his neighbor, the mystic is deprived of allowing his own self-humanized willful selfhood and overriding dominant humanistic selfish "spirit" be fully influenced and transformed into Christ's own superhumanistic Holy Spirit of utter Self-detachment and Selflessness. Because of this persistent and perduring overriding selfish have-attitude, the mystic is also deprived within his immortal soul of many habitual and actual graces which he would otherwise receive if he were completely and transformatively imbued with Christ's own Selfless be-attitudinal mindset.

The second harm is a positive one. It befalls the mystic without even his own awareness of this that his persistent overriding selfish self-attachment, especially in religious spiritual matters, brings on himself a weariness in battling and contending with this have-attitude addictive mindset. He is, again, a prisoner of his own selfish self-possessiveness. His dominant willful selfhood seeks to be in complete autonomous charge and control of his own selfhood. But, due to his overriding preoccupation with his own selfish self-interest he finds himself wearily battling himself rather than advancing in his spiritual communion with God in God's Triune Godhead. He is tormented by his own failure to gain masterful control over his own impulses and desires. He is blinded by his own self-serving ambitions, especially his religious ambitions. His best religious efforts are defiled by this overriding self-attachment and his willful self-determination to abandon himself totally to God's providential care is seriously weakened.

At this point St. John takes note of a point which St. Augustine had noted previously in his own writings. God's creation of the universe ex nihilo was less a challenge to His omnipotent power than Christ's subsequent recreation effectuated by His sacramental renewal of mankind through His own Paschal Mystery. For, God's initial creation met with no creaturely opposition whereas His subsequent redemptive recreation meets with not only some of the angels willful rebellious disobedience, it also meets with many of mankind's equally willful and disobedient resistant rebelliousness. What this notation brings to light is the disparity between God's vertical, hierarchical, ontological order of created existence, on the one hand, and the creature's horizontal, historical, ideological order of rebellious willful resistance, on the other. These two completely irreducible and non-educible orders represent the two crossbeams of Christ's cross of crucifixion: the vertical and horizontal crossbeams of the cross' cruciformity. These two orders will have a most prominent place in these commentaries on the mystagogical treatises of St. John of the Cross.

Here, anticipating a more thorough-going account later on in this commentary, it is opportune at this point to indicate that within the cruciform crux of the two opposing crossbeams of Christ's cross of crucifixion the mystic's selfhood is found on the horizontal subjective beam whereas his immortal soul is found on the vertical objective beam. The subjective-objective opposition between these two beams is an opposition between the vertical order of existence issuing from God's own divine creativity and the horizontal order of resistance issuing from the creature's willful opposition to both this fundamental order of existence and to Christ's supplemental salvific sacramental recreation of mankind's falling from grace in the Garden of Eden.

The matter of his authentic superhumanized self-fulfillment demands that he find the authentic fullness of his own abject subjective needfulness not within the supplemental subjective immanent phenomenological order of his own experiential subjectivity and self-awareness but transcendentally beyond within the non-experiential supernatural ontological objective order of God's gracious, sacramental presence within his immortal soul. That is, the mystic's authentic self-fulfillment of his own selfhood is not to be found within himself and his own selfhood which is entirely supplemental but entirely beyond in his soul which is fundamentally supernaturally alive with God's own sacramental benignant, gratuitous, graciousness. In view of this, the mystic must suffer through an enigmatic paradox. It is only in the measure that he willfully, painfully, and forcibly relinquishes his overriding possessive selfish have-attitudinal self-attachment to his own dominating self-control of his own willful selfhood that he will conscientiously find his demanding need for his own selfhood's authentic self-fulfillment fully fulfilled in the fundamental objective supernatural order of sacramental existence completely transcendent to his own subjective selfhood. Indeed, the more the mystic clings willfully and resistantly to his own selfishly self-serving willfulness, the more tenaciously he becomes a prisoner and addicted to his own selfish religious bodily self-gratification and mental self-vindication to the detriment of his willful selfhood's authentic self-fulfillment.

There is a radical difference between the subjective horizontal resistant order of phenomenology (i.e., ideology) and the objective vertical ontological order of existence. In the objective order there is no room for "make-belief" and pretense which is very much the case in the subjective order. The objective order is that of God's creation which is reality itself. The subjective order is that of man's cultural recreation which is a make-believe world of man's own fascination. This "world" of man's self-cultivation is not negligible even though it is not reality itself. For this supplemental "world" brings to a self-humanistic and self-civilized conventional completion what cannot be entirely completed in the natural order of God's creation. For example, flowers have their own natural beauty independent of any human agricultural workmanship or skill. Yet, the human skills of artfully and artificially arranging flowers in flower beds, gardens, vases, etc., bring an enhanced esthetic beautification to the natural beauty of these plants. These plants of themselves naturally and fundamentally could not bring about this esthetic enhancement without mankind's self-cultivated supplemental skillfulness. In other words, God's own creation finds supplementally its completion through mankind's industrious skillful civilized self-cultivation.

Chapter 7: The mystic is tormented by his own self-attachments.

This point emphasized by St. John directs its attention to the addictive possessiveness of all self-attachments whether they are worldly or religious attachments. When we reflect that self-attachments are found in the horizontal order of the mystic's egocentric self-assured willful resistancy, the horizontal order of the mystic's having or not having a possessive self-control over his own willfulness in contradistinction to the vertical order of existence and being which involves no such self-possessiveness, it is clear that St. John is speaking of the torment that any addiction brings on a person who is afflicted with the strangle-hold this addiction has on the addict. The alcoholic, to cite a well-known addiction, is a prisoner of his own craving and willful self-attachment to alcohol.

The mystic may be a religious alcoholic and a prisoner of his own egocentric craving and willful self-attachment to the spiritual mystical inebriation which he has discovered in his own prayer-life. Like any addiction, the mystic's self-attachment to his own spiritual inebriation prompts and urges him to crave such mystical experiences when they are missing and to revel in them when they occur. This is a torment precisely because his built-in willful egocentric resistancy (i.e., concupiscence) refuses to dispense with and let go of such addictive attachments. Yielding to such addictive attachments only reinforces the mystic's willful need for these experiences which can never authentically fulfill the mystic's craving precisely because they do not transcend the mystic's own egocentric selfish self-serving subjective egocentricity. Indeed, they only further whet the mystic's need to ex-perientially have more of what he craves and in having more to be more tormented by his addiction to this insatiable need.

Chapter 8: The mystic is blinded by his own self-attachments.

This follows logically from the previous torment described in chapter 7. When one is seriously addicted to anything and becomes a self-centered prisoner of this addiction, this person's willful mindset becomes itself biased toward favoring having this addiction. Again, the drug-addict and/or alcoholic foolishly construes that he is in complete willful self-control of his drinking and drug consumption. Further, he is self-convinced that he is better off when he is actually intoxicated than when he is sober. Similarly, the mystic who is ad-dicted to any worldly or religious attachment is prone in his willful attitudinal mindset to esteem himself to be better off with this addic-tion than without it. This warped biased mindset is further reinforced by his willful built-in resistancy (concupiscence) to tenaciously resist relinquishing this addiction. Indeed, any such addiction can only be overcome with a resolute and forcible decisiveness that pits the per-son's willfulness against its own built-in resistancy. Of course, once this resistance is actually forcibly overcome by an ascetic program of kenotic self-denial, the mystic does take possessive charge and au-thentic self-control over his own willfulness.

Chapter 9: The third harm which self-attachments bring to the mystic is that of defilement.

Whatever be the self-attachment to which the mystic is addicted this self-attachment defiles the mystic's total attachment to God. The mystic's very own selfhood no longer is orientated entirely and ex-clusively toward God whom he willfully is committed and religiously dedicated to serve. St. John has recourse to a repulsive and gross ex-ample to emphasize this defilement. Of course, the defilement is even worse because the defilement takes on the dimensions which derive from measuring it by God's own infinitude and holiness. Thus, a glass which is reserved exclusively to serve and to drink wine becomes defiled when it is covered with vermin.

Chapter 10: There is still a fourth harm which accrues to the mystic who is a prisoner of his self-attachment.

This is the harm of weakness which a person suffers in his moral character. Reverting yet again to the example of the drug-addict and alcoholic, it is clear that the virtuous power of the person to temperately partake of drugs and alcohol in the vertical order of being is seriously impaired and weakened. The person who in his soulful will is able to choose to partake of or not to partake of drugs and alcohol is virtuously (i.e., morally) strengthened in this volitional power to choose to willingly temper his indulgence. That is, he retains an even stronger volitional ability to temperately indulge or not to indulge in such intoxicating spirits. However, when in the subjective horizontal order of the person's egocentric selfish willful mindfulness, the person is possessively self-attached and addicted to these intoxicating spirits, his objective soulful will no longer retains its moral and virtuous strength to choose or not to choose to partake of these spirits temperately.

Chapter 11: Further, the mystic cannot be entirely free from the servility and servitude of his own selfishness when he retains any willful self-serving self-attachment and addiction.

Here we must distinguish between objective instinctive animal drives inherent in man's very corporeal sentient nature. These instinctive involuntary drives are directed toward goals which are beneficial to the animal body's growth, maintenance, protection, and survival. These instinctive animal drives do not of themselves impair nor imprison the soul's innate will from freely choosing to govern their exercise. Even though one's animal instinct for food is in its spontaneous hunger drive exceedingly difficult to govern, it is still governable and susceptible to being subordinate to the soul's voluntary direction. This is most evident when individuals voluntarily undergo hunger strikes which can even impair their physical health and sometimes end in death by starvation. Their instinctive animal drive for food cannot overcome their overriding freedom to govern such a drive.

In contradistinction there are subjective self-cultivated self-serving willful needs which are not instinctively inherent in the substantive corporeal body's very animal nature. These self-cultivated needs are supplemental to the fundamental substantive corporeal human body's instinctive appetitive drives for food, drugs, sex, and shelter. Thus, while a person instinctively hungers for food he can supplementally and artfully by an acquired cooking skill prepare certain foods to increase their gustatory appetency, appeal, and enjoyment. In skillfully and artfully preparing such foods, he cultivates a subjective need for such culinary pleasurable emotional feelings. This need is not an instinctive drive on the part of the substantive corporeal animal body for its own nutriment to sustain its metabolism. Rather, it is a self-cultivated and self-humanized need for a gustatory pleasure, satisfaction, and contentment which affects subjectively the person's egocentric awareness of the insubstantial physiological body's tantalizing sensuous sensitivity.

This sensational sensuality is not merely an instinctive animal appetency and passionate drive for food to nourish and sustain the body's metabolism. This sensuality is an egocentric self-serving compassionate subjective deficiency within a human person's willful somatic selfhood and somatic personality which is not directed to any objective purpose but entirely self-orientated toward one's selfhood's willful sensuous (i.e., somatic) bodily self-satisfaction and self-gratification. Hence, it is not simply an instinctive animal passionate drive spontaneously aroused to provide for the animal body's own natural well-being. It is a willfully self-cultivated compassionate self-centered and self-serving voluptuous physiological subjective sensational (i.e., kinesthetic) stimulation over and above (i.e., in addition to) the animal body's objective instinctive purposeful drive.

It is compassionate because it is not an involuntarily and spontaneously adduced affection (i.e., passion) as is the case with the animal body's instinctive drives which are spontaneously affectively aroused by appetitively sensible objects beneficial or inimical to the animal body's wellbeing. Rather, it is deliberatively and skillfully a willfully emotionally (i.e., motivationally) self-induced affectation to service the selfhood's somatic need for its own voluptuous self-satis-faction and self-contentment. These needs are motivationally self-serving inasmuch as they stimulate voluptuous feelings sensationally introduced into the nonsubstantive corpuscular body's subjective kin-esthetic physiology thereby motivationally urging and spurring on the person's somatic (i.e., sensuous) selfhood to willfully undertake whatever action is necessary to procure its own sensuous self-gratific-ation. Hence, they are compassionate precisely because they stimulate the person's egocentric self-oriented awareness and interest in his own self-serving egocentric somatic selfhood's social security and self-contentment.

It must be noted that the human person's personhood is in the vertical order of existence spontaneously dynamic in all of its innate natural operations. All of these vital operations issue radically and re-motely from the person's substantive hylemorphic nature and most notably from the human soul which is the animating substantive principle of all of the vital activity proper to the substantive human body. The proximate principle of these vital operations (viz., seeing, growing, walking, eating, thinking, willing, etc.,) are called activities of faculties because they have their own special power to act (viz., the eye for seeing, the leg for walking, the intellect for thinking, etc.,). These faculties, whether organic or inorganic operate spontaneously in virtue of the substantive body/soul's intrinsic dynamic spon-taneity. Thus, the human person in his own personhood naturally op-erates spontaneously and authoritatively in all of the operations that emanate from his own substantive dynamic nature. This dynamism is not exhausted or spent in any of its natural operations. It is just the opposite. The more these potent dynamic faculties are actually oper-ative, the more reinforced and expansively dynamic do they become. Thus, the more the intellect or the will operates actively, the more vir-tuously (or viciously) thoughtful and volitional do these faculties sub-sequently become.

The case is simply the reverse with the human personhood's self-cultivated self-humanized selfhood and personality in the hori-zontal order of his willful subjective resistancy vis-à-vis all that transcends this subjective selfhood in the objective vertical order of his own human nature. All of the functionally productive operations accruing to the human person's selfhood have a synergism that is proper to the personhood's own subjective self-serving willfulness. This synergism is not spontaneously actuated in view of a transcendent objective, goal, and purpose. It is influentially and forcibly activated by the personhood's own self-serving egocentric willful neediness. This willfulness is not innately dynamically potent. Quite the reverse. It is inherently impotent. The person's willful selfhood and self-serving personality cannot act spontaneously; it must be motivated (influentially prompted and spurred) to become active. Such willful activation is not itself a vital intransitive activity immediately beneficial to the human person's well-being. It is a skillfully functional (or unskillful dysfunctional) transitive production which is elicited only through willful effort and body or mental exertion. This willful productive action (due to its impotency) needs to be motivationally (i.e., influentially) activated. This willful motivation in the case of its somatic (i.e., sensuous) bodily deficiency (i.e., need) is sensationally stimulated by self-induced influential stirring feelings which emotionally motivate the will to exert what bodily effort is necessary to productively procure its own secure sensuous self-contentment.

It follows from the preceding exposition that the more the human person in his own willful subjective somatic selfhood (i.e., personality) motivationally subjects his own will to the advancement of his own sensuous bodily self-gratification, the more he becomes possessively attached and even addicted to the self-possessive security of this contentment. That is, the less free he is to deny himself this hedonistic pleasure and to forgo this self-induced self-serving sensuous indulgence whatever be its specification (viz., food, sex, drugs, shelter, etc.,) among worldly enjoyments or (viz., consolation, exultation, glorification, etc.,) among religious enjoyments. Furthermore, unlike the person's natural dynamism and faculties which reinforce themselves in the very exercise of their operations, this self-cultivated synergism of the person's influential self-serving willful selfhood becomes weakened and spent with its willful exertion. The selfhood's need for even greater sensuous self-satisfaction demands that the selfhood's will muster a greater willful exertion to emotionally stimulate itself to an even more industrious functional (i.e., skillful) undertaking to procure even a larger feeling of secure sensuous self-contentment. In other words, the selfhood's willfulness eventually exhausts its own emotional resourcefulness. It not only becomes a captive to its own urgent needs, it becomes increasingly captive by having these needs become increasingly needful without being potently able to satisfy their increased urgency and neediness. The person caught in this strait may falsely construe that he is masterfully (i.e., skillfully) completely in self-control. It is quite the reverse. He is a captive prisoner addicted to his own self-serving demanding needs.

So much so is this the case that St. John offers what seems at first blush to be a remarkable declaration. Venial sins are less obstacles to divine union than are any even trifling self-attachments. He sagaciously notes that a bird is as much impeded to fly if it is restrained by a hair of one's head or the bars of a cage. The point of this probing declaration is that God in His infinite power and merciful justice can remit and forgive venial sins with the proper penitential prayerful regret on the part of the sinner. On the other hand, a person imprisoned within the possessive addiction of his own selfhood's willfulness lacks within the reservoir of this own willfulness the needed willful exertion and stamina to extricate himself from this imprisonment. Indeed, it is precisely the messianic mission of Christ to free mankind from the prison of this self-centered prison and to enable mankind to experience the freedom of His own Holy Spirit. This begins in the penitent only with a total self- surrender to Christ's redemptive and liberating power accompanied by a sincere confessional acknowledgment of his utter helplessness.

Chapter 12: An assessment of the two evils of self-attachment.

Mortal sins are both totally privative impediments because of their aversion to God and positive impediments because they indicate a lack of conversion to God. Venial sins are much less impediments. Sensual attachments defile both the selfhood's somatic and psychic personality (viz., desensitizes one's emotional body feelings and prejudices one's equitable mental bearings). These attachments engage one privative affliction principally and others indirectly. Thus, vain-glory entails principally blindness and gluttony entails principally lukewarmness.

Through the practice of one virtue all of the others grow (viz. prudence, justice, temperance, fortitude)...through the resistance to one self-attachment, resistance to all others also increases. Resistance to temptation strengthens the will's willful skill to overcome its own self-centered selfish resistancy. (This is a paradox). Self-cultivated artificial needs must be differentiated from innate natural drives.

Chapter 13: Coping with the mortifications required by an ascetic Gospel lifestyle.

Two ways: active mortification and passive mortification. In the active mode, one takes the initiative in a program of self-denial. A refusal to deny one's own self is tantamount to refusing to affirm God. In the passive mode, God Himself takes the initiative to deny to the mystic all self-serving motivating religious incentives.

Two rules of thumb: a) imitation of Christ & b) fulfilling the Father's Holy Will without the benefit of any personalized religious gratifying bodily self-contentment or justifying mental self-containment.

Benefit of the total control of the four following religious experiences a) emotional feelings of joy (exultation, consolation) and sorrow (dryness and desolation) and b) dispassionate bearings of hope (inspirations, fascinations) and fear (anxieties, dread).

MAXIMS:

not the easy but the difficult

not the delightful but the harsh

not the pleasing but the unpleasant

not rest but work

not praise but criticism

not the most but the least

not the prized but the despised

not wanting but not wanting

not the best but the worse of temporary goods

not the least but the best for love of Christ

Avoid pride of life, concupiscence, and of eyes; act with contempt for one's own self, speak with contempt for one's own self, and think of one's self contemptuously. Check the text for the diagram and adages leading to the summit of Mount Carmel.

Chapter 14: "A love of pleasure and an attachment to it usually fires up the will towards the enjoyment of things that give pleasure to it. An intense enkindling of another better love (love for Jesus Christ, our Heavenly Bridegroom) is necessary to vanquish our appetite [for pleasure] and the denial (i.e., self-denial) of this pleasure."

St. John here addresses the mystic's mental mindset and selfish attitudinal attachment to the body's sensuality and self-contentment as his overriding need for self-fulfillment. An overall selfish self-serving have-more mental mindset and attitude toward the body's sensuality motivates the mystic to have pleasure as his dominant willful bodily need and self-fulfillment. The only cure and antidote for this predominant overriding addictive pleasurable mindset is a radical metanoetic attitudinal conversion. The mystic must train to renounce his selfish have-more addictive attitudinal mindset regarding the body's sensuality and to replace it with a have-less be-more messianic attitude proper to Jesus Christ's own redemptive mindset. This means that the mystic must sacrificially renounce and train to deny himself his body's pleasurable selfish sensuality and strive to adopt Christ's ascetic mindset and have-less self-denial attitude in order to have his body's endeavors become selflessly more serviceable to God and to selves other than his own selfish self. St. John does not here immediately delve into this radical cure of the body's need for sensual pleasure. But, he does indicate that such a radical antidote is called for in overcoming the body's need and demand for sensual pleasure.

This radical antidote is found in adopting Christ's own messianic be-attitudinal mindset. The beatitudes are a profile of Christ's superhero-ic, superhumanistic divinized Selfless personality.

Chapter 15: The dark night entails that the mystic be deprived of all self-serving selfish sensorial and sensuous satisfactions and self-contentment by deliberately mortifying this sensuality.

In other words, this dark night is successful in the measure that the mystic is no longer a prisoner of his own sensitivities, emotional feelings, and selfish gratifications in the body's urgent need for gust-atory, venereal, medicinal, and clothing self-contentment. An active ascetic training in self-denial enables the mystic to curb these secular bodily needs. In addition, a passive training in the "dark night of the senses" further enables the mystic to curb his body's sensual religious need for a self-contented exultation and glorification.

THE ASCENT, Book II: Chapters 1-10: FAITH IS THE MYSTIC'S PROXIMATE MEANS OF ASCENDING TO GOD.

Chapter 1: The night of the spirit.

In darkness, and secure,

By the secret ladder, disguised,

--Ah, the sheer grace---

In darkness and concealment,

My house being now all stilled.

St. John states that the mystic enters more securely within the very intimacy of his mystical encounter with God by completely tran-scending and leaving aside his dependency on religious sensational imagery and sensuous emotional feelings. When he has become purged of further needing and requiring satisfying and motivationally stimulating and comforting religious experiences to sustain his prayerful attentiveness to God, he is dispositively and attitudinally prepared to prayerfully enter into a more intimate union with God bereft of all such comforting religious feelings and stimulating sensitized sensuous exalted affections. This meditative form of prayer has served him well to arouse in himself mystical empathic religious affections toward God and the saints. On the other hand, his self-attachment to meditative prayer harbors more a selfish self-indulgent interest in this form of prayer with its accompanying religious excitement and self-contentment rather than a completely disinterested intent to prayerfully serve and do honor to God transcendent to his own personalized religious experiential sensuous self-indulgent bodily feelings and emotions.

When he reaches this advanced stage of self-purification in which he no longer clings to this long-time meditative method of praying with the focus of his prayer-life being his ability to imaginatively, empathically, and emotionally induce within himself the very feelings of Christ, His Blessed Mother, and those of the saints, he finds himself at this juncture having to prayerfully live exclusively on faith as his only guide and motivating inspiration. For, he is now bereft of all subjective personalized gratifying religious imagery and feelings of and for God and His saints. He can no longer even evoke through religious imagery of the Gospel past emotional feelings and comfort even if he would wish to do so. Religious imagery no longer avails him of any profitable religious affinity with God.

The mystic here in his helplessness to experience sincere and authentic feelings for Jesus and God-the-Father is primed to enter the night of the "spirit" in which his trusting faith in God transcendent to his own subjective religious experiential personalized feelings becomes his only succor and strength. Yet, this faith itself provides him with no intellectual illumination commensurate with his own intellect's native light of intelligibility. Paradoxically enough this faith which is a supernatural gift of God leaves the mystic plunged into a profound ignorance of God which he likens to the pitch black darkness of midnight when there is not even a glimmer of the sun's light reaching the earth. On the other hand, St. John explains, this very pitch-black darkness of faith is the perfect protection the mystic needs to hide himself from the wiles of the devil, the weakness and seductive attraction of his own flesh's sensuality, and the lure of the world's temptations along with fear of the world's intimidations. The devil's keen angelic intelligence has no power to penetrate into faith's darkness. Faith is completely alien to the devil.

At the same time, the mystic's total self-abandonment to this gratuitously given supernatural gift of faith is not only bereft of his previous religious stimulating sensuous comfortable feeling for and of God, it is also bereft of any complete intellectual intelligibility regarding God. Certainly where the mystic previously experienced a considerable ordeal and deprivation in losing his religious feelings for God depriving him of his motivation to zealously attend to God, he will now in this advanced stage of entering into a more intimate mental union with God undergo an ordeal that is far more trying, terrible, and devastating to his own subjective religious mental security and self-esteem. The ordeal of the night of the "spirit" by comparison with that of the night of the "senses" is not only gloomier in that the mystic suffers more acutely the agonizing experience of the loss of any emotional feeling for and of God, he suffers now within the innermost inward intimacy of his own mental psyche an overriding irrational foreboding and nebulous disturbing mental anxiety and dread. This robs him of the mental tranquility and serene intimacy with God which characterized his prayer up to this point.

This ever-present foreboding mental anxiety and angst peculiar to the "dark night of the spirit" is subjectively accentuated precisely because the very objective intellectual gift of faith rather than enlightening the mystic regarding God's intelligibility actually befuddles the mystic's own native intelligibility of God. God's infinite Goodness is readily intellectually intelligible. Yet, the mystic is unable to reconcile this intelligible infinite Goodness with his own subjective personalized lack of religious sensuous savor and taste for God coupled with his ever increasing mental anxiousness, uneasiness, and foreboding regarding God's retreat from him. Hence, while objectively and trustingly through the supernatural light of faith the mystic approaches

God sacramentally in the Blessed Eucharist whom he believes to be truly present in the Person of Jesus Christ, he subjectively in his self-humanized personality experiences no palpable exalted sensitized religious feeling nor any mental intimate serene and self-assured caring and concern for this divine sacramental presence.

In brief, the mystic within the subjectivity of his own religious personality is totally both in his somatic bodily sensorium and his mental thoughtfulness devoid of the bodily comfort and mental pious serenity with which he was previously wont to pray. Concomitantly with this bleak and agonizing deprivation of God's palpable and tranquilizing personalized religious experience (i.e., total religious emotional gloominess and mental wariness) the mystic's subjective religious motivation to confidently and lovingly continue to pray is reduced to blindly trusting intellectually in faith in God's own trustworthiness and benignity transcendent to and independent of the mystic's subjective personalized religious torment and ordeal of having no reassuring palpable bodily exciting or mental confident experience of this divine fidelity.

St. John is describing here both in the stanza of his poem and in his subsequent explanation of this stanza that the mystic becomes eventually at some point inescapably enveloped in the "spirit's" dark night. At this point he has advanced beyond the tribulation of the dark night of the "senses" which was very trying and disruptive to his emotional zeal and religious fervor and, now, he finds himself undergoing a more severe religiously mental disquieting uneasiness, the total inner experiential religious loss of caring for God accompanied by a vexing inability to prayerfully recollect himself in the intimate companionship of God's providential loving security. Yet, St. John insists that this stark religious experiential bleakness and isolation from God is a "sheer grace." Why? Because the mystic is now being delivered and liberated from the prison of his own religious sensuality and even from his own most intimate innermost subjective needful imperious demand to have a mentally self-assured serene carefree communion with God. Caught up with the throes of the dark night of the spirit he is now completely subjectively and willfully dependent exclusively for spiritual guidance on the transubjective trustworthy theological intellectual virtue of faith as he prayerfully continues his pilgrimage up to the summit of Mount Carmel. Indeed, at this stage of his spiritual advancement the mystic is subjectively cloaked exclusively in his hopeful willful tenuous attachment to the theological gift of faith with no other religious motivational bodily stimulation or mental comfort and succor to bolster and foster his interest in God as the paramount center of his life.

This faith itself is like the cloud in the Old Testament which guided the Israelites through the desert after their exodus from Egypt. The cloud was more than a natural formation because it served miraculously as a guide in the desert's vast waste. Hence, it was both supernatural evidence of God's divine presence and, at the same time, equal evidence of God's hiddenness. In virtue of the intellect's own native intellectual light the cloud of faith is nebulously impenetrable to the intellect's own intelligence and intelligibility. On the other hand, this very nebulosity serves as a guiding light to the human intellect which is blinded by the infinite luminosity of God's own divinity gratuitously revealed to the mystic's supernaturally illumined intelligence through the theological gift of faith. The advantage to the mystic of relying exclusively on faith as the guide to his mystical journeying to God is that he is protected by the blinding cloak of this theological virtue from the devil's influence as well as from the influence of his own subjective willful selfish demand for his own privatized religious experience of God. In other words, the mystic's former craving to sensitively feel God's exultation, on the one hand, and to mentally experience God's serenity and imperturbable security, on the other, are no longer crutches on which he can prayerfully limp along on his journey to join God on the very summit of Mount Carmel.

Faith is credulous trust in what is objectively and inherently trustworthy. Every cognitive faculty including both the human senses and the intellect are innately trusting and credulous. For, they are ordered to knowing what formally exists transcendent to their proper cognizance. The adage "seeing is believing" is simply a concise declaration of sight's credulity. One can trust one's eyesight precisely because whatever it sees is obviously and evidently seeable and visible. The very visibility of what the eye sees is itself the cause of the eye's sight and trusting act of seeing. But, the eye's sight is confined to its own formal cognition; similarly with the intellect's own insight. The eye cannot "see" sound which is formally discerned by the ear; and vice versa, the ear cannot "hear" color which is formally discerned by the eye. On the other hand, the intellect's formal object of knowability is "being;" it has no such confinement or restriction as do the senses. Furthermore, where the senses discern only the sensibility of things, the intellect can discern the actual intelligibility of all that it knows. This includes the very intelligibility of God who is minimally a "being" and maximally the very "Beingness of all beings." Such knowledge, however, is not a direct natural intellectual gazing on the very divinity of God since God remains infinitely removed from the human person's own creaturely existence.

The senses are incidentally but not essentially fallible. Being organic, they may by reason of a deficiency or defect in their organs be incidentally fallible. Thus, a blind person's sight is fallible. The intellect, on the other hand, is inorganic; it has no organ that can be deficient or defective. That is, it is essentially and faithfully infallible in its formal discernment of its own intelligibility without any incidental impediment to deflect this inherent infallibility. Indeed, it is infallibly credulously trusting regarding its own intelligible formality: being-as-such. This infallibility is stated in the principle of identity: "being is being;" contradicting this principle is both unprincipled and unintelligible. Affirming this principle, the intellect not only is cognizant of its touchstone to all of reality, being-as-such, but is cognizant of recognizing the very truth of such knowledge. Hence, the intellect's innate trustworthiness and infallible fidelity is not directly provable precisely because its formal object of cognition defies proof; it is foolproof. Only a fool would seek to prove the obviously evident. The intellect may incidentally err not in its formal cognitivity but in its subsequent reasoning. But, even here it can logically examine its formal reasoning and both intelligently detect and correct its errancy and fallacious illogical reasoning.

Supernatural faith is moreso a supernatural infallible intellectual knowledge since it has access to the patent evidence of God's very supernal divinity supernaturally revealed. This faith transforms and elevates the human intellect and its intelligence from its natural cognitive infallible insight regarding the "being-as-such" of all that exists to sharing in God's divine supremely intelligible infallible insight into the very "Beingness" of all that exists. The human bodily eye, unlike the brute animal eye, can "see" intelligently because the human soul is essentially intelligent and permeates the body's eyesight with the vitality of its own intelligence. That is, the human eye as a bodily faculty animated by an intelligent spiritual soul is endowed with intelligible sight in virtue of the human soul's own innate intelligence. Similarly, when the human soul is adoptively through baptism sublimated to the Blessed Trinity, it becomes supernaturally infused with a divine and sublime intelligibility in virtue of its sacramental assumption into God's supernatural divinity. Accordingly, when the Eucharist host is elevated at Mass, the eye sees formally the host's color, the intellect naturally sees the host as a body which is colorful, and the human person through his baptized soul supernaturally discerns the host as God's very own supreme divinity. The eye sees under the medium of physical light, the intellect under the medium of its own soul's native spiritual light, and the human person supernaturally under the divine light of God's own glory bestowed on the soul as grace. Each of these three "sights" is "for real." The consecrated Eucharistic host is colorful, is a body, and is God, the Second Person of the Blessed Trinity, Jesus Christ. Thus, the soul's intellect can "see" supernaturally in the medium of supernatural faith beyond the prowess of its own native intelligibility.

The Eucharistic host is Jesus Christ, God/Superman. This reality is not visible to the body's eye or intelligible to the soul's native intellect, but only discernible to the supernaturally sublimated soul's intelligence. The body's eyesight is faithfully trustworthy; the soul's intellect is faithfully trustworthy, and the soul's sublimated intelligence is, a fortiori, exceedingly trustworthy. Indeed, the human soul divinely infused with the infinitely lucid light of God's own Trinitarian glory "sees" unerringly the unexcelled quintessence of reality above and beyond every other formal cognition. The mystic can trust this Gospel sacramental revelation more unerringly and infallibly than he can his own senses and his own native intelligence exercised through the soul's intellect. This knowledge is entirely transsubjectively objective. The Eucharistic host is not God because the mystic subjectively bodily feels that it is or subjectively mentally cares that it is so. It is so fully independent of and transcendent to the mystic's subjective bodily sentimental zealous religious feeling, and mental solicitous pious religious caring. What is tremendously remarkable in these instances of cognitive credulous trustworthiness and fidelity is that the actual reality without any impeding intermediary is what is actually discerned, seen, and known. Through the supernatural gift of faith, the mystic is able to infallibly discern the actuality of God's Trinitarian Personal divinity. It is this supernatural faith which is the cornerstone to the Catholic Christian's mystical life.

Note that in the case of the senses the special medium of cognition proper to each sense is a created medium. Thus, for example, the natural medium of the sun's light serves as the bodily eye's medium. This is not an intermediary medium in the sense that the eye's sight must first discern light before it can actually see what is rendered visible by the sun's light. Light is a see-through medium; it is not itself visible but the medium of visibility for whatever the eye does actually see; similarly with intellectual knowledge. Its medium of knowing is the soul's own intellectual spiritual lucidity which is translucently incorporeal and in no way physical as the sun's light is physical. Yet, this medium is also created by God. On the other hand, the medium for the supernatural gift of faith is God's very own pellucid uncreated infinite divine glorious splendor. It is in the infinite luminosity of this glory that the mystic beholds intellectually the very divinity of God in beholding the resurrected "face" of Jesus Christ in the consecrated sacramental Eucharistic host and wine. In this present life the very infinite brilliance of this glory blinds the intellect whereas in the hereafter in heaven the sanctified intellect will discern that this very glory and God's divinity are one and the same supreme reality.

If the mystic's supernaturally enlightened intellect in the present life seeks to comprehend faith and the tenets of faith in terms of its own natural light of intelligibility (i.e., being-as-such), it wrestles with the mystery of theologically understanding God's infinite revealed divinity (viz., Beingness) in terms that are less intelligibly comprehensive (viz., being-as-such) than is God's own infinite divine nature. Being-as-such is the formal scope of the human intellect's intelligibility. This is a transcendental category of all intelligible categories within reality. Beingness, on the other hand, which is God's very own actual divine existence, is the transcendental reality of all realities. While this sublime Beingness is an analogous object of the philosopher's quest and the ultimate attainment of the intellect's own natural credulity and belief in its own prowess to intelligently probe the entire expanse of reality, such a divine Beingness self-revealed in its own infinite glory and luminosity is only the supernatural object of a theological faith that spawns a superhuman worship, thanksgiving, praise, and love that infinitely surpasses the human person's own native prowess. Beingness becomes the supernatural object of a supernatural faith when this same supreme reality (viz., the Trinitarian Godhead) becomes Self-revealed to mankind in salvation history encompassing the Old Testament as God-the-Father, the New Testament as God-the-Son, and the Acts of the Apostles culminating in the foundation of the Sacramental Church with the Holy Spirit as her animation.

The philosopher cognizes and recognizes that God, the Beingness of all reality, is a Supreme reality within the universe of reality as the pinnacle and unexcelled excellence of all that exists. That is, he encounters God as the summit of reality which he cannot personally encounter because of the infinite transcendence and remoteness of such a reality from his creaturely existence. In brief, God to the philosopher is the analogous end of his intellectual quest but not the beginning of his personalized experiential religious engagement. For, this Supreme Being is utterly the beginning of all created reality while having no beginning of its own. The human person's intellectual quest and philosophical search for God is over in his discovery of God's existence because he can neither objectively volitionally (i.e., personally) nor subjectively experientially (i.e., personalistically) engage such a reality that remains infinitely removed from his volitional grasp. God remains infinitely removed and beyond the human person's soulful embrace and self-humanized and self-cultivated ventures.

It is not surprising that while the very Greek and Roman cultures of antiquity did attain to a philosophical grasp of God as an ultimate monotheistic reality, there continued to culturally exist polytheistic religious practices centered on mythical gods and demi-gods who could not measure up to the philosopher's grasp of a monotheistic intelligent ultimate source of all created reality. It is only when this very ultimate divine reality personally reveals its own divinity to mankind in the Old Testament that He is humanly regarded as a Personal reality personally engaging the human person superhumanly and preternaturally. In view of this divine Self-revelation the human person becomes enabled to religiously adore, sacrificially worship, honor, obey, thank, and praise God who makes Himself superhumanly accessible to such religious worship.

This supernatural Self-manifestation of God as the Beingness of the entire universe of reality unfolds historically in the history of mankind's Biblical redemption, sanctification, and glorification. Initially, this monotheistic God is revealed to Abraham, Isaac, and Jacob as the God of Abraham, Isaac, and Jacob and the tribal families of these three patriarchs known as the chosen people of God. Additionally, this God is revealed to Moses by a divine and personal name which reveals that God is not merely a Supreme Being as the philosopher grasps intellectually, but the very Beingness of all beings, the "I Am who Am," Jehovah, the solitary God above and beyond all gods, the Beingness of all of reality and of all beings within reality that is eventually recognized and addressed as Lord. In this Self-revelation to Moses, God can no longer tolerate polytheistic religious practices. There is only one religious sacrificial practice which is suitable to this solitary, supreme, personal divine Authority. This religious program is spelled out to Moses and transmitted to the chosen Jewish people.

God is initially revealed as a Father who has providential care of his chosen people. God is further Self-revealed in the New Testament as not being merely with, for, and over His chosen people, but actually instantiated in mankind itself in the Person of Jesus Christ, God/Superman. Here, God is no longer merely the God of a chosen people but the God for all of mankind and at the service of mankind to liberate mankind from his own bondage to all that is not worthy of his innate dignity as created in the image and likeness of God. This

Self-revelation reaches its climax at Pentecost in the founding of Christ's mystical body, the sacramental Church, at which time the third Person of God, the Holy Spirit, enters within the innermost intimacy of mankind to abide and dwell in each individual human being superhumanly, superhumanistically, and superhumanely. Indeed, God is now so manifestly evident that the individual who refuses to religiously acknowledge Him condemns himself to be an enemy and an outcast that is bereft of God's own Godliness.

Chapter 2: The three stages of the mystic's purgative night of being weaned away from his own selfish subjective religious cravings.

St. John compares the mystic's own subjective personalized religious excruciating experience of his progressive prayerful loss of God's comforting presence as occurring within the three main segments of night-time. First there is the twilight phase when the lingering daylight of his religious feelings is still discernible. Then there is the peak of midnight when there is not the least glimmer of daylight either in the overhead sky or on the earth's horizon. Accordingly, there is no longer the least trace remaining of any lingering bodily religious sensitivity and feeling for God. Additionally, the mystic's mental intimacy and religious quietude and solace regarding God have also vanished from his prayer-life. Thirdly there is the dawning when the approaching daylight is ever so slightly discernible on the earth's horizon. In this dawning there returns to the mystic some ever so slight palpable intermittent bodily exalted religious sensitivity and some sedating mental intimation of God's divine presence.

It is ever so much the case that these three phases do not succeed each other with the same regularity that occurs in the natural course of a day's 24 hour span. The mystic who is subjectively locked within his own egocentric willful selfhood suffering through each of these successive night-time stages of God's retreat from his experiential consciousness, has no self-assured conviction that anyone of these stages will ever be succeeded and give way ultimately to a new spiritual dawning. Mystical time of the mystic's religious subjective prayerful experiences of God is not commensurate with the diurnal time

49

of the sun's solar orbiting. St. John's comparison is made from his own personalized mystical experience of these three phases of the increasingly severe and harrowing loss of God's symptomatic response to the mystic's prayerful attentiveness.

Twilight is the first initial phase which is identified with the mystic's loss of all sensuous emotional feelings of religious self-contented exultation and self-rejoicing. The second is identified with the mystic's subsequent loss of intimate self-assured sedate religious tranquility and imperturbable serenity. This is the peak phase of midnight which is the dark night of the "spirit" in which the mystic must rely exclusively and tenaciously on the theological gift of faith to prayerfully cling to God who presumably has completely vanished from his own experiential sensorium and cerebrum (i.e., bodily sensitivity and mental intimacy). The third phase, the dawning, arrives when the mystic begins to appreciate to the full the enormous spiritual and superhumanistic benefits he has and continues to acquire because of his loyal steadfast prayerful attentiveness to God through faith in spite of his total loss of religious zest and sensitized sublime gratification and/or religious serenity and mental religious justification. In other words, the mystic in this third phase of his mystical dawning comes to further illuminated awareness that his religious and prayerful attachment to God is an authentic love of God who existentially and sublimely transcends his own subjective personalized sensuous devotional excitable feelings and sedately serene devotional mental bearings (i.e., orientations).

The preliminary entry into the first stage in this mystical pilgrimage is known as the active phase in which the mystic himself willfully subjects himself to a rigorous program of ascetic self-denial deliberately forgoing for love of God all excessive devotional prayerful sensitized excitable self-indulging devout emotional feelings. This preliminary active stage gives way to its passive counterpart. This occurs when the mystic becomes aware that praying is no longer religiously and exultantly exciting and stimulating but very routine and humdrum. This is the case because the Holy Spirit withholds from the mystic all savor and religious enjoyment of praying in the awareness of His divine indwelling. In this phase known as the purgative and twilight phase, there is still an intermittent lingering of emotional savor accompanying prayer. But, for the most part, the former fervor and zest accompanying prayer are no longer available. It should be emphasized that the transition from one phase to the next is very difficult to discern

The other two stages are also known as the passive phase in which the mystic's own ascetic initiatives of penance and deliberate self-denial are no longer of any further avail in advancing the purification and mortification of his own selfishness and self-attachment to the religious enjoyment that prayer affords. At this stage the Holy Spirit actively intervenes more comprehensively in the mystic's prayer-life by withholding not only the sensuous subjective devotional experiential visceral feeling of God's providential presence (viz. the blackout of the senses) but also the mystic's experiential cerebral secure serenity (viz., the blackout of the spirit). The experiential loss to the mystic of all divine and sublime symptoms of God's response to his prayerful devotions is itself the crux of the mystic's bodily malaise and mental forlorn anguish. When he prays the psalm that declares that God revels, rejoices, and takes delight in His loved-ones, he himself finds neither self-assuring devotional ardor nor mental tranquility to corroborate this psalm. This devotional barrenness only intensifies his own awareness of his total subjective lack of exuberance toward God. This is the passive phase of the dark night of his experience of the total loss of God both in terms of his bodily feelings and in his mental bearing and loss of equipoise.

Chapter 3: Sacred scripture itself testifies to theological faith's primacy in the mystic's devotional union with god.

Here St. John as is his frequent wont reverts to Sacred Scripture to verify his overriding premise that the gift of supernatural faith is the proximate touchstone to achieving a perfect union with God. At the same time he points out that the normal path of the intellect's intelligible knowledge is derived from the senses. The intellect is inherently unable to gain any insight into any special color if by blindness the body's organic eyesight is prevented from first espying that specific color. If such a person born blind were told that a special flower is a colorful pink, he would be unable to intellectually contemplate the color, pink, in its very pinkishness. Of course, he could intellectually ponder that pink is a quality of the flower. But he would intellectually have no specific intelligibility of color-as-such as colorfulness since his body's eyesight is itself deprived through blindness of its natural vision of specific colors.

The same holds for the intellect itself which is blinded by the supernatural gift of faith. It cannot intellectually fathom or intelligibly contemplate in its own intelligibility Christ's divine Sonship with the Father's paternity. This special Gospel truth of God's Self-revelation is not visibly or tangibly discernible to any of the organic senses. St. John states that these divine Gospel truths regarding God and God's providential design toward creation are acquired through hearing. He does not further elaborate what "hearing" is but it is clear it is not simply a sensible discernment on the part of the ear. Rather, it is an intelligible discernment which leaves the intellect itself dumb and blind regarding the complete intelligibility of this divine Sonship since this full Gospel intelligibility not merely transcends the ear's sensibility but also the intellect's finite intelligibility.

God's Gospel Self-revelation is infinitely intelligible and, thereby, in its infinitude supernaturally transcends the intellect's own finite light of intelligibility as well as the sensibility proper to the organic senses. Accordingly, if God's Self-revelation were not made manifest supernaturally the human intellect would never have any wherewithal informative knowledge to contemplate these divine and sublime truths. Indeed, it is a Gospel aphorism that unless people first believe such Gospel hearings through the supernatural gift of faith they will not be able subsequently to intellectually seek to theologically fathom their intelligibility. Catholic Christian philosophy and dogmatic theology are based on this aphoristic premise that unless one first believe he will not accede to any intellectual understanding of Gospel revelation. Inherent in this premise is the beneficent and benevolent gift that supernatural faith bestows on a person's native intelligence. It endows this intelligence with intellectual amplitude that exceeds its own native prowess.

While supernatural faith's own divine ebullience actually dims the intellect's own natural finite light of intelligibility regarding divine supernaturally revealed realities, it compensates for this eclipse by infusing into the intellect's native intelligibility an infinite divine luminescence expanding its own intelligibility beyond the finite reach of its own finitude. This is not a contradiction. The human intellect is certainly not actually infinite in its native intelligibility. However, it is virtually infinite inasmuch as it can virtually (i.e., indefinitely) expand ad infinitum its comprehensive understanding. Supernatural faith is God's very own infinite luminescent glory graciously radiating and infinitely illuminating the mystic's spiritual intellectual soul. This divine luminosity simultaneously overshadows and blinds the human intellect's native light while supernaturally elevating its own soulful virtual intelligibility to an nth degree open to God's own actual infinitude. Of course, the human person cannot instantaneously actually assimilate God's own infinite divine intelligibility and Self-revelation. This cannot be done even through the span of eternity when the resurrected person beatifically beholds God in heaven. No creature, not even an angel, can actually intelligibly contemplate and totally intellectually infinitely fathom God's infinitude. This is possible to God's divine intelligence alone. Nonetheless, through the supernatural gift of faith the Catholic Christian can intelligibly and informatively contemplate the actual reality of the Gospel's divine sublimity which transcends in its totality both the reach of the sense's sensibility and that of the human intellect's own native intelligibility.

It is precisely this supernatural gift of theological faith which is the mystic's infallible and authoritative guide throughout his mystical pilgrimage to beatifically embrace God's very own Triune Godhead on the summit of Mount Carmel. Of course, this very same faithful guide plunges the mystic into the very abyss of darkness, a midnight darkness, precisely because it surpasses the mystic's exercise of his own native intelligence in all matters of divine Gospel revelation and the Church's sacramentality. Furthermore, this supernatural gift of faith is entirely transcendently intellectually beyond and independent of the mystic's own entirely subjective personalized religious devotional experiences regarding the Gospel's definitive dogmatic truthfulness. Hence, as the mystic's immutable anchor this faith, along with the soul's (i.e., supernatural) voluntary obedient adherence to the doctrinal formulations of this faith articulated by the Church's Magisterium, safeguards and guarantees that the mystic's entirely subjective personalized religious experiences have their origin in God's Triune Godhead transcendent to the subjectivity of the experiences themselves.

Chapter 4: The darkness of supernatural faith further elaborated.

Just as the bodily eye cannot naturally see its colorfully tangible objects without the benefit of the sun's light rays so also our own spiritual soul's native intellect cannot supernaturally exercise its supernaturally elevated intellectual sight into God's Self-revealed existence and divine nature without the effulgent radiance of God's very own infinitely luminous glory illuminating the soul's spiritual interiority. And, just as the body's organic eye cannot naturally gaze directly at the sun without becoming blind, neither can the human soul's spiritual inorganic intellect gaze supernaturally (through faith) directly at God's gracious divine radiance flooding the soul's interior without incurring its own intellectual blindness. It is in this manner that faith blinds the soul's own supernaturally elevated intellectual power when the Catholic Christian gazes directly on the Blessed Sacrament and when the mystic intellectually contemplate the articles of faith infallibly articulated by the Church's Magisterium.

From this it follows logically and inescapably, St. John insists, that all of our normal avenues of thinking, willing, sensing, feeling, imagining, conceiving and experiencing God's Gospel Self-revelation fall short of God's own triune divinity and incarnation of Jesus Christ into mankind's own flesh and blood. This being the case, it becomes incumbent on the mystic to deliberately divest himself of his usual and normal ways of exercising all of these activities when it comes to approaching God's Gospel and sacramental Self-revelation in terms commensurate with God's own sublime transcendent eminently spiritual supernatural divinity and miraculous activity. It matters not that the human intellect can philosophically by its own native intelligence grasp the very existence and divine attributes of God. Nor, does it matter that this same intelligence supernaturally elevated by faith's supernatural divine graciousness can even more eminently intelligibly and philosophically probe more acutely God's divine monotheistic nature and attributes, such theological knowledge remains more a finite human grasp of God's tremendous infinitude rather than an ample grasp of God's actual ineffable existential infinitude itself. The latter can only be intellectually grasped through the supernatural gift of faith which in this present life is blinding and only fully beatifying in the hereafter when the mystic following his physical death enters heaven.

Given the previous paragraph it is inescapable that the mystic's pilgrimage to a perfect union with God will be by a path which in no way is mapped out by human design and ingenuity. It will be by a path that is completely alien to a human person's own native intelligibility and subjective self-humanized and self-cultivated experiences. The mystic will have to learn to distrust all of his own natural inclinations, insights, feelings, instincts, intuitions, and self-centered gratifications and vindications in approaching God in terms that are appropriate God's own transcendental reality. This mystical pilgrimage will demand that he be guided by an authoritative guide who commands that he comport himself in a manner which is completely alien to his normal patterns of behavior and instinctive inclinations.

Furthermore, the mystic must be prepared to willingly and deliberately forego all of his usual ways of doing things and become prepared to follow a Gospel way which is counter-culturally completely out of sync with the world's secular rhythm. Furthermore, the mystic must become courageously and steadfastly prepared to even discount and disregard as nothing (nada) even the most divine refined theological knowledge or devotional experiences that he acquires of God inasmuch as God's own Triune Godhead exists infinitely and ineffably beyond all such encounters. So uncompromisingly rigorous is this stark nakedness and ascetic denudation counseled by St. John that he cites Sacred Scripture where Christ declares that He has come into the world to enable the blind to see supernaturally and those that see only naturally to become themselves blind regarding supernatural knowledge of divine things.

Chapter 5: Supernatural union with God engages three distinct faculties.

St. John indicates that the mystical union with God which is the culmination of the mystic's pilgrimage to the summit of Mount Carmel engages three distinctive faculties, the intellect, the memory, and the will. He does not intend to immediately expound each of these three faculties. He will do so later in this treatise. For the present he seeks to explain what this mystical union is and entails. To this point he differentiates This program ofbetween the natural union which bonds the creature to God, the Creator, and the mystical union which is the supernatural Trinitarian sacramental presence of God in the soul. This natural union is God's creativity in which every created reality comes into existence and is existentially sustained by God's omnipotence. The supernatural union begins with God's supernatural sacramental presence in the soul and culminates when the mystic's own will is in complete conformity with God-the-Father's Holy Will. Attaining to this conformity demands that the mystic forcibly strips himself of everything which is repugnant to God's Holy Will. This regime of self-abnegation must attend not only to the superficial but, moreso, to the radical impediments that prevent the mystic's own will from being in perfect union with God's Holy Will.

This program of self-abnegation is a transformative process of self-detachment from all that is not Godly. The principal agency of this transformative process is God Himself (i.e., the Holy Spirit). However, the mystic must take into account that he can cooperate with this transformative process by properly disposing himself through self-abnegation to become submissive to God's Holy Will. This pre-disposal demands that he strip himself of his inclination to be attached to creaturely enjoyments and to relying on his own resourcefulness in his pilgrimage to ascend to Mount Carmel's summit. For, the mystic must take to heart the words of Sacred Scripture which declares that only the one who is reborn through sacramental baptism as a new creature and child of God can aspire to such a perfect union. Flesh and blood avail the mystic nothing in his advancement to this union. The more the mystic through actual and habitual self-attachments depends and relies on his own native abilities, talents, and self-cultivated assets, the less is he disposed to become totally attached to the service of God-the-Father's Holy Will rather than his own. God-the-Holy Spirit cannot efficaciously and unctuously transform the mystic's own will while the mystic himself persists in resisting God-the-Father's own infinitely benevolent graciousness made manifest in the gift of His only begotten Son, Jesus Christ, who laid down His life especially for the mystic's redemption, sanctification, and glorification.

The moral of this rigorous program of ascetic self-detachment is summed up in one word, NADA, which means that the mystic who seeks to be totally attached to God's Holy Will must not be self-attached to anything that is not Godly. For, every such self-attachment constitutes an obstacle and impediment to becoming utterly attached to God Himself. On the other hand, were it not the case that God Himself supernaturally and sacramentally makes possible the mystic's complete supernatural transformative submission of his own willfulness to the Father's Holy Will through Christ's sacrificial redemptive mediation under the power of their Holy Spirit, the mystic's own self-imposed life-style of radical self-abnegation relying only on his own willful self-determination would result in his becoming more alienated from God's supernatural graciousness rather than more perfectly conformed. The key to appreciating and embracing this abstemious kenotic ascetic life-style advocated in this Sanjuanistic treatise is the pivotal role that the Beatitudes play in the life of Christ's disciples. The Beatitudes extol the Gospel wisdom that it is only in total humility that the mystic can advance to God by paradoxically retreating from his own self-reliant self-centered and self-serving resourcefulness. What is of paramount importance to the mystic is to recognize that it is not what he can do for God that really matters; rather, it is what God both can and wills to do for the mystic that really counts and is all-important. This Sanjuanistic ascetic program of total self-denial emulating Christ's own crucified immolation is based on the Gospel insight that the only overriding obstacle to attaining to a perfect union with God's Holy Will through contemplative prayer is the mystic's very own selfish self-centered self-serving willfulness.

Here St. John supplies a most ingenious and revealing example to illustrate how this selfish self-centered willfulness on the part of the mystic impedes God's Holy Will from perfectly transforming the mystic's will into God's own. Just as a window pane allows the sunlight to pass through it perfectly the more it is itself spotless, so also does God's Holy Will's own gracious effulgent benignity shine perfectly through the mystic's own will the more the mystic's own will is itself fully self-dispossessed. However, if there is the slightest smudge on the window pane it will impede the sunlight's radiance from entering the room in its full plenitude of lumination. Similarly, the slightest willful selfish self-attachment on the part of the mystic is sufficient to impede God's infinitely gracious benignity from radiating in the mystic's own willfulness. St. John also notes that the pane of glass is not itself radiance; it is the sun's light that is radiant. Yet, by participation the pane partakes of the sun's radiance by allowing this light to be suffused through its vitreous transparency. Cleaning the pane of glass does not make the sun more radiant, it merely makes possible the perfect suffusion of this radiance through the window pane. The same is the case for the mystic who ascetically and willfully dispossesses himself of his own willful self-serving selfish self-interests which offer resistance to the Holy Spirit's persistency.

The mystical life is summarily the abstemious ascetic life-style of radical self-denial in which the mystic is willfully engaged in becoming detached from everything which is an impediment to serving God's Holy will above and beyond seeking his own self-serving selfish egocentric willfulness. The degree of the mystic's attachment to the Father's Holy Will is measured by the degree of the mystic's willingness to suffer his own humiliation in the service of God. Christ's promise of peace and sublime devotional exultation are impossible to one who lack's purity of heart and a have-not denunciation of mind. The total authentic supernatural self-fulfillment which is Christ's promise to the mystic of eternal beatitude in the bosom of God's Triune Godhead is unattainable without the mystic's advancement to a culminating stage of total sacrificial self-abnegation.

Chapter 6: The theological virtues of faith, hope, and charity efficaciously and supernaturally effectuate the mystic's total self-transformative abnegation within his three faculties of intellect, memory, and will.

The three theological virtues of faith, hope, and charity respectively serve to transformatively empty and eviscerate each of these three faculties, the intellect, memory, and will, of their own native activity and eminence. The intellect's innate understanding enlightened supernaturally by faith finds itself plunged into intellectual nebulosity. The memory's mnemonic memoriality imbued supernaturally with hope becomes blunted with a chronic amnesia. The will's volitional self-indulgent satisfaction and justification supernaturally infused with charity becomes completely bereft of all selfishly self-serving self-contentment. Of course, all of this is very paradoxical. It would seem that these three theological virtues would serve to supernaturally wed the mystic to God in a perfect wedding of consummate divine bliss. Yet, St. John declares that they effectively and efficaciously succeed in thwarting the mystic's intellect, memory, and will of the normal operation proper to each. Not only is this evisceration required to advancing the mystic's pilgrimage toward God, it would seem that this interference with these three faculties would be the very reverse of what the mystic would normally expect from the supernaturally transformative efficacy of these theological virtues.

St. John will explain later more in detail why and how these three theological virtues have such a detrimental effect on the normal operation of these three faculties. What is important for the moment is that the reader must grasp that the mystical life in its supernatural transformation involves not only the mystic himself actively embracing the Gospel life-style of self-abnegation, he must expect that passively he must also undergo a rigorous supernatural humiliating chastisement administered by God Himself through God's own supernatural and sacramental embrace of the mystic in these three theological virtues. In other words, there are two completely distinct phases in the first major purgative stage of the mystical life. The first phase is known as the active one and the second as the passive one. Why? Because in the active phase it is the mystic himself who skillfully deprives himself of his own creature comforts while in the second phase it is the Holy Spirit who takes full charge of this purgation by depriving the mystic of all supernatural devotional understanding, mindfulness, feelings and bearings regarding God's own Godliness. In other words, God's ways are not mankind's normal ways of thinking, willing, and acting.

Chapter 7: The mystical journey to God is traveled on a very narrow road.

Here St. John presents in more explicit terms the Gospel declaration that the gate to heaven is very narrow. It entails a "supreme nakedness and emptiness of spirit" such that it is "only God that ought to be sought and gained." Here Christ's invitation to His disciple cannot be taken other than in its most strict and literal understanding. This invitation urges the disciple to take up his cross and to deny himself with the same resignation and total self-abnegation made manifest by Christ Himself in His own passion and crucifixion. The Gospel of Christian discipleship puts forward a radical paradox which is the very nucleus of the mystical life: unless one sacrificially surrenders his life he cannot hope to have it saved. This is the same paradox inherent in the Christian's Gospel life-style advocated by Christ when he enunciated the New Testament's renewed covenant of God with man. St. John of the Cross pulls no punches in his interpretation of the path of self-deprivation and self-abnegation that the mystic must embrace in his pursuit of a perfect union with God in God's Triune Godhead. He points out that to many of those who set out on this path have a "sweet tooth" and draw back when they are faced with the harrowing prospect of being denied any further devotional consolation and quietude in their mystical journey. The proper be-attitudinal mindset suitable to the mystic is to prefer pious aridity over pious consolation and to prefer self-deprecation over self-exultation. Otherwise the mystic will find himself actually prayerfully seeking himself in God rather than seeking God beyond his own selfish self-centered needs and demands.

St. John insists that no one can exaggerate the demanding degree of self-denudation and self-deprivation which the mystical life of the

Christian exacts on the disciple of Christ seeking to become mystically one with Christ. Furthermore, St. John further emphasizes, no one can fathom the severity and the degree of self-deprecation this ascetic life-style imposes on the mystic's egocentric self-esteem and self-importance. Indeed! It is unfathomable precisely because the very depth of a person's most inner intimate willful selfhood is itself a sheer abyss of nothingness itself deprived of the absolute everythingness which God is in the Godhead of His transcendent eternal immutable existence beyond the self's historical evanescing transiency. St. John explicitates that the mystical Gospel life entails an abstemious sacrificial self-denial and self-denudation in both the matter of devotional religious sensitive excitement as well as cerebral devotional intimate serenity. For, the mystic who strives to "save" and "salvage" and cling to these selfishly self-serving religious experiences will lose out in his pilgrimage for a perfect union with Christ. On the other hand, the mystic who willfully accepts being stripped of all prayerful devotional comfort and consolation will arrive at the "lightness" and "sweetness" of the mystical life's yoke of self-immolation and self-oblation.

St. John sums up the mystic's ascetic life-style as not one of technical skill but of one immersed in Christ's very own Gospel life-style. No student is greater than his master. Christ Himself is the consummate Master of man's wedding with God and God's wedding with man. The mystical consummation of this nuptial union with God cannot be brought about other than by, with, and through Christ Himself and His Holy Spirit alive in the mystic's own spirituality. There is no other path, procedure, or technique. Christ is the way, the truth, and the life of the mystic's ascetic pilgrimage to the summit of Mount Carmel. By His passion and death Christ suffered every possible humiliation conceivable to mankind. First, He suffered his own physical self-deprivation in his physical death. Further, He suffered His own sensitized body's excruciatingly painful death as He was scourged, crowned with thorns, and nailed to the cross. Furthermore, He suffered in His own mental intimacy an even more excruciatingly dehumanizing deprivation with the rejection by the Jews of Himself and His Gospel message. For, they were providentially prepared to recognize and to embrace Him and His Gospel Message through the Old

Testament. Finally, He suffered within His innermost intimate mental inwardness the agonizing experience within His own Self-humanized Selfhood of being without any divine solace from His Heavenly Father's benign graciousness. The Christian mystic disciple of Christ should expect no less suffering self-oblation in his own mystical journey to "put on" the heart and mind of Christ. St. John sums this up with the following sentence: "The journey, then, does not consist in recreations, experiences, and spiritual feelings, but enduring within one's sensory and spiritual constitution, exteriority and interiority, the death of the cross."

The mystical "ascent to Mount Carmel" is simply a prolonged and sustained regimen of self-denial and self-surrender in accepting the humiliating uprooting and extirpation of the mystic's own selfish self-serving willfulness. In other words, it is nothing other than the virtual death of the mystic's own selfish self-love and self-esteem. Either God's august, immutable, eternal, and infinite transcendent benevolence is the measure of mankind's ultimate excellence or mankind's finite, mutable, mortal, and historical anthropocentric self-esteem is the penultimate measure of God's Godliness and excellence. Unless the mystic suffers the death of his own selfish self-love and self-esteem he can never entertain nor esteem a love that is selflessly as lovely as Christ's own infinitely merciful friendly divine loveliness made manifest in His Paschal Mystery. The Catholic Christian mystic's Gospel life-style is to live and to experience within the subjectivity his own personalized selfhood the self-oblation of Christ's death and resurrection. The prayerful path is that of contemplation steeped in and anchored in the theological gift of faith. Indeed! The mystic cannot even skillfully enter into the experience of contemplative prayer until and unless he has already willfully accepted to suffer a complete loss of his previously stimulating and motivating emotional bodily prayerful feelings of loving and being loved by God. With the complete loss of this sensitized prayerful approach to Christ, the mystic is now reduced to prayerfully trusting exclusively on his belief of what Christ proclaims in His Gospel which, in turn, is sacramentally established in Christ's Mystical Body, the Church.

Chapter 8: Self-attachment to the intellectual is itself an impediment to advancing to perfect mystical union with God.

It is the overriding premises of Sanjuanistic mystagogical theology that faith is the proximate key to mystical union with God. Faith is a theological gift residing in the soul's intellectual power of intelligence and understanding. Yet, the intellect's own native intelligence and understanding is itself in its own normal and natural exercise an impediment to the mystic's total reliance on faith alone to guide him on his mystical pilgrimage to God. On the face of it this seems to be both an endorsement of the place of the importance of the soul's intelligence in the mystic's life together with a complete denunciation of its efficacy in perfectly embracing God mystically (i.e., piously and devoutly). To fully appreciate this seemingly enigmatic declaration on the part of St. John it is necessary to briefly expound the centuries-old traditional Scholastic Aristotelian metaphysical understanding of the causality inherent in the cognitive activity proper to the body's organic senses and the human soul's inorganic faculty of intelligence. Once the reader gains an insight into this cognitive causality he will acquire a greater admiration for the depth, the rigor, and the clarity of our Holy Carmelite Father's mystagogical theology.

The following metaphysical account of knowledge in terms of its causality is strictly objectively intellectual. In other words, it is not subjectively experiential as is the case with the experimental physical, psychological, and social sciences which are either empirically verifiable or, otherwise, mentally, historically, and/or economically demonstrable. The significant difference between the metaphysical approach and the experimental approach is that the former is holistic while the latter is piecemeal. This is not a minor difference. In a holistic metaphysical approach the subject in its integral wholeness is taken into essential account. In a piecemeal experimental approach only a non-essential fraction of the subject in isolation from the whole is taken into account. Thus, the metaphysical approach is that of the generalist while the experimental approach is that of the specialist. In a metaphysical study of the eye, for example, both the human and the brute bodily eye are organically identical in their sightly vision. In the experimental study of the eye, this is not the case. The peculiarities of the fish's physiological eyesight and vision differ from that of the eagle. Thus, the metaphysician speaks of both human and brutes as being animals (i.e., sentient beings) whereas the specialist discovers that the peculiarities of the senses of each differ considerably in their animal makeup.

Another way of attending to the radical difference between the metaphysical approach and that of the experimental sciences is to consider the subject of water. To the metaphysician the substance of water remains substantially the same whether it be an ocean of water or a drop of water; whether it be an iceberg of water or a cloud of water. In every instance the very substantive reality of water remains intact. Realistically it can be stated that water remains substantially its very same nature whether it is vast as the ocean or as tiny as a drop and whether it is liquid, solid, or vapor. This is the generalist approach to knowing water. The experimentalist (i.e., experiential) and mathematical approach is to reduce water to its fragmentary components such that each component is no longer itself substantially water. Such is the case with water explained in a mathematical ratio as two parts hydrogen and one part oxygen. It is only the mathematical combination of the two as a valence (i.e., equivalence) which constitutes water, not as a substance, but as its symptomatic make-up. In the metaphysical approach there is an ontological holistic whole that remains intact in every instance whereas in the experimental (i.e., experiential) approach there is only a phenomenological whole that appears to be a "whole" but is only a piecemeal or quasi-whole but not a real unequivocal whole. That is, it is a whole of equivocation; not a univocal whole. In brief, it is inherently unintelligible as a stable entity; it is a fabricated enterprise that appears to be an integral reality but in actuality is not so.

Attending, now, to the metaphysical examination of the activity of knowledge and knowing, it is important to explain what causally constitutes the activity of knowledge beginning with the knowledge proper to the sentient body's eye-sight. When this is adequately explained, it will become more intelligible to the reader to appreciate the full impact of St. John's premise that faith and theological faith alone is the adequate proximate touchstone to the mystic's perfect nuptial union with God in God's very own Trinitarian Godhead. Mystical theology deals with God's supernatural Self-revelation (i.e., epiphany and theophany) and the mystic's personal objective and personalized subjective encounter with God. Accordingly, the mystic must cognitively engage God on God's own supernatural and super-human terms as well as his within his own subjective personalized experiential humanistic terms. Both of these are required in order for the mystic to ultimately become wed and joined with God not only on God's own supernatural unlimited divine transcendent holistic metaphysical theocentric terms but also on the mystic's own limited anthropomorphic and anthropocentric experiential humanistic terms.

Cognition involves different causes. The cognitive faculty itself is an agency of cognition, an entirely passive agent because knowledge is not produced by the cognitive faculty that actually knows and learns something. Through knowing and knowledge the cognitive faculty is assimilated to the known object which exists independently and prior to the faculty's knowledge of it. Hence, the known object must actually informatively impact on the cognitive faculty and impart to this faculty a formative image of its own formative nature. In the case of the body's organic eyesight, this informative impact is that of a physical body's color. In the case of the ear this informative impact is that of a physical body's sound. This informative impact differs with each different organic cognitive sense. In addition to this informative causality and the cognitive faculty's passive agency there is still another active agency which explains how the apple's red color can informatively impact on the organic eye's cognitive faculty of seeing. This active agency in the case of the body's eyesight is sunlight; in the case of the ear it is the earth's atmosphere. Each separate sense has its own special medium of informative cognition.

Hence, the formal informative object of the body's cognitive eyesight is color and its proper medium of seeing is the sun's light. Now, the sun's light itself is entirely colorless; indeed, it is itself translucently invisible to the body's eyesight. It is a medium of and for the eye's seeing colorful physical bodies; it is a medium of making these colorful bodies visible to the eye. Sunlight itself is both invisible and colorless. The body's organic sight itself does not see color-as-such. Rather, it sees only specific shades of color proper to the physical bodies which are formally one or more different specific shades similarly with the ear in regards to the sounds that it detects. It does not hear the atmosphere; this atmosphere is soundless. It is the medium of hearing sounds but is itself soundless.

The human soul's cognitive faculty of intellection can also cognize and know the same colorful physical body which the sentient body's organic eyesight sees. However, the intellect "sees" intellectually and not merely optically. It "sees" this same colorful physical body intelligibly and not merely sentiently and sensibly. That is, it "sees" red-as-such intelligibly over and above the eyesight's vision of the special shade of color existing in a flower's body. Seeing intelligently red-as-such over and above the specific shade of color visible to the body's organic eyesight, the soul's intellect can intellectually differentiate between a specific color, such as the specific shade of red, and the general reality of color-as-such which is the categorical genus for every specifically different and diverse shade of color. Hence, the intellect enjoys a cognitive insight into the very essence of the physical body's red color (viz., the rose flower's red shade) over and above the sentient body's cognitive eyesight of seeing simply and only the special diverse shades of color. There is a remarkable difference between sentient cognition and intellectual cognition. One is organic and the other inorganic. Why?

Because the former's sentient knowledge (i.e., the eye's visual seeing colorful flower) is accompanied by the spatio-temporality of the flower's materiality whereas the latter's intelligible knowledge is not. The eyesight's vision of the flower is always seen as a small or large red color, a shaped immobilized or mobile red color, a smooth or rough red color, etc.. On the other hand, the intellect is able to intelligibly "see" the very as-such (i.e., essence) of red-as-such apart from its physical spatio-temporal specificity. That is, the intellect can intellectually "see" insightfully red-as-such and color-as-such apart from and in contradistinction to the special shape, configuration, number, size, distance, hue, texture, etc. of the actual red shade proper to the colorful flower.

Indeed, there is a radical significant difference between sentient and intelligent knowing. Sentient knowing is limited and restricted to the physical body's informative spatio-temporal materiality whereas intelligent knowing cognizes informatively the physical body immaterially apart from its actually existing spatio-temporal materiality. The intellect can "see" and recognize color-as-such, red-as-such, shape-as-such, size-as-such, sound-as-such, stationary-as-such, solid-as-such, fluid-as-such, etc., apart from the special material (i.e., spatio-temporal) conditions of a particular physical body. In other words, the intellect can cognitively "see" and recognize a family of special colors as belonging to color-as-such, a family of shapes as belonging to shape-as-such, etc.. The intellect can "see" insightfully what is essentially intelligibly common to each of these special informative sensibilities of all of the senses which cognitively see, hear, taste, touch, and smell the physical cosmos. Again, while each special sense is limited to being cognitively informed by its own formal object (viz., color, sound, odor, flavor, temperature, texture, etc.), the intellect can intelligibly know what is the common family essence as-such of all the special senses, the sensible-as-such apart from the spatio-temporal conditioning of each's own special informative object of sensible cognition.

The intellect's intelligible knowledge can be explained by attending to the causes of its intelligibility. The soul's faculty of intellect is itself merely a passive agency. The act of knowing and the knowledge acquired by the intellect is not the product of its own agency. It can only assimilate knowledge; it cannot productively create its own knowledge. It must be informatively activated by knowable objects independent of and transcendent to its own passive cognitivity. It is obvious from the preceding paragraphs that the intellect would never intelligibly cognize the special color of red if the body's sentient eyesight had not antecedently seen some special shade of red in a physical body. Yet, where the eye sees only a specific shade of red proper to the physical body (viz., the rose petal) which is actually red, the intellect discerns intelligibly red-as-such over and above the specific shade of red sentiently seen by the body's eyesight. That is, the intellect has an intelligible insight into the very family communality of every specifically different and diverse red shade. The intellect recognizes the reality of the family of red colors above and beyond the physical object's limited material spatio-temporal existence (viz., in the rose flower's red petal) perceived by the body's eyesight. The intellect can intelligibly recognize red-as-such independent of the actually existing red rose flower petal and independent of this petal's spatio-temporal physiological dimensionality. This means that the intellect's very own formal informative object of knowing is not that of the informative sensibility of any of each of the special senses but rather that of the as-such informative intelligibility of the sensibility common to all of senses.

This intelligibility which is shorn of all the concrete tangible spatio-temporal properties peculiar to a physical body's materiality can only be explained by an active informative agency which acts metaphysically to impregnate the faculty of the intellect with an as-such intelligible species of what the special senses informatively image in their sensible image of sensing physical bodies. Where the sun's physical light is the active informative medium enabling the body's eyesight's "to visibly see" colorful physical bodies, there is a separate intellectual metaphysical light serving as the active informative medium for the intellect's own insight to "invisibly see" red-as-such metaphysically apart from the physical body's spatio-termporal red dimensionality and materiality. The informative media for each of the special senses is a physical medium. The sun's light renders the rose flower's red petals to become visibly red. For even in the darkness of night the petals remain actually physically red but are not sentiently visible to the body's eyesight. Similarly, the human spiritual soul's own metaphysical light renders the visible red sentiently imaged by the body's eyesight to become intelligibly invisible within the intellect's own intellectual insight.

The rose flower's petal is physically red and sentiently seen to be such by the body's eyesight. The eye's informed sentient seeing of this red petal entails that a cognitive image of red be present in the eye commensurate with the physical red in the rose petal. However, this cognitive image must itself be commensurate with the eye's cognitive sentiency. For, the eye's organicity itself does not become physically red when it becomes informatively cognizant of seeing the rose's red petals. Furthermore, the flower's physical body cannot be simultaneously red and green on exactly the same surface area while the eye's sentiency can simultaneously "see" multiple different colors in one and the same act of seeing. Hence, the eye's sentient images of various colors serve as informative "see-through" images just as light itself is entirely a translucent "see-through" medium for the eye's informative seeing the visibility of a flower's physical colors. There can be no informative sensing if there is no "see-through" informative image of seeing available to the body's eyesight made informatively colorfully visible by the sun's light. The body's eyesight actually sees the rose's red petals but only through an informative medium (viz., the sentient images of specific colors) which are for the eye "see-through" informative images.

The intellect has its own metaphysical informative medium of knowing. This informative medium is both the active agency of intelligible light (viz., the human soul's own spiritual translucency) and the informative species (i.e., ideas) through which the intellect recognizes reality transcendent to and independent of its own faculty of knowing. This informative medium is one of intelligibility precisely because its object is entirely immaterial and metaphysical (i.e., not restricted to a physical body's spatio-temporal dimensional materiality). Whereas the rose flower's petals are physically and materially a special distinctive shade of red cognitively mediated by the eye's sentient image of red through which it sees these rose petals rendered visible under the sun's light, the intellect "sees" under the human soul's spiritual illumination the same red rose petals rendered intelligible through a metaphysical idea of red-as-such (which is a family communal generic reality of red). Accordingly, the intellect may intelligently and intelligibly discern that the red rose flower petal is colorfully red in the family of red colors as-such. This makes possible for the human eye to "perceive" that the rose flower's red petals are truly and essentially red because they are instances of the family of red-as-such colors. Such truthful "seeing" is not possible to the dumb brute animal's own eyesight because the brute animal's sentient soul is not fully spiritual and endowed with the human soul's intelligent spiritual insight of knowing the very substance and essence of things

Each special sense has its own special informative object of sensibility (i.e., color, sound, flavor, odor, texture, temperature, etc.) and its own active physical agent of informative mediation (viz., sunlight, atmosphere, water, vapor, solidity, climate, etc.). The same holds for the soul's faculty of intelligence, the intellect. It has its own object of intelligibility (viz., being-as-such) and its own active metaphysical agent of informative mediation (viz., the soul's own spiritual lucidity). Where the senses are unable to sense each's own informative object of sensibility apart from sensing the physical object itself (viz. the rose flower's red petal), the intellect is able to intelligently understand its own informative object of intelligibility (viz., being-as-such) apart from the intelligible object itself transcendent to its own intellectual knowledge. Thus, the intellect can understandably know that it knowingly understands whatever it actually does know through the intellectual metaphysical medium of intelligibility that is being-as-such. However, this understanding must be further clarified.

Just as the intellect understands red-as-such as the common generic essence of all the innumerable varieties of specific shades of red, it does not actually explicitly know all of these special shades instantaneously in understanding red-as-such. The idea of red-as-such is to the intellect the intelligible medium (i.e., know-through) of insight by which the intellect comprehends what is essentially generically common to every special shade of red. The same holds true for the intellect's own informative object of intelligibility, being-as-such. In knowing being-as-such (i.e., a know-through species) the intellect understands by an intellectual insight what is transcendentally and entitatively common to every existing reality (God included). In other words, the informative object of the senses is a special sensibility proper to each whereas the informative object of the intellect is its own intelligibility which can be formulated as being-as-such. In addition to understanding its own informative intelligibility, the intellect can comprehensively understand what is fundamentally and basically constitutive of every existing reality in the universe of existence, God included. Thus, in the case of the rose flower's red petal the intellect can understand that the rose plant is superficially red because red is a color-as-such and not a plant-as-such. The rose flower's being-as-such is more fundamentally a plant-as-such than a color-as-such.

In addition to its informative intelligible object of cognition, the intellect has a virtual overarching ideal informative object of intelligibility. This can be intellectually discerned by differentiating between a physical object such as the rose flower's colorful red petal, which is really physically red, and the metaphysical reality of red-as-such which is generically red but not actually any one special palpable physical shade of red, and, thirdly, the metaphysical reality of redness which is the ideal quintessence of the metaphysical red-as-such. The human intellect virtually (i.e. potentially) knows the ideal redness when it actually cognizes red-as-such. Redness is the ideal plenitudinous fullness of red-as-such. It is not actually formally and specifically any special shade of red but it is potentially every special shade of red which ever existed, ever will exist, or ever could possibly exist. Redness exists in an ideal intangible and invisible metaphysical reach of reality transcendent to and independent of the real physical cosmos of tangible red bodies. Redness is simply, solitarily, indivisibly, and immutably red. Redness is virtually intelligible because it is the very plenitude of red-as-such.

However, redness as an ideal reality is not colorfully red as is the case with the rose flower's red petal. The latter is visibly, really, tangibly, actually and mutably red while the former is invisibly, ideally, intangibly, potentially, and immutably red. Redness ideally encompasses comprehensively, immutably, and everlastingly the universe of red colors; it is universally the color, red. The rose flower's petal is specifically a specific shade of red and may cease to be red with the death of the rose plant. But the universal, redness, never passes away and can never cease to be red. However, it should be noted that this ideal redness is itself a created reality because redness does not exist in virtue of itself albeit its own ideality. It does exist ideally but it is not the ideal existence. Only God is ideally existence itself and eminently the very Beingness of all that exists in the universe of reality.

To sum up the causality of "knowing" and "knowledge," there are three causes: the material, formal, and agent causes. The material cause is the physical body which is sentiently known by the animal senses. One and the same material physical body (viz., an object such as an apple) is separately seen, heard, touched, tasted, sniffed, etc. by each of the special senses. Each sense senses by dint of its own formally informative object of sensibility (viz., color, sound, solidity, flavor, odor, etc.). There is an active informative agent proper to each special sense (viz., light, atmosphere, texture, water, vapor, etc.) which serves to mediate between the passive knowing faculty and the material object that informatively impacts on the faculty and impregnates it with its own formality (i.e., a cognitive representative image). All of these causes are also present to explain the human soul's knowledge and intellectual knowing through the faculty of the intellect.

The intellect itself is the passive agent of knowing while its material object is the same material physical body (viz., an apple) known to the special senses. The intellect's own formally informative object is not one of sensibility but one of intelligibility (viz., color-as-such, sound-as-such, solidity-as-such, flavor-as-such, odor-as-such, etc.). There is an active informative agent proper to the intellect (viz., the soul's own entirely spiritual and immaterial metaphysical lucidity, aura, entity, solubility, vaporosity, etc.) which serves to mediate between itself as a passive knowing inorganic faculty and the material object that informatively impacts on it to impregnate it with its own formality (i.e., a cognitive representative idea).

There only remains the task of explaining the radical difference between the representative image in the senses and its counterpart, idea, in the intellect. The representative sensible image is the cognitive informative medium (viz., a know-through) through which the sense senses the material object (viz., the apple). This is a representational cognitive medium. Thus, it is not the medium itself which the special senses know---the sentient image medium is a "know-through" and not a "know-what" object---; rather they know the actually existing material object transcendent to and independent of the sense itself. However, they know it (i.e., sense it) through the sentient image inhering in the sentient faculty itself. This sentient image re-p-resentationally includes all of the tangible spatio-temporal aspects peculiar to a physical body's material physicality such as its size, shape, weight, im/mutability, number, etc..

The intellect's own representative intelligible idea is the informative cognitive medium through which it cognizes the material object (viz., the apple). However, the idea in its intelligible representationality does not include in itself the tangible spatio-temporal aspects of the physical body's material physicality. The intellect is itself entirely metaphysically spiritual and immaterial and its own representational idea of the material physical object must itself be entirely shorn of all the spatio-temporal materiality proper to the physical object's tangibility. The physical body (viz., the apple) cannot cause a metaphysical (i.e., spiritual idea) in the intellect. What does effectuate and cause this intelligible informative representational idea of the physical body to impact on the intellect is the human soul's own agency of its inherent spiritual metaphysical lucidity, aura, entity, etc., serving as a cognitive medium between the two. Thus, while, for example, the sun's physical light illuminatively makes the red apple to be visibly sensibly red and optically seeable (i.e., representationally seeable via a sentient cognitive image) to the body's eyesight, the human soul's metaphysical lucidity illuminatively makes the red apple to be invisibly intelligibly red-as-such and intellectually seeable (i.e., representationally knowable via an intellectual cognitive idea).

The intellect above and beyond the senses can intellectually, insightfully, and intelligibly apprehend and know the very essence and quiddity (i.e., as-such) of all that exists within the physical cosmos. And even beyond this the intellect can cognize intellectually and metaphysically (i.e., spiritually and immaterially) what is ideally the very quintessential formality of all that exists within the physical cosmos. In the final analysis the human intellect has intellectual and intelligible access to the ideal reach of reality transcendent to the physical cosmos. This ideal metaphysical reach is the very universe of reality which is the solitary, immutable, imperishable, intangible, everlasting, quintessential formative causality of all that exists in the physical cosmos. It is itself a created reality as is the case with the physical cosmos. Yet, it is an empyreal angelic heaven by comparison with the cosmic stellar heavens that exist beyond the sphere of the planet earth located within the solar system.

In brief, the human intellect as a faculty of knowing unlike the senses can cognitively know the essence and substance of all that exists within the physical cosmos and beyond this cosmic reality all that exists transcendently within the metaphysical reach of the ideal angelic realm of reality. For, again, it can know not merely the physical color of the red apple sensibly, spatio-temporally, and physically but also metaphysically in its very essential formative intelligibility of red-as-such and even beyond this in its ideal quintessential supernal formative intelligibility of redness and colorfulness. While the intellect's knowledge has its inception in sensory knowledge it does not have its completion and perfection in such knowledge since in its own innate metaphysical spiritual intelligibility it transcends all of the limitations and cognitive physical, tangible, spatio-temporal restrictions peculiar to the senses. The intellect's own adequate formative object of intelligibility is being-as-such and through this representational informative medium of intelligibility the human soulful intellect has intelligible access even to God's own actual uncreated existence as the very ideal Beingness beyond and independent of all created beings. This intelligible access to God is natural to the human soul's own dynamic metaphysical spiritual cogent agency of informative intelligibility.

Yet this natural metaphysically theological knowledge of God remains very general, abstract, and inchoate. For example, if one were to visit a cemetery and find a tombstone which through the ravages of time is no longer legible one could intelligibly understand that a human body is buried below ground. Such knowledge is informative but only in a very abstract, vague, and obtuse manner. One does not know the deceased human person personally in the deceased person's personhood. Such is the case with the human intellect's natural metaphysical intelligibility of its theological grasp of God. Yet, in spite of the abstract generality, obtuse, and vague characteristic of this theological knowledge naturally and philosophically available to the human intellect, it is still a very valuable and trustworthy knowledge of God enabling the human person to differentiate what is supremely divine from what is inferiorly created and totally dependent on this Supreme Divinity.

God is precisely the one and only one universal supreme reality within the universe of reality. No creature's existence can be identified with God's divine eternal uncreated existence nor confused with it. But, it must be quickly emphasized, such knowledge of God and God's supreme divinity and attributes is not mediated by God's own intelligibility and infinite dynamic divine existence; it is formatively mediated by the human intellect's own informative adequate medium of intelligibility, being-as-such. God is intellectually recognized to be the very existential supreme incomparable Beingness of being-as-such. Such Beingness would be less than perfectly Beingness itself if it were not supremely intelligent, loving, knowing, simplicity itself, eternal, immutable, perfect, dynamic, solitary, etc..

The preceding metaphysical account of knowledge, knowing, and the faculty of knowing is summarily an account of the centuries-old traditional Scholastic philosophical and theological account of knowledge having its roots in the philosophy of Aristotle. It was refined and increasingly clarified through successive generations of academic scholars. St. John of the Cross would have been himself quite familiar with it since he attended notable Spanish institutions of higher education for his own intellectual formation preparing for the priesthood. Scholastic philosophy and theology were rife in such Spanish institutions. Such metaphysical knowledge is undoubtedly the underpinning of St. John's mystagogical theology in which he posits that supernatural faith is the anchor and lodestone of the mystical life. What does supernatural faith superimpose and add to the intellect's own natural metaphysical mode of theological cognitive intelligibility? It adds a supernal and supernatural informative medium of superintelligibility which is nothing less or other than God's own divine and supernatural light of glory radiating from His infinite divinity as the sun's light radiates from the sun's solarity to render the physical world to become visibly seeable to the eye's eyesight. This supernal informative medium is nothing less than God's own divine uncreated sublime light of glory graciously, gratuitously, and benignantly radiating supernaturally, miraculously, and sacramentally within the human soul's spiritual interiority.

Of course the very infinite ebullience of this divine supernatural sacramental radiance within the interiority of the human soul both overwhelms the soul's natural metaphysical informative cognitive medium of intelligibility while expansively enhancing its native intellectual insight to probe more intelligently into God's divine infinite intelligibility. For, this supernatural sacramental radiance does not representationally provide the human intellect merely with a sublime idea or theological ideas of God's actual supernal divine existence. It provides the human soul's intellect with the actual divine sublime existential presence of the uncreated supreme reality of God's Trinitarian Godhead. So ineffable and gloriously miraculously marvelous and stupendous is this gracious sacramental presence of God that the human person can only intelligently address it as a mystery (viz., a sacrament) in which God becomes supernaturally incarnated in the created nature of mankind's own creaturely nature in the Person of Jesus Christ: God/Superman. The human creature becomes a new superhuman creation. The human creature is miraculously and supernaturally enabled to intellectually directly contemplate God's supremely infinite divine effulgent glorious graciousness and Self-revealed Trinitarian Godhead.

But this is effectuated only through the theological gift of faith because the human intellect itself cannot of its own natural informative agency be the cognitive medium of knowing God through such an uncreated divine medium. And, thus it is that St. John insists that it is only through the supernatural theological gift of faith that the mystic can prayerfully commune and contemplate the very "face" of God that remains ineffably hidden beyond the mystic's human native intelligible comprehension. Indeed, the mystic's own innate finite mode of metaphysical intelligibility becomes itself an impediment to prayerfully contemplating directly and devoutly the infinite supernal graciousness of God's own Triune Godhead sacramentally Self-revealed to mankind in the Catholic Church's sacramentality. That is, it becomes an impediment if and when the Christian seeks to reduce this divine supernatural and miraculous presence to the measure of the human intellect's own finite intelligibility based on its formal object of knowing, being-as-such.

Why, then, is the mystic's attachment to his own intellectual theological knowledge an impediment to his transcendent attachment to God's own Triune Godhead made supernaturally, sacramentally, and miraculously present to the human soul's interiority in the infinite glorious merciful graciousness of His own infinite benignity? It is an impediment because even if the mystic explores intellectually and superintelligently through the light of divine faith a more supernatural theological understanding of God's divine infinite Self-revealed Godhead, such informative knowledge makes available to the mystic a more refined and theologically insightful definitive doctrinal knowledge regarding the deposit of faith of God's Self-revelation. Yet, none of these supernaturally theological informative dogmatic tenets can provide a more informative existential presence of God to the mystic than God's very own sacramental gracious divine and sublime supernatural glorious merciful Self-revealed Presentedness which enables the mystic to directly supernaturally embrace God through faith by simply lovingly gazing on God's own Trinitarian Godhead in contemplative prayer. This is the remarkable and stupendous discovery of the mystic that God in God's very own Trinitarian Godhead and Personhood is supernaturally existentially cognitively present to him within the interiority of his own spiritual soul sacramentally informed by the graciousness (i.e., supernatural grace) of God's own merciful divinity.

The significant difference between dogmatic and moral theology, on the one hand, and mystical theology, on the other, is that in the former God's infinite superintelligibility and august authoritative moral primacy of holiness are the subject of theological speculation whereas in the latter God's infinite merciful superadorable benignity becomes the object of theological veneration. Here there is a mutual complementarity. Divine supernatural dogmatic and moral knowledge of God precedes fundamentally the mystic's amicable supernatural love of God. Conversely, the mystic's amicable supernatural love of God's own infinite sublime amicability supplementally completes and brings to perfection the human person's fundamental supernatural dogmatic and moral theological understanding of God. The mystic cannot dispense with dogmatic and moral theology no more than can the dogmatist and moralist dispense with the mystic's devotional theology. The two supernatural approaches to God are mutually complementary when each precedes the other within its own proper fundamental/supplemental priority. One is a "love of divine wisdom" theologically and intellectually contemplating God's Self-revelation while the other is the very theological "wisdom of loving" willfully and prayerfully contemplating God's Self-revelation.

It must be pointed out that the "God" of the philosopher remains immeasurably and infinitely removed from his power to render Him religious adoration, sacrificial worship, praise, thanksgiving, petition, and honor. In fact, the philosopher cannot really know the very Personhood of God as such. To recognize that this "God" is the author of all of creation is a causal knowledge based on the contingency of creation itself's own intelligibility: "whatever issues into existence from non-existence cannot be the cause of its own existence." This necessitates the ineluctable conclusion that there must exist an immutable primary causation whose very existence is beyond causation. At this point in philosophical speculation it remains a moot point whether creation issues from such a beginning by necessity or by contingency. For, whether it be by one or the other the entire universe of creation remains infinitely distant and remote from such a Beginning. Further, it remains a moot point whether some segment of creation itself is eternally createdly coexistent with this Beginning or whether all of creation has come into existence in the succession of temporary stages. In other words, while such philosophical knowledge of "God" is a bona fide access to "God's" monotheistic existence and divinity, this infinitely remote "God" remains almost indifferently beyond mankind's freedom and loving reach of religious sacrificial commitment.

The monotheistic God of the Old Testament, on the other hand, is the God who from the very creation of mankind in the persons of Adam and Eve has revealed Himself as a providential companion to mankind. He is not only not infinitely remote, He is personally, religiously, and ingratiatingly present to the very subjective personalized affectionate bodily feelings (viz., heart) and intimate mental concerns (viz., mind) of Adam and Eve. When these two autoprogenitive humans fell from God's benevolent friendship, He promised to restore them and their descendents to His divine benignant graciousness. In the supernatural redemptive history of mankind this God revealed His very Personhood in successive stages of revelation as being a

Trinity of Persons. In the first stage He revealed Himself as a Father with a paternal interest and providential care for a select people with whom He makes a covenant in the person of Abraham. He subsequently reveals his very own name, Jehovah, "I AM WHO AM," which is somewhat synonymous with the philosopher's understanding of God as the Beginning of all reality. Yet, this is a personal identification of God to Moses that the God of Abraham, Isaac, and Jacob is both the author and providential Author of all creation but, moreover, the Ruler who institutes and commands a special moral and religious paternal bond between His people of predilection and Himself. To acknowledge this august sovereignty God is called Lord. This Self-revelation of the Old Testament culminates in an even more proximate and intimate epiphany when God further reveals His monotheistic deity not only to His people of predilection, the Hebrews, but also to the gentiles as incarnate in humanity in the very Person of Jesus Christ, Son of the Father. This Self-revelation reaches its climax in the further theophany recorded in the Acts of the Apostles when the Holy Spirit of the Father and the Son descends upon the Apostles at Pentecost, founders of Christ's sacramental Church, in the form of tongues of fire.

The Catholic Christian mystic is engaged with the God who is not merely the very remote impersonal Beginning of the philosopher but better known by supernatural faith as the God who as the transcendental sublime Beingness of all of reality is personally and providentially engaged with his own creature, the human person. At the same time, the mystic also engages this very same divinity personally and religiously because the mystic is supernaturally and superhumanly subsumed baptismally into the very divine infinite benevolent embrace of God's Triune Personhood. The mystic is simultaneously the adopted child of a Father who remains infinitely and paternally above and beyond his own creaturely existence; a brotherly companion to the Father's Son, who has become sacramentally infinitely below and at the service of the mystic's pilgrimage to the Father's heavenly abode; and an intimate companion to the Holy Spirit, the Father and Son's own amicable embrace actually abiding within the intimate innermost near-infinite vacuous vicissitudes of the mystic's heartfelt feelings and mindful concerns.

In brief, the Catholic Christian mystic is prayerfully in the family familiarity of the Trinitarian Personhood of God who is not merely the Beingness of all reality but inclusively its benevolent Author and providential Lord and Master. St. Paul is astounded at the immeasurable magnitude, grandeur, and amplitude of Jesus Christ encompassing the height, width, and depth of all of reality. It is in this sense that the mystic as a Catholic Christian is prayerfully enveloped in the familiarity of the infinitude of God's Triune Personhood to the extent that he is prayerfully infinitely beyond and above himself within the eternal immutable vault of the Father's paternal bosom; he is prayerfully infinitely below and beneath himself within the temporality of the Son's sacrificial filial humility; and, inclusively he is prayerfully self-enclosed within the innermost intimacy of the Holy Spirit's infinite benign affluent amorous sociability permeating the historicity of his own innermost inward selfish selfhood. Infinitude is the mark of this Triune prayerful familiarity. For, the mystic remains a mere mutable creature infinitely removed from the Father's eternal immutability even while he prayerfully experiences within the serenity and tranquility of his mindful recollection something of the Father's benignant immutable equanimity and utter simplicity. Simultaneously the mystic remains within the temporality of his own human sinfulness infinitely removed from the Son's sinlessness in the measure that he prayerfully experiences the grace and infinite mercy of Christ's unbounded forgiveness. Finally, within the innermost intimate vicissitudes (i.e., heart) of his own needful selfhood's infinitely needy willful feeling of deficiency regarding the Holy Spirit's infinite fulsome benevolent amorous graciousness, the mystic experiences a sublime selflessness within the historical horizon of his own selfishness; a divine infinite willful freedom to partake of unbounded love within the very abyss of the rebellious servitude to his own selfishness.

It is opportune to point out here even by way of simple declaration that the supernatural sacramental presence of God within the human soul's interiority also has something of a dumbing-down effect on the mystic's will and memory in addition to its miraculous dumbing-down impact on his intelligence as explained in the preceding paragraphs. This is not the place to expansively explain this dumbing-down effect on the memory and will. This will be broached later in this commentary. For the present, it is the intellect as the subject of faith which occupies our attention. The more the mystic relies on his own native intellectual intelligence to ponder and to puzzle out what is happening to him mystically in his devout pilgrimage to lovingly embrace God in a manner worthy of God's own divine magnanimity, the less the mystic will be able to efficaciously advance on his devotional pilgrimage. The reason for this is that God is not merely nor ultimately a God of intelligibility but a God of love which exceeds every attempt to confine or reduce this infinite love to some intelligible circumscription. The same holds for the memory and the will of the mystic. The more the mystic seeks to rely on his own memory's mnemonic historical memoriality and remembrance of God and his own divine experiences of God the more this very remembrance will impede his memory from becoming eschatologically and transcendentally subsumed into the vault of God's heavenly transhistorical eternal serene immutability. The more the will clings to its own willful self-serving willful selfish possessive hold of God the less it is able to enjoyably have God for its own divine and sublime blissful righteous security.

Consider the Blessed Sacrament of the Eucharist. The mystic's eyesight beholds a wafer of bread while the human intellect beholds through the supernatural gift of faith Christ's actual divinity. By reason of this supernatural enlightenment by the gifted infusion of the supernatural glory of God's own divine splendor the mystic's eyesight beholds not only a divine wafer but God's very own divinity. Were the mystic to explore this Self-manifestation of God's glory instantiated in the wafer merely within the dimensional terms of the body's eyesight, he would lose out on the august divinity of God transcending the dimensionality of the eye's sightfulness (viz., the size, color, shape, texture, etc. of the host). The case would be the same for the human intellect were it to seek to reduce the supernaturally revealed infinite Beingness of God's own divinity to the intellect's own finite scope of intelligibility, being-as-such. Normally the eye's sight is essentially trustworthy: seeing is believing. And normally the intellect's own insight is also essentially trustworthy: being-as-such is essentially that which is existing. But, in the case of the Blessed Sacrament, the Holy Eucharist, it is the very Beingness of all being that is splendidly supernaturally revealed and made manifest. Hence, the eye actually sees this sublime reality within the scope of its own visibility and the intellect within the scope of its own intelligibility. But the very sublime, supernatural, miraculous splendid manifestation of this Divinity is eminently more evident and manifestly trustworthy than is the dimensionality of the wafer's body or the intelligibility of the intellect's own insight. The consecrated wafer is exceedingly intelligible and infinitely effulgently supernaturally manifest beyond both the scope of the eye's bodily dimensionality and the intellect's spiritual intelligibility. Hence, it is eminently believable and faithfully trustworthy and manifestly so.

Chapter 9: Faith is the proximate and proportionate medium for the mystic's perfect mystical union with God.

St. John insists that faith and faith alone is the mystic's perfect superintellectual medium to attain to a perfect mystical union with God. This means that the mystic must forgo every intellectual activity which is not born of faith and faith alone. Faith itself has a dumbing-down effect on the intellect's own native intelligence just as the noonday sunlight has the effect of completely eclipsing a candle's light burning at high noon in plain daylight. Furthermore the likeness between the mystic's access to God through the theological gift of faith and the mystic's beatific vision of God in heaven is such that in the supernatural intellectual cognitive medium of faith the mystic does actually gaze on the eminence of the divine sublime splendor to God's divinity and glory while not beholding its plenitude, whereas in the beatific vision he does. Nonetheless, God's very own divine and sublime Triune Personhood is directly available to the mystic in contemplative prayer through the supernatural medium of faith. It must be pointed out that God's supernatural sacramental sanctifying grace and glorious graciousness flooding the interiority of the mystic's spiritual soul is completely like the light rays of the sun. The sun's rays are distinguishable from the sun's own substantive solarity. While the sun remains substantially the same solarity from one day to the next, the sun's rays do differ from one day to the next. This cannot be the case with God who is the quintessence of substantive simplicity. God's glorious divine radiance is not divisibly different from His divine substantivity because God is not only substantially and essentially simple, God is utter simplicity. Hence, God's sanctifying grace in the human soul is indistinguishable from God's substantive indivisible divinity and Triune Godhead.

The utter magnificence and stupefying splendor of the theological gift of faith explains why its presence in the soul's intellect leaves the mystic with a virtual intellectual blindness. Through faith God's ineffable Triune Godhead is totally in the infinite plenitude of God's utter absolute simplicity supernaturally flooding the mystic's soulful interior with God's sanctifying graciousness. This completely overwhelms the mystic's native intelligence and intelligibility. Hence, this has a dumbing-down effect on the mystic's innate intelligibility in comprehending God's Self-revelation through faith. St. John points this out as something to be expected since this same overwhelming result is reported in different places in Sacred Scripture when God makes His own divinity supernaturally manifest. The mystic's pilgrimage to advance to a perfect prayerful communion with God must be one that is pursued within the overwhelming umbrage of faith's impenetrable and ineffable nebulosity.

Chapter 10: Here St.John indicates the different modes of intellectual knowledge.

St. John indicates the different ways that the intellect arrives at its knowledge. He does so in order to examine which of these ways is conducive to the mystic's approach to God through the theological gift of faith and which impedes this mystical faith-bound approach. He will in subsequent chapters immediately following this present chapter examine and evaluate successively each of these ways.

The first distinction which St. John offers is that between the intellect's natural way of receiving its ideas and its supernatural way. The intellect's natural medium of receiving its ideas is through the sentient body's senses. Additionally, it is through intellectual reflection in which the intellect, as we have previously explained, can contemplate its own metaphysical cognitive informative medium of intelligibility, being-as-such, which completely transcends the reach of the sense's sensibility. Within this exclusively metaphysical transcendental reach the intellect reflectively can expand its knowledge upward to consider the completely ideal empyreal theological domain of reality. Its supernatural way of gaining knowledge encompasses every way that surpasses its natural approach to knowing. This supernaturally gained knowledge is further subdivided as follows.

It is subdivided into corporeal and spiritual knowledge. Supernatural corporeal knowledge is derived either through the sentient body's external special senses or through the same body's internal senses, notably the imagination including all that can be imaginatively fashioned and fancied. The supernatural spiritual knowledge, in turn, is also subdivided into two different ways of knowing. One is through distinct and particular knowledge (viz., ideas) and the other through vague, ambiguous, general knowledge (viz., ideas). He further clarifies what he includes in this distinct and particular knowledge of ideas. This knowledge includes four distinct ways of knowing by bypassing the sentient body's innate sensibility. This includes paranormal (i.e., extraordinary) visions, revelations, locutions, and spiritual feelings. The vague, ambiguous, and general knowledge is that of contemplative prayer mediated exclusively through theological faith. This knowledge is of one kind only and not further subdivided. The entire thrust of these chapters immediately succeeding this chapter 10 will address each of these ways of knowing leading up to the climax which is the mystic's form of contemplative prayer shrouded within faith's own arcane nebulosity.

THE ASCENT: Book II, Chapters 11-22: PURIFICATION OF KNOWLEDGE THROUGH VIRTUE OF FAITH

Chapter 11: Harm and impediment of supernatural objects of the exterior senses.

There are paranormal subjective experiences which accrue to the mystic beyond the usual and normal route of intellectual knowledge and understanding mediated by the exterior senses. Such paranormal experiences become inadvertently distracting obstacles to the mystic's predominant trust through faith in the Blessed Trinity's immediate available presence through the Church's sacramentality. What is clear from this presentation by St. John is that he is speaking of a "knowledge" which arrives to the mystic outside of the natural mode of intellectual knowledge. Indeed, what will become increasingly apparent to the reader of this commentary is that these paranormal experiences simply bypass the soul's native intellect and intelligence altogether. Rather, they occur within the mystic's subjective psychosomatic selfhood and not within the mystic's soul itself which is the normal objective and trans-subjective habitat for the activity of intellectual knowing and intellectual volitional willing. These paranormal experiences are the following:

Sight: visions of saints, angels, luminous splendors, etc.

Hearing: words of persons seen or unseen

Smell: sweetest fragrances

Taste: exquisite savors and flavors

Touch: extreme spiritual delight resonating as a feeling

These are not to be trusted even if they are from God. The more exterior are these paranormal phenomena the less they are to be trusted. These are susceptible to deception, especially by illusions effectuated by the devil. They are not profitable to the spirit because they are more corporeal than incorporeal. In addition, God usually communicates to the mystic spiritually (i.e., interiorly and intellectually) rather than by external paranormal phenomena. The reason for this mistrust is based on the radical difference between sensory sensible knowledge which is itself objectively trans-subjective and sensational experiences which are themselves subjectively self-orientated. Unlike the eye, the imagination is an internal and nor an external sense. When the eye beholds a red rose, it is in the very existing presence of the rose that the eye's sight is exercised. When the imagination imagines the red rose it is in the very absence of the existing rose. The eye's sightful knowledge is exercised regarding an object which evidently exists whereas the imagination's knowledge is not grounded on what self-evidently exists but only on what imaginatively exists. Hence, It is not only less trustworthy, it is susceptible to self-deception.

Bona fide philosophical natural knowledge of God is entirely immaterially intellectual transcendent to the sensibility of the exterior senses of touch, sight, smell, hearing, and taste. When the human intellect grasps intellectually that God is a Supreme Being this divinity is understood as a Being which transcends the physical and tangible domain of cosmic reality. Such knowledge is abstemiously intellectual and beyond the material spatio-temporal dimensionality which characterizes sensory knowledge. Such intellectual knowledge which is natural to the human person's intellectual spiritual soul is grounded on what is objectively self-evident to the intellect, being-as-such as that which actually exists, which is inherently beyond the scope of the sense's palpable sensibility. Such intellectual knowledge elicits a spontaneous appetitive drive on the part of the soul's intellectual will. This drive is a willful love to rightfully appropriate the object of this knowledge which is beyond the spatio-temporal dimensionality peculiar to the physical cosmos and the body's animal senses.

The special paranormal phenomena mentioned by St. John of the Cross are not the normal product of either the external senses nor of the internal sense of the imagination. Rather, they correspond to sensory experiences which are entirely subjective within the experiential subjectivity of the human person's selfhood in contradistinction to the human person's soul and animal sentient body animated by this intellectual soul. These paranormal experiences occur within the self-cultivated and self-humanized sensitized body's subjectivity and consciousness as sensational encounters that are artificially self-induced. To better grasp the paranormal entirely subjective epistemic trait of these mystical religious experiences, consider the artificiality of odors, flavors, noises, textures, and sights with which we are sensationally surrounded in our present hi-tech worldly environment. They are all orientated toward sensationally enhancing and exciting one's own subjective self-conscious bodily awareness.

When we watch a TV presentation or attend a movie theater we enter into a completely artificial environment of electronic sight and sound that is entirely sensationally subjective to the viewer and hearer. The same is the case when we use the telephone or the computer. When we detect perfume on another's person we are made aware of our own subjective bodily sensuality and sensitivity. The same holds when we touch a plastic surface which is utterly smooth or sit on a plastic cushion that is utterly soft and yielding. Our own bodily subjective sensitivity and feeling is also sensationally stimulated through artificial flavors that are introduced into food as seasoning by a chef's culinary skill. On a TV screen or in the cinema the patron is not in touch with reality transcendent to his own subjectivity. Indeed, the reality itself that is filmed need no longer be existing. The patron is entirely focused on his own bodily sensitivity, subjectivity, and feelings. This may seem strange to one reading this commentary. It would seem to be the case that viewing a film documentary of some historical event on the other side of the globe would provide the viewer with a more intimate knowledge of that event than merely hearing about it from a person who actually witnessed it. But, ontologically speaking the reality being documented on film is itself no longer existent whereas the witness who would recount it actually exists. The documentary falsely promotes the viewer's personal conviction and entirely subjective bodily consciousness of having actually personally and sensationally experienced the historical event within its very historicity; that is, experiencing the past as currently present.

Were these artificially induced experiences effectuated supernaturally and not merely artificially through human technical ingenuity, they would be somewhat comparable to the paranormal experiences which St. John is addressing as impediments distracting the mystic from clinging to God through the infallible medium of faith rather than through these epistemically misleading subjective impressionistic experiences. The mystic who revels in these sensational religious phenomena thinks very highly of himself for being singled out to experience them. The devil employs these to induce autosuggestions in the mystic. Even rejecting these will not result in rejecting their beneficial fruit if they are truly from God and, if they are from the devil, their rejection will minimize their adverse impact of agitation, dryness, vanity, presumption, etc., which occurs in their aftermath. These adverse influences will not impact the mystic if the paranormal phenomena which occasion them are ignored. On the other hand, God's own supernatural phenomena, even if they are deliberately ignored and not explicitly entertained...will still convey their beneficial influence to the mystic because their fruit will linger on even when the phenomena are absent. If a mystic persists in dwelling on these phenomena and deliberately entertaining them, 6 harms will result.

1) Faith's rigor and prominence in the mystic's prayer-life will gradually diminish and wane.

2) The mystic's attention to God's transcendent super spiritual reality will be impeded by the distractions of the self-humanized and sensationally self-cultivated body's emotional religious feelings and sensuously emotional sensitivities brought on by these paranormal religious experiences.

3) These subjective religious experiences themselves by their very sensationally sensitizing sensuous excitation will captive the mystic and take possession of the mystic's conscious attention.

4) They will focus the mystic's attention on the tactual rather than on the ethereal and the invisible.

5) The mystic will lose God's favors because he is absorbed with these religious phenomena.

6) Embracing them is tantamount to opening the door to the devil.

In rejecting these paranormal phenomena the mystic becomes better disposed toward receiving greater and more spiritual favors from God. Thus, the mystic will be humbled and less prone to be captivated by these phenomena and more hospitable toward God transcendent to these phenomena themselves. The mystic will become docile toward God and more leery of the devil, the "Beast of the Apocalypse" with seven heads warring against the seven mansions and degrees of love expounded by St. Teresa of Avila. Entertaining these paranormal sensationally sensitizing religious experiences with their accompanying compelling emotional feelings exposes the mystic to the devil's influence.

Chapter 12: Harm and impediments of imaginary objects of the interior senses.

These imaginary objects include i) natural phantasmagoria (fantasies) and their corresponding carnal affections; ii) supernatural fantasies and their corresponding emotional feelings and gratifications; iii) both natural and supernatural fantasies taken together. These latter may be the grist for mental meditative prayer but they cannot serve as the proximate medium for perfect union with God. These imaginary objects, for example, come into play when one is praying the rosary and meditating on the mysteries pictorially. Similarly, they occur in praying the 14 stations of the cross. Such tactual fantasies albeit their religious orientation are not commensurate with God's total incorporeal spirituality. These serve very well as a remote preliminary prayerful approach to God but in that they arouse fervor and zeal in the mystic. But, they cannot serve as the proximate approach to God which is the mystic's wedding to Christ. The mystic must eventually transcend these imaginary and imaginative fantasies along with their stimulating emotional religious gratification if he is to advance to a perfect union with God in contemplative prayer.

Contemplative prayer demands a medium that is commensurate with God's own immateriality transcendent to all sensorial and sensory mediation. The mystics who tenaciously cling to this meditative mental prayer of imaginative fantasizing to induce religious emotional fervor will eventually experience restlessness and aridity in their prayer-life. Eventually, the mystic must forego these religious fantasies and emotionally stirring religious feelings in order to become restfully engrossed in the pure general act of prayerful contemplation bereft of all feelings prompted by fanaticizing on sensuous sensational stimulations.

Contemplative prayer does away with imagery altogether; it is a quiet loving attentiveness to god without the intervention of any discursive reasoning.

Chapter 13: Signs indicating when prayerful meditation is to be replaced with prayerful contemplation.

Discursive meditation is not to be abandoned too soon; otherwise, the mystic will find himself regressing backward and downward toward palpable external objects of attention instead of progressing inward and upward toward intangible and spiritual realities.

(First sign) Prayerful meditation becomes dry without savor or enjoyment and relish. All fervor vanishes. Yet, St. John cautions the mystic not to abandon this meditative prayer until and unless he is fully established in the mental peace and placidity of contemplative prayer bereft of all imaginative and imaginary religious fantasies.

(Second sign) There is no longer an interest in prayerfully attending to religious objects and sacred liturgical rites merely imaginatively. The mystic's prayerful attention is not focused on what is exterior to his own subjective personality and selfhood but, rather, what includes the very intimacy of his own selfhood.

(Third sign) The mystic becomes attracted to remaining alone in loving attentiveness to God's sacramental presence and indwelling without focusing on any special experiential tactual object engaging the pensive, volitional, and memorial activity of the intellect, will, and memory.

Note well that this transition to contemplative prayer cannot be efficaciously effectuated when only the first sign is present without the second. Neither can it be accomplished if the first two signs are present without the third being in place. For, the mystic may find prayerful mental meditation difficult because of some physiological or mental disorder. At this point St. John adroitly addresses contemplative prayer itself as he has previously identified it. At the outset of contemplative prayer, he explains, the loving knowledge that is characteristic of it may not be noticeable to the mystic. This is not surprising since i) the very supernatural medium of this prayer is itself ethereally subtle and indiscernible to the intellect, will, and memory. ii) In addition, the immediate object of this prayer (viz., God's very own

Triune Divinity and Godhead) is absolutely utterly spiritual, indivisible and nontactual. When the mystic eventually becomes habituated to contemplative prayer, he will completely transcend the activity of meditative prayer itself because the former affords the mystic a calm, deeper, more enjoyable religious intimate experience of God because it is practiced without effort and avails the mystic of a peace of mind, restfulness, savor, and delight that is more spiritual and sublime in keeping with God's very own divine sublime immutable eternal divinity.

According to St. John of the Cross, mental prayer is divided into discursive prayer and contemplative prayer. The major difference between these two is that discursive prayer avails itself of the human imagination to visualize sensationally and emotionally Gospel scenes which evoke religious piety, ardent fervor, and special affection for Jesus, our Blessed Mother, the Apostles, the saints, etc.. Contemplative prayer, on the other hand, dispenses with all imagery and sensational emotional excitation.

How can one abandon one's customary manner of praying? In the first place, it must be accomplished by our willing it. This occurs when we become fatigued and weary of such prayer. It no longer invites us and beckons us to continue such prayer. It becomes more monotonous than exciting. Further, it becomes distracting and enervating. Rather than persisting in such prayer the person turns to reading spiritual material rather than attempting to meditate and to capture pious scenes imaginatively.

How can one leave one's imagination aside in prayer? In the first place, one can sustain pray more uninterruptedly with one's intelligence than with one's senses. Thus, for example, instead of trying to "picture" God, one attends to God intellectually as the "Supreme Being." Such a "Being" is totally spiritual and immaterial. That is, God is not tall nor short nor big nor small. These are all quantitative dimensions. God transcends all dimensionality. God is not colorful nor tasteful nor tonal, loud nor soft, etc.. God is totally beyond all sensibility. "God" cannot be imagined in any sensorial way. Praying to "God" intellectually rather than to some sensorial image of God leaves all of the senses, the imagination included, in a vacuum. Further, it also leaves one's religious feelings aside and completely ignored and discarded.

Such mode of prayer, at first, is completely devoid of feeling, sensation, imagery, excitement, religious fervor, zeal, and ardor. It is devoid of all religious contentment, satisfaction, and devotion. The person who is praying experiences a profound aridity, loss of prayer's familiarity, excitement, and engagement. The praying person is at a loss to continue in prayer. It is no longer an engaging activity but a bore, a burden, a chore, a puzzle too confounding to invite continuing.

Yet, this is intellectual approach is a higher form of prayer? Why so? Because "God" to whom one is praying is not reducible to any image. Not even the very humanity of Jesus Christ can capture His Divinity. His Divinity eluded the apostles even when they were eating with Him, walking with Him, and listening to Him. This "Divinity" can only be captured intellectually on its own completely immaterial and immutable terms. The sensibility of Christ's humanity changes from infancy to adulthood. His divinity, on the other hand, is eternally unchanging and unchangeable. Thus, to prayerfully ponder Jesus Christ intellectually is to be able to attentively sustain immutably and persistently a prayerfulness that transcends imaginary distractions and interruptions.

When this transcendental intellectual attentiveness is attained, the one who prays is no longer praying meditatively engaging one's religious imagery; one is praying without the benefit of religious feeling, fervor, devotion, and zeal. This sensuous vacuum is the occasion for allowing one to advance more fully into a mental prayer that is entirely mental in keeping with the mind's own total lack of sensitivity and feeling including religious feeling, emotion, and satisfactory contentment. This is the aridity and dryness which is so frequently a major obstacle for everyone who enters persistently into mental prayer. At this point, many give up prayer altogether or return to meditative imaginary prayer without advancing any further in their prayer--life. This is a very, very sad outcome.

Having entered into this dryness and achieved and sustained this intellectual approach to prayer, the pray-er is now able to mentally without emotional feeling and any sensitivity retreat into the utmost subjectivity, intimacy and psyche (i.e., mind) of his own selfhood which is devoid of all imagery. The mind is the nucleus of inactivity, repose, and tranquility. There is no imaginary sensation in the mind to excite it. There are only notions and concepts that are devoid of all sensitivity and excitement. When the mind is totally care-free, it can think clearly and calmly; that is, it can calculate in purely mathematical terms in a highly sophisticated manner. This "mind" is not to be confused with the intellect. The intellect is a faculty of the spiritual soul while the "mind" is the person's self-centered facility to calculate concerning all things which it deems important to its own social security and self-reliance. In brief, the "mind" entertains no feelings but it does entertain concerns for what it esteems to be of paramount importance to its own self-centered security. In this sense, it has mental bearings and concerns which tranquilize and sedate it or disturb and upset it.

These concerns are rooted in the mind's mortality because unlike the soul which is inherently spiritual and immortal, the mind (psyche) is humanistically humanized and spiritualized but not inherently spiritual and, accordingly, not immortal. Hence, its paramount concern which is the root of what it can and cannot bear up with is its historical mortality and eventual demise. It is very much concerned and cares about its eventual death and termination. Hence, it is always calculating ways to cope with its inner deficiency and its eventual death.

Contemplative prayer engages this mind in all of its intimacy. At the outset of this engagement the mind becomes increasingly at peace since it is aware that God, Jesus Christ, and His Holy Spirit, are its own permanent security and safeguard. It subsequently becomes disturbed and burdened with unexpected cares and concerns principally because it becomes increasingly aware that it must surrender its own self-control totally to Jesus Christ, the Master and Lord of all masterful self-control. The increasing and inevitable prospect of this creates an alarm and disorientation which is unyielding and horrendous. Such is the "dark night of the spirit." This continues until the crisis is resolved by the pray-er totally capitulating to Christ's Holy Spirit.

At this point in the life of the mystic, contemplative prayer is no longer in the least meditative; it is continuously contemplative. Why? It is no longer the mystic which is laboriously creating imaginary scenes to bolster its own religious fervor. Rather, it is Christ's Holy Spirit alive within the bosom of the mystic's mental selfhood that is prompting the mystic to willingly calculate ways to become increasingly surrendered to Christ's pneumatic influence (i.e., the Holy Spirit's presence) to the praise and glory of the Father and to the service of the mystic's neighbor. In other words, the mystic at this point is completely care-less about its own selfish self-interest. The mystic is no longer in charge of his/her own social security; this has been prayerfully turned over to Christ and the Father's Holy Spirit's magnanimity and boundless utterly reliable bounty. The mystic is mentally at peace with a profound and enduring peace that only Christ can give and sustain.

It is the hope of this commentary to expound more explicitly the difference between meditative and contemplative prayer by contrasting the somatic visceral with the psychic cerebral completely subjective polarized stages of a human person's egocentric consciousness. It is the very premise of this commentary that the mystical life of prayer engages explicitly the mystic's egocentric conscious psychosomatic selfhood not to the exclusion, however, of his hylemorphic body/soul inalienable nature. The difference between meditative prayer and contemplative prayer is that the former is steeped in the imagination's imaginary images whereas contemplative prayer is steeped in the mind's imageless inspirations. These images occur in the human body's conscious subjective self-humanized visceral sensitivity whereas the imageless inspirations occur in the human body's self-conscious subjective intimate self-humanized cerebral insensitivity. The self-humanized and self-cultivated humanized body has two polar counterparts: the soma with its sensitized emotional feelings stimulated by fantasized sensational (i.e., tactual) imagery, and the psyche with its desensitized unemotional bearings sedated by stolid non-sensational (i.e., non-tactual) inspirations.

The polar opposition between the self-humanized body's somatic stimulating sensitivity and its psychic sedate intimacy can be better grasped by contrasting the seductive sensational tactility of imaginary fantasies with their prosaic non-sensational and non-tactile polarized counterpart conceptions proper to the mind's psychicity. Three apple pies can be succulently and sensationally presented electronically on the TV screen whereas the mathematical number three in its simple symbolic notation presented on the same TV screen is bereft of the sensuality and the sensationalism of the three apple pies. The number, three, conceptualized mathematically is bereft of the tactility proper to the apple pies. Whereas the human person's self-cultivated and self-humanized bodily subjectivity can self-consciously and mentally conceptualize the number three prosaically devoid of all tactility, the same bodily subjectivity can consciously and imaginatively fantasize the number three tactually and sensationally. The latter is sensationally and excitingly stimulative in arousing the somatic body's subjective emotional feelings (i.e., sensitive likes and dislikes). The former is un-sensationally dull and unexcitingly sedative in calming the psychic body's subjective un-emotional bearings (i.e., intimate careful interests).

Furthermore, the psychic self's cerebral mental conceptual inspirations are inherently more important or unimportant than are the somatic body's imaginative fantasies likeable or unlikable. The former are non-tactual and dull but more precise and incisive whereas the latter are imprecise but more sensationally tactile. The number three, albeit its threefold content is mentally conceived to be a united threesome whereas the same number's threefold union is imaginatively fancied as a discrete threesome. In other words, the human person's subjective psyche is better able to grasp the relevance of the number three precisely and incisively with a serene bodily mental bearing (i.e., composure) that is calm and dispassionate whereas the same human person's bodily subjective soma is only able to imaginatively visualize the same number imprecisely dramatically and with much bodily excitement.

Meditative prayer engages the mystic with religious imagery that is exciting and stimulating. This provokes within the mystic religious emotional sensitive feelings of ardor, fervor, and zeal. On the other hand, contemplative prayer involves the mystic with religious inspirations that are unexciting and sedating. These evoke within the mystic religious unemotional intimate yearnings of reverence, respect, awe, piety, etc.. The former somatic feelings spur in the mystic's bodily subjectivity a religious sensuous emotional self-gratification and a righteous self-contentment whereas the latter psychic yearnings and pinings spur in the mystic's mental subjectivity a religious non-sensuous un-emotional self-justification and a righteous self-containment. Further, the three pies sensationally projected on the TV screen seem nearer "at hand" and more concrete to the mystic whereas the number three mentally conceived mathematically seems more abstract and remote. On the other hand, the three fantasized pies appear to the mystic as still exterior to his conscious egocentric bodily self whereas the mathematical number three is conceived by the mystic as intimately intrinsic to his egocentric mental consciousness.

When a religious bodily somatic visceral feeling for God is substituted for the fantasized three pies and a religious mental psychic cerebral yearning for God is substituted for the conceptualized mathematical number, three, the mystic is prayerfully within the confluence of his egocentric conscious selfhood alternatively aware of God meditatively (i.e., excitedly with a liking or unliking somatic feeling) or contemplatively (i.e., serenely with a concerned or unconcerned psychic bearing). The radical difference, however, between the mathematical number, three, and God is that the former is merely subjectively imagined or conceived whereas the God of the Catholic Christian mystic exists actually and really transcendent to and independent of the mystic's psychosomatic subjective religious emotional feelings and sensitivity, on the one hand, and subjective religious emotionless bearings and intimacy, on the other. In other words, the Catholic Christian mystic is experiencing subjectively and religiously within the psychosomatic constitution of his own selfhood God's actual Triune objective trans-subjective sacramental presence to him within his hylemorphic natural body/soul constitution by the supernatural grace of the Church's sacramentality.

The significant difference between meditative and contemplative prayer is captured by the human person's personalized experience of the number three imaginatively and illustratively encountered in the three fanciful apple pies sensationally projected on the TV screen and the same number mathematically and mentally conceived bereft of all sensational tactility. The one is sensuously and sensitively felt within the mystic's bodily somaticity whereas the other is entertained mentally without any concomitant bodily feeling within the intimacy of the self-humanized and self-cultivated body's psychicity. The somatic body (i.e., its physiology) is empirically observable through technical instruments whereas the psychic body (i.e., the willful mind) is impervious to such empirical observation. The prayerful conscious attention peculiar to meditative prayer is focal attention which is one of outward divergent exclusivity and movement since the mystic can only focus on one of the three pies at a time. By contrast the prayerful conscious attention peculiar to contemplative prayer is that of immobilized inward concentration which is one of inclusive convergence since in one and the same concept the number 3 simultaneously encloses its threefold components.

Chapter 14: Contemplative prayer versus meditative prayer.

There are two reasons to abandon religious fantasies as the focus of meditative prayer. The first is the very first sign mentioned in the previous chapter. The mystic no longer experiences an avid enjoyment and satisfaction in praying meditatively through the medium of religious icons and fanciful Gospel scenes. The second is related to the first. This style of discursive meditation has served its purpose to introduce the novice to the fervent habit of mental prayer. When the mystic is habituated to mental prayer and raising his mind to heavenly things, contemplative prayer is more efficacious in both sustaining and advancing the mystic's mindful elevation to a less taxing exercise of mental recollection beyond the imagination's distractions. When contemplation arrives, it is regressive to cling to meditation.

The second sign mentioned in the previous chapter is a further reason to relinquish meditative prayer and to advance to contemplative prayer. Pictorial Gospel imagery suffused with sensuous sensational tactility is not commensurate with God's totally intangible, immaterial, and spiritual sublimity. Furthermore, the imagination's wanderings serve to distract and impede the mystic from pursuing and enjoying the serene peace afforded by contemplative prayer. In the previous chapter, the example of the number 3 suffices to accentuate this point. Exemplifying the arithmetic number, 3, imaginatively can be done in a multitude of ways. It is a distraction to single out one way to the exclusion of the multiple other options or to seek one exemplification which is more efficacious than the others. Three apple pies, three cucumbers, three stones, three birds, etc.; there is no end to the possible examples of the number three. Mentally conceptualizing the number, 3, may be accomplished in one unitizing typeset. Of course, the imaginative illustrations are more colorful and sensationally stirring than is the colorless arithmetic 3 mentally conceptualized. Yet, the latter's conceptualization affords the person a more enduring, stable, and intuitive grasp.

The third sign mentioned in the previous chapter favoring contemplative prayer is the very activity of contemplation itself. St. John clearly emphasizes, however, that the mystic must be somewhat firmly engaged in this contemplative prayer prior to abandoning meditation altogether. Were this not the case, the mystic would be neither prayerfully meditating nor prayerfully contemplating. That is, he would be altogether out of touch with God in his mental prayer-life. Evidence of this contemplative prayer obtains when the mystic is religiously and reverently praying in a medium enveloped in obscurity and generality devoid of sensational and sensitizing sensuality prompted by sensational imagery.

The advantage of contemplation over meditation is compared to relaxation versus work and toil, being unoccupied versus being occupied, enjoying a gift over and above toiling to attain to it. St. John proceeds to describe this religious general mystical encounter with God. The clue to such mystical knowledge is its subtlety and aloofness from all that stimulates and excites the self-humanized and self-cultivated body's sensitivity. In praying to the Blessed Trinity the mystic could imaginatively fix his conscious attention on a green shamrock or conceptually fix his conscious attention on the symbolic "sign of the cross" which one makes in blessing himself prayerfully. A shamrock could be as much a reference to Ireland as it is to the Blessed Trinity. But, the cross itself is the mark of the Christian who believes and confesses the Trinity. The cross carries a religious weight and import which the shamrock does not. The cross with Christ's corpus on it is exhibited at Mass; the shamrock is not. The cross as a symbol of Christianity is more intimate to the mystic than is the shamrock. Furthermore, the bare configuration and outline of the cross offers no sensational bodily stimulus whereas the shamrock may be embellished in many ways to draw attention to its tactile sensuality. Furthermore, the Christian religious significance of the cross is more intimately relevant to the mystic than is that of the shamrock. The shamrock remains extrinsic to the Church's ritual liturgy whereas the cross does not.

Notice that St. John's brief comments distinguishing contemplative prayer from meditative prayer makes mention of the special faculty of the human soul's intellectual power which is other than that of the imagination and involves a non-imaginative activity bereft of images bearing the sensational tactility that gives rise to sensual excitement and emotional feelings. It is the contention of this commentary that these descriptions given by St. John pertinent to contemplative prayer pertain more to the human person's subjective willful mind proper to the human person's self-cultivated selfhood than they do to the intellect which is the soul's inalienable faculty of thinking. This contention will be further expatiated as this commentary proceeds. For the moment, note that St. John is describing a mystical experiential religious encounter with God in differentiating between these two modes of mental prayer. This experiential religious encounter is predominantly subjective within the subjectivity of the mystic's egocentric consciousness. Intellectual knowledge, on the other hand, is completely objective and trans-subjectively objective. It is not embedded within the mystic's subjectivity and egocentric consciousness.

Certainly, mental prayer which finds its seat within the subjectivity of the mystic's egocentric consciousness is preceded by both a natural intellectual (i.e., philosophical) and a supernatural intellectual knowledge (i.e., the theological virtue of faith) of God. Such subjective religious mental prayer has its foundation and inception objectively and trans-subjectively in faith which is not inherently experiential but abstemiously intellectual and the moreso intellectual the more it is a supernatural act of faith. The mystic's faith in the Holy Eucharist is not predicated on its sensibility but on its super-eminent miraculous trustworthy intelligibility. Furthermore, the Holy Eucharist's divine viability does not depend on the mystic's subjective religious pious reverence and zealous devotion. Rather, it is the very reverse, such piety and zeal are very much dependent on the super-intelligible divine reality of this Blessed Sacrament's divinity transcendent to and independent of such religious piety and zeal.

St. John takes considerable pains to explain why intellectual knowledge itself enters into a generality which is not available to the special senses whether these be the external senses, such as sight and hearing or the internal senses, such as the imagination. The medium of sensibility for the body's faculty of sight is formally color and its agency of seeing is the medium of light, especially the sun's solar light. The body's eyesight can discern the red rose specifically because red is a species of color which is the formal object of sight's sensibility. When the red rose is lit up by the sun's light, its specific color becomes sensibly visible to the eye. The sun's light enables the eye to see what is lit up by its solarity but the eye cannot look directly at the sun itself the source of its visibility. Indeed, it can only attempt this if it looks at the sun through a darkened glass which shields the eye from the sun's glare.

The soul's intellectual power can intelligently discern not merely the specific shades of color, such as the color red, but the very general reality of color-as-such above and beyond the special shades themselves. Color-as-such is not in its as-such generality specifically red nor any other special shade of color. It is virtually every shade of color but actually none of them explicitly. Hence, the intellect discerns intellectually and intelligibly what is common to every shade of color; namely, color-as-such. In doing so it does not ponder the physical and tangible reality of color colorfully, sensibly, and tangibly but merely entitatively, intelligibly, and intangibly as a qualitative reality which qualifies colorfully whatever physical body is actually colorful. This is the major difference between intellectual knowledge and sensory knowledge. This difference holds for all of the senses. The intellect can intelligently grasp sound-as-such intelligibly (i.e., generically) and intelligently apart from every specific tangible and special sensible sound which the ear can hear and detect explicitly.

The human soul's faculty of intellect can by Intellectual contemplation attain to the reality of color more succinctly, intelligibly, and essentially (albeit generically) than can the body's faculty of eyesight. Similarly with every other sensory bodily faculty. While the body's eyesight can only see the rose as colorfully red the soul's intellectual insight can "see" the very essence and intelligibility of the color, red, in terms of color-as-such and red-as-such. Hence, the intellect "sees" by a light which is more penetrating and lucid than is the sun's solarity. The sun's light is a material and physical illumination whereas the intellect's light is the human soul's own immaterial and metaphysical solarity. The sun illuminates the physical rose's physical trangibility and sensibility whereas the human soul illuminates the rose's metaphysical intangibility and insensibility. The former is specific and specifically imaginable whereas the latter is generic and unimaginable; it is only intelligible.

From this comparative analysis it should be evident to the reader that contemplative prayer partakes more of the activity of the human soul's intellectual faculty than it does of the human body's sensorial activities. Contemplative prayer, accordingly, is fundamentally rooted in the soul's intellect moreso than in the body's sensorial activity whether this activity be on the part of the external senses or the internal sense of the imagination. Nonetheless, contemplative prayer is not per se merely an intellectual activity. For, whereas the body's sensorial activity due to the very tangible and physical specificity of sensory knowledge gives rise to bodily animal passions and affections aroused by and centered on special and specific physical features of a physical body's color, sound, taste, odor, texture, temperature, etc., the soul's intellectual activity gives rise to a more general and non-specific entirely dispassionate (non-bodily) voluntary appetency. Whereas the human body's animal appetency is spontaneously aroused by specific colors, odors, flavors, sounds, etc., which are sensibly detected, the human soul's intellectual appetency (viz., will) is spontaneously and dispassionately indifferent to the specificity of these sensibilities. That is, the intellectual will is free and at liberty to spontaneously appetize (i.e., prefer) one color over another, or one sound over another, etc., and to reverse its appetency at will. This dispassionate freedom is rooted in the intellect's intelligible insight into the very essence and entitative quiddity of color-as-such, sound-as-such, flavor-as-such, etc..

What is the case for merely physical and tangible realities is more so the case for God who is completely intangible and metaphysically totally beyond the reach of the human body's animal sentiency. Prayer is directed toward God beyond the range of the human body's animal sentiency. That is, the more prayer is removed from the tangible and sensible specificities of sensory and imaginative knowledge, the more prayer enters into the metaphysical realm of reality's intelligibility which is commensurate with God's own total spirituality. Accordingly, contemplative prayer partakes more of a completely dispassionate volitional freely elicited sedate ethereal appetency and love for God than that which occurs within the human body's animal instinctively spontaneous passionate appetency.

Yet, St. John quickly cautions the novice mystic to relinquish meditative prayer only when he is firmly installed within the intellect's intelligible supra-sensible metaphysical reach of God. Otherwise, he will no longer be praying passionately and affectionately through his bodily sentient appetency while he is as yet unable to pray competently and more freely and at liberty at the level of the intellect's metaphysical intelligibility. Of course, the difference between approaching reality sensibly at the level of the body's animal sentiency or intelligibly at the level of the soul's supra-sentient spiritual intelligibility is the difference between walking up a hill or taking an elevator. For, where the bodily eye and its corresponding appetency can only know and instinctively react to the rose in terms of its superficial color the soul's intellect and its corresponding appetency (viz., will) can know and freely respond to what color-as-such is in its very quidditative essence. In this manner, the intellect and its willful appetency can differentiate and choose freely between the rose itself and its superficial qualitative color whereas the senses and their appetency cannot.

To the novice who is still not proficient in contemplative prayer this putting aside praying passionately with the bodily affectivity proper to sentient knowledge in order to pray dispassionately and intellectually without the benefit of such bodily affectivity…this seems tantamount to abandoning prayer itself. For, approaching the rose sentiently and sensibly (i.e., sentimentally) the person cannot but be sensibly and bodily affected by its special color whereas approaching the same color intelligently and generally in terms of color-as-such does not elicit such bodily affectivity. For this reason, such intellectually grounded prayer while more intelligibly penetrating and more noble in its volitional appetency (i.e., freedom to appetize) still seems to the novice to be less dramatic, less vivid, less stimulating, and less personally engaging in the very trappings of prayer. For this reason, it seems to the novice that engaging in such purely ethereally intellectual prayer which is beyond the sensibility of the body's sentiency is tantamount to not praying at all.

At this point our SanJuanistic text expands upon this differentiation between the specificity of all knowledge and its corresponding generality. The more general knowledge becomes and the less the knower can specifically penetrate this generality, the more paradoxically knowledge seems to be deprived of its very lucidity. Of course, the very opposite is the case. He exemplifies this in a ray of sunlight penetrating a window's transparency. When there are specks of dust afloat in the sun's ray, the ray itself becomes discernible whereas it would not be at all discernible were these specks altogether absent. In other words, the ray of light is itself inherently lucid and transparently lucid. Its general clear lucidity becomes only accessible to the eye when this lucidity highlights (i.e., renders visible) the eye's object of sight. Hence, it is the case to the eye that light itself is invisible and for that reason the eye can only view or espy it directly through a darkened glass or lens.

What is the case for our body's eyesight is moreso the case for our intellect's intellectual sight. Here, St. John addresses the intellect's natural and supernatural knowledge. Its natural knowledge is illuminated by the agency of the soul's own spiritual luminosity. Its supernatural knowledge is illuminated by the agency of God's very own infinite glorious splendor. This glorious splendor is not a mere radiation as is the sun's light, nor a mere finite illumination as is the soul's highlight; it is an infinite radiance whose utter substantive simplicity makes impossible any distinction between the generality of its luminosity and any special instance of it. Hence, it is this very divine infinite splendor in all of its august all-encompassing generality which illuminates the human soul in its pellucid splendor that constitutes the object of supernatural faith. Its very infinite brilliance is only discernible to the soul's human intelligence in the way that specks of dust enable the eye to espy the sun's rays. Specks of the human soul's own intelligible knowledge enable the intellect to espy God's infinite glorious radiance which of itself remains as dark to the intellect's intelligibility as the sun is overpoweringly dark to the sensibility of the body's eyesight.

The sun's radiation is mutable in the sense that it is not continuously daylight and it does not penetrate and render transparent every material body it illuminates. The human soul's illumination is immutable in that it is not subject to the sun's spatio-temporal variation. Yet, it is finite and cannot illuminate that which is infinitely luminous such as God's very own divinity or even the purely luminous spirituality of the angels. God's infinite luminescence, on the one hand, is so generally and infinitely comprehensively translucent that there is no special instance of it that lacks this very translucency. So much so is this the case, St. John explains, that when the mystic in contemplative prayer is transported through the medium of faith to God's supernatural Self-revelation in Sacred Scripture and in the Church's sacramentality, he is transported beyond the reach of the astronomical spatio-temporal dimensions of the cosmos, and beyond the reach of his human person's own self-cultivated historicity into the transhistorical vault of God's immutable eternity. Here the passage of time and time's temporality vanishes and the mystic can no longer measure the length of time he may be contemplatively absorbed in prayer.

By reason of such contemplation the mystic is no longer occupied with his senses, his bodily functions, his cosmic environment, and his historical memoriality. Indeed, it would seem that he is very idle and no longer busy with the affairs of the world and of his own social security. And, indeed, this is very much the case. Yet, this idle activity is more humanistically self-fulfilling and humanly noble and edifying than all of the busy engagements and business affairs that pertain to the world's development. The amnesia which this contemplation entails on the part of the mystic's memory and the special volitional love which it incites is due to God's infinite supernatural radiance that infinitely exceeds the mystic's natural intelligence and volitional appetency. Indeed, the special volitional love that this contemplation evinces is a love that is so pure and devoid of all sentient passion that the mystic is engulfed in a divine amorosity without being cognizant about anything specific and special regarding the very object of this love.

St. John does not proceed here to further clarify this presentation of contemplative prayer. He states that for the moment this account is sufficient to make his point that the mystic should not completely abandon meditative prayer which engages the senses and sensorial affectivity until and unless one is firmly ensconced in a predominantly intellectual encounter with God through the supernatural gift of faith which transcends completely the scope and range of sensorial cognition. Since theological faith which has its seat in the soul's transsubjective intellectual activity is the cornerstone for the mystic's subjective religious encounter with God, contemplative prayer which is the summit of the mystic's personal wedding with God issues from this super-intellectual encounter with God. By reason of this intellectuality the mystic enters analogously into the Trinity at the pinnacle of the intellect's metaphysical general theological reach. For, not only is God a Supreme Being, Good, True, and Beautiful; God is infinite Beingness, Goodness, Truth, and Beauty transcendent to and independent of all creation and of every creature. While the very generality of this intellectual knowledge and volitional love of God outstrips the body's sentient affectivity, it is also bereft of the imperfections peculiar to the body's sentient affectivity grounded in the material, physical, tangible, and spatio-temporal perishable environment of the body's own mortality.

It must not be mistakenly construed here that contemplative

prayer as propounded by St. John in his SanJuanistic mystagogy is restricted exclusively to the human soul and the soul's suprasensible intellectual/volitional activity. Contemplative prayer by reason of the human person's self-personalized personality also includes subjectively and supplementally the involvement of the mystic's self-cultivated and self-humanized conscious psychosomatic willful and mindful selfhood. In other words, contemplative prayer is both fundamentally, objectively, and soulfully intellectual and supplementally, subjectively, and self-centeredly consciously experiential. Suffice it to state at this point that while the intellectual in its inherent intelligibility is non-experiential (i.e., not steeped in the human person's subjective self-centered awareness), the experiential is not, in turn, objectively intellectually intelligible. This point will be expounded more at length subsequently in the course of this commentary.

Chapter 15: Contemplation for beginners.

At the outset of contemplation the mystic will be frequently reverting to meditative prayer. Contemplation itself which is completely beyond the body's sentiency will occur only for brief periods. These periods are characterized by a quiescence and serenity that partakes of God's very own eternal immutability. Once contemplation becomes habitual the three faculties of intellect, will, and memory become themselves stultified regarding each's respective normal activity. The intellect receives this supernaturally infused contemplative knowledge of God through the supernatural theological gift of faith passively illuminated by God's sublime Gracious Divine Glory just as the body's eyesight receives the sun's illumination passively. Contemplative prayer excludes in its total absorption in God every intellectual distraction involving the body's sentient imagery. For, God's divinity is neither circumscribed nor measurable by any finite measurement such as tall, taller, or tallest. God's being transcends metaphysically in His very Divinity all such dimensionality and measurement suitable to the body's sentiency. Further, the intellect does not become engaged in its own intellectual theological reasoning regarding God. Its own intellectual cogitation would itself impede the mystic's intellectual loving absorption in the stupendous reality of God's divine

Triune divinity supernaturally and sacramentally present to it.

Further, any specific recollection by the memory of the historical past or anticipation of the historical future is also excluded from the mystic's engagement with God in contemplative prayer. The memory is stultified in its memoriality precisely because the mystic engages God transhistorically within the very vault of God's immutable eternity. In sum, the mystic in contemplative prayer is intellectually absorbed with the august uncircumscribable infinite Triune Godhead sacramentally present to the soul in the limpid luminescence of God's glorious splendor. Here, absorbed with the very supernatural presence of God's Triune Godhead the mystic becomes very obedient to the Gospel's sage counsel: "Be still and know that I am God." The mystic's intellectual will, in turn, will no longer be seeking its own immortal happiness in specific practical choices engaging the mortal body's own affectivity and appetency. Its normal immortal quest for happiness will be engulfed with a supernatural refined and exquisite bliss proper to God's very own divine beatitude.

Attaining to such contemplative prayer is entirely dependent on God's supernatural sacramental Self-manifestation to the mystic. It is mediated through the supernatural theological gift of faith. It is not the culmination of the mystic's own intellectual advancement in dogmatic or moral theology. For, these disciplines are acquired through much intellectual cogitation and pondering in which the intellect's own native intelligibility is very actively engaged. What is peculiar to this contemplative prayer, on the other hand, is that the intellect's own native prowess of reasoning becomes suspended when it becomes absorbed with the overpowering presence of God's eternal Triune Godhead. Similarly, the mystic's memory itself becomes memorially suspended in a form of amnesia as well as does the mystic's intellectual will's innate appetency for immortal happiness become suspended because of its being engulfed in God's very own divine blissful beatitude.

Chapter 16: Supernatural imagery is an impediment to perfect union with God.

By "supernatural imagery" St. John most probably means supernatural fantasies which are not the object of the corporeal body's organic exterior senses which normally sense what actually exists. Rather, he has in mind the entirely concocted subjective fantasies of the somatic body's own imaginative fabrication. Now, these fantasies are the offshoot of the human person's own self-subsistent personhood's subjective egocentric self-conscious ingenuity. They are imaginary concoctions constituted of "image, form, figure, and species" peculiar to the sentiency of the extrinsic senses. Yet, unlike the extrinsic senses, the object of such imagery is not the reality itself sensed by the extrinsic senses but merely the spectacular imaginary itself concocted by the imagination. The example that St. John cites from Sacred Scripture to illustrate these fantasies confirm that they are merely subjective imaginary artifices.

Note that these paranormal fantasies are much more seductively alluring than are the paranormal phenomena of the exterior senses. The reason given by St. John for this increased allure on the part of these supernatural fantasies is that the imagery they evoke is more spectacular than are the physical objects discerned by the extrinsic senses. There is also an additional consideration for the intense allurement of these fantasies. They are entirely private to the one who self-consciously entertains them in contradistinction to the physical objects of the external senses which are public to everyone. By reason of this privacy they are more subjectively personalized and more intimate to the human person's very own subjective personality. In this way, they impact more forcibly on the human person's subjective sensitivity.

To get a better handle on these fantasies consider a Walt Disney animated cartoon movie such as Snow White, Fantasia, or whatever. These animated film fantasies had to be conjured up imaginatively before being sketched out on paper and transmitted to film and synchronized with sound effects. Anyone who enjoys the same imaginative ingenuity can conjure up for himself similar and even more fantastic fantasies. It seems quite obvious that these fantasies have their own fascination. One might view a Disney film and exclaim "fantastic" in response to their seductive affectivity. Hence, they have more charm and allure than the real physical objects of the extrinsic senses.

Now, if such animations are paranormally (i.e., supernaturally) infused into the mystic's own imagination pertinent to some article of Catholic faith or some Gospel scene or similar reference, they would have a charm and allure of their own very much more enhanced to stimulate the mystic's religious devotion than would the Disney productions on the general public.

St. John's interest in these supernatural phantasmagoria is to point out that they are not suitable media to enter into perfect communion with God. They harbor merely the spatio-temporal dimensional trappings of the senses themselves and, therefore, they are not media commensurate with God's very own intangible, nontactual, immaterial, supernal, indivisible, spiritual Divinity. Now, even when the imagination can imaginatively fancy a purely mathematical quantum devoid of the tangible features which the extrinsic senses discern in physical objects, even here this fantasized imaginary mathematical quantum is not a suitable medium to represent God's total nonquantitative Divine Nature. Picture a teacher tracing on the black board a straight line with a piece of chalk. It is an imaginary line and only imaginary. Because a conceptual line has no dimensional width and cannot support any coloration such as the white chalk. The line on the black board only fantastically symbolizes the mind's conceptualization of a straight line. It is a pure subjective imaginary fantasy. No mathematically concocted imagery adequately depicts the mathematical concept which it imaginatively fantasizes. Hence, a fortiori, there is no imagery whatsoever which suitably represents the reality of God because all fantasy entails the use of linearity in its graphic depiction.

Now, the mind's conceptualized geometric line, on the other hand, is not itself an imaginary fantasy. Yet, it is merely the human person's own subjective mental fabrication inasmuch as the human person in virtue of its self-subsistent personhood can egocentrically self-consciously mentally dream up and conceptualize a geometric line which has no physical existence transcendent to and independent of the human person's own egocentric mental subjectivity. Further, this geometric line is a constituent of all geometry and arithmetic. For, in bisecting the line yielding two separate lines, the bisection results in an arithmetic mathematical notion of two discrete quantities unlike the one line which is continuous. But, again, every notion which the self-humanized mind of the human person can conjure up is itself suffused with mathematical linear dimensionality.

Such dimensionality is entirely incommensurate with God's utter non-quantitative metaphysical simplicity. There is no quantitative measure proper to God's Divine Nature. Conclusively, then, all fantasies of the imagination and all notions of the mind's own fabrication cannot serve as proper media to cognitively know God or enter into a perfect cognitive union with God. This is the telling point which St. John is eager to convey in this chapter. Now, as a sweeping generalization, it should be noted that no mathematical knowledge is the measure of truth itself. Mathematical knowledge is only the measure of quantitative precision and exactitude. Hence, if a piece of lumber is cut to a 2-foot length, it is not truly two feet; it is precisely two feet long. If the piece of lumber is not truly wooden, it is synthetic and artificially resembling wood. That the piece of lumber is not wooden is not a quantitative consideration of mathematical precision; it is a qualitative one pertaining to the very nature of piece in question. Knowledge of God never engages a quantitative consideration.

Therefore, all such phantasmagoria even if they appear in Sacred Scripture are inadequate to the mystic's advance in encountering God supernaturally in a perfect intellectual communion through contemplative prayer. These dimensional mathematical considerations do not measure up to God's utterly nonquantitative Divine Nature of total simplicity. All mathematically couched conceptual notions and fanciful imagery are inherently deceptive precisely because their very quantitative precision instills an entirely self-conscious egocentric self-assurance that remains entirely epistemologically subjective. For, again, in the physical cosmos of reality there is no physical body which is precisely without any tolerance for error exactly two feet in quantitative measurement. To guarantee that the log is cut precisely to a two-foot length is to make a claim that appears to be correct and exacting. In reality this very precision can exist only in the mind which invents it. The log's own wooden physical composition does not allow such precision.

St. John's sagacious counsel---regarding all such phantasmagoria even supernaturally infused in the mystic's subjective imagination or mind---is for the mystic to remain self-detached from them and not to entertain and dwell on them by frequently remembering them and adverting to them. By completely ignoring them and refusing to entertain them by seeking to enjoy and to welcome them, and even to recall them to memory, the mystic succeeds in thwarting the devil's malicious intervention into the mystic's prayer-life. For, St. John insists, there is no need to strive to discern whether these phenomena are from God or from the devil. Simply ignoring them will suffice to prevent the devil's malicious interference and meddling.

Furthermore, God's supernatural divine infused knowledge imparted to the mystic in contemplative prayer is not conditioned nor modified by any specific form, idea, figure, concept, mode, dimension, or style of infusion. The knowledge imparted to the mystic in contemplative prayer is pure, and, limpid and unimpeded by any special idea of God Himself. Indeed, this is the chief characteristic of contemplative prayer. The mystic is not engaged in thinking much but in loving much. The entire thrust of contemplative prayer is be one with God's very own Triunity in a knowledge that remains as totally simple as is God's very own total Simplicity. Any special thought, notion, image, etc., that the mystic would entertain during contemplative prayer would itself interfere with this prayer itself. Any intellectual, volitional, or memorial attachment to what is other than this limpid light of Glory would interfere with this contemplative prayer itself and the perfect union with God that this prayer affords the mystic.

God's own divine and sublime knowability and knowledge is utterly infinite and not limited to any specific or special consideration. To be properly disposed to God's very own infinite medium of knowing the mystic must be divested of all activity which is naturally peculiar to his own faculties, especially the intellect itself. God has no created form or likeness which can mediate between His actual divine substantive existence and creation. The chasm between the two is infinite and can only be bridged by God's own infinite omnipotent powerful goodness, and luminescence. Indeed, St. John insists, when

God is Self-revealed sacramentally, he communicates Himself "mouth to mouth." When one shakes hands with someone else there is no medium interfering with one person's hand sensing the sensibility of the other person's hand over and above sensing the sensibility of his very own hand. In such a "touch" the medium of interpersonal cognition is indistinguishable from what is cognized. The same holds true for two wrestlers tangling with each other in a wrestling match although it is more each's mutual resistance which is discerned more than an interpersonal congeniality.

Further, there is a self-awareness of one person simultaneously aware of the self-awareness of a person other than one's very own self. This interpersonal intimacy is magnified in the act of kissing when two persons mutually volunteer to kiss each other on the lips. This is simulated with less physical intimacy when a kiss of peace is exchanged between two persons who greet each other cheek-to-cheek. Yet, this gesture of intimacy is sensible and not entirely as intimate as is the case with intimacies that are themselves entirely intangible and spiritual when two wills are wed in a common cause even when the two are not in physical contact. Here there is a willful self-surrender to a common cause that transcends the will's of both persons even while engaging the very ego-centric subjective selfhood of them both. The handshake and kiss are merely external manifestations and gestures of this more deeply subjective intangible intimacy.

The intimacy proper to contemplative prayer engages the very inmost intimate core of the mystic's own subjective selfhood sacrificially, willfully, and selflessly self-donating in a volunteer donation his very own self-control to Christ's very own total Selfless Self-surrender consummated on the cross of crucifixion. Of course, this is a superhumanistic and a superhumane act of agape love supernaturally bolstered by the very Holy Spirit of Love, the Holy Spirit abiding miraculously within the innermost intimate intimacy of the mystic's subjective selfhood (i.e., as the Sinew of the indomitable morale of his own inner spirit). But, the fundamental medium of this interpersonal intimacy is the theological virtue of faith whose proper medium of superintelligibility is the very Glorious radiance of God's own infinite sublime benignity flooding the mystic's soul with sacramental sanctifying Grace.

St. John of the Cross continues his exposition of these paranormal fantasies. He explains that they occur involuntarily and cannot be prevented anymore than a pane of glass can prevent sunlight from shining through its own transparency. Yet, by simply ignoring them the mystic will still experience their beneficial impact on his own religious conscious sensitivity if they are from God. The only way this beneficial impact can be impeded is by a lack of ascetic self-detachment on the part of the mystic. For, if the mystic becomes attached to these phenomena and their religious impact on his own sensitivity this attachment itself will become a serious impediment to his advancing to contemplative prayer and a more perfect union with God mediated by God's own Gracious Glory. The mystic should never be preoccupied with any sensation, image, idea, notion, memory, or any accompanying ravishing mystical delight. For, these would impede his immediate and direct prayerful supernatural communion with God in a more intimate union of contemplative prayer than these paranormal experiences afford. These paranormal phenomena and their religious impact can only be beneficial in the measure that they increase the mystic's total reliance on and attachment to faith as the solitary medium of perfect union with God.

The infinite light of God's Glory which is metaphysically infinitely spiritual is itself the divine medium of supernatural intelligibility Self-revealed to the mystic in contemplative prayer. The splendor of this Glory is itself devoid of all created specificity just as sunlight itself is devoid of the very colors which it makes visible in illuminating colorful physical bodies. When the soul is supernaturally flooded with this divine luminosity and glorious splendor of God's Grace, its very own natural light of intelligence may constitute an impediment to God's infinite glory in the measure that a particular person prefers to rely on his own finite native light of intelligence to fathom God's divinity rather than on the infinite luminosity of the supernatural gift of faith gratuitously given by God in the sacrament of baptism.

If the mystic wishes to seek refuge from God's infinite magnificence and luminous splendor he will retreat into the light of his own native intelligence. This occurs, for example, when the human person prefers his own man-made electric light to view a film in a dark theater rather than to bring the film out into the full light of the sun. The sun's light would be too overwhelming. The human person frequently has recourse to his own native intelligibility to penetrate into God's supernatural Self-revelation. This impedes rather than facilitating a more perfect grasp of God's ineffable Divinity. While God's supernatural infinite glory overwhelms the mystic's natural light of intelligence, it does not impair it nor impede its own operation. God's own divine Glory harbors no such deleterious effect on the soul's own spiritual nature and intellectual insight no more so than does this very same Glory incarnated in Christ's sacred Humanity do anything but supernaturally enhance this human nature.

By becoming supernaturally and sacramentally blinded in the infinite effulgent radiance of God's own Glory, the human intellect through faith becomes enabled to recognize that all that it naturally knows is merely a flicker of knowledge relative to God's own infinite knowledge mediated by the radiance of God's own Glory. This infused insight of faith is tantamount to an infused wisdom befitting God's own infinite knowledge and knowability. This infused wisdom enlightens even the intellect's own natural theological knowledge of God. It is one of the gifts of the Holy Spirit's infinite Giftedness. For, the intellect can now even better understand beyond its own innate luminous soulful medium of intelligibility that its very own natural enlightenment is itself as reflected in the faith-filled effulgence of God's luminosity merely a shadow of that Uncreated light itself as is the case for all other media of sensibility and intelligibility whether animal or angelic in the universe of creation.

It is important to further expatiate on this stupendous theological gift of faith which includes the very Glorious Life of God's Triune Godhead graciously and lavishly dispensed within the mystic's spiritual soul. A match lit during a day's high noon when no clouds impede the sun's radiance is similar to the light of the human intellect's native intelligence in the light of faith's divine luminescence. The eye can see the lit match's flame but not discern any radiance emanating from the flame. The match's flame blanches in the light of the sun's own radiance. Similarly with the human intellect's own native soulful light of intelligibility when the divine light of faith illuminates the intellect's own insight. Just as it is more the sunlight than it is the match flame's puny light that more efficaciously befits the vision of the body's eyesight, so also is it the case that the supernatural effulgent Glory of God's own divinity is more befitting to the human intellect's efficacious vision more so than is its own natural light of intelligence. The supernatural aspect of this light of faith derives from the infinite distance separating the creature from the creator. Granted that God creates mankind in His own image and destines mankind to supernaturally revel in His very own eternal bliss and beatitude, this infinite heavenly paradise is infinitely beyond the reach of mankind's own native prowess whether cognitive or volitional. Mankind can only avail himself of this paradise through God's own gratuitous benignity and Self-Revelation and not on his own. We learn through God's Self-Revelation in the light of faith that this supernatural gratuity is itself mediated Personally by the Three Persons of God's own Triune Godhead.

Chapter 17: Why does God communicate through supernatural visions accessible to our external senses?

This would seem to be foolhardy given that such visions may become an hindrance to advancing to perfect union with God in contemplative prayer. St. John's response to this question is to point out that such visions elevate the mystic's soul from a low to a high state. God orders these visions to gently accommodate the soul's own personal disposition. Thus, God proceeds from the sensory to the intellectual befitting the human being's own nature. The ascetic mystical life begins by disciplining the senses and continues on by disciplining the human soul's intelligence and volition. Thus, supernatural phenomena are presented to the exterior senses as corporeal visions of saints or holy things, very sweet odors, locutions, and extremely exquisite and delightful touches. The interior senses have their own supernatural phenomena over and above the exterior senses. These are more private and personalized and less public than are the miraculous phenomena discernible to the exterior senses. These paranormal phenomena are clearly the focus of the Gospel scenarios and special episodes in the lives of the saints which the mystic conjures up for meditative mental prayer. This prayer is discursive in the manner that the mystic may imaginatively and prayerfully fantasize the mysteries of the Rosary in the process of reciting Hail Mary's.

These religious fantasies are very conducive to eliciting pious feelings toward God and elevating the mind and heart toward heaven. Indeed, they are intended to be more transformative of the mystic's own heart and mindset toward God more so than informative of some doctrine of Catholic faith. The more the mystic prayerfully seeks to approach God the more he aspires to the entirely spiritual reach of reality commensurate with God's very own divinity. In this approach, he gradually divests himself of the tangible imaginative aspects of his prayerful life and ensconces himself in a recollected ambiance which simply transcends all that is tangible and imaginative. This ambiance is entirely intellectual and spiritual befitting God's own sublime nature of Divinity. In ascending to this ambiance, the mystic is entering into contemplative prayer and leaving aside prayerful meditation which actively engages both the external and internal senses. God who is utterly spirit is not discernible to any of the senses and, hence, is not directly sensed in the physical cosmos' tangibility. In this more elevated prayer, the mystic is more attentive to words evoking God's sublimity, majesty, grandeur, and loftiness such as goodness, beauty, truth, mercy, wisdom, almighty, etc., whose meaning cannot be adequately exemplified nor imaginatively captured in any imaginary fantasy.

The upshot of this transition from a sensory steeped prayer to a completely intellectual intelligible and non-sensory reach of prayer addressing God's divinity, essence, nature, substance, power, creativity, sublimity, personhood, will, intelligence, etc., is that the mystic's prayer-life is no longer geared to arousing his own sensitized religious feelings and emotions toward God. Such religious emotional arousals stimulated by prayerfully evoked sentient and sensational religious imagery motivate the mystic's will to become zealously active in serving God. On the other hand, what is utterly intellectual and non-sensory prayerful knowledge vis-à-vis God carries no such affective impact on the soul's intellectual will. Rather, this knowledge incites the will to remain unemotionally calm and sedately attentive to God bereft of all sensational emotional stirrings and feelings. In this transition from meditative prayer centered on religious sensational imagery to contemplative prayer bereft of all such imagery, the mystic becomes less attached to feelings and emotions of religious excitation and more attached to an unemotional, unaffected, unsensational and nonsensuous religious bearing propitious to contemplative prayer and commensurate with God's own eternal immutability.

In view of this, whether still a novice in meditative prayer or an expert in contemplative prayer, the mystic must never become attached to paranormal religious sensorial phenomena which he experiences without willing it. This for two reasons. If these are from God they will effectuate a beneficent religious fruitfulness even if they are disregarded. Secondly, the task of having to discern beneficial from bogus phenomena will not have to be undertaken. The effect of this deliberate ignoral is that these paranormal sensorial phenomena will not become an impediment to contemplative prayer itself through which the mystic communes directly with God in God's actual Supreme Existence. The only element that the mystic must derive from such supernatural sensorial phenomena is that of his increased devotion and piety toward God Himself over and beyond these religious experiences themselves.

Chapter 18-21. These chapters are to be read privately.

They provide specific examples of the unreliability of supernatural phenomena even when these are from God and not from the devil. The entire thrust of St. John's critique of these phenomena is to emphasize that the pure medium for perfect communion with God is that of the supernatural theological virtue of faith which places the mystic sacramentally in immediate direct touch with God in God's very own Triune Godhead without any created intermediary that would impede this immediate spiritual intimacy with God's very own sublime supreme substantive subsistent Triune existence.

Chapter 22: The difference between the Old and New Testaments regarding supernatural phenomena.

St. John of the Cross sagaciously notes that in the Old Testament it was most appropriate for God to communicate to the prophets through revelations, visions, locutions, etc. because the Old Testament is merely a foreshadowing of the New. However, in the New Testament the fullness of revelation is given in Christ's Incarnation and Gospel preached by the Apostles. Hence, to presently seek to be informed of God's Will by special supernatural phenomena is to arrogantly presume that the fullness of God's Self-Revelation has not been sufficiently given in Christ.

ASCENT Book II Chapters 23-32: FURTHER PURIFICATIONS THROUGH FAITH

Chapter 23: Exploration of spiritual and intellectual apprehensions.

The reality intellectually grasped in these supra-natural encounters need not be actually present to the intellect in the same manner that physical things are physically present to the senses precisely because these intellectual encounters are not mediated by the senses themselves nor by any sentient knowledge which is the normal route for the intellect's knowledge of physical things. Our San Juanistic Carmelite explains that his only interest in these extraordinary forms of apprehensions is to point out that they themselves are occasions of impeding the mystic from advancing in the spiritual life centered principally on being directed by the nocturnal light of the supernatural theological gift of faith.. Such faith is the only proximate means of gaining access to God in the perfection of contemplative prayer.

St. John proceeds to differentiate between these supra-natural encounters which are visions, revelations, locutions and spiritual feelings. In a vision the intellect gazes directly at the object it envisions in a manner similar to the faculty of sight gazing directly at its visible object. In a revelation the mystic's intellect receives a more penetrating understanding of a revealed truth which prior to the revelation it did not grasp as profoundly. In a locution the intellect receives knowledge as though it were actually heard by the body's faculty of hearing. That is, since a word is first heard by a child before it is actually recognized in reading a script, these locutions are received intellectually more by being audible than by being visible. Spiritual feelings are the supernatural volitional appetizing of tangible properties, such as flavors, odors, touches, etc., which are intellectually grasped as exceedingly intelligibly delightful far beyond any real tangible body itself.

These four types of supra-natural intellectual knowledge are called spiritual because they by-pass the normal mediation of the senses. Hence, they are more ethereal precisely because they include no tangibility proper to physical bodies which impinge on the body's sensory faculties of sight, hearing, taste, touch, etc.. Yet these apprehensions impinge on the intellect passively. That is, they are not conjured up by the intellect but rather impact the intellect passively. In other words, they are infused into the intellect supra-naturally.

St. John insists that these four different kinds of supra-natural intellectual apprehensions are all generically visions. Whereas in sentient knowledge it is only the faculty of sight that enjoys visionary knowledge, the intellect's own intellectual scope and range of knowledge is not confined to the specificity proper to each special sensory faculty's sensibility: seeing to the eye, hearing to the ear, smelling to the nose, touching to the hand, tasting to the tongue, etc.. The intellect's own intelligibility is that of the being-as-such of what is seeable, hearable, touchable, tastable, etc.. Hence, the intellect can "envision" intellectually and generically in a "common sense" way the specifically different tangibilities proper to and exclusive to each special sense. The intellect not merely "sees" colorful bodies, "hears" soundful bodies, "tastes" flavorful bodies, and "smells" odorous bodies, etc., it "understands" the very being-as-such of these diverse tangibilities in one "common sense" intelligibility.

In its generic "common sense" understanding the human person's intellectual grasp of these diverse tangibilities engages virtually one and the same "vision" or "insightful" intelligibility of the diverse sensibilities proper to each of the special senses. This is the point which St. John is emphasizing. Whereas the eye sees the red apple's colorful sensibility the body's sentient appetency reacts pleasantly to the ripe apple's red complexion. The intellect, in turn, grasps the apple's red-as-such color in its generic intelligibility in terms of the being-as-such of the apple's red color. While the eye's seeing engages the apple's sensible, palpable, tangible red color and the sentient body's appetency spontaneously finds the delicate red hue to be seductively and passionately pleasing, the intellect grasps the red-as-such in its colorful intelligibility of being-as-such beyond and bereft of the physical palpability peculiar to the apple's red visibility.

The intellect grasps the truth of the apple's red shade. That is, that the apple is truthfully colorfully red-as-such. The mystic's intellectual will spontaneously appetizes (i.e., enjoys) the apple's red-as-such color delightfully and dispassionately because it delights in the truth of the apple's color. This volitional delight is not sentiently and physiologically passionate; rather, it is a spiritual and dispassionate volition in keeping with the soul's inherent inorganic immaterial simplicity. Whereas the body's eye sees that the apple is a special specific shade of red peculiar to a particular species of apple, the intellect's eye "sees" (i.e., understands) the very truth of this specific red apple; to wit, that this specific shade of apple red (ex. gr., the red of the winesap or the delicious apple) is, indeed, an instance of the color, red-as-such.

What is the case for the vision of the body's eyesight is similarly the case for each other of the special senses. While the nose is smelling the apple's special apple odor and the sentient body's appetency spontaneously finds the subtle odor to be seductively and passionately pleasing, and the tongue in tasting the apple's flavor finds the special flavor to be also seductively passionately pleasing, the intellect grasps the apple's tangible qualities intelligibly as being tangible qualities-as-such (i.e., red-as-such, flavor-as-such, odor-as-such of the apple). The intellect grasps the truth of the apple's subtle and special color, odor, and flavor in terms of the being-as-such of these qualities in general (i.e., as-such).

That is, again, the intellect grasps that the apple is truthfully and odorously a pleasant red-as-such delicate-as-such, and sweet-as-such color, odor, and flavor proper to the peculiar species-as-such of the particular fruit being sensed. And, again, the mystic's intellectual will spontaneously, delightfully, and dispassionately appetizes (i.e., enjoys) the apple's special tangible qualities not tangibly and sentiently but intangibly and spiritually because it enjoys the truth of the apple's tangible qualities. In brief, the intellect grasps intelligently and generically what is specific to the sensibility of each of the special senses. Thus, the mystic's intellectual will's delight in the truth which is common to all of these special senses is a more exquisite dispassionate enjoyment than is the mere sentient passionate (i.e., physiological) affected enjoyment afforded the body's sentient appetency.

Lest this point of differentiation between sentient and intellectual knowledge be loss to the reader, consider the following. Sentient knowledge occurs within the physical changeability of the object that is sensed. This changeability itself is physical with the entire spatio-temporal changes attendant on it. The person in seeing and smelling the apple tree's fruit on one day senses a significant different apple tree on any different day. For, the apple tree with its ripened fruit is continuously undergoing a physical environmental change regarding its temperature, growth or decay, moisture, light, etc..

Hence, one day the tree's fruit may be exceedingly fragrant, colorfully ripe, and tasteful; and on another day, not so. The following day these vivid tangible features of the apple tree's fruit may have begun to decompose. This transiency and temporary duration of the apple tree's fruition is integrated into the sentiency of the organic senses. However, this variable fluctuation of the apple tree's fruit including its environmental conditioning, shape, size, texture, distance from the person sensing it, its temperature, enumeration, etc., are not germane to the intellect's grasp of it. The intellect's grasp as-such metaphysically transcends the spatio-temporal dimensionality of the apple tree's physical existence.

In the case of the intellect there is no spatio-temporal transiency to its knowledge. Where the nose smells the ripe apple's fragrant odor better if it is close to the apple and less well if it remains at a distance; better when the apple is fully ripe and less so otherwise; the intellect's knowledge abstracts from these spatio-temporal variations involving the apple's size, shape, texture, location, immobility, moisture, or movement by the wind, etc.. The senses, on the other hand, are immersed in the spatio-temporal conditions of the apple tree's physical existence. Thus, while the special sensibility of the senses is always fleeting and temporary, this very same sensibility is grasped intelligibly, intelligently, and steadfastly by the intellect in an as-such everlasting insightful understanding. Correspondingly, the intellectual appetite (viz., the soul's will) delights in such knowledge without suffering or undergoing any passionate (i.e., transient) affectivity.

In brief, the intellect can discriminate between the apple tree as a plant-as-such and its fruit, the apple-as-such and between the different species of apples each of which has its own peculiar tangible qualities. The intellect grasps the very truth of the apple tree and its fruit when it grasps that this tree is a substantively a plant-as-such while it is only incidentally and seasonally a fruit-as-such. Since a tree-as-such is in its as-such intelligibility bereft of all palpable and tangible sentiency, the more the intellect intellectually understands intelligibly both the apple tree and its fruit, the more general and removed from its sentient palpability is its proper intellectual knowledge.

This generality being the case with the intellect's knowledge of the physical cosmos, it is all the more so in terms of the intellect's knowledge concerning God whose existence infinitely transcends the physical cosmos' materiality and spatio-temporal dimensionality. One intellectually more perfectly understands the apple tree when it grasps that it is as a substantive living plant being. The very understanding of "substance" completely transcends the vicissitudes of the physical cosmos's physical sentient tangibility. "Substance" is exceedingly more general, intangible, and intelligibly comprehensive than is any special quality of the tree and its fruit. Further, the truth that the apple tree is substantively a plant induces in the will a more delightful dispassionate ethereal enjoyment than all the pleasure that smelling, tasting, and eating an apple can afford the body's sentient affective passionate appetency. For the soul's volitional delight regarding the apple is ever immutably enduring whereas the body's passionate delicious and delectable enjoyment is fleeting.

When a person is in the very dark of night and completely out of reach of the apple tree with its delectable fruits, this person may continue to memorially delight volitionally in the everlasting truth of the apple tree's very substance. Further, this very volitional delight does not occur transiently in the body's physiology as does the sentient appetency of the physiological pleasure which accompanies the nose and the eye's sensing the tree's ripened fruit. The will's volitional delight is not a transient enjoyment which lasts only the length of the body's physiological paroxysm which is the case for the sentient appetency accompanying the seeing, smelling, tasting, and eating of the ripe apple. Further, the intellect can discriminate between the scents proper to different species of apples. Indeed, it knows and delights atemporally and enduringly in the very truth-as-such of the tangible properties peculiar to different species of apple trees. The intellectual will, accordingly, delights in this truth not fleetingly and temporarily as is the case with the body's physiological affections but permanently "at will" without any bodily physiological movement.

Given this differentiation between sentient and intellectual knowledge, it is very important to recognize that the intellect may quite independent of the senses become cognizant of a special color or odor or sound or flavor, etc., that no sense has ever actually sensed. Of course, this would not be normally the case; it would be paranormal. Yet, it is within the compass of the intellect's own intelligibility. For it would understand insightfully that this special never-before-sensed color and scent are respectively instances of color-as-such and odor-as-such. Furthermore, it would volitionally enjoy and delight in these special instances of color-as-such and odor-as-such more exquisitely and enduringly than is possible to the senses which are steeped in the spatio-temporal variability of both the physical environment and the body's own organic physiology. The soul being inorganically spiritual is not susceptible in its proper activity to the body's mutation and variation.

Given this analysis, it is clear that there is an intellectual memory that can recall and retrieve both intellectual knowledge and its concomitant volitional appetition. This memory is a Platonic memory, however, and not a historical memory inasmuch as its activity is itself atemporal and only congruently temporal. Thus, a person may recall thinking the same thought today as on the preceding day and willing the same concomitant appetition today as on the preceding day. Still, neither the preceding day's thought and appetition nor the present day's memorial recall occur transitionally and temporally in a manner peculiar to the physical cosmos' mutational temporality and the physical body's own mutational physiology. Within the physical cosmos, changes occur within material bodies or the substantive matter of material bodies. Within the soul's inorganic immateriality, there are no such bodies to undergo physical changes. Hence, all changes are metaphysical and incorporeal. This is the case for the very activity of thinking and reasoning on the part of the intellect and volitional appetition (i.e., willing and loving) on the part of the will.

When the intellect and the will change from a power to know to the act of knowing and from the power to love to the act of loving, they do not mutate as do physical bodies including the human body's organic physiology. They change metaphysically consonant with their inorganic incorporeality. Thus if a tree is transplanted from one spot to another, it cannot occupy both spots simultaneously; it bodily changes its location and undergoes this relocation. Furthermore, this change takes time to be accomplished. On the other hand, when the intellect and will change from not-knowing to knowing and non-loving to loving, they change metaphysically and not physically. In other words, these faculties may be simultaneously both knowing and non-knowing, loving and non-loving in regard to the same object. For, regardless of whatever knowledge and whatever love that these faculties enjoy regarding the same object, this knowledge and love may be increasingly augmented regarding the same object because the potentiality of each faculty is not materially limited and physically inhibited as is the case with the potential materiality of physical bodies.

Consider another example. The body's eyesight can actually see simultaneously red and blue in one and the same vision. No physical body in regard to its corporeality may within the exact same expanse of its physicality be simultaneously red and blue. The spot that is red cannot be blue and vice versa. The reason for this is that physical matter in its materialization harbors only one formative formality. To harbor another formality it must first relinquish the one it has. The senses in their sentient organicity are not as hide-bound physically and materially as are the formal tangibilities of the physical objects they sense. Evidence of this is that the body's eyesight can "see" in one and the same act of seeing several diverse colors simultaneously.

Ancient Greek and Roman philosophers reasoned from this that the senses are able to harbor simultaneously within the organicity of their sensibility a variety of different formal tangibilities proper to each special sense's scope of sentiency. That is, color for the eye, odor, for the nose, texture and temperature for touch, sound for the ear, and flavor for the taste. Accordingly, since the eye sees, for example, simultaneously in one and the same act of "seeing" both red and green, the very tangible formalities of red and green exist in the body's eyesight not physically but organically commensurate with the eye's sentient organicity. These sentient formal red and green colors existing in the eye's organicity are the informative media (i.e., images) through which the eye sees red and green colorful bodies. The eye does not formally see these images themselves; it sees through these informative images the very colorful bodies from which these informative images derive by way of a mediating agency which is sunlight for seeing visible colors, water for tasting soluble flavors, air for hearing audible sounds, etc.. The Medieval Scholastics---and St. John of the Cross also---adopted this account of knowledge. In sum, all knowledge is effectuated by representative media of information and an agency effectuating this information.

The remarkable difference between the exterior special senses and the interior sense of imagination is that whereas the former can sense the formal tangibilities of physical bodies only in the actual presence of such bodies the interior sense of imagination can imaginatively image these very same tangibilities in the absence of such physical bodies. Thus, whereas the special senses do not sense their own mediating informative images but only the physical bodies harboring these formalities, the imagination can, in turn, image these representative formalities apart from the physical bodies themselves.

The intellect, in turn, acquires its own informative ideas of the physical cosmos through the senses but not with the tangible restrictions peculiar to the physiological organicity proper to the senses. Whereas the eye sees through its own sensible formality of color specific colors in their formal informative imagery, the intellect "sees" through its own intelligible formality of being these same informative specificities in their as-such generality. Thus, the intellect grasps intellectually the rose's specific roseate shade of color in terms of the general representative informative idea, red-as-such. Further, the intellect grasps "red" intellectually in a more generic informative idea, color-as-such, since red-as-such is a species of color-as-such. In a further generic informative idea, quality-as-such, the intellect grasps intellectually that a color-as-such is a species of quality-as-such. In a still further more generic informative idea, an incidental essence-as-such, the intellect grasps intellectually that a quality-as-such is incidentally an essence-as-such. For, the rose bush is essentially-as-such a rose botanical plant even apart from its colorful red hue and its aromatic bouquet odor which are merely incidental essences (viz., qualities) of its efflorescence.

In accord with the preceding analysis it should be manifest to the reader of this commentary that the intellect's intellectual knowledge and understanding of the sensibility of the special senses can become increasingly intellectually and concomitantly volitionally refined. Whereas the rose flower or the rose bush is able to emit a limited aromatic fragrance and bouquet commensurate with its physical limitation and that of the environment where it is planted, the intellect's understanding of this fragrance includes no such physical conditioning or limitation. The intellect grasps the very as-such intelligibility of the rose flower's aromatic scent and colorful hue among its other features. Furthermore, it grasps it beyond the limitation of the rose bush's physical location and material limitation. It grasps it as-such in all of its immutable generality and commonality to the point that it grasps that this odor and this color are floral odors and floral colors, plant odors and plant colors, living odors and living colors, incidental odors and incidental colors, etc., vis-à-vis the rose bush's very substantive botanical nature, etc.. In this manner, these soulful faculties remain simultaneously both potentially unknowing and knowing, unloving and loving because their potentiality for knowing and loving remain unlimited regarding the very same object. Accordingly the change from unknowing and not-loving to knowing and loving is a metaphysical and not a physical change.

To recap this previous analysis, all knowledge whether sentient or intellectual occurs through a medium. This medium is twofold: informative and one of agency. The sentient representative informative medium is an image whereas the intellectual representative informative medium is an idea. The informative agency on the part of the special senses is different for each sense. For the eye it is the sunlight that renders physical colorful bodies to be visibly colorful to the eye; to the ear it is the air's atmosphere that renders physical sounding bodies to be audibly tonal, etc.. These informative agencies are themselves physical because the informative image they impart to the senses retains something of their physicality; to wit, the spatio-temporal features peculiar to the sensibility of the senses. The intellect's informative agency is incorporeal and metaphysical because its informative medium, the idea-as-such, is completely bereft and stripped of all corporeal limitations.

This analysis follows the Aristotelian mode of philosophical resolution by reason of the four causes: the material, formal, agent, and final causes. St. John of the Cross's understanding of this causal analysis is commensurate with his philosophical and theological education based on the Scholastic tradition which was prevalent at the time in the Spanish schools of higher education. Within this Scholastic approach to knowledge, the human intellect completely without the prior intervention of the senses can on its own accede to a purely intellectual knowledge entirely bereft of any and every bodily sentiency. This occurs with the color, red, when the intellect attains to the ideal realm of the existence of redness. Redness is the ideal totality of all possible and actual shades of reds include both those which have existed and cease to exist and those which will exist and do not yet exist.

Redness is the ideal red color because it comprehends the totality of all diverse shades of red without itself being actually and explicitly any one specific shade itself. In other words, it is virtually every specific shade without actually and explicitly being any one to the exclusion of any other one. Furthermore, it is everlastingly and immutably red; eternally so if it were concreated consistent with God's own eternity. It is necessarily red because it is immutably so. That is, it is ideally perfectly red because it is lacking in no special shade of red. It is not itself in its instantiated ideal existence actually one shade of red to the exclusion of another shade. Were it such, it could not by this instance of redness be any shade other than this specific shade. Finally, the real actual palpable, visible, color of red that the body's eye can see in seeing the red apple is less perfectly red than is the ideal reality of red intelligible to the soul's intellectual eyesight. Why so? Because the former is a limited red shade whereas the latter is an unlimited number of red shades.

In other words, the more general and impalpable is the intellect's knowledge (i.e., the more vague and indistinct) the more comprehensibly intelligible is its knowledge of whatever it actually knows. The same axiom applies to the intellect's knowledge of God. The more metaphysically invisible, intangible, and impalpably general is the human person's intellectual knowledge of God, the more intelligible does its knowledge apprehend and comprehend God's own sublime, ideal, and totally spiritual supernatural existence and nature. It follows from this that the mystic who in supernatural faith attains immediately and directly without any impeding created informative mediation or agency God's Triune Personhood does so in the utmost general and impalpable terms.

Taking this analysis a step further, it should be increasingly obvious to the reader that the more general the intellect's knowledge and the will's love of their object is, the more knowledgeable and loveable are their corresponding activities. For to know that the rose's scent and hue are scents-as-such and colors-as-such, living-as-such, qualities-as-such, incidental-essences-as-such, etc., is to be able to both understand and love them more perfectly and unaffectedly than is the case for sentient knowledge and sentient appetent affective love that have no access to this general metaphysical level of knowledge and love. Transposing all of this to God, the more general and universal is the mystic's love and knowledge of God, the more exquisitely intelligible and appetible is the mystic's soulful divine knowing and loving commensurate with God's own supernal infinite utterly spiritual immutable divinity and Triune Personhood.

Thus, again, to know that God is not merely intelligible but intelligibility itself and not only loveable but loveliness itself is to become enabled to love God more intelligently and more lovingly. Further, to know that God is not merely a being-as-such but the very Beingness of being-as-such is to both intelligently contemplate (i.e., know) and to volitionally appetize (i.e., to love) God in a Godly manner befitting God's very own supreme unexcelled existence. This is why our Carmelite mentor is repeatedly insisting that contemplative prayer occurs precisely when the mystic is absorbed with God vaguely and enamored with God in a manner that cannot be conveyed in any specific and special mode of loving and knowing.

Lest the reader of St. John's mystagogical text and of this commentary overlook the purpose of this exploration of these supra-natural "insightful" apprehensions, it is simply to point out that they are occasions for the mystic who receives them to become so infatuated with them that they become occasions to be distracted from living out the mystic's prayer-life exclusively within the nocturnal ambience of faith's own supernatural light, the only proximate informative entry into God's own Triune divine nature. The inerrant fidelity of this light keeps the mystic prayerfully attentive to the revelation of Christ in the Church's sacramentality, Sacred Scripture and Sacred Tradition interpreted and promulgated by the infallible authority of the Church's Magisterium. In this way the mystic is protected from any deception which may attend these peculiar extraordinary supra-natural visions he is exploring and discussing here.

Chapter 24: Two kinds of supra-natural, spiritual visions.

Visions themselves are further subdivided into two kinds: those that are substantively incorporeal and those that are corporeal. As an example of the latter he cites the entire Book of Revelation. This is the vision of the New Jerusalem, the Church triumphant in heaven rejoicing in union with Christ as the Lamb of God and the eternal light that illuminates all the saints and angels. This awesome and stupendous vision is seen and recorded by St. John, the Evangelist. St. John of Cross states that it is by a special supernatural illumination

129

(other than the beatific vision) which enables the Evangelist to intellectually enjoy this vision.

Note, that this supra-natural vision is grasped intellectually by the Evangelist. Yet, it is described largely pictorially, figuratively, and metaphorically. That is, the vision itself is intellectual but its rendition within the mindful self-consciousness of the Evangelist transforms the vision into spectacular imagery full of symbolism that needs further interpretation to one who reads the Book of Revelation. Hence, the objective intellectual mode of contemplating this vision differs from its subjective descriptive translation which the Evangelist conjures up from within his own personalized self-conscious mindfulness.

He gives as examples of incorporeal visions those that would enable the mystic to have access to the very substantive essence of God's divinity, angels, and human souls. Such visions are not available in this present life of Christian pilgrimage. They are accessible only through the beatific vision in the life of immortality after death with the resurrected body. It would seem however, that such lofty visions might have been the case for St. Paul and even Moses in the old Testament.

Turning again to corporeal visions which are still patterned after the Book of Revelation, St. John of the Cross stipulates that the offshoot of these is a superlative experience of mystical delight. These visions are intellectual insights into supernatural realities physically depicted. These religious experiences evoke in the mystic quietude, illumination, exultation, delight, purity, love, humility, and an ennobling edification toward God. These differ both in degree and selection.

The devil can through autosuggestion effectuate these visions. But not with the same clarity nor with the same spiritual residue. An example of the devil effectuating these visions is the devil showing to Christ all the kingdoms of the earth. When these visions are influenced by the devil they are followed by an extreme affective aridity and heightened self-esteem. These visions are not suitable to either contemplative prayer or to a perfect union with God because their knowledge of creatures is not commensurate with God's very own divine being and knowledge. However, these visions are not an impediment to contemplative prayer providing the mystic does not become infatuated with them and tenaciously attached to them.

St. John of the Cross adds an important clarification proper to contemplative prayer. The greater is the mystic's fixed installation in the darkness of faith the greater is his growth in the fervor of supernatural hope and love. In other words, the less prone the mystic is to trust in his own religious experiences (viz., these visions) the more he is prepared to trust in God's Sacramental and Self-revelation in Sacred Scripture and Tradition as testified to by the Church's Magisterium. He also points out that the spiritual religious supernatural love that is born of this faith is not emotionally felt precisely because it is itself entirely spiritual in keeping with the human soul's own intellectual spirituality. However, sometimes its vivacity also resonates in the body's somaticity. It is imperative in progressing toward and in maintaining contemplative prayer to seek to live exclusively in the darkness of faith and to avoid everything that interferes with its austerity.

Chapter 25: Nature and kind of revelations.

Revelation is the disclosure of some hidden truth or mystery whether these be past, present, or future. Revelations are intellectual inasmuch as hidden truths are made more lucidly and intelligently manifest. These revelations are hidden mysteries about God and about God's creatures. When they pertain to God they engage articles of faith which involve God's own divine nature such as the Trinity. When they pertain to God's works they often address promises and threats spoken by God through His prophets.

Chapter 26: The two kinds of knowledge of naked truths: the proper conduct of the mystic in their regard.

Intellectual truths are exceedingly delightful and rapturous because in having them the mystic delights in attributes of God's very divinity. These are His omnipotence, goodness, sweetness, mercy, wisdom, etc.. These delights are ravishing beyond speech. These revelations never deal with particulars and they can never be expressed other than in the most general of terms.

This is the type of knowledge available in contemplative prayer. It is not a knowledge about God. Rather, it is knowledge of God Himself. It is knowledge that derives from a perfect prayerful union with God. The devil cannot meddle here. He tries at the sensory level but the upshot is not a buoyant religious spiritual joy. It is rather a severe dryness. The devil cannot penetrate into the human soul's interiority. One instant of this supernal delight afforded by God is sufficient to eradicate all of the venial sins which a lifetime of dedication could not efface. It must be emphasized that this knowledge available in contemplative prayer is not merely the philosophical musing of God infinitely removed from the philosopher's pondering. This knowledge gained through contemplative prayer is mediated through the theological virtue of faith enabling the mystic to gaze on God's Trinitarian Godhead present through the Church's ministers, Sacred Scripture, and the Church's sacramentality.

So intimate is this sublime encounter with God it is nothing short of a divine sublime touch where the medium of knowing God is the very presence of God's own divinity (i.e., God's infinite glorious radiance) which is not mediated by any creature or created informative represenatation. Note that this knowledge is more spiritually and volitionally inebriating than it is intellectually illuminating. That is, the extreme divine delight is more overwhelming than is the mystic's comprehension of God as the fountainhead of this delight. For this knowledge is more akin to the beatific vision even though it is enveloped in the umbrage that accompanies it in this present life of faith's intellectual insight into God.

These delights are gratuitously received from God. Sometimes they arrive out of the blue and resonate beyond the soul's own sanctuary into the body's subjective sensitive somaticity and intimate psychicity. Other times they arrive during the mystic's soulful prayerful recollection and linger only as a soulful ecstasy. They cannot be self-induced or anticipated. St. John points out that the mystic here need not become self-detached from these delights since they are the very goal of his prayerful spiritual pilgrimage to enjoy a perfect union with God. From this it follows that only the mystic who is self-detached from all that is not God Himself is susceptible to experience these delights within the psychosomatic resonance of the subjectivity of his somatic body and psychic mind. Even if these sublime revelations allow the mystic to elucidate the articles of faith more explicitly, he cautions the mystic not to desire such elucidations because this very quest for such enlightenment may divert the mystic from the overall impact of faith. This overall impact unites the mystic so directly and personally with God's omnipotent infinite Godhead that the mystic cannot but remain overpowered by God's glorious brilliance and, thereby, find his intellect eclipsed in the umbrage of this majestic splendor.

The other kind of revelation pertaining to creatures is less delightful precisely because it is a knowledge of what is inferior to God. This knowledge pertains to prophecy and discernment. It remains entirely interior to the soul itself. Here St. John admonishes the mystic who has these experiences to place less credence in them than he would in the confessor to whom he reveals them. The reason for this is that it is imperative for the mystic to rely more on the credence of faith alone rather than on his own understanding and mystical experiences.

This kind of revelation is an infused knowledge exemplified in the infused charisms and Church ministeries mentioned by St. Paul in Sacred Scripture. It is a knowledge peculiar to the prudence dispensed by a very holy person who has a gifted purity of heart and can discern the hearts and minds of others. Such an individual can discern the hearts of others by observing and interpreting their personal characteristics and behavior. This discernment may even include supra-natural knowledge regarding future events.

Again, this knowledge comes to the mystic unsolicited. St. John again cautions the mystic in regard to such supra-natural knowledge to be wary of the devil's meddling. This diabolical deception is recognizable because it is effectuated through the imagination's excitation. The mystic, for example, may learn of the sins of another for the purpose of defaming the other and causing mischief. If a mystic becomes attached to these forms of revelation they will become an impediment to his advancing to contemplative prayer and a more perfect union with God rooted exclusively in faith. Thus, the mystic is advised to remain aloof from such knowledge even when receiving it unsolicited. It is preferable to remain quietly composed in the darkness of faith proper to contemplative prayer itself.

We may at this point infer two singular points. The first is the point that contemplative prayer does not bypass the intellect nor is it confined to merely intellectual knowledge. Intellectual knowledge coupled with the soul's volitional love are fundamental to contemplative prayer. Both are entirely spiritual, inorganic, and beyond the body's physiological constitution. Given this foundation, contemplative prayer in its very essence transcends the body's sentiency and affectivity. It is not surprising, then, that the mystic who is absorbed in contemplative prayer becomes oblivious to his environment and to the passage of cosmic time and even of the historical events taking place. The contemplative movements are fundamentally spiritual metaphysical atemporal, and transhistorical.

Supplementally and incidentally contemplative prayer engages the body's psychosomatic self-humanized subjectivity. It is not merely the soul that engages in contemplative prayer; it is the human person principally, individually, and inalienably. This human person is not constituted of the soul alone; but is constituted substantively of the body and soul. While the soul is the dynamic life of the body, it is endowed with an inherent life of its own in virtue of its own inorganic and incorporeal vitality that transcends the body's corporeality. The human person in his subsistent unique and inalienable personhood avails himseflf of this soulful dynamism as well as of the body's soulfully energized organic animated animal and botanical dynamism. Still, there is still a supplemental and additional dimension to the human person's personhood. This is its subjective synergism in the human person's self-cultivation of his psychosomatic body's self-serving productivity. This self-humanized self-cultivated psychosomatic body finds its genuine and authentic personalized self-fulfillment not in the artificial products of its own personification but, rather, in the (supernatural) perfection of its own natural constitution; principally in the human soul's immortal existence and supernatural restoration to its mortal body through the mediation of Christ's resurrection and ascension into heaven.

In view of this subjective synergism and psychosomatic subjectivity, the human person's self-cultivated body has its own need to partake and to participate in the soul's inherently spiritual intransitive activity of contemplative prayer. Furthermore, since contemplative prayer is fundamentally and inherently supernaturally spiritual (i.e., infused and suffused with God's very own Triune divine supernatural benevolent and merciful Personal gratuitous graciousness), the person's superhumanized self-cultivated bodily subjectivity (i.e., psychosomatic personality) seeks its own genuine and authentic personalized confident self-fulfillment not in its own subjective selfhood nor in its own transitive artificial cultivations, but in the plenitude of the human person's objective nature's supernatural destiny (viz., God) and that nature's pluperfect intelligible conscionable faithful governance toward that divine destiny as well as its volitional intransitive loving enjoyment of its arrival at this destiny.

In view of the preceding paragraph, the supra-natural volitional joy and spiritual delight flooding the soul overflows into the human person's bodily psychosomatic subjectivity as its proper personalized bodily sensitized spiritualized self-contentment and religious mindful intimate self-containment. For this to take place it is imperative that the human person within the subjectivity of the selfhood of his own personhood be both heartfully (i.e., bodily) and mindfully (i.e., mentally) totally sacrificially surrendered in his subjectivity to his selfhood's self-fulfillment in the human person's objective supernatural order transcendent to his own self-possessive subjectivity. In other words, if the human person in his mystical life tenaciously clings to his subjective religious heartfelt sensuous self-contentment and to his subjective mindful impassive religious self-containment, he will become distracted and deterred from seeking God objectively, intellectually, and principally through the supernatural medium of faith.

Chapter 27: The second type of revelation: secrets and mysteries.

The first of these pertain to God Himself in His Trinitarian Godhead. The second pertains to God's creation. These, then, center on the Catholic deposit of faith and what can be derived from this deposit. Sacred Scripture itself abounds in examples of prophecies about the future. These revelations also continue to take place even today inasmuch as some mystics are foretold about the time of their death or the fall of a nation. Another kind of such a revelation occurred at Lourdes and Fatima. In Lourdes our Blessed Mother's Immaculate Conception was revealed. This is a truth already inherent in Sacred Scripture but only implicitly. At Fatima future events were prophesied.

The devil is a very bothersome meddler in these revelations. He may begin by revealing authentic truths as a way of later misleading the visionary. Again, St. John offers a stern admonition regarding these revelations. Even if their clarity regarding the truths pertaining to the deposit of faith leaves no room for doubt or deception, it is still preferable for the mystic to abide in the abstemious darkness of faith inherent in contemplative prayer itself. For, in the latter the mystic continues to advance toward a perfect prayerful union with God Himself. He adds still another admonition to the mystic receiving such revelations. If this mystic becomes enamored with these, he becomes susceptible to being exploitatively deceived by the devil's intrigues. Again, St. John stresses that the night of faith in quiet resolute prayer of contemplation is an infallible path to a perfect union of love with God's own divine loveliness.

Chapter 28: Supernatural locutions received by the spirit.

These are of three types: successive, formal, and substantial. Successive locutions are words and reasonings received and deduced while the mystic is prayerfully recollected. Formal locutions are very distinct and formal words received notably from a party other than the mystic himself. Substantial locutions are words which impart to the soul the very power to enact what they exhortatively signify.

At this point it seems important to explain what the "spirit" signifies here for St. John of the Cross. It means that the locutions are distinctively beyond the reach of sensorial supernatural communications. In this sense they may be supernaturally disclosed directly to the soul's intelligence or directly to the human person's egocentric mindful self (in virtue of the human person's personhood). For, it is the case that the intellect is the human person's soulful faculty informed with ideas while the person's mindful self transforms itself by mentally fabricating speakable notional words befitting such ideas.

But, in either case, whether it is the intellect receiving objectively supernaturally infused ideas or the mind consciously, subjectively, and superhumanistically experiencing words consonant with these infused ideas, both of these receptions are suitably locutions as described by St. John of the Cross. The activity of reasoning intellectually with a supernatural facility and clarity beyond the mystic's own habitual ability is one that differs markedly from the subjective mind's mindful superhumanistic mode of rationalizing. The intellect reasons syllogistically whereas the mind rationalizes logistically with a mathematical catalogical (i.e., typological) logic different from its metaphysical ontological counterpart in the intellect. More can be said about this at a later point.

Chapter 29: Successive locutions.

When recollected in contemplative prayer, the mystic proceeds with his thoughts and judgments in such an easy and facile manner that it seems to him not to be himself but another person that is facilitating his thoughts and reasoning. This "other" can be easily construed to be the Holy Spirit indwelling within the inner inmost mental and heartfelt recesses of the person's selfhood.

Note, St. John cautions, that these thoughts and judgments themselves need not harbor any formal deceptions. Yet, the reasoning which ensues from them may be conducted naturally by the intellect's own native intelligence. In this case, they are subject to illogical conclusions. In another caution, St. John points out that any personalized attachment the mystic may have to these locutions may result in a false exalted self-esteem that God is speaking directly to him. Such self-esteem militates against the proper attitude of self-denial and mortification which should be the mystic's proper approach to God.

Why then must the mystic remain self-detached from these locutions? It is because in the normal course of events the Holy Spirit's Gospel instruction is given through the committed theological virtue of faith. By this route, the mystic receives holistically and integrally what he is to learn and understand of the mystery of Christ. In any event, it is clear to St. John that the slightest attachment the mystic may have to these locutions poses the prospect of their becoming an impediment for him to proceed forward to a perfect union with God in contemplative prayer based totally on faith's blinding luminous splendor of God's very own divine Glory (i.e., Graciousness). Note, again, that blind faith is not blind because it is wanting in intelligibility. It is blind because the intelligible evidence it presents (viz., God's infinitely radiant Glory) is super eminently and awesomely intelligible to the point of overpowering the human intellect's own native light of intelligibility.

It should be also noted again that the human intellect on its own is able to metaphysically at the ideal reach of reality ponder the reality of God in terms that are completely beyond the reach of the senses. This native prowess proper to human intelligence is itself aggrandized in the supernatural light of faith. Thus, while naturally metaphysically recognizing the existence and reality of a Supreme Being of Beingness endowed with attributes commensurate with this supremacy, the human intellect in the light of faith can more lucidly and clairvoyantly marvel at the incomprehensible mystery of the Blessed Eucharist in which Christ is sacramentally incarnated in His Church in His glorified Body, Blood, Soul, and Divinity.

The lifestyle of the mystic should be less that of anticipating and reveling in paranormal religious experiences and more that of the sage who lives a life of mortification and self-denial in imitation of Christ's very own lifestyle of humility. The devil can also meddle with these locutions. This is very evident in the case of heretics and also in the lives of those who have made a pact with the devil.

Conclusively, these locutions may originate in three separate sources: the Holy Spirit, the intellect's own natural insight, and the devil. There are some general signs of discernment which can assist the mystic to differentiate between these. If they derive from the Holy Spirit their beneficent effect will be the mystic's experience of an increased love, humility, and reverence for God. If they derive from the intellect itself, the soul is left dry and empty. However, this is also the same effect that results if they originate from the devil. It is difficult to discern between the two. Indeed, St. John points out, the devil can induce tears in the mystic. In the final analysis the abiding effect that locutions have when imparted by the devil is distinctively different from the benign effects these locutions have when influenced by the Holy Spirit. The deleterious effects they impart to the mystic when they derive from the devil are dryness, self-love, false humility, self-esteem, and vanity. St. John's final counsel is for the mystic to remain self-detached from them.

Chapter 30: Interior locutions.

These are experienced as coming from another and not from the mystic himself. These are not solicited. They arrive out of the blue. Ordinarily, they shed light on some special teaching. Sometimes they are accompanied by acceptance and at another time by repugnance, especially when they are directives and summons from God requiring considerable humiliation for the mystic to comply with them. When these locutions originate from the devil, they include a readiness on the part of the mystic to accomplish them for the mystic's own personal aggrandizement. These locutions differ from successive ones because they include with their directions the element of persuasion (i.e., conviction) and readiness to expedite their execution. In any event, St. John cautions the mystic to challenge these locutions because they bear directives which are not essential to the Catholic faith. Therefore, they could be diabolical deceits. They should be confided to a reputable confessor.

Chapter 31: Substantive locutions.

These impart to the mystic an immediate efficacy to enable the mystic to carry them out with great dispatch. If God commands the mystic, "do not fear," the mystic abruptly becomes undaunted. The mystic need not aspire to receive these exhortations and commands. Further, he need not seek to become self-detached from these locutions. The efficacy inherent in these commands cannot originate with the devil unless a person has already surrendered himself utterly to such diabolical influence. Hence, the mystic cannot be deceived by such commands when they originate from God. Further, the devil cannot interfere with God's own influence. Certainly, the devil can influence the mystic by autosuggestion because as the father of lies he can falsely present things as charming and enchanting. However, his influence is no match for God's almighty power. St. John concludes by declaring that mystics who receive such exhortations from God are happy indeed.

Chapter 32: Spiritual feelings.

These are of two kinds: volitional feelings of the will within the soul's very interiority and those that are even loftier. These are more proper to the will than they are to the intellect. Yet, they enhance the intellect's own proper knowledge. They are unsolicited and arise at any instant. They are gratuitous. Some are distinct and brief and others are prolonged.

These spiritual unctions may be impeded by the intellect itself if the mystic becomes more attentive to trying to intellectually understand them rather than to merely passively entertain them. The mystic should not aspire to have such feelings because the devil can meddle here also. The mystic should have toward these elevated religious exultations an attitude of meek resignation, humility, and passivity. It should be noted that while St. John speaks of feelings here and provides no explicit examples to describe these spiritual feelings, he more than likely is not addressing mystical ecstatic exultations and consolations which are rooted in the senses since he is speaking within the context of the intellect transcendent to the senses. Of course, it is the case that such exultations may be essentially volitional and not sensuous even while resonating within the somatic body's subjective sensitivity. In any event, they impact on the intellect itself to the point that they fortify its acumen in regard to recognizing the source of these experiences.

This marks the close of St. John's examination of all paranormal mystical forms of knowledge imparted intellectually. He insists that this examination is comprehensive. There are no other supernatural phenomena intellectually transmitted other than these.

ASCENT Book III. PURIFICATION OF THE MEMORY THROUGH THE THEOLOGIAL VIRTUE OF HOPE

Preliminary to the exposition of the memory

The role and place of memory in St. John's mystagogical writings.

Here as in the preceding pages of the *Ascent*, St. John continues to explain how and why the activity of memory, like the faculty of the intellect must, in turn, be purged of all of its proper memorial activity as a preliminary for the mystic to enter into contemplative prayer. It is very much the case that St. John does not make it a point to define the memory itself no more than he does to define the intellect. But, it is the task of this commentary to spell out more explicitly what these two faculties entail along with the faculty of the will. In the measure that the mystic understands the operations peculiar to these two faculties and the will along with them, he will become more competent in understanding the ascetic program St. John proposes as a necessary preliminary step of actively becoming better disposed to enter into contemplative prayer itself and in contemplative prayer to accede to a perfect union with God's Trinitarian Godhead.

Three distinct cruciform orders inherent in the human person's constitution and spiritual life.

Here, it is vital to bring to the reader's attention that there are three distinct cruciform orders inherent in the human person's constitution and spiritual life in which the mystic is seeking to cooperate with God's grace received in Baptism and through it to become more perfectly conformed by its efficacy to Jesus Christ's Sacred Heart and beatitudinal mindset. The cross's vertical order is hierarchical. That is, its prioritization is that of the superior to the inferior, the ordinate to the subordinate. This is the natural order of the dynamics of existence. It is the order of nature and supernature, the order of human-kind's own dynamic substantive body/soul nature and of the Sacramental Church's supernatural divine grace.

The uppermost primacy of this order is God's transcendent sovereign subsistent existence in God's ideal imperishable transcendent and immutable abode of eternity in existential opposition to the posterior lowermost reach of this order which is the cosmic existence of that which is merely temporary and materially perishable in time's duration. In his substantive corporeal nature, man partakes of both the perishable cosmos and of the imperishable everlasting heaven of the angels in his substantive incorporeal nature (viz., his spiritual soul). In brief, mankind naturally participates in both the lowest subordinate and the highest ordinate reaches of the hierarchical vertical order of created existence. This order is objective for it exists independently of the intellect's knowledge of it and the will's volition toward it. Indeed, the intellect's knowledge is directly ordered to knowing this reality itself in all of its reaches. By reason of His Incarnation Jesus Christ, God/Superman, the Uncreated/creature, is both the Author and the hierarchical synthesis of all of creation which He incorporates within His human nature.

The cross's horizontal order of self-humanizing articulture is historical. Its own prioritization is that of domination versus subjugation, the master versus the slave, the dominant versus the recessive. This is the cultural order of the synergistics of resistance. It is the order of culture and religion, the order of humankind's synergistic psychosomatic self-humanization and superhumanistic Christian skillful self-mastery and self-control carried out in the sacrificial ascetic program of self-denial proposed by the Catholic Church's Gospel lifetyle summarized in the evangelical counsels of poverty, chastity, and obedience which, in turn, epitomize the Gospel lifestyle of the beatitudes.

There is no absolute primacy in this historical order. Every priority is preceded indefinitely by an anterior priority. Secular history's past is always preceded by a prior more ancient immemorial past and history's future is, in turn, always succeeded by a posterior stage of futurity beyond the immediate future of tomorrow. Secular history is not merely moments of time or time's transient duration. Time exists in the objective cosmic order of temporal existence. History transpires in the subjective order of humankind's egocentric self-de/constructive self-humanization and self-eventuation.

This historical expiration and evolution is horizontally subjective and does not occur in the vertical order of existence. Man's human nature is not naturally historical; it is naturally hierarchical. That is, humankind is the wedlock of both the angelic created heaven's spirituality and the cosmos' materiality.

There is no evolution in the substantive nature of humankind from the creation of Adam & Eve to their progeny in the last individual that ever will be procreated. Ontological reality is constituted of dynamic actualities becoming more or less actual and actualized in terms of their natural potential. History, on the other hand, is a de/constructive process of mankind's self-humanization forcibly, fatefully, and willfully exerted through the synergetic construction of events and their eventuation. These events do not eventuate purposefully as dynamic actualities developing in a manner proper to the natural substances of the physical cosmos but eventuate kinetically to the dys/advantage of mankind's self-serving self-humanization and self-actualization.

History is a self-cultivated story of evolving stages that unfold in mankind's productive social self-actualization. There is no history in the vertical ontological order of creation or in the subsequent immortal existence of the human person following the body's death. Every human person is constituted of the same substantive common nature. There is no historical evolution in this nature itself or in the prolongation of this nature through human procreation. There is, however, an evolution in humankind's artificially self-cultivated egocentric self-humanization. This evolution takes place historically within the individualized subjectivity (i.e., selfhood) of each human person's collective and individualistic egocentric self-subsistent personhood.

In the Book of Genesis there is conflated together two separate accounts of creation. One is unmistakably theocentric. That is, this account of creation is ahistorical. It is hierarchical. Each successive day of creation is succeeded by a higher and superior superordinate order of existence culminating in the creation of mankind as the bond between the angelic and the cosmic orders. The other account is unmistakably anthropocentric. That is, this account of creation is historical and is given as unfolding from within the innermost experiential egocentric subjective self-awareness of Adam himself involved in a primeval stage of innocence and a subsequent fallen stage of guilt.

The priority peculiar to the historical order itself is not one of purposeful ordination and destination. Rather, it is one of an egocentric influential self-serving fateful orientation and polarization. There is an idealistic orientation in polar opposition to its realistic counterpart and vice versa. These polar opposites parallel somewhat the ideal/real ordination-subordination in the objective ontological hierarchical vertical order. However, they are themselves in their polarity in the case of mankind's selfhood opposed to each other as the dominant self is opposed to its subservient self; and, vice versa. Hence, this polar opposition is not hierarchically of corporeal matter (viz., a body) versus incorporeal spirit (viz., the soul), or time versus eternity. It is a polarized psychosomatic bi-polar corpuscular tension within the very subjective egocentric personality and selfhood of each individual person.

This personality consists of an insubstantial somatic visceral corpuscular body and insubstantial psychic cerebral mind which are in polar contention with each other. This personalized body is not corporeal; it is corpuscular. That is, it is not dynamically and holistically organic (viz., one and the same substantive body throughout all of its vital organic existence and activity). It is anatomically and kinetically synergized into a complex of disparate organisms which are, in turn, composed of microscopic cells, molecules, atoms, etc., forming the subject of biochemistry and modern experimental studies. This personalized mind, in turn, is not spiritually incorporeal as is the case with the human soul's intellect. Indeed, this mind cannot function without the healthy functioning of the brain and its neurological connections.

The vertical hierarchical order of the cross is at cross-purposes with its horizontal-historical counterpart. Christ's humanity which is crucified to the cross is pinioned within these cross-purposes. He spans the hierarchical vertical order of eternity and temporality, on the one hand, and the historical order of history's immemorial past and future, on the other. He is both transcendently beyond the cosmos's temporality in His Personhood which exists from all eternity and immanently within the momentary time of the cosmos' temporality by reason of His human nature. Again, He is both prefigured and anticipated at the very dawn of salvation history in the Old Testament and incarnate in the eschatological culmination of this history in the New Testament. Further, He continues to be suspended on the cross-purposes of this cross of crucifixion throughout the on-going history of the members of the Sacramental Church which He founded as recorded in the Acts of the Apostles, the Epistles and the Book of Revelation.

The disciple of Christ who is not greater than the master is likewise within his own personhood suspended on this same cruciform order of cross-purposes. The vertical objective hierarchical order of the human person's natural constitution is at cross-purposes with the historical order of his cultural subjectivity. He can only reconcile the two in the very same way that Christ Himself reconciles the two disparate orders within His own self-surrender to His Father's Holy Will which requires that He die to His own subjective Selfhood in order to both surmount its historical demise in order to achieve its authentic historical self-fulfillment eschatologically beyond history within the transhistorical realm of the Father's own eternal abode, the heavenly Jerusalem.

This triune cruciformity peculiar to the branches of the cross is the key to this commentary on the mystical life of prayer. The objective natural order is inherently metaphysical and ontological. Every reality within this order consists of a holistic energetic entity which is constituted of a whole of excellence. The whole always exceeds its constitutive parts. Thus, while the human person's nature is substantively constituted of a substantive material component, the body, and a substantive immaterial (i.e., spiritual component) the soul, this holistic substance is not reducible to its component parts. In other words the nature of the human person is not half and half or any other ratio; it is wholly material and wholly spiritual. While the soul is not material and the body is not spiritual, the integral human nature is holistically both spiritual and material. Further, this is the case for any incidental component of the soul and body. The human soul which is the vital principle and animation of the human body is wholly, indivisibly, and holistically alive in every part of the body.

On the other hand, the subjective cultural order is inherently paraphysical and phenomenological. Every consideration in this order consists of a non-holistic piecemeal synergistic enterprise which is only a quasi whole. For, whatever the whole may be that is encompassed, it is always reducible to the sum of its component parts. Thus, the anatomical parts of any of the body's physiology are what constitute that anatomy's make-up. There is nothing more to the heart's make-up than its anatomical components. One cannot state of the heart's ventricle or artery that each is wholly the heart; each is only a component part of the heart. There is no holistic anatomical heart in contradistinction to its anatomical parts. There is no metaphysical whole and holistic entity in the subjective cultural order; there are only paraphysical enterprising "wholes" that synergistically, anatomically, and organizationally function as a quasi whole.

In the objective vertical order there can be no substitution of any component of a natural organic holistic whole. The human person's substantive body cannot be replaced by another available body. Similarly for the human soul. Further, no natural part or component of this substantive body, even a non-substantive component, such as the body's bodily arm or leg or eye or ear, etc., can be substituted for and replaced with another leg, eye, ear, etc.. It is quite otherwise in the subjective horizontal order. This is so precisely because there is no organic holistic whole; there is only a piecemeal quasi whole constituted of its component parts. In this case, a component part may be substituted artificially by an alternative part. Thus, the eye's cornea may be replaced with an artificial cornea or a portion thereof.

The full import of the preceding differentiation between the objective metaphysical and the subjective paraphysical orders cannot be overemphasized. In the objective natural metaphysical and ontological order every part of the eye's organ is organically one and the same faculty of sight. Thus, while there are two separate organs of sight there is but one entitative energetic holistic faculty of sight and one intransitive holistic operational act of seeing proper to every constitutive part of that faculty. It is quite otherwise in the subjective artificial and cultural paraphysical and phenomenological order. In this order, there is no faculty of sight but only a facility of seeing which is a mechanistic synergistic facility rather than an organic faculty. Any part of this mechanism (i.e., organism) of seeing may be replaced or supplemented by an artificial part or mechanism. Thus, for example, there is the artificial optical lens whether it be a telescopic or microscopic lens which further facilitates the mechanism of sight's vision. Further, it is not this subjective mechanism of sight that actually sees; it is simply this subjective mechanism that facilitates the objective organ of sight's actual seeing.

Further evidence of this is the artificial making of a camera which duplicates the subjective synergistic mechanism of sight. The camera can artificially capture the visualization of objects more perfectly than can the mechanism itself of sight. Yet, the camera cannot itself energetically "see" its own visualizations (i.e., photos). These are actually only energetically seen by the objective faculty of sight. In other words, the metaphysical and ontological order of nature is fundamental and nonsubstitutable in its fundamentality. The paraphysical and phenomenological order of culture is supplemental and ancillary to the fundamental order and cannot itself substitute for the fundamental order itself; it either supplementally facilitates and brings to perfection the metaphysical order's own operation or aborts altogether the fundamental order by substituting for it and supplanting it rather than supplementing it.

The human person encompasses both an objective order of nature and a subjective order of culture. It is one and the same human person fundamentally and naturally that supplementally and artificially brings its own objective nature to a completion and perfection subjectively and culturally which is not possible to that nature considered merely naturally, objectively, and fundamentally. This interplay between a person's objective nature and subjective self-cultivation involves cruciformly the vertical and horizontal branches of the cross. Each of these two branches are at cross-purposes with each other. Their reconciliation constitutes their cruciformity when they are juxtaposed to each other. Their reconciliation can only be achieved supernaturally and superhumanistically through Christ's very own crucifixion and self-oblation on the cross that was raised on Calvary.

It is the purpose and objective of this commentary to expound the mystagogical writings of St. John of the Cross within the framework of this cruciformity. This means that the dual objective and subjective constitution of the human person including the reconciliation of these two orders must be dialogically taken into account and reconciled with each other pursuant to the reconciliation effectuated by Christ Himself in the context of His divine Personhood incarnate in mankind's human nature and culturally brought to perfection within the subjectivity of His own compassionate Sacred Heart and beatitudinal mindset. Thus, there is a triune cruciform order which dialogically permeates this commentary as the reader will discover as he proceeds forward.

The human person's bodily objective/substantive corporeality versus its subjective/insubstantive corpuscularity.

The human person's substantive body considered objectively remains one and the same body from the instant of conception to the instant of death. This is the corporeal substantive holistic body which is irreducibly more than the sum of its bodily parts. This corporeal substantive body exists at the very instant of the conception of a person's existence and endures throughout the human person's earthly lifetime. In this very instant a human person's conception this substantive body at the very outset of its development is substantively a living mineral, zoological, botanical, human body. It is one and the same substantive human body that undergoes and sustains all of the developmental changes that occur to the human person throughout that person's lifetime.

Yet, this body subjectively considered lacks this irreducible substantivity. It is reducible to the fragmentary anatomical and biochemical components into which it is analyzed. This anatomical and biochemical insubstantive quasi corpuscular body is reducible to the sum of its organistic, cellular, microscopic molecular and atomic parts. Furthermore, in terms of these fragmentary parts, this "body" is continuously, transformatively and processively morphing. Consider as one example which is typical for all other instances of the body's anatomical and physiological make-up. The body's blood is spoken of as a vital fluid and vitally important for the nourishment and metabolism of the body's organs and organisms. This fluid is made up of living cells. These cells themselves are made up of other components such as proteins, water, glucose, HDL, LDL, & VLDL, leukocytes, erythrocytes, platelets, etc.. These components themselves are further reducible to biochemical molecules which, in turn, are explicable in terms of atomic and subatomic components. These cells are continuously morphing into cellular transformations. There are different blood types in different individuals.

In brief, the human body considered subjectively, phenomenologically, and insubstantively is never one and the self-same body other than metaphorically in a "make-believe" acceptance. Indeed, every person can subjectively verify for himself that the body of which he is subjectively aware is a different body from one day to the next and frequently from one hour to the next and indubitably from one year to the next. Considered objectively, ontologically, and substantively, on the other hand, it is one and the self-same body in a literal real-belief acceptance that undergoes all of the developmental changes that occur minerally, zoologically, botanically, and humanly. The substantive "body" exists in the vertical order of existence while the latter insubstantive "body" resists such holistic enduring existence in the horizontal historical order of resistance. Further, it is one and the self-same human person that is both aware objectively and reflectively of his substantive body and self-aware reflexively of his insubstantive quasi-body.

One and the same human person who is in the objective vertical ontological order constituted and aware reflectively and intelligently of being constituted of a dynamic energetic soul/body substantive nature which is common to every other person is simultaneously in the subjective horizontal phenomenological order mindfully and self-consciously aware of having a kinetic insubstantive synergetic mind/body self-cultivated selfhood in a polarized sociability with selves other than his/her own self. In the objective order the person's body is constituted of an intelligent animal sentiency and affectivity whereas in the subjective order the person's body consists of a sensationally sensitized emotional somatic sensorium in polar opposition to an ideationally desensitized unemotional psychic cerebrum.

Quite possibly the brain is the most crucial synergetic mechanism for the human person's personalized mindful psyche. The mind's psychicity differs from its bodily polarized somatic counterpart precisely because its own self-conscious psychicity is devoid of the conscious sensuality, feeling, tactility, sensitivity, sensations, etc., proper to the somatic body's anatomy. Both the somatic body and the psychic mind are accessible to the human person only through a reflexive conscious attention to each.

Indeed, the body's somaticity can be consciously felt in the diversity of its anatomical organisms when these organisms themselves draw attention to their sensitivity, whereas the mind's psychicity, in turn, engages a self-consciousness which is entirely devoid of every kind of sensational sensitivity and feeling.

This disparity of consciousness accentuates the polarized tension between the body's soma and the mind's psyche. The somatic body's own insubstantial fragmentary anatomical organizational functions are directly empirically observable and manipulable through hi-tech sophisticated equipment and biochemical control. In direct contrast to this, the psychic mind's own insubstantial fragmentary thoughts, notions, conceptions, inspirations, and fabrications resist hi-tech observations and direct biochemical manipulation. Because of this, the mind's psychic functions are entirely subjectively private and beyond the empirical scrutiny of anyone other than the egocentric personality itself which is privately aware of its own intimate thoughts, schemes, inspirations, & dreams.

There is a have/have-not paradox in the polar tension found in every personality's psychosomatic selfhood. When one is attentively conscious of the body's outer somatic feelings and motions, one is inattentive to the mind's inner psychic bearings and motionlessness. And vice versa. When one is attentively motionlessly absorbed in one's thoughts, one is inattentive to the body's sensations and motions. In other words, when one is preoccupied with the one, the other is neglected. One cannot be simultaneously fully attentive to both. That is, if one is to mentally attend to mathematical calculations, one is to sit down and cease engaging in an athletic game or manual work demanding a close control over the body's skillful movement. On the other hand, if one is actively engaged in a physical sport, he cannot in this action be calmly carrying out mathematical calculations.

One's psychosomatic personality is fraught with paradoxes. One might construe that an individual engages his consciousness in the most exacting and strenuous way in an extrospective awareness in which the body's mobility and agility is the focus of his attention such as in playing a contact sport or grappling in a wrestling match. This is not the case. This extrospective stage and phase of consciousness is best described as a simple and basic focal awareness. Paradoxically enough one is intimately and intensively more conscious of one's own selfhood when one is completely oblivious to the body's movement, feelings, sensitivities, and sensations while completely introspectively self-absorbed in an entrancing hypnotic concentration. This self-absorption is best described as a subconsciousness because it is below the threshold of one's empirical observation. A semi-conscious stage is one that is partially conscious and partially subconscious as is the case with one playing a musical instrument while attending to a musical score. Another example of this semiconsciousness is the card game of contract bridge.

A bridge player must be subconsciously mentally attentive to calculating the mathematical grouping of the cards he holds in his hand in combination with his partner's cards partially revealed in the opening contract bidding even while he consciously hears and attends to his opponent's contractual bidding. This bipolar tension inherent in the psychosomatic personality of every human being lends itself to extreme ideologies which are irreconcilable to each other. Thus, on the one hand, there is the guru in the Orient who through transcendental meditation construes that mankind attains to the zenith of its self-humanized selfhood when the psychic mind's self-absorption is entirely bodiless and assimilated to a global consciousness. If this bodiless spiritualistic union with a global consciousness is not attained in one's lifetime the human psyche returns through rein-carnation to another lifetime and this cycle continues until a complete global consciousness is eventually attained.

On the other hand, here in the Occident, there is the technocrat who through hi-tech efficiency construes that mankind attains to its zenith of self-humanized selfhood when the somatic body is entirely reconstructed as a mindless robot capable of stupendous mechanical feats and a prolonged life that is indefinitely sustained through bio-physical intervention and hi-tech instrumentation. The model for this is the robotic bionic invulnerable superman of films equipped with hi-tech senses and remarkable resistance to withstand gigantic phys-ical and electronic forces.

Memory in St. John's mystagogy is the center of the human person's historical evolution.

St. John states that the memory as a faculty of the soul. Yet, he describes it otherwise. The only memory which is endemic to the soul is the Platonic memory that is the storehouse for ideas which are com-pletely devoid of the spatio-temporal accoutrements proper to physic-al bodies. Such a memory recalls the intellect's own ideas and intel-lectual reasoning within the residuum of the intellect's own intelligib-ility and accompanying volitional velleity. This memory excludes the person's objective animal body's sentiency and affectivity, on the one hand, and the same human person's subjective self-humanized sensit-ized emotional bodily feelings and emotionless mental bearings, longings, and yearnings, on the other hand.

Given that St. John within his own cultural setting had no expli-cit knowledge of egology and the human person's self-subsistent per-sonhood's own subjective psychosomatic personality and selfhood, the soul was the only logical source of the memory's memoriality for him. All vital activity was ascribed either to the substantive human body's organicity or to its corresponding substantive inorganic soul. Such activity was explained as deriving from faculties. These faculties operate instinctively and spontaneously by reason of each's own in-nate power and prowess rooted in the body and soul's inherent ener-getic substantive dynamism. Such is the case for the corporeal body's

152

senses and instinctive appetency, on the one hand, and for the inorganic soul's intellect and will, on the other.

It is very important to grasp the Scholastic metaphysical tradition's understanding of faculty as employed by St. John of the Cross. The radical agent in every human being's human activity is the self-subsistent person. It is one and the same induplicable unique and unsubstitutable person that conceives, grows, sees, thinks, wills, walks, breaths, etc. However, this self-subsistent person acts dynamically in two different metaphysical orders of activity. One is substantive while the other is ancillary to this substantive dynamism. The human person must be dynamically, existentially, and substantively human prior to additionally perfecting and enhancing its dynamic substantive nature operationally. Thus, the human person is naturally (viz., soulfully) substantively intelligent and free at the instant of conception prior to actually and self-subsistently engaging in intelligent and free activity (viz., thinking and willing). In the activity of thinking and choosing the substantive soul does so through ancillary faculties (viz., ancillary powers) that act incidentally in virtue of the soul's substantive intelligent and free nature. These faculties are innate to the soul itself and are also incorporeal because the human soul itself is utterly immaterial and inorganic in its vital operations. Thus, these faculties (as well as all faculties including sensory ones proper to the corporeal body) operate spontaneously and dynamically in virtue of the human person's substantive dynamic hylemorphic nature.

Now, unlike the memory which St. John describes, these faculties operate within the objective ontological order of existence. The memory of which St. John speaks, however, does not itself function in the objective ontological order. It belongs to the human person's subjective phenomenological order. It is confined to the subjective historical horizontal ideological (i.e., phenomenological and epistemological) order of resistance rather than to the objective order of existence. Furthermore, the memory is not a faculty; it is a facilitator/facility. Faculties have an energetic intransitive spontaneous dynamic operation of their own whereas facilitator/facilitating functions function only kinetically when they are prompted to do so. These facilitator/facilitating functions produce transitively some serviceable product and/or function under the human person's forcible willful self-controlling influence and prompting. Further, they function synergistically by un/skilful control only in conjunction with what they transitively make happen or produce. Faculties, on the other hand, operate intransitively and energetically in virtue of their own innate spontaneous dynamism.

Thus, the faculty of sight spontaneously sees even if the human person does not consciously attend to this act of seeing. This inattention occurs when a person may be absorbed in his own thoughts and be oblivious to the physical action his sight is seeing as he sits in the stadium as a spectator at a sporting event. On the other hand, the functional anatomical organism of sight works or fails to work as an optical sensor only when it is being deliberately consciously attended to. This attentiveness occurs, for example, when the same spectator's attention is suddenly awakened by the crowd's roar he may attentively strive to focus his eyes on the field of action to catch the event that prompted the roar. This focal attention forcibly and willfully engages the anatomical function of optically controlling and focusing and making the eye's object transformatively more seeable and not merely informatively seeable as it is the case for the innate faculty's power of seeing. Further, this attentive willful focus may be rendered even more functionally and skillfully proficient by the additional use of binoculars to view the sporting spectacle more sharply.

At this point of trying to optically focus his eye, he is no longer attentive to his mental reverie and is very much aware of the focal flexibility or inflexibility of his optical vision. In this awareness he is more subjectively attentive to the eye's anatomy itself as an optical function moreso than he is aware of it as a faculty of seeing the sporting action on the field. Indeed, this subjective/objective difference is accentuated if the spectator resorts to his binoculars to get a close-up view of the action. The binoculars further facilitate the eye's subjective anatomical function of transformatively seeing while the objective seeable reality itself (viz., the athletic game) remains informatively very much the same with or without the use of the binoculars. That is, the athletic activity and the faculty to see this activity intransitively remains the same naturally, informatively, and objectively even while the viewer subjectively manipulates and transitively controls the eye's artificial optical functioning facilitator (viz., the binoculars).

Reverting, now, to the memory itself. There is something of a facultative instinctive memory as an internal sense in brute animals. It operates in conjunction with the animal's imagination. It is obvious that brute animals are endowed with a brute memory in view of their conditioned behavior. A dog, for example, can in response to previous training both obey and anticipate the trainer's signals. There is some measure of memory in evidence here in this humanly controlled behavior and not only here but even of animals left alone in their own native environment. A similar instinctive sensorial memory (viz., an inner sense along with the imagination) attendant on associatively remembering simple imagery and sensible affections may also be present in the bodily objective animal nature of human beings. But, such instinctive memory is not historical.

Historical memory recalls the past as past or anticipates the future as future. There is no evidence for this in the conduct of animals. The past as past is a segment of time that is gone by and no longer exists. Similarly, the future as future is a segment of time not yet existing. Such history invites reminiscence for the past and anticipation for the future. This memorial reminiscent or anticipatory activity is not centered in the vertical order of existence. It occurs exclusively in the subjective horizontal order of resistance; that is, a resistance that resists the ontological reality itself of existence. Evidence that brute animals have no historical memory is manifest in the total absence of memorials and relics that they do not artificially construct and fabricate to commemorate either their past or to anticipate their future.

Reminiscence and anticipation are themselves polarized functions not of a faculty of memory but a facility/function of memorizing which is a willful commitment to keep something in one's memorial archive and to associatively recall it at will. In other words, the memory is not an innate faculty at all which operates spontaneously apart from one's willful domination of it. It is a skillful self-cultivated function which works under the will's dominant influence and facilitated self-control. The memory consisting of "memories" recalled is an archival storehouse and remembering is clearly an associative skill of retrieving these memories in conjunction with a memorial past or future event. The more skilled is one's associative processes, the more adept one is in remembering and recalling to mind prior past experiences and anticipating planned and projected future experiences.

Memory's anatomical organistic mechanism is quite likely the brain as is the case with the psychic mind itself since a serious impairment to the brain is sufficient to impair one's memory as well as one's consciousness as is the case for a person enduring a prolonged coma or suffering from amnesia. Memory is more often identified with the historical past rather than the historical future because the future's eventuation has not as yet a factual record of events whereas the past has. Yet, in the measure that the future as future is factually recorded, it is mnemonically remembered. Thus, a person who has purchased a money bond which will financially mature in 20 years has a factual mnemonic record of the future as future which he fully anticipates and remembers futuristically.

Now, the polar difference between the past-as-past and the future-as-future is that one is a backward regressive self-orientation while the other is a forward aggressive self-orientation. The historical past invites a regressive self-orientation and mindset because one tends to hold the memorial past as a static series of events done and over with whereas the historical future invites an aggressive self-orientation because its upcoming kinetic eventuation is still under the direct domination of the will's manipulative influence. Yet, paradoxically, the polarity between the historistic past and the futuristic future influence each other. The futurist tends to anticipate and interpret the future in terms of the past whereas the historicist tends to review and interpret the past in terms of the future. Indeed, the very subjective egocentric personality of the human person is markedly dominated by either a historistic attitudinal bias or its polar opposite, a futuristic attitudinal bias.

Indeed, entire nations in their civilized cultural self-orientation and social group political mindset may be dominated by one or the other of these bipolar historical self-orientations. Without a doubt the United States of America in this year 2004 is dominantly a futuristic minded nation accepting without question that it is willfully fated to serve as the vanguard for the world's global democratization and economy. Further, these two dominant polarized typological historical mindsets demand a lifestyle suitable to each's attitudinal bias. The personality of the historicist is customarily conservative and traditional in what he values and esteems whereas that of the futurist is notably liberal and experimental in what he values and esteems. This attitudinal bias is not itself morally rooted. It is an amoral consideration rooted in the human person's subjective egocentric personality and its subjective willfulness to socially promote the bias of its own dominant self-interest and to demote and discredit the bias of its polar opponent. For, each polarized opponent esteems that its own bias is more advantageous to its own civil, social, and political security than is its polar opposite. In the United States both biases have politically materialized into a polarized bi-partisan political system.

Time must not be confused with history. There is no historical memory in the hierarchical order of time's temporality. Time itself exists entirely in the objective ontological realm of reality. Time itself includes its own temporal past and future. But both are presently existing as a present-past and a present-future in every moment of time's temporal momentary duration. Of course, time may be measured differently by different individuals and by different standards of measurement. But the actual passage of time's temporal duration exists independent of one's measurement of it. Indeed, the actual existence of every moment of time is durationally concomitant with eternity's timeless instancy. For every moment of time, be it a second, a minute, an hour, a day, a month, a year, etc., is in its present durational existence concomitant with eternity's durationless and timeless instancy.

This aspect of time is vital to contemplative prayer. Because, the mystic who successfully enters into this prayer finds himself absorbed in eternity's timelessness in every instant that this prayer is fully contemplatively absorbed in the Blessed Trinity. His intellectual memory remains oblivious to any memorable historical past or future eventuation extraneous to the intellect's timeless intellection. Hence, in contemplative prayer the mystic is suspended between time's momentary durations and eternity's timeless instancy. In this contemplative prayerful suspension, the mystic is oblivious to the momentary transition of time's temporality while he completely transcends history's non-existent historistic and futuristic chronologies.

Neither is history to be confused with time's temporality. Strictly speaking, again, there is no history in the vertical ontological order precisely because reality itself in its hierarchical existence is entirely transcendent to and independent of one's egocentric self-centered consciousness. History, however, is not independent of one's subjective egocentric self-centered consciousness. If one entirely forgets the past, one's own personality is obliterated. This is the case whether it involves one's individualistic or one's group social history. A loss of one's historical roots is tantamount to losing one's cultural self-cultivated personality, orientation, self-esteem, and the wealth that accrues to that personality's historical culture. A person of Irish descent, for example, living in a country other than Ireland still regards himself as an offshoot of the Irish culture and history.

Within a personality's self-cultivated egocentric subjectivity, the human person cannot simultaneously and concomitantly be conscious of the soma and the psyche together. Due to the polar tension between these two, conscious attention to the one entails a complete inattentiveness to the other. In view of this, there is a twofold antipodal consciousness. One is extrospective engaging the somatic body's mobility, sensations, and sensitivity and the other is introspective engaging the psychic mind's immobility, and intimate insensate impassivity. Paradoxically, when one is absorbed in the mind's thoughtful impassive bearing (i.e., poise and composure) one is unaware of the body's passivity and feelings. Inversely, when one is focused on the body's sensations and passivity, one is impervious to the mind's own impassive thoughtfulness.

In other words, an introspective personality is dominantly turned inward whereas an extrospective one is dominantly turned outward. The one tends to be melancholic and pensive while the other tends to be sanguine and active.

Now, in between a total introspective psychic impassive self-absorption usually manifested in an hypnotic trance in which one's consciousness of the body's somatic sentiency is entirely ignored and a total extrospective self-sustained somatic passive hyperactive athletic engagement in the case of a basketball player actively playing in which the mind's inner thoughts are, in turn, entirely ignored, there is an intermediate posture that combines and fuses the former with the latter. Hence, from a totally subconscious dormant to a totally conscious active stage of consciousness, there is a semiconscious stage in which one is simultaneously attentive to both the mind's psychic thoughts and the body's somatic movements. This is occurring at the very moment that I am typing out these sentences. The automatic movement of my body's fingers in typing is coordinated with the autocratic placidity of my ruminating mindful thoughts.

Corresponding to this extrospective and introspective outer and inner awareness, there is also an historical backward regressive and forward progressive self-orientation within the human person's self-humanized egocentric psychosomatic personality. The introspective historistic psychic personality tends to be dominantly defensive, idealistic, conservative, pessimistic, and retrogressive while the extrospective futuristic somatic personality tends to be dominantly aggressive, realistic, liberal, and optimistic. It is not unusual that the idealistic person is frequently retrospectively reminiscing about the "good old days" when things were allegedly more normal while his realistic counterpart focuses prospectively and habitually on the future that promises a never-ending improvement of upward progress and mobility. This egocentric conscious memorial backward and/or forward-looking self-orientation, and mental horizon is prompted in different personalities by the underlying optimistic or pessimistic attitudinal bias that is the dominant mindset of that personality.

This attitudinal bias itself is not a faculty but an overarching prismatic frame of mind mindset at the service of a personality's partisan overriding self-interest and self-esteem. This attitudinal bias facilitates a personality's willful self-serving decisions regarding its own social welfare favoring its own autonomous (i.e., self-sufficient) security and partisan (i.e., selfish) self-interest. This prejudicial attitude is possessively a have/have-not viewpoint favoring a personality's self-serving partisan (i.e., selfish) advantage. This prepossessive attitude is entirely subjective and entirely predetermined by a personality's dominant ideological stance regarding what is advantageous to securing and insuring its own personalized autonomous social security. The two antipodal overriding attitudes are that of the pessimist peculiar to the idealistic mindset and that of the optimist peculiar to the realistic mindset. Hence, a personality's memorial self-orientation is predetermined by its own dominant overarching pessimistic or realistic frame-of-mind attitudinal outlook and outreach. The mindset of the pessimist is slanted idealistically inward toward the historistic past whereas that of the optimist is slanted realistically outward toward the futuristic future.

A person's memorial consciousness is canted toward that historical bent suiting its own personalized attitudinal bias in behalf of its dominant partisan self-interest. This may change with age since a young person normally has his future ahead of him while an older person has his future already unfolded in the past. A young person tends to be optimistically free-wheeling and liberal-minded while an older person tends in the opposite direction to be more pessimistically cautious and conservative. A young person is futuristically forward looking while the older one is historistically backward looking. It should also be, again, noted that this overriding attitudinal bias regarding a personality's partisan autonomous self-interest is keyed to a person's social security. Hence, it simultaneously engages both his individualistic and his partisan collective self-interest in regard to the social groups of which he is a member.

Of course, this attitudinal paradoxical have/have-not bias is entirely a self-humanized and willfully self-cultivated self-serving overriding interest that motivates the person in all matters pertaining to the personalized social welfare of the person's own selfhood. The proper Christian attitude for the mystic following Christ's very own superhumanized mindset, is not a biased have/have-not attitude of possessively having what accommodates one's dominant ideological self-serving autonomous partisan social self-interest, but a paradoxical be-attitude of total self-detachment in the horizontal cultural subjective order of resistance in order to be totally possessively self-attached to God existing in the vertical natural objective order of existence.

This self-sacrificing be-attitude is nothing less than the Gospel lifestyle of living the evangelical counsels of poverty, chastity, and obedience promulgated by Christ and made manifest in His own Gospel Lifestyle and Deeds culminating in His Paschal Mystery. Paradoxically, this have-not self-sacrificing be-attitude transcends all ideological self-serving partisan self-interests and all manner of prejudicial attitudinal biases rooted in these polarizing autonomous partisan selfish self-interests. Of course, the Christian be-attitude is not one of a self-serving latent hostility toward others but one of a selfless hospitality vis-à-vis others. The merely humanistic have/have-not attitude favors and promotes its own selfish advantage to the disadvantage and the detriment of its polarized opponent. Idealistic and realistic ideologues who are prisoners of each's own respective partisan ideological have-attitude are not only mutually opposed to each other, they are in polar opposition to each other. This is the overriding difference between a have/have-not merely humanistic attitude and a Christian superhumanistic be-attitudinal frame of mind that emulates Christ's own Gospel lifestyle of sacrificial self-denial and ascetic mortifications at the Gospel's behest of participating in a royal superhumanizing social service that is entirely highlighted by Christ's very own sacrificial Selflessness.

Of course, on a purely humanistic plane, it is possible for a policeman, a statesman, or a fireman, for example, to exhibit an unselfish have-attitude of volunteering to sacrificially risk his own life in behalf of a cause (viz., the common good of the defenseless) which transcends and exceeds his own partisan self-serving self-interest in his own autonomous social security. This, however, is not entirely a selfless be-attitudinal mindset but merely an unselfish one. Unselfish to the extent that one's own life is sacrificially forfeited in the defense of a cause that transcends one's own selfhood. But, still only partially sacrificial inasmuch as a trained policeman has considerable assurance of his own competence and personal safety in successfully coping with dangerous situations and criminals.

Christ's sacrifice, on the other hand, is totally Selfless explicitly because His own innocence had nothing to profitably gain or to guarantee regarding the social security of His own Selfhood. Furthermore, His overriding superhumanizing motivation consonant with His

Messianic be-attitudinal frame of mind was to serve His Heavenly Father's Holy Will and not His own putative needful deficient social security. Indeed, it is imperative for every disciple of Christ to adopt the same superhumanistic Messianic be-attitude of royal Selfless sacrificial universal redemptive service to mankind at the behest of God-the-Father's Holy Will. It is precisely within the context of Christ's priesthood that the Christian disciple's baptismal mindset is superhumanistically configured to Christ's own Paschal Mystery celebrated in each Eucharistic commemoration.

Of course, Christ's Selfless sacrificial oblation to the Father could have had some element of a self-serving motivation inasmuch as His own human and self-humanized body was subject to death and corruption. By reason of His oblation, dying, and death, His own body was subsequently resurrected and ascended into the heaven of His eternal Father's glory. In view of this very Paschal Mystery there is, accordingly, a self-serving motivation in all who live out their baptism to the full and find their own self-fulfillment in participating in Christ's Paschal Mystery.

In other words, the simply self-centered humanistic selfhood is needfully deficient regarding its own social self-sufficiency and security. Of course, this needful deficiency is the direct offshoot of original sin. We would not know or even suspect this were it not for divine revelation. Because of this deficiency within the very nuclear core of every person's self-subsistent personhood (viz., a person's selfhood and subjective personality), this person's selfhood needs to provide for its own self-sufficiency (i.e., autonomy) by functionally (i.e., willfully) cultivating artificial services which selfishly cater to the sustenance of this needful deficiency. One cannot help but be selfishly self-attached to serving one's own needful selfhood. This slavish serviceable self-attachment to one's own selfhood can only be masterfully transcended and overcome by Christ's very own Masterful sacrificial Selfless Service consummated on the cross of His crucifixion. Left to its own selfishly self-cultivated humanism mankind remains selfishly self-centered and a prisoner of its own selfhood.

Memory's memoriality and the mind's psychic mindfulness.

Memories are rooted and stored in the subjective personality of the human personhood's egocentric self-awareness. What is of uppermost concern to this egocentric personality is its autonomous self-assured social security which is entirely partisan and in no way communal with a communality that is endemic to the family community prevalent in the vertical ontological order of existence. Neither the egocentric psychic mindful self nor its corresponding somatic bodily self are of themselves engaged with the transcendent communiverse of being-as-such beyond the reach of their own personalized respective subjectivity and self-centered selfhood. The human person's self-subsistent personhood is not in its subjective egocentric consciousness interested in reality itself transcendent to its subjective personalized autonomous social self-interest. In its completely self-reflexive awareness it is egocentrically self-absorbed and self-concerned with its own autonomous social security and overriding partisan (i.e., selfish) self-interest.

Of course, in his mere reflective (i.e., non-reflexive) awareness the human person does attend to the activity of his objective nature (i.e., its substantive body and soul) transcendent to the subjectivity of his own egocentric selfhood. However, when his consciousness is not overtly reflective but entirely reflexive and self-absorbed with his own egocentric selfhood, he is oblivious to the metaphysical communiverse of reality transcendent to his ideological selfhood's own subjectivity. He is either wrapped up in the dream world of his own inner psychic thoughts or the fantasy world of its own outer somatic imagery or, again, conjunctively with both simultaneously as is the case with the one who is immersed in some fine art endeavor.

This inward psychic consciousness is typically a backward historistic memorial awareness while its outward somatic counterpart is typically a forward futuristic memorial awareness. This difference is explained by the typical attitudinal bias to which each is respectively self-attached. The inner sphere of psychic awareness ingeniously idealizes fabulous thoughts while the outer somatic sphere contrives to realize these thoughts in fantastic enterprises. Take, the mathematical circle, for example. The mind idealistically conjures up the perfect circle (i.e., a self-enclosed curved line) and, in turn, this is imaginatively displayed on the blackboard with a large "O" symbolically realizing and imaginatively illustrating the mind's idealistic ideation. A circle is a curved linear configuration fabricated in the mind's psyche devoid of the physical tangible features of color, odor, temperature, flavor, solidity, texture, sound, etc.. It is exclusively a paraphysical mathematical extended unidimensional linear continuum devoid of everything that is not germane to its sheer quantificational spatial extensionality.

This psychic ideation of a mathematical circle is not the ideation of an entity; it is, rather, the ideation of a non-entity. The circle is not a being-as-such; rather it is a non-such-being. There is no-such-being in the physical cosmos transcendent to the psychic mind's own ideation nor in the metaphysical reach of reality which is utterly non-spatial and non-quantifiable. It is a mathematical enterprise rather than a metaphysical entity. It resists existing outside of the psychic mind's own conception of it. How can the psyche dream up such fabulous mathematical fabrications as the circle?

It is because the psyche itself is entirely entitatively empty of every being-as-such. That is, it is itself in its very psychicity a non-entitative emptiness and spatial vacuity. From this embryonic nullity the mind magically makes something out of nothing. This mental "nothing" is deprived of and in need of reality itself to transcend its own vacuity. But, the something which it makes smacks also of its own psychic embryonic nothingness. In other words, a circle is composed of a curved line whose linearity itself is deprived and devoid of every physical feature existing transcendent to the mind's own psychicity. This psychic vacuity is no more mysterious than is a hole in the ground which is brought about by a shovel removing the soil from the same location leaving a lack of ground which is construed to be a hole. Such a "hole" is not a thing-as-such; it is a non-such-thing. Yet, it is very much this non-such-thing which is required to accommodate a telephone or fence pole, for example.

Accordingly, the psychic mind can enterprisingly conjure up some quasi-thing (i.e., the mathematical circle) out of its own lack of being something (i.e., its own non-entitative emptiness). And, again, the artifictional "something" which it notionally fabricates is an enterprising mathematical non-entity. An entity is endowed with an identity such that it cannot existently be other than what it is. The color, red, cannot be half-red and still be red. The same red rose may be different shades of red in each of its red petals. Nonetheless, each different shade is holistically the color, red-as-such. Each petal is holistically red or not red at all. A green apple may cease to be green and become a ripe red. But the color green itself, cannot become red. Green and red are entitative colors that cannot exist other than entitatively as the unit-entity-identity which each is.

This unit-identity does not pertain to mathematical notions. Every geometric linear notion is an enterprise made up of both an extended and inextended continuum. This is not an issue of an entitative being's existence existing simultaneously as an inextended continuum (viz., point) and as an extended continuum (viz., segment line). It is an issue of notionally simultaneously subconsciously having and not-having together the ambiguous absurdity of polarized opposites that resist existence itself transcendent to the cocoon of the mind's dematerialized (i.e., mathematical) psychic vacuity. This polarized mathematical absurdity (i.e., of a circle) is a non-entitative artifictional enterprise.

In turn, the human person in his somatic consciousness can symbolically exemplify imaginatively this mathematical conception with an "O" or with a word, circle (in English). In this manner the psyche dreams up a fabulous idealistic phantom specter, the circle, whose paraphysical nontactual configuration can only be conceived and intuited by and within the selfhood's psychic mind. In turn, the selfhood's somatic body inventively fantastically imagines the circle's realistic spectacular counterpart which can be tactually traced on the blackboard and empirically inspected and perceived to be the exemplified artifactual mathematical circle that was artifictionally conceived.

Entitative realities contrasted with non-entitative enterprising undertakings.

The notional nontactual phantom non-such-entity circle is the intuitive typological exemplar and archetype for all non-such-circles while its imaginary phenomenal "O" counterpart on the blackboard is its figurative artifactual exemplification that can be tactually empirically perceived and detected. Neither the notional circle nor its tactual counterpart exists in reality transcendent to the human personality's subjective egocentric psychosomatic selfhood. Both are entirely make-believe. One is noumenal and nuclear while the other is phenomenal and symptomatic. Why? Because the conceived circle is a linear mathematical quantitative continuum devoid of any identifiable entitative unit-identity being-as-such.

An entitative reality cannot be dissected and dismembered into fragmentary fractional parts. The entitative red-as-such color, for example, remains holistically red-as-such in every instance of its instantiation. A rose red is red-as-such, a tulip red is red-as-such, a strawberry red is red-as-such, etc.. Furthermore, each separate petal of the rose bud, the red tulip, or the red berry is itself holistically red-as-such. This is not the case with the line since one segment of its linear continuum has extension while another (viz., the point) has not. Yet, both are crucial to making up its linearity.

In other words, the metaphysical reality of red-as-such is a holistic identifiable unit entity that retains its holistic unit identity in every instance of its instantiation. On the other hand, when a circle is cut up into its arc segments, no arc segment itself is a circle. It remains merely a fragmentary segment of a circle. Accordingly, there is no community family of circles in the circle's segment parts whereas there is such a family unity community in all the variable instances of the specific variable hues and shades of the color, red-as-such.

Every example of a circle---there are no actual instances since a non-such-circle does not exist outside of the mind's conception of it--- is itself a non-such-circle. This paradox pervades the entire horizontal order of subjectivity. The imaginary "O" on the blackboard symbolizes a circle figuratively and symptomatically but is not itself the notional circle which it exemplifies. The notional circle is devoid not only of physical attributes but even of all tactility and is completely imperceptible whereas the phenomenal circle on the blackboard is tactually visual and perceptible. The notional rotund circle is both half concave and half convex.

Yet, the concave half is circular but not a circle and similarly with the convex half. The notional circle is ambiguously both rotund and oval. Yet, an imaginary rotund circle is not oval and vice verse. In other words, the noumenal spectral circle intuited by the psychic mind is transparently (i.e., implicitly) all that the mind intuitively reads into it. By contrast the phenomenal spectacular circle fantasized by the imagination is explicitly and symptomatically only one facet of what the mind intuits. This disparity between the psychic and the somatic is typical of the paradoxicality that permeates the entire psychosomatic order of mankind's subjectivity since there are no entitative realities in this self-cultivated horizontal order of resistance (i.e., resistance to existence). There is no general entitative unit-identity name nor proper name for whatever is notionally or imaginatively artificially fabricated and cultivated in this horizontal order. Thus, the very term, circle, considered simply in the context of its own terminology, is a functional pseudonym; that is, a non-name, a phony-name, a tag, a label, a nick-name, etc.

Any term is only literally and truly a name when it formally signifies an entitative reality transcendent to the term itself, a reality that is a unit-entity-identity in the vertical order of existence. Accordingly, the mathematical term, circle, is a quasi-name, a nick-name since there is no such entitative reality in the objective realm of existing entities outside of the psychic mind's notion of it. Yes, there are rotund round realities such as the apple, the pear, the peach, the stone, etc. But, they are not constituted of circles albeit the circularity of their rotundity. Their circularity is merely a psychically abstract mathematical notional feature of their physical rotundity. If the apple itself were cut up into minuscule pieces until it were nearly pulverized, no one piece would be itself a circle. Why? Because the apple itself is a solid physical substance that can be pinched with the teeth when eaten and with the hand when grasped whereas a circle is constituted of a mere paraphysical unidirectional dimensionality which has length but no width. A circle cannot be pinched. It is a mathematical non-such-thing rather than a metaphysical thing-as-such (i.e., being-as-such).

What is the case for the mathematical term, circle also is the case for any term considered merely in its terminological horizontal context as a fabricated notion in the egocentric self's subjective subconscious psyche. Confined exclusively to the psyche's subjective mental skillful fabrication every term is semantically meaningless. Hence, it can be assigned any conventional meaning at random since it is itself a mere phantom pseudonym, a mere nick-name. However, the same term becomes a real name when it designates a reality, a being-as-such, in the vertical order of existence. The term, red, considered itself reflexively and semantically in its terminological composition in the horizontal order of its notional psychic fabrication is not itself a unit-entity-identity. For, the separate letters r-e-d are not themselves each red. This term, red, becomes a real name and not merely a pseudonymous semantic term when it signifies a transcendent reality in the vertical order of existence that is actually an identifiable unit-entity reality such as is the case with the reality of the color, red-as-such.

The idealistically conceived non-such artificial fictional circle enjoys dimensional length but no width. It is a unidimensional phantom ideation, a noumenal intuition. It is intimately transparently discernible to the mind's psychicity but otherwise eerily elusive and occult to the body's sensitized somaticity. Its realistic imaginary symbolic figurative phenomenal counterpart on the blackboard must have tactual width to be factually seen. Hence, it is not actually itself a circle. It is an apparent circle but not a transparent one as notionally conceived. That is, it deceptively appears to be what it is not. The noumenal circle cannot be found outside of the psychic mind's conception of it. This notional non-such-circle, accordingly, is precisely, exactly, and transparently a linear non-entity whereas its imaginary symbolic counterpart is only imprecisely, inexactly, and apparently the symptomatic appearance of this same non-entity. The fanciful figure on the blackboard is not itself the notional circle which it symbolizes and the notional circle, in turn, completely resists the prospect of existing outside the mind's own psychic dematerialized (i.e., mathematical) abstract vacuity.

In epistemological terms, the mind's noetic circle is a delusion if the human person misconstrues that there is such an entitative reality transcendent to and independent of the mind's own psychicity. Further, the body's imaginary figurative circle is an illusion, again, if the human person misconstrues that there is such an entitative reality transcendent to and independent of the body's own somaticity. One's subconscious self-centered poise and mental bearing is more securely convinced and self-justified in precisely describing its intuitive experiential awareness of a circle in stark noumenal mathematical terms moreso than in phenomenal imagery. Consider how notionally compact is the expression of a four million-billion-sided figure is and how impossibly difficult it would be to draw this imaginary figure on a blackboard slate. Notionally this many-sided figure is not perfectly rotund; yet, its imaginary exemplification, were it possible to imagine, would seem to be actually rotund.

Such noumenal knowledge is that of the Gnostic. It is very occult albeit its mathematical precision because it escapes the empirical investigation and inspection proper to the senses. It is gnostic because it emphasizes the subjective priority of knowing over and above the reality itself of what is knowable. Such gnosticism erroneously measures reality in terms of its own delusional notions. Such notions themselves because of their mathematical matrix are inherently ambiguously indefinite and paradoxically enigmatic. Such notions are themselves, albeit their nonsensicality, romantically useful. The wheel itself of every vehicle which moves by rotating on an axle is itself the product of a conception of a mathematical circularity. A machine is frequently the working of many circular cogs that mesh together and spin around on each's own axis without moving about from place to place. In this they resemble the mind's own immobilized mental movement.

Mathematical knowledge constrasted with metaphysical knowledge.

Of course, in reality outside of the mind's own notionality and the imagination's own fantastic imagery, there are real substantive physical bodies that are really circular. But, their circularity, again, considered apart from their corporeality is itself purely an abstract notional non-entity. This non-such-entity that marks the circle is the

169

very hallmark of the personhood's own self-humanized psychosomatic personality. A personality's genius is its own plastic creativity to fashion a make-believe world from which the human person can cultivate its own personality and personify and personalizes itself by making something out of nothing (i.e., fabricating a non-being-as-such). This is the root of its resourceful inventive ingenuity which allows a person's personhood to inventively, functionally, and experimentally fabricate a wheel and to continue to processively, stage by stage, to implementally improve on this fabrication.

All the worlds of culture are fabricated out of the framework of purely mathematical phantom notions. Simply stop to attend to the configuration of these type-set words themselves printed here in this commentary and recognize that they have the semblance of curvilinear mathematical configurations of their own. Reverting to the circle, again, consider the artificially constructed wheel which is circular to facilitate its rotation with a minimum of resistance. It originates from within the psyche's noumenal phantom ideations which are idealistically mathematically precise and exacting but unobservable to any egocentric empirical self other than the self that mentally conceives them within the intimacy of its own psychicity.

The wheel itself that allows an automobile to move with minimal resistance is the phenomenal appearance of the non-such-circle but never with the precision of its notional counterpart. Yet, it is publicly observable not by the psychic self but by the somatic self that handcrafts it and utilizes it to facilitate its own mechanized automotive automatic self-mobilization from place to place. The symbolic circle on the blackboard, on the other hand, allows two separate psychic selves to telepathically communicate interpersonally with each other with a minimal of resistance since one and the same semantic symbol conventionally signifies each's personalized intuition of the non-such-entity that is the mathematical circle.This very interpersonal intuitive telepathic psychic communication is socially sufficient to prompt the delusion that a circle actually exists transcendent to one's subconscious mental intuitive conception of it. Consider yet another example of the innumerable phantom notions which haunt our every day life's cultural endeavors. The American dollar bill is such an example of the subjective cultural order of having resistance in opposition to the objective natural order of existent beings. The dollar bill in one's pocket is a have/have-not non-entitative enterprise. It is both an artifictional and an artifactual enterprise simultaneously. I am its owner, it's in my pocket. This is fictional. I am not its owner, it is already promised as payment for something I purchased yesterday. This is factual. Indeed, the American Dollar bill is a pseudonym which both has and has not simultaneously the meaning which is conventionally assigned to it. It is inherently ambiguous as is the case for any non-such-being which is mathematically measured and calculated. That is, it is ambiguously fictionally mine while it is in my pocket, yet factually not mine since I already have spent it and owe it to someone else as payment for what I purchased.

This ambiguity is the paradoxical absurdity that not only haunts mathematical non-such-beings but also the entire worldly reach of the horizontal order of mankind's self-cultivated self-humanization. The very notion of a line ambiguously includes both its curvature and its rectitude in every segment of its linearity. It is simultaneously the case that the shortest distance between two points is not only a straight line but also a curved line when there is an obstacle intervening between the two points. Mathematics is itself engimatic as is the entire order of mankind's horizontal historical subjectivity. This entire order of mankind's self-humanization may be subdivided into three mutually polarized nuclear self-cultivated centers summed up in the three timeworn arts, the liberal, mechanical, and fine arts.

The threefold arts are a keystone to the human person's psychosomatic make-up.

The liberal arts are those whose artificial product is principally inwardly psychically a communicable symbol, the mechanical arts are those whose product is principally outwardly a handcrafted tool, and the esthetic (i.e., the fine arts) are those whose product is a combination of the previous two, a playful toy. This triad of artificial cultural centers can be illustrated in examining the profile of a musical work. First, there are all of the musical symbols which are artifictionally and notionally designed by the psyche's functional skillfulness. Then there are the musical tones themselves imaginatively construed as mimically implementing the body's own musical tonality and resonance. Further, there is the musical score itself composed by a master musician whose composition is incubated in the psychic mind of the composer. Then, there is the handcrafted musical instruments themselves executed by the somatic body's handy mechanical craftsmanship. The musicians that actually perform the musical composition must both adeptly interpret the musical score displayed on the sheet music and skillfully handily play the musical instruments in accord with the musical score.

Thus, the musical piece's composition involves a mental musical mastermind, its implementation a masterful musical mechanical craftsman, and a master musical virtuoso performer. Or, even if there are not one but many collaborative masterful musical artisans, there must be one who masterfully oversees the others. Thus, there is a mastermind superintending all the composers, a master mechanic supervising all the mechanical experts crafting musical instruments, and a master conductor maestro conducting all the musical performers performing an orchestral piece, for example. In brief, there is neither one universal world nor communiverse of music. There are many worlds and their only bond is their interpersonal intersubjective communication and collaborative association with each other.

The language of music as an instance of a fine art has no family community identity significant terminology and intelligible objective conversation as is found in the ontological vertical objective reach of reality's metaphysical communiverse of beings-as-such. Music has only an expressive interpretative notational symbolic terminology (viz., the musical score) facilitating an experiential non-intelligible group cooperative interpersonalized functional musical communication (viz., an orchestra's instrumental performance) within a polarized field of psychosomatic performing selves as is found in the subjective typological worlds of musical events. There is no innate faculty of musical composition or rendition in humankind's egocentric psychosomatic subjective selfhood. There is only the musical functionary artificially cultivating and performing in a notational symbolic audible language a musical experience artificially facilitated by the confluence of the purely symbolic musical score itself and the musical instruments interpreting the score. The upshot of the communication in musical language is simply to experience subjectively within the self's interpersonal communication its very own psychosomatic harmonic entirely subjective musical resonance.

There may be an association of composers who have the same group functional partisan esthetic compositional self-interest. There may be an association of musical craftsmen who produce musical instruments having their own group functional partisan esthetic hand-crafted self-interest. There may be an association of musicians with their own partisan esthetic virtuoso self-interest. There may be a group association of financial entrepreneurs who finance these musical productions at all levels. There may be academies instructing neophytes aspiring to become skilled in each of these three tripartite fields of music as a fine art.

In other words, there is no one universe of music nor one universal musical language. There are only many variable worlds of music with no family community identity to unite them. This family unity identity is reserved for the vertical order of reality based on what is entitatively being-as-such as the semantic intelligible meaning of words. Music is itself composed of many musical artificial non-such-beings (viz., notes, tones, instruments, instrumental notations, composers, performers, conductors, etc., each of which are all functionally mind-crafted and/or hand-crafted skills to symbolically, organizationally, harmonically, vocally and instrumentally control audible sound tonalities in purely mathematical non-entitative enterprising quantified dimensional measurements. As previously pointed out, mathematical calculation is not based on metaphysical entities but only on fictional non-entitative notional enterprises. Music is an excellent example of a completely subjective self-humanizing horizontal order of non-intelligible experiential communication within the fine arts which ingeniously synthesizes in one and the same artistic rendition mankind's subjective psychosomatic personality and interpersonalized social selfhood.

Certainly, music engages sounding musical tonalities and not merely musical symbols outlined symbolically on a scale. Music's tonalities play directly on one's somatic emotional sensitivity and psychic emotionless intimacy. The purely figurative symbolic language of musical scores facilitates a telepathic communication among all the member musicians of an orchestra performing the same composition. All the members of an orchestra under the direction of a conductor are all telepathically of one mind in performing a magisterial score. That is, they are not "single-minded" in the sense that there is a common unit-entity-identity of one and the same musical reality. There is no-such-reality. No more so than there is such a reality in a mosaic artfully created by the juxtaposition of different colored tiles.

The audible musical tonality itself of a musical composition technically played on various musical instruments evokes a musical emotional or emotionless empathy among all those who both perform and partake of its musicality. A musical theme or melody may be either somatically emotionally exciting and stirring or psychically emotionlessly sedate and soothing. The gamut and variations of one's subjective interpersonal tonal empathic psychic ethos and/or one's tonal empathic somatic pathos captured in musical forms are too nuanced and variable to be categorized. Indeed, the range and nuance of one's empathic somatic feelings and psychic bearings may be functionally described in terms of the specific conduct they may evoke and provoke. One may be sad and morose and collectedly quiet or glad and joyful and dancing about. But, the somatic feelings and psychic bearings themselves defy categorization precisely because they are not cognitively informative but conatively transformative. They are modulations of one's subjective egocentric conscious selfhood and not of one's objective soulful cognizance.

The Christian mystic's own religious empathic somatic feelings (i.e., sensitivities) and psychic bearings (i.e., composure) are also susceptible of being expressed and modulated in musical tonalities and melodies. It is quite notable that the music that has traditionally been most suitable to Sacred Scripture in the Catholic Church's Latin rite has been Gregorian plainchant whose roots are found within the ancient Greek and Hebrew cultures. Plainchant is more like a lullaby that one would sing to a child at nighttime. It is not a musical tonality whose conative resonance and import is expressed independently of the words of the Gospel. Hence, it is subjectively conatively supplemental to the more objectively fundamental cognitive text of Sacred Scripture. Singing the Alleluia in plainchant is not merely the conative musical expression of one's own subjective religious feelings of exultation, it is, moreover, an objective cognitive salute of praise recognizing God's grandeur and majesty as the source of this religious exultation.

Mathematical knowledge is inherently ambiguous.

Mathematics and all its calculations are in themselves paradoxically unintelligible. This unintelligibility is rooted in their quantitative factors which are themselves non-entities. Every mathematical factor whether geometric, arithmetic, or their combination, is enigmatically absurd and unintelligible. One can understand intelligently why they are unintelligible. But, again, such understanding is not itself a mathematical knowledge or understanding. It is a paramathematical knowledge and understanding. A geometric line as noumenally conceived is not clear-cut in its conception. It is enigmatically and absurdly very ambiguous. It is composed both of a unilateral extended continuum (viz., the segment line) and a non-extended continuum (viz., the point). That is, every line is composed of extended segment lines and non-lines or points which are, on their own terms, inextended continua separating and connecting these extended line segments.

Hence, a line both has and has-not simultaneously quantitative linearity. That is, if a line is composed only of points, it is inextended. And, if it composed only of segments without tangential points, it is not a continuous geometric continuum but an arithmetic discrete continuum. For, if the segments are not tangentially connected by joint connections (viz., points), they are discontinuously discretely connected. A line is composed of both a positive line (viz., a segment) and a negative line (viz., a point); one component is extended and the other inextended. This is the root for the plus and the minus in mathematics and the positive-negative digital polarity that prevails throughout the entire reach of the horizontal cultural order of resistance and is the basis for mathematics' own algebraic logistics and logical enigmas.

Were this have/have-not polar opposition of a geometric line both having and not having extended components an issue of actual existence in the ontological order, it would be a contradiction and, hence, impossible. Since, it is only a polarized opposition in the horizontal have/have-not artificial cultural order of resistance it is an enigma and puzzle but not a contradiction. It is the enigmatic puzzle and absurdity endemic to mathematical constructs and thinking that is typical of all artificial constructs and mankind's self-humanized undertakings in the horizontal order of every human being's self-cultivation. The manifold worlds of mankind's historical self-development are themselves fraught with this engimatic polarizing have-have not absurdity.

There is still another example of this mathematical ambiguity which prevails throughout all of the subjective artificial worlds of humankind's self-cultivated self-humanization. A geometric line noumenally considered in the psychic mind is ambiguously and implicitly simultaneously both straight and crooked. When a segment line is symbolically and phenomenally imagined within the somatic body's imagination, it is either straight or bent in any one segment of its extension but not both in any same segment of its extension. Hence, the explicitation and application of theoretical math in all fields of the experimental social and physical sciences engages insuperable conundrums which are inherently the unintelligible absurdity endemic to mathematics itself. Theoretical math intuitively engages both the curved and rectitudinal line simultaneously while applied math differentiates between the two separately.

Another example of this enigmatic disparity between theoretical and applied math is the triangle. In purely psychical terms, the mind intuits the triangle as a three-sided unidimensional linear polygon. In this intuition every type of triangle is implicitly contained and noumenally (i.e., transparently) discerned as one and the same triangle. However, when this notional triangle is itself sensationally and phenomenally (i.e., apparently) exemplified in imaginary configurations within the body's own somaticity, the ambiguity inherent in this notionality becomes quite manifest. For, the isosceles, the scalene, and the equilateral triangles all differ from each other as special types of the notional triangular polygon. In other words, the notional triangle is not a holistic unit-entity-identity. It is a mosaic figurative-unified-enterprise. It is not an entitative being-as-such; it is an enterprising non-such-being (i.e., a make-believe entity).

In brief, mathematical knowledge is literally not knowledge at all in the sense of knowing what actually exists and could not otherwise exist. When a line is conceptualized its curvature or rectitude remain unknown since a conceived mathematical line is ambiguously both. This inherent unknown ambiguity is proliferated wherever mathematics is applicably the normative standard measurement for every field of study in the horizontal cultural order of resistance. This includes the fields of social and political study, economics itself, all fields of commercialism, all fields of the physical experimental sciences, all fields of psychology and psychiatry, history, the fine arts, etc.

There is still another enigmatic feature of mathematical conception and its inherent enigmatic logistic reasoning. The line in its very psychic conception is clearly unclear regarding its indefinite length. It is impossible to define a line for its very components are themselves resistant to any definite or definitive identification of length. Is a line a short length or a long length? It is both simultaneously and ambiguously. For, no line can be cut into such small segment lines that these small segments could not be further segmented into even smaller segments. And, conversely, no line is never so long that it could never not become actualizeably even longer ad infinitum. In other words, a line is microscopically indefinitely and interminably minute and equally ambiguously macroscopically indefinitely and interminably momentous.

Hence, when one examines the cosmos purely mathematically as does the experimental physical sciences of physics and astronomy, it is both indefinitely microscopically minute and indefinitely macroscopically gigantic. In the former case it is composed of molecules which dissolve into non-tactual insubstantial atomic particles and these in turn into sub-atomic particles ad infinitum. In the latter case it is composed of celestial planets and stars which are combined into systematic clusters as the solar system, nebulae, galaxies, and groups of galaxies ad infinitum. The only obstacle to probing further into these cosmic reaches is the limitation of the hi-tech instrumentations which inhibit this further critical probing. On the other hand, when this same physical cosmos is examined not mathematically as is the case with the experimental physical sciences previously mentioned but simply in the tangible physicality of the natural substances which make up this cosmos, there is no such indefinite ambiguity.

The natural substantive elements of fire, air, earth, water, and vapor are definitively and entitatively definable. The very planet, earth, is not itself in its planetary astronomical mathematical consideration a physical reality at all. It is merely in astronomical terms an extended plenum globular quantum in the vast extensive vacuum of space (i.e., a positive location in polar opposition to its negative non-localized spatiality). The planet, earth, as a physical reality is constituted of a variety of physical substances each of which is a definitive entity-as-such and not merely a non-entitative enterprise that can be mathematically construed.

In brief, the metaphysical natural vertical order of reality is not to be confused with its mathematical artificial horizontal counterpart. Both are tenable when the fundamental-supplemental priority proper to each is fully respected. The natural order is fundamental while the artificial/culture order is supplemental. A disorder arises when the supplemental is forcibly and inordinately made to supplant and to eliminate the fundamental altogether. An example of this forcible supplanting of the order of nature by the order of culture is the issue of evolutionism clashing with creationism. When evolutionism is proposed as an all-encompassing fundamental account of reality, reality itself becomes enigmatically unintelligible. However, when it is proposed supplementally as an historical evolutionary unfolding rather than as a dogmatic ism, its inherent enigmatic conundrum remains still compatible with creation's fundamental inherent intelligible account of reality.

The threefold arts are prototypes of the different spheres of mankind's cultivated worlds.

This liberal, technical and esthetic triad of artificial self-cultivated centers that typify all of our subjective worlds of culture also engages the memory in which we are especially interested in our pursuit of elucidating the mystagogical writings of our Carmelite Holy Father, St. John of the Cross. The mind's psychicity is the artificial incubator of what is paradigmatically artifictional in the worlds of culture. The body's somaticity is the artificial laboratory of what is experimentally artifactual in the worlds of culture. Each is in polar opposition to the other. The fictional explains the factual fictionally whereas the factual establishes and verifies the fictional factually. A theory remains fictional until it is tested and proven to successfully work factually. A fact remains inexplicable until it is theoretically explained in a fictional workable account that meshes with other proven working accounts.

Artifiction engages the psychic mind's conceptual rationality which is intuitively a mathematical mode of reasoning in which the fragmentary whole is equivalent to its fragmentary parts. The standard of such reasoning is one of contractual and agreeable equivocation and equivalence. If two selves arbitrarily agree that a dozen eggs can be exchanged for $1.00.00 then the eggs are equivocally equally exchangeable for 100 cents. When the trade-off actually occurs and is perceived to be such by the senses it becomes empirically an artifactual event. Certainly, the American dollar bill, the organization of the eggs into a set of a dozen, the contractual agreement itself to trade-off the dozen for the dollar, the actual exchange itself, etc., are all artificially contrived non-such-beings. These are eventful enterprises, not entitative actualities. They are conscious self-humanizing interpersonalized cultural events which considered historically have a willful agreeable contractual eventful mythical past that is over and done with and a willful agreeable contractual future that remains to eventually factually occur whenever the same agreeable trade-off is re-enacted.

An artifiction is any mental ideation and conception formulated and calculated by the mind's psychicity. It is fictional in the sense that it is occult and hidden from any direct empirical sensory inspection and perception. This noumenal mental conception serves as a prototypical model. When a building architect dreams up a design model for a new home he functionally (i.e., skillfully) drafts a blueprint of this design to guide the builders who construct the residential structure. The prototypical model itself remains noumenally hidden in the architect's own mind. The handcrafted blueprint itself usably serves as the phenomenal imaginative artifactual manifestation of the noumenal design. The home itself becomes the usable facility which is the product of both the mind's artifictional and the imagination's artifactual proficiency. The mind's conceptions themselves cannot be sensistically and sensitively detected not even by the particular personality that invents and entertains them. An artifaction, on the other hand, is any bodily sensation and imaginary image fashioned within the body's somaticity.

In a chronological order, it would seem that a building's master plan, blueprint, and archetype take precedence over the drafting of the blueprint itself and the building's actual construction. Normally, a house is not built until the blueprint is completed. With its completion the building of the house commences. The building's plan is designed mentally by the psychic self before it is drafted in a blueprint outline. This psychic self is the architect. The building's structure is mechanically constructed by the somatic self, the technician. This mechanical self is the mason, the electrician, the carpenter, the plumber, etc.

It must not be overlooked that the architect cultivates his mental architectural psychic designing functional skill in the very process of successfully producing a manageable blueprint of this design. The mechanical craftsman, in turn, cultivates his bodily functional mechanical skill in the very process of successfully deploying handcrafted tools to build the designed structure. There are no innate potent energetic faculties in the horizontal cultural order of subjectivity. There are only impotent inertial aptitudes that synergistically become kinetically skillful functions in the process of successfully cultivating productive serviceable facilities.

The human person synergistically cultivates his artistic skills in the process of successfully cultivating the products of these skills. The normal path for a person to acquire each skill is the program of apprenticeship where the novice is trained to imitate the master who is already skilled in his trade. Further, typical functioning skills are not themselves exchangeable with other types of skills. The carpenter cannot apply his own skill skillfully in the task of constructing what the stonemason can skillfully construct. Furthermore, the architect's skill cannot be substituted for the technician's skill and vice versa. Given the preceding chronological order in the building of a house, it seems plausible that the human person in its self-subsistent person-hood is not only inwardly and introspectively conscious of his own psyche and its abstract idealistic hidden mathematical paradigms for designing the building's blueprint, he is simultaneously retrospect-ively conscious of mentally remembering the calculations in prepar-ing the house's blueprint and he can, in turn, memorially recall the process of synthesizing these calculations together to design one in-tegrated structural blueprint.

In doing so, he can repeatedly revert to these calculative mental notions and remember them (i.e., retrieve and re-gather them togeth-er) as an eventuation of the historistic past (i.e., of recalling to mind previously dismembered events and now remembering them in one overall synthetic eventuation culminating in the blueprint). The not-able hallmark of the memory is that it is a storehouse and an archive of past dismembered events and eventuations which may be historic-ally remembered as having been previously dismembered. We might term this a diachronic memory.

In the case of future events and eventuations, the process of re-membering and dismembering is merely reversed. But, in its reversal, the focus of memory is more preoccupied with the somatic body's own constructive skillful functions of prospectively building the ar-chitect's blueprint into successive stages of membered piecemeal con-structive events scheduled ahead into the future. Whereas the archi-tect has to retrospectively design the house to fit agreed-upon spe-cifications, the craftsmen have to projectively construct the house in projected time-schedule stages to end up with the overall blueprint plan. They begin their construction by keeping the overall blueprint in mind (i.e., remembering it) whereas the architect designed the building by visualizing each section as fitting into the whole pattern (i.e., dismembering it). This may be suitably termed a synchronic memory.

Memories are fraught with paradox.

Memories themselves whether they are retrospectively of the past or prospectively of the future are, like everything else in this phenomenological order of subjectivity fraught with paradox. When one reverts to the past it seems that one remembers things simply "as they were." The case, however, is that one remembers them from one's own personalized fragmentary experience which remains fragmentary precisely because the entire context and framework of every personality's subjectivity is fragmentary in keeping with mathematics' own quantitative fragmentation. The historistic past is always fragmented into years, days, months, eras, epochs, etc., that can be associatively calculated.

One's memory is itself always a fragmentary egocentric conscious enterprise undertaken within a more overarching social group consciousness of which each conscious self is a member. An American's memory will differ from a Chinese's memory. Opposing combatants in a war will remember the same war differently depending on whether one is a victor or a victim of the war. Again, there is no one-world order in the subjective and intersubjective reaches of the horizontal order of culture. Neither is there a one-world memory or bank of memories. The memories recorded by a popular magazine's photographs focus on one aspect of the world's culture and make possible photographic relics recalling to mind that special aspect. Magazines of special interest focus on distinctly different cultural aspects. These magazines serve to recall to mind historical past events when these publications themselves are out of print and no longer current.

Another paradox of memory is that a person may choose to willfully and attitudinally fixate his mindful attention and social self-interest historistically on the past or futuristically on the future. One advanced in years may prefer to relive the past rather than to live in the present and, inversely, young individuals may prefer to live in their future expectations rather than to live in the present. Secular history has no hierararchical transhistorical upward purposeful direction. It is restricted to an horizontal backward and forward fateful self-orientation. Of itself history is a memorial record only of events and the process of events in their eventuations (i.e., evolution and revolution). An actual reality's existence is never an event or eventuation. It is an actuality that enjoys a status of permanent or temporary existence. Further, it is either an essential substantive actuality or an incidental non-substantive actuality (viz., the apple's red color).

It should be noted that the psychic mind's own function is exclusively one of association, disassociation, and exchange. In these associations it links together and disjoins whatever it wills to exchange. Again, the psychic mind's hallmark is not excellence but equivalence, mathematical equivalence. Thus, one American dollar for two French francs is an acceptable equivalence when it is willfully (i.e., contractually) agreed to be exchanged in this ratio. Indeed, exchange is the principal function of the mind's calculations as the cornerstone of its own intuitive calculations. Intuition is its key to all of these exchanges when the mind intuitively discerns the equivalence or nonequivalence between whatever it wills to have willfully (i.e., forcibly) and contractually exchanged. The incentive behind such exchanges is the profit and advantage this exchange yields to the one who agrees to it (both intrapersonally and interpersonally). This profitable factor is the incentive that induces agreement between parties. It is the very influential motive that is thematically the subject to rhetorical discourse.

The overriding concern in such exchanges is strictly one of equivalence which is subject to interpretation. This intuitive exchange is the keystone to intuitively interpreting the Old Testament in view of the New. Thus, for example, the story of the bronze serpent erected to cure the Jewish people of the OT from the poisonous venom of serpents who bit them, becomes an allegorical story, par excellence, for the New Testament's insight into the interpretation of Christ being lifted up on the cross of crucifixion as the savior of all mankind poisoned by the venom of their own sinfulness. There is no moral value inherent in this trade-off. But, note, that there is always a self-sacrificial element in this trade-off and a paradoxical tension inherent in every exchange. For example, 1 is agreeably equivalent to 1/3 + 1/3 + 1/3. But, if it is so divided, then it cannot be in this exchange identical with a different ratio such as 1/2 + 1/2 even though the two ratios are themselves equivalent to each other. Thus, if a father gives an equal share to both his 3 sons and 2 daughters, the recipients themselves will receive unequal portions. Hence, if 1 is exchanged for 3/3, it sacrifices in this exchange its immediate prospect of being exchanged for 2/2 although the two ratios are equivalently 1.

The threefold liberal, mechanical, and fine arts are, again, the fulcrums on which pivots the artificial cultivation of mankind's social self-humanization and communicable exchange. The intellect's objective ideas and the mind's subjective ideations are liberally exchanged and manageably controlled through the artifictional cultivation of the linguistic symbols of meaningful communication and cooperative group associations. The intellectual will's purposeful intentions and the mind's mindful will's own motivations are mechanically and technically exchanged and exploitatively controlled through the artifactual cultivation of tools and utilities of material construction and group builders. Finally, the former two are synthetically and esthetically exchanged, managed and exploited, through the combined cultivation of artificial media of artistic creation made manifest through special implements that facilitate the self-humanized body's own grace and handiness.

The key difference in this threefold artificial self-humanizing self-cultivation of one's personality is the facilitated social (i.e., exchangeable) usage inherent in the product of each's respective psychic, somatic, and combined psychosomatic constructs. The liberal artisan fabricates a usably useful product (viz., a linguistic symbol); the technical artisan constructs a usably useless product (viz., a paint brush); while the fine arts artisan constructs a compound useful/useless product. Thus, the very term, paint brush, is a useful linguistic expression which the wordsmith fashions to communicate the mind's ideation. The actual paint brush in the hand of a house painter is a handcrafted utility tool that is useless other than for special tasks of applying paint for protective purposes. A similar paint brush in the hands of an artistic painter is more of a toy than a tool which the artist toyfully (i.e., handily) deploys to creatively depict an esthetic scenario (i.e., a mental ideation).

In the worlds of man's cultural self-humanization there is an exchange currency at the level of the psychic self's artificially cultivated industrious associations. This exchange currency is money which as an official tender authorized by the government facilitates the artifactual commercial exchange of social goods and services. This tender currency is itself further facilitated by the artificial cultivation of bureaucratic social groupings that manage and regulate the minting and the banking of such monies and monetary exchanges at all levels of society. There is concomitantly an exchange currency at the level of the somatic self's artificially cultivated industrialized self-materialization. This exchange currency is electricity which facilitates the artifactual exchange of physical matter's natural resourceful energy into a harnessed reservoir of synergistic force utilized in multiple ways to facilitate mankind's self-mastery over his own somatic body's corpuscular materialization. In between these two upper and lower exchange currencies, there is the electronic media of mass communication for exchanging of ideas, news, business, entertainment, employment, diplomacy, education, discussion, information, sales, etc.

Within the superhumanistic order of mankind's historical Christian salvation, sanctification, and glorification, the cultural self-superhumanizing exchange currency of both the mystic's psychic and somatic selves is the Precious Eucharistic Body and Blood of Jesus Christ who Selflessly surrendered Himself as a volunteer scapegoat to die a death of sacrificial immolation as a ransom at the service of all humankind's liberation from its own sinful servitude. Thus, where the coin of the secular realm carries the imprint and motto of the nation and its political leaders serving as the legal tender for all commercial exchanges, the coin of Holy Mother the Church's sacred realm is the Catholic Church's sacramentality which carries the imprint and ritual motto of the Blessed Trinity. In this sacral exchange the very human and self-humanized psychosomatic selfhood of man is exchanged for the superhuman and superhumanized Selfhood of Jesus Christ, God/Superman.

Where mankind's industrious skill manages to self-humanizingly transform its own psychic selfhood into multiple associative modes of interpersonal exchange facilitated by legal tender and also as well to successfully self-humanizingly transform its somatic selfhood into materialized modes of ever-increasingly complex techniques of self-manipulation facilitated by electricity, Holy Mother, the Church's salvific and sanctifying sacramentality serves mankind by super-self-humanizingly transforming mankind's own psychosomatic selfhood into Christ's very own Selfhood facilitated by the Giftedness of God-the-Father's Holy Spirit. In other words, the Divine Economy brings about a transformative exchange in which mankind's own selfhood is transformed into Christ's divinized Selfhood with such a superhumanistic self-mastery that mankind's self-serving selfishness becomes transformed into Christ's Selfless service.

Returning more explicitly to the subject of our memory, it should be clearer now that the memory which is described and engaged in St. John's writings is more of a skillfully self-cultivated function of the person's selfhood than it is an innate faculty of the soul. A faculty operates spontaneously of its own prowess and its activity is never transitively productive. It remains intransitively non-productive. A function (as an exercise of a skillful facilitator) works only when it is willfully (i.e., forcibly) prompted to do so. Its functioning when successful results transitively in producing a serviceable product. In the process of producing such a product the function itself becomes successfully transformed into a skillful self-serving function. For example, the corporeal body's organic faculty of sight never alters what it actually sees in its act of simply gazing at something.

On the other hand, the corpuscular somatic body's anatomical sensor of visualization optically functions effectively only in the measure that its very act of visualization is willfully manipulated to facilitate its optical "seeing." The faculty of sight is the power   to informatively see. A person who is blind is still endowed with this faculty even when its actual operation is impeded by some anatomical defect and deficiency. Hence, there is a radical distinction between sight as a sense faculty and sight as a sensor function.

The human body's objective corporeality versus its subjective corpuscularity.

When the eye's innate power to see is impeded by a cataract that clouds over the eye's anatomical lens, a surgical removal of the cataract does not restore the faculty of sight. This faculty is innate to the human body's substantive holistic corporeality. With the removal of the cataract, sight's anatomical and physiological mechanism is able to function properly to facilitate seeing. This surgery transforms the eye's anatomy into a functioning facility facilitating the faculty's actual seeing. Another instance of this transformative functioning is when one willfully squints to better peer at something.

In other words, a faculty operates efficaciously by spontaneously and informatively enhancing its own operative power of seeing whereas a functioning sensor functions effectively by first becoming transformed to facilitate its own functioning. Again, another example. The body's legs are a faculty of the corporeal body's own mobility whereas a bike is a body's mechanical facility facilitating the corpuscular body's mechanized mobilization. The human body's corporeality moves intransitively by its own legs without artificially and forcibly moving anything else to do so. The human body's corpuscularity is moved transitively (i.e., artificially) by moving (i.e., peddling) the bike's mechanized mobility which, in turn, enables the cyclist's body to be more easily transported in a momentous motion. That is, one part of the body, (i.e., the legs) moves another part (i.e., the torso) artificially by first productively moving (i.e., peddling) the bike's mechanism.

In the vertical order all human vital activity operates intransitively (i.e., non-productively) while in the horizontal order all self-humanized actions function transitively (i.e., productively). A vital intransitive activity issues spontaneously from a faculty while a self-vitalized function engages artificially fabricated facilities, facilitators, sensors, etc. Again, by way of another example, vertically the procreative sexual powers do not artificially fabricate a human offspring, they engender and beget an offspring since the newly conceived offspring remains immanently in its conception, birthing, bearing, nurturing, housing, education, etc., a child (i.e., equal in dignity) and not a product of its parents parenting throughout all of its life.

Whatever is productively constructed is serviceably useable for the one who makes use of it. The offspring of human parents is always a protégé of the parents and not normatively an indentured useable slave nor, worse still, a mere utilizable facility. Granted that professional athletes are traded as functional facilitators, a parent does not give birth to an athlete but to a person who chooses to function as a professional athlete later in life.

In any activity issuing from a faculty, the faculty itself is enhanced by the ensuing activity. The faculty of sight becomes itself inherently more informatively seeing when it actually sees. Similarly with every other cognitive faculty. In any function of a facilitator, the artificially fabricated product of the facilitator must be put to a self-serving useful profit that does not necessarily benefit the facilitator itself. Thus, in the case of the bike, again, the beneficiary of the function of peddling is not precisely the legs themselves which normally tire from the effort of peddling. And neither is the beneficiary the bike itself. The beneficiary is the body's torso whose local movement is momentously facilitated by peddling the bike. Thus, peddling is a productive function while simple walking is a non-productive activity, an operation. Of course, walking on a tread-mill becomes a function rather than an operative activity precisely because the mechanism itself facilitates the walking rather than do the legs themselves acting naturally as the human body's mobilizers. On a treadmill the legs maintain the body's stability but do not of themselves propel the body's mobility.

The reason much time is allotted to these radical distinctions between the person's vertical order of nature and its corresponding horizontal order of culture is to emphasize that all the activities of the human person in the vertical order emanate spontaneously and dynamically from its own substantive body/soul dynamic nature and are intransitive (i.e., non-productive) activities emanating from special faculties proper to the body and soul respectively. These activities redound immediately to the holistic benefit of the faculties themselves and the body/soul's own dynamic wellbeing. This is also the case with brute animals in each's own respective nature. When the spider weaves its web, it is not artificially producing it. The web instinctively and spontaneously emanates from its dynamic nature. If it were producing the web, the web itself would be a product of its own artificially constructed mental design of the web and subsequent skillful implementation of crafted tools to fabricate this design. Furthermore, it would be progressively seeking to modify and to improve on this design in the construction of successive webs.

In contradistinction, all the personalized self-cultivated functions of the human person which issue from its self-subsistent personhood in the horizontal order of culture are artfully (i.e., skillfully) crafted transitive productions which, in turn, serve to increase the personhood's self-humanized autonomous (i.e., self-reliant) social security. The very production of such serviceable facilities entails the cultivation of a function (artful skill) in the process of their production. That is, the carpenter becomes a skillful carpenter in the process of designing and making a hammer and saw and then, in turn, deploying them skillfully to construct something. There is no innate carpentry faculty as there is an innate faculty of eyesight. There is only a facilitator propensity of self-accommodation which becomes a skillful function in skillfully producing a product accommodating the facilitator.

In other words, in the vertical order of human nature, the human person does not work while in the horizontal order of artfully cultivating his self-humanization, the human person does forcibly work. For, the vertical order is that of a dynamic and energetic operational existence while its horizontal counterpart is that of a synergistic kinetic effort to overcome an inertial resistance. Every transitive productive project entails a willful conscious effort and exertion on the part of the body's somatic mobilization and willful conscious self-controlled effort on the part of the mind's psychic conceptualization.

Objectively, the person's corporeal substantive body/soul dynamism acts without effort. Thus, in simply seeing or walking there is no effort. One need not make one's self walk. But in focusing one's eye (viz., peeking and peering) or in peddling the bike an effort is involved. One needs to make one's self forcibly engaged in these transformatively productive actions. The importance of this distinction is that it enables one to fully appreciate the remarkable difference there is between the human personhood's subjective mindful and willful make-do personality in comparison to the personhood's objective soulful personal intellectual and willing operational doings. The former willfully consciously artifictionally fabricates its thoughts and willfully cultivates an artifactual skill in the process of transformatively producing something whereas the latter's intellect is informatively directly impregnated with its knowledge of reality and becomes cognitively strengthened (i.e., virtuous) the more it assimilates that knowledge through its own logical reasoning and cogitation.

Further, the latter's will efficaciously attains the very purposeful end which it willingly intends by simply willing it. A person in jail may be more efficaciously free than a person out of jail who is addicted to alcohol precisely because the jailbird efficaciously wills not to be a drunkard. Further, the soulful will's own volitions are spontaneously and not forcibly elicited. Intellectual reasoning does not take place under the domineering control of the soul's willful influence. Rather, it spontaneously thinks and reasons in virtue of the intellect's own facultative spontaneity and prowess. On the other hand, the psychic mind's conceptualization takes place under the mindful will's influential self-control and self-determination. When one "makes up one's mind" one does so forcibly under the will's own self-determination and self-control.

The objective soul's intellect and intellectual activity versus the subjective self's mind and mindful functions.

The perfection of intellectual knowledge is the holistic truth of being-as-such just as the perfection of the soul's willful volition is the common good of being-as-such. The intellect does not arrive at the truth because the soul's intellectual will forcibly wills it to do so. Quite the reverse. The soul's will itself ought to obediently and morally choose to will rightfully what is objectively the truth of its choices (i.e., the truthful common good of being-as-such). The moral rectitude of the will's free choices is established by the truth of being-as-such. This is its conscience. On the other hand, in the case of the personhood's subjective mindful personality and mindful will in the horizontal order, the selfhood's mind is not perfected by the truth-as-such of being-as-such. Paradoxically enough its self-fabricated thoughts

190

harbor only the no-such-truths of its own conceptual non-such-beings (i.e., ideations).

Recall that the proper fabrics of the psychic mind's thoughts are always mathematical non-entities and calculative enterprises. Mathematical reasoning is itself an enterprise since it deals with non-entities. There is no truth-as-such in mathematical thinking. There is only an exactitude or lack of such precision. $2 + 2 = 4$ is not a truthful equation but an exact balance and equivalence between two different factors or combination of factors. The key to mathematical reasoning is the mental skill of intuitively and accurately associating one factor or combination of factors with others that differ. Thus, any factor or combination may be exchanged with any other providing they are calculated to be precisely equivalent. If the will forcibly and arbitrarily determines to mindfully establish a different mathematical equivalence such that 1 is not equal to 1 but rather to 2, then $2 + 2$ would be equal to 8. Not truthfully but merely correctly, exactly, and precisely according to a prior willful agreement.

The major difference between the soul's intellect and the self's psychic mind is that the former objectively and spontaneously thinks and knows the very entities of reality itself whereas the latter subjectively is merely conscious of its own enterprising self-cultivated fabricated thoughts. Thus, when the soulful intellect thinks of red-as-such, it is thinking communitively and entitatively of the very family reality of the color red. Concomitantly when the self's egocentric psychic mind is subjectively conscious of the term, red (viz., r-e-d), which it consciously fabricates and associates with the intellect's thinking about this family color, red. The very term itself as conceived by the psychic mind is a non-such-red. That is, r-e-d spelled out terminologically is not itself the entitative color, red-as-such. The term itself is semantically meaningless.

Not only does the self's psychic mind skillfully and consciously fabricate words corresponding to what the intellect is thinking, it can store and recall these words from its store of memories and in turn associate these words with what they originally signify in the intellect's knowledge. Indeed, there is a concomitant parallel engagement between the soul's intelligence and the self's psyche integrated by the human person's very own self-subsistent personhood. While the self-subsistent person's personhood actually thinks intellectually, the same personhood is concomitantly psychically conscious of such thinking and psychically fashioning a semantic term corresponding with the intellect's thinking.

But, what is remarkable is that the term, r-e-d, is itself merely as a semantic term or composite linguistic expression, a non-entity, a non-being-as-such. It is a skillful fabrication of the self's psychic mind. Indeed, this fabrication is an important skill precisely because the human person could not communicate the intellect's thoughts to another person without the means of such artfully fabricated terminology whether it be spoken, written, or mimicked by the body's gestures. The very grammar that makes for correct speech is a skillful fabrication of the self's conscious psychic mindfulness. The soul's intellect itself does not entertain such notional fabrications. Its thoughts are entirely objectively engaged with the very existing entitativeness of reality itself. Yet, the human person must skillfully mentally fashion and imaginatively fancy significant semantic terms to correctly communicate to others what the intellect conceives.

Certainly, it is the legacy of any culture to transmit through their own artificial self-humanization from one generation to the next the artful skills constructed in that culture. Thus, a new-born babe does not have to invent the alphabet to learn to speak. It merely has to memorize the alphabet and artfully by rote become experientially familiar with its correct grammatical usage. Similarly, in the course of history the historian too memorially deconstructs past eventuations into a series of events (as one learns the alphabet) and subsequently reconstructs these fictionally in one overall account.

The historian supports this fictional story of the past by factual documents recorded in the past. This fictional account of history is factual in the measure that factual documents are supplied to support this account. This fictional account remains fictional in the measure that it is a plausible interpretation of these documented events. Anyone's autobiographical personal history recorded in a diary format is an account of that person's personalized memorial experiences. A nation's national history is only memorially experiential. Those citizens who actually experienced the events of the past can only, in turn, memorially relate these experiences to the new generation of citizens. The new generation cannot themselves, actually experience these memories. This is another paradox of the memorial order of subjectivity. Paradoxically, there is no *Truth* in history; there is only proof. Truth is found only in the vertical order of existence and not in the horizontal order of resistance.

The objective ontological order versus the subjective ideological order.

Now, the reader of this commentary can appreciate how this differentiation between the objective vertical ontological order and the subjective ideological (or epistemological or phenomenological) horizontal order is so very important in appreciating to the full the mystagogical writings of our Holy Father, St. John of the Cross. The intellect itself is the proper faculty to initiate a direct knowledge in faith of God in contemplative prayer in terms of and in the actual presence of the very actuality of God's very own Triune Godhead. The memory, on the other hand, as St. John explains, is also involved in the mystic's supernatural and sacramental encounter with God in contemplative prayer. Not primarily and fundamentally as is the case with the intellect, but secondarily and supplementally through the theological virtue of hope. And, therefore, as it is the case that the personhood's own mindful egocentric selfhood is the very core of its memorial egocentric consciousness, it needs itself also to undergo a special purgation preliminary to the mystic's entry into contemplative prayer.

That is, its involvement with contemplative prayer entails the total suspension of its normal memorial secular world de/construction function just as the intellect's own natural involvement in contemplative prayer entails the suspension of its own native intellectual activity. Thus, it is imperative that the mystic deliberately (i.e., willfully and forcibly) by the human personhood's own subjective willful mindful self-control cease to consciously concentrate on the mind's own associative remembrance of both past events and/or anticipation of future ones. Indeed, it is imperative that the conscious function of remembering becomes entirely vacant and suffers total amnesia.

Why? So that the mystic's full conscious attention will not be reflexively attentive to its own self-conscious egocentric rememberances of the historistic past or the futuristic future. What is crucial in contemplative prayer is that the personhood's egocentric self be reflexively and consciously submissive to the reality of God's own sublime objective sacramental supernatural Graciousness superintelligibly present to the intellect's faith filled prayerful soulful contemplative gaze. Just as the intellect itself can only intellectually engage God in contemplative prayer by the theological virtue (strength) of faith enabling it to cognitively participate in knowing God's superintelligible Personhood beyond its own intellectual strength, so also the self's egocentric memory can only consciously engage God in such contemplative prayer by the theological virtue (reinforcement) of hope. That is, it can consciously and hopefully train itself ascetically by self-denial in advance of contemplative prayer to consciously transcend its own mindful self-fabricated remembrance of past gone or future upcoming historical events and eventuations which would only serve as distracting impediments to contemplative prayer's consummation: beholding and worshipping God's Triune Godhead sacramentally and graciously present to the mystic's soulful embrace.

When the human person in his own self-subsistent personhood is left to attend to his own subjective self-serving remembrances, he is hopelessly out of touch with the reality of God's eternal subsistence that transcends not only the egocentric confines of a person's own subjectivity but, moreover, the very horizon of history's historicity. The mystic in contemplative prayer sacramentally encounters not merely God's Supreme Divine Nature but the very Triune Personhood of this Supreme Nature. God is creatively present to every creature by His omnipotent power of His Divine Nature but even more perfectly present to the mystic by the miraculous personal presence of His own Triune Personhood as is the case with every Christian in a state of Grace baptized into the Church's Trinitarian sacramentality.

Certainly, this total amnesia prescribed by St. John of the Cross will be the occasion in the mystic's life for considerable awkwardness in living out a mundane life involving routine activities and responsibilities. Our Carmelite Holy Father addresses this embarrassment and responds to it. Yet, it does not dissuade him from insisting on the total suspension of all conscious memorial remembrances in order to engage more fully in the exercise itself of contemplative prayer. Indeed, it is the case that the mystic is to prepare and anticipate contemplative prayer by actively self-inducing ascetically this memorial forgetfulness and oblivion. And, indeed, this is not an impossible task however difficult it may seem. It is a matter of skillful training in willfully controlling one's own reflexive somatic consciousness and psychic subconscious attentiveness to one's own historicity.

Furthermore, even if the typical Catholic Christian is not anticipating entering into contemplative prayer, it does not behoove one emulating Christ and His Gospel lifestyle to place his confidence in a historistic past which is no longer existent nor in a futuristic future which need never exist. The theological virtue of hope instills in the disciple of Christ a confidence which is not egocentrically vested in one's own autonomous social self-reliance but transcendently in Christ's bodily resurrection. For, one's self-centered autonomous memorial self-awareness, as is the case with every historical aspect inherent in the horizontal order of one's subjectivity, is susceptible to dissolution with the body's death. Left to itself and its own resources, the personhood's subjective personality is hopelessly unable to transcend its own historical demise. Therefore, every hope that one places in any guarantee which itself issues from this historical order of subjectivity is a vain and foolish hope. Without Christ's resurrected immortality one's own psychosomatic personalized experience of life in all of its historical social dimensions would remain hopeless.

In the transition from meditative prayer to contemplative prayer which entails transcending altogether the imagination and its imagery, the self's conscious attention must not be reflexively concentrated on its own egocentric psychic selfhood to the exclusion of what engages the intellect's object of super intelligibility, the actual sacramental presence through Grace of God's very own Triune Personhood. In remaining attentive to the objective reality of God's sacramental Triune gracious presence in the soul, the mystic's very own self-centered egocentric mindfulness will become confidently conscious and certainly convinced through the theological virtue of hope of transcending secular history itself and history's fateful eventual inevitable demise. In other words, the human person through its own self-subsistent personhood will subjectively and religiously experience hopefully in contemplative prayer what it could never experience on its own if it remains exclusively within the historical hopelessness of its very own reflexive memorial historical self-conscious subjectivity.

It must be emphatically and unequivocally understood that this willful deliberate ignoral of one's own psychic secular memorial conscious self on the part of the mystic in order to become better disposed for contemplative prayer is not to be confused with the contemporary account of "centering prayer" which entails that the psychic mind itself be purged of all notions to the point of blanking out completely in order to become passively receptive to assimilating God's infused inspirations. St. John's insistence on the memory's willful suspension is a purgative prerequisite, indeed, to entering into prayerful contemplation but not to the point of suspending or stultifying the mystic's own personalized awareness altogether as might be the case of one entering into a self-induced hypnotic trance to become completely oblivious to the somatic body's sensations and feelings, on the one hand, and the objective universe of reality, on the other. The seat of contemplative prayer is not the person's subjective selfhood; it is the person's objective soulful intelligence and intellectual will enlightened by the theological virtue of faith.

This amnesia required by St. John is a willful submission and conversion (i.e., a metanoia) of the person's selfish self-centeredness to the objective reality which transcends the historicity of its own subjectivity. It specifically is not a person's willful concentration on its own egocentric self's reflexive inner mental impassive self to the detriment of its outer somatic compassionate self. A person's selfhood in its historicity can only of itself attend to the world's historical secular eventuation of events; it is of itself unable to attend to the actuality of existent realities and their actual transhistorical metaphysical development. The seat of contemplative prayer is not a person's subjective selfhood but rather a person's objective soul. Contemplative prayer is fundamentally ontological and only supplementally phenomenological. In this way the human person's self-subsistent personhood becomes able within its own egocentric subjectivity to religiously, willfully, mystically, and conscientiously surrender its own selfhood with its self-centered prejudices and submissively offer its very bodily mortal self sacrificially to the service of the objective truth of God's supernatural sacramental presence through Grace in the soul's immortal transcendence beyond the historical subjectivity and historical transiency of the mystic's own mortal selfhood.

It must be pointed out that the intellect's natural knowledge in terms of being-as-such transcends all of the tangible conditions of the physical cosmos including time's temporality and the quantitative dimensions of physical substances such as their distance, number, size, shape, location, etc. Thus, such intellectual knowledge is already naturally disposed to reach even the theological height of God's own eternal heaven of supernal transhistorical and timeless existence transcendent to all of creation. Hence, even on a natural plane, the human person's subjective personality can be consciously disposed to yield and submissively surrender itself to a transhistorical reach of reality transcendent to its own mortal historicity. Of course, it must be understood that one and the same person within his own personhood sacrificially yields and submits his subjective self-attentiveness and self-interest to his objective selfless intellectual attentiveness to an absolute and eternal truth transhistorically transcendent to his own creaturely mortality.

The worlds of the human person's humanistic self-cultivation is not to be confused with the universe of God's creation.

Now, the self-subsistent human personhood's subjective personality can self-consciously in conjunction with other selves other than itself deliberatively in its own enterprising way constructively cultivate its own social self-humanization processively within historical stages of development without ever transcending the back and forward orientation of history's own horizon. This self-humanization and all of its secular worldly achievements is entirely artificially subjective and itself distinct from the universe of reality existing in the ontological vertical order. The very secular hi-tech worlds of culture within which persons earn their living wages are themselves in our contemporary democratic civilizations atheistically divorced from the ontological theocentric vertical hierarchical order of reality. This is the notable crisis of our contemporary age in Western civilization: a technocracy devoid of a moral compass and deliberately oblivious to and antagonistic to God's moral authority in the objective metaphysical, hierarchical natural order of existence.

There is no subjective phenomenological one-world history comparable to ontological reality's total objective unity which attains its universal epitome and culmination in God's own unicity as its capstone. The prospect of there being many different universes beyond the compass of the universe in which mankind presently exists is as plausible as the prospect of there being many supreme Beings existing apart from each other. God as a Supreme Being has no equal and, certainly, no duplicate since God is the totality of existence outside of which there is only nothingness speaking negatively and relatively (since there is no existing reality that exists independent of God's own existence). God exhausts the total plenitude of existence since God is not merely uniquely existing but, moreso, the very uniqueness of existence itself. There is but one God. God cannot be duplicated nor cloned. God is totally simple and totally unitively simplicity itself. Indeed, God's very existence is the infinitude of existence.

Everything that can be attributed to God is God; for, it is compatible with both God's simplicity and God's infinite existence. Accordingly, what is not God simply does not inherently exist; it exists only derivatively in virtue of God's very own existential uniqueness. Accordingly, there are not two separate universes of reality since every reality that is not God exists only in virtue of God's universal uniqueness. There is not in the subjective fields of mankind's self-humanized cultures one overall world of mankind's own artificial fabrication. There is no-such one-world history. Such a prospect of an evolving one-world history is itself a utopian figment of the psychic mind's own fabrication.

The world of mankind's own historical self-cultivation is ineluctably a many-faceted make-believe world. An "as if" enterprise rather than an "as is" reality. Hence, while there is a universal pinnacle of Be-ingness (viz., God) in the ontological natural vertical order of reality there is no equivalent pinnacle of non-beingness in the artificial ideo-logical horizontal historical order of culture. Of course, there is a psychic awareness of the non-such-beingness of the psychic mind's own subconsciousness. But, it is neither a pinnacle nor the culmina-tion of the artificial non-such-being of the manifold worlds of man-kind's own self-cultivation. Paradoxically enough, this subconscious awareness of the psyche's own empty nothingness is itself the nadir of mankind's own willful obstinate resistance to reality's total plenit-ude of God's very own divine existence. It is very important to appre-ciate that the typical introspective engagement of the psychic mind is involved with its own enterprising mental notions and fabrications which are themselves only impotent artificial non-such-beings (i.e., non-entities).

In the case of the centuries-old religions of the Far East such as Buddhism or Hinduism, the monk's introspective transcendental meditation is centered on the egocentric psyche itself and not merely on its psychic mental ideations and notions. And the oriental monk attains to the nirvana (i.e., the nadir) of the psyche's own non-such-beingness when he subconsciously willfully obliterates and ignores even the psyche's own thoughts and thoughtfulness. That is, he be-comes completely psychically self-consciously self-absorbed in the very nothingness and emptiness of his own selfhood's psyche. He thus finds himself subconsciously enveloped in the very pith of an ig-norance even deprived of an awareness of its own selfhood as a sub-ject of awareness.

This nirvana, of course, is completely antithetical to what consti-tutes contemplative prayer for the Catholic Christian mystic who be-comes reflectively (not self-reflexively) trustingly contemplatively and prayerfully in faith consciously hopefully emancipated from the inhibiting prison of his own selfhood's mortal historicity and sub-jectivity and, thereby, utterly ecstatically (i.e., beyond his own self-hood) absorbed in the very Triune Personhood of Beingness itself. This is, indeed, the case even when the Christian Catholic mystic is not experiencing subjectively any ecstatic religious bodily feeling of sublime exultation or any mental bearing of serene consolation. The very confident and hopeful thrust of contemplative prayer transports the Catholic mystic beyond the parameters of his own moral historical selfhood. In contemplative prayer the mystic is ecstatically "beside and beyond his self" and transformatively inside the Giftedness of the Holy Spirit of Christ's very own Super-Self-humanized Selfless Selfhood.

It should be pointed out that the vertical ontological order is entirely orthodox. The holistic truth of the intellect and the family common good of the intellectual will cannot be other than what is in conformity with and identified with the truth of being-as-such. Thus, the very being of the color, red, in the red apple cannot truthfully be red other than in terms of the being-as-such of red-as-such. A particular red flower is not truly red because it resembles another red flower. It is truly red inasmuch as it is an instance of the family of red colors: red-as-such. Furthermore, the red flower cannot in any aspect of its red color be red as an instance of red-as-such and simultaneously not be red (viz., some other color). This simply could not exist and, hence, could not be authentically true-as-such. What could not be true-as-such could neither be good-as-such since the good-as-such is in its turn the very value which makes what is true-as-such to be worthwhile. It is only at the intellectual transhistorical level that the metaphysical foundation of reality can be intelligibly understood in terms of the transcendental unity, truth, and inherent value of being-as-such. What is transcendentally and transhistorically the case as-such is incumbent on every instance of every existing being regardless of the status of that existence.

In direct contrast to this, the horizontal historical subjective ideological order is entirely paradoxical. Its mode of consciousness is not one of knowing but, moreso, one of not knowing and of ignorance. It is the case that its own conscious self-awareness is not conversant with reality that exits transcendent to and independent of its own consciousness. Rather, it is conscious only of its own fabrications. The self's psychosomatic consciousness is one of nescience rather than one of cognizance; it is one of the absence of reality rather than one of reality's presence. Yet, this reflexive self-consciousness is very important as a supplement to the human person's soulful intelligence, intellectual and sensorial knowledge. It becomes problematic when the human person deliberately by willful self-control and self-deception substitutes this cultural order of subjective mortal historical consciousness for the natural objective immortal and transhistorical order of reality itself and, thereby, completely contraceptively and abortively deliberately eliminates and ignores altogether the fundamental primacy proper to the ontological order itself.

We should also note that it is not the subjective psychic mind nor the somatic body themselves which consciously function in fabricating artificial objects facilitating each's respective self-awareness. That is, it is not the psychic mind that fabricates its own notions and ideations nor the somatic body that fabricates its own imaginary fantasies.

 Rather, it is the human person who egocentrically functions in virtue of its own self-susbsistent personhood. It is this very personhood that is psychically subconsciously or somatically self-consciously productively functioning. There is no egocentricity in this consciousness in the sense that there is some ego which is a substantive component of a person's psychic or somatic consciousness. The paradox here is that this "ego" is simply a pronominal term which symbolizes and stands for the person's self-subsistent personhood's own self-conscious selfhood. It is a ubiquitous term for the pronouns, "me, myself, and I," which are all sobriquets for the human person's personhood personified in its own subjective personality and its personalized projects.

There is another way to explain the "ego's" paradoxicality. Consider a room off a hallway or corridor. One enters the room through a door and exits through the same door to return to the hallway. This door is both an adit and an exit threshold. This threshold is neither inside nor outside of the room itself or the hallway itself. It is merely the entry-way or the exit-way to both. This is the case for the ego in regard to both the psyche and the soma. It is the threshold between them. Just as one cannot see the inside of the room unless one is outside; neither can one see the outside of the room unless one is inside. Of course, this is paradoxical. It explains alienation. If one is inside the room as an outsider one is an alien. Again, if one is outside of the room as an insider, one is a native and not entirely an outsider. A person's psychic ego paradoxically misconstrues that it has telepathic intimate access to anyone else's psyche and psychic thoughts and bearing (i.e., equipoise, attitudinal self-interest, and mental composure); especially if the person regards the other self as an alien. Similarly, a person's somatic ego paradoxically misconstrues that it has sympathetic access to everyone else's soma, somatic sensations, sensitivities, and feelings; again, this is especially so if the other is seen as an alien. Similarly, one can only look historically backward from a forward position and, conversely, one can only look historically forward from a backward stance.

Psychic consciousness is mindfully self-orientated inwardly and introspectively toward the mind's own psychic noumenal notionality or self-orientated outwardly and extrospectively toward the physiological body's imaginary somatic phenomenal sensationalism. In either case, this inward psychic concentration and its antipodal somatic outward focus are polar opposites in the selfhood's own psychosomatic egocentricity. These reflexive stages of consciousness engage the non-beings-as-such of their own respective psychic or somatic skillful functioning fabrication. A human self-subsistent personhood's egocentric subjective psychosomatic personality is not mindful of reality itself when it is reflexively absorbed and preoccupied with its own selfhood. However, when it is reflectively (but not reflexively) concomitantly aware of the activity of the human soul's intellect and will including the corporeal body's organic sense's and instinctive appetites, the self's personality is conscious of what is transcendent to its own historical memorial selfhood and self-cultivated egocentric subjectivity.

When it reflexively concentrates on its own psychic spectral notions and/or focuses on its own somatic spectacular phenomena it is solipsistically out of touch with reality itself. In these cases it is reflexively conscious only of the non-beings-as-such of its own artificial fabrication. In other words, in these cases it memorially reverts to its own past notional events or adverts to its own projected future somatic imaginary eventuations. For, the historic past is that which actually exists no longer and the futuristic future is that which need never exist. It is the case that a relic of the past or a life-insurance policy referring to one's future death are really themselves only historic and futuristic tokens of the selfhood's ephemeral and evanescent mortality.

In other words, that which these historical tokens respectively testify to (viz., the historistic past and the futuristic future) are not themselves ontological realities. They remain artificial figments of a human person's own subjective self-cultivation. For, their value is not one of being-as-such; it is one having no-such-being. In the present moment in which they are consciously attended to by anyone, they exist only as tokens of the past that are no longer existing and a future which need never exist. They may be appreciated as antiques or as guarantees of future wealth and security available to one's surviving beneficiaries in the case of a life insurance that matures when a person dies. But, such appreciation is entirely subjective and the appreciative worth, accordingly, of these tokens of the past and future remain subjectively with the persons who treasure them and those who certify and guarantee them; not with the tokens themselves.

Contemplative prayer engages the mystic in both the hierarchical and historical orders of his own personhood.

Contemplative prayer while it occurs in time is not itself subject to time's temporality, nor is it encumbered with the physical tangibility of substantive bodies, nor hobbled with the cosmos's physical quantity of location, size, number, shape, mutation, etc. Neither is it weighed down with history's own historistic or futuristic horizontality which are subjectively outside of the realm of reality itself. Indeed, contemplative prayer is itself more centered on the ideal reality of atemporal and transhistorical eternity, God's very own abode, beyond the finitude of the heaven and earth of creation. For, contemplative prayer unites the mystic supernaturally and sacramentally with the very Triune Personhood of God's own Divinity Self-revealed in the Church's sacramentality, tradition, and Sacred Scripture.

There is no created intelligible medium that mediates the Catholic Christian mystic's prayerful communion with God's transhistorical and timeless substantive existing divinity present to the Christian mystic in contemplative prayer. St. John states unequivocally that only God can self-manifest himself to humankind to enable mankind to be so sacramentally wed to Him that in the theological gift of faith it is God-the-Father's very own infinitely superintelligibile Trinitarian Personhood that the mystic mystically beholds and lovingly adores through Christ, with Christ, and in Christ, God/Superman, in the power of their Holy Spirit.

Now, it might be objected that Christ's very own created humanity cannot serve as a proper medium in contemplative prayer to unite the mystic immediately and presentedly to God's Triune family Personhood. After all, St. John of the Cross himself insists that no created medium can intervene between the mystic and God's own Supreme Godhead in contemplative prayer. Well, it is the case that Christ's very own humanity, body and soul including His Selfless Self-divinized super-humanized Personality exist in virtue of His Divine Personhood's total infinite uncreated divine subsistency. Hence, Christ's human nature is not merely a creaturely existence mediating the mystic's contemplative prayerful union with God. It is a creaturely existence that subsists Personally through Christ's divinely subsistent Personhood. That is, it is a glorified divinized human nature and divinely Self-cultivated super-humanized Personality whose very subsistence is that of God's own Filial Personhood. For, again, these creaturely aspects of Christ's fully human nature and fully super Self-cultivated Personality do not exist subsistently in virtue of a created subsistent nature such as is the case with creaturely human beings, they exist in virtue of the infinite eternal divine subsistence of Christ's Personhood as the Son of the Father.

Note that this is analogous to the existence of the color, red, in the apple that is red when it is ripe. The apple's red-as-such color is only an incidental reality to the apple's substantive nature. For, the apple before it is a ripe red apple is actually not red. This incidental color of the apple which exists incidentally still inheres and exists in virtue the apple's substantive existence. Similarly Christ's divinized human nature is not only not an impediment to the mystic's direct gazing on the Son's divine Personhood in contemplative prayer, it actually facilitates this contemplative prayerful gaze itself because it is through Christ's divinized and subsequently glorified human nature in resurrection that the Second Person of the Trinity's infinitely subsistent Personhood is made supernaturally and miraculously manifest to the mystic's contemplative gaze.

Further, as is the case in receiving the Blessed Sacrament of the Eucharist the mystic's one personality is consummately and religiously assimilated into Christ's Mystical Body as a member of that ecclesial Body, the Church, to become sacramentally and transformatively enabled to enter into mystical communion with God's eternal Triune Godhead. Our holy Carmelite Father's description of contemplative prayer in the *Ascent* and elsewhere leave no doubt that it is God in God's Triune Personhood that the mystic lovingly embraces in contemplative prayer. Or, rather, there is no doubt that through the theological virtue of faith it is the Trinitarian Personhood of God's own Godhead that lovingly embraces the mystic to its own divine bosom in contemplative prayer.

There is yet another paradoxical aspect to this self-humanized subjective order of culture's artificiality which must be emphasized relative to contemplative prayer. The more subjectively personalized is one's conscious experience of reality, the more self-assured, convinced, and self-confident one becomes of knowing reality itself transcendent to these artificially self-cultivated experiences. A person in a movie theater experiencing personalistically an unfolding drama of Christ's crucifixion is more self-assured and convinced of having witnessed the actual reality of this grim and cruel ordeal than he would otherwise be in only reading of it in a Gospel account. This pseudo-confidence is rooted in the subjective will's self-possessiveness rather than in the objectivity of the evidence which is offered in such a movie dramatization. Thus, the report in Sacred Scripture that Christ was crucified is less subjectively electrifying in its experiential sensational and sensitized vividness than a movie dramatization which allows one to personalistically and empathically experience for himself this dehumanizing cruelty inflicted on Christ.

Paradoxically enough, the more self-confident, convinced, and entrenched one becomes in one's own artificially self-induced religious experiences, the less reliable are these experiences themselves in revealing the truth of reality's own objectivity. St. John of the Cross is repeatedly cautioning the mystic not to mistake his own mystical experiences for the transcendent reality itself of God's own Godhead. He contends that these finite experiences themselves are entirely subjective and never measure up to the infinite reality itself of God's own sublime Divinity. Hence, he cautions the mystic against becoming self-attached to these subjective mystical experiences. Any such attachment to religious experiences of God become themselves an impediment to entering fully into contemplative prayer in order to become unitively attached to God's sublime Divinity objectively transcendent to the subjectivity of these religious experiences.

This pseudo self-confidence, certitude, and conviction fostered by subjective religious experiences also give rise to another paradox. This very self-confidence itself rooted in the self-subsistent personhood's own autonomous selfhood induces a doubt about the reliability of one's own religious experiences. Indeed, a total self-reliance on the precocity of one's own egocentric subjective selfhood invites a serious doubt about the prospect of actually knowing reality as it actually exists transcendent to one's own subjective experience of it. For, these experiences themselves remain solipsistically confined within the subjective selfhood that experiences them. Accordingly, the more personalized are one's experiences of anything, the more these experiences are prone to sewing doubt in the one who experiences them regarding their actuality. This is very much the case for the dreams that one experiences, especially if these dreams anticipate future events.

This brings up an even more surprising paradox. Truth cannot be proven for it need not be proven. The very truth of whatever is judgmentally true is itself obviously and evidently true beyond proof. Thus that the red rose is actually red-as-such is evidently, obviously, and inerrantly judged to be so beyond all doubt. Indeed, what is objectively, intelligibly, sensibly, evidently, and impartially such is truly so beyond one's subjective experience of it. A sensory faculty cannot err in what pertains to its own holistic sensible principle of information unless it is incidentally handicapped. Thus, the faculty of sight cannot err in seeing what is colorful since its formal object of information is color-as-such. Yet, if the faculty's optical organism malfunctions by being color-blind, the faculty can still see in the context of bleak black-grey-white color-like shading. And the intellect itself is inerrant in what pertains to its own holistic informative principle of intelligibility, the truth of being-as-such. Conversely, what is partisanly and subjectively personalistically experiential is itself in its very cultic enigmatic paradoxicality absurdly unintelligible.

For, paradoxically enough, experience is rooted in one's own egocentric psychosomatic consciousness and consciousness itself is not a cognizant knowing but, rather, a nescient conative empathic and/or telepathic quasi-knowing through subjective somatic sensitized feelings (viz., liking or not liking) and subjective psychic intimate bearings (viz., caring or not caring). Both fall short of the reality itself which they empathically or telepathically experience. Furthermore, one's visceral emotional somatic experiences are in polar opposition to one's psychic cerebral emotionless experiences. The reality of marriage, for example, is the lifetime heterosexual one-flesh living of two persons of the opposite sex committedly bonded in marital love for a lifetime. The subjective experience of many married couples is completely other than this reality itself. Hence, if marriage is identified by a married couple's subjective experience of it, it will be different for each spouse within the same marriage.

Up to this point in this segment of this commentary it is mainly one's subjective egocentric self-cultivated self-humanization which has been the center of our attention. The reason for this is that one's memory itself is historically an offshoot of this psychosomatic egocentricity. It behooves us now to attend, even if it is rather briefly, to mankind's super-cultivated super-humanization as manifested in Christ's very own Supreme Personhood's own divinized human nature and egocentric subjective Personality. Certainly, Christ is not subject to any of the sinful afflictions of original sin other than the dying and death of the body's mortality. Hence, His divinized psychosomatic egocentric Personality and Personalized subjectivity is not itself subject to any of the built-in willful inhibitions of resistance peculiar to the offspring of Adam & Eve who inherited by original sin such residual willful resistance and rebellion vis-à-vis the objective order of existence.

Jesus is not willfully and selfishly egocentrically Self-attached to any of His own personalized subjective experiences to the point that such an attachment would constitute an impediment to being transcendently Self-attached directly to the Holy Will of God-the-Father. That is, Christ's own super-personal-humanized egocentric Selfhood is in no wise selfishly egoistic or partisanly egotistical in pursuing its own partisan selfish self-interest. Jesus' Super-self-humanized Personality is entirely Selfless in its egocentric Selfhood's somatic emotional feelings (viz., likings) and psychic emotionless bearings (viz., concern and cares).

The Catholic Christian mystic in contemplative prayer addresses directly Christ and his own Heavenly Father's Holy Will through the mediation of Christ's own crucified immolation and obedient Selfless Self-surrender to this Holy Will. It is clear from Sacred Scripture that Christ, God/Superman, is Himself the superintelligible sacramental medium for the mystic's direct and perfect communion with God-the-Father's Holy Will. This sacramental medium is, accordingly, God Incarnate in the Second Person of the Blessed Trinity. Yes, Christ's humanity is created; it is not eternal; it is created in time and overarches the entire expanse and span of history's historicality. Yet, His humanity itself whether not-yet-glorified before His resurrection and now glorified as it is such in the Blessed Sacrament of the Eucharist is not itself an impediment to the mystic's perfect mystical (i.e., religious) communion with the Godhead's ineffable Triunity.

Indeed, in the resurrection at the end times, the mystic's own corpreal body along with its corpuscular self-humanized somatic materialization and concomitant psychic dematerialization will be resurrected into the glory of Christ's very own divinized egocentric psychosomatic Bodily Personality. This very superhumanized Personality of Christ is the mystical Body of the Sacramental Church which incorporates within its resurrected glory the glorified bodily personalities of all the saints-to-be in Heaven.

Contemplative prayer engages the mystic's eschatological

memoriality.

Note, again, that the total amnesia prescribed for the mystic's secular historical memories preliminary to fully entering into contemplative prayer is not to apply to the mystic's memory of the Gospel and Church history of His own redemption and glorification. The history of Sacred Scripture and the history of the Sacramental Church's own saintly pilgrimage toward its eternal destiny in heaven is not to be confused with the purposeless selfishly self-serving fatality of secular history. Sacred history is providentially destined to a purposeful Selfless transhistorical culmination that not only outlasts secular history's fatalistic doom but also continues on in an everlasting indefeasible transhistorical existence when secular history ceases. Doomsday marks the termination of secular history and the everlasting beginning of sacred history's heavenly reign. Hence, wouldn't it be expedient for the mystic's memory to be actively preoccupied with the Gospel's historical account while deeply absorbed in contemplative prayer?

Here, again, St. John of the Cross in responding to this question would insist that faith as the cornerstone of contemplative prayer would not exclude the Bible from the mystic's amnestic kenosis. Bible History---whether of the Old Testament, the New, or the Acts of the Apostles and the other sacred writings subsequent to the New Testament---is not confined to the historistic past or even the futuristic future. Some of it is, such as the crossing of the Red Sea in the flight of the chosen people from their enslavement in Egypt, etc.. This is a genuine historical event even in the sense of secular history. This historical event is itself past and gone. Yet, the typological and anagogical significance of this event outlives the event itself. This significance continues to resound even today in the Church's on-going sacramental existence and ministration.

Neither does the resonance of this Gospel typology and anagogy remain exclusively within the subjective order of the Catholic Christian's egocentric historical reminiscence. Indeed the typological significance of the Gospel's historical events, especially in the Old Testament, is that they foreshadow both futuristic and transhistorical realities which outlive these events themselves. Thus, the miraculous crossing of the sea which divided into steep walls of water to form a passage of escape for the Jews of the Old Testament figuratively and futuristically foreshadows the sacrament of baptism which literally liberates the human person from his sinful enslavement to his own egoistic selfishly self-centered self-serving selfhood. This liberation enables the human person within the integrity of its own constitution and personhood to baptismally enter into Christ's own Paschal Mystery and to sacrificially subjugate his own subjective personality to the service of God and his neighbor beyond the confines of the historical selfishness of his own subjectivity fallen from grace by the original sin of Adam & Eve.

Would it not be propitious for the mystic to reminiscently ponder Gospel accounts and passages in his contemplative orisons? Yes! The "yes" is because the contemplative prayer which St. John is proposing for the mystic is one in which the mystic in theological faith and hope gazes directly at the supremely eminent glorious reality of Christ Incarnate actually sacramentally present to the mystic as Christ exists resurrectionally and everlastingly in the bosom of the eternal infinite subsistence of God's Triune Godhead. So awesomely grandiose and stupendously magnificent is this Supreme reality of God's sacramental wedding to mankind and mankind's sacramental wedding to God's Godhead through Christ's mediation that the special, particular, concrete Biblical historical and memorial attention to this wedding---which is dogmatically true in the rigor of its divine Gospel revelation---becomes a facilitator to gazing directly on the majestic transhistorical grandeur of Christ superintelligibly and supernatually present to the mystic in All God's sublime Magnificence and Glory available to the mystic in contemplative prayer. It is better for the mystic to gaze trustingly and to confide hopefully and prayerfully in God's awesome sublime infinite totality and incomprehensible utter total simplicity than to attempt to intellectually digest or experientially and hermeneutically capture this Glorious miraculous luminescent Reality of infinite Graciousness into Gospel bites and specific religious reminiscences. This would be tantamount to attending a sumptuous banquet and eating the hot dogs which one has brought along for the feast. It is more pleasing to God that the mystic in contemplative prayer be absorbed in the infinite eternal incomprehensible munificent magnificent Subsistency of God's very own merciful Trinitarian Godhead than to be attentive to the mystic's finite comprehensible intellectual grasp or subjective personal religious hermeneutical scriptural exegeses of the Bible. Yet, in contemplative prayer which finds its source and culmination in the Blessed Sacrament of the altar, the mystic's objective hierarchical status of being supernaturally and sacramentally elevated and the mystic's subjective historical process of becoming historically Biblically integrated into God's very own Godhead coalesce.

There is still an important point regarding memory that needs our attention before turning to the texts of St. John's *Ascent* dealing with memory's purgation. The memory is not confined to recalling the knowledge of past and future conceptual and imaginary events. This recall also entails remembering the specific somatic emotional feelings and psychic emotionless bearings which accompanied these events. This is especially the case with autobiographical events whose occurrence is recorded in a diary by the person who experiences them. Yet, memory also includes remembrances of past and future events which occur outside of one's very own personalized experiences of them. Such a memory is mediated through the experiences of others, of course, and such a memory could still empathically arouse a somatic sensitized feeling of utmost urgency and/or a psychic bearing of utmost intimacy when that memory is brought back to one's attention.

In brief, memories are not without their own somatic emotional affectivity and passivity, on the one hand, and psychic emotionless impassivity and non-affectivity, on the other. St. John of the Cross shrewdly sizes up these memories in the light of the influence they exert on the subjective will's own volitions, commitments, and decisions. This self-centered will's inadvertent partisan possessiveness becomes increasingly more transparent in the ensuing part of this commentary attending to the actual text of our San Juanistic Carmelite's mystagogical writings.

ASCENT Book III. Chapters 1-15 PURIFICATION OF THE MEMORY THROUGH THE THEOLOGIAL VIRTUE OF HOPE.

Chapter 1: The purification of memory and its activity.

We have come to the point of examining specifically the 15 chapters presented by our Carmelite Holy Father addressing the purgative purification of the memory preparatory to entering into contemplative prayer and perfect union with God. Of course, it must be kept in mind that in this segment of the *Ascent* St. John is presenting the active phase of the mystic's self-mortification. The passive phase will be undertaken in the treatise of the Dark Night of the Soul following the *Ascent*'s conclusion. The objective here is to enable the mystic to have confident recourse to the theological virtue of hope rather than to place any confidence in his own self-assured initiative in approaching God. The more the mystic is attached to his own memories in the horizontal order of resistance the less docile and disposed he is to become attached to the reality of God's own supreme eminence in the vertical ontological order of existence transcendent to the subjectivity and horizontal (i.e., historical) order in which these memories are rooted. He addresses three kinds of memories: those that are natural; those that are supernaturally focused on the imagination's imagery; and, those that are entirely spiritual and bypass the imagination altogether.

Chapter 2: The memory's natural remembrances.

It is vital to surpass the natural functions of memory in order to enter into the supernatural activity of contemplative prayer. When the mystic is fully absorbed in contemplative prayer this is not conducted by the mystic; it is conducted by God Himself. In contemplative prayer the mystic encounters God through the supernatural virtue of faith "face to face" in the incomprehensibility of God's own infinitude. Becoming attached to one's memories in the measure that these memories are rooted in the historical subjectivity of the mystic's selfhood inhibits a total attention and self-attachment to God in lieu of becoming attached to these memories themselves. Indeed, these memories become a distraction and an impediment to the mystic's total self-abandonment to the supreme reality of God's Triune Godhead supernaturally and sacramentally existing and accessible through faith within the interiority of his own soul. By natural memories St. John indicates all memories which entail remembering and calling to mind outer objective sensibilities of the senses including the passionate affectivity they arouse in the mystic's corporeal sentient body. What must be added to these objective sensibilities are also the subjective sensations that are experienced subjectively within the somatic body's own physiological makeup including the sensitized emotional feelings they, in turn, arouse.

Inasmuch as these memories involve the mystic's objective sentient corporeal animal passions including the mystic's subjective corpuscular emotional compassionate feelings, the memory which is engaged here is not the Platonic memory which transcends all objective sensible affectivity and subjective sensitive sensations. This Platonic memory is strictly ethereal and operative within the soul's own incorporeality bereft of all sentient tangibility and sensitive tactility. Plato alludes to this memory when he seeks to explain the origin of the intellect's ideas. Given that these ideas (viz., green-as-such) are inherently bereft of all physicality which is not the case for the green shrub, the green grass, the green emerald gem, etc., they cannot have their origin or cause in the physical bodies that are the objects of the animal body's sense of sight. The idea, green-as-such, is intellectually pondered apart from physical bodies which are colorfully green. Every idea intellectually pondered is metaphysically spiritual and incorporeal. It transcends the reality of physical bodies and cannot be derived from whatever is physical. Plato reasons that the human soul which intellectually ponders its metaphysical ideas remembers them from an immortal existence prior to becoming incorporated in a physical body.

Since the memory which St. John describes involves objective sentient instinctive passions and subjective sensitive self-induced emotional compassions (i.e., feelings), this memory is not strictly speaking the soul's intellectual memory. For the purpose of this commentary we need not explore the brute animal's instinctive memory which in no wise is intellectual. This leaves us with the historical memory which has been sufficiently elaborated in the earlier part of this commentary.

Memories that engage both of these objective sentient and subjective sensational sensory forms along with their affections or disaffections are incompatible with contemplative prayer itself precisely because such prayer in its intellectual context transcends all the temporal and palpable lineaments of the senses. Contemplative prayer is oblivious to all such sentiency and to all the emotional affectivity and sensuality peculiar to such sentiency. He provides the example of someone involuntarily swooning when overcome with rapture in contemplative prayer. As long as this swoon lasts, the individual is not conscious of any of the body's sensations and, correspondingly, is oblivious to its sensibility, sensations, and their accompanying emotional affectivity. So much so is this the case that the swooner also loses track of the passage of time and the current flow of history. This example is adduced to point out that contemplative prayer does not engage the senses nor the somatic body's own sensations and sensitivities.

This total amnesia proper to contemplative prayer poses a problem for everyday living and functioning. St. John agrees that this is a real problem. The mystic who is orienting himself to enter into contemplative prayer becomes absent-minded regarding everything that is not vital to this prayer itself. Yet, this is necessary because the one who begins to live the mystical lifestyle of contemplative prayer will find his own memory entirely under the influence of the Holy Spirit. Hence, he will remember what the Holy Spirit prompts him to remember and will be oblivious to all else otherwise. He also adds that this is the very way which our Blessed Mother, Mary, was guided by the Holy Spirit in her daily life not only in spiritual matters but also in mundane affairs. In other words, the mystic who is by adoption a "son of God" will be influentially led by the Spirit of God. The overall point of this self-imposed amnesia is to recognize that a Christian mystic's lifestyle is not under his own direction but under the transformative influence of the Holy Spirit.

An objection is posed to this rigorous program of self-denial. It would seem that St. John is asking a mystic to accomplish what is in itself impossible. That is, to naturally surpass by his own initiative what actually transcends his initiative. St. John agrees that this is humanly impossible. Only God can introduce the mystic into the sublimity of contemplative prayer which involves total amnesia. Yet, he urges the mystic to become ascetically disposed to become absent-minded as a preliminary to fully entering into contemplative prayer itself. He recommends that for the mystic the memory of everything involving the senses and their accompanying sensuality is to be forcibly (i.e., willfully) ignored by the same effort that one makes to forcibly recall them to mind. This is the case whether these memories are merely earthbound or even heaven bound and heaven sent. In other words, it matters not whether the mystic who is anticipating and training himself to enter into contemplative prayer remembers and brings to mind mundane or religious past (or anticipated future) sentient images and imagery along with their attendant affections and feelings; both are to be dismissed and disregarded. He must deliberately dismiss them by willful acts of self-denial and self-detachment. Otherwise, they remain as impediments, distractions, and hindrances to his advancing to contemplative prayer.

Chapter 3: Three harms which ensue in failing to achieve this absent-mindedness.

Two are positive and one is privative. The first is concerned with the things of the world; the second with the devil; and the third with the impact this failure would have on contemplative prayer itself. The first harm pertaining to the world is simply the consideration that all such memories harbor the manifold imperfections inherent in the world's worldliness: the mystic's own selfish attitude, feelings of antipathy and resentment, dalliances, intrigue, falsehoods, rancor, etc.. All of these are liable to contaminate the mystic's own inner disposition and, per force, his own feelings and attitude which would inhibit him from entering into contemplative prayer. St. John insists that any attention to these is bound to subtly and adversely influence the mystic's own outlook toward God.

In response to the objection that a total ignoral of the world's events would be detrimental to the mystic's prayerful regard for the world's salvation, St. John responds that it is better for the mystic to silence his insistent need to attend to his own self-serving interests and mundane business affairs and to allow God to speak to him in solitude. In the final analysis, St. John insists that complete absent-mindedness is a blessing because all the wanderings of memory and all of the distractions that are attendant upon these wanderings are, thereby, eliminated in one fell swoop. So much so is this the case that even religious memories of the mystic's emotional feelings of attach-ment to God should be forgotten. In this forgetfulness, St. John insists, God will flood the mystic with an ocean of peace and tranquility proper to contemplative prayer itself.

It is not amiss here to pause for a moment and to reflect on St. John's urgent counsel to the mystic to become skillfully trained in this absent-mindedness as a necessary preliminary to advancing to con-templative prayer. In view of this it is quite notable that when one ad-vances in age one's memory fails even without such training. The reason is that an elderly person is both less adept in recalling a multi-tude of minute details to manage his life and less forward-looking in terms of his secular life's future opportunities. In view of becoming more stably installed in contemplative prayer and less attached to the memories of one's life, it would seem logical that it would be much easier for an elderly person than for a young person who is still pre-occupied with making his way in the secular world of business and in the trade or profession in which he earns his livelihood. Yet, paradox-ically enough, while the older person suffers a diminution of memory, he also clings tenaciously to special memories and becomes almost habitually accustomed to reliving and to mentally residing in the memories of the past. On the other hand, a younger person is not weighed down by the past memories of his life. Yet, on the other hand, the young person is paradoxically weighed down by his me-morial attention to his future expectations.

Chapter 4: The second kind of harm pertains to the devil's influence in such memories.

If the mystic entertains such memories the devil can have a field day with the mystic's feelings, pride, vanity, fears, etc. For the devil can influentially control the imagery and feelings such imagery evokes and through this control manipulate the mystic's own lifestyle even to the point of fooling the mystic into mistaking the mere appearance of things for the very reality itself. We know from our previous exploration of memory as a function of our personality's egocentric subjectivity that it is very much the case that a sensational spectacle that is merely an appearance of things and not their very substance can have a far greater impact on one's personalized experience of it than can the reality itself. Such is the case for a documentary movie which presents an artificially sophisticated staged account of some story which seems to the movie-goer to be a most realistic personalized experience of that very reality itself. Yet, the movie-goer remains really very ignorant of the reality itself that the movie is purportedly depicting. The mystic who entertains such memories places himself directly within the deceitful influential manipulation of the devil himself.

Chapter 5: The third kind of harm derives from the prospect that the distractions afforded by memories present an impediment to the mystic's advancement in moral and spiritual perfection.

St. John's reasoning here is very basic. We can only sensually desire and detest what we intelligently and conscionably know to be desirable and detestable. If we conscionably govern our sensory knowledge we are already in a position to govern the desires and detestations which they arouse. With the governance of these objective sentient affections and disaffections, on the one hand, and the ascetic elimination of these subjective sensuous sensitized affectionate or disgruntled feelings, on the other, the mystic is in a better position to be sufficiently in charge of his own conduct to be able to efficaciously exercise his intelligence and intellectual will without hindrance and distraction from the affections of his objective sensibility and from the emotional feelings of his subjective sensitivity.

Since the moral virtues of temperance and fortitude are directly under the mystic's soulful volitional governance the body's objective sentient passions themselves are, thereby under the direct governance of the mystic's intelligence and will when the mystic is properly disciplined by the virtues of temperance and fortitude. Regarding the mystic's subjective sensuous emotional feelings and sensational imagery (whether these are mundane or spiritual), these are subject to the control of the mystic's mindful willfulness. In this respect, these feelings and imagery are well-in-hand for the mystic only in the measure that he is skillfully and ascetically trained to disregard them and even to suppress them by self-detachment and self-denial.

On the other hand, when the objective intellectual moral discipline is missing and the subjective mental self-control is also missing, the mystic becomes the prisoner of his own objective sentient affections and subjective sensitized feelings. For, he becomes manipulated and exploitatively dominated by them. This is a form of addiction. Since the stirrings of such passionate affections and correlative emotional feelings detract from the mystic's reflective attention to his soulful intellect's own spiritual transcendence and inhibit the mystic from enjoying subjectively mental serenity and tranquility, they are severe impediments for the mystic to advance to contemplative prayer.

Hence, any willful attention devoted to the recalling of such sensory and sensational episodes detracts from the mystic's prospect of even advancing to contemplative prayer which is a spiritual good leading to perfect union with God. Since contemplative prayer intellectually engages God's very own superintelligible immutable infinite incomprehensibility, the mystic must forgo altogether not only the fickle affections and feelings conjured up by remembering specific mundane sentient and sensational encounters but even the ones conjured up by religious sentient and sensational encounters. The mystic must skillfully train himself to mortify his sentient and sensational memories in the same way that he mortifies his external senses.

Chapter 6: The benefits of total amnesia regarding sentient and sensational memories.

The benefit of being rid of such memories is an undisturbed serenity of mind and peace of soul along with the benefit of a clear conscience. Further, the mystic is not open to tempting autosuggestions inducing impure thoughts and occasions for sin. Recollected in this tranquility the mystic is properly disposed to be led by the Holy Spirit. Even from a therapeutic consideration, a person troubled with emotional agitations is in a worse position to cope with them by continuing to be exposed to sensational stimulations. Even if the mystic is thrust into the most disturbing situation, he is better served to remain calm and collected than to become emotionally stirred up. It would seem much easier for one cloistered in a monastery to engage in such ascetic training since there are a minimal of sensationally sensuous and sensitizing distractions to engage the senses. One engaged in our ultra-modern work-a-day world with its neon lights and incessant barrage of sensational phenomena would find it exceedingly more difficult to be shielded from the garish and seductive mundanity of the secular world's influence. Yet, what is impossible to be accomplished by the secular mystic on his own is possible to be accomplished through God's grace even within the honky-tonk of the world's madcap and often morally corrupt environment.

Chapter 7: St. John now turns to consider supernatural phenomena previously examined in an earlier part of this Ascent.

Such supernatural phenomena previously spoken of as visions, revelations, locutions, and sentiments engaging the imagination's imagery leave memories in their wake. These memories not only engage vivid imagery, figures, forms, etc., they also involve stirring affective sentient passions and emotional sensitive feelings. Now, it is important to bear in mind that these supernatural phenomena may come directly from God. Hence, they need not in themselves be injurious to the mystic. Yet, St. John cautions that the mystic is not to become attached to the memory of these paranormal phenomena by becoming fixated on their imagery, forms, figures, and emotional affectivity and feelings. If the mystic is to do so, this fixation itself becomes an impediment to contemplative prayer precisely because the mystic's self-centered will's tenacious possessiveness of these mystical experiences prevents the mystic from approaching God in contemplative prayer solely on the strength of theological hope which is a super-confident expectation of possessing God alone and not anything which would serve to substitute for this divine sublime possession. Only when the mystic is completely dispossessed of any attachment to these special subjective mystical experiences will he be properly disposed to advance to contemplative prayer and, accordingly, to give objectively total prayerful attention to God alone transcendent to the subjectivity of these experiences.

It is noteworthy that all of these considerations proposed by St. John pertaining to the self-control of one's memories involve skills that are artificially acquired only in the process of "making something happen." Thus, for example, a carpenter acquires the skill of carpentry only in the process of constructing something that actually works when it is tested. The mystic who is sorely tempted to repeatedly recall to mind and heartfully relive the uplifting and exhilarating sensational and emotional religious experiences he recently had can only dispel this memory by skillfully attending to and adverting to something different in his religious prayer-life. In the measure he succeeds he cultivates a skill to keep his attention addressed to the sacramental reality of God present to him. If he repeatedly recalls this experience to mind and unduly dwells on it, he is in this very activity failing to strive to attend to the eminent reality of God supernaturally and sacramentally present to him within the objective interiority of his soul and within the subjective inner intimacy of his own submissive selfhood. Attending in faith to the stupendous and overwhelming reality of the supreme graciousness of this divine and sublime presence is more essentially the crux of prayer than relishing and reliving memories of bygone religious experiences.

Chapter 8: There are five kinds of harm involved in the mystic's lingering on the memories of these extraordinary mystical experiences that engage the senses.

1) The mystic will be deluded in mistaking the natural for the supernatural. 2) He will be prone to priding himself in having such experiences. 3) He will be opening himself up to the devil's deceptions. 4) He will be impeding his advancement to encounter God through the theological virtue of hope. 5) He will entertain a far less exalted view of God than is warranted.

Regarding the first harm, its root is grounded in the inadequacy of sensory imagery to serve as an adequate medium for learning the very truth of supernatural things. We can recall that the medium and standard for knowing the truth of things is knowledge that is completely intellectual and metaphysical transcendent to all sentiency. If the mystic relies on visions which are predominantly sensational to judge of what actually supernaturally transcends their sensational éclat, he will misjudge the completely spiritual non-sensational reality of God's own suprasensible Divinity. The very sensational vivacity of such imagery will itself deceive the mystic to mistake these mystical experiences as coming from God while they could be actually coming from the devil. The solution here is to completely forget about these mystical experiences. As previously indicated by St. John, if they do come from God they will leave a beneficent and benevolent affectivity within the mystic's own visceral somaticity even while he chooses to ignore them.

Chapter 9: The second kind of harm: falling into pernicious vanity about these extraordinary mystical experiences.

They foster a self-indulgent pride if they are not entirely ignored. And what is so pernicious about this pride is that the very persons who continue to resurrect memories of these paranormal experiences become themselves insouciant to their own puffed-up self-esteem. Such mystics become smugly self-satisfied with themselves and their vaunted intimacy with God. As an antidote to this spiritual vanity, St. John offers two counsels. a) Authentic virtue is found in self-denial and self-contempt, and being even despised by others. b) All of these exalted extraordinary mystical experiences count for nothing compared to a single act of genuine humility. Humility does not allow the mystic to dwell on his own goodness but only on the goodness of others.

Chapter 10: The third harm stems from the devil and the control that he can exert over the mystic who dwells on these sensorial memories.

The devil can convince the mystic of the authenticity of these mystical experiences by the very sensational vivacity they exhibit and stirring emotional feelings they induce. Further, such conviction is entirely rooted in the mystic's own self-centered subjectivity. It is not a conviction based on any objective evidence transcendent to the mystic's own egocentric subjectivity. Paradoxically enough, the more certain the mystic becomes of the authenticity of these entirely subjective mystical experiences, the more this assurance is rooted in the mystic's solipsistic self-possessive self-enclosed selfhood. Even when these mystical encounters are directly from God, the devil can tamper with these by further emphasizing the intensity of their sensual sensitizing impact to trap the mystic to become infatuated with them. The outcome of this mystical infatuation is that the mystic becomes preoccupied with these experiences themselves rather than with God who transcends them. When the mystic becomes attached to these experiences he becomes a dupe of the devil's deceptions and ever more confident in his own mystical prowess than in the reality of God transcendent to his own subjectivity and selfhood.

Chapter 11: The fourth harm: they impede the mystic's advancing in the theological virtue of hope.

Perfect union with God in contemplative prayer is not mediated by any sentient, sensorial, or sentimental stimulating imagery and emotional feeling. For, the more the mystic hopes and relies on these sensorial mystical experiences by resuscitating memories of them as a means to advance in his mystical encounter with God, the more the mystic places his confidence on his own self-reliance and resourcefulness rather than on God's own initiative. In this way he deprives himself of the theological gift of hope which demands that he totally rely on and prayerfully confide in God's own gratuitous initiative to advance to perfect mystical union. By confidently living and praying in the power of this theological hope the mystic is supernaturally enabled to confidently and even with full conviction be wed to God's immortal and eternal existence and Triune Godhead transcendent to and independent of his own ephemeral and fleeting mystical subjective experiences. For, through theological hope the mystic seeks more to be objectively wed to the God of consolation than to his own subjective private consolations of God.

Chapter 12: The fifth harm: they lead to base and improper judgments regarding God.

God's magnificence is incomprehensible, incomparable, and ineffable. Any willful attachment to these mystical experiences derivative of the senses inadvertently prompts the mystic himself to judge God in the context of these experiences which are infinitely removed from God's immeasurable immaterial suprasensible immensity. God is naturally knowable to the human intellect by philosophical insight and reasoning. This   knowledge is a bona fide knowledge inasmuch as one intellectually grasps that God is a Beingness of Absolute Primacy transcendent to all of creation. However, this knowledge itself remains finite inasmuch as it acknowledges God's infinity to be infinitely beyond this theological knowledge itself. This intellectual acknowledgement and recognition of God's infinitude by the intellect's own finite grasp of it is not self-contradictory. This is a human knowledge of God and not a divine one which is supernaturally revealed.

It is similar to knowing that the ideal reality of the color, redness, is formatively virtually every shade of red that could ever exist in the real cosmic reality of physical red colorful bodies. Yet, in knowing this, the intellect is not actually and specifically cognizant of all the multitudinous varieties of red shades that are virtually included in the ideal color of redness itself. Such knowledge is one of generality and not one of specificity. Indeed, this is the knowledge which is propitious to the theological virtue of faith. St. John insists that the mystic who actually in contemplative prayer gazes directly through faith on God in a "face to face" encounter intellectually knows God in a very abstruse, recondite, vague, and general manner that cannot be translated into any specific knowledge. This generality peculiar to philosophical intellectual knowledge probing the metaphysical ideal realm of reality is similar to the knowledge which is peculiar to the mystic who encounters God through faith in a "face to face" sacramental encounter involving only a vague recognition of Him.

God in contemplative prayer anchored in the theological gift of faith is supernaturally knowable to the mystic's human intellect even in his present pilgrim state of wending his way to heaven, the New Jerusalem. Again, this knowledge is available through the theological gift of faith and the benevolence of God's very own infinite Graciousness gratuitously and generously bestowed on the Christian in baptism along with the other sacraments. In other words this supernatural knowledge of God's actual infinity and Triune Godhead is not known merely virtually as the ideal color, redness, is known virtually. Through faith the mystic is in actual intellectual touch with the eminent infinitude of God's Triune Godhead. It is impossible for the mystic to intellectually assimilate the infinitude of this sublime reality made supernaturally and sacramentally present to the mystic through God's very own infinite Graciousness. The mystic must in dazed awe gaze directly in faith on this Triune Personhood while not attempting to intellectually "size up" God's infinite eminent awesomeness by comparing God with his own puny subjective religious experiences.

For, engaging in the latter would be tantamount to sizing up God by what is infinitely inferior to His majestic grandeur (i.e., the actuality of God's infinite Personal eminent sacramental presence alive in the mystic's soul). Furthermore, St. John points out, the mystic who clings to his memories of these mystical experiences is prone to have confidence in himself and his own religious experiences rather than hopefulness in his indestructible revival of his mortal bodily selfhood. For, this fondness to dwell on these memories increases the mystic's prayer-life in his own vincible egocentric self-confidence rather than hopefully through the theological gift of hope in Christ's manifest invincibility revealed in His resurrection from physical death. The theological gift of hope enables the mystic to transcend the historical hopelessness of his own self-conscious subjectivity rooted as it is in the body's mortality. This hope enables the mystic from within the vulnerability and deceptiveness of his own historical experiential subjectivity to confidently rely on the infallible objective faith-filled trust he has in God's transcendent fidelity and omnipotence.

By rekindling in his memory these religious experiences the mystic blinds himself to the utter hopelessness of his own self-humanized subjective ephemeral historical selfhood. Just as the human body unlike the human immortal soul is subject to death and corruption, one's subjective psychosomatic personality is likewise hopelessly subject to the same fate. It is foolishness to place any confidential hope in one's very own selfhood even if this self is privy to supernatural religious experiences. The theological virtue of hope is itself only confidently hopeful when its hope is entirely faith-bound; that is, entirely based on God transcendent to the perishable hopelessness of the mystic's own historical subjective selfhood. There is still another point that reinforces St. John's insistence that the mystic must completely forgo trusting and relying on his own mystical memories, even sublime ones derivative from the senses, as a preparation to entering into contemplative prayer. The ultimate objective of the mystic is not merely to know God in the very actuality of God's infinitude but, moreso, to possessively love God in a manner commensurate with God's very own infinitude. In this regard, the mystic's knowledge fails because the human intellect itself cannot intellectually on its own totally assimilate God's infinitude even when the mystic directly encounters this infinitude through faith in contemplative prayer. The intellect must be supernaturally bolstered and even shielded from God's infinitely glorious supernal luster by the theological gift of faith.

On the other hand, the mystic's volitional love of God through the theological virtue of charity, can actually lovingly beyond the intellect's touching God through faith possessively love and cherish God's Triune infinitude not merely by hoping to embrace God as the Beloved object of this love but by actually doing so. For, whereas the truth of intellectual knowledge contributes to the perfection and enhancement of the knower, the beneficence of volitional love enhances the lover in the measure that the lover is in the actual possession and enjoyment of the beloved. Of course, this possession of God is commensurate with the beloved's own goodness. Hence, the mystic's volitional love bolstered by the theological gift of charity in contemplative prayer attains to the very Beloved sublime object of this love, God's Triune Godhead, more perfectly than the intellect in faith or the memory in hope can do so.

Still it is precisely through the theological gifts of faith and hope that the mystic's volitional love of God in charity is supernaturally mediated. In a mystical sense the crux of this love is not that the mystic have his own subjective devout experience of it but that he comport his life and life-style in a manner which is redolent of this sublime love. God merits to be loved for His own sake and not for the subjective mystical experience which this love may impart. For, the mystic himself becomes honorable and lovable for lovingly cherishing, loving, honoring, and adoring God for His own sake who is the fountainhead of all loveliness. This supernatural love (i.e.,charity) is a love of friendship; it is a love of benignity in which the mystic bolstered by the Holy Spirit's own supernatural giftedness embraces God not for his (i.e., the mystic's) own personal partisan benefit but for God's glory, blessing, and benediction. That is, the mystic returns God's benevolent love with a commensurate supernatural love bestowed supernaturally on the mystic by God.

It is propitious here to attempt to clarify the supreme and supernatural, sacramental reality of God's Triune Graciousness within the baptized Christian. When the sun's radiance makes visible our planet, earth, the flower's colorfulness is made visible. Apart from the sun it remains invisible. This visibility does not physically change the flower's actual existence and nature. Whether visible by the sun's light or invisible in its sunless darkness, the flower remains a colorful plant. The sun's radiance enables the flower's color to be actually seen and enjoyed by the human person's animal's sense of sight. God's Graciousness is analogous to the sun's radiance. There is a major difference, of course. The sun's rays are incidental to the sun's substantive solarity. It is the same sun that radiates from day to day. But each separate day's radiance differs from day to day. In God's case, His divine radiance and glory is not distinct from His divine substantivity. God is utterly simple; there is no incidental or ancillary attribute in God. Whatever is attributable to God is God. Hence, God's supernatural Graciousness within the interiority of the Christian's soul is not merely an incidental ray of His infinite Goodness; this Triune Graciousness is God in His Triune Personhood!!

Now, this glorious radiance of God's infinite glory does not reside in the soul's interiority as a bird in its nest. It is more like the sun's radiation rendering the flower visible. This divine Graciousness renders the finite and creaturely spiritual soul to be superspiritually divinized without ceasing to be a creaturely soul. The Gospel speaks of this as the human person through its soulful sacramental enlightenment by God's supernatural gratuitous Graciousness becoming a "child of God."

What this "graciousness" affords the mystic's soulful intelligence is a vision which is a divine vision because it is illuminated not by the mystic's own native soulful spiritual luminosity but by God's own divine glorious and infinitely luminous radiance. Thus, in the light of this divine glory the mystic through the supernatural gift of faith exercises a divine insight and not merely a human insight, a divine wisdom and not merely a human wisdom, a divine knowledge and not merely a human knowledge.

In other words, the mystic's soulful intelligence and will are supernaturally endowed with a supernatural medium of divinely envisioning all of created reality including the very sublime divinity of God's own Triune Godhead. It is in the very supreme luminosity of divine lucidity that the mystic exercises in faith his native soulful intelligence and will. This could not be exercised without the supernatural gift of faith which both shields the soul from the infinitude of God's infinite radiance and enables the mystic to soulfully gaze directly at this ineffable pellucid medium. The mystic in the very presence of the Blessed Sacrament of the Eucharist is through the gift of faith gazing directly on Christ's divine infinitude incarnate through a comparable infinite humility in the very humus of the consecrated host and wine. In gazing on the Eucharist in faith the mystic is gazing on Christ's own glorified human body miraculously wedded to the Godhead's own divinity.

By gazing through faith on the Blessed Sacrament, there need not be any artificial electric light or natural sun light to enable the mystic's bodily eyesight to see the consecrated host. The host may be hidden in the tabernacle and only evident to the mystic by the vigil light that serves as a sentinel to alert everyone to the Blessed Sacrament's presence. After all, the artificial electric light and the sun's natural light are infinitely less luminous than the luminosity of God's own august divinity. It is not surprising that Christ's spoken word is the only communication He left with His apostles and disciples. He did not Himself have recourse to communicating through His own written words. After all, He who speaks the "words of God" (viz., the Gospel) is the very "Word of these words." Accordingly, in the Blessed Sacrament and the liturgical celebration of the Eucharist, there is not only the spoken words of the Gospel (viz., the words of consecration, the "word of God") there is, moreso, the very "God of these words" (i.e., the Blessed Sacrament).

We do not light a match or a candle in the noonday sun to enable us to improve our body's eyesight. These lights are no match for the sun's translucent lucidity. Similarly, when the soul's intelligence is illuminated by God's very own divine luminescence, the intellect does not have recourse to its own native soulful illumination to improve its insight into God's divine luminescence. The supernatural gift of faith is sufficient to enable the human soul's intelligence to avail itself of the gratuitous gift of God's sacramental Graciousness serving as the supreme mediating excellence illuminating the mystic's supernatural intellectual vision and insight.

Chapter 13: Advantage of ignoring the imagination's imagery even when such imagery is supernaturally received.

In addition to avoiding the 5 kinds of harm previously mentioned, there is the advantage of praying calmly without the distractions and emotional excitement occasioned by imagery. Thus, the mystic would not have to discern between authentic (coming from

God) and inauthentic fantasies (coming from the devil). And, in this regard, the mystic would not have to consult with a confessor to seek assistance in this discernment. In addition, the mystic will not be wasting his energy on these subjective distractions. Rather, he will be spending his time ascetically detaching himself from these kinds of mystical experiences and, in the process, become better mentally disposed to enter into contemplative prayer enabling him to encounter God beyond all imaginative and imaginary forms, figures, and shapes which are not, of themselves, commensurate with knowing God in terms of God's very own intangible and sublime Divinity. It is preferable to remain entirely bereft of such sensational imagery in one's prayer-life even if this means remaining in limbo regarding all special religious emotional consolations, feelings, and bodily contentment.

An objection is posed. If the mystic willfully rejects reviving and reminiscing in these religious consolations which come from God, wouldn't this foster a harmful pride in the mystic who might think that he is self-sufficient and can do without them? The reply by St. John is the same as previously given in an earlier part of this *Ascent*. When these are received passively (i.e., without deliberately evoking them or by deliberately remembering them or otherwise deliberately reviving them and dwelling on them) their beneficial result and impact on the mystic will endure even when the mystic actually disregards them.

This is excellent advice. Consider, for example, the prospect of one having to pass through a park each day to reach his office. In this passage he can enjoy the flowers without stopping to pick them or to tend to them. His arrival at the office will not be delayed and his passage will be made more delightful by the presence of the flowers. If he stops to pick and tend to the flowers, his arrival at the office will be delayed.

Hence, undue attention to supernatural religious feelings and emotions becomes a distraction whereas simply allowing them without deliberately attending to them eliminates the problem of their obstructing the mystic's ascetic advance toward God in contemplative prayer. St. John sagaciously points out that deliberately attending to these religious feelings even when they are supernatural involves an entirely human initiative, not a divine one. The mystical life is not advanced by the mystic's human initiative. Rather, it is advanced by God's very own divine initiative. Hence, by inordinately attending to these spiritual feelings, the mystic is stymieing the Holy Spirit's initiative. Again, since religious emotional feelings are stimulated by sensational imagery, they address merely the outer peeling and rind of the mystical life. The very fruit and substance of the spiritual life transcends all such sensational imagery.

The more the mystic depends on his own initiative to become spiritually and religiously emotionally stimulated, the more he is impeding the Holy Spirit's own supernatural initiative. The Holy Spirit influences the mystic directly and intimately without the benefit of such emotional stimulation. Indeed, the mystic's mystical advancement toward God is more a divine act of supernatural transformation effectuated by the Holy Spirit than an act initiated by the mystic himself. Accordingly, all of these involuntary supernatural emotional religious feelings evoked by specific sensational imagery should be welcomed by the mystic in the measure that they are conducive to the mystic becoming more enamored with God as his own Beloved. When this is the case, the mystic may remember such experiences in the measure that they foster a greater love for God. Otherwise, he should ignore them entirely.

The figures and imagery which induce such amorous supernatural religious emotional experiences are so sensationally impressive that the mystic can readily recall them without effort, so states St. John. And, again, when they are recalled simply to further stimulate the mystic's love for God, they are very beneficial. Still, St. John counsels, when this love for God is enkindled in the light of faith, the images and figures themselves are to be left aside. At this point, St. John differentiates between images impressed on the soul and those impressed on the imagination. As previously indicated in this commentary, the human soul's faculty of intelligible information is the intellect whereas the body's faculties of sensible information are the senses. The intellect is inorganic where the senses have organs. The intellect's proper knowledge naturally transcends all imagery. Thus, again, in knowing red-as-such, the intellect need not "see" any actual special shade of red. Rather, it knows all specific shades of red as pertaining holistically to the family entity of red-as-such.

In other words, the intelligibility of red-as-such transcends the actual specific imaging of different shades of physical tangible bodies. The specific shade of the apple's red color is sensibly tangible whereas the holistic color of red-as-such is intangibly intelligible. In other words, the intelligible reality, red-as-such, is more knowable intelligibly than is any sensory image of red precisely because the latter is a restricted knowledge directed to a special but restricted object. The former is an unrestricted knowledge which overarches without eliminating all the restricted sensible forms of knowing peculiar to the senses.

Within the subjective psychosomatic egocentric order, one can differentiate between a mental conception and its corresponding imaginative depiction. This has already been previously mentioned in this commentary. The psychic mind's ideation of mathematical notions differs from the somatic body's imagination of them. Thus, the mental notion of a geometric line differs from the imagination's figurative symbol for it (viz., "__"). The notion conceptualizes a line as a spectral nontactual phantom whereas the imagination's imagery depicts the line as a spectacular phenomenal imaginary symbol. One is fabulous (i.e., entirely fictional) and the other is phenomenal (i.e., entirely factual). The fictional line is confined to the mind's nontactual notionality and the factual is exemplified in the body's sensational and tactual imagery. The fictional is not tactually detectable to sensory empirical inspection whereas the factual is empirically inspectable. Further, the fictional is noumenal (i.e., transparent) whereas the factual is symptomatic (i.e., apparent but not transparent). In its transparency the fictional concept is nontactual like a phantom or spook while in its tactual appearance, the fanciful image only "seems" to be phenomenally like to its ghostly conceptual counterpart.

In mentally conceiving of a line, the mental conception ambiguously includes simultaneously both a rectilinear and a curvilinear line. In that a line is an extension between two distinct points, the same extension may be simultaneously both a rectilinear and curvilinear extension. The one does not exclude the other. In other words, a conceptual line is either/or and both rectilinear and curvilinear simultaneously. The imaginary line, on the other hand, is either the one or the other but not both simultaneously. Thus, the imaginary line can only imitate but never completely instantiate its conceptual prototype.

Now, when the somatic body's sensational sensitivity and the psychic mind's intimate notionality are supernaturally and paranormally transposed as is the case with the mystic's subjective religious experiences, the results are intensively magnified. The mystic's religious notions become considerably spookier and eerier ghostly phantoms whereas the imagination's imagery becomes exceedingly more spectacularly sensational. The impact of these religious notions is that the mystic experiences them more intimately than simple mathematical notions are experienced while the mystic experiences their sensational religious imagery more sensitively than any other prosaic and profane sensational imagery. The effect of these religious notions is that the mystic is made more intensively aware of his own psychic intimacy while the effect of his enhanced religious imagery of these religious notions, he is made more intensively aware of his own body's ultra somatic sensitivity.

Consider, for example, the Old Testament's mention of the apple tree as the tree to be avoided by God's decree. Here the apple tree is spoken of figuratively, metaphorically, and notionally only. What God is addressing to Adam & Eve and forbidding them to exercise on their own is their own self-centered and selfishly self-serving willful mindfulness. He is not explicitly condemning a physical apple tree as poisonous and toxic. This tree in the Old Testament is the very paradigmatic womb of original sin which is the human person's personalized willful and mindful rebellion against God's Holy Will. This is the "tree" which spawns the fruit of mankind's fall from grace and the onset of the body's corruptibility and death.

Advert now to the New Testament's mention of the same "tree!" Now it is the wood of the cross on which Christ is crucified. This tree is not merely the notional figurative non-sensational tree of Adam & Eve's intimate mindful and willful self-serving selfishness. This tree includes the sensational sensitivity peculiar to the human person's bodily imagery and selfhood. Christ's crucifixion on this New Testament tree involves His own body's sensational sensitivity, feelings, and emotional dis/contentment. By Selflessly offering His own bodily pain and excruciating suffering and death to honor and respectfully obey His Father's Holy Will, Christ restores to the human body a life beyond corruption and death available in His resurrection from death and ascension into heaven.

Where Adam and Eve's tree paradigmatically is the "tree of death," Christ's tree is enigmatically and paradoxically the "tree of life." Where Adam and Eve ruptured mankind's intimacy with God resulting in the body's decay and death, Christ's suffering of the body's dying and death restores and reconciles mankind's intimate life with God. Certainly, Christ was not crucified on a live apple tree. Indeed, the wood of the cross is not that of a living tree; it is itself that of a defunct tree. On the other hand, the intimacy with God that Adam and Eve originally enjoyed in the Garden of Eden was a living intimacy.

The entire point of this exegesis is to contrast the human person's notional and psychic willful intimacy with its total absence of bodily sensitivity with the same human person's imaginary and somatic (i.e., bodily) willful sensitivity which, in turn, harbors no mental intimacy. These psychosomatic dichotomous and bipolar constructs of every person's subjective personality are culturally the domain of mathematical computation. When they are superhumanistically transformed with religious import they magnify both the intimacy and the sensitivity that is peculiar to the self-cultivated   human personality.

It matters not, however, whether these supernatural religious experiences are centered exclusively in the sosomatic body's sensational sensitivity or in the psychic mind's notional intimacy, what is important is that the mystic be able to discern whether they are authentically from God or from the devil by reason of their lasting impact. Those from the devil which occur within the imagination leave a dry and arid aftermath whereas those from God leave a lasting comforting and consoling residuum. Those, on the other hand, which occur exclusively within the psychic mind's intimacy always leave a beneficial residual effect of enduring serenity whenever they are remembered and recalled to mind. The underlying reason for this is that purely psychic devotional notional thoughts (viz., comparable to mathematical notions) are impassively emotionlessly soothing and pacifying and not motivationally exciting.

What is clear in this differentiation between contemplative prayer and meditative prayer is that the former completely transcends the sentient boundaries of the objective corporeal body's sentient affectivity and the subjective corpuscular body's psychosomatic sentimentality. In other words, the stable seat of contemplative prayer is principally the intellectual soul and not the self-humanized psychosomatic self. Certainly, it is the human person who is personally engaged in contemplative prayer; it is not exclusively the soul that is so engaged. For this reason the spiritual and inorganic delightful supernatural resonance of contemplative prayer may by a surplus effusion overflow into the human person's subjective self-cultivated psychosomatic selfhood.

Chapter 14: Spiritual knowledge in the memory.

Here St. John has in mind the type of supernatural revelations previously examined in ch. 26 of Bk II. These are supernatural intellectual revelations directly of God or directly of creatures. Since they are intellectual, they do not directly engage sensorial imagery and fantasies. However, since the mystic may recall these revelations to mind, they are at this point in the *Ascent* mentioned by St. John of the Cross in view of their being remembered or recalled to mind. From all that has preceded in this segment of this commentary devoted to memory, it should not be lost on the reader that historical memory itself is not a faculty of the soul. It is a function of the self-subsistent human personhood's own self-cultivated egocentric selfhood. Yet, this memorial function is able to recall what the intellect grasps precisely because the person's historical memory functions associatively in conjunction with the intellect's intelligent thinking and concomitant volitions.

That is, the human person by dint of his own subsistent personhood both thinks and wills objectively, soulfully, and intelligently while fashioning subjectively, intuitively, artificially, and historically the terminology and temporization of this intelligent thinking. The psychosomatic self's mnemonic aids to recall the intellect's utterly spiritual supernatural thoughts need not be sensorial images such as are religious icons that are created and entertained in the somatic body's imagination. Rather, these may be the psychic mind's noumenal notions such as words which have no meanings other than those derived from the intellect's knowledge which they nominally and mnemonically mimic.

Regarding these supernatural revelations, the ones that are directed toward creatures should be remembered only to the extent that the mystic's affective love for God strengthens the mystic's trust in God transcendent to and independent of this subjective affectivity. When they fail in this regard, they should not be deliberately recalled to memory. On the other hand, St. John explains, those revelations which are immediately directed toward God are efficaciously beneficial and conducive in their subjective experienced affectivity to increasing the mystic's trust of God in faith whenever they are memorially recalled to mind. For, he explains, they are originally experienced by the mystic as God's divine and sublime mystical touches. Hence, the mystic remembers them and recalls them to mind for their conative religious transformative impact on the self's willfulness rather than for their religious cognitive information concerning God.

It must be emphasized to the reader that these sublime touches are not principally divine subjective sensitized religious emotional feelings which, indeed, are stimulated by sensory imagery in the body's sensational somaticity when they do occur. Rather they are divine profound religious tranquilizing intimate affluences born of notional intimations in the psychic mind's noumenal psychicity. They serve not to stimulate but to sedate the mystic's willful selfhood and to stabilize and reinforce its amorous concern for God. They are born of a direct supernatural touch with the Triune Godhead of God's Supreme ineffable Divinity sacramentally indwelling within the soul's interiority.

Again, it is well to point out to the reader what exactly is this spiritual interiority of the human soul. The human soul is entirely spiritual, immaterial, and inorganic. Hence, one should not attempt to understand it in reference to a physical body's interiority. It is not essentially located within any physical place other than in reference to the substantive corporeal material body which it animates. Of itself considered simply within its own spiritual constitution, it cannot be understood other than spiritually. Hence, its interiority is not, in regard to the universe of reality which it can both intelligibly know and amiably love, an inside interiority as opposed to a reality existing outside and independent of it. This interiority is not bounded by any inside/outside polarity. Again, this interiority is not like a pocketbook which can physically contain different contents which are stored there. Such emptiness only obtains within the material universe of reality. This interiority is entirely spiritual and is distinct from the entire universe of reality existing apart from this interiority as one drop of water is distinct from the entire ocean from which it is taken.

Of course, this analogy fails to completely encompass the soul's spiritual interiority because the drop of water and the ocean are both physical. Yet, when the drop of water is extracted from the ocean, it is obviously differentiated from the ocean itself even though it becomes indistinguishable from the ocean when it is returned to the ocean's water. Such is the status of the soul's interiority. What it knows and loves from within the intellectual and volitional prowess of its interior vitality is whatever exists transcendent to this interiority in the universe of reality. This interior vitality may itself be increasingly supernaturally revitalized by God's very own eminent Personal divine vitality proper to His Triune Godhead. This is the indwelling of God's merciful Graciousness sacramentally endowing the baptized Christian with God's own Life and elevating the Christian to act in virtue of God's own divine and divinizing vitality as a "child of God."

Furthermore, it must also be appreciated that the knowledge to which the spiritual soul has access is fundamentally channeled through the senses. Unless the corporeal body's eye first sees a very specific and special shade of red which is diversely different from every other shade of red and every other shade of color, the human soulful intellect could not conceive nor intellectually contemplate red-as-such above and beyond the body's eyesight. Indeed, the intellect would have no knowledge at all of the color, red, in its very specificity of red-color-as-such in contradistinction to every other shade of color. If a person is born color-blind and can never optically see any special color, its soul cannot intellectually have an insight into any special color-as-such. However, it may still intellectually grasp and understand what is intelligibly color-as-such; namely, that which is a visible quality of a physical body.

Of course, it remains ignorant regarding the specificity of color-as-such. In fact, even in the case in which the human person never personally sees a specific shade of color, he may intelligibly and intellectually understand what someone else is describing, such as a shade that is sky-blue-pink, for example. For, while the specificity of this shade escapes the soul's intellectual intelligibility, it does not escape its intelligibility that this special unseen shade is a specific instance of color-as-such.

Chapter 15: A general rule governing the memory's use for mystics.

St. John explains the paradox inherent in the theological virtue of hope which is vital to the mystic's entry into contemplative prayer which is the proper medium to engage in perfect union with God. Hope is directed to what is not yet possessed in the fullness of its actual existence. In view of this, the more the mystic relies on his own mnemonic possession of God through recalling special supernatural religious experiences, the less hope he has of possessing God existing independently and transcendentally beyond the historical memory of these experiences. At the same time, the less he is prepossessively attached to remembering these religious experiences, the more hopefully in the theological virtue of hope he is able to aspire in faith to actually possessing God transcendently in the eminent totality of God's Supreme Existence both in this life through faith and in the next life beyond faith.

To appreciate the role of theological hope regarding the person's historical memory, it is important to differentiate between the soul's objective intellectual willful possession of God and the self's subjective mindful willful possession. The soulful will's drive toward God is to lovingly possess God appropriate to God's own infinite truthful loveliness; this is a dutiful obedient worshipful love which the will ought to observe because of God's supreme worthiness. There is no other love befitting God's supreme infinite Goodness. The self's willful love toward God, on the other hand, is a need to possessively appropriate God to fulfill its own lack of loveliness; this is a self-serving imperious love.

The soul's willful objective love is an orthodox meritorious love. There is no sacrifice involved. The soul loves God appropriately and volitionally when it dutifully loves God adoringly above all other loves. In this it does not slight any other being, including its own self. The theological gift of faith enables the mystic to actually love God appropriately in the supremacy of God's existence transcendent to and independent of the mystic's own being. On a purely natural plane of love, the human person cannot love God in a manner befitting God's infinite loveliness because his very creaturely finitude precludes this. God supernaturally endows the human person's dignity with His own divine gratuitous graciousness thereby enabling him to requite God's infinite benignity with a comparable dignity. Faith enables the human person to know God in a divine way surpassing his own human finitude.

The self's willful subjective love is a paradoxical love. The self loves God volitionally by appropriating God sacrificially dispossessively and self-detachedly; that is, it loves God not for its own selfish self but, rather, for its own selfless self-fulfillment. In other words, the mystic's selfhood does not willfully dutifully love God obediently and appropriately as does the soulful will befitting God's own Infinite Goodness. Rather, it loves God affectionately and appreciatively (viz., it prizes and treasures God) when it wills to possessively have God not for its own selfish service but to have itself sacrificially serve God unselfishly and selflessly. Since the mystic's self cannot accomplish this self-detachment on its own apart from God's graciousness, the mystic in theological hope aspires to sacrificially love God beyond its own resourcefulness to do so. Christ accomplishes selflessly and self-fulfillingly in His own sacrificial crucifixion what mankind cannot accomplish on its own. The mystic hopefully enters into this accomplishment by willfully sacrificially surrendering his own willful subjective self-control to the masterful Selfless self-control of Jesus.

In conclusion, St. John is eager to differentiate himself from the iconoclasts who wish to remove all religious objects from within the Church. He insists that the total amnesia regarding the sensorium which he recommends to mystics is not to be confused with this iconoclasm. On the contrary, sacred icons are very conducive to a prayer life that lifts the mind and heart to God. The program of deliberate skillful forgetfulness which he is counseling the mystic to adopt is simply a prudential program of making wise use of religious imagery to advance in love of God and to transcend such imagery when it impedes this advance itself. The issue of forgetfulness is more one of self-detachment than it is one of amnesia or forgetfulness. Since our historical memories are entirely subjective and rooted in our self-centeredness, the more we are self-attached to them the less we are attached to God that objectively transcends them.

It is more vital to the mystic to attentively attend to God's merciful sacramental gracious Personal presence in the soul's interiority than to remembering and savoring anew past remembered or future anticipated mystical experiences within the subjectivity of one's own psychosomatic selfhood. The devotional subjectivity of the mystic's selfhood whether it be exterior devotion felt within the body's somatic sensitivity or an interior impassive devotion from within the mind's psychic intimacy, such devotions remain always subjectively distinct from God's objective transcendence to these devotions. It matters not within this devotional subjectivity whether the mystic actually experiences or remembers God by way of recalling or anticipating this mystical experience, both the actual experience and its remembrance are not to be confused with God's own supreme reality transcendent to this subjectivity.

St. John makes no mention of the remembrance of past sins as a hindrance to advancing into contemplative prayer and perfect union with God's Trinitarian Godhead. Both in baptism and in the sacrament of reconciliation the mystic is miraculously transformed into a "new creation." Reminiscing on one's past sins certainly meditatively arouses in the mystic a greater commitment and resolve to increasingly esteem Christ for His redeeming sacrificial love made manifest in His Paschal Mystery. This is more so the case the more the mystic prayerfully ponders the suffering Christ endured in His passion and crucifixion to purchase the mystic's redemption and remission of sins.

Yet, such prayerful reminiscing is more at the level of meditative prayer rather than contemplative prayer. Meditative prayer involves sensory imagery and bodily feelings and emotions and is not itself a hindrance to contemplative prayer; rather, it is a propaedeutic to contemplative prayer. It is only an impediment when the mystic clings and remains attached to meditative prayer's sensitized bodily feelings and contentment rather than abandoning it in order to advance to contemplative prayer's greater intimacy with God devoid of all such devout bodily emotional resonance.

ASCENT, Book III, THE PURIFICATION OF THE WILL THROUGH THE THEOLOGICAL VIRTUE OF CHARITY

Preliminary to the exposition of Charity

The will is purified through charity.

At this point in this commentary, it is propitious for the reader of this commentary to turn to read in its entirety the text itself of our Carmelite Holy Father's *Ascent*. In this Book III, chs. 16-45 inclusive, he masterfully explains and scrutinizes in great detail the will's self-abnegation and ascetic lifestyle preliminary to advancing through charity into God's Trinitarian family embrace in contemplative prayer. Again, it is important to remind ourselves that the *Ascent* is the active approach to contemplative prayer in which the mystic on his own initiative pursues apprenticeship training under the supervision of one who has already mastered this training.

In our case, the masterful Doctor of Mystical Theology supervising our own ascetic training is St. John of the Cross. The passive phase of this ascetic training comes in *The Dark Night*. When we have set ourselves to the task of training our will to the master's prototypical program of self-denial outlined in the *Ascent*, the Divine Master Himself in the Person of the Holy Spirit will take Personal charge of bringing our feeble attempts to their proper conclusion and consummation. This passive phase of the mystical life is described for us in the *Dark Night*. For the present, it is the active night which is in the forefront of our attention. This is the night in which the mystic takes the initiative to mortify and chastise the will to enable it to become disposed to love with an amicable love of charitable friendship beyond its exploitative selfish self-attachment and self-interest.

The will is purified through charity. Charity, of course, is God's very own supernatural benign and benignant love and loveliness alive in the Christian in the Person of the Holy Spirit. It is a divine love that becomes incarnated into our human history in the Person of Jesus Christ, God/Superman. It is this very same divine love that is graciously imparted to Christ's disciple inasmuch as this disciple through baptism is incorporated into Christ's Mystical Body, the Sacramental Church. It should be noted that our Carmelite Holy Father cites Sacred Scripture, as he frequently does, to pinpoint the prominent place that charity has in the life of Christ's disciple. He cites Moses' command in Deuteronomy: "You shall love the Lord, your God, with all your heart, and with all your soul, and with all your strength." I submit that this command entails that the mystic's love is a cruciform love. Vertically, the mystic is to love with his soul, horizontally with his heart, and cruciformly with all his strength.

Consonant with this Scriptural citation the mystic's prayer-life and love-life are to be patterned on the cruciform format of St. John's mysticism. Charitable love is the intersection and reconciliation (i.e., the crucifixion) of two separate vertical and horizontal loves. Fundamentally, objectively, and vertically it is a love emanating from the mystic's soulful obedient intellectual will. In addition, it is supplementally, subjectively, and horizontally a love emanating from the mystic's self-centered, self-serving psychosomatic will. When these two will's are mutually reconciled and integrated in the mystic's life

241

through the cruciform reconciliation mediated by Christ's own crucifixion, there ensues the cruciform integrality of a covenant love of mutual friendship between God and man which is more vital and vigorous for being more integrally integrated.

The marvel of this very austere and carefully detailed program of self-denial and willful mortification proposed by St. John in these chapters is its concentration on the selfhood's self-centered psychosomatic will in contradistinction to the soul's intellectual will. While still speaking of this self-centered will as though it had its residency immediately in the substantive spiritual soul, he proceeds to ingeniously outline in great detail a strict training of willful self-denial that does not immediately engage the moral virtues of justice, prudence, temperance, and courage germane to the soulful intellectual will's dutiful observance of the Decalogue, but engages the self-centered sacrificial ascetical skills of self-denial and self-detachment conducive to living the superhumanistic lifestyle demanded by the "beatitudes." These beatitudes demand that one live and love God not merely fundamentally, voluntarily, and obediently in the letter of the Decalogue as indicated by the Old Testament, but supplementally, committedly, and sacrificially in the spirit of the New Testament evidenced by Christ's very own Gospel lifestyle made manifest in His Paschal Mystery and enunciated in the beatitudes: blessed are the poor in spirit, the meek, the mourners, the hungry, the merciful, the pure in heart, and the peacemakers.

This beatitudinal Gospel volitional ascetic life-style complements the rigorous moral virtuous obligatory prescriptive and proscriptive morally virtuous life-style spelled out in the Old Testament's Decalogue. This beatitudinal lifestyle not merely obligates Christ's disciple to act obediently and virtuously to what is honorable and worthy of such obedience as conscionably and objectively befits the soul's intellectual will, it further insists that the disciple must sacrificially volunteer to die to his own selfhood's resistance to this obligatory love. The beatitudes enumerate the different manner and ways that this dying, self-detachment, and self-emptying must by ascetical training be inculcated into the Christian's life.

It is clear that the follower of Christ must voluntarily will to dutifully obey the commandments, the Decalogue. He is duty-bound to love God worshipfully above and beyond every other love. This is a fundamental love that emanates from his soul's intellectual will which is a love that is a purposeful drive for what is inherently an immortally finalizing good (viz., happiness) that both epitomizes and consummates this love. The primary and ultimate supreme objective goal of this love ought to be directed toward God since God is the unsurpassable infinite plenitude of Goodness. On a natural plane, the soul's intellectual will is a drive for immortal happiness; on a supernatural plane, it is a drive for the holiness of happiness which is God's very own Triune Personal eternal beatitude.

It is not sufficient that the disciple of Christ love God dutifully and soulfully, he must also love God appreciatively, heartfully, and mindfully. This heartfelt and mindful love does not engage the mystic's soulful objective impartial intellectual will but the mystic's self-centered self-serving subjective psychosomatic partisan will. This will is not a purposeful drive for an objective goal that fundamentally finalizes and consummates this drive; this will is a self-serving need for what serviceably and supplementally compensates for the need's deficiency. Needs are volitional bodily sensitive visceral and/or mental insensitive cerebral voids that demand self-centered, self-serving, self-fulfillment.

In addition to these two disparate loves, the disciple of Christ is to love God with all his strength. This strength is brought about by combining together and integrating these two loves with each other in a complementary way which reconciles the two with each other. This is accomplished by the cruciformity of Christ's cross of crucifixion. The fundamental voluntary dutiful love incumbent on the intellectual will and the supplementary sacrificial committed love incumbent on the psychosomatic will combine to yield a volunteer self-determinate love of amicability that is both meritoriously dutiful and sacrificially self-controlled. Of course, these three loves are each in turn elevated, consecrated, and consummated at a superhuman, superhumanistic, superhumane order of loveliness commensurate with God's own graciousness and holiness.

It is also to be noted that these two disparate wills, the mystic's soulful will and his self-centered psychosomatic will correspond respectfully to the cross' vertical and horizontal cross-beams. Their coalescence and reconciliation correspond to the cross' cruciformity. These two disparate wills are exercised by one and the same person. The fundamental will is exercised in view of the person's sovereign dynamic energetic intelligent and free nature and the supplemental will is exercised in view of the same person's influential synergistic self-cultivated and self-centered autonomous personality. The fundamental will attains its moral perfection when the person objectively matures into a sovereign character that is morally courageous, temperate, just, and prudent. The supplemental will achieves its influential momentum when the same person developmentally becomes charismatic through self-detachment and self-commitment to a service surpassing its own self-centered selfish autonomous self-interest.

Where the mystic's soulful will must be supernaturally elevated to love God not merely with human but with the superhuman moral virtues of justice, prudence, courage, and temperance, the mystic's selfhood psychosomatic will must be superhumanistically transformed to love God serviceably and heroically with ascetic skills over and beyond its own needy selfish social self-interest. This entails a Gospel self-emptying, a dying to self, and an ascetic program and training of deliberate and decisive self-denial and self-detachment involving this will's heartfelt emotional feelings of joy, sorrow, hope, and fear.

Joy, sorrow, hope, and fear examined more closely.

In his typical terse and straightforward manner, St. John states that the only joy, sorrow, hope, and fear which befit the Christian mystic's self-serving psychosomatic will are the ones which are willfully centered on serving and honoring God. Any other center of such emotional influences (viz., one's own selfish self-centeredness) detracts from God and dishonors Him rather than serving Him. He further explains that a masterful self-control over any one of these basic emotions entails a comparable control over the others. In view of this symmetry he only explicitly explores the emotion of joy and the willful rigors of subjugating its joyful influence to the service and honor of God. He assumes that the mystic will successfully control the other emotions when he successfully subjugates this emotion exclusively to the service of God's own honor and glory.

St. John gives a clear-cut description of this emotional feeling of joy. He states that it is "a satisfaction of the will with esteem for an object it considers fitting." He further explains this description. "The will never rejoices unless in something which is valuable and satisfying to it." He further differentiates between an active and a passive joy indicating that the one is under the will's self-control while the other is not. He attempts no further clarification at this point. However, it seems clear that the active joy is willfully self-induced and self-controlled whereas the passive one is not.

This definition of joy strictly applies to the enjoyment of God. That is, it is a joy that is fitting for God's own divine blissful delight and enjoyment. Therefore, the satisfaction which it provides to the mystic is one for which the human person has a self-esteem (i.e., a self-appreciation) which is fitting and compatible with God's own supreme transcendent sovereign primacy. Such a joy and satisfying feeling of enjoyment would have to be entirely selfless; not merely unselfish relative to another self but fully selfless befitting God's supremacy that is transcendent to the human person's self-centered selfhood. Yet, it would still be a subjective enjoyable self-centered compassionate bodily feeling and/or dispassionate mental bearing because the mystic values and appreciates (i.e., enjoys selflessly) God because of the righteousness God gratuitously and graciously supplies to the person's selfhood.

These four affections of joy, sorrow, hope, and fear are spoken of by St. John of the Cross as emotional feelings. This commentary takes the liberty of also extending these four affections to emotionless bearings proper to the selfhood's mindful will in contradistinction to the selfhood's heartfelt will. These two wills are in polar opposition to each other. Neither is a faculty of the human person's selfhood. Both are facilitators of the human person's self-serving selfhood. They function motivationally and self-servingly by influential promptings. They do not operate spontaneously and intentionally (i.e., purposefully) in virtue of their own power to act. Feelings are centered on the corpuscular body's outward somatic sensitivities be they comfortable/pleasant or uncomfortable/unpleasant. Bearings are centered on the corpuscular body's inward psychic intimacies be they convenient/equilibrious or inconvenient/disequilibrious.

The selfhood's heartfelt will seeks its own satisfying social self-contentment and enjoys this more fully in sharing it empathically (viz., sympathetically) with associate selves who experience the same enjoyment. Sadness arises when there is the experience of a dissatisfying social self-discontentment. Hope is the expectation of a future satisfying self-contentment and fear of the loss of such a satisfying self-contentment. The selfhood's mindful will seeks its own vindicated social self-containment and enjoys this more fully in sharing it empathically (viz., telepathically) with associate selves who experience the same enjoyment. Sadness arises when there is the experience of a disconcerting social self-non-containment. Hope is the expectation of a future vindicating self-containment and fear the loss of such a vindicating self-containment.

The selfhood's heartfelt will is influentially motivated by what stimulates and excites the will to bodily action while the selfhood's mindful will is influentially motivated by what sedates and lulls the will to mental quietude and serenity. Hence, the heartfelt will enjoys what is thrilling and is sad when there is a lack of such stimulation. It hopes for such stimulation when it lacks it and fears downcastfully to be without it. Similarly the mindful will enjoys what sedates and calms its mental serenity while it is sad and troubled when it is distraught and lacking in such mental composure. It hopes for such sedation and serenity when it lacks it and it dreads being without it. The selfhood's heartfelt will enjoys what is likeably pleasant and comfortably stimulating while the selfhood's mindful will enjoys what is carefully agreeable and circumspectly correct.

Prior to exploring with St. John the different instances of emotional joy which are fitting or not fitting to render honor and service to God, it is very important to emphasize that these emotional heartfelt feelings and mindful bearings are entirely subjective within the mystic's somatic self-cultivated autonomous personality and not objective within the mystic's sovereign personal animal nature. The human person's sentient dis/affections proper to his animal sentient nature are instinctive spontaneous involuntary passions which are amenable to and subordinate to the person's soulful intellectual will. Thus, a person's faculty of sexuality is an instinctive procreative drive and faculty with its own proper venereal passion and venereal pleasure. The moral governance of this venereal pleasure is not directed to completely suppress or eliminate this animal pleasure. Rather, the moral governance of this venereal pleasure and the exercise of this sexual drive requires that its exercise and venereal enjoyment be tamed and modulated in view of its innate purpose and goal; namely, to procreate new life and to engage in an amicable partnership with one's spouse. It is not morally virtuous to completely suppress this venereal pleasure and enjoyment within the marital union of a man and a woman.

On the other hand, the emotional venereal bodily feeling which a human person experiences subjectively within the awareness of his body's sensational venereal sensitivity is subject to his willful self-control. It does not emerge spontaneously and instinctively; it is willfully self-induced, it is willfully self-controlled, and it may be willfully self-suppressed. This emotional feeling of venereal pleasure and enjoyment is not purposefully directed to a procreative end and to a marital partnership. It is entirely self-centered and self-serving to the point of providing a person's self-cultivated somatic selfhood with a sensitized bodily self-satisfied, self-fulfilling venereal feeling of self-contentment.

An example of this venereal pleasure is the feeling of lust that a man may have for a woman. Without even engaging the woman or entering into a relationship with her, this feeling of lust is entirely a subjective venereal emotional feeling of pleasure willfully self-induced and willfully exploitatively entertained. This feeling of venereal self-contentment is sinful precisely because it is entertained independently of and in rebellion to the objective conscionable moral order of what is fittingly appropriate for a person to engage in the marital act of sexual intercourse reserved for the intimacy of a couple respectfully wedded to each other and committed to uphold each other's dignity and integrity.

The will that is involved in controlling, inducing, and exploiting this venereal sensational sensitive feeling and emotional influence is not the person's objective soulful intellectual will but the same person's subjective psychosomatic self-centered will. St. John himself never explicitly adverts to this will in his own mystagogical writings but it is clear from his descriptions that he is implicitly adverting to such a will. He had no formal academic instruction or education pertaining to the human person's egology. This was not developed in his century of learning. The person's soulful intellectual will is a faculty that acts spontaneously, purposefully, and energetically on its own initiative. The same person's psychosomatic self-centered mindful will is a facilitator that acts motivationally (i.e., when influentially prompted), purposelessly (i.e., self-servingly), and synergistically (i.e., in conjunction with other skillful mental and bodily components).

At this point St. John differentiates 6 different types of emotional joys over which the will can exercise self-control to the point of orientating these emotional joys toward God as deploying them at the service of God or, failing in this, deploying them at the service of the willful selfhood's own selfish self-esteem and self-satisfaction to the detriment of serving God's honor. These 6 types of joys are temporal, natural, sensory, moral, supernatural, and spiritual. We can easily recognize and differentiate between each of them because St. John subsequently describes the conduct peculiar to each as well as the specific activities which they engage. There can be no doubt that this description of the will's self-control fits to a "T" the selfhood's self-centered consequential and sacrificial psychosomatic will rather than the soul's antecedent obligatory intellectual soulful will.

In other words, again, there are effectively two different wills that are articulated in St. John's anthropology. While he himself does not take pains to explicitly identify or differentiate between the soul's objective intellectual will and the self's subjective self-serving will, he effectively cultivates this distinction in his text by the description and entailments he ascribes to the "will."

There are four emotional compassionate bodily feelings and/or mental bearings which St. John imputes to this self-serving psychosomatic will: joy, hope, fear, and sorrow. Joy is the kingpin in these four compassions. They are compassions because they are empathically self-referential. That is, given that they are self-centered and self-serving, they entail an intra and interpersonal empathic resonance. Hence, a person becomes conscious especially of his own bodily sensitivity and sensuous erogenous satisfaction and contentment (or, dissatisfaction and discontentment) when he is conscious of his body's sensitivity under the influence of this joy or lacking it. At the same time, a person is susceptible to empathically and sympathetically induce such pleasurable emotional sensuous feelings in selves other than his own selfhood and to be himself susceptible to be seduced when he intuitively (viz., associatively) discerns these joyful sensual feelings in a self other than his own self.

These feelings are compassions precisely because of the pathos and sufferance they evoke in their interpersonal personalized resonance. The simple instinctive passions, on the other hand, which occur objectively in the human person's animal sentient body, harbor no such self-referential interpersonal personalized resonance, sufferance, and pathos. A simple instinctive passion (viz., hunger for food's nutriment) rises spontaneously and involuntarily prior even to the person's voluntary assent to it whereas an emotional compassionate feeling (viz., need for food's gustatory enjoyment) is stimulated and suffered only through one's self-conscious willful attention to it. In other words, an instinctive passion rises involuntarily whereas an emotional compassionate feeling arises when it is deliberately stimulated and self-induced. It is subject to willful self-control, self-suffering, and exploitation.

Indeed, when the human person becomes captive to these emotional compassionate feelings and loses willful mastery over them, they are considered to be pathological and detrimental to the person's emotional and mental health. This is the very point which St. John emphasizes in regard to these compassionate emotional feelings. The mystic must exercise a complete masterful and skillful control over them by becoming self-detached from them. Otherwise, he becomes possibly addicted to them and loses mastery over them. This self-detachment entails that the mystic simply suppresses them and prevents them from exercising a captive, seductive, and addictive influence over himself.

The bodily feeling and/or mental bearing of pleasurable joy is the kingpin to the other three. By ascetically willfully denying himself any gustatory pleasurable emotional feeling in eating, the mystic controls not only this enjoyable feeling in eating but also the additional feelings of hopeful future gustatory joys, fears of not having or losing such gustatory feelings, and sadness in eating without such gustatory enjoyment. This emotional feeling of gustatory pleasure (or displeasure) harbors no element of moral propriety or impropriety. It harbors merely an empathic feeling or pathos of satisfaction and contentment or dissatisfaction and discontentment.

These compassionate sensitive feelings are compatible with the person's self-centered somatic bodily heartfelt will. They must be distinguished and differentiated from the same person's self-centered psychic mental mindful will. This latter will harbors and entertains dispassionate intimate bearings (i.e., composures). Here the ethos is not one of the body's empathic sensuous sympathetic sensitivity but of the mind's empathic austere telepathic intimacy.

It must be further noted that the objective animal instinctive appetites include not only concupiscent but also the irascible appetites (i.e., drives) of anger and hatred. The subjective volitional self-cultivated needful emotional feelings and/or emotionless bearings enumerated by St. John are exclusively concupiscent and not irascible. Concupiscent instinctive objective animal passions require tempering while irascible passions require bolstering. The four subjective emotional compassionate feelings and/or bearings enumerated by St. John require not mere tempering but frequently complete suppression to be brought under the will's masterful self-control.

Furthermore, subjective compassionate emotional bodily feelings harbor an empathic interpersonal influential pathos which impact not only on the self that self-induces and self-controls these feelings but also on selves other than one's own self. A person with a joyfully emotional pathos charismatically, empathically, and seductively induces a similar compassionate pathos in selves other than his own self who are susceptible to such a pathos. If other selves are not empathically susceptible, they are antipathetic and not sympathetic. Any residual enduring (i.e., long-lasting) pathos, be it a compassionate feeling of joy, sadness, hope, or fear can be described as a pervasive mood or temperament which typifies the dominant charism (or lack of charism) that distinguishes a person's personality.

Similarly, subjective dispassionate emotionless mental bearings harbor an empathic influential ethos which impact not only on the self that self-induces and self-controls these bearings but also on selves other than one's own self. A person with a joyfully emotionless ethos charismatically, empathically, and seductively induces a similar dispassionate ethos in selves other than his own self who are susceptible to such an ethos. Again, if other selves are not empathically susceptible, they are antipathetic and not telepathic. Any residual enduring (i.e., long-lasting) ethos, be it a dispassionate mental bearing (composure) of joy, sadness, hope, or fear can be described as an entrancing sentiment which typifies the dominant charism (or lack of charism) that distinguishes a person's personality.

The intellectual soulful will and self-centered psychosomatic will differ.

There is a radical difference between the objective soulful and subjective self-centered wills. This difference can be stated as follows. The soul's intellectual will voluntarily (i.e., freely) and personally (i.e., individually) is morally responsible for what it conscionably appropriates. It exercises its will sovereignly without reference to any subjective bias or self-interest. In contrast, the self's self-serving will volitionally (i.e., decisively by commitment) and personalistically is amorally conscientiously self-accountable in appropriating possessively whatever it deems important for its own autonomy to assuredly secure its own biased self-serving self-sufficiency. The former volitional freedom and love is conscionably governed by what is purposefully reasonable for the will to choose in order for its choices to attain to the will's innate drive for excellence (viz., happiness). The latter volitional freedom and love is conscientiously prompted and motivated to possessively pursue what is self-servingly profitable and advantageous for the will's own skillful self-reliant self-control and

251

self-fulfillment (i.e., viz., its social security).

It cannot be sufficiently emphasized that the intellectual will's love transcends all sensory affections and passions peculiar to the corporeal animal body's sensibility in the vertical order of existence. Hence, the intellectual will does not voluntarily exercise its choice because it is fond of or affected by what it chooses. Its choices transcend such affections. The intellectual will is intelligently informed by what is intelligibly objectively good-as-such and not by what is sentiently good. Hence, it is informatively enlightened by what is conscionably the morally right choice in terms of the intelligibility and truth of the choice itself.

The same human person, on the other hand, is not innately endowed exclusively with an intellectual willful appetite. Its own corporeal body is endowed with instinctive appetitive drives that affectively and passionately stimulate the body's autonomic nervous system to engage in bodily movements purposefully directed by these instinctive drives. Certainly, these instinctive drives with their passionate affections impact on the intellectual will's own purposeful choices. But, only subordinately and not directly. The human person's intellectual will may choose to prefer to indulge the animal body's gustatory enjoyment over the permanent truthful joy that such gustatory enjoyment is only temporary and injurious to the body's health. Yet, in such an immoral indulgent choice the human person remains radically free to temper the body's gustatory enjoyment of food in spite of the will's diminished freedom to cease indulging in such immoral gluttony.

By way of contrast the selfhood's subjective self-serving psychosomatic will with its volitional deliberative element of controlled reflexive consciousness and pathos is permeated with the conative emotional (i.e., influential motivational) feeling of dis/satisfaction peculiar to the somatic body's sensitivity and with the conative bearing of non/justification peculiar to the psychic mind's intimacy. The selfhood's psychosomatic will is a will that volitionally cares for, is interested in, and is concerned about the object of its volitional commitment, endurance, and self-control. Its self-centered and self-serving love lovingly and affectionately (i.e., conscientiously) transforms its object into an interesting and important prized object.

The intellectual will is obligated to love what is appropriately (i.e., conscionably) loveable independent of the will's own love for it. It remains free not to love what it is obligated to love and may freely choose not to love what it is conscionably obligated to love. The loveable object's loveliness is not born of the will's love for it. Rather, the intellectual will's own love is informatively measured by the object's intelligible truthful loveliness. If the object of what it freely chooses to love is noble, the will's love is morally noble. If the object is ignoble, the will's love in choosing to love this object is immorally ignoble. In other words, its fundamental conscionable love is directed to possess its object appropriate with its object's inherent worthwhile value.

It is simply the reverse for the selfhood's self-serving psychosomatic will. Whatever it loves it appropriates possessively to suit its own willfulness. The object of its love becomes valuable precisely because it is possessively willfully appreciated and prized for its self-service. The will's very self-attachment to the object bestows on the object a serviceable useful value which is not inherent in the object itself apart from its usage corresponding to this service it provides for the self-centered will. This selfhood will's own love is sentimentally or temperamentally one of self-interest, self-concern and a liking and caring that is partisanly self-involved. It is not an informative love. Rather, it is a transformative love which transforms the object of its love into a valuable and important object precisely because of the selfhood's appreciative love and need of it to fulfill the deficiency in its own needfulness. Sacred Scripture addresses this love when it declares that where one's treasure is there also is one's heart.

Furthermore this volitional appreciative or depreciative love is a conscientious prejudicial and not a conscionable judicious love as is the case with the love proper to the intellectual will. That is, it is a self-centered love that is influential both intrapersonally within the selfhood's own self-serving willfulness and interpersonally vis-à-vis the willfulness of other selves. The intellectual will's love is caused by what is purposefully good and intentionally loved in view of that purpose. This is an intentional love which is manifestly informatively intelligible but not self-consciously experiential no moreso than is the spiritual soul itself self-consciously experienced (viz., sensitively felt or intimately intuited).

The selfhood will's self-oriented love is under the dominance of its have-attitudinal mindset and framework. This mindset is the prejudicial overarching framework of what the selfhood's will deems to be of utmost importance to its own autonomous (i.e., self-reliant) social security. This importance includes both a bodily feeling of self-satisfied automatic self-contentment and/or mental bearing (i.e., composure) of self-justified autocratic self-containment. It is transformatively an unintelligible but very experiential careful and concerned love inasmuch as the personhood's self is very much self-consciously personalistically self-involved with its own enduring bodily emotional feeling of un/fulfilled dis/contentment and/or enduring mental bearing of un/fulfilled self-non/containment. This selfhood's willful bodily sensitivity and/or mental intimacy become increasingly intensified when the mystic experiences in the *Dark Night* the trying ordeal of the senses and the spirit deprived of their respective self-righteous bodily feelings and mental bearings.

It is important to note that the person's willful selfhood prejudicially in terms of its own dominant self-orientated have-attitudinal mindset loves carefully, caringly, interestedly, fondly, favoringly, likingly, preferably, appreciatively (i.e., experientially) and conscientiously (or, the converse) whatever it decides as having importance or no importance for its own overall historical self-interest and autonomous social security. This biased mindset (whether idealistic or realistic, pessimistic, or optimistic) predetermines its motivating bodily feelings and mental bearings which it volitionally harbors and entertains toward itself and empathically toward selves other than its own self. In this sense, the person's selfhood's willful love is a transformative and not an informed love. That is, again, it transforms the object of its love into a treasured, interesting, and important serviceable useful object available for its own use to advance its own social security.

This transformative love in view of the selfhood's interest in selves other than its own self is, again, an empathic love through which the self's willful bodily self sympathizes with the feelings of others compatible with its own bodily temperament and alternatively through which the self's willful mental self telepathically sides with the bearings (i.e., outlook) of others compatible with its own mental sentiment. By reason of this empathy in which the person's willful self favorably or unfavorably associates its own self-serving self-orientated interests with other selves conditioned by its own overarching have-attitudinal mindset, this transformative empathic love serves as a conative quasi-knowledge.

This empathic love is the prospect of experientially substituting one's own self for another self and to consciously feel sympathetically within one's own somatic body the feelings which others feel or to subconsciously entertain telepathically within one's own psychic mind the bearings (i.e., inspirations, cares, concerns, preferences) which others psychically experience within themselves. This empathic love is prejudicially transformative inasmuch as it appreciatively increases or depreciatively decreases the willful selfhood's self-regard and self-esteem toward others who are objects of its concern and care. Thus, a self may be unsympathetic toward the feelings and apathetic toward the bearings (i.e., outlook) of others who are considered to be aliens to its own biased have-attitudinal mindset.

This influential motivational un/appreciative love is experienced as a conscious "feeling" (i.e., bodily sensitivity) in the case of the somatic will and as a subconscious "caring" and "concern" (i.e., mental intimacy) in the case of the psychic will. This somatic feeling and/or psychic caring are both entirely egocentrically subjective; the feeling and/or caring are motivationally prompted and influenced by what attitudinally is of paramount solicitous importance to the selfhood's own willful self-reliant social security. An emotional feeling stimulates and excites the somatic selfhood's willful bodily sensitivity to take action to make happen whatever seems necessary to secure and prolong the body's pleasurable self-contentment.

On the other hand, an emotionless (i.e., impassive) caring sedates and calms the psychic selfhood's willful mental intimacy to defend and protect its self-contained self-righteousness. The significant difference between these two is that sensitized enjoyments of pleasurable self-contentment are diffused symptomatically and superficially throughout the selfhood's extrinsic visceral body while a mental intimate righteous self-containment penetrates noumenally and profoundly to the selfhood's intrinsic cerebral core.

The selfhood's psychic and somatic wills are polarized.

To better grasp the polarity that differentiates the willful selfhood's psychic self from its somatic self within each personhood's subjective egology, consider a glass of water. What makes the glass a container of water is not its composition as glass. It is its hollowness and emptiness as a container. Pewter or some non-glass plastic container may be similarly configured to successfully contain water. What is crucial to these water containers is that they be empty and hollow configurations. If they are solid, they cannot contain water. What is emptiness? It is a lack and a deficiency, a deprivation. That is, it is a deprivation of whatever is lacking to fill the emptiness. It is a non-entity inasmuch as it is a lack of what is entitative. Hence, it is a non-such-being which in the absence of what it lacks is simply a no-such-entity. Where does such a non-entity "no-thing" originate? In the mind's vacuity. Certainly not in water itself whether it is contained in the glass or existing outside of the glass which can contain it. Emptiness is merely the absence of something that can fill it. In this sense, it is a quasi-being because it is considered merely in reference to a being which it is not.

Another example of this emptiness is a donut-hole. Assuredly, the dough removed from the donut's center is itself some-thing and not a no-thing. Yet, the donut that has a hole in it is lacking dough at its center. This lack is not itself an entitative being-as-such but a non-such-being. This non-such-being arises in the psychic mind's notionality which it conjures up from its own blank psychic emptiness. The notional mathematical configurations which the mind conjures up within its own psychicity are compatible with its own psychic blank emptiness since they are themselves devoid of all objective physical tangibility and all subjective physiological tactility (i.e., sensational imaginary imagery) and feelings peculiar to the somatic body's neurological sensitivity. In brief, a glass is a container of water not inasmuch as there is a content of water in the container. It is a container

256

inasmuch as it is empty of all contents especially water, in this case. Its emptiness cannot be perceptually, tactually, and empirically detected. It can only be conceptually, non-tactually, and mentally (i.e., rationally) intuited. Such rationality, of course, is not reasonable; it is unreasonable (i.e., fashionable and mythical).

Accordingly, the selfhood's psychic self willfully possesses its self-reliant vindictive social self-containment when it is emotionlessly, impassively, sedately, and immutably self-absorbed within its own intimacy and rationality, fully immune to the somatic body's sensitivity. And, vice versa, the selfhood's somatic self willfully possesses its own self-reliant sensuously enjoyable self-contentment when it is emotionally, excitedly, and sensitively fully self-absorbed and mobilized and impervious to the psychic mind's inert intimacy and blank rationality. This psychosomatic polarity within the selfhood's own willfulness is a negative-positive have/have-not opposition. To be aware of one is to be oblivious of the other. Psychic subconscious mental awareness is statically, impassively, and emotionlessly dispassionate while somatic bodily consciousness is kinetically emotionally compassionate.

Thus, conceptually a dozen is statically and precisely a group of 12 while perceptually it may be kinetically 12 eggs, 12 donuts, or whatever one's selfhood decides to group together as a dozen. Hence, a paradigmatic and archetypical dozen is, on the one hand, conceptually an empty carton with 12 empty pockets to accommodate 12 factors. This is purely, exactly, and correctly a mathematical model. On the other hand, it is not conceptually but imaginatively imaged as 12 eggs assembled within a carton or removed from the carton's 12 pockets.

In this instance of the 12 dozen eggs the psychic selfhood's will is self-reliantly socially self-justified because the dozen group of eggs are precisely in mathematical terms equivalent to any other dozen group justifying the mind's willful demand and rationale for a precise equivalence between one egg carton and another. All egg cartons are precisely the same. This is an example of the mathematical equivalence which is the underlying rationale for all exchanges, trades, and associations fabricated by the psychic mind's self-controlled willful social equity. At the same time, the somatic selfhood's will is enjoyably self-gratified because the dozen group of eggs are pragmatically in consumer useable terms equivalent to a week's full-course of meals with eggs for breakfast, eggs for making a cake, and eggs for other similar recipes satisfying the body's satiation and needs.

Hence, while the mathematical nontactual measurement of an egg-carton remains statically, idealistically, remotely, and usefully exactly equivalent, the psychic will is socially self-justified and vindicated. And, while the size of each of the dozen eggs vis-à-vis each other are kinetically realistically, apparently, and only approximately and tolerably equivalent (i.e., never exactly so), the somatic will is socially self-gratified with their pragmatic usage over a period of time.

The polarized psychosomatic will's self-containment/contentment differs in that the psychic selfhood's willful vindication is devoid of all sensational sensuality, sensitivity, emotion, excitement, feeling, and somatic kinetic bodily motion. Hence, its willful mental social self-contained intimate bearing (i.e., composure and posture) is non-sensational, insensate, intimate, impassive, emotionless, and auto-suggestively sedate. The somatic selfhood's willful sensitive contented gratification is replete with sensational, sensuous, sensitized, emotional exciting feelings. These polar differences are characterized by a negative and positive opposition in the horizontal order of possessive having. To have one is to suffer the loss of the other. This involves a sacrifice. One has to be sacrificed in favor of the other.

This sacrifice entails a paradox endemic to the horizontal cultural order of resistance. The selfhood's psychic will's self-containment is socially secure when the human person experiences a mental self-reliant intimate sedate insensate imperturbable calm whereas the selfhood's somatic will's self-contentment is socially secure when the same human person experiences a bodily self-reliant sensitive sensuous sensational excitement. Correspondingly, a human person's psychic mental self resists relinquishing the social security of its mental serenity including its telepathic personalized affinity with associates (i.e., other selves) who volitionally have and are committed to the same idealistic mentality and ideological attitudinal mindset fostering this serenity. Similarly, a human person's somatic bodily self resists relinquishing the social security of its bodily excitement including its compassionate personalized affinity with associates who volitionally have and are committed to the same realistic mentality and ideological attitudinal mindset fostering this excitement.

There is, then, a paradoxical have-have/not polar opposition between the selfhood's willful psychic and somatic have-attitudinal mindsets and dominating self-interests and attitudinal commitments (i.e., surrender) to what they deem to be of paramount importance for each's respective self-reliant social security. When it is fully and willfully the psychic selfhood that is of paramount concern, it is a cerebral self-justified self-control of its own subconscious mental immobilized psychicity which prevails. This willful psychic self-absorption is completely empty of the somatic body's sensational sensitivity and mobilization. This is an egocentric self-possession in which this psychic selfhood is completely detached (i.e., completely dispassionate) from the somatic body's sensational sensual sensitivity.

And vice versa, when it is fully and willfully the somatic selfhood that is of paramount concern to the person's self-subsistent personhood, it is a visceral self-gratified conscious self-control of its own body's exciting somaticity and sensitivity which is preferred and prevails. This willful somatic self-absorption is completely oblivious to the mind's dispassionate notional intimacy. It is completely attached to its own sensual sensitivity. To have one is to sacrificially forgo and dispense with the other. This paradox pervades the psychosomatic egological subjectivity of the human person's willful conscious selfhood's freedom of self-control. Given this polarity inherent within the subjective personality of the human person, it is no great surprise that a national personality committed to a socialistic form of civilized government finds itself at loggerheads with a neighboring national personality committed to a capitalistic form of governance and civilization.

The objective soulful and subjective self-centered will's respective freedom.

The standard for the intellectual will's exercise of its freedom of choice and its attainment to the perfection of its freedom is that of excellence. This excellence is nothing less than the holistic and total possession of the good-as-such itself (viz., happiness) in its immortal reality that ultimately subsists only in God who alone is absolute infinite Goodness. This natural common standard of excellence is an absolute catholic universal immortal transhistorical standard common to every individual human that ever exists. This will's objective (viz., happiness) is achieved only when an individual's particular possessive voluntary choices are conscionably (i.e., morally and reasonably) appropriate to and consonant with this ideal standard of excellence.

By contrast, the standard for the selfhood's self-serving and self-controlled will's exercise of its freedom and its self-fulfillment is one of social equivalence. This equivalence is perforce a piecemeal possession of what is in one's biased attitudinal mindset esteemed to be of utmost importance to insure a social self-reliant autonomy not only intrapersonally within one's own psychosomatic selfhood but also interpersonally vis-à-vis other selves. This standard of equivalence is a social conventional standard of willful contractual agreement and consensus in all exchanges willfully agreed upon. This will's self-fulfillment is reached when its self-serving decisions conscientiously succeed in guaranteeing its own autonomy (viz., social security) within itself and vis-à-vis selves other than its own selfhood.

Of course, this self-fulfillment must be considered both horizontally and vertically precisely because it involves a human person who is fundamentally existingly (i.e., ontologically) a sovereign immortal transhistorical communal nature and has only supplementally and existentially (i.e., phenomenologically) an autonomous mortal historical self-cultivated sociability. If the psychosomatic will's self-fulfillment is considered merely horizontally, it can be only supplementally and not fundamentally become self-fulfilled since this selfhood is itself only a supplemental need and requirement for the human personhood's own self-fulfillment. Considered merely horizontally, the psychosomatic will is incapable within its own resources of providing its own selfhood with a total self-fulfillment. It is paradoxically in its own polarized psychosomatic selfhood inherently in a have/have-not polar opposition within itself, i.e., a polarized tension.

It can only overcome and resolve this tension by finding its total fundamental self-fulfillment in the transcendent vertical order of existence. In order to accomplish this, it must paradoxically willfully die to (i.e., relinquish, renounce, and abandon) its own selfish biased have-more attitudinal mindset and self-serving self-reliant self-centered social autonomy. This self-denial, however, is only the preliminary stage of its self-fulfillment. It must be completed by a complete willful conscientious self-surrender and total be-attitudinal commitment become conscientiously self-surrendered to the personhood's own moral conscionable transhistorical immortal communal happiness in the objective vertical order of existence.

This willfully committed self-humanizing self-fulfillment, however, cannot be fully consummated without the mediation of Christ's super-humanizing Paschal Mystery and the charitable Gift of His Holy Spirit abiding within the innermost core intimacy of the Christian's psychosomatic willful selfhood. Ultimately the willful selfhood finds its total self-fulfillment in living beyond its own selfhood's social subjectivity with a joy and enjoyment that is objectively God's very own Triune beatitudinal eternal family bliss. Indeed, it is the very premise of this commentary that the soul and the self's wills are both distinguishable from each other in terms of a vertical-horizontal ordering but also compatible and complementary with each other in terms of the cruciformity proper to Christ's cross of crucifixion.

The soul's intellectual will---in the vertical order of the human person's own intelligent and free human nature---reaches its conscionable maturity in the person's development of his moral character strengthened by the four moral virtues of justice, prudence, temperance, and fortitude elevated to a superhuman theological excellence. This occurs in the hierarchical order within which the human person's own immortal soul partakes of a spiritual order that transcends the physical cosmos and supernaturally aspires to partake of what ideally is God's very own eternal divinity and benignity. This cannot be accomplished without the moral virtues of justice, prudence, fortitude, and temperance elevated by grace to the ideal standard of God's very own supernatural perfection of Goodness. Christ stipulates that His Heavenly Father is the standard of excellence for His disciple's moral perfection.

These moral virtues including the punitive discipline they entail contributing to the mystic's moral character are fundamental to the mystical life of contemplative prayer. However, the mystical life cannot find its consummation and perfection merely in obediently exercising its intellectual will to dutifully love what is not only supremely worthy of love, supernaturally revealed, God Himself in His Triune Godhead. The mystical life supplementally demands that the very selfhood of the person consciously commit, surrender, and conscientiously sacrifice its own subjective self-serving biased mindset and selfish self-interest and humanistic autonomous historical social security in behalf of this very conscionable love of God transcendent to its own selfhood's historical mortality.

The intellectual soulful will's moral character vs the selfhood psychosomatic will's charisma.

This self-sacrifice and ascetic self-mortification itself is not an issue of the mystic's moral character but moreso of the mystic's charismatic personality of charitably, superhumanistically, and sacrificially giving of himself wholeheartedly to the social service of God and his fellowman in contraposition to striving exclusively for his own autonomous selfish social security.

This dedicated service requires an ascetic skill and training proper to the Holy Spirit of the beatitudes: blessed are the poor in spirit. Blessed is the mystic who is self-emptied of the captivating self-humanizing egoistic morale and resolve of his own self-serving domineering partisan psychosomatic attitudinal ideological mindset. It is only when he is conscientiously rid and stripped of this crippling and self-alienating self-serving dominating humanistic morale (i.e., spirit) subservient to his own biased mindset that he is authentically free to be at the service of God without any further restriction, self-restraint, or self-controlled impediment.

Accordingly, the Christian mystical life is objectively, conscionably, and morally an issue of moral virtue supernaturally elevated by God's sacramental graciousness. Subjectively, conscientiously, and in view of the Holy Spirit's superhumanizing influence and beatitudinal morale proper to Christ Himself and His own messianic mindset, it is an issue of an ascetic Gospel lifestyle of prayerful self-denial which cannot apart from the Holy Spirit's own subtle indomitable influential morale (viz., a sacrificial charitable love for the Father's Holy Will) be consummated and brought to completion. Of course, it is Christ Himself who through His own crucified immolation makes superhumanistically possible this ascetic dying to one's selfish self in order to live to God beyond the prison of one's own selfish self-centered selfhood and subjectivity.

This dying and self-denial is a sacrificial love while charity is itself a self-giving love of friendship emanating primarily and gratuitously from God's own infinite gracious and magnanimous supernatural and superhuman loveliness. The selfhood's will must sacrifice its own biased selfish self-cultivated, self-humanizing have-more mindset and self-interest in order to serve God selflessly as a companion to Christ in sacrificial surrender to Christ's own Masterful Selfless Service rendered to God-the-Father in behalf of mankind's redemption, sanctification, and glorification.

This sacrificial love is a have-have/not polarized love. To predominantly have love equivalently for one's own historical moral social selfhood is to be deprived of having a love that excellently serves God transhistorically beyond and above the selfish needs of one's own social subjectivity. And, vice versa, to have a love that is totally transhistorically at the service of God is tantamount to being deprived of one's own self-centered selfish associative self-love. Certainly, there are degrees of difference here. One may be predominantly in love with God and minimally in love with one's own self-interest that detracts from a total surrender to God's primacy. Or, vice versa.

However, the goal of the Catholic Christian mystic is to pursue a perfect prayerful union with God in this life as a pilgrimage climbing up Mount Carmel and in the next as an eternal total enjoyment of God. God is infinitely perfect. Eternal beatitude brooks of no imperfection nor detraction from God's own infinite loveliness. Hence, the struggle for the mystic's willful selfhood to prayerfully, sacrificially, and superhumanistically become in his own charismatic Christian subjective personality "another Christ" never ceases until the very moment of his physical death.

Christ's own Self-immolation makes possible the mystic's own sacrificial charitable (i.e., selfless amicable) love for God-the-Father entailing his own ascetic dying to self. It is Christ's Holy Spirit alive within the very heart and pith of the mystic's psychosomatic selfhood that influentially prompts and superhumanistically influences the mystic in union with Christ's ecclesial sacramentality to faithfully wed together this personalized subjective sacrificial conscientious immolative and oblative personalized love with the personal conscionable objective obedient conscionable love of God. In this cruciform wedding of the two loves there ensues---through the Holy Spirit's personal embrace of the Father and the Son's mutual love---the amicable charitable love in which the mystic by sublimation enters into a mystical communion of friendship with the Triune Godhead through Christ's very own superhumanistic Selfless sacrificial loveliness.

This loveliness to the casual spectator appears as the foolishness of the cross while to the mystic it is nothing less than the mystic's own selfhood entering cruciformly, oblatively, and resurrectionally into heaven integrated into Christ's own resurrected ascension. In this regard, the Virgin Mary's own bodily assumption into heaven remains as the model and mother to the mystic's pilgrimage. This mention of Mary is not merely an anecdotal appendage to the mystic's pilgrimage. For, Mary is the mother of the Christian's baptismal life into the Trinity. She is the Mother of the Church's sacramentality as she is the Mother of Jesus, the Church's Head. It is as a baptized member of the Sacramental Catholic Church that the mystic becomes himself sacramentally enabled to enter mystically into Christ's Mystical Body, the Sacramental Church.

The reason, then, that the selfhood's own self-serving egocentric willfulness is able to ascetically die to its own selfish social self-interest is prompted by the supernatural virtue of love (viz., charity) which motivationally spurs on this selfhood to purge itself of its own selfishness. This divine charitable love is nothing less than the Holy Spirit of the Father and the Son abiding within the very recesses and nuclear core of the innermost intimacy of the self's willful psychosomatic selfhood. So subtly and docily delicate is the Holy Spirit's charitable influence on the selfhood's willful self that it is virtually indiscernible to the mystic whether it is under his own motivational influence that he willfully suffers his own demise or under that of the Holy Spirit. This same pneumatic subtlety also reigns when the mystic subsequently in contemplative prayer becomes charitably consumed with the Triune Godhead's beatitudinal joy.

What seems beyond dispute, however, is that there are two separate phases of this dying to self in St. John's mystical theology. In the active phase being expounded here in the *Ascent,* it is the mystic himself who is in charge of this austere program of self-immolation. Here, certainly, the Holy Spirit's influence is also present but less in evidence. In the *Dark Night* the mystic himself is no longer in charge of the ongoing and continuing process of self-oblation. This is the passive phase in which the Holy Spirit's influence is more in evidence and more pronounced. The basic difference between the active and passive phases hinges on this issue of who is in charge and has control over the purifying purgative process itself: the mystic's own willful self or the Holy Spirit's own influential prowess? Nonetheless, whether it be the active or passive phase of this purgation of the mystic's self-centered psychosomatic selfhood, the Holy Spirit's influence is so subtle and delicate that the mystic seems unable to differentiate and to discriminate between his own willful self-control and that of the Holy Spirit's

As previously stated, the selfhood's psychosomatic will is itself dichotomously polarized paralleling the dichotomy peculiar to the personhood's egology. Of course, this dichotomy is not explicitly found in the writings of our Carmelite Holy Father no more than is the selfhood's will in contradistinction to the soul's intellectual will explicitly found in his texts. Yet, it is hoped that the reader of this commentary will discern that St. John's mystical account dovetails with this commentary's expatiation of the will and the intellect's cruciformity. Hence, when St. John speaks of the emotions of joy, sorrow, hope, and fear and in the context of his explanation of joy, it seems that it is either a somatic self-willed emotional feeling of self-satisfaction and self-contentment which he is describing or a psychic self-willed emotionless bearing of self-justification and self-containment. In either case, this joy is very much a self-serving, self-controlled, and self-centered subjective volitional experience of honoring and serving God amicably in a friendship beyond the self's self-centered historical social selfishness. God who exists in the vertical ontological order is the transcendental center of these bodily feelings and mental bearings of joy, sorrow, hope, and fear.

The opposite of this somatic self-satisfaction would be an unwelcome bodily feeling of dissatisfied self-discontentment; and the opposite of this psychic self-justification would be an unwelcome mental bearing of non-vindicated self-non-containment (viz. a disequilibrium). While joy and sorrow occur in the very presence of what motivationally volitionally prompts and influences these feelings and bearings, hope and fear occur in the very absence but possible presence of what motivationally prompts the loss and absence of these feelings and bearings. Thus, hope would be a confident future anticipation of eventually possessively having self-satisfying feelings and self-justifying bearings. Fear, on the other hand, is the lack of confident anticipation of having future self-satisfying feelings and self-justifying bearings with this difference. Emotional bodily feelings of fear involve and engage the actual loss of self-contentment (viz., emotional dejection) whereas the emotionless mental bearing of fear is a dread, trepidation, and anxiety (viz., emotionless discombobulation).

St. John proceeds in a masterful way to explore the self-serving motivations that are incumbent on the affectionate enjoyment of temporal, natural, sensory, moral, supernatural, and spiritual objects. He meticulously identifies the special interest peculiar to each of these enjoyments. He proceeds to evaluate the detriment that ensues from having a self-centered selfish self-gratifying and self-justifying enjoyment of these objects and the benefit in becoming self-detached from these enjoyments. The criterion for measuring these detriments and benefits is to ascertain whether they are conducive to increasing or decreasing one's affection for God transcendent to the selfhood's selfish self-centeredness.

Further clarifications regarding the selfhood's soma and psyche (heart and mind).

What is a bodily feeling? It is a sensitized sensational stimulation of contentment and/or discontentment (i.e., pleasure and/or pain) concerning whatever one attitudinally likes and/or dislikes. It is consciously experienced within the anatomical body's subjective sensitive somaticity. It contributes to one's autonomous somatic willful selfhood's self-reliant enjoyable self-contentment (i.e., comfort) or sorrowful self-malcontentment (i.e., discomfit). It is entirely subjective and personalistically discernible from within one's self-reflexive awareness of the somatic body's neurological sensitivity. It may be observed empirically and indirectly by technical instruments.

What is a mental bearing? It is a sedate inspirational intimation of self-containment and/or self-discontainment (i.e., easiness and/or uneasiness) concerning whatever one is concerned for and cares about, and/or is indifferent to. It is subconsciously experienced within the cerebral mind's subjective psychicity. It contributes to one's autonomous psychic selfhood's self-reliant self-containment (i.e., self-sufficiency) or self-noncontainment (i.e., self-insufficiency). Again, it is entirely subjective and is not discernible apart from one's self-reflexive subconscious awareness of the psychic mind's own psychological intimacy. It is not empirically detectable even with technical equipment.

Feeling and bearing are antipodal. Feelings engage the willful somatic body's sensuous sensitivity while bearings engage the willful psychic mind's insensate intimacy. Both deal with the selfhood's taking a willful grip and self-controlled hold of itself; that is, a willful, mindful, and wholehearted self-control of its own body's functional sensitivity and/or mind's functional intimacy. Failing this self-control, feelings and bearings involve the uncontrolled and, possibly, uncontrollable sensitivities and intimacies proper to the self's bodily somaticity and mind's psychicity. However, since the will is egologically polarized between its inner psychic and its outer somatic selfhood, it must sacrificially forgo willful control over its somatic body if it decides to skillfully exercise expert control over its psychic mind. And vice versa if the reverse is the case. Of course, this is a paradox. And this paradox is entirely subjective within the egological polarity that persists between the selfhood's psychic willfulness and its somatic willfulness. Feelings tend to motivationally stimulate the somatic will to bodily kinetic action whereas bearings tend to motivationally sedate the psychic will to inertial mental somnolent inaction.

The reason for this is rooted in the polar difference that marks the somatic body from the psychic mind. The somatic body's physiological functions are manipulative whereas the psychic mind's psychological functions are managerial. Both are self-serving serviceable functions that artificially (i.e., willfully) fabricate self-serving products of convenient service facilitating the body's own manipulative function and/or facilitating the mind's own managerial function. Thus, the human body's hand in addition to being the focal faculty of touch is also manipulatively a mechanical tool that can proximately in a hands-on fashion grip, pound, screw, scratch, pull, push, facilitated by an appropriate tool, etc. By willfully fabricating artificial tools the body's own manipulative somatic selfhood becomes robotically and artificially further functionally mobilized.

The psychic mind, on the other hand, exercises a remote managerial self-control rather than a proximate manipulative and mechanical one. Its own willful self-control does not proximately but only remotely engage whatever it seeks to manage. In addition to being centered in the neurological organ of the brain, it also managerially functions by fabricating communicative symbols that can conveniently command functional attention from selves other than its own self, "help," "stop," "come," "go," "stand," "sit," "wait," etc.. By willfully fabricating artificial symbols conveniently communicating its own will to others it remains itself immobilized while managerially mobilizing other selves into serviceable action. That is, it can manage the actions and activities of others while remaining itself quite immobilized in its own self-controlled mental managerial comportment.

Note that the manipulative tool and the managerial symbol are artificially self-serving conveniences. They are not inherently or naturally good-as-such or valuable-as-such apart from their usage; they are lacking in a value of their own apart from their exploitative usage. They are useable goods which are only functionally and self-servingly (i.e., socially) good. In reality they are non-such-goods and not good-as-such as is the case with any good and valuable reality in the vertical order of nature. They are quasi-goods inasmuch as they are deployed to the advantage of their user. In other words, they are functionally good inasmuch as some person possessively avails him self or her self of their functional usage. Such conveniences have no innate purpose; they have only a serviceable usage dictated by the actual use to which they are exploititatively deployed.

A common pin, for example, may be fabricated simply to baste the hem of a skirt which a tailor or seamstress is sewing. On the other hand, it may be used for many other functions. In this regard it is not being abused or misused since it has no purpose inherent in its nature. It is not a natural entity; it is an artificially fabricated enterprise. It may be exploititatively deployed for any serviceable function other than the special one for which it was fabricated. It is valuable and prized only in the measure that it successively serves some productive function. If it is possessively owned by an individual person, its usage by another person in opposition to the owner's wish may, in this sense, constitute an abuse. But, this abuse is not a misuse of the convenience itself but rather a transgression on the owner's own ownership of the convenience.

This difference between a serviceable functional entirely subjective self-cultivated quasi-good and a natural objective good-as-such is paramount here in differentiating between the intellectual will's striving for the excellence of happiness and the selfhood's will striving for the equivalence of its own social security in its self-sacrificial contractual agreements within itself and with other selves. The former is attained by possessing what is reasonably, absolutely, and conscionably appropriate (i.e., practically good-as-such) to the attainment of the soul's immortal happiness (i.e., excellence) while the latter is attained by possessively appropriating what is willfully, conscientiously, relatively, and sacrificially used to provide for the selfhood's own self-reliant social security (i.e., an exploitative useable quasi-good). A valuable natural good is endowed with an inalienable purpose while a prized self-serving fabricated quasi-good is a purposeless convenient tool or symbol that may exploitatively and conveniently function at the behest of the person who uses it.

On this point, some tools and symbols are so precisely functionally fabricated that their exploitative usage is very limited. Such is the case, for example, for the screw which is so small in size as to be part of a wrist watch. It cannot be successfully deployed to any other usage. A wrench, on the other hand, may be deployed for many different usages. The same holds for symbols. Some, again, are so precisely functionally fabricated that their exploitative usage is very limited. Such is the case, for example, for the French word, vert. It is not deployable in its special significance in any language other than French. And, if it is, it may be used with a significance that is entirely different.

On the other hand, certain symbols in classical Greek retain their significance and meaning whenever they are used; for example, the term, paleo. Regardless of these usages, every tool and every symbol are inherently functionally useless until they are successfully used in whatever serviceable usage they are deployed. In this usage, their social conventional consensus comes into play. This is nothing other than a willful agreement among different selves or within one and the same self to deploy these conveniences agreeably

The selfhood's psychosomatic will versus the soul's intellectual will.

Contrasting these quasi self-cultivated artificial goods in the historical order with the natural goods existing in the vertical hierarchical order of the universe, consider the apple that grows on the apple tree. This apple, quite apart from its inherent nutriment available to the person or animal that eats it, enjoys an innate inalienable purpose. It contains the seeds for the apple tree's regeneration and proliferation. In this regard the apple is inherently valuable and good precisely because of the inherent purpose which it naturally fulfills. Eating this apple and destroying its seeds is tantamount to terminating the apple tree's proliferation and regeneration. This is similarly the case with the human embryo from the very instant of its conception and inception as the zygote offspring of the male sperm and the female human egg. It has not only an innate temporal purpose similar to the apple's regenerative seeds, it has an everlastingly immortal purpose that outlives even its bodily mortality. In other words, its very immortal destiny militates against its being used exploititatively for any person's self-serving convenience. It is never a mere quasi conventional good prized and appreciated simply for its serviceability; it is an inherent valuable good quite independent of whether a person appreciates and values it for its proper intrinsic worth.

The human person's intellectual will loves (i.e., freely wills) the apple intelligently for what it intrinsically is in the order of nature. Accordingly, it willingly loves and lovingly enjoys the apple when it loves it truthfully and appropriately in view of its inherent nature and purpose. In this sense, it willingly respects the apple for what it is. It may both choose to eat the apple and preserve its seeds for planting, or it may wantonly destroy both the apple and seeds together. In the former case, it willingly and conscionably and sentiently enjoys the apple's tangible flavor and nutriment and in the latter, it unconscionably enjoys its own muscular willfulness. On the other hand, if the apple is plucked and baked as an ingredient in an apple pie, the same human person's intellectual will freely enjoys the apple's artificially increased tasty succulence. However, this enjoyment is short-lived because the apple as a consumable (i.e., destructible) good offers only a temporary and transient willful enjoyment. Yet, it is an authentically good willful enjoyment since the will loves the apple appropriate to its own intrinsic worth.

The preceding example of the apple is the kind of conscionable respect that primitive people have for their environment which they have not learned to cultivate much beyond its natural growth. A more cultivated civilization that has learned to cultivate the very apple tree that grows apples regards the apple artificially grown as a product of its own artificial cultivation. When this occurs, the apple is no longer merely inherently (i.e., naturally) a valuable good-as-such entity in the horizontal hierarchical order of existence but additionally and artificially a valued no-such-good enterprise in the vertical historical order of resistance. The apple in this latter case is not merely naturally an object of the human person's soulful intellectual will and enjoyment but also an object of the same human person's self-centered subjective mindful self-possessive will. The apple is not merely objectively intellectually and willingly enjoyed for what it appropriately and truthfully is in its own nature, it is additionally willfully possessively willed and possessively enjoyed for its own self-serving exploitative usage to its owner's economic social security.

In this latter sense and usage, it is only a quasi relative social commodity no-such-good that can be exchanged and substituted for something else to the advantage of its owner who possessively and willfully owns it. Its willful enjoyment by the human person's subjective self-centered willfulness is additionally and very subjectively more than a mere sentient sensible enjoyment; it is a sensuous sensitized enjoyment because it is the fruit not of the tree but of the human body's subjective self-serving will forcibly exerting its willfulness over the mechanical body's toil and labor struggling to cultivate an apple orchard in a soil that offers only resistance to this labor working with only primitive tools. The manifest difference between the intellectual will's objective sentient enjoyment of the apple and the self-centered subjective will's sensuous enjoyment is that the former is temporary consonant with the apple's temporary and destructible nature while the latter is historically and processively enduring consonant with the will's own self-possessive willful social security.

In other words, the human person's objective intellectual will is by its very nature purposefully and spontaneously ordained to love an immortal and everlasting good-as-such (viz., the common good) which is truthfully appropriate to every human person's intellectual will. This finalizing objective immortal value is inherently valuable not merely for the service it renders but, moreso, for its own intrinsic worth. This value is a holistic entitative general value that is not reducible to any instance of it. The apple is merely an instance of this general good-as-such; it is not equivalent to this transcendent and transhistorical good-as-such. This transcendent good-as-such is an excellent metaphysical good (viz., happiness) that exceeds every instance of its pursuit.

Indeed, there is only one instance of this wholesome good-as-such which is completely unexcelled. This is the instance of God that is the infinite plenitude of this communal good-as-such which is the natural common good for every existing human individual person's soulful will. This transcendent finalizing good-as-such is the very root of the human will's inherent freedom. The human person is necessarily ordained to love this good-as-such as the very finalizing objective of its every voluntary choice. This is its immortal destiny and happiness and joy to be able to freely love whatever it loves within the ambit of the conscionable truth of this transcendent wholesome communal good-as-such and what is appropriate to its inherent excellence. Indeed, this is the root of the person's moral right to happiness and its moral obligation to respect this inalienable right in every other individual. Failure to honor this right is a failure to willingly and freely respect in general justice the inalienable rights of others as sovereign persons with regard to the conscionable governance of their own conduct.

The same human person's subjective self-centered will is not ordained to love any such transcendent immortal worthiness. Hence, it is not inherently ordained to love appropriately (i.e., truthfully and conscionably) what transcends its own self-centered willfulness. It is rather geared to self-serviceably love appropriating possessively (i.e., conscientiously in a self-possessive ownership) whatever it is that it loves throughout its historical transitional span of life. In other words, its love is peculiarly an addictive love. This subjective will of a human person's very psychosomatic selfhood is conscientiously geared to cling to its own addictive willfulness. Paradoxically enough its own selfishness is both its strength and weakness. We know from the revelation of Sacred Scripture that the subjective personalities of Adam and Eve were not originally created with such a selfishly self-centered will. This will became so as a result of their original sin which all of mankind has inherited.

The singular difference between the same human person's objective soulful will and his subjective selfhood's will is that the former is inherently a purposeful intelligent appetitive drive for a communal objective transcendent immortal goal and the latter is a purposeless unintelligible need for a mortal socially self-serving self-fulfillment. The former is a spontaneous freedom that is dutifully (i.e., conscionably) obligated to truthfully choose what is appropriate to its own immortal finality (i.e., sovereignty). The latter is a prodded and prompted freedom that is forcibly (i.e., conscientiously) activated to possessively appropriate what accommodates its own socially secure (i.e., autonomy and self-reliant) self-fulfillment. When the soulful will chooses well it morally strengthens its willingness to choose rightfully. This strength is a moral virtue. When it chooses otherwise, it weakens its willingness to choose rightfully; this weakness is a vice.

In the case of the selfhood's will, whatever it wills decisively it wills selfishly, possessively, agreeably, and conscientiously. This possessiveness is, indeed, a reinforced willful agreeable self-attachment. This agreement is entirely self-centered with one's own self exclusively or socially among several selves. The more forcibly decisive is this self-serving willfulness the more self-controlled it is; and the less forcibly decisive, the less self-controlled it is in its own willfulness.

In the case of the farmer exploitatively cultivating an apple orchard to economically provide for his family's welfare by selling the apples in the market place, he may justifiably take considerable pleasure and satisfaction in the successful crop and profit he realizes from the result of his skillful toil and labor. Yet, St. John of the Cross points out that such a pleasurable enjoyment is not conducive to the farmer's religious and pious union with God which is the objective of the Catholic Christian's mystical life. Why not? Because this joyous self-possessive affectivity deriving from the farmer's own skillful industry detracts from the farmer's joyful appreciative affectivity toward God for the primacy of His providential bounty and benignity contributing to the successful cultivation and harvesting of the apple orchard.

St. John meticulously elaborates on the privative harm that such self-humanizing indulgence brings upon the farmer by diminishing and stunting his pious and religious regard for and appreciation of God's providential primacy in his life's agronomical work. The more affectionately delightful satisfaction the farmer has for his own skillful handiwork and his successful harvest, the less affectionate devout appreciation he has for God who is the Author of the apple's existence and beneficence. The least affection the farmer has for his own handiwork's agronomical harvest is sufficient to bring about in him a dullness of mind regarding God's primacy in his life and work. This is St. John's observation. And the more intense is the farmer's self-possessive affectionate enjoyment of his own skill and agronomical handiwork, the more harmful this is in depriving him of a proper affectionate appreciation for God's primacy in his life and work. He may progressively neglect his spiritual devotions directed toward God, and even come to abandon all interest in God. His own greed for the material success he has realized in his farm may bring him to affectionately prize, treasure, and rejoice in his own material wealth in the place of affectionately treasuring and rejoicing in God's own bountiful graciousness.

The antidote to this seemingly inconsequential joyful satisfaction that the farmer initially takes in his skillful handiwork in bringing about a bountiful harvest and reaping a considerable profit in the market place is to completely forego and to suppress such affectionate selfish joyful satisfaction at the very outset; to nip it in the bud. If he cannot suppress and forego this selfishly self-centered joyful satisfaction and contentment at the very outset of his agronomical success, he will be less able to squelch it when it becomes increasingly intense with future harvests. By squelching it, he does not become prone to greedily, selfishly, and self-possessively cling to the profit his bountiful harvest provides him. He acquires a liberality and freedom from the captivity of his own selfishness. He acquires a better judgment of the true value of his harvest and his other farm possessions. He will gradually discover that his sensitive bodily emotional feelings will be more within his masterful willful self-control rather than finding himself addictively captive to their seductivity. In brief, the more unselfishly he is self-dispossessed of his own affections, the more liberally and masterfully he can enjoy his own bodily sensitive emotional feelings without being captive to their sensuality. Consequentially, this farmer's heartfelt bodily sensitive affectivity and emotional feelings will be more readily at the selfless service of God than selfishly the sensual belt of his own addictive captivity.

The freedom proper to the soulful intellectual will is inalienable because it is innate to the human person and remains intact even when through the body's mortality and death the immortal soul survives. The freedom proper to the selfhood's will is alienable precisely because with the body's demise the human person's subjective personality also perishes. Indeed, any person's personality may be loss to

275

that person if he suffers a severe case of amnesia. The freedom peculiar to the soul's will entails no sacrifice nor does it involve any reference to the human person's selfhood. Hence, there is neither possessive attachment nor dispossessive detachment in the exercise of its freedom. Moral virtue is virtuous because it is the will choosing what is reasonably and truthfully appropriate to will; immoral vice is vicious because it is the will choosing to will what is inappropriate and false.

There may be incidentally a forcible coercive influence that diminishes the intellectual will's voluntariness in freely exercising its choices. This can occur when, for example, the instinctive animal bodily appetite is so overtaken with an imminent fear to the body's safety and well-being (viz., when attacked by a wild animal or threatened by a gun-wielding bandit) that a person out of fear chooses to will a course of conduct which it otherwise would not voluntarily undertake. Another separate incidence arises when a human person's self-centered will's selfish heartfelt and/or mindful willfulness overrides and inhibits the intellectual will from exercising its own fundamental conscionable truthful freedom of choice. For example, a farmer who has become so greedily and affectionately self-possessively attached to his own agronomical possessions that he no longer objectively and conscionably recognizes his fundamental responsible, dutiful, and conscionable freedom of choice to religiously honor and thank God for his prosperity.

The freedom proper to the selfhood's self-control entails a sacrificial decision. This is peculiar to the very selfishness of its self-centeredness. This willful freedom is psychosomatically ambivalent. If the human person decides to become righteously self-attached to the body's gratification and contentment as its overriding self-interest, it will sacrifice the mind's righteous justification and containment. How so? The more engaged is the person in the body's excitement the less he is preoccupied with the mind's serenity; and, vice versa, the more self-contained and serene is the mind's comportment, the less the same person is engaged with the body's excitement and contentment. This sacrificial aspect is endemic to the human person's subjective selfhood's psychosomatic volition.

That is, the body's excitable emotional sensitive feelings must be forcibly and sacrificially suppressed if the human person is to avail himself of a serene and self-contained mental comportment. And, vice versa, this mental comportment must be forcibly (i.e., willfully) sacrificed and forgone if the human person is to indulge in the body's sensational excitement and stimulation. Willful self-attachment and self-detachment involves a self-possessiveness and self-dispossessiveness which is not the hallmark of the soul's intellectual will. It is, however, typical of the selfhood's self-centered willfulness. To give expression to the body's excitement is tantamount to suppressing the mind's serenity; and, vice versa.

There is still another important difference between these two wills. The soul's will loves intentionally inasmuch as its volitions emerge spontaneously, purposively, and naturally from its willfulness. The selfhood's will, on the other hand, loves motivationally inasmuch as its volitions emerge only when its willfulness is strenuously prompted and prodded. Again, the soul's willful intentions are purposefully directed whereas the selfhood's willful motivations are purposelessly needfully self-serving. In other words, the soul's will is a purposeful drive that is goal directed whereas the selfhood's will is a purposeless need that is self-served. Further, the soul's willing volitions are causally determined and finalized by the purpose to which they are directed while the selfhood's willful volitions are urgently influenced by the body's emotional sensational sensitivity, on the one hand, and/or by the mind's emotionless inspirational intimacy, on the other. In sum, the soul's volitions emerge spontaneously by virtue of the soul's energetic vitality whereas the selfhood's volitions emerge only by prompting in virtue of the person's self-centered psychosomatic impotent synergism.

The human person in his personhood is objectively personal and subjectively personalistic.

The human person is personally sovereignly consciably responsible for his soul's volitions whereas the same person is personalistically conscientiously autonomously accountable for his self's volitions. Why so? This is so precisely because in the former case an act of the soul's will is that of a sovereign independent person acting within a hierarchical community of sovereign persons. In the latter case an act of the selfhood's will is that of an autonomous interdependent personality acting within a historical grouping of socially autonomous (i.e., self-reliant) personalities. In other words, the human person in the hierarchical order of nature is a sovereign independent person within a family of persons whereas in the historical order of culture he is an autonomous interdependent personality within a social grouping. The human person's soulful will harbors an innate inalienable fundamental finalizing immortal freedom whereas his selfhood's will harbors a supplemental ancillary conditional (i.e., contractual), alienable and mortal freedom.

Consider the individual who is a citizen of a country with a fully developed highway system. Fundamentally, the person is radically free by an inalienable intellectual freedom of choice inherent in the immortal soul to drive his car however he will on the open highway. Supplementally, the person is only contractually free to drive his car by an alienable freedom of self-control derivative of the culture of the country of which he is a citizen. By reason of his fundamental freedom he is conscionably and personally responsible for the operation of his vehicle. By reason of his supplemental freedom he is conscientiously and personalistically accountable for the operation of his vehicle. If he violates a culturally established highway regulation, he may be legally deprived of his self-serving freedom of self-control. However, his fundamental freedom of choice remains intact. It is a natural inviolable freedom and not a culturally contracted alienable freedom.

The fundamental/supplemental difference between these two freedoms becomes more apparent when one considers the adage that man is not made for work but, rather, the reverse: work is made for man. In other words, work is at the service of mankind. Mankind is fundamentally the human person who immortally transcends the historical horizon and worlds of his own laborious work. Yet, the human person supplementally cultivates his own personality through work undertaken within the horizontal order of his historical autonomous social self-fulfillment. His historical self-orientation is an evolving supplemental never-ending task whereas his transhistorical immortal destiny and ordination is a fundamental finality. Foolishly the human person may live to endlessly work but such a life-style does come to an end whereas the human person himself continues to immortally outlive this life-style.

St. John himself does not explicitly speak of the mystic's egological selfhood and subjective psychosomatic willfulness. Yet, he does especially speak of the human person's subjective need to self-control his own body's emotional sensitive feelings and mind's emotionless intimate bearings. Further, he does not take special pains to differentiate between what is inherently good-as-such in the hierarchical order of God's creation and what is an artificially fabricated artificial quasi good-as-such in the historical order of mankind's recreative worldliness. Yet, what he does have to say explicitly encompasses the mystic's psychosomatic selfhood and this selfhood's self-control of (i.e., possessive attachment to and dispossessive detachment from) its own emotional bodily feelings and emotionless mental bearings in the matter of temporal, natural, sensory, moral supernatural, and spiritual goods. Regarding this he sweepingly declares that every self-centered selfishly self-serving bodily righteous self-contentment (viz., exultation) and/or mental righteous self-containment (viz., validation) which detracts from God's objective and transcendent service, honor, and glory impedes the mystic's advancement to a perfect loving amicable union with God in contemplative prayer.

This impediment arises precisely because the mystic becomes selfishly self-attached to his own body's subjective selfishly self-possessive sensitive emotional feelings of righteous exultation and/or to his own mind's subjective intimate emotionless bearings of righteous vindication moreso than to the primacy of God's righteous holiness who transcends the very subjectivity of these experiences.

The gist of this sweeping and all-encompassing position advanced by St. John is that the mystic who becomes selfishly self-attached to God's gratuitously imparted spiritual graces and gifts, exalted emotional feelings and/or profound emotionless bearings exploits them for his own edification rather than for God's greater glory. It is one thing for a carpenter to take a satisfactory emotional feeling of contentment and to seek a just wage for himself in remuneration for his skillful workmanship; it is another thing for a mystic to take a satisfactory religious emotional feeling of selfish self-contentment in his own mystical prayerful experiences of God. The carpenter's self-contentment is the product of his own skillful craftsmanship whereas the mystic's mystical self-contentment gratuitously received from God is not a product of his own prayerful craftsmanship.

St. John's position in regard to both the carpenter and the mystic's self-centered emotional affectionate feeling of self-contentment is that if the same person is both a carpenter and a mystic, both's attitude of selfish self-centered affectionate contentment is not conducive to arriving at a perfect religious self-detached affectionate communion with God's Triune Godhead. Such selfish self-centeredness leads both the farmer and the mystic to an affectionate disregard for God who transcendentally exists beyond both's willful self-centered subjectivity.

The issue, then, of the will's need for purification addresses the will of the mystic's subjective willful self-possessive psychosomatic selfhood rather than the soul's intellectual will. The issue pivots on the following sweeping premise. The mystic who subjectively exploititatively uses his religious experience of God for his own selfish self-interest and self-aggrandizement exploititatively and basely makes use of God rather than sacrificially placing himself at God's service. On the other hand, the mystic who subjectively and prayerfully denies himself these bodily self-satisfying religious feelings and/or mental self-justifying religious bearings sacrificially serves and honors God selflessly. Such a mystic is not motivated to pray by some selfish self-serving bodily religious emotional stimulation or by some mental religious emotionless consolation. Rather, in the absence of such selfishly self-centered motivations, the mystic's prayer-life is prompted exclusively, sacrificially, and selflessly to prayerfully praise, honor, adore, worship, thank, and to petition God. Such a mystic's prayerful experience may be gratuitously rewarded with bodily feelings of stimulating exultation and mental bearings of profound serene sedation. Nonetheless, these stimulations and sedations are not the motivational proddings that prompt and sustain his prayer-life.

In brief, the only influential satisfying somatic feeling and justifying psychic bearing of righteous self-enjoyment---including the three other feelings and bearings mentioned by St. John of sorrow, hope, and fear---which the mystic is able to conscientiously entertain that is compatible with God's very own infinitely adorable holiness is a religious enjoyment motivated by Christ's very own Selfless charitable and agape love which sacrificially is devoid of every selfish self-serving consideration. Certainly, attaining this consummate stage of perfection and sacrificial self-immolation is impossible to the mystic on his own initiative and within his own subjective humanistic resources. But, what is impossible to man is possible to God. The mystic in the active stage of ascetic purification takes willful steps to ascetically deny himself his own selfish self-prompting inducements to pray. In the passive stage, the Holy Spirit completes this purification by withholding from the mystic every righteous somatically self-satisfying and/or psychically self-justifying prayerful enjoyment.

The mystic who does eventually attain to mystical union with God's Triune Godhead through contemplative prayer and who does experience subjectively ecstatic religious transports of divine bliss both within the sensitivity of the body's willful somatic emotional feelings and the intimacy of the mind's willful psychic emotionless bearings is no longer in willful self-control of these righteous rapturous self-contentments and self-containments. These enjoyments are neither motivationally self-induced nor self-educed for the selfish self-serving benefit of the mystic's own possessive willful somatic righteous self-satisfaction or willful psychic righteous self-justification. The mystic is no longer possessively selfishly self-attached to these religious feelings and bearings and committed to their self-control. These are exquisitely purely charitable feelings and bearings of love for God and the mystic's fellowman completely devoid of any and every taint of egocentric selfishness. They both originate and culminate in the Blessed Trinity. The very cultic selflessness of these mystical experiences is itself the mark of their superhumanizing Christianizing influence issuing from the Holy Spirit's exquisite docility and Christ's own exquisite meekness characteristic of His Selfless Sacred Heart.

The Catholic Christian mystic---like every disciple of Christ---is called to strive for God's very own divine perfection and holiness. St. John of the Cross outlines the active steps of an ascetic training in which a disciple may regiment and train himself in a program of mortification and self-denial preparatory to reaching a saintliness measured by God's own Holy Godliness. This program will reach its culmination when God Himself in the Person of the Holy Spirit takes over this program of purification. This self-mortification is spelled out in the Beatitudes beginning with "blessed are the poor in spirit." This beatitudinal spirit of poverty and self-denial under the Holy Spirit's docile influence must submissively and processively grip the very heart and the mind of the selfhood's somatically sensitized willfulness and willful psychic intimations to enable the mystic to become transformed into Christ's very own superhumanistic Personality of meekness, poverty, righteousness, mercy, purity, solicitude, and peace steeped in His redemptive beatitudinal messianic mindset.

In the process of this ascetic training, the mystic will succeed in attaining to a masterful Christian selfless self-control only by surrendering himself (i.e., a willful sacrificial commitment of self-dedication and conversion) and his own humanistic partisan have-attitude to Christ's beatitudinal Messianic non-partisan mindset. In so doing the mystic must resistantly contend with and forcibly (i.e., willfully) suppress those emotional feelings and emotionless bearings of his psychosomatic selfhood that are typical of the secular world's domineering will to possessively control and to safeguard at all costs the self-reliant security of its own socially selfish autonomous selfhood.

The reader should be reminded that while the selfhood's will is psychosomatic and is, accordingly, subject to its own inner dichotomous polarized tension, it is the human person in terms of his own personhood that is one and the same individual that exercises this psychosomatic willfulness. The selfhood has no substance nor essence of its own as is the case with the selfhood's body/soul substantive hylemorphic nature. It will be seen when this commentary advances to the "dark night" that this psychosomatic willfulness corresponds to the dark night of the sense in its somatic sensitivity and the dark night of the spirit in its psychic intimacy. These are two separate orders of purification each of which has its own peculiar characteristics and stringencies.

ASCENT, Book III, Chapters 16-45 THE PURIFICATION OF THE WILL THROUGH THE THEOLOGICAL VIRTUE OF CHARITY

Chapters 16-25: the mystic's enjoyment of temporal and natural goods.

In chapter 16, St. John first addresses the mystic's enjoyment of temporal goods relative to the enjoyment he owes to God's own glory and exultation. He identifies these temporal goods as riches, status, positions, awards, children, relatives, marriages, etc. He makes it clarion clear that the mystic---including the laity who are not religious nor members of the hierarchy---must not exploititatively seek a selfishly self-serving enjoyment in these goods. Doing so detracts from the prospect of having an entirely selfless mystical enjoyment of God redounding to God's glory and to the mystic's own honor of re-joicing in God honorably befitting God's own infinite Goodness.

He further adds a most wise insight regarding selfish self-centered enjoyment. It is blinding while self-centered selfish sadness disposes one to see properly. That is, a sensitized feeling or intimate bearing of self-centered enjoyment blinds the mystic to his real transi-ent historical misery, insecurity, finitude, and vulnerability vis-à-vis God whereas sadness makes him more aware of his temporal mortal condition and his need for God's protection and mercy. The upshot of selfishly enjoying temporal goods is that such enjoyment detracts from his being entirely at the service of God without regard to his own confining selfish self-interest.

The harm that befalls the mystic who fails through mortification and self-denial to become purified of his selfishness in the enjoyment of these temporal goods is his increasing alienation from God's friendship and love. This alienation is first of all, privative from which there ensues negative and positive alienations. This privative alienation from God has four degrees which become progressively worse. The first is that of backsliding in which one's subjective mindful willful attitude towards God becomes blunted and clouded regarding the ontological moral conscionable order of truthful reality itself transcendent to the mystic's own subjectivity.

The second degree stems from the first. There ensues a withdrawal from spiritual exercises and the religious and liturgical things of God. The individual becomes lukewarm. He becomes more selfishly self-conscientious regarding his own concupiscent enjoyments and personalized self-possessive interests and less attitudinally respectful of his moral conscience and his advancement in moral virtue and justice, especially the justice he dutifully owes to God. He becomes careless and tends to his spiritual exercises only by rote and mechanically and not piously and reverently.

The third degree is the complete abandonment of God. Here the individual allows himself to fall into mortal sins. He becomes a slave to the world's allurements and dead to his conscionable obligations to God. Such persons are notably greedy for the world's plaudits, pleasures, and self-centered securities. In their greed they are never fully satisfied. The more absorbed they become with the world's securities the less conscious they are of God's own blessings and their conscionable obligations toward him. They have become prisoners of their own selfish self-centered affections.

The fourth degree is that of idolatry. In the place of God the individual now unabashedly adores and worships the world's promises of comfort, ease, and social security. Here the individual is more a captive of his own avarice than any other vice. Money has become his passion. So much so are these individuals a slave to money which they idolize that many persons who suffer the loss of such wealth become prone to suicide.

St. John proceeds to indicate the benefits which abound to the mystic who denies himself a selfishly self-indulgent enjoyment of temporal goods. This ascetic self-detachment is a matter of the mystic modifying and changing his heartfelt willful self's overriding dominant attitude. This entails a metanoia conversion from a have-more possessive humanistic attitude to a dispossessive have-less attitude.

This dispossessive attitude is the attitude to have less possessively in the horizontal and subjective order of having in order to be more in the vertical and objective order of being. Unless one by a total commitment and self-surrender sacrificially foregoes his own selfish self-serving humanistic have-more self-control attitude in favor of Christ's superhumanistic selfless redemptive be-attitude (having less possessively in order to be more existentially), one remains enslaved within his own subjective self-controlled possessiveness.

It is in this self-sustained selfish self-control that a person finds his personalized self-guarantee of his own worldly autonomy and social security. This autonomous humanistic spirit is in direct polar opposition to Christ's Holy Spirit of sublime humility and submission to the Father's Holy Will. The more one's psychosomatic selfhood is selfishly self-controlled in its enjoyment of temporal goods the less it is masterfully dispossessed of its own selfishness and properly disposed in its own self-humanizing spirit to be submitted to the Mastery of Christ's own Holy Spirit of docility.

Hence, it is crucial that the mystic dispossess and detach himself from even the least selfishly self-indulged enjoyment of temporal goods. For, being unable to become so detached in very little things, it becomes even more difficult for him to become detached in larger things. The spiritual profit which the mystic acquires in this self-detachment is a self-humanizing beatitudinal mindset and spirit of largesse, generosity, and liberality that is Christ's very own Holy Spirit. Further, this liberality will be accompanied by a more open-minded access to the intellect's transcendent clarity of reasoning, the mind's very own rest & tranquility, a peaceful confidence and hope in God, and in the selfhood's will itself a fully conscientious authentic psychosomatic self-centered selfless enjoyment of God that consists of God's own beatitudinal bliss rather than the will's selfish self-serving enjoyment. St. John continues with a bevy of blessings which the reader may read in the actual text itself.

In the subsequent chapters our Carmelite Holy Father diligently and wisely examines the same topic of the will's psychosomatic autonomous sensitized emotional feeling of righteous self-contentment and intimate emotionless bearing of righteous self-containment in terms of the five remaining types of enjoyable goods: natural, sensory, moral, supernatural, and spiritual. By natural goods he means, beauty, grace, elegance, bodily health and similar bodily endowments. He includes also endowments in the soul such as common sense, discretion, sound judgment, etc. Here again, any selfish self-indulgent enjoyment of these goods detracts from the mystic's submissive selfless enjoyment of God's own joy. The person with physical beauty can become vain by enjoyably prizing this comeliness over and above God's own divine beauty. The mystic must seek to rejoice in the enjoyment of God through these natural goods and, thereby, detach himself from any selfish self-enjoyment deriving from these goods themselves.

It is notable that any inordinate selfish self-indulgence in the enjoyment of any of these six types of goods brings about the same harmful privative alienation from God by self-inducing within the mystic's own self-humanizing willful mindset and morale a spiritual lukewarmness regarding God. In addition, each separate type of selfish self-indulgent good induces its own selfish special harms further alienating the mystic from God. St. John stipulates that fornication is the special harm inflicted on the mystic's psychosomatic willfulness for the person who seeks his own self-centered selfish enjoyment in natural goods. He lists 6 principal types of such harm.

The first is vainglory, presumption, pride, and a disdain for one's neighbor. The second is a lustful sensuality. The third is a self-induced perception which is susceptible to flattery. The fourth impacts the intellect because one's self-absorbed domineering morale and dominant have-attitude of selfish self-indulgence prejudicially blinds the mystic's partisan selfhood from being submissive to the intellect's objective and impartial conscionable reasoning. The fifth is the mind's willful self-absorption in trivial amusements. The sixth is the eventual disgust and abhorrence of all things pertaining to God.

It is notable that here St. John mentions that the selfhood's willful self-cultivated domineering have-more attitudinal morale (i.e., humanistic spirit) becomes more absorbed and interested in the sensual satisfaction of the somatic body rather than with the insensate justification of the psychic mind. Instead of being recollected, it will be dissipated. The direct benefit that the mystic derives from a selfless self-detachment in regard to these natural goods is a humility regarding its own self-reliance and a self-sacrificing charitable regard toward others. One who fails to ascetically deny his own selfish selfhood ends up by fatally denying God's own primacy. Another important benefit is that the mortification of the sensuality peculiar to the senses brings considerable inner calm and recollection to the mind. In brief, self-detachment here brings about a release from the self-addictions that occasion temptations and trials, and an increase of prosperity in the practice of the moral virtues.

Sensory goods involve sensitized exciting emotional feelings of self-contentment. These are willfully self-induced through both the exterior special senses and the interior sense of imagination. Of course, St. John himself does not differentiate between objective sensible passionate enjoyments of the corporeal animal body which are the involuntary offshoot of appetitive instincts, on the one hand, and subjective sensual compassionate emotional feelings in the selfhood's self-humanized corpuscular body. These latter emotional feelings are willfully self-induced to motivationally stimulate and activate the corpuscular body to engage in some artificial productive exploitative manipulation. From the context of the *Ascent* and the description of the human person's selfish self-indulgent enjoyment of sensory goods, it seems clear that St. John has in mind the entirely subjective and motivationally self-induced and self-controlled sensuous sensitized emotional feelings occurring in the body's neurological somatic physiology which are only discernible through a self-conscious awareness.

Regarding these sensuous sensitized religious emotional feelings, St. John stipulates an overriding principle. In the mystic's mystical encounter with God through contemplative prayer in which God in God's Triune Godhead is holistically sacramentally supernaturally mystically present as mediated by Christ, this contemplative encounter transcends the reach of both the senses considered sensibly as faculties in the objective order of sensing and the senses considered sensually as functioning sensors in the subjective order of sensation. If these sensuous sensitized religious emotional feelings (which are entirely subjective and reflexively consciously experienced by the mystic) are not deliberately and decisively self-induced but merely the overflow from the soul's own objective spiritual exuberance, they are not under the mystic's self-control. In such a case, they provide for the mystic an additional motivational reverential inducement to prayerfully rejoice in God's own bliss over and above the soul's own volitional spiritual dutiful delight.

If, however, they are motivationally selfishly self-induced, they constitute an impediment to the mystic's perfect union with God. To insure that the mystic is neither confused nor confounded by these feelings of righteous contentment he postulates a principle of discrimination. Where the feelings are conducive to the mystic's self-aggrandizement, they are clearly self-induced. Where they increase the mystic's exultation in and prayerful enjoyment of God, they are instigated by God. Indeed, if the mystic himself experiences a hunger and a need for these sensual emotional feelings, he should detach himself from them. For, instead of this hunger liberating and freeing the mystic from his own religious selfish self-attachment, this hunger only binds his somatic will more securely to his own self-aggrandizement and self-satisfaction at the expense of God's own honor and glory.

The harm that this self-aggrandizement incurs to the mystic is manifold. In general it is a lukewarmness of spirit and a blindness toward what is conscionably upright transcendent to these comforting righteous feelings. Much harm is brought on through such self-indulgence. These are vanity, mental distraction, inordinate covetousness, indecency, interior and exterior lack of composure, impurity in thought, and envy. St. John further specifies the sins which these harms induce in the mystic who yields to selfish self-indulging in sensuous sensitized religious emotional feelings. The reader may read his specific account of these many sinful kinds of conduct which are the outcome of this selfish self-indulgence.

Chapter 26: The enjoyment of sensory goods.

In chapter 26 he proceeds to indicate the spiritual and temporal benefits which accrue to the mystic who is ascetically self-detached from these sensuous sensitizing righteous emotional feelings regarding sensory goods. The mystic regains a recollected composure toward God and is no longer dissipated through the miasma of his senses. When he retreats from the subjective self-humanized body's sensuality, emotionality, and sensational sensitivity he retreats inward within the mind's insensate, emotionless, and intimate sanctuary. Of course, this retreat remains confined to the mystic's psychic selfhood. For, to withdraw from the body's somaticity is to advance into the mind's psychicity. They are in polar opposition to each other. To have and become consciously ensconced in the one is to be deprived of the other.

But, St. John of the Cross does not explain contemplative prayer (which is an intellectual supernatural union with God in faith) in terms of the psychic selfhood's willful mental subconscious self-awareness. Contemplative prayer is entirely within the objective vertical order of God's existence. The psychic willful mental self is entirely within the subjective horizontal order of the mystic's resistant humanistic bodily self-cultivation. Contemplative prayer transcends the selfhood's mental psychicity as well as the selfhood's bodily somaticity. Hence, what St. John implicitly insinuates here is that the mystic must not only become unselfishly self-detached from the somatic self's selfish sensuous emotional bodily feelings but also from the psychic self's selfish insensate, emotionless mental bearings as well.

For, even though the psychic mental willful selfhood itself is not motivated through emotional, sensitized, sensational imaginary religious feelings, but by its own proper emotionless, insensate, inspirational thoughtful religious bearings, nonetheless these bearings are fashioned within the mystic's self-humanized body's subjectivity since the mind itself is non-functional if the brain is severely impaired. How so? Any severe concussion to the brain is sufficient to bring about a severe comatose loss of one's complete reflexive psychic self-awareness. St. John concludes this section by noting that the more the mystic in this life becomes unselfishly self-detached from both psychosomatic willfully self-induced and self-controlled exuberant righteous feelings and calming righteous bearings, the more increas-

ingly exquisite will be his own glorious reverential enjoyment and rejoicing in God's own bliss when he reaches heaven precisely because
he self-sacrificially surrendered himself to God through Christ's own
cross of crucifixion.

Chapter 27: The enjoyment of moral goods.

In chapter 27 St. John addresses moral goods and the religious
enjoyment that is proper to them. Moral goods include the four cardinal moral virtues of justice, prudence, chastity, and fortitude including each's proper activity. The works of mercy also are included
(which are corporal and spiritual), piety, civility, and good manners.
Moral goods are not serviceable goods which are somewhat quasi-
goods in the measure they profit the individual who avails himself of
their self-serving usage. Moral goods are inherently good-as-such
within the vertical order of the existence of nature transcendent to the
horizontal order of cultural resistance. The psychosomatic selfhood
that willfully and self-indulgently prides itself in having these moral
goods cannot objectively practice these moral virtues efficaciously.
Hence, if the subjective willful psychosomatic selfhood is to find
righteous enjoyment in these moral goods, it can only do so by willfully dispossessing itself of its own exploitative usage of them for its
own self-aggrandizement and security.

St. John goes so far as to extol non-Christians for not only practicing these moral virtues but also for priding themselves in these practices even without the benefit of supernatural grace afforded by the
Sacramental Church. Christians, on the other hand, should practice
these in the light of their faith in the supernatural order of directly
and self-submissively glorifying God alone. Hence, the Christian's
motive for the psychosomatic willful religious enjoyment of practicing these moral virtues must be paramountly to render service to
God and not to indulge in the selfish self-centered religious enjoyment of these practices. So much so is this service to God's transcendent glory important for the psychosomatic will's underlying motivation for its religious self-rejoicing in these moral virtues that if the
mystic fails in this regard by lacking complete selfless self-detachment from the religious self-satisfaction and self-justification in the

practice of these virtues, he thereby lacks the motivation of charity which characterizes all Christian love. Charity requires that the mystic be a companionable friend to Jesus committed be-attitudinally with Him in love to the same messianic mission which is the world's salvation.

St. John then proceeds in chapter 28 to enumerate seven kinds of harm which a selfish self-indulgent righteous enjoyment of these moral goods can incur. The first is vanity, pride, vainglory and presumption. Of course, this would be the case where the mystic is making use of objectively morally good conduct to willfully and selfishly aggrandize his own psychosomatic selfhood. One might protest that it is not possible to objectively be morally just and upright and subjectively gloat and brag over such conduct. But, certainly, this is possible because the very psychosomatic motivation which may induce one to willfully make possible such conduct as engaging in philanthropy by one who is very wealthy is precisely the public honor and esteem which will follow from such largesse when the donor's identity is made known.

The second is that one's psychosomatic self becomes prone to prejudging that his neighbor's activities are not as grandiose as his own. He, therefore, cultivates a disdain for them and an enhanced self-esteem for himself. The third harm is that the mystic now seeks his own selfish self-aggrandized righteous visceral satisfaction and cerebral justification through his own accomplishments. The fourth is that the mystic's reward will not be forthcoming from God. The mystic will have reaped his own reward. The fifth harm is the failure to advance in the perfection of holiness. The sixth is the lingering delusion that only the works which supply righteous self-satisfaction and self-justification are worthy works. Others are not. The seventh is that the self-indulgent perpetrator of these works becomes intractable to others and cannot follow prudent counsel.

Chapter 29: speaks of the benefits that derive from one's self-detachment from religiously self-indulging in these moral goods.

The first is an escape from the temptations and deceits of the devil. The second is a greater mental equipoise and conscionable balanced judgment in engaging in these good works. The third is that the mystic actually adopts more readily Christ's very own be-attitudinal mindset, humility, docility, and poverty of spirit. The fourth is that the mystic becomes more prudent in his work. The fifth is that the mystic becomes more pleasing to both God and his neighbor alike and is freed from a host of vices.

Chapter 30: The enjoyment of supernatural goods.

Chapter 30 addresses supernatural goods and the manner in which the mystic may subjectively rejoice in them. He gives a list of what these goods themselves are. They are goods which exceed the natural talents and faculties of man's own activities. These are wisdom and knowledge (i.e., the gifts of the Holy Spirit), special graces such as faith, healing, working miracles, prophecy, knowledge such as the discernment of spirits, interpretation of words, and the gift of tongues.

He makes an important distinction to differentiate between these supernatural goods and the subsequent spiritual goods to be later examined. Supernatural goods engage the mystic with selves other than his own self whereas the spiritual goods engage the mystic with God Himself and God, in turn, with the mystic alone. St. John further stipulates that these supernatural gifts provide two different benefits: temporal and spiritual. A temporal benefit is the physical healing made possible by the gift of miraculous healing, for example. A spiritual benefit redounds to the mystic's increased knowledge and love of God.

St. John sagaciously notes that the supernatural goods that provide merely temporal benefits need not be and are not necessarily subjectively motivated by charity (viz., an increased friendship with Christ). They are gifts freely given by God quite apart from the charitable worthiness of those who receive and exercise these gifts. Given, then, that they are not crucial to the selfhood's psychosomatic will becoming both in its own sensitivity and intimacy transformatively united with Christ's very own super-Self-humanized divinized sensitivity and intimacy, it follows that the recipient of these gifts may efficaciously exercise them even though lacking in Christ's very own utter Selflessness. Yet, if they are to benefit the operator of these gifts as well as the beneficiary who receives their miraculous results, the operator himself must charitably enjoy them without any selfish self-interest motivating this enjoyment.

There are three types of harms that the mystic incurs who without charitable joy exercises these supernatural gifts rendering miraculous temporal benefits. These are self-deception, a weakening of faith, and vanity. The element of self-deception enters because these paranormal temporal benefits could be effectuated by the devil and not by God. A lack of charitable religious enjoyment in exercising such a gift could cloud the issue of whether it is God or the devil that is effectuating the miracle. A selfish religious enjoyment other than an enjoyment motivated by charity prejudicially blinds the operator from judging impartially and disinterestedly regarding the source of the miracle and it also prompts the operator to impetuously exercise this supernatural power without a completely self-detached reservation. Further, if these are from the devil their operator finds himself performing the devil's work.

In the second harm it is theological faith itself which is weakened. When the operator fails in performing his miracles, others may lose faith in God. Additionally, by trusting more in these miracles than in the theological virtue of faith, the operator's own faith becomes weakened. Furthermore, God never works such miracles other than to promote faith when such miracles themselves seem to be the only avenue to awaken faith in others. The third and final harm is that of vanity. The operator of these miracles is susceptible to vanity if he rejoices in them apart from entertaining the selfless religious enjoyment proper to Christ's own Selfless charity.

Chapter 32 explains the two principal benefits which accrue to the mystic who has detached himself from every self-indulgent religious enjoyment when engaging in these supernatural gifts and graces. The first is the mystic's increased fervor and attention to praising and extolling God rather than seeking his own self-aggrandizement. The second follows from the first. By reason of praising God the mystic himself experiences within himself a greater divine religious exultation. The mystic comes by the first benefit precisely because of the sacrificial have-have/not polar opposition inherent in the person's own psychosomatic willful selfhood. To have a less selfish self-possessive religious enjoyment of God is tantamount to having a more selfless less self-possessive religious enjoyment of God. In view of this self-detached self-denial the mystic gains by having a more exultant religious experience of God that is purified and purged of all selfishness.

Now, this have-have/not polar opposition is not merely within the horizontal order of the person-hood's willful egocentric subjective psychosomatic selfhood. Assuredly, there is this polarity within the willful selfhood's psychosomatic egological subjectivity. Yet, the polar opposition here in terms of advancing in the self-centered religious enjoyment of God that is both fully objectively a spiritual soulful praise of God's own glory and simultaneously subjectively the mystic's willful selfhood experientially glorying and exulting in this praise of God's glory...this polar opposition is between the horizontal order of the mystic's self-conscious selfhood's subjectivity and the vertical objective order of the mystic's soulful intellectual cognizance and spiritual joy mediated through theological faith in God's Triune gracious sacramental presence.

In other words, the more the mystic is fully consciously and willfully absorbed in God existing in the vertical order of existence transcendent to the willful selfhood's own egocentric self-centered awareness in the horizontal order of resistance, the more the mystic's willful selfhood is itself ecstatically transported in its own religious experience of God beyond the subjectivity of its own selfhood to partake in Christ's very own Selfless superhumanized resurrected Bliss which is consonant with praising, adoring, and treasuring God's Triune Godhead befitting that Godhead's very own glorious divinity. Of course, this is tantamount to having arrived at the third stage of perfect union with God to which the mystic is wending is way in this pilgrimage up to the pinnacle of Mount Carmel. This present purgative stage of self-denial is a preparatory stage to advancing to this perfect union through contemplative prayer.

Ch. 33-45: The enjoyment of spiritual goods.

We reach St. John's exposition of the sixth and final type of good, the spiritual good, engaging the selfhood's religious self-enjoyment. This exposition extends from chapter 33 to the *Ascent*'s concluding chapter 45. Our Carmelite Holy Father notes at the very outset of this exposition that the mystic's hunger for religious sensitized sensuous emotional self-satisfaction frequently leaves neither space nor time for religious intimate insensate emotionless self-justification. Within the context of this entire ascetic purgative program pertaining to the will's religious self-enjoyment, it is being construed in this commentary that St. John does not explicitly here have in mind the radical difference between the sensory instinctive appetites and the intellectual will's spirituality in the objective vertical order of existence. Rather, he has in mind the difference in the subjective horizontal order of resistance between the selfhood's willful psychic emotionless and somatic emotional self-centered religious experiences.

Immediately St. John describes what is peculiar to spiritual goods. These are motivating influences that urgently facilitate the mystic's attentive conversion to God and, in turn, God's own communication to the mystic. He immediately divides them into delightful and painful motivations. And these, in turn, are further subdivided into those that are distinctly recognized and those that are vaguely recognized. He proposes to leave the examination of the painful motivations to his treatise, the *Dark Night*. In this present treatise of the *Ascent*, he proposes to tackle the delightful motivations that are clear and distinct.

It will become increasingly evident what constitutes the difference among clear and distinct spiritual delightfully motivating goods when St. John in subsequent chapters enumerates them and reviews each one in turn within its own ambiance and usage. St. John offers no examples to contrast the distinction he makes between clear and distinct spiritually motivating goods and ones that are vague. This distinction would seem to pinpoint the difference between meditative and contemplative prayer inasmuch as the former focuses on imagery and the latter transcends such imagery because of its purely intellectual approach to God. The mystic in contemplative prayer encounters

God in God's Triune Godhead in a vague and obtuse knowledge proper to theological faith.

This knowledge through faith and its ensuing subjective religious delight is vague and obtuse precisely because this encounter through theological faith is one in which God in the totality of His infinite divine Trinitarian Godhead's divine glory is sacramentally and supernaturally made manifest to the mystic. God's infinite glory is too august and majestically and infinitely splendid to allow the mystic to intellectually assimilate and digest in one gulp. Hence, this knowledge remains vague and indistinct because, again, the august splendor of God's infinite glory overwhelms the intellect's own natural medium of intelligibility.

Following this brief description and division of spiritual goods and the willful selfhood's self-centered religious enjoyment of them, mention is made of the mystical enjoyment which accrues to the mystic from the intellect and the memory. He refers the reader to the first two books of the *Ascent* in which these two faculties and their operations were meticulously examined including the proper approach the mystic should have in conducting his selfish self-indulgent religious enjoyment regarding their activity. This same purgative counsel of self-denial applicable to the intellect and will still holds here for the mystic in dealing with spiritual goods derivative of the intellect and memory.

In chapter 35 St. John further subdivides spiritual delightful goods into four types: motivating, provocative, directive, and perfective. The *Ascent* ends with his explicit examination of motivating and provocative types of spiritual goods. We may assume that the directive and perfective goods are taken up in the *Dark Night*. However, this need not be so since the latter treatise undertakes to explore the spiritual painful goods. Without further delay we may, along with our Carmelite Holy Father, address the motivating goods which are statues, paintings of saints, oratories (i.e., shrines) and ceremonies (i.e., paraliturgical exercises).

The reader of this commentary may refer to the actual text of the *Ascent* to appreciate to the full our Carmelite Holy Father's counsel to the mystic's religious self-centered religious enjoyment regarding sacramentals, paraliturgical celebrations, and homilies. What St. John finds disturbing is that many individuals are more self-attached to these sacramentals themselves than to the sublime transcendent reality toward which they are directed. These spiritual sacramentals, paraliturgical celebrations, and homilies (including homilists) can motivate the mystic to greater religious fervor, piety, zeal, and devotion toward God, the Sacramental Church, and the saints. Inasmuch as they do so, they are very beneficial for the mystic to advance to a greater love of God and a more perfect union with Him in the measure that the mystic does not idolize these sacramentals and devotions themselves precisely because of the self-centered religious somatic selfish satisfactions and psychic selfish justifications which they afford him.

Here ends, then, the *Ascent* rather abruptly. St. John immediately launches forth into the *Dark Night of the Soul*. The ascetic program of self-denial and self-detachment from the mystic's own selfish self-centered religious experience of self-satisfaction and self-justification will continue. However, the program will not be under the direct charge and willful control of the mystic himself. Rather, it will be undertaken on the part of the Father and Son's Holy Spirit abiding within the innermost inner nuclear recess of the mystic's subjective selfhood's own psychosomatic willfulness.

The task is for the mystic to yield and surrender to the Holy Spirit his own selfishly self-centered self-humanizing domineering spirit (i.e., self-assured self-humanizing morale) of self-control and self-reliance willfully dedicated to the service of his own partisan have-more attitudinal mindset. The mystic's willful self resists any self-surrender of its own willfulness. This resistance is entrenched in the original sin of the garden of Eden. While the sacrament of baptism removes this sin and replaces it with divine grace, the effects of this sin linger in one's selfhood which resistantly opposes relinquishing altogether its own self-centered self-secured partisan selfishness.

Both the *Ascent's* active and the *Dark Night's* passive phases of this initial period of purgation will reach their climax when the mystic's own self-humanized domineering spirit will be eventually successfully surrendered to the Holy Spirit's super-humanizing humility, meekness, and docility characteristic of Christ's very own Selfless Sacred Heart and Messianic redemptive mindset. This will usher in the second phase of the mystic's pilgrimage up the slope of Mount Carmel. This is the illuminative phase in which the mystic comes to appreciate more fully the wisdom of Christ' cross on which he has been ascetically suffering the dying and death of his own partisan selfish willful selfhood and experiencing its redemptive liberation and coming to birth into the sacramental life of Christ's very own Selfless Selfhood. This illuminative phase is most auspiciously delineated in *The Spiritual Canticle.*

ASCENT FIRST APPENDIX

The soul's intellectual will vs selfhood's will.

Up to this point in this commentary, the intellect and the memory have been the center of attention of the mystic's Gospel ascetic lifestyle (i.e., of self-denial). St. John of the Cross diligently proposes an active ascetical purification of intellectual and memorial activity preliminary to advancing to contemplative prayer and a perfect union with God's Trinitarian Godhead in faith and hope. We have noted with our Holy Carmelite Father that contemplative prayer entails an eclipse of the intellect's natural thinking to accommodate the supernatural light of glory illuminating its theological virtue of faith. We have also noted that an amnesiac blackout of the memory's actual remembrances is also incumbent on the mystic entering into contemplative prayer. We have taken considerable pains to expound the prowess and activity peculiar to both the intellect and the memory. It behooves us now to do the same regarding the will and to anticipate that the will, in turn, must suffer an austere curbing of its own volitions anticipating the mystic's advancement to contemplative prayer.

Previously we have emphasized that the San Juanistic account of mysticism must be examined in its cruciformity which means the height, width, and depth of the cross's very own cruciform configuration. Thus, height is the vertical hierarchical order, width is the horizontal historical order, and depth is the cruciform intersection of the cross's vertical beam with its horizontal beam, the intersection of history's ephemerality with hierarchy's eternality in an eschatological culmination of the historical in heaven, the New Jerusalem.

The vertical beam, as previously noted, engages the intellect as an innate faculty of the human soul while the horizontal beam engages the mind as an egocentric self-cultivated psychic functioning consciousness of the human personhood's selfhood. The intellect is entirely objective inasmuch as its intellectual activity engages all real and ideal reaches within the ontological universe of reality, God included. The psychic mind is entirely subjective inasmuch as the center of its egological attention is solipsistically its own notional fabrications and their concomitant willful motivations. We took considerable pains to emphasize that the substantive soul's intellect is not to be confused with the non-substantive self's egocentric psychic mind. The human person in its self-subsistent personhood both objectively thinks intellectually and is concomitantly reflectively aware of this thinking. In addition to this concomitant reflective awareness, the same personhood is able to subjectively, reflexively, and introspectively retreat within the very bosom of the mind's psychicity and become entirely (viz., hypnotically) oblivious to everything transcendent to this mindful egocentric concentrated self-absorption.

We also took considerable pains to emphasize that the substantive corporeal body's sensory faculties are not to be confused with the non-substantive self's somatic body's anatomical sensors. The human person, again, in its self-subsistent personhood both objectively sentiently senses and is concomitantly subjectively somatically aware of this sensing. Again, in addition to this concomitant reflective awareness, the same person is able to subjectively, reflexively, and extrospectively consciously retreat within the very viscera of the anatomical body's somaticity and become exclusively preoccupied and focused on one or another anatomical sector's mal/functioning to the exclusion of other sectors. Thus, there are two different orders of consciousness. One is a reflective consciousness concomitant with every cognitive and appetitive activity of the human person's in/corporeal substantive nature in the hierarchical order. The other is a self-reflexive egological consciousness in which the same personhood becomes self-absorbed within the subjectivity of its own selfhood in the historical order.

Thus, while the objective act of gazing at visible objects concomitantly includes a reflective consciousness that is not in the least egocentrically subjectively self-absorbed, there is a subjective act of reflexive consciousness focused entirely on the eye's own anatomy and sensitivity. This happens, for example, when one is deliberately winking or blinking one's eyelids, rubbing one's eyeball to relieve an irritation, or squinting to minimize the sun's glare or, again, to peer more intently at a minute object . This reflexive consciousness of the corpuscular (i.e., anatomical, physiological, biochemical) body's own somatic sensitivity is focused subjectively egocentrically and self-consciously on the eye's own anatomical functioning as an optical sensor moreso than as a faculty of seeing a visible object transcendent to this optical organism itself.

In other words, we have taken considerable pains to emphasize that vertically the human person's entirely objective innate substantive spontaneously energetic dynamic nature is co-constituted of a corporeal physical consubstantial material body and an immaterial consubstantial spiritual soul as one holistic compound substance. In this matter, the human person's self-subsistent personhood naturally and spontaneously acts dynamically and energetically through the faculties (viz., senses, instinctive appetites, intellect, and will) endemic to that intelligent and free nature. In turn, this same person's personhood in its self-cultivated self-subsistent personhood is subjectively in the horizontal order a polarized nonsubstantive egocentric awareness which is either consciously focused on the corpuscular body's somatic sensitivity and anatomical mal/functioning or subconsciously concentrating on the mind's psychic insensitivity and psychological mal/functioning.

In either case the person's self-subsistent personhood is subjectively aware of its own psychosomatic egological selfhood. Within this subjective and horizontal order of the human person's self-cultivated non-substantive egocentric selfhood there is only an inertial non-spontaneous synergism typical of a car which requires a battery's electric spark to ignite its engine. When this ignition occurs, the engine functions automatically on its own and will continue to do so until its fuel is consumed. If the fuel is not replenished it will no longer function.

Less this comparison of a personhood's egocentric selfhood with an automobile be considered an exaggeration, simply consider the case of a person with an irregular rhythmic heartbeat. An artificial electronic pacemaker can be delicately and surgically installed to monitor and to stimulate the heartbeat insuring that its beat be more rhythmically regular. Indeed, this electronic device makes it possible for an individual to consciously feel within the somatic body's own anatomy more secure and more self-assured of his own body's resiliency and physique. Indeed, this electronic device provides a personhood with a more secure automatic self-control of the body's anatomical mechanistic functioning. The upshot of this difference between the objective ontological order and the subjective ideological (i.e., phenomenological, epistemological) order is that the former operates spontaneously in virtue of its own innate energetic power (i.e., faculty) to act whether this be a cognitive activity of knowing or an appetitive activity of desiring.

The latter subjective egological self-cultivated selfhood functions or malfunctions only automatically and mechanically in its somatic bodily sensitized consciousness or autocratically and psychologically in its psychic mental nonsensitized subconsciousness. In either case, each's respective functioning, like the car's motor, requires a spark to ignite and/or control its functioning. In other words, a personhood's own selfhood can only synergistically function inasmuch as it is forcibly made and moved (i.e., sparked motivationally) to function in conjunction with concomitant factors.

Thus, while in the objective ontological order the substantive corporeal body's appetitive instinctive sensorial desires and the incorporeal soul's appetitve intellectual will operate spontaneously in view of the cognitive information presented by the senses and the intellect, it is simply the reverse in the subjective phenomenological order of the self-subsistent personhood's nonsubstantive somatic body and psychic mind's egocentric self-serving needs. The intellectual will is an appetitive drive to appropriate what is beneficial to the perfect completion toward which this drive is purposefully directed. A drive is always purposefully goal and end-directed. A drive is analogous to an agent that enjoys a power to act spontaneously. It differs from the agent itself in that the agent can spontaneously initiate an acitivity but of its own agency it can not purposefully direct that activity. This difference can be illustrated with a rider and a horse. The horse is the agent which enjoys the power to move about rapidly from place to place. The rider purposefully directs the horse to reach a preordained goal. A drive is a purposive agent whose purposeful goal is its power to spontaneously consummate, finalize, and bring closure to its activity. In other words, an appetitive drive is basically a love for what befits and is appropriately beneficial to that love. A drive and its purpose are homologous to each other. There is no drive without an intrinsic purpose and no purpose without a latent drive.

The intellectual will is just such an intelligent appetitive drive. That is, it is an informed drive, an informed purposeful love. This is also the case for the corporeal body's instinctive appetitive drives. However, these are not intelligently but only sentiently informed. On the other hand, the self-subsistent personhood's self-cultivated selfhood's own willfulness is not a spontaneous drive naturally in love with what purposefully completes and benefits its drive. Rather it is a self-serving need (i.e., a want, a deficiency, a lack, a wish) that purposelessly requires and demands for its own self-possessive serviceable use whatever supplementally serves to overcome its own lack and deficiency. The human person's willful selfhood is not an appetitive drive but a self-centered egological deficient need.

Consonant with this need the human person's selfhood willfully demands and artificially contrives to transform its deficient have-not need into a self-sufficient have-no-need. Hence, this need is immanently a self-centered self-love for what usably and purposelessly (i.e., self-servingly) functions to provide for the selfhood's autonomous (self-sustained) social security. It is not, therefore, a transcendental love for what is purposely and appropriately beneficially loveable for the selfhood's complete well-being. Rather, it is a truncated and transformative love whose very craving and deficient need artificially and craftily transforms its purposeless object of love into a useable self-serving convenience to offset its own social deficiency and lack of self-sufficiency.

In view of this very important differentiation, it must be appreciated that the selfhood's will functions synergistically. Briefly, it functions forcibly by being made to function. It does not function spontaneously. It is not a potent faculty but an impotent facilitator that functions to supplement its deficiency. The selfhood's will forces itself to function; that is, it makes itself function by prompting and prodding (i.e., motivating) itself to physiological bodily action or psychological mental inaction. The expression "make up your mind" confirms this. This synergism is typical of the car's engine which is a synchronization of gears and mechanisms that mesh together. A person's selfhood functions synergistically by artificially fabricating serviceable-products to supplement its own needs and deprivations. In the process of fabricating these services it synergistically fabricates its own skillful functioning and corrects its mal/functioning throughout the successful duration of this experimental process.

In view of this important distinction, the entirely objective substantive soul/body faculties operate naturally, energetically, spontaneously, and intransitively (i.e., non-productively) within the range of each's own proper competency. In this respect the intellectual will operates informatively under the intellect's input. On the other hand, the entirely subjective insubstantive selfhood's psychosomatic dys/functional will operates artificially, synergistically, influentially, transitively, and transformatively (i.e., productively). Whatever beneficial good the intellectual will purposefully loves exists independent and transcendent to that love itself. On the other hand, the selfhood's will first must "move itself" (i.e., motivate itself) to productively and artificially transform the object of its need into a self-serving convenience that offsets this need's own deficiency. That is, it must be forcibly and influentially motivated (i.e., activated) to overcome its own crippling inertial deficiency. It must artificially transform itself and artificially personalize itself into the role of a functioning self-starter motivated by whatever it requires to overcome its own inertia. This motivational influence may issue from its own self or even from a self other than its own self.

Either way, this motivational influence is a self-starter, a self-serving stimulus in the case of the somatic will and a self-serving palliative in the case of the psychic will. The somatic will is prone to productive action while the psychic will is prone to productive inaction. This proneness in each must be artificially prompted and primed to "move" from bodily inaction to action and from mental action to inaction. The somatic body must be sensationally and emotionally stimulated (i.e., moved to action) while the psychic mind must be inspirationally and emotionlessly sedated (i.e., moved to inaction). The body kinetically functions productively and with much forcible effort and exertion when it is in action. The mind inertly functions productively with little forcible effort and exertion when it is inactive.

The reason for this polarity between the body's kinesis and the mind's inertia is that the convenient serviceable functional product of the body is the fabrication of a facility (viz., a tool) to extend the body's own maneuverable mechanical self-control. On the other hand, the convenient serviceable functional product of the mind is the fabrication of a facility (viz., a symbol) to extend the mind's own manageable noetic self-control. The product (viz., the tool) of the body's functioning is both palpably external and proximate to the body's serviceable usage while the product (viz., the symbol) of the mind's functioning is both impalpably internal and remote to the mind's serviceable usage.

But, again, this motivational influence even in issuing from the human person's own selfhood is not energetically and spontaneously instigated. It is synergetically and influentially (i.e., forcibly) prompted. The deficient need as a lack is not a fundamental lack but a supplemental one. It is not a simple lack of food, sex, drugs, and attire which are fundamental goods and not merely supplemental quasi goods. Rather, it is a lack of the artificially required facilitating conveniences to effortlessly procure and possessively have these nutritional, sexual, drug, and clothing provisions as its very own self-sustaining possessions thereby guaranteeing its own self-contented autonomous social security. The basic natural drive to eat an apple to nurture the person's corporeal animal body is artificially supplemented by serviceably filling a need, for example, for a ladder or elongated pole to easily reach the apple in the tree. This need is a deficient lack and the artificial fabrication of a ladder or an extended stick is a self-serving implement that self-fulfills that need. Deers love apples but do not construct ladders precisely because they are not endowed with a self-subsistent human personhood's self-conscious awareness of its own deficiency. That is, they are not endowed with a self-serving willfulness to possessively have what is needed to supplement their deficiency to readily have the apples available to them.

This lack demands not a causal agency initiating the psychic self to mentally and thoughtfully design a ladder and subsequently the somatic self to handcraft its fabrication for future use. This lack demands an influential motivation that sparks the willful self to overcome its crippling lack and to supplementally artificially mentally design and handily fabricate working social services and tools supplementing this lack. Some selves never construct a ladder and never cultivate an advanced sophisticated society of social services and equipment. They continue to shimmy up the tree to harvest the apples. Other selves willfully cultivate such services to facilitate their lack of cooperative communication and tools to facilitate their lack of mechanical facilities.

Some social groups of persons advance in their self-cultivation and socialization in the measure that they become increasingly more synergistically sophisticated in the skillful mastery of their dys/functional psychosomatic selves as they become increasingly more functionally skillful the more successfully they artificially supplement their selfhood's social deficiencies by cultivating increasingly more intricately manageable bureaucratic communicable services maximizing human coordinationthrough speech and increasingly more complex maneuverable mechanisms that minimize the body's exertion and effort.

These useable services, again, are twofold. One is the service of symbols fabricated mentally by the psychic self and the other service is that of conveniences fabricated handily by the somatic self. The symbols facilitate the human person's remote managerial social self-control through communication of the psychic self's mental notions with other selves and the handcrafted facilities facilitate the same human person's proximate manipulative self-control through mechanisms suitable to the body's members. The mind's fabricated symbol is the telepathic medium of social communication whereas the body's fabricated tool is the empathic medium of social incorporation. There are, therefore, within the human person's personhood two separate wills, the antecedent objective intellectual will objectively proper to the human person's natural soul and the consequential will subjectively proper to the same personhood's psychosomatic deficient autonomous social self-subsistence.

The antecedent will is essential to the personhood's sovereign moral personal responsibility to govern the destination of its own freedom of choice regarding its immortal happiness which is common to the family of human persons. The consequential will is crucial to artificially providing for the same personhood's personalized amoral autonomous (i.e., self-sufficient) social security. The antecedent will is morally responsible for the personhood's personal "doings" freely elicited in view of its common family immortal good-as-such (happiness) while the consequential will is amorally and agreeably accountable (to itself and other selves) for the same personhood's personalized "making" itself free from the indigence of its own crippling deficiencies (i.e., needs).

Accordingly, the freedom peculiar to these two wills is inherently an equivocal freedom. That is, the freedom proper to the antecedent will is an inalienable freedom of independence and of choice to personally prioritize and govern its own means-end choices relative to its ultimate-end of happiness (i.e., the communal family immortal good-as-such). The freedom proper to the consequential will is an alienable freedom of self-control to personalistically take possessive charge over its own freedom to rid itself of its own social indigence, dependency, and deficiency (i.e., need) by artificially cultivating whatever services that cater to overcoming such indigence.

The former freedom is fundamental whereas the latter is supplemental. Furthermore, the former freedom engages volitions that are intentional and purposive. Why did you do this? A purpose is intended. It aims at something to be done in an intransitive operation that does not terminate in an artificial product distinct from the operation itself. The latter freedom engages volitions that are motivational and self-serving. What made you do this? A motivation is the influence which prompted the making of something. It explains what usage and service one expects from a transitive production resulting in an artificially fabricated product. Eating is not fundamentally a productive activity inasmuch as the beneficiary is the one who eats. Eating with a fork is supplementally a productive activity inasmuch as the one who eats does so with greater facility which the fork makes possible. Fabricating the fork historically precedes supplementally the service of using the fork. Yet, fundamentally, eating itself purposefully takes hierarchical precedence over the historical order of fabricating and using a fork to eat.

When the two freedoms respectively observe each's own proper fundamental-supplemental orders of priority, they complement each other. However, when the supplemental order willfully undermines, overrides, curtails, and substitutes itself for the fundamental order itself, there ensues a grave rebellious antimoral and antinomian disorder within a person's own personhood. This occurs when a personhood's possessive self-interest and self-attachment to its own dominating have-attitudinal selfish self-interest in the horizontal order prejudicially blinds the same personhood's attentiveness to its prior moral obligation in the vertical order to observe what is conscionably nobly and honestly upright and morally appropriate. The food that one eats, the apple for example, is inherently nutritional whether one eats it or not. The fork, on the other hand, is serviceably self-servingly useable (i.e., social) only if one first fabricates it to make it available and secondly if one actually makes use of it.

The apple is informatively a good-as-such independent of one appetizing it. The fork is a non-such-good which transformatively becomes a serviceable somewhat-good in the measure that it is usably fabricated and usably used. The apple is a family community good since it can actually benefit any member of the animal family (i.e., both brutes and humans) which would eat it quite apart from whether it is this or that family member that actually does eat it. The fork, on the other hand, is only beneficial to the one who actually possessively owns it and makes use of it as a social service (i.e., a self-serving product).

Is it possible for one to value a fork and to consider it more important than an apple? Certainly. It is possible to fabricate a fork in gold which is not made to facilitate eating but simply to serve as an award for a service rendered. The one receiving this award could cherish it not because it is fundamentally valuable in terms of its gold but because it supplementally commemorates, for example, the public recognition of a person's years of superb service as a chef. It is possible to possessively esteem what is merely a man-made non-suchgood artificial service over and above what is naturally and fundamentally a good-as-such.

In other words, this rebellious disorder occurs whenever in the horizontal order of having-more the willful self selfishly and possessively appropriates for its own selfish self-serving self-sufficient needs whatever it wills for its own self-control while ignoring altogether in the vertical order of being-more the intellectual will's duty to possess appropriately, judiciously, and conscionably whatever the human person wills to possesses. Thus, if by way of hypothesis the person owning the gold fork would refuse to let it be used to enable someone to eat who could not actually eat without its use, this denial would be because one's supplemental self-possessive love for having the fork completely ignores and overrides the more fundamental dutiful love of morally and conscionably respecting the basic appetitive drive for nourishment which sustains life. In other words, a human person's fundamental existence is inherently more important than any serviceable implement that supplementally assists in maintaining that person's existence.

The overriding difference between the meritorious love proper to the antecedent will and the sacrificial love proper to the consequential will follows. The intellectual will by its very informative nature is purposefully directed to possessively love what is conscionably (i.e. dutifully) appropriate to love to enable it to honestly reach its will's ultimate goal (viz., happiness), the immortal holistic good-as-such. The selfhood's will, on the other hand, by its very purposelessly self-serving orientation and self-transformative culture conscientiously (i.e., imperiously) demands to appropriate possessively for its own selfish self whatever it needs for its own selfhood's self-sufficiency. The former is a dutiful love for what the will is morally obligated to love. The latter is a sacrificial love for what the will must forcibly love above every other consideration to secure its own autonomous social self-sufficiency and self-control. The former is an act of choice which remains free to reverse itself even in the very act of choosing. The latter is a selfish self-serving decision that is forcibly and dominantly self-imposed. This very decision must sacrificially give up what is incompatible with its dominant selfish self-interest for self-control. For example, if one seeks to become the world's champion tennis player, he must sacrificially forego becoming the world's champion golfer; and vice versa.

St. John of the Cross's insistence in this section of the *Ascent* on the will's purification as a preliminary ascetic training preparatory to the mystic's advance to contemplative prayer most certainly engages the consequential will of the person's self-cultivated and self-humanized subjective selfhood and not the antecedent will proper to the person's soulful nature. The antecedent will's own volitions are conscionably judicious and upright when the mystic is united with God in contemplative prayer and, thereby, virtuously meritorious because of their dutiful obedience to what is noble and honestly good-as-such. There is no reason to curb such volitions. If they are not morally upright, there is every reason not to curb them but simply to confess them in the confessional and to abandon them rather than curbing them. On the other hand, the consequential will's volitions are selfishly self-centered and the person's selfhood is very liable to become selfishly and possessively self-attached to them. It is precisely this excessive self-attachment which must be curbed and curtailed.

The personhood's soulful intellectual will is superior to and superordinate to the body's instinctive sensorial appetites. That is, the body's instinctive appetites are hierarchically subordinate to the intellectual will's own volitions. The will does not dominate these carnal instincts. Rather, it subordinates them to its own volition as a brute animal is tamed and domesticated through discipline and sometimes even adopted as a pet.

It is quite otherwise with the personhood's self-centered and self-serving will. The selfhood's will is itself within its own selfhood dichotomously polarized into a psychic and somatic willfulness parallel to the egological polarized dichotomy prevailing within the personhood's own egological self-consciousness.

The selfhood's psychically dominating have-attitude willfully selfish self-serving partisan interests are in polar opposition to those of its somatic counterpart. This polar opposition within the person's very selfhood entails an insuperable sacrificial possessive have-have/not paradox that is peculiar to the person's subjective freedom of self-control. For if the self is possessively and dominantly in careful charge of its own psychically orientated self-interest, it must perforce forfeit, forgo, and subjugate its somatic self-interest to this psychic domination. And vice versa if the reverse is the case. To possessively have and commandeer the one psychic or somatic self-interest is to be sacrificially deprived of its polarized counterpart. Furthermore, the very artificially fabricated self-serving object of the will's psychosomatic self-fabrication and self-possession is not something which is an inherently valuable good-as-such. It is a paradoxical no-such-good apart from the selfhood's personalized possession and serviceable usage to overcome its own social lack and need of its own autonomous social security.

Any object of the intellectual will is inherently a good-as-such quite transcendent to and independent of the will actually loving and choosing to love it. It is simply the reverse with the selfhood's psychosomatic will. Whatever it willfully decides to possess for its own selfish self-serving usage is a no-such-good apart from the will's actual serviceable usage of it. It is this very self-serving usage that transforms the no-such-good into a loved and cherished object. In brief, whatever the intellectual will fundamentally loves is loved because it is inherently loveable whereas whatever the self's psychosomatic will supplementally loves is loved because it is serviceable. In the fundamental love, the will adds nothing of its own velleity to the beloved's lovability whereas in the supplemental love, it is the will's cherishing and prizing the beloved that makes it loveable.

Hence, both horns of the dilemma "do I love you because you are beautiful or are you beautiful because I love you" can be answered in the affirmative providing each is placed in its proper priority. The beauty that precedes love is a fundamental beauty inherent in reality transcendent to and independent of the lover. The beauty that succeeds love is a supplemental beauty which is bestowed and imparted by the lover's preferential affection for the object of its affection.

Both loves and both senses of beauty are compatible with each other when the fundamental takes precedence over the supplemental love fundamentally and when the supplemental takes precedence over the former supplementally. Thus, one fundamentally loves the rose flower because it is beautiful independent of such love and supplementally the same rose flower becomes increasingly beautiful because it is affectionately cherished and cared for by its owner in a special way. The fundamental love of the rose is naturally meritorious inasmuch as the lover naturally benefits from the rose's innate beauty. In the supplemental love in which the rose-lover cherishes and prefers the rose to all other flowers, it is the rose which benefits from this tender preferential cultivated care which sacrificially gives up all other flowers in attending to the rose.

Within this same vein it is well to also note that the intellectual will is informatively an intellectual will. It can only love what is intelligibly presented to it as truthful. In other words, it is impossible to love what it does not in a preliminary way informatively know to be truthfully such as it is. This informative knowledge is a conscionable moral practical knowledge because it presents to the will what informatively the will should practically will in any instance of its purposeful choices in order to be authentically true to its own innate freedom of choice in governing its own ultimate immortal destiny.

Again, it is entirely the reverse with the self's psychosomatic purposeless selfish self-serving will seeking its own sufficient managerial and/or exploitative self-control. In servicing its own need to possessively take charge and control to overcome its own autonomous self-deficiency, it must (i.e., it is imperative) that it transformatively functionally artificially fabricat whatever is necessary to supplementally over come its own social insecurity (i.e., lack of autonomy) and self-insufficiency. It must conscientiously provide for its own social security by transforming its deficient needy not-having self into a self-sufficient selfhood having-no-need. In the process, the willful self must skillfully function to artificially transform itself by productively making possessive use of its own serviceable products. In this manner it functions to self-cultivate and to self-humanize its own personality to transform its self-deficiency into a self-sufficiency.

Of course, this willful functioning (viz., making do) could just as well be dys/functional. And, indeed, this willful functioning is an exploratory, evolutionary, experimental process of trial and error in striving to conscientiously (i.e., wholeheartedly) contrive to transformatively fabricate whatever is necessary to facilitate its own social self-sufficiency (i.e., autonomy). Indeed, it remains dys/functional throughout this entire experimental process up until the moment it actually does succeed in transforming itself by successfully fabricating self-serving useable services and conveniences. When this occurs the self has skillfully succeeded in self-cultivating transformatively its own facilitating functional self-serving psychosomatic personality.

Again, the subjective selfhood's will is a psychosomatic will paralleling the egocentric self's psychosomatic egology.

Hence, it is a self-polarized impotent willfulness needing to be forcibly and influentially started (i.e., motivated) to overcome its own deficiency. The psychic self's motivational incentive differs from its somatic polarized counterpart. It is motivationally moved to inaction rather than to action. For it is in its own mental inaction that it is conscientiously in self-possessive charge and control of its pensive reflective self. It is otherwise for the somatic self's motivational incentive. In its turn, it is in its own bodily action that it is conscientiously in self-possessive charge and control of itself. The psychic willful self is bent on providing for its own autonomous self-contained justifiable pensive self-control whereas the somatic self, in its turn, is bent on providing for its own autonomous self-contented satisfactory robotic self-control.

In view of this dichotomous polarized difference the psychic self is motivated and prompted to transformatively self-cultivate its own impassive emotionless immobilized cogitative inaction. For, in the fabrication of its own self-serving symbols to telecommunicate through speech its mental notions, it is best served to remain serenely and hypnotically immobilized in its own subconscious introspective notional thoughtfulness. The somatic will, on the other hand, self-cultivates its own compassionate emotional activation and mobilization. For, in the fabrication of its own self-serving utilities to facilitate its body's functional maneuverability, it is best served when its bodily members are alertly and consciously mobilized. Just as the soul's intellectual will is a purposeful drive to will what transcends its own nature the selfhood's psychosomatic will is a purposeless selfish self-serving need to decisively artificially cultivate for its own immanent personalized partisan psychic and/or somatic advantage whatever is conducive to securing and insuring the control of its own autonomous immanent self-fulfilled psychic justifiable self-containment or somatic satisfactory self-contentment.

In other words, the human personhood's self-centered will finds that the psychic mind's notional fabrications and the somatic body's implemental fabrications are motivationally interesting not because they are actually inherently important (viz., good-as-such) in themselves but, rather, because they are serviceable (viz., non-such-goods) in ministering to the selfhood's psychosomatic need to become securely, autonomously socially fully self-reliant. The selfhood's psychosomatic will prizes and esteems these artificially cultivated services to be important for its own immanent partisan selfish self-serving self-sustainable self-fulfilling usage and advantage.

Let an example be given to immediately bring home this point more forcibly. The musician who composes a musical piece possessively prizes this composition as the product of his own musical genius. He is motivationally prompted to compose this score to exhibit his esthetic musical genius and to, therefore, justify profiting financially from it to provide for his own autonomous social security. The musical piece which is committed to some parchment to allow musicians to become familiar with it and to perform it is in itself actually no more important or worthwhile than the parchment on which it is written. If someone possessively treasures the musical piece as a musical masterpiece, its precise value issues from this appreciation itself which the human self's self-serving will appreciatively invests in the composition. In brief, it has no inherent value of its own apart from the partisan service which it renders in fulfilling a needful lack, want, and deficiency on the part of the self that self-servingly treasures it. What it supplies to the selfhood's lacking deficiency is a personalized experience of being esthetically amused and bemused when the musical score is performed.

In other words, the musical composition is valuable not because it exists on a parchment independent of this evaluation. It is valuable precisely because it is willfully possessively prized, cherished, and treasured by the self who initially willfully composed it and by the self who subsequently willfully is bemused and entertained with its charming melody.

Thus, its value is entirely subjectively a self-cultivated arbitrary worthwhile value owing to the human selfhood's own deficiency which possessively needs the service of such a cultivated item to supplementally fulfill its own deficiency. And, it becomes influentially increasingly valuable in the measure that more and more egocentric selves actually appreciatively possessively prize, cherish, and treasure it for the esthetic service it provides for their own social autonomous (i.e., self-sufficient) selfhood.

Of course, again, if the musical piece is an excellent specimen of its musical genre yielding a most satisfying musical emotional enjoyment, this is an added incentive motivating a self's will to possessively prize and treasure it all the more. It is not inherently a good-as-such benefiting anybody in a community that chooses to appropriate it. It is transiently a no-such-good which becomes socially an artificially cultivated useable and serviceable value in the measure that it serves to fulfill a needy deficiency which possessively values and treasures it to supplement this deficiency. A ripe apple in the first century BC was as inherently beneficial to anyone who ate it as is the case today for a ripe apple at the outset of the twenty-first century. A musical composition socially valued at this early period need not have any appreciable value today in the twenty-first century since this early music has become outmoded by later musical scores. Or it may have an antiquarian value all of its own to muscicologists.

Furthermore, just as the objective substantive corporeal body is endowed with its own organic sensory faculties, the senses, these in turn, have their own sensorial appetitive purposeful instinctive sensorial drives distinct from the will's intellectual appetitive drive. These sensorial instinctive drives are fourfold and purposefully directed toward the corporeal body's holistic well-being: food, sex, drugs, and attire. Food is for the body's nourishment, sex, for its procreation, drugs for its healthy vigor, and attire (viz., clothing) for its protection against the elements. These sensorial appetites manifest themselves in the corporeal body's locomobility. A brute animal body including the human sentient body moves from place to place, that is, walks, runs, crawls, etc., for the purpose of procuring its body's food, sex, drugs, and attire; that is, its nutriment, proliferation, vigor, and protection.

Supplementally within the somatic body's own anatomical physiology there are sensor organisms supporting these fundamental instinctive sensorial drives. This supplementality is similar to the optical sensor anatomical organisms supporting the faculty of sight and the auricular sensor anatomical organisms supporting the faculty of hearing. Over and above these sensor anatomical organisms there is within the intelligent animal which is the human person, other needed and required self-cultivated somatic supplemental supports to artificially service and facilitate the basic instinctive drives inherent objectively in the substantive body's corporeality. These supplemental self-cultivated supports are not present in brute animals. They have no egocentric subjectivity; they have no face which is the surface appearance of a subsurface self-possessive egocentric self-awareness (i.e., selfhood).

Were humans similar to brute animals and not needing self-cultivated artificial wherewithalls to supplement their substantive corporeal body's basic instinctive appetites, humans would never industriously busy themselves cultivating the many sophisticated tools, implements, machines, mechanisms, industries, businesses, etc. which further serve to artificially cultivate fields of agronomy, pharmacy, clothing, buildings, etc. supplementally supporting the substantive body's fundamental instinctive appetitive drives. It is one thing to walk through a field to pluck an ear of corn from the corn stalk to feed the body's instinctive appetitive drive for nutrition and quite another to artificially cultivate an agronomical system of growing and successfully farming corn.

This artificially self-cultivated needed supplemental somatic support is entirely willfully self-serving and subjectively self-centered. In that it is a supplemental self-serving need, it is itself purposeless. Hence, in its role as a supportive social serviceability, it serves the selfhood's willful need to functionally ingeniously devise and fabricate whatever may be deployed to supply for its deficient need. The field of corn cultivated by the farmer is more than a simple naturally nutritional good-as-such which in itself it inherently is. It is supplementally an artificially cultivated agronomic commodity which the farmer possessively needfully (i.e., self-servingly) treasures and prizes to support, safeguard, and foster his own agronomic enterprise and his family selfhood's autonomous economic social security. As a commodity, it is an artificial no-such-good until it is actually sold at market value and its financial worth and profitable gain is established.

The more artificially successfully cultivated is the abundant succulent, and nutritious yield of the farmer's corn crop, the more profitable is the farmer's own somatic self-satisfaction and self-contentment with his agronomical endeavor. Indeed, the farmer's motivational incentive to emotionally stir himself (i.e., his selfhood's somatic will) to toil with much effort to produce and harvest such a corn crop is precisely the profitable gain he anticipates to automatically (i.e., technically through the usage of hi-tech physiochemical products and mechanical equipment) fulfill his self-satisfying need to provide for himself and his family his own autonomous economic social security and the security of his agronomical enterprise. In the process of fulfilling this need, he productively (i.e., artificially) enlarges a good-as-such crop, the nutritional corn, which through further process shows up on someone's table as a breakfast cereal.

Paradoxically enough, the agribusiness of corn crop farming is both that of both growing a crop which is purposefully, fundamentally, inherently, nutritionally a natural good-as-such and supplementally, profitably, transitionally, and self-servingly an artificial no-such-good commodity which becomes serviceably good to the farmer who owns it and profits from it when it is sold in the futures market. The corn crop as a self-cultivated agronomical commodity is not inherently worthwhile other than in its social self-serving functional usability to supplement a self's needful deficiency.

That is, it is paradoxically serviceable in one respect and utterly non-serviceable in another respect. As a fundamental good-as-such it is a non-serviceable community vegetable which is inherently nourishable to any animal body which avails itself of its nutritional value by eating it. A kernel of corn itself is entitatively and essentially an embryonic corn stalk which left to its natural dynamism would develop and grow into a mature stalk with many more ears of corn. As a basic vegetable it naturally is nutritional to the animal body; not serviceably or usably so, however. For, even if it is never actually eaten it still remains nutritional. It is only useable and serviceable as an artificial commodity in the measure that it profitably satisfyingly fulfills the farmer's needful selfhood's self-demand for its own possessive self-assured autonomous economic social security for his family and his agronomical enterprise.

The selfhood's willful self-serving needs are never holistic as is the case with the substantive body's purposeful instinctive appetitive drives for food, sex, drugs, and attire. The ear of corn inherently, intransitively, and directly benefits the substantive body's entire substantive growth and homeostasis the instant it is eaten. It is a natural family community good-as-such for both the community of brute animals and the community of mankind, the intelligent animal. The corn crop as a social cultivated artificial no-such-good commodity does not directly benefit the farmer himself who farms it but only indirectly, transitively, and functionally inasmuch as the money it procures profitably safeguards and serviceably provides for the farmer's autonomous economic social security.

The corn crop as a self-cultivated agronomical commodity is not an inherent family community natural good-as-such but a social artificial transient no-such-good product apart from its actual possessive functional usability by the farmer who sells it for a monetary profit and subsequently by whoever purchases it to use as fodder for animals, food for humans, and/or fuel for automobiles. In other words, as

317

a commodity it is not naturally a family community good which holistically benefits not only the individual substantive animal body that consumes it for nourishment but holistically the entire community of bodies which is communitively stronger because this one body is holistically nourished with it. Instead, as a commodity it is a serviceable useable artificial no-such-good which socially benefits the self or selves that selfishly self-centeredly possessively owns and self-servingly profits from its exploitative usage.

Again , to amplify this account, consider the innate instinctive drive that the corporeal body has for food as a nourishment. The hand must mechanically move the food to the mouth. Utensils such as cutlery facilitate eating. Thus the human self has need (i.e., demands and requires) such cutlery to facilitate eating. Hence, cutlery is fabricated to supplementally facilitate this self-service of eating. But, what is useful in serving one type of food is not in serving another. Cutlery is important not because it is valuable quite independent of eating but precisely because it is a mechanical and technical tool to handily and skillfully facilitate transferring the food to one's mouth.

In other words, willfully devised subjective self-serving needs ordinarily supplement innate fundamental purposeful objective instinctive appetitive drives in the same way that art imitates nature and bring nature to a peak of perfection which nature on its own is unable to achieve. Similar to cutlery, there are a host of self-serving cooking utensils willfully and artificially devised to technically and mechanically facilitate the somatic self's bodily preparation of food to become both easier to digest and more palatable to one's taste. The important point here is the radical difference between the corporeal substantive body's objective natural appetitive instinctive facultative drive for nourishing food and its corresponding non-substantive anatomical body's egocentric subjective artificially self-cultivated willful needs for artificial utensils and recipes facilitating procuring, preparing, and seasoning the food for a more self-satisfying, self-contented, and self-fulfilling gustatory enjoyment and satiation.

Now, in the objective ontological order the substantive corporeal body's innate drives are spontaneously informatively stimulated by sensorial knowledge. These informative sensorial stimulations incite passions and affections instinctively mobilizing the body to some form of locomotion directed to the purpose of the drives themselves. Thus, the smell of food stimulates the body's autonomic hunger motor drive for nutrition. This stimulation is a passion and affection precisely because the corporeal body itself involuntarily undergoes a passionate movement which instinctively incites its autonomic motor mechanism to locally move toward the source of the odor in order to eat.

These passions and affections themselves are involuntary in the sense that they are not voluntarily aroused. Yet, they are subordinate to the intellectual will's own volitional governance of them. That is, the intellectual will does not evoke them but its innate freedom of choosing to directly govern the person's own personal communal holistic wellbeing endows the will's own intellectually informed volitions with a superordinate commanding governing power over the body's instinctive appetitive drives. Now, these appetitive passions are either concupiscible or irascible. The concupiscible passions purposefully and instinctively incite the pursuit of what is pleasant to the animal sensory appetite and the irascible passions purposely and instinctively incite the body to aggressively contend and to cope with whatever difficult obstacle impedes the concupiscible appetite's successful pursuit of what is pleasant. Hence, each complements the other in its own respective fundamental, supplemental priority. The concupiscible is fundamental and the irascible is supplemental.

The concupiscible passions are those of sensorial love for what is pleasantly good and hate for its opposite. Joy is the possession of this good and sorrow is the possession of its opposite. The pleasant attracts and the unpleasant repels. Hence, the two instinctive concupiscible autonomic bodily motor movements are those of passionately advancing toward what is pleasingly pleasant and retreating from what is painfully unpleasant. The irascible passions purposefully and instinctively contend with difficult obstacles impeding either the body's pursuit toward the pleasant or retreat from the unpleasant. Thus, the passion of anger instinctively moves the body to overcome the obstacle. When this contention is not successful there follows the passion of frustration along with the body's retreat from its original pursuit. The alternative passion of dread (or fear) occurs when what is unpleasant is present and the body instinctively seeks to retreat from it. When this escape is not possible there ensues the passion of despair.

Brute animals exhibit all of these passions and affections in their instinctive animal behavior. The human animal, unlike the brute animal, is intelligent and can intellectually grasp the purpose inherent in these passions and can, accordingly, through the intellect's intelligent volitional appetite subordinate these passions to the intellect's normative conscionable rule and governance. Since these passions are purposely ordered to the holistic (i.e., overall) well-being of an animal's life, brute animals of different species instinctively (i.e., passionately) behave purposely in view of the preservation and procreation of their own species. In the case of a human person's animality, these sensorial passions instinctively purposefully pursue the body's holistic overall well-being but neither to the detriment of the soul's well-being nor to the detriment of the person's overall (i.e., body/soul) holistic well-being. Hence, their spontaneous instinctivity is subject to being tamed and domesticated in a way similar to taming wild animals.

Of course, wild animals are not all equally susceptible to being tamed. The human person's animal body is inherently susceptible to such domestication precisely because it is hierarchically subordinate to the human soul's spiritual ascendancy. When these passions are reasonably (i.e., habitually) domesticated, they are brought under the sway of the soulful will's volition and the rule of the intellect's reasonable conscionable governance. Basically, the concupiscible passions require reasonable restraint in their taming because they are prone to excessively succumb to the pleasure afforded by food, drugs, sex, and attire. The irascible passions require reasonable bolstering in their respective taming because they are prone to retreat from engaging in difficult and threatening circumstances. Thus, the passion to eat is tamed and tempered by reasonable disciplined moderation whereas the passion of anger (coping with a difficult obstacle) is tamed by reasonably boosting up and bolstering the anger to strengthen its vigor to overcome obstinate obstacles.

When the tempering and boosting are reasonably based on the instinctive purpose of each passion their domestication becomes habitually the chronic behavior of these passions, the moral virtues of temperance and bravery are bred into the moral character of the will's freedom to habitually and readily choose to govern the behavior of these passions relative to what is conscionably beneficial to the body's holistic well-being with a view to the entire person's immortal holistic well-being (viz., common community good). Failing in this, the moral character of the will's freedom to intelligently govern these passions is weakened and becomes immorally vitiated with the result that the body's holistic well-being is jeopardized including the person's overall immortal holistic moral upright communal wellbeing. It cannot be sufficiently emphasized that these sensorial instinctive appetites are inherently purposeful drives for the body's overall well-being stimulating the body's autonomic nervous system to exercise a bodily movement toward the object of the instinctive drive.

Thus, the instinct for food is a purposeful drive to nourish the body; sex is a purposeful drive to procreatively renew the body's vitality in its offsprings; drugs is a purposeful drive for the body's healthy vigor; attire for the body's protection. These instinctive purposes are not themselves directed toward sensorial pleasure and away from pain. The purpose of one's appetitive instinctive drive for food is nutrition; it is not for the gustatory pleasure of eating or for the avoidance of the starvation pains from not eating. The gustatory pleasure is an ancillary incentive to eat but not itself the purpose of eating. Indeed, in the subjective phenomenological order this informatively ontological objective carnal pleasure (or pain) that is an ancillary surplus inducement supporting the instinctive sensorial drive's inherent purposeful objective...this carnal pleasure becomes transformatively the artificially self-cultivated motivating influence (viz., emotional compassionate feeling) compelling the selfhood's somatic will to engage in a supplementary functional action that fulfills its self-serving need for its own satiating sensual satisfaction in the matters of food, sex, drugs, and attire. This subjective emotional sensual compassionate feeling (i.e., of pleasure and/or pain) is itself not merely an objective sensible instinctive pleasure peculiar even to brute animals, it is a sensuously sensitized artificially self-cultivated emotional feeling of pleasure that resonates in the corpuscular body's somatic sensational sensitivity.

To appreciate this radical difference between an objective sentient passion of pleasure and its subjective compassionate emotional sensitized feeling, compare the enjoyment of a natural orange with that of an artificial orange-ade. The affected feeling of refreshing delicious pleasure afforded by the orange's juicy sweetness is derivative of the orange itself. The orange itself is actually refreshingly juicy and sweet. The orange-ade, on the contrary need not itself be actually sweet in its artificial concoction containing an artificial sweetener. Yet, it is experienced in the body's somaticity as exceedingly satisfyingly sweet principally because it is more convenient to portably carry with one's self a small packet of this orange-ade concoction to mix with water than it is a dozen oranges. The refreshment and pleasurable feeling of sweet satisfaction one experiences from the artificial orange-ade does not objectively derive from the ade itself but, rather, subjectively from one's symptomatic (i.e., phenomenological) experience of it.

Brute animals, for example, do not take any special artificial preparation of cooking or seasoning their food prior to eating it. They do not boil, bake, fry, or roast their food prior to consuming it. Neither do they season their food nor prepare gourmet meals by following sophisticated recipes. The art of cooking is entirely a self-cultivated self-humanizing skill motivated (viz., emotionally stimulated) by the selfhood's somatic willful need for its own self-serving sensuous sensitized satiated pleasurable satisfaction in consciously experiencing subjectively for its own self's satisfaction within its own body's personalized somaticity the enhanced purposeless self-serving pleasure afforded by food, sex, drugs, and attire.

The moral virtue of temperance in the objective ontological order cannot be practically developed unless a person actually eats and partakes of food. One is not temperate by completely abstaining and fasting from food nor by eating as a glutton would eat without any moderation or restraint. The moral virtue of temperance is practically developed in the very activity of eating moderately to consciably achieve the purpose of nourishing the body. This cannot be achieved without informative knowledgeable education to discipline the body's normal nutritional daily intake which varies with a person's development and growth. This moral discipline of temperance must be one of moderation since left to its own devices a person will eat only the foods which suit its own palate. Such a moderation affords a person a modicum of gustatory pleasure which affectively prompts one to eat as an added ancillary incentive to engage in eating for the purpose of nourishing the body and sustaining its homeostasis.

In the subjective phenomenological order of one's somatic skillfully self-cultivated self-serving conscious experiences regarding food, sex, drugs, and attire, there is no moral consideration nor conscionable discipline governing one's pleasurable sensuality, self-contentment, and sensitized emotional compassionate feelings. This moral practicality rules and governs the human person's innate sensorial instincts in the objective ontological order of nature but not the human person's self-humanized selfhood in the subjective phenomenological order of culture. The self's willful somatic insatiable need for and procurement of sensuous sensitized satisfying enjoyable experiences in the matter of food, sex, drugs, and attire is never-ending precisely because it is a purposeless entirely self-serving need to procure for itself and to have its own autonomous social self-sufficiency.

Indeed, it is precisely the conscious experiential awareness of emotional feelings of sensitized sensual pleasures that motivates the will to forcibly engage in an action that procures these pleasures for its own personalized satisfying and gratifying self-contentment. These sensitized sensuous feelings are so emotionally (i.e., motivationally) compelling and sensitizingly stimulating that the self's somatic will can only control them by a training that demands and requires that they be resistantly repressed altogether. Otherwise, the will becomes addictively self-attached to them and cannot resist their emotional influential compulsion.

In resisting them the subjective self's somatic will must (it is imperative) forcibly resist making unrestricted use of the artificial conveniences that elicit these sensitized sensuous emotional pleasures. This means in the matter of attire a modest attire, in the matter of food a basic fare and periodic fasting, in the matter of drugs health-directed pharmaceuticals, and in the matter of sex a firm resolution to sacrificially resist at times strong sexual emotional impulses in marriage, and to accept periodical abstention reserved for a covenant marriage.

Whereas in the objective order moral virtue is acquired by a practical informative discipline of following a middle modicum between immoral extremes, in the subjective amoral order proper self-control is acquired by a transformative skillful ascetical training of abstemious mortification and self-denial that proceeds from a stage of apprenticeship to that of self-mastery. In the process of acquiring this masterful self-control, the somatic will must resistantly repress its emotional impulses by denying to itself its own self-indulgence in entertaining the sensational imagery inciting these emotional feelings and in refusing to make use of the self-devised conveniences which cater to these sensuous pleasures.

The intellectual will objectively domesticates the passions intelligently by normatively and conscionably subordinating them to the holistic purpose proper to the human person's holistic communal family immortal well-being. When this moral order is habitually inculcated by discipline into a person's lifestyle this person becomes morally temperate and brave in all the body's concupiscible and irascible passions and affections for food, sex, drugs, and attire. Otherwise a person becomes passionately and excitably immorally intemperate and cowardly regarding his instinctive craving for food, sex, drugs, and attire. Of course, being temperate in food means moderation, in sex it means chastity, in drugs it means sobriety and in attire it means modesty. Concomitantly in all of these it also means the courage to cope with difficult obstacles and serious temptations to conduct one's life conscionably.

One is morally chaste outside of marriage by refraining completely not only from heterosexual intercourse but also from any sexual engagement including entertaining sexual fantasies. Within marriage one is chaste by restricting one's heterosexual intercourse to one's own spouse and by practicing periodic continence and respecting one's procreative faculty's openness to its life-giving power. One is morally sober in regards to all forms of drugs when the drug itself apart from impending death is not allowed to impair the intellect's sound reasoning. One is morally temperate in one's attire when one dresses modestly and comports one's self not to alluringly incite the sexual appetite of others.

It should also be pointed out that one's moral conscience includes both an objective intellectual cognizance of the practical truth-as-such of one's voluntary conduct (i.e., what the will ought purposely to choose in governing its own choices) as well as one's subjective awareness of the obligation inherent in this practical judgment. That is, conscience is both fundamentally and informatively objectively truthfully cognitive as well as concomitantly conscious. The person's personhood is both cognizant objectively of the moral obligations inherent in its intellectual will's freedom and aware of these moral obligations. This awareness is not egocentrically self-reflexive, however. It is merely a concomitant awareness. Yet, this awareness has a subjective overtone precisely because the personhood in the subjectivity of its egocentric selfhood is not completely divorced from the person's objective moral obligations.

Now, let us focus on the human body's self-humanized and self-cultivated entirely subjective nonsubstantive materialized somaticity. This is not a fundamental but a supplemental order. The somatic body is not the substantive fundamental corporeal holistic body that exists transcendent to one's experience of it. This somatic body resists one's personalized experiential conscious feeling of its sensitivity. This somatic body is not endowed with tangible properties but only with tactual sensations. It harbors no purposeful innate instinctive faculty drives. Rather, it harbors only self-serving self-cultivated demanding needful proclivities and propensities (i.e., deficiencies). For example, the proclivity to run fast rather than to merely walk is self-served by the artificial skill of taming and riding a horse.

Now, the personhood's "self" like the "ego" is not an entity. It is a pronominal reference to the human person's self-subsistent personhood taking personalized possessive charge and control of its own self-serving freedom. It is not the "self" that has needs; it is the human person's self-subsistent personhood that subjectively culturally willfully fabricates for itself civilizing self-serving useable conveniences to accommodate and transform its have-not needful deficiencies into a have-no-need social self-sufficiency. The human person's willful selfhood is psychosomatic paralleling his objective hylemorphic nature's body/soul constitution.. This willful selfhood is entirely a supplemental self-serving needful impotent propensity (i.e., deficiency). This willful self is not endowed with innate fundamental energetic faculties that operate spontaneously as is the case for the personhood's objective substantive body/soul dynamic nature. This willful self is the self-subsistent personhood's unskilled synergistic psychosomatic deficient needful impotent proclivity and propensity to willfully (i.e., self-centeredly) acquire what it possessively lacks to insure its own social self-sufficiency and self-reliance.

Indeed, this needful lack becomes transformatively and experimentally a skillful function in the process of successfully producing, fabricating, and cultivating useable conveniences to facilitate its autonomous own social self-sufficiency. In the case of the somatic self, it handily cultivates bodily implements (i.e., tools) and mechanisms facilitating the body's automatic social competent self-manipulation. In the case of the psychic self, it ideationally cultivates mental terms (i.e., symbols) and bureaucracies facilitating the mind's autocratic social communicative self-management. This psychosomatic synergistic willful selfhood functions experimentally to become expertly and masterfully adept in cultivating and making use of serviceable conveniences to successfully procure for itself its own autonomous social security.

Thus, returning to the natural instinctive drive for food, the need to forage for food and to prepare food for digestion, etc., spawns the artificial making of tools for hunting, cultivating, and serving food, etc. These tools, in turn, artificially enlarge the somatic body's own mechanical and technical self-manipulative control of its own self-competency to conveniently and satisfactorily nourish itself. Eating is natural but eating with a fork or chopsticks is artificially conventional. Such utensils facilitate the artificial process of eating and supplement the self's need to self-servingly cultivate such technical specialized artificial functioning skills as the hunter, the cook, the waiter, the butcher, the farmer, the grocer, etc., which are all supplemental technical skillful functions serving the substantive corporeal body's basic appetitive instinctive drive to eat for the purpose of nourishing the body.

The major difference between what is simply artificial and what is a more sophisticated cultural willful need is the degree of self-sufficiency and self-reliance that is peculiar to each. A spoon still requires the body's handy skillful utilization of it. Etiquette requires not merely the spoon's simple utilization but a style of usage which comports with a conventionally adopted manner of eating. An automobile, on the other hand not merely artificially supplements and supports the human body's spontaneous mobility as is the case with a cane or an artificial leg, it completely substitutes for this spontaneous mobility by allowing the rider in a car to be locally conveyed from place to place without even engaging the body's own natural mobility. The human body remains stationary while the car is automatically and robotically moving along from place to place.

Now, where the substantive corporeal body in the objective order is instinctively aroused by affective passions to move about from place to place to fetch food, for example, the non-substantive corpuscular somatic body in the subjective order is compassionately (i.e., emotionally) spurred and willfully self-motivationally stimulated and excited to both artificially fabricate and artfully deploy conveniences to both facilitate fetching food and preparing it tastefully to insure that it will provide the maximum gustatory self-satisfying pleasure and nutritional satiation. These artificially self-induced stimulations are sensitized feelings of emotional compassions pertaining not only to food, but also to sex, drugs, and attire. It is very important for the reader of this commentary to appreciate to the full that these emotional compassionate feelings are entirely subjective and self-consciously willfully artificially self-induced. They are not spontaneous involuntary concupiscent animal affections of hunger existing objectively in the corporeal body's instinctive passionate purposive drive for nourishing food. They are willfully and consciously self-cultivated and entirely self-serving physiological stimuli to motivate the personhood's self-controlled willfulness to become kinetically active in fabricating conveniences to cater to the somatic body's need for competent self-controlled and self-satisfying self-manipulation.

The selfhood's (i.e., personhood's) own self-cultivated self-humanizing willful need is itself an impotent have-not deficiency in the horizontal order of having. It is a willful need to possessively have and acquire what it does not innately possess. This willful need is not an instinctive faculty drive for food, for example, in the vertical order of being that is innately able to spontaneously and autonomically activate the corporeal body's mobility to walk in search for food. This willful self, on the contrary, must be forcibly motivated, influenced, and induced by an emotional impetus to engage in a productive action to facilitate its autonomous masterful self-control over its own bodily manipulation. This emotional impetus entails a synergistic coordinated productive skillful functioning not only within its own intrapersonal selfhood but also interpersonally in conjunction with other selves.

Again, in the subjective order of willful consciousness, the impetus of the self-induced emotion kinetically activates the personhood's own willful inertial selfhood to forcibly make itself (i.e., motivationally move itself) to supplementally skillfully improve its own body's anatomical automatic manipulation. Thus, it is more self-gratifying and skillfully productive in planting and growing a crop of corn to artificially cultivate the soil by shoveling than it is to dig the soil with one's bare hands. Hence, the step of artificially fabricating a shovel antecedent to planting and eating a crop of harvested corn seems more fundamental than the act itself of planting the corn and eating it. Indeed, it is historically and supplementally self-servingly prior in time to the actual planting and eating of the corn. But it is not fundamentally prior in purpose in the proper order prevailing between the subjective supplemental and objective fundamental orders themselves. For, the subjective order's purposeless artificial willful self-serving needs, self-facilitation and self-produced facilities are supplemental to the objective order's fundamental purposeful instinctive drives. The corn naturally recycles its own nature fundamentally prior to the farmer's supplemental cultivation of it. But, in the enterprising functional synergistic process of artificially self-cultivating self-serving artificial useable conveniences to cultivate the corn, it happens that this subjective self-serving order of culture which is supplemental to the purposive objective order of nature can succeed in willfully completely substituting its own cultural supplemental priority for the fundamental priority proper to nature itself.

This occurs, for example, when a paraplegic's legs no longer anatomically and physiologically function. Certainly, the faculty to walk is unquestionably impaired by this dysfunctional breakdown. But the faculty itself is not completely extirpated. One retains, for example, the faculty of sight even when the anatomical functions of the organisms of sight completely malfunction. Otherwise, there would be no meaning to saying that someone is blind. Being blind entails the inoperative exercise of a faculty which one continues to have even when its physiological function is impaired. In the case of the paraplegic, a wheelchair or a mobilized motor-vehicle not merely supplements for the fundamental faculty of walking but completely substitutes for it altogether. Not all such amoral substitutions, however, can be morally warranted.

For example, in the instance of the heterosexual faculty of sex. The actual bodily seminal movement of heterosexual intercourse between marital spouses cannot be artificially substituted for by a process of artificial insemination. The normal copulative insemination effectuated in marriage results in the conception of nascent human life in the female heterosexual organism. This normal insemination may be technically artificially facilitated in the amoral horizontal order of subjectivity thereby dispensing completely with the normal connubial act of copulation. This is technically feasible in the supplemental order but it is not morally warranted considered from the fundamental objective vertical order of nature. The reason for this is that the conjugal act is not exclusively and reductively an egocentrically self-serving productive facilitating function serving and servicing one's own subjective willful selfhood. Its objective innate purpose transcends the subjective order's utilitarian and pragmatic sense of technical self-serving sexual facilitation and autonomous manipulative self-control and self-gratification.

In the case of heterosexual marital conjugal acts, these are not merely a technical robotic function of each spouse's respective somatic body's anatomic sexuality automatically facilitating venereal self-contentment. Rather, it is fundamentally the complementary hetero-sexual organic procreative faculty itself which is mutually engaged between the husband and wife in the act of marital intercourse. Hence, heterosexual intercourse is not reducible to the transitive supplemental function of mechanically (i.e., automatically) and anatomically bonding the seminal sperm/ovum bodies together but, moreso, fundamentally in the intransitive procreative act of engendering new life. The seminal bonding along with the functional self-cultivated artificial implemental skills facilitating this bonding cannot completely substitute for the fundamental connubial marital embrace itself. This reciprocal marital connubial act of copulation is and remains fundamentally and primarily a dynamic procreative activity of the human person's intrinsic heterosexual nature and heterosexual faculty of procreation. The offspring's lifelong existence conceived of this marital copulation is both sovereignly initiated and educationally consummated in that marital heterosexual communal family embrace which is and remains its sovereign parental source and authority for the offspring's birth, nurture, and education throughout the entire life of the offspring. For, the offspring of this conjugal procreative union is itself a person distinct from the parents themselves and not merely a self-serving utilitarian serviceable exploitable commodity (i.e., a byproduct of a synergistic process of reproduction).

This offspring remains immanently within the physical and moral authority of both parents as the fruit of their parentage in their conjugal union as "one marital body." The very purpose of the heterosexual drive proper to each human spouse is to physically join two distinct heterosexual spouses into one physical bodily communal family embrace preparatory to engendering one (or more) offspring whose life is germinated from the intercourse of this sexual fusion. The substantive spousal bodies in the objective order engaged in conjugal union transcend the somatic anatomical body's nonsubstantive subjective order of serviceable anatomical functions. It cannot be sufficiently emphasized that whereas in the objective order the instinctive appetitive heterosexual drives are purposefully directed toward procreation and not concupiscently toward the passion of venereal pleasure. On the other hand, in the subjective order the deliberately self-induced emotional compassions of sensitizing venereal excitement and sexual stimulation serve motivationally to urgently influence and compel the human person's egocentric inertial willful self to kinetically become bodily engaged in a self-serving sexual intercourse culminating in the personalized experience of venereal pleasure and self-contentment. The experience of this venereal pleasure need not be reciprocated between the spouses no more so than is the actual experience of conception experienced by both spouses. Yet, even if it is not, the unitive element of reciprocal willful sacrificial marital self-surrender of each spouse's own somatic anatomical sexual function and sensitivity submitted to the service of the other self makes possible a mutually empathic emotional feeling of self-fulfilled self-contentment. The cook who prepares a meal feels empathically the contentment of those who eat and relish the food carefully prepared for their enjoyment.

Objective procreative instinctive sexual passions and affections are inherently communal and are purposefully holistically beneficial for the bodily replication of both the heterosexual partners themselves and, additionally, holistically beneficial for the entire family of individuals in whatever kingdom it is whose heterosexual corporeal bodies engage in sexual intercourse. After all, every species of animal is strengthened by the increase and prolongation of the members of that species. This, certainly, includes the family of human beings. By contrast, artificially self-controlled and subjectively contracepted self-induced self-humanized emotional venereal compassions (i.e., excitations and stimulations) along with the artificial prophylactics and pornographic images that heighten these artificially self-induced venereal emotional feelings...these sterile lifeless self-induced stimulating venereal emotional compassions are socially infectious. Just as a person crying empathically elicits sympathy from others and just as tear-gas induces tears in those who are exposed to it, artificially self-controlled selfishly self-centered contracepted venereal excitations along with the contraceptive devices and pornographic images that induce them provoke empathically in other selves similar selfishly self-centered venereal sensual stimulating sensitivities.

The radical disparity between the objective substantive corporeal body's natural intransitive dynamic operative procreative vitality versus the subjective insubstantive corpuscular somatic anatomical body's transitive functional artificially (i.e., contracepted) controlled facilitating synergism is starkly made manifest in differentiating between heterosexual intercourse in marriage open to life and asexual contracepted intercourse whose very procreative vitality is artificially stymied. There is one faculty of sight and hearing and smelling and touching but two separate anatomical functioning organisms proper to each of these faculties. When the faculty of sight sees the apple on the tree branch, it does not see two separate apples viewed by each separate optical organ, it sees but one apple.

Similarly, there is but one heterosexual faculty of sex but two separate complementary male/female anatomical organisms. In the objective order the faculty of sex is fundamentally procreative and in the subjective order the anatomical functioning organisms supplementally facilitate the coition which is integral to the heterosexual marital act of procreation. These anatomical organisms are quasi-productive fe/male functions of germination and insemination requiring the anatomical fusion of husband and wife in the marital embrace. These are supplemental and not fundamental to the marital act. For, in the menstrual cycle of the woman's organic germination she is not continuously fertile. Yet, the marital act remains fundamentally and essentially a procreative act and supplementally a unitive act of mutual volunteer serviceable self-donation even when the act is consummated outside of the period of the woman's fertility.

In the fundamental analysis, it is not the faculty of sight that sees, it is the underlying person that sees through the faculty of sight. The optical organisms themselves do not see at all, they merely facilitate the act of seeing analogous to the lens of one's binoculars or camera which facilitates the act of seeing by artificially visualizing the object seen. Binoculars and cameras themselves do not see but they do improve the visualization of what the faculty of sight actually sees. Similarly, it is not the heterosexual faculty of sex that procreates; it is the underlying person that procreates. And, in the case of human heterosexuality, it is a parental person of opposite complementary facultative authority that procreates the offspring. The heterosexual faculty is not reducible to the biological organs of sex no more than is the faculty of sight reducible to the anatomy of the optical organs. One may lose one eyeball and still have the faculty of sight. One may suffer the loss of both optical organs and still have the faculty of sight which remains blind because of the anatomical impediment. The faculty of sight is not reducible to the organs albeit sight's need for the proper functioning of the organs facilitating the act of seeing.

In the case of the human heterosexual faculty of procreation, both progenitors must concur in their marital embrace that they are not merely embracing anatomically but mutually voluntarily and personally thereby mutually authorizing that their procreative marital embrace is inherently open to the potential offspring which is its vital objective purpose and fruition. This reciprocal authoritative self-surrender is imperative not only for the conception and birth of their offspring but also for its subsequent rearing and upbringing. Asexual (i.e., homosexual) intercourse which is a purely anatomical intercourse of same-sex couples is today in our contemporary age permissively very prevalent in society. Indeed, it is lauded as an alternative lifestyle to marital heterosexual intercourse. But even heterosexual intercourse in marriage becomes asexual when it is implemented by artificial contraception whatever be the artificial method of inhibiting the intercourse itself from normally fulfilling the procreative purpose of sexuality itself.

By engaging in this artificially controlled asexual intercourse in marriage, heterosexual spouses are living a life which is commensurate with homosexuality. For, both the overriding self-serving have-attitude and the underlying motive of venereal self-satisfaction inherent in asexual intercourse (i.e., contracepted intercourse) are geared to engaging exclusively in the subjective experience of the somatic body's venereal pleasure completely supplanting and culturally substituting for the natural procreative vitality proper to heterosexual intercourse itself. This asexual activity is exclusively socially selfishly self-centered and confined to the social horizontal order of having. It is inimical to the vertical transcendent family order of the common-good of the community of mankind. It is rooted in a contraceptive mentality and dominant self-serving have-attitude which self-righteously and egocentrically esteems and values its own entirely subjective ego-centric self-controlled autonomy over every other consideration. It impugns the dignity and decency of the human person's transcendent sovereignty and rebelliously resistantly undermines the moral order itself whose foundation is the objective metaphysical order of reality and existence.

This artificially self-controlled sterile sexuality pursued exclus-ively for one's own selfish venereal sensual self-satisfaction inhibits the somatic selfhood's willful need for genuine self-fulfillment by emotionally forcing it to urgently and automatically succumb to its own selfish self-serving satisfaction to the exclusion and detriment of its own authenticated integrity. In brief, it makes its user addictively a prisoner of its own venereal lusts. The mere convenient availability of any artificial contraceptive facility self-induces the demanding need for its usage facilitating the emotional sensuous experience of selfishly self-gratifying venereal sensuality.

Yielding to this imperious "need" automatically induces a com-pulsive addiction which many experts today in the fields of the ex-perimental physical and social sciences mistakenly claim to be genet-ically rooted in the homosexual's chromosomatic makeup. Such is the emotional force of such a venereal self-attachment that it symptomat-ically seems to have been genetically inherited. Yet, were this actually the case, the homosexual so afflicted would cease to be fundamentally a human being. For, a human being is inalienably endowed with an immortal soul intellectually and responsibly free to conscionably gov-ern its own conduct antecedent to and transcendent to its subjective need to artificially supplement its own psychosomatic deficiencies.

ASCENT SECOND APPENDIX

The organic corporeal versus the anatomical corpuscular body.

The exclusively societal and non-communal aspect of the self's artificially self-induced and self-controlled subjective compassionate emotionality in all areas pertaining to food, sex, drugs, and attire should not be overlooked. When a fork is artificially fashioned, it need not be the self-same self who fashioned it that actually utilizes and possesses it as its very own property. It may be utilized by many selves other than the self that fabricated it. The very availability of the fork to facilitate eating socially stimulates an emotional compassion (i.e., empathy) to possess the fork for one's own personalized self-service and usage. The same holds for artificial sexual contraceptives whether they are plastic, mechanical, or chemical. To observe one riding about in a car is tantamount to wanting one's own self to have a similar automotive experience.

The fork artificially facilitates one's pleasurable enjoyment of eating. This infectious aspect of a personality's subjective sensual emotions should not be ignored. Furthermore, the facilitated enhancement of the pleasure of eating with a fork artificially transforms a mere sensorial pleasure into a sensuous sensitizing self-serving Epicurean satisfaction that is consciously somatically and empathically felt by other selves. It is in this sense that such entirely subjective amoral sensitizing sensual emotional compassions along with the artificial contrivances that facilitate them are very socially influentially infectious. Monkey see, monkey do. Indeed hysteria and panic which grips and inflames a crowd of people issues from uncontrolled empathic infectious emotional outbursts. One who hysterically yells "fire" in a crowded room empathically instigates an hysteria in its occupants who are all seized by the fear of being trapped.

In the objective order, human instinctive sensorial passions are entirely holistically communal and beneficial for the family common good of mankind even when they benefit individual families individually and not as members of social groups. The individual's substantive corporeal welfare benefits the entire family community whether it is the human family or merely the families in the animal kingdom of brute animals. This is the case in matters of food, sex, and drugs. For a well-nourished, procreatively vital, and healthily vigorous body is in a position to enhance the common good not only of his own person, his own immediate family, but the larger extended community family of mankind as well. This is also the case for the brute animal regarding the species of which it is a member.

Returning, again, to human procreation, the instinctive carnal heterosexual passions themselves stimulate and excite spouses to physically move toward each other in an intimate connubial procreative embrace. Under normal conditions neither the passions themselves nor the ensuing marital procreative embrace are restricted merely to a socially contraceptively lifeless self-serving selfish venereal sensitized sensual pleasure confined to the married couples themselves. On the contrary, the anticipated procreative fruit of the sexual passions spurring on an intimate spousal embrace culminates eventually in the birth of one or more offsprings which enlarge and enhance the metaphysical common good not only of the immediate marital family but of the larger community of which the family is the bedrock and cornerstone. It is morally untenable that the offspring of this marital union could be construed to be a mere byproduct of this marital union and susceptible in a pragmatic or utilitarian sense to be treated as a commodity that could be experimentally exploited, commercially traded and disposed of as one would discard a used automobile.

Contrast this, again, with artificial asexual contraceptive self-control and artificial insemination. This reduces the marital act to a robotic function technically (i.e., artificially) inhibiting or facilitating the merger of a male's sperm with a female ovum deliberately and artificially divorced from the natural heterosexual embrace of the parents themselves. This eliminates altogether the natural marital fusion of one and the same heterosexual parental faculty joined with its integral complementary fe/male organic counterparts. Furthermore, it disregards the reality that the sperm and the ovum themselves respectively naturally merge in virtue of their parental authoritative wedded personhood's heterosexual intransitive vitality. In brief, this artificially cultivated asexuality is resistantly and transitively transformed into an entirely serviceable self-serving productive process divorced from its intransitive existential purposeful procreative vitality and authoritative heterosexual parenthood.

The sperm and ovum are not products of the functioning of their parent's sexual anatomy no more than is the faculty of sight and its act of seeing a mere function of the eye's anatomy. For, again, it is the person that sees through the faculty of sight; it is not the anatomical organs of sight that actually see. Similarly it is the parents who conceive through their sexual heterosexual faculty. The sperm and ovum respectively spontaneously merge in virtue of their spontaneous motility engendered by their parental intransitive heterosexual procreative energetic sexual facultative dynamism. In an artificially self-controlled contraceptive asexual engagement, the process becomes exclusively a socially self-serving exploitable lifeless venereal experience of selfish self-gratification facilitated through imitating copulation. Same-sex couples claim to have even a more socially agreeable venereal experience since the procreative element is automatically excluded from their homosexual non-marital embrace.

To artificially, in artificial insemination, divorce the ovum and the sperm from the actual sovereign authority of their heterosexual parental progenitors is tantamount to exploitatively treating these seedlings as by-products of sexual conduct. The upshot of this is that the authentic heterosexual parents of the conceived offspring become artificially divorced from their legitimate offspring. The offspring, in turn, becomes alienated from its bona fide parents. Furthermore, the very integrity of the parental heterosexual faculty of procreation becomes artificially disintegrated and violated by the very individuals who engage in its parental activity. The embryonic offsprings themselves unwittingly become exploitable serviceable by-product commodities of conception in the same manner that an automobile emerging from an automated assembly line becomes a commercial commodity for sale to any buyer who wishes to purchase and make use of it for his own convenience.

Given that the automobile might be a lemon, it could be pirated for scrap. The same would apply to the embryonic offspring which becomes susceptible to being pirated for the serviceable use of the embryo's vital organs and biochemical plasticity. A product is in one sense or other a socially self-serving utilizable exploitable convenience whether it be a tool to be handily manipulated or a cryptic symbol to be mentally meaningfully managed to advance one's self-communication. When a car becomes used up it is scrapped altogether. Similarly with the presumptively defective human embryo. As a mere useable social commodity it may be abortively scrapped at will by anyone adopting a contraceptive have-attitudinal mindset.

In the interplay between the fundamental soulful will's intransitive volition and the supplemental selfhood's willful transitive volition, the latter takes precedence over the former only supplementally (viz., instrumentally), but not fundamentally. Thus, again, when the farmer cultivates the apple orchard for his own economic profit, he does supplementally by his own artificial productive working skill enhance both the growth and proliferation of apples; he does not abortively decrease and/or even suppress altogether the growth and proliferation of the very apples he is cultivating. The same must hold for the issue of sexual conduct proper to marriage. The fundamental soulful will's volition morally wills to engage conscionably in marriage when it dutifully obeys the "truth" of sexual intercourse's own vitality; it freely engages in a purposefully life-giving intransitive activity. That is, like the apple which is not a product of the tree but its fruit which perpetuates and proliferates the tree's own species and vitality, marital sexual intercourse conceives the embryo which is the same fruitful species and vitality of the parents' marital embrace perpetuating the "marital body's" integral procreative vitality.

The farmer's supplemental entirely purposelessly self-serving willful volition to artfully and skillfully exploit the apple tree's prolific vitality does not countermand nor abort the tree's fundamental vitality and fruit. Rather, it supplements and enhances the tree's natural vitality. The farmer's selfhood's will is motivated by his own profitable self-serving incentive to guarantee his (and his family's) own convenient and comfortable self-centered social security by transitively working and laboring to plant more trees and to safeguard and enhance their fruitful growth and proliferation. The farmer's laborious skillful work is transitively productive whereas the very growth of the apples on the apple-tree is intransitively non-productive. Similarly with the marital procreation of children. The parental sexual embrace itself is naturally and fundamentally a non-productive intransitive volitional activity while the skillful work and toil that supplementally provides a comfortable and convenient dwelling and furnishings to accommodate and safeguard the new-born life is very much itself a productive transitive volitional transaction.

Of course, the marital sexual embrace does not involve exclusively the person's soulful will; it also engages the person's animal instinctive sexual passions. At the same time, it must be further pointed out that objective sensorial carnal passions are subject to the will's domestication in a manner analogous to taming wild animals. This taming is not effectuated by suppressing the body's carnal passions altogether but by subordinating and subjecting them to the rule of the will's own volition. A person's volitional moral character is acquired by tempering the body's concupiscent passions and emboldening its irascible ones. A married couple is not sexually chaste by refraining altogether from marital intercourse nor is a married couple brave for acting without fear. A person's moral character is volitionally formed when the carnal passions are disciplined and tamed according to the purpose of their own instinctive drives.

In the case of the human person's self-centered will, it is not a matter of moral character but of his overriding attitudinal mindset. This attitudinal mindset is a person's dominant and paramount volitional outlook and outreach regarding the self-serving importance of everything that pertains to procuring and safeguarding his own selfish social security. The issue here is not one of being morally upright and immortally happy in the hierarchical order of existence but of having one's own self-assured security in the mortal historical order of resistance. In the former order the soulful will's volitions are inherently potently efficacious, meritorious, responsible or blameworthy and irresponsible; the will is intentionally honest in whatever it wills if it efficaciously and honestly wills to be honest. If it wills to be dishonest, it is quite dishonest in whatever it wills.

It is quite otherwise with the selfhood's will's volitions; they are inherently important but inefficacious. When the human person wills for its own bodily selfhood to be sensuously comfortable and satisfactorily self-contented, its own volition is impotent; its volition is merely a wish until and unless it forcibly and willfully "moves" itself to laboriously and with much effort to constructively and productively make whatever is required to procure and provide the conveniences its own body needs and requires (i.e., demands) to insure such contentment. What is it that "moves" this selfhood's will to engage in a productive self-serving action? In the case of the psychic heartless mindful will it is whatever selfish emotionless motivational bromide that sedates and stabilizes its mental caring; and in the case of the somatic mindless will it is whatever selfish stirring emotional motivation that stimulates and excites its bodily feeling.

In regard, then, to the marital act of sexuality, the soulful objective will intentionally wills to procreate new life in the measure that it wills honestly and efficaciously and conscionably the very objective goal of sexuality. If it wills otherwise, it is willingly irresponsible and immoral (i.e., dishonest) in its own volition. Its volition's responsibility may be diminished if its total freedom is curtailed by a terrible and terrifying fear which the human body passionately endures. In regard to the same marital act of sexuality, the selfhood subjective will motivationally wills to procure its own selfish sensuous venereal satisfaction. Of itself, this motivation is amoral; it is neither inherently an honest nor a dishonest goal. Indeed, it is not a purposeful goal at all; it is entirely a self-serving purposeless service. Indeed, without this subjective motivation there need not be any engagement at all in the procreative purpose of sexual intercourse in marriage. The objective life-giving purpose of sexual intercourse is fundamental whereas its subjective willful need to secure for itself and its spouse their own selfish venereal self-satisfying contentment is supplemental. Marriage affords both to the married couple when the fundamental and supplemental dimensions complement each other.

This complementarity is overturned or subverted when the supplemental willful motivation contravenes and artificially aborts the fundamental will's natural purposeful intention. This occurs, for example, when through artificial contraception the intercourse of the married couple is artificially prevented from achieving its natural conception of new life or the newly conceived embryo's life is itself abortively exterminated. These two antecedent and consequential wills may be at odds with each other in one and the same facultative marital body when one spouse intentionally wills the sexual intercourse to be open to new life while the other spouse motivationally wills to artificially and skillfully contravene life in order to have an uninhibited guarantee of venereal satisfaction and contentment in a fundamental/supplemental complementarity.

When this complementarity is subverted, one's subjective motivational will becomes increasingly imperiously and selfishly self-addicted to venereal pleasure. When this selfishly self-centered subjective willful mindset overrides the objective soul's conscionable volition, the human person becomes blindly & rebelliously oblivious to the voice of conscience and to the soulful will's moral responsibility. In view of this, it is of utmost importance that a married couple practice mutual volunteer periodic abstinence from sexual intercourse precisely to willfully inhibit each's respective self-serving subjective will from cultivating the rebellious mindset of imperiously demanding and becoming self-addicted to venereal pleasure as the overriding motive to enter into their marital embrace.

In view of this, marital chastity cannot be maintained without a concomitant periodic ascetic self-denial and volunteer willful and forcible abstention from the venereal pleasure which accompanies sexual intercourse. The completely celibate life that priests and religious volunteer to live is itself the very safeguard and guarantee for married couples that marital chastity is not only merely possible but actually and efficaciously feasible between spouses. Indeed, in view of the spouse's hopeful expectation of their marital intercourse contributing to God's joyful honor and glory and not merely their own selfish honor and glory, it is imperative that they not become addictively attached to the venereal pleasure inherent in their marital embrace.

A completely humanistic attitude is always a dominant and dominating self-serving selfish overriding willfulness to esteem as important whatever seems most conducive to advancing a person's autonomous self-controlled social security. Since a human person's selfhood is psychosomatically and antipodally fashioned, his dominant have-attitude is unwittingly and competitively pitted against its psychosomatic opponent. A human person's subjective personality is usually dominantly pessimistic-idealistic or competitively optimistic-realistic in its have-attitude outlook and outreach. A pessimist is attitudinally regressively defensive and conservative-minded in his basic have-attitudinal outlook and outreach. The realist is attitudinally offensive (i.e., aggressive) and progressively liberal-minded. Each ideological have-attitude is antipodally at odds with the other.

The pessimist's attitudinal personality and life-style self-control is the mind's cerebral emotionless calculations overriding the body's visceral emotional stimulations. The realist's attitudinal personality and life-style self-control is simply the reverse. The pessimist places more security in operating from the control booth of his bodiless and heartless telepathic mind whereas the optimist's control center is the body's mindless empathy. Pessimists think alike whereas optimists feel alike. The former are motivated by emotionless inspirations while the latter are motivated by emotional stimulations. The pessimist prefers to be guided by a careful and righteous bearing whereas the realist prefers as his guide a comfortable and gratifying feeling.

The prototypical personality and life-style of the realist/optimist is that of the playboy and/or playgirl hedonist whose dominating and domineering humanistic have-attitude overrides and rebels against the restrictive obligations inherent in the objective moral order. In contrast, the prototypical personality and life-style of the idealist/pessimist is that of the puritan whose dominating and domineering humanistic have-attitude overrides and rebels against the permissive latitude inherent in the objective moral order. This liberal mindless personality and hedonistic attitude is more often and more frequently tolerated and fostered in Western civilizations whereas its conservative mindful counterpart is more frequently found in Far Eastern civilizations.

Each prototypical lifestyle and paramount attitude is prejudicially biased toward its own self-centered selfish partisan outlook and blind toward that of its opponent. Indeed, each prototypical attitude accuses its opponent of being prejudicially one-sided and sectarian. Furthermore, each respective attitude and overriding personality in the measure that it promotes its own supplementarity to the exclusion of the objective fundamental metaphysical moral order promotes and underwrites a completely secular dictatorial humanism to the detriment of the human person's transcendent immortal destiny beyond the reach of his subjective historical social mortality.

The hedonistic personality becomes humanistically, addictively, and selfishly self-attached to and a prisoner of its own bodily sensuous sensitized feelings of luxurious comfort and gratification. The puritanical personality becomes, in turn, humanistically, addictively, and selfishly self-attached to and a prisoner of its own mental impassive intimate bearing and caring for its Spartan rectitude and vindication. Neither of these opposing lifestyles is graced and fortified with an objective moral character. Both are prejudicially buttressed with each's own partisan attitudinal mindset and built-in bias. Each is an enemy and foe to the other. The hedonist tyrannically demands that his own lifestyle be automatically catered to by a robotic automation self-service whereas the puritan tyrannically demands that his own lifestyle be autocratically catered to by a bureaucratic automation self-service.

The dominant self-humanizing spirit in the traditional Far Eastern civilization is not that of the sensationalism peculiar to Western civilization of artificially stimulating and stirring up the somatic self's self-indulgent sensuous emotional feelings. It is that of concentrating on the sedating psychic self's self-calming nonsensuous emotionless mental static bearing and self-composed equipoise. The prevalent have-attitude of this somnolent lifestyle is not focused on the body's somatic physique, sensitivity, suppleness, and sensitizing feelings of emotional stimulation but on the psychic mind's mystique, intimacy, sedateness, and emotionless placid impassive self-composure.

This abstemiously ascetic lifestyle of the East is simply the reverse of the robust lifestyle prevalent in the West. It should be noted that the very lifestyle in the East is cultivated, supported, and promoted by the native civility and civilization proper to these Eastern cultures. Of course, this radical differentiation between the East and West is becoming more blurred with the ever increasing advance of the economic homogenous globalization of all cultures. Nonetheless, it is significant that this Eastern lifestyle of the hypoactive recluse antipodal to the Western lifestyle of the hyperactive activist serves as a revealing stereotype of the two polarized extremes proper to the self-subsistent personhood's subjective psychosomatic personality sociability and social autonomy.

Both of these antipodal lifestyles are skillfully mastered through strenuous self-transformative training. The one's training is focused externally and extrospectively on the somatic body's physique, emotional feelings and mobilization. The other one's training is concentrated internally and introspectively on the psychic mind's mystique, emotionless bearings and immobilization. Of course, the somatic body is willfully involved in the training proper to each of these two exemplary lifestyles. In one case one's egocentric self is conscious exclusively of the body's somatic needs in a robotic mindless/body fashion whereas in the other one's egocentric self is subconsciously exclusively concentrated on the mind's psychic needs in a bodiless/mindful hypnotic fashion impervious to the body's somaticity.

Paradoxically enough the austere ascetic personality of the East is more intensively conscious and intimately centered in its own selfhood moreso than is the case for the athletic robust personality of the West. Precisely because a subconscious hypnotic stage of egocentric consciousness is not merely partially aware of the self's extraneous extrospective somaticity which can be empirically observed and even controlled by others through hi-tech equipment. The hypnotic self is subconsciously fully conscious of the self's intrinsic introspective noumenal psychicity which is occultly hidden from everyone else and from everyone else's direct control. By way of contrast, the robust athletic personalized self is consciously absorbed with the prowess and athletic posture of the somatic body's sensitive feelings, physique, and athletic resiliency. This athletic posture reveals only a phenomenal symptomatic appearance of a selfhood's authentic nuclear personality. It is only the austere ascetic personalized self that is able to subconsciously experience within the psychic mind's utmost intimate posture the very nuclear noumenal transparent selfhood of its own nuclear personality.

Again, a way to grasp the antipodal difference between the psyche's inner static noumenal transparency contrasted with the soma's outer kinetic symptomatic appearance is to first consider mentally quantified mathematical extensions (viz., geometric continuous extensions and arithmetic discrete extensions) devoid of every tactual feature discernible to the senses. Secondly, consider the imaginatively fashioned mathematical symbols in the body's soma figuratively and symbolically exemplifying the psyche's mathematical notional conceptions.

The discrepancy between the noumenal arithmetic "one" and its symptomatic counterpart imaginative appearance immediately comes to the forefront. A mental arithmetic numerical "one" is not itself a solitary discrete unit entity but a discrete unified aggregate enterprise made up of fragmentary components. Thus the mental arithmetic "one" is implicitly equivalent to any possible combination of its fragmentary segmentation such as $1/2 + 1/2$ or $1/3 + 1/3 + 1/3$, etc.. Further, the psychic mind can intuitively discern these possible fragmentary equations in conceiving the nuclear core of the arithmetic "one."

Its tactual imaginary symbolic exemplification cannot depict this nuclear core in its noumenal vacuity and nullity which includes an indefinite number of fragmentary possibilities but not their actualized and explicit possibilization. The imaginative symbol "one" is only a symptomatic appearance of its mental model. For, in its core it is not explicitly any fragment of itself nor any combination of these fragments. The archetypal "one" conceived by the mind's psychicity is ambiguously both an arithmetic discrete "one" and a linear geometric "one."

The archetypal "one" is null and void of all explicit fragmentation. Indeed, the archetypal numerical arithmetical "one" is precisely a 0. Why so? Because, it is the prototypical typeset of all subsets. It is possible to calculate with an 0 additively and subtractively. For, $0 + 0 = 0$ and $0 - 0 = 0$ are notional numerical prototypical equivalences in which one zero is added to or subtracted from another one zero to yield mathematical equations of a numerical "one" that is inherently fragmentary. In its imaginative arithmetic symbol it appears explicitly as a solitary unit entity which it is not. For, it is a mathematical enterprise of implicitly unified fragments that are either explicitly in an aggregate or segregate unification.

This is simply another paradox peculiar to the subjective selfhood's bipolar psychosomatic personality and willful selfhood. To better grasp this differentiation, it would be more apropos to symbolize the numerical one in the following manner: $1 + 0 = 1$ and $1 - 0 = 1$

to capture more accurately its noumenal nuclear fragmentary core.

Where the psychic mind may lucidly and transparently intuitively discern many implicit enterprising fragmentary mathematical combinations in one and the same core noumenal discernment, the somatic body's imagination can only in an extended series of explicit imaginary symbols capture this fragmentation not intuitively in one mental discernment but symptomatically and imaginatively in explicitly examining separately each of the separate fragments together with the arithmetic "one." Thus, the equation $1 = 1/2 + 1/2$ is implicitly psychically discerned intuitively and transparently in concentrating simply on the arithmetic "one" alone. This implicit noumenal discernment does not eliminate nor preclude other multiple latent equations inherent in the same "one." Yet, its explicit symptomatic phenomenal depiction in the imagination explicitly excludes other equivalent possibilities.

It is not amiss at this point to emphasize that the numerical mathematical one is a fragmentary one and not a unitary holistic one which is the case for the metaphysical one in the vertical order of existence. The human corporeal body, for example, is a unitary organic body. That is every segment of the corporeal body is unitively one and the same corporeal body be it a physiological member or even a segment (viz., a cell) of this member. Thus in the vertical metaphysical order every entity is an organic unit entity regardless of its complexity whereas in the horizontal mathematical order every mathematically measured and standardized enterprise is merely organizationally unified. For, there is no overall holistic unitary organicity in its organization. Every organization, thus is either explicitly mechanistic if the somatic body be considered or implicitly bureaucratic if the psychic mind's own arrangement be considered.

Again, this anomaly regarding the subjective numerical mathematical "one" versus the objective metaphysical "one" is another instance of the radical difference that differentiates the vertical from the horizontal order. The mathematical one is called "one" pseudonymously. That is, it is only a name-tag. For, it is not a unit entity that retains its entitative unit identity in every instance of its usage. It is not a univocal term but an entirely equivocal one. Hence, it is merely labeled "one" because there is no instance of its usage that it need have exactly the same fragmentary aggregate (viz., geometric) or segregate (viz., arithmetic) combination. Thus, it is a queer or quasi paradoxical "one."

This is moreso the case in its prototypical notional conception by the psychic mind since the mathematical 0 is a nuclear core "one" amenable to any and every fragmentary combination that the psychic mind can intuitively conceive. In sum, equating 1 with two halves $1/2 + 1/2$ is merely one of a myriad of equations which the psyche intuits in the vacuous nuclear core of the aggregate and/or segregate numerical notional "one." In brief, the psyche can noumenally intuit transparently (i.e., see through) within the empty nuclear core of the arithmetic "one" its multiple fragmentary possibilities whereas the imagination symbolizes symptomatically and apparently this aggregate numerical number instantially rather than holistically.

Another instance of this disparity between the notional conception of a mathematical quantum and its imaginary exemplification is the geometric line. Notionally, the line is ambiguously and simultaneously implicitly both ortholinear and curvilinear. The vacuous distance between point x and point y when these points are not coincidental is a distance that is spanned simultaneously and implicitly be a straight and a curved line. On the other hand, when the imagination symbolically images a line, the line that it images cannot on one and the same segment of this line be both ortholinear and curvilinear.

By reflecting on the previous analysis it can be readily appreciated that the notions and conceptions of the psychic mind are very much spooky specters and ghostly phantoms. Of course, such phantoms are merely dream-like and not at all real. There is no such phantom "0" transcendent to and existing independent of the psychic mind's own psychic intimacy. Such spooks as eerie as they are, are merely the figment of the psychic mind's own nontactual psychicity. It would be more accurate to speak of such phantoms as spiritualistic but not spiritual.

This noumenal mathematical fabricational intuitivity on the part of the psyche is most probably the radical source of the Gnosticism which bedeviled the early years of Christianity. Of course, the term, gnosis, has as its etymological root the Greek term, noesis, which signifies the mind's mental knowing. Gnosticism is rooted in this noumenal mathematical transparency peculiar to the subjective mind's nontactual vacuity. In reflecting on this it is revealing that the very paraphysical static sterility peculiar to mathematical notions and ideations is the same nullity and vacuity which is the very spatiotemporal core of the mind's own psychic intimacy. The psychic mind is completely statically nontactual and, hence, not detectable to any sensory empirical inspection. It is also well to take note that the so-called Enlightenment rationalism of the 18th century took its cue from the psychic mind's noumenal mathematical intuitivity.

Hence, the paradox of Gnosticism also includes its psychically self-enclosed rationalistic agnostic bent and radical skepticism. The renowned French philosopher, Rene Descartes, was deeply mired in this mathematical agnosticism. He explicitly recognized this mental solipsistic closet in which he had sealed himself and vainly tried to escape from it. He is known as the philosophical father of the modern mind and the Enlightenment which inherits and propagates this philosophical agnostic rationalistic solipsistic skepticism. Descartes sought to escape the hermetically sealed closet of his own psychic mind by conceiving a phantom notion of God as the greatest conceivable reality in the universe. He intuitively reasoned that this notion must be caused by God Himself since it is too grandiose to have been merely invented by his own psychic mind. Alas! Such a notion is, indeed, a mere figment of the self-humanizing psyche. Later avowed atheistic humanists recognized this and concluded that Descartes had ingeniously proven rationalistically that God is an invention of the human mind. This, then, is the subjective introspective nuclear static inertial core of the selfhood's psychic willful selfhood.

When one's selfhood seeks to take masterful self-serving charge and self-control of this very core, its motivation to do so is not to emotionally stimulate itself to action but, rather to emotionlessly statically sedate itself to remain in a trance of inaction conducive to hypothetical (i.e., dubious) musing which theoretical math demands. This inner static vacuity is precisely what one experiences in willfully hypnotically retreating to this subconscious psychic inner selfhood. This retreat is not achieved without considerable transformative skillful hypnotic training involving a complete eclipse and ignoral of the somatic body's imaginary fancies, sensitivity, and tactual feelings.

The first step in this training is to control one's physical environment to facilitate an introspective hypnotic somnolent retreat without having distractions impinging on the somatic body's sensitive feelings and sensual stimulating emotions. Indeed, the traditional library located on a university campus was the typical refuge where a student would retreat to find the silence required to be isolated from the sounds and activity engaging the senses and the body's own movements. Before the advent of the radio, the TV, the movies, the computer, etc. with their visual graphics and audible sounds, the book's printed word was the normal medium of communication. In this medium, the eminence of learning and knowledge appealed to an intelligible insight and employed terms that transcended the AV range of electronic communication with its electrifying audio-visual sensational stimuli. Within this inner sanctum of the traditional library it was possible to both objectively think intellectually in metaphysical terms and subjectively to muse mindfully in mathematical terms without the eye and the ear's distraction.

With today's mass media of electronic communication in the place of the written word "what you now see and hear is what you get." In other words, one's pedagogical education today is geared toward an empirical observation rather than to an intellectual insight proper to the discipline of metaphysics. Both abstemious intellectual contemplation and mindful mathematical theoretical musings are no longer commonplace as academic activities. Traditionally, the word, "being," conjured up a hierarchical rank of reality that transcended the reach of the physical tangible cosmos and sensory knowledge. In our contemporary culture in Western civilization the typical student's range of interest and curiosity is confined to the horizon of the senses and the empirical data afforded through them.

The second step in gaining introspective self-mastery over one's own psyche is to inwardly transcend the imagination's tactual imagery in order to concentrate on the psyche's nontactual vacuity. The motivation of this inward horizontal (not vertical) retreat is to masterfully take charge of the very core of this self-serving psychicity itself and not merely to master its mathematical notions. Indeed, the third step is to void the psyche of all of its mindful notions and to remain subconsciously statically and hypnotically transfixedly absorbed fully in its blank spatiotemperal static vacancy and void. When one masterfully, artfully, willfully, and mindfully achieves this psychic nullity he has become fully self-servingly in charge and in self-control of the inner intimate nuclear core of his own selfhood. But, paradoxically, he does so only by alienating himself from his polarized counterpart, his corpuscular body's somatic willful sensitive self.

And also, paradoxically enough, he becomes statically and transfixedly more solipsistically a complete prisoner of his own mental selfhood and addictively more captive to his dominant have-attitudinal humanistic spirit and "never-say-die" morale (i.e., his willful commitment to achieve and to maintain this autocratic masterful self-control over his own completely self-centered mindfulness). This transcendental inwardness is not a self-fulfillment that transcends the horizontal order of the self's own subjective egocentric selfhood and self-experienced supplemental deficiency. Rather, it is a self-centered self-serving autocratic self-detachment from experiencing the body's somaticity (i.e., sensitivity and movement) and a total self-attachment to the mind's psychic intimacy in which one is completely enveloped in one's own personalized selfhood. When this hypnotic stage of psychic self-mastery is attained in Buddhism, it is referred to as nirvana in which the self is impervious to the somatic body's deficient needs and sensitized feelings and emotions and, thereby, is released from the toil and labor peculiar to the body's own painful exertions, efforts, and trials.

In this peak experience the ascetic's consciousness is psychically willfully (i.e., forcibly) self-enveloped not in a one-world consciousness for there is no one-world reality in the subjective artificial order of mankind's self-cultivated self-humanization. The experience of total nullity afforded in this horizontal transcendental self-absorption is that of a "motionless body." It is not that of an objective levitational spiritual delight or joy peculiar to the soul's intellectual will. For, this utter inward psychic notional vacuity is statically the subconscious experience of the total absence and the complete deprivation not merely of the body's somaticity but of reality itself transcendent to the horizontal order of the human person's noetic self-cultivation and self-humanization.

This experience of nullity within the very core of one's own self-hood is an experience of the selfhood's own self-possessed psychic will willfully deprived of reality itself transcendent to its own egocentric subjectivity. This psychic absence and void is experienced as "nothingness" and as a willful nihilistic resistance to reality itself transcendent to the subjectivity of one's own selfhood in the objective order of existence. Most notably, it is a peak experience of the utter absence of the very summit and pinnacle of reality, God's very own Beingness.

The hypnotic experience of nirvana is certainly a relief from the somatic body's own physiological tensions, feelings, sensitized sensuous pains and pleasures, etc. But, it is not an encounter with any reality in the vertical order of existence transcendent to the egocentric self's solipsistic subjective willful resistant selfhood. Can a person enter into this nirvana, sustain it, and even communicate with others from within its vicissitude? Yes, there is an empathic telepathy between one psychic self and another. Certainly, it is not typically a sensitized sympathetic or antipathetic feeling which is infectiously socially experienced when one somatic self temperamentally empathizes with another somatic self through compassionate feelings reinforced by a handshake, a hug, a kiss, and similar body contact.

Rather it is a telepathic non-sensitized mental communication involving one's psychic bearing and self-composed equipoise which dispenses with the body's symptomatic emotive expressions and gestures. It is an empathic communication which has recourse to cryptic symbolic notations which are intuitively mutually intersubjectively recognized by two separate psychic selves. Persons playing the game of bridge are telepathically communicating with each other in bidding their cards. Musicians playing the same musical score telepathically communicate with each other through the score's cryptic musical symbols. For the meaning of these symbols is exclusively mentally intuited and discerned.

Of course, this telecommunication could not take place easily while a person is hypnotically in a trance or coma. For, the body's sensitivity is suspended. It may very well be that a person in a trance is susceptible to be alert to special sounds which are telepathically cues to his own entrancement. These are mantras which exercise a special hypnotic influence over his own psychic willfulness. This is an influence to which he has willfully subjugated himself.

It must be pointed out that while in the objective order the intellectual will is informatively governed and obligatorily directed by the intellect's conscionable knowledge, the order is reversed in the subjective order. It is the psychic mind or the somatic body which are transformatively oriented by the selfhood's self-serving partisan overriding have-attitudinal willful self-interest. Thus in the case of the psychic self, the mind's mathematical notions do not mindfully follow the mind's own consciousness. The mind is entirely subservient to the will's self-serving domination. Thus, if "1" is equated with a 2/2 fraction rather than with a 3/3 fraction this is not a mindful reasonable matter. It is transformatively a forcible matter under the will's mindful self-controlling willfulness and domination. That is, it is the will that determines this and not the mind's consciousness.

However, in the case of the soul's intellect it is its own reasonable logic which is operative and not the will's influential domination or causal determination that prevails over this logic. The color, green, is not really colorfully and truly green because the intellectual will wills it to be so. It is so independent of the intellectual will's volition. The intellect insightfully grasps the reality of the color, green, and recognizes the truth of this color fully independent of the will's volition or interference. It is most notable that objectively the soul's intellectual knowledge is informatively cognitive and the human person is conscious of this intellectual insight and informed cognition. The opposite is the case within the subjectivity of the selfhood's psychosomatic "knowledge." Both the human person's somatic and psychic self-conscious knowing is pervasively one of consciousness that is devoid of informed cognition and the human person is cognizant of this void.

To subjectively have a love for something because one has a bodily feeling for it and/or a mental caring and concern for it is tantamount to transforming the object of one's love into a valuable, treasured, and precious object. What is important and interesting here is not informatively the object of one's love but rather temperamentally and/or sentimentally the subject that bestows a preferential transformative value on that on which he is willfully attached.

Where the somatic selfhood is dominated by an overriding willful have/have-not attitude committed to its own automatic autonomous self-gratifying sensuous self-contentment the psychic selfhood is dominated by an antipodal overriding willful have/have-not attitude committed to its own autocratic autonomous impassive self-justifying self-containment. The two willful selves are in polar opposition in a negative-positive tension with each other. For the human person to be self-possessively and mindfully in charge and in self-control of its psychic self-contained notional personality is tantamount for it to have no interest in its somatic counterpart. And the reverse is the case for the human person in taking possessive charge and mindless control of its self-contented sensational personality.

The human person's self-humanized dominant spirit (i.e., egocentric nuclear self) is inflated with a domineering self-confident selfish morale when its willful self-serving resolution and commitment to take charge of its own willfulness succeeds in subjugating one part of its polarized selfhood to its counterpart. Thus the psychic willful self's self-serving ascetic spirit of domination becomes increasingly boosted in its own self-confident morale, pluck, and spunk the more securely ensconced it becomes in its own inertial static emotionless serenity which is achieved only in the measure that the somatic selfhood's emotional excitation is forcibly deliberately suppressed and expunged. And, vice versa, the somatic willful self's domineering self-serving robust spirit becomes increasingly boosted in its own self-serving confident morale, spunk, pluck the more securely ensconced it becomes in its own kinetic emotional excitation which is achieved only in the measure that its counterpart's psychic selfhood's emotionless serenity is mindlessly ignored and forcibly expelled from its focal consciousness.

The impact of this triumphant humanistic spirit (i.e., morale) of successful domination on the selfhood's psychosomatic self-motivation is considerable. The triumphant somatic self's emotional feelings become increasingly enthusiastically and even euphorically elated and inflated. When, however, this same robust personality's own attitudinal partisan self-interest in its own sensual self-gratifying automatic self-contentment becomes forcibly subservient and suppressed by some other self's psychic domineering personality, its own emotional excitation becomes notably deflated, depressed, and morose. This robust personality experiences serious pathological unemotional depression and dejection when it becomes subjugated to the will of another self's psychic domination. The depth of this depression is determined by the degree of this personality's resolve and determination to relinquish its own self-cultivated preferred activist lifestyle.

The reverse occurs when the psychic self's triumphant spirit of domination successfully prevails over its own somatic counterpart. Its emotionless self-contained autocratic bearing becomes increasingly clairvoyant and even visionary. When, again, this same ascetic personality's own attitudinal partisan self-interest of ethereal self-justifying autocratic self-containment becomes forcibly subservient to some other self's somatic domination, its own emotionless placidity becomes notably anxious, discombobulated, and agitated. This placid and introverted personality experiences serious disorienting disturbing vague anxieties and irrational forebodings. The depth of this worry and the severity of its impact on the individual who experiences it are ascertained by examining the resolve or lack of resolve of his self-attachment to stick to his self-cultivated preferred austere lifestyle.

This completely humanistic self-cultivated personality with its domineering "spirit" is charismatically infectious. One who successfully (i.e., willfully) cultivates a dominant and domineering personality whether it be psychically or somatically centered exercises a commanding motivating leadership within any group setting. This domineering personality is empathically socially influential in boosting the morale of any group regardless of the size of that group. The particular individual personality whether it be a psychically austere or a somatically robust personality exercises a considerable charismatic influence on its peers in advancing its own respective idealistic utopian passivism or realistic pragmatic activism. An athletic or martial humanistic "spirit," for example, of "never say die" and "never give up" is considered to be the spark which infectiously creates an intrepid team spirit or "esprit de corps" which enables a sporting or combat team to successfully contend with and overcome even a daunting opponent.

The humanistic "spirit" of this personality is the spine, the spunk, the pluck, the heart, the morale, and the intimate core of the willful self's own self-serving selfhood. It is a have-attitudinal spirit of domination which is at odds with its antipodal have-not attitudinal counterpart which is subjugates and subdues. This humanistic spirit is at the service of a self-cultivated personality's own ideological bias whether it be psychically the self's own imperturbable defensive-minded passivism typical of a socially secure romantic autocratic self-containment or somatically the self's own excitable offensive mindless activism typical of a socially guaranteed pragmatic automatic self-contentment. This humanistic "spirit" paradoxically harbors a partisan selfish conservative or liberal bias. Each polarized bias is willfully self-resistant to its opponent's own ideological slant. The conservative minded passivist is dominantly a psychically introverted personality whereas the mindless liberal activist is dominantly a somatically extroverted personality.

It must be also pointed out that the selfhood's willful selfish commitment and attachment to its own overriding have-attitude and partisan self-interest is not comparable to the intellectual will's own love for whatever it wills to love. The intellectual will's volitional love is a drive which is purposefully destined for what is inherently loveable and immortally good-as-such. The selfhood's willful love, on the other hand, is a need for what is purposelessly and self-servingly usably a self-centered partisan (i.e., selfish) self-orientated love. Hence, in this self-orientation the egocentric will's self-love is not directed to what is naturally good-as-such but, rather, for the artificial no-good-as-such which becomes usably good only in the measure that this selfhood avails itself of its advantageous service.

The selfhood's will does not love something causally and purposefully because it is attracted by its inherent worth and value.

Whatever the self needfully loves is an artificial no-such-good that becomes serviceably good and worthwhile only in the measure that the self willfully possessively demands its service and makes use of it. Hence, while the intellectual will informatively loves the good because it is inherently beautiful the selfhood's will's self-love transformatively makes the object of its love to seem beautiful precisely because he possessively cherishes this good to service his own deficient needs. "Do I love you because you are beautiful or are you beautiful because I love you?" The answer is both. But, only when one love is fundamental and prior to the other fundamentally while the other love is supplemental and prior to the other supplementally and not fundamentally. Thus, a diamond ring is supplementally loved inasmuch as it is designed by the jeweler to be beautiful through carefully cutting, polishing, and mounting it in a proper setting. The very love that the jeweler has for it transformatively brings about its scintillating sparkle. When worn by a person who is fundamentally beautiful the ring supplementally enhances this natural beauty and grace. In other words, a person's fundamental natural beauty may be supplementally adorned with a diamond to further enhance this natural beauty.

But there is a radical difference between the natural beauty of the person and the artificial beauty of the polished diamond ring. The latter is artificial because it artfully enhances the natural beauty of the person. It is artificial because it is artfully designed and used to serve as an adornment. To employ, on the other hand, the human person's natural beauty merely to show off and to model the diamond in a jewelry story is an abuse and an affront of the person's dignity. Why? Because it places the person's fundamental natural beauty at the service of the diamond to advance its sale by the jewelry store. In other words, it inverts the fundamental-supplemental order of what is valuable and what only has value.

A ripe apple is nutritionally a fundamental good-as-such even when it is not actually loved or eaten by anyone. A rough diamond is a no-good-as-such until it is supplementally made useable (viz., humanized) and put to use as an adornment. It is the jeweler's affectionate love (i.e., feeling and cherishing) for the diamond that artfully transforms it into a cut, polished, and mounted ring in a special setting. The apple is a natural good-as-such apart from anyone loving it whereas the diamond is artificially good only through someone affectionately cherishing and artfully transforming it to serve as an adornment for his own self-serving usage. A natural good does not become increasingly good the more numerous are the individuals who love it whereas an artificial self-cultivated no-good-as-such becomes increasingly valuable the larger are the number of individuals who covet it. The importance of this difference cannot be overemphasized.

In the intellectual will's volitional choices there is no self-centered prejudicial consideration of affectionately caring for and having a concerned self-interest and predilection for the object of its choice. Its choices are objectively, judiciously, and impartially informed by the intellect's conscionable access to the truth-as-such of these choices. On the other hand, the selfhood's will is prejudiced by dint of its own partisan attitudinal self-interest in the object of its willfulness. It carefully, souciantly, and caringly evaluates every object in view of its own self-serving needs and attitudinal bias. Hence, whether it is the psychic or somatic willful selfhood's self-serving needs and bias that are consciously involved, each respectively evaluates and cherishes the worth of the objects of its love in term of its own commitment to its own overriding dominating have/have-not attitudinal bias and self-interest.

The somatic willful pragmatic self entertains strong exciting emotional feelings and sympathetic empathy toward objects and other selves that serve its dominant attitudinal need for automatic sensuous self-satisfaction and self-contentment whereas the psychic romantic willful self entertains a strong sedating emotionless bearing and telepathic empathy toward objects and other selves that serve its own dominant attitudinal need for an autocratic ethereal self-justification and self-containment. Furthermore, the very kinetically alert personality is motivated by excitable emotional feelings that tend to be consciously sustained by moods prolonging these feelings. The very static inertial somnolent personality, on the other hand, is motivated by a sedate emotionless calm bearing that tends to be subconsciously prolonged by trances characteristic of one daydreaming.

357

There is still another prototypical personality intervening between these two cerebral utopian and visceral pragmatic mindsets. This third personality is an esthetic one. Thus, the three major fields of the arts, the liberal, the technical, and the fine have each a prototypical personality personifying each field. Each's specialized function characterizes the attitude and mindset of each personality.

The liberal art's product's criterion of success and achievement is precision and exactitude. That of the technician is efficiency and convenience. And that of the esthete is harmony and grace. All three are self-serving inasmuch as they have no innate purpose transcending the egocentric personality that cultivates them. The esthete personality is a hybrid of the other two. That is to say, the esthetic personality cultivating the fine arts derives its own theories from the cerebral reach of the liberal arts. And, in turn, it derives its instruments of executing these theories from the technical arts. In terms of these theories the esthete himself must be resolutely trained to abide by cerebrally ascetic regulations and language that demand mathematical precision and exactitude pertinent to his own artistic field. In addition, he must be astutely trained to technically master the instruments peculiar to expressing the medium proper to his own artistry.

In this manner, the esthete engages simultaneously his cerebral psychic mental calculation and his visceral somatic bodily mechanism to effectuate his own personification of a fine art-form. The esthete is not committed entirely to the psyche's complete introversion or to the soma's complete extroversion which is the case respectively for the liberal artisan and the technician. He partakes of both in a more moderated form. Thus, the esthete is not formally a mathematician; yet, his own special language peculiar to his specialized field of artistry is mathematically regulated. On the other hand, he is not formally a technician actually engaged in making the artistic instruments of his own artistic deployment; yet, he is required to skillfully master the use of these instruments. The esthete is a personality that is captivated by one or more of the fields of the fine arts and has cultivated a skillful familiarity with the esthetic symbols and tools proper to this artistic field of endeavor. In so doing, he is simultaneously committed to acquiring an autocratic esthetic self-justification in the correct interpretation and use of the language and symbols regulating his artistry and an automatic esthetic self-gratification in the skillful deployment of the tools proper to this artistry.

There are many different major fields of the fine arts such as dance, poetry, painting, sculpture, music, theater, etc., including the many genres peculiar to each. Music is an excellent example of the esthetic personality since it demands both the composition of a musical score that is symbolically mentally justified due to its exacting mathematical precision together with its execution on a musical instrument that is skillfully played to gratify one with pleasing tactual sensational feelings interpreting the musical score itself.

Reflecting on the subject of music as a fine art and on the esthetic personality that is predominantly committed to this esthetic lifestyle, it is possible to fine tune our appreciation of the polarized dichotomy and disparity between the psychic self's enchantment with its own emotionless impassivity versus the somatic self's fascination with its own emotional excitement. Plainchant is a music that hymnally intones the Gospel, notably the psalms. Its modulated rhythm, dulcet sounds, and lullaby-like intonation do not play on arousing or stimulating one's visceral emotionality but rather play on reinsuring that one's visceral somatic self remains completely subjugated to the mind serenely elevated in prayerfully hymning the psalms to God. The lively rhythm, strident drum beat, and syncopated melodies of popular songs do play directly on arousing and stimulating one's visceral emotionality. These stir one to dance about or, at least, to mark the sprightly beat with the stamp of one's foot. What this difference reveals is that different genres of music allow for un/emotional nuances and modulations that are too subtle to capture in words.

The range and gamut of these un/emotional dys/affectionate intimate bearings and sensitized feelings range from the psyche's emotionless dreamlike enchantment to the soma's frenzied emotional excitation. Words fail to capture this vast gamut of completely subjective motivational rhythms and beats ranging from emotionless psychically enchanting spell-binding dulcet airs to emotional pulsating somatically stirring heart-thumping melodies.

What is the motivational upshot of this vast range of musical emotional/emotionless rhythms? In the vertical objective order of nature, a person's appetitive drives are spontaneously and informatively aroused to actuate the body's mobility at the sensorial level and, correspondingly, spontaneously and informatively aroused to actuate the soul's will at the intellectual level. No artificially self-induced motivation is required to forcibly prompt or nudge their arousal and actuation. They act spontaneously. The sensorial drive acts instinctively while the volitional drive acts freely by choice.

In the subjective horizontal order of culture, on the contrary, a person's self-cultivated psychosomatic needs are transformatively (i.e., motivationally) reactively incited to psychic inaction and somatic action. This is because the person's selfhood is impotent to act spontaneously on its own and must be moved (i.e., motivated) to inaction or action. The impetus within the subjective horizontal order of resistance is to willfully, forcibly, and influentially (i.e., motivationally) transform the selfhood's own supplemental deficiency from not-having to having a self-sufficiency and thereby overcoming its own deficient ineptitude. This is the exact reverse of the fundamental informative appetitive arousal which is the case in the objective vertical order of existence.

The radical difference between these two orders is that the objective order is energetically spontaneously dynamic whereas the subjective order is synergistically reactively enervating. That is, the one is innately and fundamentally potent while the other is supplementally impotent and only self-acquisitively competent. That is, the latter needs supplementally to be impulsively moved (i.e., self-started and motivated) to become in/actuated. The singular difference between the objective and subjective orders is that the former is cognitively informed regarding the existing reality that transcends it while the latter is consciously transformed regarding its own willful self-resistance. Consciousness in all of its reflexive stages of egocentric awareness is a non-cognitive manner of knowing. Indeed, it is a conative experiential knowing. What this means is that a personality becomes consciously transformatively knowledgeable about something through the somatic emotional feelings and/or psychic emotionless bearings that it is aware of having and entertaining regarding some

360

thing and someone else.

By reason of its self-cultivated sensitized somatic feelings and intimate psychic bearings it "knows" by becoming aware of having emotional and/or emotionless attachments or detachments toward something or someone. Hence, its knowledge is not informative; it is persuasively and transformatively dys/informative. It is in this sense that one may interpret the axiom that "love is blind." This is an axiom that is warranted in the subjective order of culture alone. For, this self-love emanates not from an innate appetitive drive that is directed toward what is informatively naturally good-as-such but from a need that is orientated toward culturally transforming what is no-good-as-such into an exploitable useable self-fulfilling service. In this conative self-centered awareness a personality has an emotional sensitized self-conscious "feel" and "like" or "dislike" (i.e., extrospective orientation) for something or someone somatically experienced as an exciting urgency or alternatively a "regard" and "esteem" or "disregard" for someone or something psychically experienced as a calming concern. In either case, it is not an informative cognitive conscious awareness that is experienced for the object or person of one's self-esteem or self-disesteem but a dys/informative nescient awareness that prevails in the subjective order.

One's subconscious mental "bearing" toward whatever one has a special cerebral attachment is always weighed carefully in terms of one's mental psychic prejudicial attitudinal mindset that insists on employing a remote mathematical scale of precision as the measure and standard of what it finds socially, politically, and acceptably suitable to its own psychic bearing and autonomous security. This mindset is exemplified in the current feminist mindset which insists that the female is the equal of the male precisely because substitutively she can functionally replace the male in everything that he undertakes. On this basis, the woman's needful psychic claim to what is equitably "just" demands that she be legalistically, socially, and politically entitled to function in all of the roles and offices to which the male has access. This "equitable" justice is nothing less nor other than the mathematical calculation that equates two static factors with each other (viz., 2 + 2 = 4).

In polar opposition to this, one's conscious somatic "feeling" toward whatever one has a special visceral attachment is, in turn, assessed caringly in terms of one's prejudicial somatic bias that insists on an imprecise utilitarian scale as the proximate measure and standard of what is socially, legalistically, and politically acceptable to willfully insure one's social security. This visceral mindset is, in turn, exemplified in the current mindset of religious tolerance which is prevalent in the United States. This mindset demands that any religious denomination be regarded as equivalent to any other because substitutively each functionally services the emotional needs for the religious self-gratification of its own members. In view of this visceral mindset regarding the equality of religious denominations and services it is the semi-official policy of the United States government to banish all religious factions from participating in the public political forum. In so doing, it advances a secular religion "of no religion." That is, it promotes legislatively a policy of penalizing any religious denomination that utilizes its own religious resources to drum up votes for a special candidate or issue. In effect, this is tantamount to establishing politics itself as the state religion.

Of course from a mere cultural viewpoint remaining entirely within the order of subjectivity, all three robust, esthetic, or ascetic prototypical personalities and lifestyles are amoral. The foundation for morality is not to be found in the subjective horizontal phenomenological order itself. It is rooted in the objective vertical ontological order and is based on what is innately and purposively good-as-such. The subjective order is restricted to evaluating what is purposely no-good-as-such precisely because this useable good is esteemed and deemed to be good only in the measure that it supplementally transforms the willful selfhood's own needful deficiency into a bodily self-satisfied and/or mental self-justified self-sufficiency. Nonetheless, any cultural custom, personality, or lifestyle even when it is inherently amoral, such as is the case with the lifestyle of a professional athlete, becomes itself either complementary to the moral order or antimoral and inimical to the moral order. The difference between the two is ascertained by having recourse to the principle of subsidiarity. Since the horizontal subjective order is supplemental to the vertical objective order's fundamental priority, it is ancillary to the moral order itself. When through this supplementarity it brings the fundamental order to a completion and perfection beyond the resources inherent in the order of nature itself, it complements the natural objective order.

However, when it self-servingly succeeds to culturally substitute itself for the natural order's own innate activity and in so doing undermines the objective order's fundamental priority, it becomes anti-moral and inimical to morality itself. Hence, a professional athlete whose personality is based simply on abiding by the rules regulating his own athletic enterprise makes of his entire lifestyle itself a recreational sport. Such an overriding dominant sporting have-attitude has for its premises that all rules are self-servingly conventional as contractually agreed upon by the parties involved regulated by such rules. Likewise, all major life-issues by one committed to this sporting lifestyle are resolved by arbitration. The only authority this sporting lifestyle acknowledges, then, is an arbitrary one that rules and governs with decisions that are always subject to revision.

This sporting lifestyle could not acknowledge nor obey a divine authority such as God is nor recognize a moral order transcendent to its own attitudinal self-interests. Such a lifestyle is incompatible with the objective order of morality which is not a sport and does not abide an overriding dominant sporting mindset and freewheeling self-subservient have-attitude as the capstone to mankind's life endeavors. Such a dominant sporting attitude, then, along with its self-subservient humanistic sporting "spirit" of "live and let live" is rebellious against the moral order itself and is not merely immoral but rebellious flaunting an entirely anti-moral, antinomian, anti-Christian spirit inimical to achieving an authentic self-humanized self-fulfillment.

On the other hand, the lifestyle which does not rebel is moral in the measure that it, by the principle of subsidiarity, supplements and complements but does not altogether substitute for the objective vertical moral order itself. The antinomian attitude willfully surrenders to the anti-moral precept that the only authoritative governor is that of the arbiter and the umpire. A democratic government succumbs to this antinomian mindset when its supreme court does not recognize a higher moral authority than itself and acts merely as an arbiter mediating arbitrarily between minority and majority bi-partisan subjective self-serving needs, parties, and interests.

There is another major difference between objective sensorial passionate affectivity and subjective sensuous emotional compassions. The former purposefully arouse the body's appetitive instinctive drives to autonomically move the corporeal body from place to place pursuant to the objectives of these drives (viz., food, sex, drugs, and shelter). The latter self-servingly impact the self's will to forcibly (i.e., motivationally) have it move itself as a corpuscular bodiless motion. In other words, animal passions do not directly impact the human soul's will in the objective order whereas the self-cultivated self-humanized sensuous emotional compassions in the subjective order do impact directly and forcibly on the self's own egocentric subjective willfulness and self-serving self-cultivated needfulness.

This sensuous emotional compassionate impact forcibly sensitizes and motivates the somatic will to kinetically move itself to action to serve its own self-cultivated needfulness. This action is not the corporeal human body's mobility to spontaneously move its body members to get about locally from place to place in pursuit of food, sex, drugs, and attire. Rather, it is the somatic will's very own bodiless kinetic mobilization that the emotions influentially and forcibly arouse and actuate. The selfhood's somatic will is a self-serving wishful need which is deficiently impotent to supplementally fulfill its own wishes. It must be forcibly moved to productively and synergistically undertake an action which functionally will supplementally service this needful deficiency. It is part of the paradox of the horizontal order of subjectivity that the human personhood's willful self-volition is inherently impotent. The order of subjectivity is that of transformatively making dreams come true in a make-believe world of self-cultivated artificiality. This selfhood's subjective will may willfully wish to move effortlessly over land in lieu of walking or running. But, its willfulness can only be implemented by first fabricating a vehicle to accomplish this.

To effectuate this wish the will itself must be first motivationally "moved" to fabricate a mechanism such as a bicycle or to procure one already man-made. What motivationally "moves" the will to this self-serving productive effectuation are the emotional empathic compassions which excitably sensitize its own somatic willfulness and others to kinetic action. But, before the self's will can factually glide and ride effortlessly over land as a motionless body peddling a bike or riding an automobile, its very own willingness must itself first become kinetically motivated to act by an emotional "bodiless motion." This is exactly the sensuous urgent influential motivational impact that sensitized emotional compassions have on the self's somatic will. They occur and are subjectively experienced and felt in the body's somaticity as "bodiless motions" occurring immanently within the confines of the self's corpuscular anatomical body.

Now, this difference between a corporeal body in local movement and the corpuscular body's bodiless motion is the difference between human nature's substantive corporeal material body in the objective order and its self-cultivated non-substantive corpuscular materialized somatic quasi-body in the subjective order. Thus, again, when a person walks down the street the walking is intransitively the holistic body's movement from place to place. The body moves spontaneously autonomically by instinct or voluntarily at will. Nothing is produced in this walking. On the other hand, when a person peddles a bike down the street, the body ceases to be a physical substantive body moving holistically from place to place. It becomes a bodiless motion forcibly converted to the bike's own cyclical mechanized motion. This motion is productively, and transitively mobilized by the biker's legs peddling the bike's mechanized mobility under the impetus of the self's own willful needful wishful volition to move about more rapidly, supplementally, and conveniently under the impetus of the bicycle's mechanism.

The effect is that cycling involves an anatomical body mobilized in a mechanical motion. This cyclic mechanical motion is not the result in the objective order of the soul's will spontaneously choosing to move (i.e., to walk) or autonomically moving by instinctive reflex but of the selfhood's willfulness in the subjective order of deciding to forcibly move itself (i.e., exert itself) to first fabricate or procure a self-serving mechanism that artificially and artfully facilitates its own selfhood's moving as a motionless body. It is by the motivational urgency of the emotional compassions and the incentive of possessing the facilitation of having a motionless body that the will is sensitized and emotionally motivated to forcibly exert itself to a productive kinetic action. That is, these subjective sensitizing emotions unlike their objective sensorial passions do not directly activate the corporeal body's spontaneous autonomic physical movement. Rather, they motivationally stimulate (viz., as a bodiless motion stimulation) the will's self-serving determination to forcibly (i.e., motivationally) bestir itself to undertake the task of having a mechanism that transports the human body automatically and not merely autonomically from place to place.

The supplemental advantage of the bike over the simple natural activity of walking is that the human person can willfully control and technically manipulate the motion of its own somatic body subjectively without objectively involving the holistic substantive corporeal body itself. Hence, by merely technically willfully (i.e., forcibly) controlling subjectively an anatomical part of its anatomy (viz., the legs peddling the bike) it can control the remainder of the corpuscular body's anatomy to artificially move in a bodiless motion above and beyond its natural corporeal mobility. Thus, the objective human substantive corporeal body remains immobile riding on the bike while the subjective somatic anatomical corpuscular body mechanically peddling the bike forcibly pushing the peddles facilitates the bodiless motion under the forcible self-determination of the self's own self-educed sensitized emotionally induced willfulness to do so.

Of course, this artificial technology can build upon itself as is the case with the automobile, the boat, and the airplane. In this case, a bodiless motion becomes ingeniously refined to the point that the occupants of such vehicles are automatically, artificially, and forcibly transported in a bodiless motion through a minimally resistant void (viz., land, air, water, airless space, etc.) while their substantive corporeal bodies remain naturally immobile and at rest.

This "bodiless motion" is peculiar to one's consciousness of the subjective corpuscular body's somaticity. The pulse of one's heartbeat and the movement of blood through one's heart and veins is experienced as a pulsating current. Yet, by microscopic analysis the blood it-self is composed of minute antibodies (i.e., cells) some of which are known as platelets. These are spoken of as antibodies because they are not substantive physical bodies but, rather, non-substantive paraphysical chemical quasi-bodies (viz., molecules). They are particles which in movement are bodiless since the movement is that of a fluidity and not of a solid physical body moving locally from place to place. Such paraphysical bodiless movement pervades the entire reach of the physical experimental sciences. And, it also per-meates the bio-chemical composition of the human corpuscular body's somatic subjectivity.

Consider, for example, the substance of water whose natural en-ergetic dynamism is its solubility. Water is identified to have three physical different states, liquid, solid, and gas. That is to say, when its solubility is actually such it is a liquid, when it is only possibly liquid but still solid it is a frozen ice, and when it is in an intermediate stage such as vaporous clouds, it is a gas. In each of these three stages of physical change water is endowed with tangible physical properties. Ice melts and dissolves into water as do the clouds and foggy mists when they turn to rain.

But, water in its dynamic solubility is never reducible to what it is not physically in its tangible palpable properties discernible to the exterior senses of the substantive corporeal body. However, we learn in the experimental science of electrochemistry that water is reducible to a molecular antibody composed of two parts hydrogen and one part oxygen. These molecules of water are themselves composed of more minute atomic antibodies. Why antibodies rather than physical substantive bodies? Because molecules themselves are not described in terms of the physical properties proper to the physical substance of water in its three physical states. These molecular particles of hydro-gen and oxygen are quasi-bodies because they are described in purely mathematical terms of their atomic components of density, weight, valence, number, mass, configuration, spin, polarity, etc. In other words, these minuscule molecular atomic particles constitutive of H20 are themselves composed of more minute subatomic particles such as the neutron, proton, and electron. All are mathematically described in purely intangible corpuscular terms proper to the psychic mind's artificial fabrication of mathematical nontactual conceptualized non-beings-as-such.

The experimental physical sciences explain that it is precisely these corpuscular antibody particles that reductively make up the human somatic corpuscular body's biochemical physiology. These particles themselves in their microscopic realm of the microcosmos move in the manner of a bodiless motion precisely because they are described noumenally and mentally in the mathematical terms of the experimental sciences as the nuclear make-up of what one empirically and subjectively experiences phenomenally in feeling the somatic body's sensitivity. Thus, for example, when we experience on a thousand different radios dispersed around the earth's globe the same sounding voice electronically radiated from one and the same transmitter, it is physically impossible for the voice of one speaking to the transmitter to be physically simultaneously in a thousand different places. Yet, it is electronically possible and efficiently feasible for this same voice to be heard radiophonically through a thousand different radios physically dispersed around the earth's globe. What one learns from this is that there is physical space of physical location such that the same corporeal physical body cannot be simultaneously located spatially in two distinctly different places at the same time.

In contradistinction to this, there is cyber non-physical, non-tangible, tactual space that is itself devoid of physical location. This allows for non-physical corpuscular tactual anti-bodies to undulatingly replicate themselves telephonically in different physical occupational locations through the electronic vacuity of cyberspace. And, not only telephonically but also televisually. Cyberspace, then, is a mathematical space with a dimensionality (i.e., the fourth dimension?) lacking physical tangible properties. This cyberspace is a marvelous electronic medium of telecommunication permitting and facilitating the same physical voice transmitted from one physical place on the globe to globally resound on a thousand other physical places radiophonically tuned in.

What is impossible through physical space has become feasible electronically through cyberspace which is devoid of all physical corporeal tangibility. Just as the physical voice moving through cyberspace becomes electronically transmitted to a thousand different physical places radiophonically, a physical body photogenically moving electronically through the cyberspace of television becomes transmitted to a thousand different physical places having a thousand different televisual sets. Again, what is physically impossible becomes electronically feasible. What, indeed is transmitted? Certainly, it is not a physical corporeal body in physical space that is transmitted. This is impossible; bilocation is impossible. It is a corpuscular antibody that is transmitted which is described mathematically and is itself devoid of any tangible physical property of its own.

In other words, an electronic body (viz., an electron) is itself a minute corpuscular quasi-body that is composed of particles mathematically described which are intuitively discerned by the corpuscular self-humanized body's psychic mind. It is no wonder, then, why these minute anti-bodies escape the objective corporeal body's natural senses even while they are experienced subjectively and consciously as the corpuscular somatic body's sensational "bodily motion" feelings especially when one accidentally touches an electronic "live wire" and feels an electric shock. In the objective physical universe a substantive body can occupy only one physical place at a time. It may move or be moved from one place to another but this local motion itself demands that the two places be physically different and distinct from each other.

Yet, by electronic radio and TV transmission the very same sound and image can simultaneously phenomenally occupy multiple different physical locations around the earth. The electrons moving in an electric current that transmit these electronic sounds and images...are each of these electrons the self-same electron moving from the transmitter to the receiver in multiple transmissions? This is an impossibility in the vertical objective metaphysical natural order of being and existence; but a seeming possibility in the horizontal subjective paraphysical microcosmic mathematical order of culture and resistance.

Or, is it the case that an electron is cloned and replicated umpteen times in the twinkling of an eye; that is, in the time that it takes one speaking into a microphone at the transmitter station to the time it is broadcast on different radio and TV sets around the world? Is this electronic process of cloning and replicating electrons over immense cyberspace distances what occurs in electronic transmission? It is hypothesized that such radio and TV electronic transmissions are sent in varying wavelengths. Is it one and the same replicated wavelength stretching for thousands of miles in cyberspace or a multiple different number of replicated wavelengths which transmit the same voice and image through cyberspace? Or, again, is this transmission effectuated by one and the same electron or a series of replicated electrons traveling electronically through cyberspace? It would seem that a radio transmission is an electronic wave that is both an inextended electron (viz., like a point on a line) undulating as a wave-length over a vast extended distance in the twinkle of an eye. That is, it is a wavicular particle antibody that remains an inextended particle electron extending itself as an undulating wave over a vast linear vacuous expanse of cyberspace. The conception of radio and TV electronic transmissions in terms of electron particles traveling in wavelengths through cyberspace explains noumenally in conceptualized mathematical terms what an auditor and viewer phenomenally and empirically experience when they are listening to the radio and watching their TV sets.

This electronic movement in cyberspace is an insoluble enigma that is peculiar to the mathematical synthetic and analytical structure that pervades the entire subjective reach of the human person's self-subsistent personhood's artificially self-cultivated egocentric selfhood. The human person's subjective corpuscular somatic body is itself purportedly composed of mathematically conceived microscopic molecular and atomic particles (viz., tactual but intangible antibodies) which are themselves composed of materialistic features described in precise mathematical spatiotemperal noumenal nontactual terms discernible exclusively by the mind's psychic intuitivity. Further, these microscopic particles are the chemical rudiments of biological cellular and microbic living matter while they themselves are explicitly lifeless.

This means that what the human person's selfhood subjectively tactually experiences as the corpuscular somatic body's phenomenal sensitized feelings and sensations are paradoxically enough explained in noumenal terms that are discernible exclusively to the selfhood's psychic intuition of nontactual mathematical conceptions. Of course, mathematical geometric lines and arithmetic numerals are themselves neither living nor tactual nor dynamic. They are inertly static and organizationally non-living. Such also is the case for molecules and their submolecular atomic composition. It is no fluke that an atomic bomb if left to itself would never explode nor implode; it would remain merely a dud as long as it is not activated and detonated. Yet, these corpuscular microscopic nontactual insubstantive antibody atomic particles along with the electron and the photon have in our modern culture completely substituted for and eliminated altogether the substantive corporeal tangible bodies of the physical universe.

A typical university educated individual today does not approach an apple tree and its fruit as a substantive reality whose holistic substantive dynamic energetic nature is not reducible to its microcosmic biochemical components. Similarly, the same individual today does not approach either the adult human person himself or the newly conceived human zygote as a holistic substantive dynamic energetic living nature that is irreducible to its nonliving microcosmic biochemical components.

Indeed, the somatic body's corpuscularity experientially makes itself empirically accessible to the human person's self-subsistent personhood only in the measure that this selfhood is extrospectively conscious of feeling its own body's sensitized sensations. This corpuscular body's anatomy and physiology considered exclusively in its corpuscular terms of the biochemical experimental sciences is reductively the product of man's own materialistic self-humanization and self-cultivation. The more the human person's subjective personhood synthetically and analytically through its own artificial ingenuity probes experimentally and reductively the substantive materiality of the person's objective corporeal body's tangible physical materiality through hi-tech equipment empirically interpreted within the framework of plausible synthesized hypothetical mathematical theories, the more mankind succeeds in materializing (i.e., pulverizing) and exploiting the inherent dynamic material energy of these holistic bodies into minute corpuscular static synergistic antibody insubstantive particles known as molecules, atoms, electrons, photons, and their ilk, etc.

In the pulverizing process of this empirical reductive exploration, the human body's own objective substantive holistic dynamic living corporeality becomes subjectively increasingly anatomically fragmentized and physiologically corpuscularized into non-living biochemical microscopic antibodies. Yet, in this subjective egocentric consciousness of feeling the corpuscular body's somaticity this corpuscularity is experienced (when one becomes experimentally conscious of distinctive parts of the body's anatomical and physiological somatic complexity) as "bodiless motions." Explaining the experience of this "bodiless motion" is no different than explaining the cyberspace motion of electric light, heat, and radio TV electronic transmissions, etc. Electricity is explained as a stream of electrons which is phenomenally experienced in an electric shock as a fluid current of "bodiless motion" rather than as a movement of small particles such as occurs when sand passes through an hour-glass. In accidentally touching an electric "live wire" one does not experience particles of electricity, one experiences a jolt of electric current. In other words, one experiences a "bodiless motion" and not minute microscopic bodies in motion.

Again, even at the risk of belaboring this point, the entire reach and psychosomatic makeup of the human person personhood's egocentric subjective self-subsistent self-cultivated selfhood is enigmatically permeated with the paradoxical surdity inherent in mathematics itself. Every mathematical quantum is simultaneously and ambiguously both a congregated (i.e., continuous, geometric) and segregated (i.e., discrete, arithmetic) aggregate. The mathematical spatiotemporal continuum is not a metaphysical entity in the objective natural universe of existence, it is a non-entitative paraphysical enterprise in the subjective world of mankind's self-humanized cultural resistance. In other words, this man-made cultural order of worldly resistance is itself resistantly opposed to the objective natural order of existence proper to the order of God's creation.

The self-serving will of a personhood's psychosomatic subjectivity willfully and forcibly attends to one mathematical aspect to the exclusion of the other. This is the case when pure geometry is willfully calculated apart from arithmetic considerations and vice versa. A mathematical linear antibody is both a continuum of extended contiguous segments (viz., lines) and inextended segments (viz., points). An arithmetic serial antibody is both a continuum of extended discrete segments (viz., integers) and inextended segments (viz., zeroes). In other words, each is the antipodal reverse of the other. Any mathematical continuum may be examined geometrically or arithmetically. Indeed, both are explored simultaneously in trigonometry. This enigma accounts for the considerable dichotomous disparity which demarcates the willful selfhood's psychic noumenal conceptual experiences from its somatic phenomenal perceptual ones.

Recall that a rotund apple is not constituted of an indefinite number of circles laminated together. Yes, its rotundity is circular but it is also tangibly a living dynamic rotundity that continues to spontaneously expansively grow as long as the apple continues to mature and ripen on the tree. One cannot pinch or touch a circle. It is not only lifeless, it is not tangible to the body's hand and it is not tactually touchable even by the imagination's imaginary imagery of it. It is intuitively noumenally discernible exclusively by the mind's own nontactual psychicity. What is the case for the circle in terms of the apple's rotundity is also the case for the atom and other non-living microscopic antibodies vis-à-vis the human body's substantive corporeality. That is, the human body's substantive tangible corporeality is not constituted of intangible only tactual antibodies.

The upshot of this corollary on "bodiless motion" is to emphasize that sensitizing emotional compassions are subjectively extrospectively consciously experienced as forcible impulsive excitable sensual sensitized urgings which the human person's selfhood's own self-serving somatic will needfully elicits to motivationally stimulate its own will to kinetic action to overcome its inherent inertial resistant impotency. In the make-believe dream world that is the horizontal order of subjectivity, the human selfhood's will can psychically willfully wish to live in a utopia of flying effortlessly through the sky. However, it cannot fulfill this dream without first expending a considerable exerted bodily effort and considerable toil to somatically realize and bring about the fabrication of a viable aircraft. To forcibly engage itself in this somatic effort of experimentally constructing an aircraft, it needs to be emotionally sensuously stimulated (viz., motivated) to engage in a sustained kinetic bodily exploitative transaction of planning and constructing one.

ASCENT THIRD APPENDIX

Affective passions vs compassionate emotions: three prototypical personalities.

Sensitive emotional compassionate bodily feelings motivationally stimulate the self's willful self-serving somatic need (i.e., requirement) to manually make, to have, to own, and to functionally avail one's own self of possessively procuring utilizable conveniences to pragmatically facilitate its willful artificial self-control and manipulate its own body with ease, comfort, and a self-gratifying self-contentment. These emotional compassionate feelings, accordingly, are self-willfully provoked to sensuously urge and impel the somatic will to kinetic action. These sensitive emotional feelings emerge from the somatic self's own demand (i.e., imperative need) for useable facilities that functionally and conveniently (and, possibly automatically) serve the selfhood's somatic needs to move about sensationally more rapidly and effortlessly. And, again and again, this willful selfhood's self-serving deficient need is itself skillfully transformed into a self-cultivated self-sufficient manipulative somatic skill in the process of cultivating and exploitatively using such useable artificial conveniences. The subjective selfhood's dichotomous psychosomatic will is not an innate faculty; it is an inbred self-cultivated propensity which is skillfully transformed into a competency in the process of experimentally cultivating artificial workable tools and symbols.

Intimate emotionless telepathic bearings, on the other hand, motivationally sedate the self's willful self-serving psychic need (i.e., requirement) to mentally make, to have, to own, and to functionally avail one's own self of possessively devising schematics to pragmatically facilitate its willful artificial self-control and management of its own mind's inventive self-containment as well as the minds of other selves. These emotionless telepathic bearings are self-willfully invoked to impassively compel the psychic will to somnolent inaction (viz., pondering and musing). These intimate emotionless bearings emerge from the psychic self's own demand (i.e., imperative need) for useful schematics that functionally and suitably (and possibly autocratically) serve the selfhood's psychic needs to have fully realized its inspirational wishes to effortlessly communicate its own wishes. And, accordingly, this willful selfhood's self-serving deficient psychic need becomes itself skillfully transformed into a self-cultivated self-sufficient manageable skill in the process of cultivating and exploititatively applying (i.e., testing) such useful sketches.

It should not be surprising to the reader of this commentary that the selfhood's own self-serving will is psychosomatically dichotomous and antipodal. This is in keeping with the selfhood's polarized egology. The human person's egocentric awareness of both its own somatic body's "bodiless motion" sensitized feelings and anatomic functions, is a simple extrospective empirical (inspectable) awareness whereas the same human person's egocentric awareness of its own mind's "motionless body" bearings and mental functioning is a complex introspective unobservable awareness. And, whereas bodily emotional feelings are sensitively experienced as a continuous or pulsating fluid current feeling of "bodiless motion", their mental counterpart emotionless bearings are intimately experienced as bearing discrete notions afloat in a "motionless body" (i.e., a stream of consciousness).

In other words, the human person's extrospective awareness of the body's subjective somaticity is similar to one observing the fluidity of a river's current while an introspective awareness of the mind's subjective psychicity is similar to observing the passing objects afloat on the river's current. In both cases, the "motion" is not that of a physical body that both undergoes and sustains the movement which it undergoes. The movement is not ontologically of an actually existing stable and substantive body; it is phenomenological of a seeming

375

process of movement. On the one hand, the human person experiences sensitized bodily feelings as a "conscious" current fluidity devoid of particles and on the other hand, the same human person experiences intimate bearings as particles afloat in a current of consciousness.

Having differentiated within the subjectivity of the human person's egocentric selfhood the difference between his bodily feelings and his mental bearings, it is very important to further differentiate between the same person's objective sentiency proper to his animal nature's substantive body and the subjective sensitivity proper to his self-humanized nonsubstantive body's sensitivity. The human person's animal body's affectivity differs markedly from his self-humanized body's somaticity. The former undergoes objective passionate movements (viz., dys/affections) which are conducive to physically and spontaneously moving the animal bodily from one place or position to another (viz., walking, running, swimming, stretching, climbing, crawling, etc.) for the purpose of arriving at the body's instinctive drive for nutrition, prolific prolongation, healthy vigor, and protection. The latter undergoes subjective compassionate motions (viz., dys/affectionate feelings) which are impulsive urgings to kinetically (i.e., by exertion) to engage in artificial manipulations (viz., handy fabrications) that serve to alleviate and appease (i.e., satisfy and gratify) the human self's somatic deficiency (i.e., need for socially secure self-sufficient sensuous sensitized self-contentment).

These subjective emotional compassionate feelings are forcefully and directly influential on the selfhood's willfulness whereas their objective instinctive passionate counterparts are not. The latter only indirectly affect the soul's intellectual will. They directly affect the animal body's purposeful instinct for its holistic corporeal appetitive well-being. The former directly impact sensitively---and not merely sensibly and sentiently--- the person's own somatic selfhood. They do not stimulate an instinctive drive for a good that is purposefully common to every living body in the same family of the animal having that drive. Rather, they stir the body's needful want to forcibly exert itself to busy itself artfully and productively to overcome its own body's deficiency and social insecurity. Now, any and every self-cul-

376

tivated handy artificial tool fabricated to relieve a person's bodily self-deficiency becomes socially serviceable to not only the self that ingeniously and laboriously fabricates it, but to any self other than the self that skillfully crafted it. In brief, any self-cultivated facility and utility is automatically a social artifact.

Basic objective animal instinctive passions are purposeful carnal drives which are affectionately attractive or disaffectionately repelling by what inherently and purposely benefits or harms the entire body's holistic well-being. They are not imperiously compelling and their dys/affectivity ceases when the purpose of the drive is consummated. This is not the case with subjective sensuous artificially self-induced purposeless self-serving emotional motivating compassionate feelings. They have no intentional inherent purpose but only a motivational self-serving forcible influence on the selfhood's imperative need to provide for its own somatic comfortable and self-satisfying social security. They only do not cease their influential pressure and impulsive urgency on the self's willfulness even when the will accedes to them, they continue to increase this pressure the more attentatively the will reactively capitulates to them.

For example, it is more urgently, effortlessly, and sensuously compelling to be entertained by a movie, a TV show, or a computer production to artificially view an apple than it is to explore and investigate the countryside on one's own in search of an apple orchard. An apple on the tree is no where near as appetitively enticing as is a TV commercial artificially displaying an apple in electrifying colors on the TV, videocassette, movie, or computer screen. The latter artificially cultivated depiction of the apple is not merely sentiently appealing as is the case with the ripe apple on the tree in an orchard. The sensationally televised apple is sensuously seductively influentially and artfully compelling. For, it is not merely a naturally good food such as is the apple on the tree which affectively stirs the corporeal body's innate drive to sample its nutritional savor; it is artfully and sensationally depicted so as to artificially induce emotional compassionate sensuous feelings that directly (i.e., motivationally) influence the subjective self's will to possessively entertain and to enjoy the apple for its own sensuous self-indulgence. The motive here in the

TV transmission is not merely to have one eat the apple for the body's nourishment but to possessively have and own it to be conveniently and sensuously enjoyed at one's leisure in lieu of eating the apple itself.

If the example of the natural apple on the tree compared with the artificial apple on the TV or movie screen seems rather lame and tame, substitute for it a pornographic depiction of the human body in its place. The human body's sexual enticement between married spouses retains its objective purposefulness even while it affectively, mutually, and passionately stirs the spouse's instinctive animal drive to procreatively proliferate their own marital vitality through their offsprings. The pornographically displayed human body's sexual enticement to the casual voyeur retains nothing of its objective purposefulness. Rather, it arouses not spontaneously the animal body's instinctive life-giving passions but stirs up self-cultivated sensitized subjective feelings of venereal pleasure which the human person can subjectively artificially entertain self-indulgently within the subjectivity of his own self-humanized and self-centered somaticity. The very temptation of such pornographic depictions sensationally rendered through television and movie media is that these are artificially divorced from the very objective purpose inherent in the human corporeal body's sexuality.

The person whose domineering have-attitudinal lifestyle is realistically and artificially that of the playboy or playgirl seeking to cater to the somatic body's subjective needs, conveniences, comfort, sensuality, security, etc., is influentially emotionally compelled to procure and possessively own this electronically sensationalized audiovisual apple (or pornographic depiction) for its own self-serving selfish sensuous self-gratification. "You owe it to yourself" is the theme of the TV commercial. That is, the personality of this narcissistic lifestyle does not seek to possessively and willfully own this product because it is intrinsically good and nutritionally valuable vis-à-vis the corporeal body's natural instinctive drive for nutriment (and the proliferation of life).

It motivationally willfully seeks to possess this product (viz., the pornographic depiction) because it is selfishly self-servingly worthwhile to manipulatively and exploitatively allow this personality a complete self-control over its own body's somatic sensitized sensuous feelings of comfort and somatic social automatic self-gratification. This corpuscular "body" which is subject to a person's artificial manipulative self-control is no longer the objective substantive corporeal body that is animated by a spiritual substantive soul. It is a corpuscular insubstantive body lacking holistic substantive organicity. Objectively in the ontological order the person's sexual faculty is a faculty (i.e., in inalienable power) of the human person's substantive body to beget life. Subjectively in the phenomenological order, the person's sexuality is a psychosomatic needy social deficiency which becomes a skillful self-fulfilled self-assured conscientious sensuous self-gratifying self-sufficiency only in the stability provided by the marriage of heterosexual spouses. Otherwise, its sexual psychosomatic needy social deficiency is overcome by the human person becoming willfully and ascetically completely self-detached from these emotionally gratifying feelings of venereal sensuality including all occasions that tantalizingly seduce such feelings.

In other words, it is anatomically speaking, a somatic body that can be experimentally analyzed and fragmented into the multiplicity of its microscopic miniscular parts, organisms, functions, sensations, cells, and biochemical microscopic cellular and molecular components. It is entirely a subjectively nonsubstantial phenomenological quasi-body inasmuch as it is the body which subjectively one can consciously phenomenally somatically experience and/or subconsciously psychically noumenally explain in purely quantitative mathematical terms commensurate with the terminology of biochemistry and biophysics.

One does not take an aspirin to relieve a headache because the aspirin itself is painless. It is because the subjective conscious symptomatic experience of the aspirin's chemical conscious effect on the body is the disappearance of the headache's pain and discomfiture. Aspirin is not objectively a natural good-as-such herb or drug that is naturally beneficial in what it actually is as a pharmaceutical curative agent. It is a no-good-as-such self-cultivated self-humanizing pharmaceutical which is serviceably usably quasi-good in the measure

379

that it promotes symptomatically the experience of a relief from pain when it is consumed. An apple is inherently a nutritional good-as-such. An aspirin is not inherently painless. Some persons do not even experience relief after taking one or more aspirins. Some experience relief for a period of usage and not after an extended period of usage. An aspirin is subjectively a private social artificial no-good-as-such medication associatively linked with a specific chemical compound that experimentally (i.e., experientially) and symptomatically relieves a headache. Frequently, the psychic autosuggestion of impending relief is more curative than the aspirin's actual chemistry on the somatic body's neurological complexus.

In other words, aspirin is not a good-as-such as is the case with the apple on the tree for anyone who procures it. It is an artificial no-good-as-such medication precisely because its symptomatic relief depends on the variable unreliable private subjective somatic experiences which one has of it. Different pharmaceutical companies make competitive claims of relief for differing brands of medications they place on the market.

Furthermore, where natural sensorial purposeful instinctive passions are chronically transient both in brute and human animals, their sensuous compassionate artificially self-induced subjective emotional counterparts are tempered by the somatic body's own somaticity (i.e., sensitized conscious feelings of them). Of course, the somatic body is only "alive" when the human person in its self-subsistent personhood is extrospectively consciously focused on its own emotional feelings. When one is conscious of objectively seeing an apple in a tree, one's reflective consciousness is on the apple itself and not subjectively and egocentrically on the optical eye's anatomical organism.

When one becomes extrospectively aware that one's eyesight is failing, one's conscious attention is subjectively egocentrically focused on the somatic body's anatomical optical physiology rather than on any visible reality itself that transcends the somatic body's subjective symptoms. However, when one becomes introspectively fully reflexively self-conscious of one's psychic inner mindful self and fully concentrates on the mental activity and notions of this inner psychic self, one is altogether oblivious to the somatic body's sensationally sensitized feelings and sensuous emotional compassions (viz., to its sensitized aches and pains along with its sensuous emotional excitement and feeling of pleasure and pain).

Subjective emotional compassions are consciously felt and linger in the somatic body as sensitized sensuous feelings which give rise to lingering temperamental conscious moods. Somatic consciousness is not transparently colorless as is the case with the sun's sunshine. Somatic consciousness is pervasively colored by lingering moods of sensitized feelings which issue from the dominant emotional overtone that prevails in the body's physiological somaticity. Certainly, these temperamental moods are also conditioned by the somatic body's own physiology which is genetically inherited.

Thus, one's somatic body may be predominantly tempered by a melancholic, phlegmatic, irascible, or sanguine biochemical disposition and humor. Further, these moods may be exploitatively manipulated by mood-inducing drugs. Yet, the moods themselves are residually the prolongation of one's dominant self-induced compassionate emotions and sensitizing feelings. A personality which is narcissistically dominated by a hedonistic attitudinal mindset, seeking to prolong and self-sustain emotionally elated periods of excitements, is prone to emotional depressions when these excitements run their course. Emotions are empathically socially infectious. In the pathos and pathology of these emotions, one who is emotionally antipathetic (i.e., a subjectively self-induced antipathy) and not merely passionately (i.e., objectively) angry, this emotional antipathy infectiously, compassionately, and empathically evokes the same emotion in selves other than one's own self.

This is the very objective of play-acting and rhetoric in politicians and preachers; namely, to induce the audience to empathically adopt the same emotions as the ones entertained by the actors and orators themselves. On the other hand, natural instinctive passions and affections are not socially empathic or seductively infectious. Panic in crowds bringing about an uncontrollable hysteria is also clear evidence of the empathic compassionate infectious sociability peculiar to emotions.

Radically, a personality's overriding willful attitudinal mindset underwriting its self-adopted self-serving lifestyle is the trigger that controls the somatic body's susceptibility to certain emotions. The full impact of these emotions is experienced by the self's self-serving will-fulness which is sensuously sensitized by these emotions to forcibly and urgently yield to their impulsive sensuality. And, since these emotions are infectiously and empathically social, it is moreso often the case that they are deliberately self-induced to influence emotional reactions in selves other than the one-self who induces them to thereby evoke them in others. This explains why an apple on a tree is merely appealing but not seductively tempting while the TV apple's sensational artificial presentation is sensuously seductive. The apple's natural sensibility naturally (i.e., spontaneously) attracts an instinct-ive carnal appetite to itself as an appetible object transcendent to the appetite itself while the TV apple's artificial sensationalism awakens the viewer's sensitized awareness to its own subjective selfhood's deprivation and urgent need for an automatic appetizing self-gratific-ation. The one is affectively and sentiently appealing while the other is affectionately and sensuously seductive.

Thus, one can deliberately induce and feel pity for one's own self when such pity will further elicit a sympathetic feeling from others. It goes without saying that one who behaves in front of a TV camera is more conscious of one's own self than is the case when the camera is not present. The attitude of one on live TV or radio is interpersonally focused. Not in the sense of being focused as a nonpartisan person appealing impartially to another person to pass on information re-garding the speed limit on a stretch of road, for example. But, rather, in the sense that the TV announcer's own subjective have-attitudinal personality and bias engages intersubjectively the subjective have-at-titudinal personality and bias of other selves within the listening and viewing range of the TV transmission.

The one who appears live on TV is a personality who is self-aware of his or her own selfhood speaking televisually and empathic-ally appealing to other selves in the audience who are also empathic-ally aware of the speaker's own selfhood and personality. Of course, the empathy on the part of the televiewer may be sympathetic, anti-pathic, or even apathetic, depending on whether there is or is not a symbiosis in attitudes between the emcee speaking and those audio-visualizing the transmission. What is most consciously focal in this intersubjective encounter is the convergence or divergence of each selfhood's own partisan self-serving prejudicial attitude including the ensuing affable emotional resonance or unfriendly emotional dissonance on the part of the TV patrons. Of course, it is a given that the very audience that is admitted to the live TV broadcast is usually sympathetic to the biased attitude of the host.

A person's lifetime career pursuit is the keystone to deciphering and discerning an individual's personality. A career is not a vocation which is a calling to nobility transcendent to a personality's self-orientation. This vocational calling appeals to one's human ideals and explicitly engages one's upright moral character. The moral order is grounded in the vertical hierarchical ontological order of existence. Neither is a career explicitly a commission which means being appointed and being sent to carry out an assigned task. This involves being vested vicariously with an authority to carry out an assigned task. A commission may be undertaken by an individual or a group. A commissioner is one who authoritatively appoints and sends another individual or group to undertake a specified task.

A career is something akin to a commission in that it involves a being sent by one's own self in the successful pursuit of an overarching and sometimes a life-long task. A career is strictly an undertaking that is self-assigned and self-appointed. Therefore, it is self-servingly self-orientated and very much typical of the horizontal historical order involving the selfhood's paramount commitment to its own autonomous egocentric social security. The task envisioned in a career enjoins a period of preparatory training in which one becomes skillfully adept and, hence, something of a professional master in becoming able to pursue the task's successful completion.

If a career is explicitly a religious one, it is that of an appointed minister. It would seem that one is known as a minister in view of the project which one is sent to carry out. Yet, the term minister is employed even for secular pursuits as is the case in the public service of governmental officials, a minister of the interior, for example. In any event, every career has its role-models and occupational involvement which usually serves to financially support one's own welfare and autonomous social security whether it be that of a diplomat, an actor, a banker, a mechanic, a salesman, a home-maker, an educator, a fireman, a broker, a secretary, a soldier, a fisherman, a janitor, a plant worker, a miner, a carpenter, a pharmacist, a medical doctor, a lawyer, a journalist, an athlete, a musician, a research scientist, etc.

All of these manifold careers have three overarching role-models patterned after the three distinctive creative arts: the liberal, the mechanical, and the fine arts. Preparatory study for one majoring in the liberal arts are the humanities usually taught fully at the college level in university settings; for the mechanical arts it is the technical fields which are usually taught in institutes of technology; and for the fine arts it is the esthetic fields which are usually taught in academies focusing on music, dance, painting, writing, design, acting, etc.

What this reveals is that in the broadest of terms those specializing in the humanities tend to be predominantly introspective while those specializing in technology tend to be extrospective and their intermediary tend to be a hybrid of the prior two. Therefore, there are in these three fields of the creative arts archetypical role-models for all individuals majoring in one of these three fields characterizing their career pursuits. One's gainful career occupation and employment provides a profile of one's personality but does not identify one's sovereign dignity as a person. The radical difference between a human person and a self-humanized personality is that the former is inalienably human by nature while the latter self-cultivates its alienable dominant personality in view of its specialized functioning in conjunction with others dedicated to the same service.

One majoring in the liberal arts is predominantly an introspective cerebral self while one majoring in the mechanical arts is predominantly an extrospective visceral self. The one majoring in a fine art is intermediately both cerebral and/or visceral depending on whether he is more inclined to creatively initiating and authoring a fine art endeavor or performing a known artwork such as an actor. A cerebral introverted personality is more subconsciously mentally and psychically self-absorbed since the professional creative product of the humanist remains immanently within his own cerebration. Most humanists tend to be autocratic and to work alone although they do have their own professional associations. The thrust of their humanist endeavors is not their written or composed works but the serviceably useful creative ideas and schemes which these works exhibit. A visceral extroverted personality is more consciously somatically self-absorbed with his own physique since the professional expert product of the technician engages the exerted automatic functioning of not only his own body's members but also of the tools and mechanisms which he craftily employs and services. Technicians tend to be automatic both in their own professional work habits and in their crafted products some of which are produced by automation. Most technicians tend to work in specialized groups and to belong to professional associations reflective of these specializations. The thrust of their technical endeavors are the serviceably useable tools and mechanisms which they fabricate.

The intermediate personality in the field of fine arts may be both cerebrally introverted and/or viscerally extroverted. A creative innovator, such as a composer, a poet, a choreographer, a painter, etc., may be predominantly introspective whereas an accomplished performer such as a concert pianist, an actor, a dancer, a cartoonist, etc., may be predominantly extrospective. One who occupies a role which is midway between each of these antipodal roles would have a personality which partakes of both the introvert and the extrovert.

The completely subconsciously self-absorbed introverted humanist personality is preoccupied not with what appears phenomenally on the very tactual surface of things that impinge on the somatic body's feelings and sensations but with intuitive noumenal ideations which escape empirical investigation and scrutiny. The exact reverse is the case with the completely consciously self-absorbed extroverted technical personality who is preoccupied with the phenomena at the tactual surface of the somatic body's feelings and visceral exertions. A person's alienable autonomous personality is self-humanized, self-orientated, and socially self-constructed in the horizontal order of history's eventuations whereas a person's inalienable sovereign personhood is naturally human in the vertical order of an eternal hierarchically ordered universe.

A human person's sovereign personhood is neither duplicable nor exchangeable with another person whereas a human person's autonomous personality ceases with the cessation of his functioning within the role of the paradigmatic model he was previously emulating. That is, his personality's function may be duplicated and replaced by a self other than his own self in which case he may no longer function in this role. Of course, he may train for a different function but in so doing he changes his personality when he changes from one paradigmatic role model to another. The tragedies of life occur when a personality is unable to make such a radical shift.

It should be noted that the somatic extrospective surface personality of the technician is easily alienated from his own self-appointed role model precisely because his own lifestyle and mannerism may be easily imitated by a self other than his own self who can readily impersonate his own behavioral traits, skills, and peculiarities of speech, occupational habits, movement, attire, posture, etc. Indeed, the somatic surface empathic self feels at home with like-minded personalities sharing the same attitudinal bias, skills, and feels himself to be alienated in the company of those who do not behave in a like-minded fashion. Further, a feeling of alienation can occur when very menial differences, such as clothing, style, occupations, residence, physical characteristics, taste, race, height, etc., occur. In such instances the personality not fitting in with special groups and settings harboring similar characteristics will feel itself alienated (i.e., an outsider). A complete alienation occurs when a person migrates from his ingrained national culture to one which differs in language, religion, customs, etc., from his own natal family.

On the other hand, the psychic subsurface introspective personality of the humanist is less likely to experience an alienation from his own selfhood even in the company of those who have an attitudinal bias different from his own. In this instance the psychic self tends to regard others as aliens rather than his own selfhood as alienated. The reason for this is that the introspective egocentric self is entirely "at home" in the inner intimacy of his own attitudinal bias. He regards others who do not share this bias as aliens. This "at home" mindset and mental bearing (i.e., equilibrium) has its anchor in the personality's introspective retreat into the very inmost psychic intimacy of his own selfhood. By reason of this it should also be noted that the humanist is less prone to socializing with others than is the case with the technician whose very skill engages the collaborative skill of others.

It should not be loss on the reader of this commentary that everyone's own personality historically passes through its youthful preoccupation with its own body's kinetic somaticity to its more mature and older concentration on its mind's static psychicity. Young people are more extroverted and physically active whereas older people are more introverted and passively inactive. In a culture which idolizes youth as is the case in the USA of the third millennium, every person of note maintains a youthful physique which futuristically and artificially is conditioned to retain its youthful flexibility and mobility. In a culture such as ancient China which idolized and revered the age and maturity of its elder citizens even after their death and departure, it is exactly the reverse. Here Confucianism held sway with its adages and its peculiar cultic animism of the departed still inhabiting domestic dwellings. Physical exercises focused aerobically on the body's own mechanical mobilization precisely to allow the mind to be unencumbered with the body's functioning.

It must also be observed that personalities that are predominantly introspective are, accordingly, more emotionlessly tranquil and impassively detached from the somatic body's emotivity and feelings. It is just the reverse with personalities that are predominantly extrospective. These are more readily susceptible to being urgently influenced and attached to their somatic body's emotional feelings and sensitized stirrings. Again, note that subjective emotions, feelings, sensitivities, moods, temperaments, etc., are not of themselves morally good nor morally bad. However, inasmuch as they supplementally by the principle of subsidiarity support and reinforce what is objectively morally (i.e., conscionably reasonable) appropriate for the corporeal body's holistic wellbeing, they are morally compatible. Failing this, they undermine the moral order itself and thus they are not merely immorally bad, they are antimoral and antinominially antimoral in the sense that they deliberately rebel against the objective moral order itself and against the author of this moral order, God's supreme moral authority and the natural law supernaturally revealed in the ten commandments.

Again, it is extremely important to emphasize that the self-humanized personality of a human person's self-subsistent self-cultivated personhood is not to be confused with the personhood itself. One's personhood exists in the vertical order of existence. It is innately endowed with a dynamic energetic compound substantive nature: matter and spirit. The human person's substantive body and soul are not separate substances. Each are co-substantive principles of one and the same holistic substance, the human person's substantive compound intellectually free nature. One's personhood itself is inalienably and incommunicably (i.e., inexchangeably) uniquely (i.e., induplicably) identical with its own substantive self-subsistent existence. God Himself cannot create two separate persons whose proper personhood is duplicated or cloned.

The subjective self-humanized egocentric psychosomatic personality, on the other hand, is in the horizontal cultural historical order of resistance and not in the objective natural vertical hierarchical order of existence. This personality as previously stated is exchangeable, duplicable, and non-identical with itself. It is self-humanized in the sense that a particular person born in the Republic of China is educated in a Chinese language and culture which is the self-cultivated civilizing product of the Chinese self-humanizing genius. The typical Chinese personality resists emigrating from its own culture to live in a culture alien to its own.

The same is the case for any individual forcibly exiled from its own native culture. In the case of such an exile the individual is forced to exchange its cultural birth-right for a culture that is alien to its own self-civilized personality. It matters not that one born into a specific culture has not itself prior to its birth contributed to that culture's development. This civilized culture is still the birth-right of the neonate who inherits not only the genetic features of his parents but also their self-cultivated cultural features as well. In any event, one's self-cultivated personality is alienable unlike one's personhood which is inherently inalienable.

Those who confuse the human person's objective personhood

with the person's subjective ephemeral alienable functioning personality abolish abortively, apodictally, and ignominiously the person's fundamental inalienable and immortal dignity, sovereignty, and nobility. This serious and grave ignominy frequently occurs whenever a person's personality is not yet functional as is the case at conception with the nascent embryo and when a person is in a coma. One's personality cannot become self-cultivated and self-humanized until and unless the person becomes aware of itself and its own psychosomatic selfhood. At conception there is not yet such a full-blown self-awareness. And, one in a state of a coma is no longer in command of this full-blown self-awareness. Yet, there is a human person at the first instant of its embryonic inception because the newly conceived embryo in the first instance of conception is substantively spontaneously and holistically the sovereign author of its own growth and development. On the other hand, no one remembers the months spent in the mother's womb precisely because in this fetal stage the human person's own psychosomatic personality is not conscious of its own selfhood. One's recollection of one's first memory indicates fairly well the time when one's own personality begins to be aware of itself and to mature.

Further, individual human persons cultivate different personality skills and functions. One is customarily stereotyped and characterized by such artificial entrepreneurial skills. Special personalities are known as carpenters, clerks, cooks, lawyers, politicians, managers, musicians, actors, athletes, bankers, teachers, celebrities, and nobodies, etc.. Such trade-marks and professional occupations indicate a type of personality related to that person's skillful social function. There is no such personality which is indispensable in the precise role with which it is occupied. For example, there is no politician that cannot be replaced by another politician.

Hence, every functioning personality is exchangeable by another personality that can readily impersonate that same function. Sometimes the exchange improves the functioning and sometimes not. Such functions themselves become exchangeable such as the function of bike-building becomes exchangeable for car-building. However, the functional skills themselves are not exchangeable. Each personality is acquired in the process of mastering a skillful function. A professional athlete skillfully trained in basketball cannot without further training become a skilled tennis player.

Finally, a personality is inescapably dichotomous. Indeed, every personality is inextricably itself bi-polar in its own psychosomatic make-up. As previously indicated this bipolarity permeates all of the complex self-cultivated worlds in the horizontal order of the human person's subjective egocentric historical self-humanization. This polarity is ineluctably peculiar to the surdity inherent in the polar structure itself of mathematical quantification. There is no one-world culture or one-world history or one-world functional occupation, or personality, or whatever. There is no overall universal unity in the subjective order of culture. There is only a radical polarized disunity which is overcome by unionization, i.e., socialization, association, and collaboration.

Every cultural world historical enterprise has its antipodal counterpart opposing it. The make-believe idealistic utopian world of the psychic mind's conceptual dream is in polar opposition to the realistic mundane utilitarian world of the somatic body's sensational fantasies. The psychic self itself mentally fabricates noumenal transparent phantom mathematical specters which are inextricably ambiguously absurd in their lack of any identifiable holistic unity. The mathematical "one" itself is an enterprising quasi-one and not an identifiable holistic unit entity. That is, it is equivalent to any fragmentary resolution of itself. $1 = 1/2 + 1/2$. And the somatic self, in its own turn, fabricates phenomenal imaginative spectacles and specimens of these mathematical notions. These imaginary spectacles remain no less absurd than their notional exemplars which they exemplify.

When one holds a 3-foot yardstick in one's hand, one somatically misconstrues that one is realistically perceptually visualizing and holding in one's hand an exact mathematically precise 3-foot piece of wood. This is impossible. It is an illusion. The yardstick is only proximately a "handy" 3-foot standard of measurement. It approximates the remote precise mathematical 3-foot measurement which the psychic mind intuitively conceptually constructs. There is always a more-or-less allowable tolerance built in for every product which is made according to some mathematical measurement. This tolerance is endemic to the psychic self's absurd and delusive mind which construes that a precise 3-foot measurement could actually exist transcendent to and independent of the subjectivity of the mind's own vacant and vacuous conceptualization. The mental artifictional prototypical yardstick in the self's psyche allows for no mathematical imprecision. Nonetheless, its handy artifactual counterpart crafted in the somatic self's hand demands a tolerance and leeway for its own imprecision. The psychic exemplar serves as the remote paradigmatic precise mathematical model while its somatic exemplified counterpart serves as the proximate but imprecise specimen of this model.

This psychosomatic bi-polar disparity between the psychic self's precise idealization and the somatic self's imprecise realization pervades the entire reach of the subjective order of mankind's self-humanized psychosomatic personality. It cannot be sufficiently re-emphasized that this subjectivity is entirely amoral. Morality itself is to be found in the objective metaphysical order of existence. This objective order harbors no such tolerance in matters of morality. Morality is not an issue of mathematical precision but of metaphysical practicality in regard to the truthful purposeful goal of human conduct. The end-means goal of human conduct is not an issue of mathematical precision but of metaphysical purpose. The intellectual will's choices are purposefully intentional; that is, goal-directed. To choose gustatory and gastronomic pleasure as the end-goal of eating is immoral because it is out of order with the objective end-goal of eating itself which is to nourish the body. The subjective selfhood of the human person, on the other hand, is motivated to eat precisely because of the self-serving gustatory satisfaction that a gastronomically delicious meal affords. And this gastronomic fare is subjectively deliciously satisfying because it is prepared with mathematical precision dictated by the recipe. Objective morality (viz., right or wrong) is a matter of purpose while subjective morale (viz., cheerful satisfaction or cheerless dissatisfaction) is a matter of self-centered service.

Now, this subjective self-centered amoral gastronomical skillful (i.e., artificial) service is more often the commanding incentive (i.e., boosting morale) urging one to eat, but it is not the objective purpose (i.e., the moral norm) governing the act of eating. If this incentive is not checked, its very self-serving willful attachment to the gustatory sensuality that gourmet food supplies will override the objective purpose of eating. In this case, it becomes not merely immoral but sensuously antimoral. It becomes rebellious to the very morality that is inherent in the activity of eating. When it is forcibly and willfully kept in check through self-control such that it does not interfere with the objective purpose inherent in the act of eating, it morally complements rather than rebelliously supplants the very purpose itself of eating.

The human person in its very personhood is objectively and naturally endowed with a soulful spiritual intelligence and will which operate spontaneously. This very same personhood is subjectively and culturally self-humanized with a spiritualistic willful mind which must be automatically and/or autocratically prompted to function. Where the person's soulful intellect and will are faculties which spontaneously operate in view their own potency (i.e., power), the same person's selfhood's willful mind is an impotent facilitator that functions only when it is prompted to do so by a suitable incentive (i.e., motivation). This willful facilitator is itself a polarized willfulness parallel to the psychosomatic polarity inherent in the person's selfhood's own egology. And, again, just as the ego serves as a threshold demarcating the ego's subconscious inward orientation from its outward conscious orientation, so also the very SELF of one's own selfhood serves as a threshold demarcating the inner psychic willful idealistic self-serving partisan selfhood from its outer somatic willful realistic self-serving partisan polarized counterpart.

The difference between these polarized partisan attitudinal selves is discernable in the products which each fabricates. The product (viz., the symbol) of the idealistic morale attitude is romantically usably useful whereas the product of its realistic morale attitude counterpart is pragmatically usably useless. Of course, again, this is a paradox inasmuch as the romantic self's exemplary static creative notions (viz., mind crafted symbols) are usably useful because they are not actually used up when they are put to use whereas their pragmatic counterpart (viz., hand crafted tools) become themselves usably useless because in their usage they become used up and worn out and no longer useable.

This paradox seems irrational and bizarre at its face value. Yet, it is endemic to the paradox that prevails throughout this horizontal order of subjectivity proper to the human person's psychosomatic selfhood (viz., his self-humanized personhood). Consider the cup as a container. It is fully usefully useable only when it is empty. When it is full it can no longer be used because its usefulness has been used up. A brand new automobile is usefully useable when its odometer is 0. When there are 200,000 miles on the odometer the auto is uselessly useable because it has been used up. It has become worn out. To conservatively retain the cup's static usefulness it must remain idly empty on the shelf. To liberally make use of the cup's uselessness it must be utilized fully as a tea-cup, a coffee-cup, a milk-cup, a beer--cup, etc., and become uselessly worn out in the process.

In other words, the mental conceptual useful mathematical blueprint static model die of any tool serves negatively as a paradigm for what is implementally positively handcrafted as a working tool patterned after its prototypical model. The model remains fictionally functionally useful even after the tool is fabricated and factually tested and experimentally proven to be serviceably kinetically useable. When the tool is functionally utilized, however, it becomes eventually useless because it wears out. On the other hand, the same static conceptual mathematically designed prototypical blueprint die remains usefully functional as a model to have the worn out tool replaced.

The romantic self willfully conjures up exemplary useful notions whereas the pragmatic self willfully devises useless tool-like exemplifications of such notions. One might construe from the previous paragraph that the idealist has the upper hand over the realist because of the useful longevity of the prototype over the handcrafted tool. But, is it not the pragmatic realist who makes serviceable and profitable use of his tools and equipment? Plans and designs mentally conceived remain merely conjectural until they are actually tested and found to be workable. On the other hand, would not one find it more lucratively profitable to possessively own the patented chemical formula for regrowing hair moreso than a bottle itself of this formula? Yet, again, the formula without the actual bottled product remains useful while the bottled formula itself cannot outlive its useable usage.

The partisan willful self-serving static useful advantage which the romantic has is in diametric polar opposition to the useless advantage of the pragmatist. Of course, the further irony and paradox is that any attempt on the part of the romantic ideologue to live exclusively, autocratically, and regressively within the static Shangri-la of his own conceptual idealistic fictional paradigmatic historistic paradise (viz., a radical and absolute conservative fundamentalism) is utterly futile. Its pragmatic counterpart attempts with equal futility to live robotically, exclusively, and progressively in the cornucopia of its own perceptual realistic factual kinetic megalopolis with its vain promise of automatic conveniences expansively improving into the future (viz., a radical and liberal relativism). In other words, each polar ism is very dependent on its opponent's ism in spite of each's proper priority vis-à-vis its opponent.

Again the very "self" of a person's subjective selfhood is not substantive. It is insubstantive. It is not the SELF that forcibly (i.e., imperiously) will's its own partisan selfish self-interest and dominant autonomous self-centered social security. It is the human person's self-subsistent personhood that wills its own partisan selfish self-interest be it a romantic or a pragmatic self-serving self-interest. And, again and again, this self-interest is not of itself a moral good nor an immoral bad self-interest. It is an amoral self-serving advantage commensurate with the person's own have-attitudinal mindset. It is to the positive advantage of a batter in a baseball game to safely hit the ball and get on base whereas it is to the negative advantage of the pitcher who controls the ball to strike out the batter. That is, it is to the advantage of one to have a hit and to the other to have a no-hit. This bipolar opposition between each opponent's willful partisan self-interest also paradoxically involves a comparable bi-polarity within each player himself. The batter may empathically assume for a moment the pitcher's role and attitude and deliberately fail to get a hit to accommodate the pitcher. The pitcher, in turn, may himself empathically assume the batter's attitude and serve up a hittable pitch to accommodate the batter.

It behooves us now to examine the selfhood's willful psychic self in polar opposition to its willful somatic self which we have previously explored in expounding the role of the compassionate sensuous emotions in motivationally stimulating the self's will to action. And as we have emphasized that the insubstantive subjective corpuscular somatic body is not itself a holistic substantive energetic bodily entity but, rather, a pluralistic synergetic systematic insubstantive corpuscular enterprise (i.e., a bodiless motion); it is in a parallel way the case that the self's somatic will is only kinetically active (i.e., willfully and forcibly in motion) when it emotionally self-stimulates and activates its own self in the service of its own partisan dominant autonomous social security in procuring and providing for itself its very own automatic self-satisfaction and self-contentment.

In examining its willful psychic counterpart, we can anticipate that it will be self-motivated in direct polar opposition to this kinetic emotional stimulating sensuous sensitizing impetus which influentially motivates the selfhood's willful somatic self to needfully require and even to demand whatever bodily effort is necessary to fabricate and/or to procure for itself whatever utility which will facilitate its own autonomous (i.e., self-subsistent) self-gratification and satisfactory self-reliance. Hence, in lieu of a "bodiless motion" it is a "motionless body" which predominates to forcibly engage this selfhood's psychic self-serving willfulness. Again, note, that in the subjective order of culture there is no causation there is only historical eventuation, flux, and forcible influence which is required to overcome any resistance to the will's own self-serving willfulness. Theroot of all such resistance is, paradoxically enough,theself hood'svery own willfulness.

Unlike the soulful intellectual will's own purposeful willingness which is potently existentially spontaneously efficacious in attaining whatever it intentionally wills, the selfhood's willful self is impotently resistant to every influence that is not compatible with its self-centered self-serving partisan biased self-interest. Whatever the soul's will chooses to intentionally will is intentionally goal-directed finality and finalizing for the will's own choice. This is the efficacy inherent in the will's willingness to prioritize whatever it wills to be final. Since by its very innate volitional potency it necessarily wills the immortal and communal good-as-such which is rooted in the transcendent existing metaphysical reality of being-as-such, the soulful will is inherently at liberty to will whatever it optionally wills to purposefully attain its innate drive for its communitarian good-as-such (i.e., its very own happiness) which is the common goal of every member of the family of mankind.

Thus, if the will chooses the enjoyment of food as its overriding end-end to attain to its ultimate natural immortal goal of happiness, food and all that attends it, especially the gustatory enjoyment of eating, becomes optionally finalized as the will's top priority. The soulful will needs no influential sensitizing emotional excitation, stimulus, and prodding to forcibly influence its choice of this option. Its very choice is immediately efficaciously intentionally finalized simply by willing it. Of course, this choice is only fully a morally good act of choice if it itself is not deprived of the appropriate conscionable truth of its choice. In the matter of choosing to make food's enjoyment its top priority, the will is choosing unconscionably to do so. Food is nutritionally valuable to the corporeal body's holistic wellbeing and even its sentient enjoyment is suitable to this same body's well-being. But it is not of itself of holistic value to the incorporeal soul which is hierarchically a superior immortal reality to that of the body's mortality. In sum, its very sentient enjoyment is not of the uppermost priority to the human person's immortal holistic well-being.

In other words, the soulful intellectual will is innately free to spontaneously and efficaciously causally and purposefully choose its own intended means to attain to its ultimate finality and immortal well-being (viz., happiness). Obviously, if the will opts for food's sentient enjoyment as its uppermost means to attain its ultimate immortal wellbeing this, again, is an inappropriate immoral choice because the human person's uppermost enjoyment is not found in the sentient enjoyment of food that nourishes the body but in the food that nourishes the soul (viz., the truth of what is good-as-such). The body itself is not the consummate component of the human person's substantive nature. Its perishable materiality is hierarchically subordinate to the soul's imperishable spirituality.

It should be noted that in the natural order of the intellectual will's ultimate immortal finality, God is the virtual and not the formal (viz., informative) immortal communal objective (viz., the good-as-such). Just as humanity virtually includes ideally but not really every possible and actual individual human being in the universe of creation, God's divinity virtually includes ideally but not really every possible and actual good in the universe of creation. The individual, Peter, is really human but not ideally humanity itself. Humanity is human-as-such and Peter is a human-as-such. But, humanity is not reducible to Peter nor is Peter identical with humanity.

In a similar vein, the human intellectual will necessarily is destined by its own finality and finalization to will the communal immortal good-as-such (viz., happiness) in all that it chooses to will. Its real choices are particular instances (viz., a means-end) of the holistic good-as-such (viz., an end-end); and in that they are, they rightfully and ethically partake of the communal good-as-such. However, if they are chosen not as instances (viz., means-end) but as instantiating the holistic good-a-such itself (viz., an end-end), they are incompatible with this holistic good and unethical. In this manner, if the will chooses eating and the gustatory pleasure of eating as an overriding finalizing good, it unethically and immorally does so.

The human intellectual will in every particular instance of its choices virtually but not formally wills God (viz., the ideal universal transcendent Goodness) overriding the communal good-as-such. God's divinity is virtually the very holiness of the human intellectual will's immortal happiness. God, however, is the eternal holiness and not merely the imperishable holiness of mankind's imperishable happiness. Furthermore, unlike humanity which albeit its virtual ideality is not a unique human-as-such, God's divinity is the very uniqueness of the good-as-such.

In this differentiation, it is possible for the human will to preferentially by choice love humanity in the place of any one unique individual human being and claim by this that it is loving every human being without exception. But, in doing so, it does not love human individual beings actually but only virtually and potentially. The human will cannot will to preferentially by choice love God (viz., the very Goodness of the good-as-such) in the place of all particular instances of the good-as-such (viz., food and the enjoyment of tasting and consuming its nutritional beneficence) and claim, thereby that it is loving without exception every instance of Goodness. For, God is not only uniquely the very plenitude of Goodness but the uniqueness of Goodness.

In sum, while God is the virtual ultimate objective of every free choice elicited by the soul's intellectual will, God is not naturally the formal objective of the human will. In view of this, the will in freely choosing God preferentially over and above every other choice must choose God not as merely the virtual ideal reality of the good-as-such, but as the very universal eminence of the communal good-as-such. Hence, while the human will is not free regarding the communal holistic immortal good-as-such (viz., happiness) which it necessarily wills in all that it chooses, it is free regarding the universal eminence of the good-as-such which is God. God is the very Beingness of all reality and, uniquely, the very Goodness of all reality. By freely choosing to love God preferentially in the place of every other existing good, the human person does not love, thereby, every created being virtually but not actually. On the contrary, the human person loves God in contradistinction to every created being including its own unique created existence. That is, it naturally and freely loves God as an eminent universal eternal end-end and not merely necessarily as its own formal communal imperishable objective end-end.

Now, turning our attention to the subjective amoral order engaging the selfhood's self-serving willfulness. This willfulness is not competently and fundamentally efficacious; it is incompetent. It only becomes competent by undertaking to overcome its own deficiency experimentally productively, supplementally, and laboriously with much effort and exertion. It may wishfully will to have whatever it wishes but it can only fulfill this wish by successfully fabricating or procuring a self-serving convenience to fulfill its wish. But, it cannot enter into such a production without first "moving itself" (i.e., motivationally) as a self-starter to initiate such an undertaking. That is, it must "move" itself to overcome its own impotency. After all, it is in its very willfulness deficient and must supplement this deficiency by making some self-serving usable convenience to offset it. This demands that the selfhood's psychosomatic will be self-motivated.

This self-motivation in the somatic willful self is automatically influenced by stimulating emotional feelings while in the psychic willful self it is autocratically influenced by sedating emotionless bearings. This is so because the somatic willful self is a mindless robotic body whereas the psychic willful self is a bodiless phantom mind. A robot functions mechanically and kinetically through the meshing of its many mechanical parts proximately self-controlled. A phantom functions telekinetically and bureaucratically through a remote self-control. A mechanical robot must overcome its own inertia to actively function whereas the bodiless spook must overcome its own kinesis (i.e., stirring) to function actively. This explains why the psychic will's entrancing motivation is one of sedation and the somatic will's motivation is one of thrilling stimulation. The selfhood's mind thinks well in the serenity of a calm mental vacuum whereas its body functions better when it is full of kinetic exertion.

In this self-motivation the selfhood's psychosomatic willfulness becomes self-attached to its motivational influential bodily feelings and mental bearings that prompt its volitions to competently seek its own self-sufficient bodily gratifying self-contentment and/or mentally justifying self-containment. The more forcibly attached is the selfhood's will to these influential motivations, the more self-determined it is to by exertion and/or inertion to overcome its own incompetent deficiencies. The issue here is not one of the soulful will spontaneously causing and sponsoring its own reasonable choices but of the selfhood's will forcible influencing its own self-controlled self-determinate decisions. Hence, the more sensationally sensuously sensitive is the self-induced emotional feeling motivating the selfhood's somatic willfulness, the more selfishly self-attached and self-determined is its somatic willfulness to self-possessively exert its body to procure its own self-gratification.

And, alternatively, the more inspirationally notionally intimate is the self-adduced emotionless bearing motivating the selfhood's psychic willfulness, the more selfishly self-attached and self-determined is its psychic willfulness to self-possessively inert its mind to procure for itself its own mental justification. Indeed, the selfishly irrational self-serving influential force of such motivations is such that they blind the selfhood's willfulness to the moral order itself which transcends the horizon of its historical supplemental self-conscious egocentricity.

Reverting, again, to the intellectual will, its powerful volitional efficacy to directly choose the finalization of its own choices and to subordinate all the body's instinctive sensorial appetites to this same finality is not an alienable or transferable responsibility. Indeed, even when the human person irresponsibly and immorally subjugates the will's freedom to a finalization which is not in keeping with the conscionable truth of that finality itself (viz., eating exorbitantly as a gourmand and glutton for the sake of its gustatory pleasure and gratification alone), the will's inalienable freedom to choose otherwise remains intact. Most assuredly, the spontaneity of its freedom to choose to redirect its own finalization away from gluttony is vitiated and weakened by its own failure to choose appropriately in the first place to eat simply to nourish the body. Nonetheless, its freedom of choice is not altogether lost. The will remains inalienably free to redirect its priorities whenever it efficaciously wills to do so.

But, it cannot be overemphasized that what can blind the person's intellectual will from truthfully and conscionably even knowing the moral rectitude and immoral crookedness of its pending choices of prioritization in the objective order of existence is the selfhood's very own willful subjective prejudicial attitudinal partisan slavish self-attachment to its own selfish lifestyle. When the selfhood's self-serving will is willfully selfishly and predominantly self-attached to one of the three following lifestyles, namely, its own robotically robust, symbiotically esthetic, or ghostly ascetic cerebral lifestyle, this self-attachment while strictly supplemental becomes by default the fundamental overriding value in the human person's self-esteem and life-style. Such an over-weaned subjective self-esteem artificially abruptly contravenes and preempts the person from attending to his objective moral and conscionable order of obligation.

How so? Because this partisan attitudinal prejudicial selfish self-attachment interferes with the intellect's completely impartial and trans-subjective ability to judge the objective truth of the matter. When the person's personhood is willfully reflexively self-preoccupied, self-attached, and self-absorbed in the influential experience of its own somatic conscious emotional urgent feelings (viz., selfish likes and dislikes) and/or psychic subconscious emotionless panic bearings (viz., selfish cares and concerns), the person remains resistantly impervious to its transcendent immortal destiny and moral conscionable communal responsibilities and duties in the objective intelligible hierarchical order of existence.

The spontaneity proper to the soulful intellectual objective will is not shared by the selfhood's own subjective self-serving will. The selfhood's willful subjective volitions must be forcibly motivationally primed and prompted precisely because this psychosomatic will is incompetently impotent to achieve its own self-serving wishfulness other than through a forcible exertion and effort in which it becomes competently skillful in producing something which makes possible the facilitation of its wish. After all, the selfhood's willful volitions are not purposefully goal-directed; they are exclusively purposelessly self-serving; they lack any inherent finality or finalization.

Accordingly, the selfhood's psychosomatic will needs to forcibly make itself motivationally will whatever it decides to possessively will because it further needs (i.e., demands and requires) to make a useable artificial convenience and to employ this convenience to offset its own incompetent self-serving deficiency. When a particular nation becomes technologically and bureaucratically very adept and advanced in its self-humanized civility, the very motivational industriousness of its citizens may become lax by the luxury this industriousness affords its citizens. Simultaneously, the very moral tenor and character of the citizens may also become lax due to emphasizing the subjective technological order to the detriment of the objective moral hierarchical order and the fundamental primacy of the soul's intellectual will.

In the objective vertical order, the soul's intellectual will is a purposeful drive whose voluntary choice is intransitively non-productive. In choosing to eat the will does not make use of food to nourish the body. Eating is not exploitatively the serviceable social usage of food. It involves the very consumption of food which is assimilated intransitively to the corporeal body's very own vitality. Eating itself does not involve the corporeal body's own transitive transformation. Rather, it involves the corporeal body's own intransitive enhanced vitality. Certainly, one might have to transitively toil to productively cultivate the food as is the case with farming. But, the actual act of eating is itself intransitively naturally beneficial to the body without the body exercising any forcible exertion. Eating is not a functionally transitive productive engagement. It is inherently an intransitive operation which is beneficial to the corporeal body's holistic well-being.

In the case of the psychic will's mental fabrication and production of useable useful notional symbols, they have to be socially communicated to become serviceably self-serving to the will's psychic need to overcome its own incompetent deficiency to communicate its own mental wishful volitions to other selves. In the case of the somatic fabrication and production of useable useless implements, these have to be successfully deployed to be serviceably self-serving to the will's somatic need to overcome its own incompetent deficiency to effectuate its own bodily wishful volitions. The will's mindful notional symbols are inspirationally useful differently in different situations. The mathematical notion of a dozen is not restricted to measuring out only a dozen eggs; it may also measure out a dozen donuts as well as other items. The instrumental fabrication of a cardboard carton with 12 cubicles to transport eggs is another application of the notional symbol of 12. A different size carton with 12 cubicles may be fabricated to transport a dozen donuts.

The quantificational meaning of "dozen" is merely mentally meaningful; it is a willful fabrication of the mind. Yet, it may be applied to different products willfully fabricated by the body's handy craftsmanship. The mathematical meaning of a "dozen" is inherently conventional and purposeless; it is entirely self-serving to the persons who avail themselves of its meaning which is arbitrarily agreed to by the persons who make use of it.

In other words, all artificial constructs are inherently without purpose. They are entirely self-serving whoever socially takes possession of them and employs them for their own self-serving devices. Artificial constructs are transitively created because the products of such constructs remain as an accretion to the one who constructs them. Furthermore, they have no natural purpose attributable to them as do entities-as-such in the hierarchical order of existence. They are artificial non-entities-as-such exploitable at will. Their usability is left open to any selfhood's willful self-possessive actual serviceable social use of them. In this sense, any artificial self-humanizing and self-cultivating production, whatever it may be, is a transitive self-transformative transaction. Not only is something artificially fabricated in such a transaction but the very self exploitatively deploying this fabrication becomes itself transformatively impacted by it.

A table fork's use is not restricted to eating. One does not abuse a table fork by scratching one's back with it. It is an artificial no-good-as-such enterprise which is useable for whatever use one willfully possessively decides to make of it for one's very own advantage. What is willfully important is that one be possessively the social owner of the artificial useable no-good-as-such product to dominantly determine for its own self the serviceable use of that item. Thus, any notion fabricated by the psychic cerebral self's ingenuity may carry any meaning which that same self willfully and possessively determines for its own usage. The mathematical numeral "1" may arbitrarily mean 2/2 or 8/8 or any other fraction providing this meaning remains precisely consistent in all of the ensuing mathematical calculations.

Indeed, if one consider the simple symbol of 0 merely as the ingenious creative notion of the mind's own psychic womb's tactual vacuity, it is a most cryptic sign. For, of itself it is a meaningless enterprising non-entity-as-such until and unless it is artificially and arbitrarily invested with a specified meaning. In mathematics, it signifies an arithmetic zero. In meteorology, it signifies a full moon. In modern social anthropology it signifies the female in contradistinction to the male. In other words, its very enterprising purposeless meaninglessness allows it to be exploitably and self-servingly useable at the behest of which-ever self decides to possessively assign it a socially useable meaning.

The very ethnicity of languages reflects the willful arbitrary self-possessive appropriation and assignment of meaning to terms that have been artificially self-cultivated in that ethnic society and tradition. The terminology in the language of French is ethnically different than the terminology of Chinese. Of course, when such terminology not reflexively subjectively but reflectively objectively signifies an entity-as-such in the hierarchical order of existence transcendent to the term itself, this term ceases to be an arbitrary term because its literal significance itself is that of an entitative reality which is existentially entitled to its own family generic and proper specific name. The term ceases to be merely an artificial symbol of the selfhood's psychic ingenious self-cultivation; it becomes literally a name for what entitatively exists in the hierarchical order of existence transcendent to and independent of the name itself.

It is precisely for this reason that certain French terms can be readily translated into certain Chinese terms signifying the same objective meaning transcendent to the terms themselves. Because the meaning in both case existentially indicates and signifies one and the same entitative reality transcendent to the terms themselves. On the other hand, the very same term carries equivocally different meanings within the horizontal order of resistance even within the same ethnically homogeneous society because the same term is willfully self-determined by those who self-possessively apropriate this term for their own usage.

Thus, the word, freedom, itself means whatever meaning the willful users of this symbolic term require that it mean to service their own needful self-serving requirements. Freedom in an athletic context bears a different meaning than freedom in the field of experimental science. Usually the prevailing meaning is forcibly determined by the dominant "will to autonomous power" in a society that controls the channels of cultural information and communication. These, of course, are notably the electronic media of mass communication, the press, the schools, the body politic, and the prevailing ir/religious cultural commitment of its citizens.

In the horizontal order, the selfhood's psychosomatic self-serving willfulness is itself a deprived need whose self-serving willful actions are transitively, artificially, and productively serviceable only in the measure that some self (i.e., any anonymous self) actually makes use of the product of these actions. Someone's willful self needs to mentally design a wheel before its successful deployment can be bodily tested. The design itself remains within the psyche's mental inwardness. Someone's bodily outward selfhood needs to somatically handcraft a wheel and test its functionality before its mental design can be usably validated. Its implementation and deployment are undertaken by the willful self's outward bodily physiology. In brief, the selfhood's self-serving willful neediness is not fully self-served in producing artificial conveniences whether these are mentally symbolic terms or bodily instrumental tools. It must socially take possessive self-control of these to fully service its dominant psychic or somatic willful neediness.

Of course, the very same person's personhood may both psychically and notionally design a wheel's model in mathematical graphic terms and somatically fabricate and handcraft an instrument of this model in wooden or metallic materials. Yet, both the design and the instrument may possessively be appropriated and usably deployed by a self other than the self that conceived and handcrafted it. In other words, all artificially self-cultivated artifictional and artifactual products are socially not-good-as-such until they are possessively owned, controlled, and exploitatively used by the one who socially possesses them. There is here paradoxically an inevitable have/have-not polarity permeating the entire social structure in the horizontal order of resistance. There are those who possessively have and are considered the rich and those who possessively have-not and they are considered the poor. This is the overriding difference between a natural family communal good-as-such entity in the objective hierarchical order and the artificial social no-good-as-such enterprise in the historical subjective order.

The apple is naturally and morally a good-as-such not because it is possessively appropriated by the person who eats it but precisely because in possessing it one appropriates its nutritional good-as-such value which is beneficial to and for the entire community of which that individual is a member. Brute animals instinctively possess and consume the apple appropriate to the holistic family communal well-being-as-such of their species. The human person freely possesses the apple appropriately when he chooses to eat its nutriment commensurate with the holistic wellbeing of his own personhood and the community of persons of which he is a member. It is the case that anything that is an entitatively valuable good-as-such in the hierarchical order of existence not only benefits the individual that avails itself of that good, it also benefits the entire species of which the individual is a member.

It is simply the opposite of this in the historical order of resistance dealing with any enterprising non-such-good usable artificial thing. The person who possesses a hammer, for example, benefits enormously from having the use of this special tool. On the other hand, others who are dispossessed of this hammer do not share this beneficence. That is, any good in the natural order is inherently a family community good or an instance of the common good proper to the family of human beings. Contrariwise, any quasi artificial good in the social order of mankind's self-cultivated humanization is of benefit exclusively to those who arbitrarily and conventionally have a claim on it.

The subjective horizontal artificial self-cultivated order takes precedence over the objective vertical natural order supplementally but not fundamentally. Thus, historically, the psychic conception of the wheel and the corresponding somatic perception of its implementation supplementally take precedence over the fundamental movement of walking as a means of moving one's corporeal body locally from place to place. For, in order to move locally in a bodiless motion (viz., bicycling) to supplementally facilitate the corporeal body's natural movement (viz., walking) from place to place, the fabrication of this facility takes chronological precedence over the corporeal body's natural ability to walk.

At the same time, the fundamental non-historical natural ability to walk still fundamentally and purposefully takes precedence over its supplemental self-cultivated historical counterpart of artificially moving on a bicycle. Why? Because one may functionally peddle a bike and still remain stationary in the same place. The bike's own stationary bodiless motion functions to serve a selfhood's willful purposeless need to facilitate and kinetically actuate the somatic body's own somaticity (viz., bodiless motion). The somatic self can be willfully self-content and self-satisfied with this exercise of the body's subjective somaticity even when the bike remains stationary in the same place. If, however, the cyclist peddles himself locally from place to place this is a purposeful movement precisely because the soul's intellectual will has purposefully chosen to locally advance from one place to another place or to locally retreat from one place to another in which case the corporeal substantive body cannot remain simply stationary in place seated on a mechanical bicycle's bodiless motion.

Here there is the intersection and possible clash of the intellectual will's objective purposeful intention and of the selfhood's subjective willful self-serving purposeless motivation. When the self's subjective purposeless self-serving motivation supplements the soul's objective purpose the self and soul's two wills complement each other. When the self's subjective motivation trumps and supplants the soul's objective purpose, the two wills conflict. And, if they do not conflict, it is because the intellectual will has become dominated and suppressed by the selfhood's will. The person's supplemental willful selfhood motivationally, forcibly, and self-possessively overrides the person's fundamental soulful reasonable purposeful will. In this instance, if someone asks the cyclist, "where are you going?" the answer would be "no where; I am just joy riding." The self's willful motivation has overcome the soul's willful purpose. If such behavior were not merely a temporary excursion but a protracted life-style, one would judge the person to be demented. However, this would be only partially the case. For the dementia is not due to the person's lack of mental prowess but, rather, it is due to the suppression of the soulful will's fundamental objective purposeful conscionable primacy.

The human person's psychosomatic willful self must be self-coordinated to successfully achieve its own supplemental self-fulfillment. When a bicycle is artfully psychically conceived, it still needs to be artfully handcrafted and fabricated. The somatic self's will emotionally sensitizes and forcibly influences itself motivationally urging itself to kinetically and decisively forcibly overcome its somatic body's own resistance to engage in the difficult labor and toilsome work to build a bicycle or to work to acquire the means to purchase one already built.

This emotional motivation is simply reversed in the case of the self's psychic self-serving willfulness. It is not emotionally stimulated and excited; rather, it is motivationally prompted to remain emotionlessly calm and without any excitement or perturbation upsetting the serenity of its autocratic self-reliant mental self-containment. That is, it is motivated to resist anything that will disturb its own self-serving inertial emotionless complacency. The bicycle's notional design is accomplished effortlessly in this psychic arena of unruffled tranquility and the psychic self serves its own partisan self-interest by remaining mentally inertly self-justified in conceptualizing the transparent mathematical precision of the bike's notional design. That is, its own psychic self-interest is best serviced and served by resisting every outside intrusion that threatens to disturb its own willful inner mental stability.

In other words, instead of willfully needing to be motivationally excited and stimulated to become kinetically active to overcome the somatic body's resistance to laborious work, it now needs to be motivationally sedated and calmed to remain inertially stabilized befitting its own psychic inwardness. In other words, instead of becoming motivationally willfully kinetically aggressive as is the case with the selfhood's somatic willfulness, it becomes motivationally willfully inertially defensive. Accordingly in the psychic self's willfulness there is no sensuous emotional excitation to motivate its own self-serving useful serviceability and its underlying dominant have-attitude of procuring for its automatic social security its own self-contained convenient psychic relaxation. There is, rather, the polar opposite of these motivational emotional influences and somatic need for convenient comfortable self-contentment. In other words, in the psychic self's willfulness there is no sensationalism, no emotional excitation, no sensational sensitizing imagery, no temperamental moody lingering emotional compassions, no sensuous sensational sensitizing feelings, and no ensuing comfortable somatic self-contentment to motivate its own self-importance and psychic self-esteem.

Befitting its psychic polar opposition to its somatic counterpart, there is, instead, a stoic notionality, an emotionless impassive sedation, an inmost intimate intimation susceptible to inspiration, a sentimental lingering entrancing romantic spell, an imperturbable balanced mental bearing (i.e., equipoise), self-contained in a mental envelope of self-assured self-justification motivating its own idealistic have-attitude of procuring for its self's psychic self-control an autocratic self-contained social security and self-esteem.

There is yet another very important aspect of this horizontal order of artificial no-such-good useable social services facilitating the selfhood's willful needy self-serving autonomous self-control. It is the aspect of exchange between one personality and another. The self-cultivated mental skill of the architect designing the model wheel may negotiate a trade with the self-cultivated skill of the mechanical technician handcrafting its instrumental deployment. That is, it may take a long time for a person to cultivate a skill. This requires sacrificing the cultivation of other skills while he is busily engaged in mastering his own craft. Accordingly, the product of one skill may be traded for the product of another. This is inevitable in the polarized fabric of everyday society. Members of any society are socially interdependent and socially members of groups whose function is homogeneous.

This grouping is in no wise a purposeful family grouping but a merely functional purposeless self-serving process of fabricating useable products and skillful services. Trading one's own serviceable products for another's involves bartering and a very cumbersome mode of economic social transaction and communication. Hence, an artificial medium of economic communication and transaction is accordingly invented and socially agreed upon to further facilitate this exchange. This is money. Money's economic serviceability is precisely its mutually agreeable usefulness to conveniently facilitate the exchange of "goods and services."

It should not be overlooked that money itself as a legal tender for commercial exchange is itself the product of both the psychic cerebral self and the somatic visceral self. The dollar that is equal to 100 cents is only such in the mind's mathematical calculation of it. For, the actual dollar bill is paper while the 100 pennies are possibly copper. These are not materially and somatically equivalent but they are mentally so. The actual symbols on these monetary bills and coins have a significance that is merely mentally intuited. Further, their tangible features, such as their color and their material composition are handcrafted by the body's technical somatic functionality.

Hence, money itself becomes an overriding artificial useable social none-such-good precisely because it facilitates its possessor's need for autonomous self-control to oversee that its own self-interest and dominant overriding partisan have-attitude is served in its exchange of goods and services with others. It is more advantageous to one's own autonomous social self-interest to possessively own money than to own any specific commodity or skill whether it is a significant symbolic document (viz., a tock or bond), a serviceable architectural skill, a serviceable technical skill, or a deployable tool. For, the owner of money can possessively procure for himself all of the previously mentioned artificial serviceable none-such-goods without having to engage in the entrepreneurial process itself of cultivating them. What is facilitated by the symbols of language in simple communication of thoughts and ideas is also facilitated by monetary symbols (viz., money) in the economic exchange of commodities and services.

Both of these modes of communication are still further facilitated by the electronic media of mass communication involving the telephone, the radio, the TV, the computer, videocassettes, CD's, newspapers, movies, magazines, etc. This medium not merely facilitates the previous mentioned exchanges but actually exercises an overriding control of these exchanges themselves. And, since this is itself an artificial serviceable social none-such-good, the very slanted signification of its language, its imagery, its prioritization of issues, the focus of its interests, its seductive format of entertainment, its instantaneity of dys/information, its globalized range of reach, etc., all this serves to advance and to promote its own built-in self-serving prejudicial biases whether these be oriented toward the "right or left." That is, these electronic media of mass communication foster a national ideology which is either idealistically and pessimistically a historistic status quo mindset peculiar to socialism or realistically a futuristic mindset of progressive activism peculiar to pragmatic capitalism.

Now, electricity serves as a dominant and domineering medium of communication facilitating an exchange between the different fields of the experimental physical sciences in particular. It is itself an artificial serviceable social none-such-good convenience which facilitates an exchange between the data and language of nuclear physics and molecular chemistry whether this is organic or inorganic chemistry or biochemistry. Further, electricity facilitates an exchange in the sophisticated electronic utilities of social habitation, the electronic utilities of the family homestead (viz., stoves, refrigerators, furnaces, etc.), industrial production of manufactured goods, the functioning of the departments of government, banking, commercialism, advertising, etc.. In brief, it is a social serviceable none-such-good precisely because it may be self-servingly utilized for any willfully self-possessed needful usage. Hence, the possessive social ownership of so-called power plants productive of electricity exercises a dominant controlling influence on society at large. All of these various socially utilizable cultivated services are supplemental to the fundamental moral order in the vertical order of existence. Again, where they supplement rather than supplant the moral order itself they are not only compatible with the moral order but they actually complement this order. Where they actually supplant the moral order itself they become rebelliously antimoral and not merely immoral.

An immoral act is an intentional act of disobedience by the intellectual will in the hierarchical order of existence. Such an act of disobedience vitiates the will's own vigorous spontaneity in freely choosing to obediently will what it morally and conscionably ought to will to enhance the rectitude and vigor of its own freedom of choice to choose what is conscionably upright and noble. However, such disobedience does not undermine the moral order itself as does a motivationally self-serving selfish act in the horizontal historical order of resistance which willfully and deliberately preempts the moral order itself.

As an example, a newspaper or a movie deliberately lionizing decrepit human behavior effectively undermines the fundamental order of reality and curtails truth itself. This is not merely immorally unconscionable; it is antimorally rebellious in defiance of the common good-as-such which in the vertical order is the overriding standard of measuring and normalizing human conduct. This does not mean that the media of mass communication must restrain itself from depicting and dramatizing conduct that divorces itself from morality, it means that such conduct ought not be dramatically or subtly promoted in its defiance of morality. The electronic media of mass communication is itself in all of its facets inherently prone to emphasizing and promoting its own ideological bias devoid of a moral compass precisely because it is itself an artificial social none-such-good utilizable mode of communication.

Again, a mere cryptic symbol ingeniously cerebrally self-cultivated by the human personality's psychic self is in its very artificiality nonsensical and meaningless. It remains such until and unless it is used as a symbol for an entitative reality that completely transcends the symbol itself and its horizontal order of mankind's self-humanized self-cultivation. One may, certainly, speak intelligently and sensibly through the electronic medium of mass communication. But, the medium itself just as the mere cryptic symbol itself of the psychic mind's own fabrication is inherently amoral, not moral.

To wit, the hi-tech electronic media of mass communication today can expertly and efficiently depict the most minute functions, physiology, and anatomy of the human body more sensationally and dramatically than ever could be accomplished in all of the previous annals of human history. The human body itself in its simple anatomical constitution is neither morally good nor morally bad; it is amoral. This pertains also to the body's sexual anatomy. Yet, to blatantly depict through the media of mass communication intimate sexual conduct simply as though it were depicting a mere anatomical function is tantamount to ideologically, abortively, and artificially demean and contracept the moral order itself. Such flagrant pornographic depiction flouts the moral virtue of chastity and temperance as well as the moral virtue of prudence. Why so? Because such sexual activity is reserved for the marital chamber.

The graphic depiction of sexual conduct outside of the marital chamber infectiously and empathically promotes its imitation by others outside the bonds of marriage. This is itself a form of pornography promoting a self-righteous self-justifying vitiating and degrading rebellious antimoral decrepitude. In our current society, this is a commonplace. It is symptomatic of a culture that no longer seeks to supplementally complement the moral order of nature through its self-humanizing skillfulness. Rather, it seeks to stridently overthrow and replace it altogether with its own antimoral antinomianism. This is legally permitted under the spurious umbrella of freedom of speech. But, a freedom which is euphemistically free (i.e., rid of) moral rule is a decadent and debasing freedom which rebels against the moral order itself. Such legalization can only prevail in the absence of a ruling moral authority.

Again, at the risk of being monotonously repetitious, the human opposition within itself. There is an inner tension between its psychic motivational autocratic social self-interest and its antipodal somatic automatic social self-interest. The psychic self subconsciously experiences its own motivational emotionless dispassionate needs as an immobilizing "motionless body" whereas its somatic self counterpart consciously experiences its own motivational emotional compassionate needs as a mobilizing "bodiless motion."

In sum, the psychic cerebral self willfully resists any intrusion to disturb its immobilized self-contained self-possessed autocratic selfhood whereas the somatic visceral self willfully insists on overcoming any resistance to obtaining for itself its own mobilized self-contented self-possessed automatic selfhood. Just as the person's self-subsistent personhood's willful psychic self-contained self motivationally and defensively resists emotionlessly any outside intrusion threatening its inside dispassionate self-contained autocratic serenity, its antipodal willful somatic self-contented dichotomous self counterpart motivationally and aggressively resists emotionally any obstructive impediment to its outside compassionate self-possessed sensuous self-contentment. One might in this comparison be tempted to presume that the psychic selfhood's partisan self-interest is dispassionately unbiased in opposition to the somatic selfhood's self-interest which is compassionately biased in behalf of its own have-attitudinal self-interest.

The dispassionate aspect of the psychic self's own emotionless motivation is its empathic impassive social resonance not its lack of a biased and prejudicial conative slant on behalf of what is usably possessively profitable to facilitate its own autonomous autocratic self-containment. The social empathy evoked psychically is a telepathic commiseration which is not an issue of communicating and experiencing interpersonal feelings sympathetically or antipathetically but of communicating and experiencing interpersonal bearings telepathically and apathetically.

I fully realize that the preceding statement strives to comprehensively contrast the psychic self's empathic dispassionate bearing with the somatic self's compassionate empathic feeling. The presentation of this comprehensive comparison is very unwieldy and wordy as is the case with much of this commentary. Yet, it is so to bring home the complexity of this empathy which functions differently within the intrapersonal dichotomy of man's psychosomatic personality. Feelings are infectiously social in that persons communicate with each other not only in words but also conationally through compassionate sensitized feelings that provoke sympathy or antipathy at one level and also through dispassionate intimate bearings that evoke telepathy or apathy at another.

A preacher who is very self-composed, emotionlessly detached and somewhat aloof from his auditors will empathically communicate with those who telepathically confide themselves to his reflective demeanor, composed bearing, and attitudinal mindset of self-assured autocratic reserve. Contrariwise, a preacher who is attached to emotional expostulations and gestures thereby striving with exciting stories to sensitize and touch the feelings of his auditors will empathically communicate with those who sympathically confide themselves to his own dramatic style, gestatorial deportment, and aggressive attitudinal mindset of automatic self-assured enthusiasm.

The upshot of this nonverbal conative psychic impassive cerebral intimate rhetorical communication, on the one hand, and its antipodal somatic compassionate visceral rhetorical communication, on the other, is their competitive opposition. To engage in the cerebral managerial style is tantamount to opposing its visceral manipulative counterpart style. The former evokes a confident self-justified attitude of intimacy between the speaker and the auditors upholding what is rational and devoid of feeling whereas the latter provokes a confident self-satisfied attitude of sensitivity between the speaker and the auditors upholding what is visceral and devoid of abstract ratiocination. The former prefers generalizations and charts whereas the latter prefers exemplifications and imagery.

The very point here of pitting these two opposing rhetorical lifestyles against each other is that the strength of rhetorical communication is not in presenting what is inherently and objectively intelligible independent of one's bodily feelings (viz., subjective likes and dislikes, tastes and distastes) and/or mental bearings (viz., subjective caring and not caring, concern and unconcern) but in couching one's material in what is influentially persuasive because one is attitudinally and prejudicially and personalistically committed to the importance of the cerebral style's inertial stability over the visceral or, vice versa, the importance of the visceral style's kinetic activism over the cerebral. An attitude is a prejudicial overriding and domineering self-serving partisan mindset that evaluates everything in view of what is of paramount importance in promoting, procuring, and safeguarding one's own personalized social security and selfish self-interest.

The rational, romantic cerebral dispassionate style evokes a self-confident intimate telepathic companionship in which a historical backward attitude upholding what is traditionally tried and true is of utmost importance. This style defensively upholds what is traditionally customary and what can be propounded in generalized terms. This style appeals to those who are attitudinally committed to what intuitively is a matter of thoughtful justified concern to everyone without exception. This is suitable to a majority will attitude. The irrational, pragmatic visceral compassionate rhetorical life-style, on the other hand, provokes a self-confident sensitized empathic companionship in which a historical forward-looking futuristic attitude prevails as that which is of utmost importance. This style aggressively promotes the promises the future holds and offers concrete examples to punctuate its thrust. This style appeals to those who are attitudinally committed to what intuitively is a matter of sensitive satisfactory comfort. This, in turn, is suitable to a minority will attitude.

The influence of these antipodal rhetorical life-styles is that the adherents of each exercises a fully partisan and prejudicial evaluative and discriminating role not in view of what is objectively cognitively intelligible but, rather, in view of what is subjectively conatively unintelligible and evaluated exclusively in terms of the subjective mind's cerebral thoughtful abstract self-serving generalized concerns (i.e., mental bearing), on the one hand, or in terms of the subjective body's visceral concrete tender self-serving tastes (i.e., bodily feeling), on the other. This subjective psychosomatic conative artistic approach may either override and eclipse the objective intellect's cognitive understanding or, it may supplementally support and complete the latter. The principle thrust of the intellect's objective cognitive knowing is to intelligibly inform the intellectual will whereas the thrust of the subjective conative knowing is to influentially (i.e., forcibly) transform and reinforce the selfhood's volitional self-serving bodily feelings and/or mental bearings.

Stylistic communication is the further paradox that the reinforcible willfulness of the human person's subjective psychosomatic selfhood entails a sacrificial trade-off freedom between its managerial and manipulative self-control. If the person's willful psychic self is to prevail in securing for itself its own partisan self-controlled autocratic inward freedom regarding its own inner notional unperturbed mental inertial tranquility and to empathically impart this to others, the person must sacrificially forego attending to his somatic self. And vice versa, if the person's willful somatic self is to prevail in securing for itself its own partisan self-controlled outward freedom regarding its own outer self-contented sensitivities and feelings and to empathically impart this to others, the person must sacrificially forgo attending to the self-controlled freedom of his psychic inner self.

And what is more intriguing still in the forgoing description of the two antipodal rhetorical styles is the conative element of communication which is not strictly speaking an informative style of communication but a transformative one. For, the empathic impact and social resonance peculiar to these two antipodal styles is their subliminal motivation to empathically transform the feelings and bearings of others to have them conform to the speaker's own attitudinal mindset.

Again and again, the selfhood's psychosomatic self-serving will-fulness is not---as an artful facilitator, facilitating function, produc-tion, and product---itself morally good or immorally evil. It is pre-dominantly amoral. Its self-serving willful have-attitudinal overarch-ing ideological partisan self-interest is supplemental to the moral good of the human person's intellectual will. The entire objective hier-archical order of nature is fundamentally prior to the supplementally subjective historical order of culture. Morality resides objectively on its metaphysical foundation, being-as-such, and on the will's own purposeful finality, the transcendental common family good-as-such. Morally upright choices elicited by the intellectual will are conscion-ably and informatively certified by the intellect itself as practically true-as-such or impractically not true-as-such. This conscionable in-tellectual judgment is not the offshoot of the will's own velleity but the completely non-partisan impartial adjudication of what authentic-ally pertains to the practical truth-of-such of the will's choices.

The subjective self's willful historical order of culture is compat-ible with the moral order in the measure that it supplements without altogether supplanting it. Accordingly, any artificially self-cultivated useable rhetorical communication---whether it is a liberally useable, esthetically useable, or technically useable style---cultivated exclus-ively for the sake of its own partisan self-interest is not warranted if it is not compatible with the moral order itself even if it is user-friendly or user-convenient. No exclusively artificial self-humanizing en-deavor is sincerely humanizing and conscientiously warranted when it does not uphold the objective moral order itself metaphysically transcendent to its own artificial subjectivity in the order of culture. When, in its exclusivity, the artificial subverts the moral order itself as is the case with pornography, for example, it not only is not morally warranted, it is rebelliously anti-moral and anti-Christian. It is not in-tegrally and authentically self-humanizing; it is dehumanizing in that it debases the sovereign dignity of the human person's self-subsistent immortal transcendent personhood.

On the other hand, the subjective selfhood's own willful psycho-somatic self-serving selfhood harbors the very self-humanizing "spirit" of mankind's own autonomous (i.e., self-reliant) dominant need for its own self-possessed social security. This self-humanizing spirit is the very mettle, the grit, and the spunk of the self's willful self-serving resolute resolve and ingenuity to forcibly contend and resistantly cope with every obstacle that threatens its own dominating partisan attitudinal mindset. The vigor of this morale is the resolve of the selfhood's own willful self-determination to dominantly psychically and/or somatically forcibly impose its own self on whatever resists its own partisan self-interest and self-esteem.

When the morale of this humanistic "spirit" supplementally complements the moral order inherent in the soul's intellectual will, there is a complementarity, solidarity, and compatibility between the subjective self's self-reliant self-possessed social security and the objective soul's moral happiness (i.e., general justice as the root of mankind's inalienable rights). In such a case there is cruciformly an integration and reconciliation between the practical truth-as-such present in the vertical order's conscionable morality and the self-humanistic spirit exhibited in the horizontal order's conscientious morale.

Of course, this can only occur when the willful psychosomatic self's own self-reliant social security is not selfishly, competitively, and partisanly self-possessed. Such partisan selfish self-possessiveness and self-attachment whether intrapersonal or interpersonal exhibits a self-alienating morale and self-dehumanizing spirit which is incompatible with the practical truth-as-such proper to the soul's moral conscience.

This self-humanizing willful spirit of the person's psychosomatic selfhood is the very nuclear core and heart of a person's personalized personhood. We may speak of a dispirited spirit or a spirited spirit. This is tantamount to speaking of a heartened or disheartened spirit. A spirited spirit is full of its own willful self-determination to resolutely and forcibly persist in having its own dominant partisan attitudinal mindset prevail over its adversaries. A dispirited or demoralized spirit is one whose willful self-determination and courageous pluck is lacking. In such a case, such a dispirited personalized selfhood would be irresolute in its own commitments and lacking in both zeal and self-confidence (i.e., hope). Paradoxically enough, a spirited spirit is not only resolved to persist in its firm commitment to its own dominant attitudinal partisan mindset but to willfully resist any mindset opposed to its own outlook and outreach. When it loses this spirited spirit, it becomes dispirited, demoralized, and in its somatic willfulness seriously depressed. In its psychic willfulness it becomes seriously anxious. Note well that this self-humanizing willful spirit in its bolstered courage or disheartened discouragement is not itself a moral virtue or vice. This spirited courage or dispirited discouragement is a matter of having or not having a sufficient self-confidence and self-conviction in forcibly having one's own partisan interest and dominant mindset prevail over one's adversaries.

It is also part of the paradoxicality of this self-humanizing spirit that due to the original sin that each human inherits from its first parents, Adam & Eve, this self-personalized spirit persistently willfully resists welcoming Christ and His Heavenly Father's gratuitous gift of their Holy Spirit's superhumanistic submissive selfless-humanizing ingratiating morale proper to Christ's very own entirely Selfless Personality, Sacred Heart, and paradigmatic redemptive beatitudinal mindset.

Indeed, it is the entire thrust of this commentary to delineate with utmost discretion the selfhood will's innermost nuclear self pursuant to St. John's own advocacy of the need to purify and purge its will of its own partisan selfish self-attachments preparatory to advancing to perfect union with God's Triune Godhead in contemplative prayer. This self-humanized spirit of the human person's own personhood is marked by the mettle and self-determination of a personality's mental have-attitude to willfully, convincingly, and indomitably (i.e., resistantly) oppose whatever is inimical to its own dominant attitudinal mindset and autonomous partisan social self-interest and security.

Its have-attitude is either that of the romantic pessimistic idealist or the pragmatic optimistic realist. Each is in polar opposition to the other. This polarity makes itself notably manifest in a democratic form of government which is committed to a bi-partisan political mindset that tolerates membership in both politically polarized parties. The vigor of the morale of this spirit makes itself known in the selfhood's resolute self-determination to resistantly sacrifice one side of its own dichotomous makeup and personality in favor of its polar opposite side which it esteems to be more important in advancing its own social security.

Hence, again, the spirited morale or demoralized dispirited lack of morale will directly influence the psychic cerebral self's impassive obdurate inflexibility or tractable laxity in defending or abandoning its own domineering idealistic romantic have-attitude and committed orientation toward his own autocratic social security. And, in turn, it will also directly influence the somatic self's emotional excitability or unemotional diffidence in promoting its own domineering realistic pragmatic have-attitude and committed orientation toward its own automatic social security. In either event any personality that exudes an abundance of morale is charismatically enabled to wield an enormous empathic social influence over others who share its same have-attitudinal outreach whether it be exercised telepathically at the psychic level of communication or exercised sympathetically at the somatic level of communication. A personality's morale serves as a spark-plug to socially influence and bolster the morale of others.

And, yes, there is a bipartisan self-humanized hybrid spirit sandwiched in between the two polarized extremes of utopian idealistic pessimism and utilitarian realistic optimism. For, between the idealistic psychic exemplar and its realistic somatic implementation, there is the intermediary task of realistically exemplifying and testing the exemplar and, in turn, its counter task of explaining and interpreting the specimen in terms of its exemplar. In other words, between the autocratic architect who designs the house and the technocratic carpenter who builds it, there is the intermediary position of the engineer who oversees the house's construction following the architect's master blueprint and, at the same time, takes care to justify the house's structure in terms of the blueprint's contractual drafted outline.

This same bi-partisan self-humanizing spirit of autonomous freedom of self-control may be found in the intermediary personality of those commissioned to exercise authority in a tripartite division of democratic political rule. First, there are the congressional personalities that psychically and cerebrally formulate the society's legal regulations and draft its basic charter and constitution. Secondly, there is the executive personality that somatically and viscerally is required to forcibly safeguard and uphold these regulations and constitution with armaments of combat if need be. Thirdly, there are the judicial personalities who are appointed to both judicially uphold the spirit of these regulations and constitutions and to judicially interpret their juridical applicability in moot situations.

It is not surprising that some judges attitudinally may be judicially idealistically conservative and historistic (i.e., inflexibly inward and pessimistically backward oriented) in their adjudications of a society's constitutions and by-laws, while others are realistically liberal and futuristic (i.e., pliably outward and optimistically forward oriented) in their own adjudications. What is peculiar to the social personality of every secular civilized political democracy in Western civilization is that its morale and self-humanizing spirit are completely confined to the horizontal order of mankind's self-cultivated self-humanization. Such civilities are not empowered to legislate fundamental morality but to supplementally regulate the civility of one's self-cultivated self-humanization in support of the moral order by the principle of subsidiarity.

ASCENT FOURTH APPENDIX

Concluding observations.

When the two objective and subjective orders cruciformly complement each other the human person's objective moral conscience and subjective personhood's conscientious morale dovetail. When they remain at odds with each other, a person's subjective willful egocentric self-conscientious morale deliberately substitutes its own domineering spirit of autonomous freedom of self-control for the moral order's fundamental dutiful sovereign freedom. When it does forcibly effectuate this substitution, its self-righteous morale and conscientiousness is resistantly rebellious regarding the moral order itself. And its dominant rebellious morale itself, however self-conscientiously (i.e., self-righteously) it is socially shared and legalistically upheld throughout the members of civil society, it remains a dehumanizing antimoral, anti-natural, antinomian, and anti Christian conscientization.

The autonomy of the secular state is supplemental to the fundamental sovereignty of the person's own self-subsistent immortally transcendent personhood morally and responsibly exercised in virtue of its own intellectually free nature and sovereignty. Within its own supplemental autonomy the secular state can by the principle of subsidiarity supplement the natural moral order and family common good-as-such with its own civilized cultural exploits and legislation providing this supplemental action brings the natural moral order to a point of perfection which it is unable to attain on its own initiative. Otherwise, this supplemental priority on the part of the secular State usurps the fundamental authority inalienably inherent in the moral order itself transcendent to the cultural order of the human person's subjectivity. This fundamental moral authority resides inalienably in each individual citizen's sovereign immortal and transcendent personhood.

Thus, for example, one's artificially self-cultivated indomitable spirited conscientious morale to champion the cause of socially legalizing artificial sexual contraception including its aftermath, procured abortion, cannot on the force of its own social willful contractual self-determination in the political arena disguise its own secular anti-moral and anti-Christian biased have-attitude of sexual promiscuity. In the case of sexual artificial contraception the subjective amoral order of culture becomes belligerently antimoral when it seeks to trump and substitute itself completely for the objective moral order of natural heterosexual procreativity. The objective moral order's author and authority is God who created the universe.

Such technically proficient and legalistically sanctioned artificial sex contraception is subjectively egoistically willfully selfishly self-serving precisely because it artificially thwarts what is objectively the natural heterosexual procreative instinctive inalienable purpose inherent in the conjugal act itself. Artificial contraception of sex's procreativity automatically, deliberately, and forcibly, reduces the intransitive heterosexual activity of intercourse to an exclusively non-procreative transitive asexual (i.e., homosexual) self-serving anatomical function of lifeless venereal sensuality between consenting partners. Given the hi-tech chemical technical feasibility and authorized legalization facilitating such artificial contraception the accompanying self-induced emotional venereal fervor, enthusiasm, and empathic exuberance in support of this aberrant asexual copulation becomes infectiously intensified and socially sanctioned.

Why so? Artificial contraception guarantees one's subjective somatic self an automatic convenient self-assured selfishly self-serving freedom of manipulative self-control over the body's sensitized and sensualized venereal pleasure overriding and preempting its innate life-giving purpose. When this procedure is further safeguarded and self-assured by having it legally sanctioned, it becomes euphemistically known as "safe sex."

Furthermore, one's egocentric social selfhood's spirited hedonistic have-attitudinal mindset and morale committed to securing its own political autonomous self-control over its own sexual conduct is self-righteously reinforced and safeguarded when the body politic sanctions the legalization of artificial contraception and procured abortion. Legalized artificial sexual contraception so guarantees a selfhood's conscientious self-righteousness that its supporters are blind to its blatantly antimoral and anti-Christian dehumanization in denying the natural proliferating purpose of sexuality itself and even in denying legal protection to the offspring of sexual intercourse.

Indeed, the very heart and core of the selfhood's willfulness is its demanding need to artificially cultivate prophylactic conveniences and services to facilitate the entrepreneurial security of its own self-reliant social autonomy. No one has a natural need for an automobile. However, the moment such a vehicle is manufactured, its utilization cultivates a social need to have and to own and to use such a vehicle for one's own accelerated convenience. Recall that the carpenter becomes a skillful building functionary only in the process of successfully building a structure working skillfully with carpentry tools.

Similarly, a self-humanized personality becomes a skillful asexual functionary only in the process of procuring and making skillful use of something instrumental facilitating an asexual venereal anatomical function. In this completely subjective self-cultivating context the sexual organs themselves become merely instrumental facilities to conveniently automatically facilitate self-serving selfish venereal experiences. A lifetime commitment of partners committed to such asexual conduct does not in the least alter or modify the patent partisan selfishness that motivates such conduct.

It is not in the least surprising that the frequent by-product of this asexual artificially controlled intercourse (viz., a newly conceived embryonic human being) is itself exploited for the self-serving needs of selves other than the selves themselves engaging in such intercourse. We have an ongoing legally sanctioned business of cloning and artificially inseminating human life in the laboratory outside of the mother's womb for the explicit purpose of experimentally advancing the scientist's further exploitative self-serving selfish control of the earliest stages of human conception. So culturally and subjectively solipsistically self-enclosed is this purely subjective self-serving functional experimental approach to human sexuality that the procreation of human life is no longer even a principal consideration in providing sexual education to society at large. Such education is typically devoid of attending to the moral foundation proper to human sexuality.

There is no innate procreative faculty of sex in the subjective order of culture. There is only the selfhood's willful claim and demand to be artificially equipped with a sexual function to facilitate and service its own self-serving willful somatic need for convenient automatic venereal asexual satisfaction and secure self-contentment. When this asexual functioning is further facilitated through the procurement and usage of hi-tech prophylactics one's selfhood's willful needful claim and demand for automatic venereal asexual self-controlled self-contentment is emotionally automatically self-induced and socially conscientiously reinforced.

What in the objective order is a driving sexual appetite for a procreative good (i.e., the offspring) which is naturally beneficial to the entire community even when one family begets the child, becomes in the cultural subjective order an artificial demanding need for what is not naturally an inherent good-as-such but only artificially a self-serving serviceable no-such-good that proves to be seemingly good only in the measure that some personality makes use of its asexual facilitation for its own egocentric selfish experience of venereal sensual satisfaction. Every such artificially contracepted no-good-as-such act of intercourse is a social antimoral venereal asexual quasi-good that can be utilized only to someone's self-centered selfish advantage. It itself makes no contribution to mankind's family common good transcendent to the social order itself. In the objective metaphysical and moral order of human conduct, the natural purpose of such heterosexual intercourse is an immortal common good which is inherently beneficial to the entire family community of mankind even when only one family avails itself of this good: namely the prospect of a newly conceived human being.

Further, where in the objective order venereal pleasure is not the purpose of a person's natural animal (i.e., carnal) heterosexual appetitive drive, it is precisely this very asexual emotionally sensitized venereal pleasure itself which is artificially and technically self-induced to motivationally urge and even compel the self's will to succumb to its artificially self-induced need to automatically guarantee its own contracepted somatic venereal self-contentment and satisfaction. There is an adage in this country of the USA that accompanies almost every product that is manufactured and sold which underwrites the purchaser's need to have its own self-centered self-controlled autonomous social security fully insured beyond any doubt. Satisfaction guaranteed or your money back. Natural instinctive animal passions and affections for food, sex, drugs, and shelter do not impinge directly on the soul's intellectual will. Further, when these natural appetitive drives attain their purpose, these drives themselves abate and become quiescent. This is evident from the corporeal body's motor reflexes. When one has walked to the tree to procure the apple to eat, one can sit down and rest under the tree while eating the apple.

On the other hand, artificial sensitized feelings of emotional compassions self-cultivated in the process of constructing automatically self-serving technical facilities and services regarding food, sex, drugs, and shelter do impinge directly on the subjective selfhood's self-serving willful needfulness. And, when these technically devised artificial facilities are in place, they facilitate not an abatement and quiescence for the self's willful artificial self-serving need for food, sex, drugs, and shelter but an increasingly intensified emotional sensitized automatic demand for the self's increased and intensified nutritional, venereal, drugged, and stylish convenient sensual self-contentment. The very establishment of a fast food outlet automatically induces an artificial demand and need for its convenient services that automatically provide sensuously succulent servings. A natural sensorial appetitive drive instinctively actuates the corporeal body's autonomic nervous motor reflexes which are still subordinate to the soul's intellectual will's own appetitive drive and the intellect's insight regarding the conscionable truth of what is practically (i.e., morally) right and not right for the corporeal body's holistic well-being. The moral conscionable object of the soul's intellectual will (viz., the intellect's appetitive drive) is the (conscionable) drive to possess what the intellect judges to be truly appropriate for the human personhood's integral holistic immortal well-being-as-such.

In this appropriation the intellectual will conscionably deems that the body's perishable sensorial goods (viz., nutrition, procreation, health, and shelter) are relatively good whereas the soul's own imperishable intellectual good (viz., the ideal transcendental reality of Goodness itself) is an absolute imperishable noble and honest good. Thus, the former are judged to be pleasurable goods whereas the latter is judged to be an eminent honest good. The noble good can be appropriately willed for its own sake as an end-end whereas a perishable good may be appropriately willed merely as a means-end. Consider a simple example. Compare a red delicious apple to a green granny apple. Which taste is superior to the other? Both flavors of the green and red apples are perishable when the apples themselves decay and are scattered like dust by the wind. Both kinds of apples are nourishable fruits.

The conscionable truth of the merit of their distinctly different flavors is to be found not in tasting them but in intellectually recognizing that the imperishable ideal of flavorness itself includes every possible flavor without distinction. In other words, one apple's flavor is not more flavorful than the other in spite of the distinctive difference between each. Yes, one may find one more delicious than the other, but this is entirely a subjective personalized self-satisfying estimation that is not a norm for what is true-as-such. Flavor is not essential to what constitutes an apple as a nutritious fruit. Conscionably, one may practically enjoy both flavorful perishable apples without falling prey to judgmentally exalting one above the other. For, one has conscionably chosen the noble truth that justly judges the comparable merit of the flavor of both different species of apple in the light of the ideal imperishable ideal reality proper to both.

Of course, if one tastefully prefers one flavor over the other, this is not a conscionable matter. It is merely a gustatory matter. If one makes this a paramount matter, this becomes unconscionable. One is disciplined early in life to eat nourishing food which is not exactly palatable to one's taste. In so doing, one is being disciplined in properly forming one's conscience. Within this conscionable assessment, all the body's sensorial goods and the soul's intellectual good are intrinsically and naturally valuable goods. Yet, the sensorial appetitive goods are only relatively good precisely because the intellectual will's innate drive to freely choose to eat, to enter into a marital heterosexual union, to take drugs, and to wear clothing is rightfully morally good inasmuch as the will's free prudent choices to engage in these sensorial appetites are both moderately and courageously chosen pursuant to the purpose of these respective instinctive drives themselves.

The purpose of eating is not gustatory pleasure but the body's holistic nutritional metabolism and well-being. One does not eat for the sake of eating but for the sake of nourishing the body. The purpose of human sexuality is not venereal pleasure but the procreation and perpetuation of the human race. These drives are not end-ends in themselves but means-ends toward the human personhood's integral holistic immortal wellbeing. The will's innate finalizing immortal end common to every human being is the transcendental communal family good-as-such of the metaphysical reality of being-as-such mediated intellectually by truth-as-such.

This transcendental metaphysical family immortal good-as-such is precisely transcendental because it holistically includes every special particular good of the sensory instinctive appetites without being reducible to any one or all of them. It is not a social (i.e., group) but a communal (i.e., family) good-as-such. It exists only in the vertical hierarchical order. Every distinctive kingdom is naturally endowed with its own communal-good-as-such. This is the case for inanimate substances, plants, animals, and human animals. That is, what is commonly and innately good and beneficial for a drop of water (viz., its evaporability) is such also for the entire ocean. That is, if it is good for the drop to evaporate into air and return as rain, so also is this the case for ocean water. If it is good for one plant to nourish itself in the earth's soil, it is good for every plant. Similarly for mankind.

But, the plant's innate common good is not imperishable whereas mankind's intellectual appetitive common good is imperishably immortal as the soul itself is immortal. Now the imperishable ideal intelligible goodness of the human will's communal good-as-such is an imperishable noble and honest moral good over and above all the real perishable sensible goods because it virtually exceeds in perfection all of the specific perishable less noble goods of the sensorial and vegetable appetitive drives. Of course the plant's drive is not sensorial. The intellectual will's free choices regarding food, sex, drugs, and clothing are morally good (i.e., virtuously temperate) when the will freely chooses to partake of them with moderation compatible with their holistic purpose regarding the corporeal body and the human person's self-subsistent personhood's holistic well-being.

Thus eating is morally good when the will deliberately eats fittingly and purposefully to nourish the body. If the human person eats otherwise, this is immorally unbefitting the human body's holistic homeostasis and the human person's sovereign morally responsible freedom of choice and authority to govern its own conduct. This is not an issue of dieting to improve the body's physique. It is an issue of the practical moral conscionable rectitude of strengthening the intellectual will's power to choose what is morally upright befitting the dignity and sovereignty of the human person's responsible freedom to govern its own conduct.

It is not morally virtuous for the will to deliberately refrain from eating altogether. This would harm the body's own homeostasis. Neither is it morally virtuous for the will to deliberately eat simply because of the gustatory pleasure that eating affords. This is an added inducement and motivation to eat but it is not the purpose of eating. A morally virtuous person eats temperately with moderation befitting the body's actual holistic nourished well-being which will differ when a person is young or old. The choice of choosing and acting morally responsibly may appear at first-blush to be a kill-joy morally and conscionably forbidding the simple pleasures of life. It is just the reverse. This conscionable engagement in pleasurable goods insures that they remain joyfully pleasurable rather than joylessly so. This matter of moral virtue holds in all of the sensorial concupiscible appetites.

In the case of the irascible appetites it is not a case of restraining their sensorial passions from overindulging but, rather, boosting their sensorial passions to cope with difficulties for the purpose of overcoming these obstacles. Hence, one is morally brave in passionately contending with a difficulty which fearfully threatens to vanquish the brave person. Such bravery is a moral virtue precisely because the difficulty is itself a barrier to easily and successfully reaching -- without passionately contending with one's own forbidding fears and the obstacles that arouse them -- what is morally and purposefully good for the brave person. The will's free choices are more than temperately or courageously morally good when the will freely chooses to honor all inalienable human rights including, for example, the inalienable right-to-life, the right to religious freedom and worship, the right to travel and even to migrate, the right to assemble, etc.. Such choices are morally just and partake of justice itself.

Justice is an ideal equality of honest and noble excellence in which an individual's conscionable choices are commensurate with upholding the inalienable dignity of humanity itself, the ideal reality of every human being as the universal unity of all mankind that metaphysically transcends and overrides all of the specific differences differentiating one human person from another, such as sex, size, age, ethnicity, nationality, religion, race, etc. Choosing and acting in the name of humanity is a noble and honest imperishable good that can be honored and chosen for its own sake and not merely as a means to an end. In this sense, such a choice to honor the ideal of humanity itself befits the virtue of justice. Because in this honorable choice all human person's are equally honorable and honored with an honor that is itself morally honorable for its equity of justice and respectability.

Such noble honor and the free choice to honor such nobility is particularly clear-cut in the case of one's regard and choice of action vis-à-vis the helpless such as the infant and the aged. Their inalienable human dignity is not diminished in spite of their helplessness and infirmity which is peculiar to their stage in life. If one does not in the name of humanity respect their sovereign integrity, one is vitiating his own freedom to honestly choose what is noble and upright. One's freedom becomes self-incriminatingly dishonored when one freely and unconscionably acts against humanity itself. When such a crime is so heinous that it violates the inalienable freedom of not only one but many human beings, such as is the case with a holocaust, it is considered to be an abominable crime against humanity.

The intellectual will's freedom of choice is a meritorious and dutiful freedom. Because when such choices are conscionably freely elicited responsibly---not from sensorial coercive passions provoked by fear or blinding emotional sensitizing sensuality, or bigoted blinding biases occasioning ignorance---the will's innate freedom is strengthened (viz., virtue) to choose what it is morally obligated to choose in honor of the integrity due to this freedom itself. Hence, it dutifully and meritoriously chooses to enhance and increase its own freedom to be increasingly free to choose to act morally in an upright manner consistent with the intellect's conscionable judgment on what is truthfully practically good (i.e. a conscionable authentic choice). Of course, this same freedom is weakened and vitiated (viz., vice) when the will chooses, for example to honor eating itself (viz., gluttony) as an end-end rather than as a means-end and to disobey the conscionable practical truth-as-such of eating's own purpose which is to holistically nourish and sustain the corporeal body's homeostasis.

The inherent fundamental benefit of eating temperately is not only the body's nutritional well-being but also incrementally the pleasurable gustatory enjoyment (albeit temporary and perishable) and satiation accompanying it. Similarly the fundamental benefit of willingly choosing to honor and respect the practical conscionable truth of eating's proper purpose not only morally upholds the rectitude and nobility of conscience itself but also meritoriously redounds to the will's own habitual fiber and moral upright character of exercising its freedom. This moral character itself merits for the will its own proper volitional spiritual rejoicing and delight in the conscionable rectitude of its own exercise of freedom. The virtue of justice is the will's own strength to willingly (i.e., freely) choose what is truthfully (ideally) excellent in that such a choice is equitably beneficial to both the person who freely elicits this choice and to every other person in the community of mankind who also partakes of freedom's ordination to the communal good-as-such.

Thus, returning to the hierarchical prioritization of the good-as-such (i.e., value) of food and of eating, by truthfully choosing to comply with the intellect's conscionable recognition that the purpose of eating is a means-end good (viz., the body's holistic wholesome nutrition), the will chooses a family communal practical (i.e., ethical) good-as-such (viz., the truth-as-such) of eating and in addition also benefits from its ancillary incremental good which is the gustatory pleasure of eating and satiating the body's hunger.

Hence, it justly, honestly, respectfully, and dutifully opts to abide by the intellect's conscionable practical truthful judgment regarding eating which the will is obliged to dutifully choose to further enhance its own freedom to be free from any choice which would vitiate (i.e., weaken) its conscionable power to freely honor is own inalienable dignity of its own sovereign personhood. If it had chosen food as a superordinate end-good rather than as a mere subordinate means-good it would have dishonestly and unjustly disobeyed its own well-formed conscience enunciating the practical moral truth regarding the authentic value and purpose of eating. In failing to choose the conscionable good-as-such it would initiate within its own bodily carnality the disordered vice of gluttony and within its own will the concomitant vice of dishonest ignobility and injustice toward the will's own integrity.

There is still one additional moral cardinal virtue, the virtue of prudence. In addition, then, to temperance in the concupiscible sensorial appetites and courage in the irascible appetites and justice in the will itself, there is the cardinal moral virtue of prudence in the soul's intellect. This virtue indicates that moral conscionable judgments are not merely apodictic judgments similar to mathematical applications. A dozen eggs or a dozen apples is merely the axiomatic application of the mathematical number 12 to grouping together in equal amounts both eggs and apples.

One's choice to eat is morally temperate when one chooses to eat for the purpose of nourishing the body's holistic nutritional well-being. But, this varies from one person's body to another and within different stages of the same person's bodily growth. Hence, the intellect prudently recognizes that there is no mathematical measurement axiomatically regulating this variation. The conscionable practical moral assessment regarding the quantity and quality of food to be eaten is prudently judged relative to a person's own body's homeostasis. The more expert is one's informed knowledge regarding this homeostasis, the more prudentially precise is one's conscionable judgment regarding what is morally appropriate in the amount and kind of food one ought to eat.

These four cardinal virtues and their derivatives are the fundamentals for what God's Holy Will is for Christ's disciple. These are fundamentally vital to the moral rectitude of the will's upright exercise of its inalienable freedom of choice. So much so are they conscionably normative for the human person's own sovereign conduct as an intellectually free nature, they are through divine grace elevated supernaturally beyond man's innate ordination to the ideal of Goodness itself to the superordinate supernatural ideal of God's very own Holiness. Be ye perfect as your Heavenly Father is perfect is the Gospel standard of conscionable moral rectitude announced by Christ Himself. God supplies the supernatural grace to enable the human person's inalienable intellectual will to be super-ordained to God's very Holiness (i.e., the eminence of Goodness) above and beyond its own innate ordination to the immortal family good-as-such. This divine and sublime Holiness is the very perfection of the immortal family good-as-such existing in its unexcelled divine eminence. This is the family of the Blessed Trinity, the Triune Personhood of God's very own Godhead.

We learn this through divine revelation. The supernal sublimity of such knowledge of God's Trinity exceeds the human intellect's native intelligence to naturally fathom this revealed mystery but it does not exceed man's supernaturally enlightened intelligence (through faith) to recognize the superintelligible reality of this mystery. Faith neither nullifies nor contradicts the human intellect's native intelligence. Rather, it expansively dilates this intelligence to enable it to gain an increasingly more acute intelligible insight into God's infinitely intelligible Divinity. This dilation will continue throughout the Christian disciple's immortal resurrection throughout the unending extent of God's eternal existence. It must be further appreciated that Christ's disciple and especially the mystic who seeks in this present life of the pilgrim an intimate union with the Triune family of the Blessed Trinity within the maternal sacramental ecclesial bosom of the Blessed Virgin's Immaculate Carmelite Heart, is not only created in the image and likeness of God, but is sacramentally through grace supernaturally elevated to intimately partake of God's very own Trinitarian life. This experiential partaking of God's Trinitarian Life within the subjectivity of his own intimacy is made available to the mystic supernaturally by the Paschal Mystery of Christ's very own God/Superman Personality sublimated to and integrated into the very Godhead of God's Trinitarian Personhood.

Within this sacramental elevation, what was previously simply an immoral or moral meritorious character of the exercise of his freedom now becomes a sinless or sinful character. He now not merely ethically dishonors and/or honors God's supreme sovereignty in obeying or disobeying the integrity of his moral conscience, he now veritably woundfully sinfully dishonors and/or mercifully sinlessly honors the Sacred Heart of the God/Superman, Jesus Christ, who graciously made Himself vulnerable to such conduct when in the Incarnation He identified Himself with mankind's own vulnerable freedom. Indeed, the conduct of Christ's disciple is either supernaturally holy with Christ's own holiness or sinful with the sin of the one who betrays His superhuman, superhumanizing friendship and amity. One cannot on the merely natural level attain to God's beatitudinal glory precisely because the limit of one's natural intellectual access to God is man's own finite knowledge of God's infinitude. Such knowledge is an authentic understanding of God. Yet, it is a virtual knowledge and not an eminent formal knowledge of God's own infinitude. For example, to know that in a grave their lies the remains of a human person is not to know that person eminently but only virtually in general terms (viz., human, mortal, deceased, young, male, a farmer, etc.). In God's supernatural revelation the Christian is supernaturally able intellectually through faith to gaze directly on the very sacramental eminence of God's infinitude (viz., face to face) and, thereby, freely supernaturally act in virtue of that infinite eminence with the supernatural graciousness mercifully afforded by that same Triune Godhead.

Turning, again, from the objective order of morality to the subjective order of the willful selfhood's self-cultivated conscientious morale. The subjective artificial order of self-cultivation cannot substitute for the moral virtues. The prospect of taking some fat-reducing chemical pills to minimize the somatic body's adipose as a substitute to practicing the moral virtue of temperance in eating is morally unacceptable. For, such a self-controlling palliative approach further reinforces one's immoral gluttony rather than supporting the person's practice of moral temperance in the matter of its conscionable practical purpose of eating. Were these chemical pills such as to reduce a person's subjective somatic bodily craving for food and not threaten the body's own homeostasis, this would support a temperate virtue of eating but not substitute for it altogether. In a complete turn-around antithesis to the soul's intellectual will, the self-subsistent personhood's selfhood self-serving will is not ordained nor driven by any purposeful objective possession. It is motivated to possess not what is reasonably appropriate to be morally and ethically (i.e., reasonably intelligibly) possessed.

Rather, it is motivated to appropriate possessively whatever it seeks to socially have for its own personalized usage. That is, it is statically (i.e., psychically cerebrally) or kinetically (i.e., somatically and viscerally) motivated to forcibly and influentially have for its own social self-serving personalized availability whatever is conducive to guaranteeing its own self-centered psychic and/or somatic social autonomy (i.e., self-secured self-reliant subsistence).

Hence, its self-serving self-cultivated purposeless needful motivation is simply the adverse of the intellectual will's own innate purposeful conscionable drive. The objective hierarchical vertical order is the order of being and existence whereas the subjective historical horizontal order is the order of having and resistance. The hierarchical metaphysical order is one of purposeful ordination and subordination whereas the historical paraphysical order is one of a purposeless self-serving dichotomous selfish self-orientation. If the psychic selfhood's partisan needful self-interest is dominant its polarized somatic counterpart is subjugated to its own domination and vice versa. Hence, its self-serving needfulness is always caught up in a have/have-not polar opposition and self-alienation of competing partisan self-serving needs and serviceable orientations at odds with each other.

The human person's subjective selfhood's psychosomatic will is motivated to appropriate possessively (i.e., securely, partisanly, and personalistically) rather than to possess appropriately (i.e., purposefully) and personally (i.e., in view of its common family immortal good-as-such). That is, again, to appropriate irrationally, absurdly, and enigmatically consistent with the paradoxical mathematical surdity and polarity that prevails through all of the self-cultivated worlds of the self's self-centered horizontal, historical order of subjectivity.

This means that the useable social artificial non-such-goods that are willfully skillfully self-cultivated are themselves not normatively measured by the immortal family communal good-as-such but by the historically mortal social non-such-goods which can only become profitable in their personalized actual serviceable usage and possessive exploitation explicitly by that anonymous someone who possessively makes use of these for its own willful self-serving personalized advantage.

Hence, the very cultivation of such serviceable quasi-goods (viz., a house or a car) may not only not profitably serve the self who skillfully laboriously fabricates them but can increasingly deprive this very self's own skillful labor from profiting from his own handiwork. The builder need not profit but only become an impoverished builder of a house if he cannot inhabit his own dwelling nor receive some suitable compensation in exchange for its construction. For, again, the artificial construct is not inherently (i.e., naturally) a community good-as-such. Rather, it is a serviceable social non-such-good which is only profitable to the anonymous self or selves who actually possessively and personalistically make use of it. This self-possessiveness is not a moral (i.e., reasonable and appropriate consideration) but an amoral irrational, accountable peculiarity of the selfhood's own purposeless selfish self-serving willful needfulness (i.e., deprivation).

In the place of moral responsibility there is an amoral accountability and liability inherent in such a subjective personalized possessive ownership. Since these artificially self-cultivated social non-such-goods have associated with them exploitative values, one who possesses the ownership of such goods is accountable to other associates who are inadvertently implicated in this personalized possession. Thus, one who possesses a membership in a golf club and plays golf is accountable for his conduct on the golf course to the managers of the course and to his fellow players. He is liable to being banished from the course if he violates the regulations controlling professional conduct. Such a violation is not a moral issue but an amoral breech of a socially contracted regulation pertaining to a personality's (viz., a player's) self-control over his own personalized possession.

In other words, any service able artificial fabrication (whatever it may be) must be appropriated possessively and personalistically (as a social non-such-good) and not merely possessed appropriately (as a communal good-as-such). That is, the self needfully willfully demands to possessively own for his own personalized (group) availability and usage this fabrication in order to profitably avail himself of its services. This needful claim to personalistically possess is forcibly and influentially reinforced by the will's self-induced compassionate emotions which motivationally force it to possessively pursue what guarantees to satisfy its own needful (i.e., deprived) autonomous social security.

The somatic compassionate emotions which the will's selfhood willfully self-induces are motivationally evoked to kinetically activate the will's self-serving need to possessively secure for its own selfhood's usage whatever is required to guarantee (i.e., reassure) its own autonomous social security in the matter of sex, food, drugs, and attire. Hence, these self-induced venereal, gustatory, narcotic, and stylistic sensual emotional feelings motivationally do not actuate the self'-s somatic body's autonomic motor reflexes -- as is the case with the corporeal body's instinctive carnal passions in the objective order of existence -- they stimulate the selfhood's own imperious willful need to exert itself to provide for its own personalistic (i.e., selfish) autonomous social security (i.e., egocentric self-sufficiency) in the subjective historical order of resistance.

It is in this sense that the self is consciously aware within its body's own subjective visceral somaticity of experiencing its own self-induced sensuous emotional feelings of, for example, gustatory pleasures as "bodiless motions" motivationally exciting, and stirring his selfhood's will to kinetic action to possessively have whatever guarantees its own self-serving self-satisfied and self-contented satiated gustatory social security. Thus in the case of food the experience of consciously feeling a sensitized emotional excitement of eating succulent gourmet foods impels the will to possessively have not merely these foods themselves for its immediate consumption but even the facilities such as the special cooking utensils and seasonings, etc., which artificially facilitate the gourmet's preparation of such succulent dishes.

Unlike the carnal appetitive passionate drives in the objective order which are instinctively directed toward the body's holistic well-being over and beyond the sensorial pleasure they afford, these subjective compassionate sensuous emotions incite the selfhood's will to needfully (i.e., automatically) enthusiastically demand to consciously experience the intensification of sensual pleasure itself within the somatic body's visceral somaticity. Paradoxically enough, this sensual emotional compassionate experience and sensitized feeling contributes to the self's freedom of self-control only by emotionally forcibly compelling the self's will to become more possessively self-attached to these self-serving sensualities and the artificial utilities which automatically facilitate their preparation.

In other words, motivational somatic sensitizing sensuous emotional compassionate feelings, on the one hand, and motivational psychic intimate nonsensuous emotionless dispassionate bearings, on the other are seductively compelling for the somatic self and seductively subtly alluring for the psychic self; that is, slavishly self-captivating. One becomes unwittingly not only seductively captivated by the force of these motivational self-orientated visceral feelings and cerebral bearings, one's selfhood becomes enslaved to their insistent demands. In brief, one becomes slavishly self-attached to them.

In addressing the subjective egocentric self's psychic willfulness in contraposition to its somatic willfulness, it is not stirring and exciting sensuous emotions which motivationally compel the will to kinetic action. It is simply the reverse of these emotions that motivate the will's self-serving need for possessively guaranteeing its own autonomous psychic social security. Of course, this emotionless and placid inertia of the psyche was already indicated in an earlier paragraph of this commentary. What is significant in subconsciously experiencing the mind's calm and sedate psychic emotionless equipoised bearing and serenity is that this intimate tranquility is experienced as the exact opposite of the "bodiless motions" of the somatic body's emotional stirrings. This serenity is experienced as a sedating emotionless calm of a "motionless body."

This inner emotionless calm of the psychic cerebral willful self does not motivationally stir or excite the will to kinetic action. Rather, it motivationally sedates and calms the will's psychic self to remain autocratically in an inertial static stage of self-induced somnolence. This is the exact reverse of the somatic self's motivationally self-induced excitement automatically spurring it to kinetic action. Just as the somatic self's willful needs for an automatic socially secure self-contented lifestyle prompt it to emotionally mobilize its bodily efforts to fabricate or procure for itself serviceable tools facilitating this lifestyle, the psychic self's willful needs for an autocratic socially secure self-contained lifestyle prompts it, in turn, to emotionlessly immobilize its mental ingenuity allowing it to fully concentrate on fabricating or procuring for itself serviceable symbols and nomenclature facilitating this lifestyle.

It is important to fully appreciate that a symbol in the horizontal order is inherently meaningless and insignificant whereas the same symbol in the vertical order is inherently meaningful and significant. Terminology is not fabricated by the soul's intellect but only by the self's mind. The intellect is completely passive regarding its knowledge and ideas of the existing universe of reality. The psychic mind is completely active regarding the fabrication of its own ideations and concepts which resist existing transcendent to the mind's own solipsistic immanency. A symbol in the horizontal order carries only a metaphorical figurative meaning whereas the same symbol in the vertical order carries a metaphysical literal meaning.

Consider the term, freedom as a self-cultivated artificial terminological symbol. Freedom in the objective order signifies an inalienable faculty (viz., the intellectual will) which acts spontaneously intransitively (i.e., non-productively) under its own impetus. In the subjective order it denotes an alienable function (viz., the psychosomatic will) which transitively (i.e., productively) prompts itself motivationally (i.e.,un/emotively) to in/action. It is alienable precisely because it is in polar tension within its own psychosomatic volition. Freedom in the objective order is fundamentally a moral freedom in which the will is both responsibly free and obligated (i.e., duty-bound) to exercise its freedom in virtue of a communal metaphysical family standard that is morally binding on this freedom. This is a freedom of sovereign rule in which the human person is not governed other than by a common law which is germane to that freedom itself. This is a royal sovereign freedom inasmuch as the person is primarily and fundamentally responsible to his own conscience objectively formed by "right reason" for the rectitude of this freedom's exercise.

Freedom in the subjective order is supplementally an amoral freedom in which the psychosomatic selfhood's will is socially and punitively accountable to selves in addition to its own self in the exercise of its freedom. It is not a freedom of sovereign governance but a socially interdependent freedom of self-control to provide for the psychosomatic self's self-reliant personalized social security. This is a contractual freedom issuing from the self's own indigence and psychosomatic need to artificially cultivate and procure for itself supplemental conveniences to serviceably fulfill this need. This is a democratic freedom inasmuch as the person's own selfhood is required supplementally to conscientiously strive to abide by the terms of its social contract. Of course, freedom in the subjective order is through and through a paradoxical have/have-not polar psychosomatic dichotomy.

If the psychic willful self has its own freedom its polar opposite somatic willful self does not. And vice versa. Therefore each's respective antipodal freedom is alienable (i.e., can be lost). Consequently, this freedom of self-control is a sacrificial freedom. Further the selfhood's purposeless self-serving willfulness is not an innate drive; it is a socially deficient need demanding consequentially both a self-cultivated skillful productive function and a corresponding functioning facility to cater to this need. Hence, it is not a power that spontaneously acts; it is an impotency that requires a prompting and motivational forcible influential impulse to sedate its psychic self's resistance to becoming statically impassive and inactive and/or a motivational forcible influential impulse to excite its somatic self's resistance to becoming kinetically compassionate and active. Further it is not morally conscionable but amorally conscientious in keeping with its own psychic and/or somatic conditional arbitrary contractual requirements for which it is liable and accountable.

Accordingly, commensurate with the psychic selfhood's self-serving imperative need to become securely socially justifiably selfishly (i.e., partisanly) self-contained, it must be subconsciously motivated to influentially (i.e., emotionlessly and dispassionately) mentally resist every attempt to disturb or disrupt its statically immobilized inner orientated autocratic self-possessed selfhood. Conversely, commensurate with the somatic selfhood's self-serving imperative need to become securely socially gratifyingly selfishly self-contented, it must be motivated to influentially (i.e., emotionally and compassionately) overcome every bodily resistance that would impede its kinetic outer orientated conscious automatic self-possession.

In other words, where freedom objectively means a freedom to

440

act morally and responsibly in a community of responsible law-abiding individuals, subjectively it means an amoral freedom to contractually and conscientiously manage and control one's lifestyle as an autocratic bodiless mind and/or to contractually and conscientiously manipulate and control one's lifestyle as a mindless bodily automaton.

In the subjective order, freedom means not a spontaneous power to choose and to govern one's own immortal destiny but, rather, an impotent polarizing instigated possibility of decisively controlling the outcome of one's own personalized fate in conjunction with selves other than one's own self. This impotent self-control, however, can only be influentially psychically idealized and/or somatically realized. For, self-possession ambiguously means personalized ownership and control of what is serviceably useable in support of one's freedom of self-control. What serves one's own selfhood is ambivalent with a have-have/not paradoxical polarized ambivalence. If one spends one's self in cultivating a masterful skillful control of several languages, for example, one sacrificially forgoes cultivating a masterful skillful control of industrial equipment employed in manufacturing plants. For, what is idealistically socially serviceable at the level of the liberal arts is usefully usably self-serving while what is realistically serviceable at the level of the technical and mechanical arts is uselessly usably self-serving.

Certainly this is a paradox of the polarized have-have/not order of ownership. The polyglot who has mastered several different languages will very likely be usefully serviceable throughout his lifetime since these languages involve the speech common to everyday communication. But, the highly specialized technician masterfully skilled in operating hi-tech industrial equipment finds his skill to be useless the moment the specialized mode of industrial manufacture is superseded by a more economically automated process.

This is a conundrum, of course. But it is the conundrum which besets the meaning of freedom in the subjective order of the human person hood's purposeless self-serving self-cultivatedself-humanized self-possessed freedom of self-control. It is a freedom of social serviceable autonomic self-control which when left to its own self-determination not merely captivates its possessor but paradoxically imprisons its possessor within its own have-have/not polarity. If one achieves an autocratic idealistic and romantic fateful self-control of one's own historical eventuation then one in the process of this fateful pursuit of one's own autocratic social security must forego possessively pursuing an automatic realistic and pragmatic fateful self-control of one's own historical eventuation. To provide further evidence of this pervasive irony built into the entire reach of this subjective horizontal order of the human personhood's self-cultivation, consider the national hi-tech progressive futuristic pragmatic self-orientation of a country like the USA at the dawn of the third millennium of Christianity. This national pragmatic culture is hide-bound to ingeniously, industriously, politically, commercially, experimentally, economically, educationally, etc., amorally and progressively transform itself into an ever-increasing and more intensive robotic lifestyle automatically serviced by self-serving utilities.

It is bent on successfully continuously re-inventing itself and superseding its own selfhood. It is a lifestyle of automated self-cultivation. What was serviceable in one generation becomes junk in the next. There is no authoritative vertical moral order of conscionable governance to oversee this self-propelled futuristic pragmatic democratic technocratic humanism. In its total and slavish preoccupation with possessively controlling the historical fate of its own self-possessed freedom of self-control, it is exhaustively projecting and self-deconstructing itself into a dehumanized selfhood of automated robots.

The upshot of this meticulous examination of the subjective selfhood's own subjective paradoxical self-serving willfulness and psychosomatic bipolarity is the fuller appreciation that the egocentric psychosomatic selfhood of the human person's self-subsistent personhood is not equivalent to nor parallel to its dynamic human nature's body-soul substantive constitutional counterpart. The psychosomatic personality is itself respectively the self-humanized self-cultivated psychic dematerialization and/or somatic materialization of the human person's substantive corporeal body in the objective order of existence.

Thus while the somatic body's corpuscular somaticity is consciously sensitively experienced and felt focally and kinetically in its fragmentary parts (viz., its functional physiology) as a "bodiless motion," the psychic body's corpuscular psychicity (viz., its functional psychology) is subconsciously intimately experienced statically by a mental concentration as a "motionless body." Indeed, it seems that it is the neurological brain moreso than any other part of the human corpuscular body that is suitably the psychic self's dematerialized corpuscular organism.

Now, Christ's very own super-self-humanized and super-self-cultivated Personality in its egocentric selfhood partakes of no egoistic partisan self-serving selfishness which is peculiar to mankind's fallen nature after original sin. Christ's very own attitudinal willful mindset is not captive to a selfish self-serving needful willfulness as is the case with all human creatures save our Blessed Mother, Mary, Christ's own mother preserved from original sin and its aftermath.

Accordingly, Christ does not manifest any selfish self-serving partisan self-interest in the mindset of His own be-attitudinal Self-esteem. Indeed, Christ's own Messianic mindset is not a have/have-not humanistic attitude typical of mankind's own self-humanized dichotomous personality. Before being supernaturally elevated into God's Triune Godhead, humans are in their own self-humanized personality and mindset either dominantly idealistically pessimistic or dominantly realistically optimistic in their overall self-esteem and overriding have-attitudinal commitment to their personalized partisan autonomous social self-interest.

Paradoxically, if a person is predominantly one type of these two self-serving attitudinal mindsets he is attitudinally at enmity with the other by reason of the polarity inherent in his own dichotomous psychosomatic personality. Mankind of itself cannot completely transcend its own self-humanizing partisan self-centered selfishness. In the subjective order of resistance, humans are humanistically slavish prisoners of their own self-serving freedom of self-control. This is the offshoot of original sin as revealed in the Book of Genesis. As previously noted, there is no artificial function or role model peculiar to one's own personality that cannot be functionally exercised by a personality other than one's own self substituting its selfhood for one's own self. One's personality is confined to the subjective historical order of events, eventuations, happenings, and functions which are dichotomously artifictional and/or artifactual.

The artifictional is a rational theory which theoretically cannot establish its own empirical validation without reference to the artifactual. On the other hand, the artifactual is an empirical factuality which cannot rationally explain itself without reference to some artifictional theory. In brief, the selfhood's psychic willfulness is interdependently allied with the selfhood's somatic willfulness albeit the mutual polarized opposition prevailing between the two.

This subjective order of resistance is not the order of existence with its existential activity. This existential order includes the reality of causation, real changes which are radically substantive changes and less radically mere incidental ones. This same order of causation includes agencies which are potentially endowed with powers that spontaneously act, vital activities which are intransitive non-productive operations, and destinations which are purposely finalizing. The subjective order of resistance is the order of having no actual existence of its own and needing such actuality for its own total self-fulfillment. This order is one of fatality in that what happens occurs not by happenstance but forcibly and fatalistically by a self's self-determination to have it happen. There is no causal destination but only a self-centered self-serving orientation. The only finality here is not a purposeful teleological finality but a historical self-serving purposeless one in which the ensuing consequence of one's influential forcible willful self-controlled self-determination (i.e., the result) is considered to be final.

Granted that, for example, eating is itself naturally a vital intransitive purposeful activity that inherently benefits the one who eats, mankind must cultivate the food that is to be eaten. This cultivation itself is not naturally but artificially undertaken and the skillful agricultural toil of this cultivation which engages mankind's self-humanization is a transitive function that cultivates a product (viz., a cornfield) which by dint of such cultivation becomes a social commodity that benefits the one who actually possessively owns the produce and can dispose of it to his own self-serving partisan self-centered advantage.

Mankind is a prisoner of its own social self-serving psychosomatic selfhood. In the subjective order of resistance there is no family communality. There is only a self-cultivated group functionality inasmuch as those exercising one and the same function are associates by dint of their interchangeability with each other and their associated partisan self-serving self-interest. In the subjective order there is no family community there are only factional or fictional competitive groupings in polar opposition to each other.

The moral freedom of choice in the objective order is meritorious because the person of upright moral character merits being honored and respected whereas a downright immoral character does not. The amoral freedom of self-control in the subjective order is not a meritorious freedom but a sacrificial freedom. Indeed, the very meaning of freedom is equivocally different when spoken of in each's different order. Fundamentally in the natural order, mankind's freedom is inalienable even when he immortally survives in heaven or in hell. This is why hell is so fiendish. It deprives a person of the full exercise of his inalienable freedom to sovereignly govern his own life and conduct. Supplementally in the cultural order, mankind's freedom is paradoxically alienable by dint of its own selfishly self-serving functional psychosomatic dichotomous exercise.

The real issue of freedom is the super-superhuman and super--superhumanistic liberating freedom which Christ Himself purchases for mankind at the price of His own Body and Blood when He redeems mankind by becoming humanly incarnate and subject to the influence of mankind's own invidious slavery to the victimhood of its own freedom of self-control. Not only does Christ gratuitously substitute His very own super-self-humanized super-self-cultivated personality for that of every human being's personality, He invites every human to substitute for its own personhood's personality that of His own Divine Personhood's divinized subjective superhumanized Selfhood. It is only by freely entering into this ecclesial covenant that mankind can be liberated from its slavery to its own freedom of self-control that has been out of control by reason of Adam & Eve's original sin.

In this covenant it is not enough that man become supernaturally fundamentally free in the objective order of his natural hierarchical existence by the supernatural gift of God's graciousness and gratuitous sacramental Life. He must also become supplementally superhumanistically free in the subjective order of his own self-cultivated resistance. The secular resistance that mankind humanistically experiences in socially safeguarding his partisan self-serving self-alienating selfish have-attitude must be replaced with Christ's very own superhumanistic resistance to all such selfishness. Mankind's Christian superhumanistic self-fulfillment does not consist in safeguarding his own selfish self-serving secular overriding self-commitment to his have-more attitudinal self-interest but, rather, in sacrificing this selfish attitude to willfully embrace a be-attitudinal commitment and Messianic mindset that radically sacrifices and submits one's very own selfhood itself to the providential care of the Father of Christ's Masterful Selfless-Selfhood.

This is the Christian commitment to willfully and selflessly have less in the subjective cultural order to further facilitate the self's own selfhood to be more fully and perfectly self-surrendered and self-fulfilled in the fundamental objective supernatural order of the Catholic Church's sacramentality found only in the objective hierarchical order of existence beyond the historical horizon of mankind's possessive selfhood of self-humanizingself-cultivation.

This Christian humanism is nothing short of the ascetical life of self-denial and the way of the cross which the Christian sums up in the practice of the three evangelical counsels of chastity, obedience, and poverty. Christ has not come to be self-served but to serve selflessly as the Servant of all mankind. This total selfless-service demands an unstinting superhumanistic self-denial and self-detachment from one's own secular self-humanizing partisan (i.e., selfish) self-interest. It is entirely counter-cultural to the completely secular worldly culture that voluntaristically and preemptively divorces its own amoral aspirations from the transcendent objective hierarchical order of morality.

This superhumanistic self-denial is impossible to man himself and his only possible to God who has accomplished it for all mankind in the Person of Jesus Christ. It is precisely this Christian counter-cultural resistance to secular society's own entrenched self-serving partisan domineering have-attitudinal selfishness that Christ's very own providentially super-self-humanizing Selfless service gratuitously grants to mankind to make possible his liberation from his own self-victimizing slavery to his own selfishly self-serving polarized willful psychosomatic selfhood.

Hence, in direct counter opposition to secular society that insists that man must not only not curb his freedom of selfish self-control and partisan self-determination but rather intensify its willful domination, Christ's superhumanistic wisdom counsels that mankind can only find its authentic self-fulfillment not within its own self-cultivated subjective supplemental partisan order of resistance but transcendentally beyond it in the objective order of existence. The subjective cultural order is a hypothetical make-believe world of a conditional and consequential if-then logic based on the selfhood's conditional willfulness. If a than b; posit a, than b fatefully follows; debit b, than a does not fatefully follow or occur. The nexus between a and b is not a causal one; it is a conditional willful influential forcible fateful nexus of the will's own dominant willful self-determined self-control. If the will is self-determined to have b it must posit a. If it is not self-determined to have b it has not posited a. This is not a purposeful but a purposeless self-serving elenchus.

In diametrical opposition to this, the natural objective order is completely believable on its own terms. Its terms and terminology are not hypothetical nor suppositional but categorical. It is not an "as if" make-believe situation but an "as is" existential status. When a and b are causally connected it is not a willful self-determination that connects them but a causal nexus in which b is dependent on a for its coming-to-be and for its existence. The subjective order is required to supplementally complete by the principle of subsidiarity what the objective order cannot accomplish naturally on its own. But, this completion must supplement and not abortively altogether supplant the fundamental moral order of existence.

Does this self-denial then demand that the Christian humanist possess nothing at all of what he himself functionally cultivates or negotiates to advance his own autonomous social security? No! It means that a Christian humanist cannot become possessively selfishly self-attached to what he laboriously earns and skillfully owns. He cannot become captive to his own subjective needs. This does not mean that he cannot be an owner and have possessions required for his own self-humanistic secular personalized cultivation. This does not mean that he cannot collaborate with others in group functional skillful productive work and ownership.

What it does mean is that the purely humanistic overriding selfish (i.e., partisan) self-serving have-attitudinal mindset and secular humanistic spirit of willful domination must itself be resisted in its very willful self-serving slavish self-alienating needfulness. This domineering secular humanistic spirit that willfully resists all that impedes its own pursuit and selfish self-possession of its own autonomous social security must itself be resisted through, with, and in the power of Christ's own Holy Spirit of Resistance. This Holy Spirit supernaturally and sacramentally abides within the very pith, the nuclear core, the mindset, and the heart of the super-self-humanized Christian personality's psychosomatic selfhood.

Indeed, this Holy Spirit of Christ's very own superhumanistic Personality is the throb of Christ's charismatic Sacred Heart; this Holy Spirit abides within the inmost inner intimacy of Christ's Selfhood's Selfless Willfulness. The Holy Spirit of this Sacred Heart is not one of willful domination and commitment to its own autonomous partisan self-esteem but one of willful docile submission to God-the-Father's Holy Will of supreme sublime benevolence.

The secular self-humanizing domineering spirit committed to its own have-attitude self-controlled self-interest and needful claims must yield to the Christian super-self-humanizing Holy Spirit of willfully submitting be-attitudinally to Christ's Masterful Selfless-service in liberating mankind from the prison of its own slavish self-alienating domineering competitive self-control. This means that the Christian's overriding be-attitudinal mindset must be metanoetically converted from possessively being attached to its own self-cultivated possessions to dispossessively having no selfish attachment to these

448

possessions themselves. This selfish self-riddance enables the Christian to be more superhumanistically attached to the supernatural sacramental reality of God's Triune Godhead in the hierarchical order of existence transcendent to its own subjective selfhood.

This also means that one's slavish humanistic attitude of resistant hostility toward one's socially competitive polarized opponents must become by complete metanoia conversion a liberated super-humanistic be-attitude of hospitality resisting the selfhood's willful selfish proneness to safeguard its own partisan social security rather than to sacrificially, submissively, and humbly be selflessly at the missionary service of prayerfully cooperating with Christ in mankind's redemptive liberating entry into the kingdom of God.

The Christian asceticism of this lifestyle is much more radical than the ascetism peculiar, for example, to the Buddhist lama in Tibet. Christ's asceticism is not only not seated nor ensconced within the bosom of one's very own subjective psychic autocratic selfhood deliberately alienated from and impervious to its personality's somatic alter ego. It is an asceticism in which, paradoxically enough, one's selfhood cannot find its self-fulfillment within its own supplemental egocentric cultural subjectivity but only beyond the deficiency of own emptiness within the vertical hierarchical order of its authentic self-fulfillment. The selfhood's empty need is not a need for its own self. It is a need for what completely transcends its own selfhood's vacuity.

This is a reality that is the very antithesis of the selfhood's emptiness, a reality that is the very fullness of reality itself: God's own divinity and Triune Godhead. Hence, this asceticism demands that both the psychic and somatic self-humanized selfhood willfully resistantly ascetically oppose its own partisan willful selfishness in order to superhumanistically transcend its own imprisonment and self-alienation. This is not humanistically possible to man alone but it is sacrificially superhumanistically possible by Christ's very own Paschal Mystery of sacrificial mediation incarnated in His Catholic Church's sacramentality.

Failure to become self-resolved and superhumanistically resolute to follow Christ's invitation to pattern one's lifetyle on the Gospel's Way of the Cross is tantamount to substituting one's self-serving self-cultivated needs into self-righteous claims. When these self-serving social needs in the horizontal order of resistance are both emotionally and/or emotionlessly promoted as self-righteous legitimate claims sanctioned into civil law, their stridency demands that they be substituted for mankind's inalienable moral rights in the vertical order of existence. For example, the legalized accessibility of artificial birth control medications and prophylactics egregiously advances the woman's right to artificially control her body's fertility and pregnancy even to the point of having legal recourse to procured abortion.

This abomination of legalized procured abortion which is currently in practice among many nations in the world today most clearly makes manifest the gravity of the selfhood's attachment to its own willful domineering have-attitude self-commitment and to its own autonomous partisan somatic self-satisfaction and/or psychic self-justification. This autonomous self-attachment preemptively blinds not only an individual but an entire social have-attitude mindset to the primacy of the moral order itself transcendent to society's willful autonomy. The Christian be-attitudinal mindset and self-commitment (viz., attachment) must not be the secular mindset of having more of one's own partisan social autonomous self-reliance but rather one of sacrificially having less autonomous self-reliance in order to be more self-fulfilled beyond the vain futile emptiness of one's own supplemental selfhood.

This Christian ascetic program of self-detachment is precisely what our Carmelite Holy Father, St. John of the Cross, prescribes as the purgative program required for the will in the theological virtue of charity to facilitate the selfhood's will's entry into contemplative prayer. In contemplative prayer the mystic becomes totally attached to our Heavenly Father's Holy Will and not to his own self-centered partisan selfish willfulness. This attachment can only come about by a preliminary skillful training in ascetic self-detachment. Our Holy Father in his consummate masterful mystagogical counsels explains the advantages and the drawbacks to one's failure to become completely self-detached in the cultural subjective order of one's freedom of self-control.

Here it seems most fitting to bring to mind Christ's Gospel clarion clear statement of the heterodoxic cruciform order that reconciles the fundamental vertical order of existence with the supplemental horizontal order of resistance. Our Lord declares that "the first will be last and the last will be first." In the order of initiation the order of existence is prior to that of resistance. In the order of completion the order of resistance is prior to that of existence. In the fundamental order the Christian is morally obligated and duty-bound to superhumanly love God's primacy above and beyond any other love. In the supplemental order the Christian is urgently exhorted by an overriding superhumanistic morale to sacrificially and submissively cherish and treasure God for His own sake and concomitantly to likewise cherish and treasure his neighbor as he himself is treasured by Christ.

In the Old Testament it is the Decalogue that is the moral law of dutiful obedience to God's Holy Will. This is fundamental and first in the vertical order of existence. In the New Testament it is the Beatitudes that spell our the Holy Spirit's heartfelt and mind bent morale of sacrificially cherishing above and beyond one's own autonomous selfhood the Father's Holy Will as mediated by Christ's own Paschal Mystery in which He gratuitously substitutes His own Selfless Selfhood for mankind's selfish personality. By participating in this exchange the Christian skillfully becomes an expert in the prayerful art of superhumanistic self-denial as paradoxically spelled out in the Beatitudes. Blessed are the poor, the meek, the persecuted, the pure, the suffering, the hungry, the peacemakers, and the merciful.

That which is historically and supplementally last in the New Testament, the Beatitudes instilled in the Christian disciple's be-attitudinal messianic mindset, becomes first in the order of perfection and completion. In other words, when the supplemental historical order's own selfless self-enamored priority completes and perfects the hierarchical fundamental order's dutiful priority, this order of resistance resistantly selflessy complements the order of existence. Thus, there is an orthodoxy in the order of existence whose fundamentally is never supplanted. There is also a paradox in the order of resistance which remains enigmatically paradoxical when the Christian superhumanistically skillfully commits himself to Christ's very own Gospel be-attitudinal lifestyle commitment to His Heavenly Father's Holy Will.

The heterodoxy consists in the self-resolution and reconciliation of the two orders that cruciformly ensues when the priority of one order complements the priority of the other.

What this commentary has been at some pains to explain is that it is not the soul itself that suffers the vicissitudes of the mystic's dark night of the senses and the spirit. It is one's subjective willful psycho-somatic selfhood that suffers the dark night's vicissitudes. The night of the senses occurs in the somatic self's conscious experience of its own body's somaticity and the night of the spirit occurs in the psychic self's subconscious experience of its own mind's psychicity. This is the thrust of this protracted exposition on the selfhood's needful will in contraposition to the soul's intellectual will.

COMMENTARY ON
THE DARK NIGHT
OF THE SOUL

Preliminary reflections to the exposition of the Dark Night.

The Dark Night is in organic continuity with the Ascent.

The Dark Night is in organic continuity with the *Ascent*. The difference between the two derives from placing one's self in the perspective of the person who takes control of the mystic's commitment to live out the Gospel's ascetic life-style of self-denial commensurate with Christ's own messianic redemptive beatitudinal mindset and example. In the *Ascent*, it is the mystic who takes the initiative in an astute training program of self-denial while in the *Dark Night* it is the Holy Spirit residing within the deepest recesses of the mystic's own selfhood who takes the initiative to complete this program of ascetic self-denial undertaken by the mystic. Alive and undetected within the inner-most intimate recesses of the selfhood's personalized mindful psychosomatic will, the Holy Spirit of God-the-Son and God-the-Father, the Spirit of Truth and of Christ's utter Selflessness withholds from the mystic's religious experience every religious bodily sensuous stimulating selfish satisfying self-contentment and every religious mental impassive pacifying selfish justifying self-containment. Bereft of these much needed reassuring religious experiences and motivational influences, the mystic experiences such a religious emotional aridity and apathy, on the one hand, and religious emotionless discombobulation and stupor, on the other hand, that continued prayerful attention to God becomes a harrowing and uninviting and even repugnant prospect and exercise.

As previously noted in the commentary of the *Ascent*, a religious emotional feeling of satisfying self-contentment and/or a religious emotionless bearing of justifying self-containment are the key self-serving and self-initiating religious motivations prompting the human person's subjective mindful will to become prayerfully engaged with God as a reality to be self-servingly treasured and appreciated. The soul's objective intellectual will is spontaneously and dynamically operative while the person's subjective selfhood's psychosomatic will functions autonomously (i.e., self-reliantly) only through sensitizing, sensational, sensuous stimulations (viz., emotional feelings) which kinetically activate the somatic will to productive bodily action, on the one hand, and through intimate, notional, insensate, pacifications which statically sedate the psychic will to mental quiescence, on the other, conducive to creative musing.

At the very end of the *Ascent*, St. John presents to the mystical novice the proper manner of sacrificial self-denial in which he must become expertly self-trained in order to both enter into a full-fledged contemplative prayer communion with God's Self-revealed Triune Godhead and, thereby, achieve his authentic selfhood's self-fulfillment by being transformed into Christ's very own utterly sacrificial Selfless Selfhood (i.e., Christ's super-self-humanized charismatic Personality). He indicates in the examination of temporal, sensory, natural, moral, supernatural, and spiritual goods the strict necessity for the mystic to sacrifice his own personalized self-aggrandized somatic self-gratification (i.e., smugness) and psychic self-justification (i.e., boasting) as the necessary condition to experiencing gratuitously and religiously in the exercise and enjoyment of these various goods God's very own Triune exultation and consolation respectively in the will's somatic and psychic selfhood.

What St. John indicates in the concluding section of the *Ascent* is that the mystic may, in every stage of his prayerful life advance to a perfect union with God's Triune Godhead in contemplative prayer, or basely exploit God to foster his own selfish self-serving psychosomatic religious needs and thereby further alienate himself from God, or preferably, deliberately deny his own selfish religious self-interest in

454

order to selflessly serve God's sovereign Godhead and thereby sincerely advance to a more perfect union with God. This selfish self-serving self-centeredness is the greatest obstacle to the mystic's perfect union with God. He is always prone to exploiting God for his own self-aggrandizement rather than sacrificially denying his own selfish religious needs and placing himself totally at the service of God's Holy Will. The *Ascent* indicates the ascetic steps of self-denial in which the mystic must be actively trained to become better disposed religiously, sacrificially, and piously toward serving God zealously and with a total commitment befitting Christ's very own Personality of total sacrificial submission to His Father's Holy Will.

This ascetic Gospel life-style has for its model Christ's very own passion and crucifixion. The mystic is invited not merely to imitate Christ, but to become an "*alter Christus*" another Christ as a full-fledged member of Christ's sacramental Church; Christ's very own mystical body. The element of heroic self-sacrificial self-denial endemic to the mystical life is crucial to attaining to a perfect union with the Father through Christ in the power of their Holy Spirit. Of course, this ascetic life-style is undertaken only within the supernatural theological virtue of hope vested in Christ's resurrection and ascension into heaven. For, while the soul is immortal, the body is not. And, one's selfhood is rooted in the body's substantive corporeality which perishes with the person's physical death. Further, the person's selfhood is itself couched in the body's insubstantive psychosomatic corpuscularity which continues throughout the mystic's lifetime from the instant of conception to the instant of physical death to undergo continuous transformation.

The mystical life entails intense suffering.

In sum, the mystical life entails an intense suffering which occurs precisely within the very egological subjectivity of the person's self-subsistent conscious willful psychosomatic selfhood. This suffering involves kinesthetically the somatic body's sensitive sensual comfort (or discomfort) and kinetic movement, on the one hand, and anesthetically the psychic mind's impassive static equilibrium (or, disequilibrium), on the other. Indeed, this psychosomatic polarity within the personhood's will is the very context within which the *Dark Night* unfolds in terms of the purgation of the senses, on the one hand, and that of the spirit, on the other, as described in our SanJuanistic Carmelite text.

Even at the risk of a monotonous repetition, it is important to point out that this subjective egocentric self-awareness peculiar to the human person is a consciousness which is not present in brute animals. Such creatures do undergo the passions of pain and pleasure in their sentient animal bodies. They do not have any egocentric self-awareness in their passions and sentient affections. This self-awareness is characteristic of the human person alone who in virtue of his own subsistent unique inalienable intelligent and free personhood is able to consciously in a self-conscious awareness take willful charge and mindful control over his own personhood's personalized egocentric selfhood. This subjectivity is the field of suffering in which the human person experiences psychosomatically in a very personalized manner his substantive corporeal body's somatic sensational sensual sensitivity and/or psychic notional nonsensuous impassive intimacy.

Not even angels, who are pure bodiless spirits, are endowed with such a subjective psychosomatic selfhood. Certainly, God who is absolute spirituality is bereft of such a selfhood. Christ inasmuch as He is human has such a selfhood along with its self-humanized and self-cultivated divinized personality. What is crucial for the reader of the commentary to appreciate is that this suffering peculiar to the human person's selfhood is pervasively a social affair that is both intrapersonal and interpersonal. For, the key to the selfhood's mind (in contraposition to the soul's intellect) is its intuitive associative grasp in mathematical calculations of a balance between opposing factors that are juxtaposed with each other in an equivalent ratio. This allows for substitutivity and exchange. A person through his own personalized selfhood can associatively, psychologically, empathically, and pathologically substitute his own emotional bodily feelings and emotionless mental bearings for a self other than his very own personalized self. Accordingly, he can suffer alone or empathically and compassionately commiserate his suffering with other selves and vice versa. The human person cannot exchange or transfer his personhood with another; as a person he is induplicable and non-substitutable. But, he can empathically share his personality's subjective bodily feelings and mental bearings with a self other than his own self. This involves a non-cognitive conative communication that is entirely intersubjective and interpersonally personalized.

Spiritual suffering peculiar to mysticism, however, whether it is a psychosomatic joyful jubilant righteous suffering or a doleful and woeful unrighteous suffering, can be associatively and intuitively fully shared with God incarnated in Jesus Christ since its root and source is God's very own divine and holy righteousness. But, this is not feasible apart from Jesus Christ since God in His own substantive transcendent and eternal divinity is not another human self or selfhood. This leaves the Catholic Christian mystic with Christ and His saints, notably our Blessed Mother, Mary, and fellow mystics as those with whom he may interpersonally empathically share his own un/righteous suffering.

Of course, this empathic shared suffering is precisely what Christ superhumanistically and superheroically experienced in His passion and crucifixion. He not only personalistically experienced and empathically suffered the suffering of each of His redeemed followers, He empathically substituted as a volunteer scapegoat His own sufferings for those of all He redeemed who, in turn, are invited in return to share their own sufferings with Him. Indeed, this actual substitutive sharing does occur vividly and willingly in those who suffer the stigmata of Christ's crucified wounds as victim souls.

This religious suffering is entirely subjective and private within the egocentric self-awareness of the Catholic Christian mystic. Yet, its root and source is entirely transubjectively transcendent to this subjectivity. For, it is rooted in both a need for and lack of (i.e., an ache and longing for) God's very own divine holiness in the hierarchical order of existence. But, God in God's majestic transcendent divinity (viz., God-the-Father) cannot personally requite the mystic's yearning ache and longing. For, again, God is not in God's divine transcendent nature a self-centered selfhood. However, Jesus Christ, God/Superman both can and does requite the mystic's pining and thirst for divine righteousness and fulfills this imperative need which the mystic himself is impotent to procure and provide on his own behalf.

Since Jesus Christ is principally the theistic root of the mystic's own religious superhuman sufferings (whether these be pious exultant jubilations or forlorn abject lamentations), he finds himself to be largely alone in experiencing and suffering them especially because their chronological unfolding does not coincide with the religious maturation of other mystics, not even with those with whom he may intimately associate on a spiritual level of communication. It is a paradox of the spiritual life that the more the mystic becomes ascetically transformed within his own personality into that of Christ's Selfless Messianic Personality, the more difficulty he experiences in communicating interpersonally with others from within the depths of his own total consecration to Christ.

It must also be re-emphasized that these sufferings are entirely experiential and confined to one's personalized self-awareness. Certainly, this personalized subjectivity is also the very secular domain of the world of culture cultivated by mankind's self-humanizing enterprising industry. This seems very paradoxical and it is. Christ in the Gospel declares that He does not seek to remove the mystic from the world but to remove the world's self-centered self-serving selfishness from the mystic. Experience is a highly personalized subjective affair that is not cognitive but conative as noted previously in the commentary on the *Ascent*. By reason of this conation the person who self-consciously experiences something remains experientially ignorant of the very nature of that "something" but is very much aware of experiencing a positive or negative feeling or bearing (i.e., care and concern) and self-serving interest vested in that "something."

The mystical life is not explicitly cognitive; it is explicitly conative.

The mystical life inasmuch as it is experientially personalized, subjective, and conative partakes of the same features peculiar to all human experience. That is, it is not explicitly cognitive but it is explicitly conative. That is, it is an affective awareness that remains ignorant and almost insouciant regarding the actual nature of the object for which it has special affectionate bodily feelings and mindful concerns. Such affection remains experientially blind and disinterested regarding the actual nature of the object of its affections (or, disaffections). Certainly, such subjective affections may complement the mystic's prior objective intelligent knowledge of the object of his affection.

Fundamentally, one cannot love what one does not intellectually antecedently know. But, supplementally, one cannot seek to love (better) what one does not affectionately and empathically love. In the supernatural order, faith takes precedence over charity fundamentally while in the same supernatural order charity takes precedence over faith supplementally. That is, the mystical life of divine love is initiated fundamentally in the soul's objective intellectual order of faith transcendent to the human person's subjective experiential selfhood. On the other hand, this same divine love is consummated and brought to perfection in the selfhood's experiential subjective order of compassionate (i.e., empathic and sacrificial) love supplementally transcending the human person's soulful obedient love.

This fundamental-supplemental prioritization is part and parcel of every person's ordinary life. Two persons of the opposite sex may objectively know and casually respect and associate with each other for a long period of time. Indeed, this time may be extended over a period of years. Such knowledge is fundamentally objective. Each intelligibly recognizes the other to be of the opposite sex endowed with specific talents, traits, virtues, and skills. Such knowledge, however, does not prompt them to seek any special interpersonal relationship and accord beyond the companionship and buddy-buddy friendship and interpersonal amity that obtains between young men and women enjoying companionship with their own genders.

Suddenly, out of the blue, each may mutually become very affectionately interested in the other. This affectionate interest brings to supplemental perfection and completion their mutual objective fundamental knowledge of and respect for each other. How so? By prompting and arousing a more inquisitive and interested inter and intrapersonal quest to become familiar not with each other's fundamental reality but with each other's supplemental subjective personality and private foibles which remain remarkably alien and unknown to each other even through further communication. This mutual affection and empathically aroused affectation spurs further mutual inter and intrapersonal exploration which is not cognitively revealing but, rather, cognitively puzzling the more conatively vibrant it becomes.

If this amicable mutual interest further blooms into a marital union, the two become intimately aware of each other's reciprocal conative affectivity which remains not only inherently non-cognitive but mysteriously more intriguing precisely because it is not objectively intelligible nor logical why each would sacrificially forego each's own respective personalized selfish self-interest and self-importance in favor of the other.

The mystical life parallels this purely natural and humanistic interpersonal union. Yet, it accomplishes this supernaturally and superhumanistically and, accordingly, with an ever increasingly intriguing and unintelligible reciprocal sacrificial affectionate supplemental empathic exchange. Certainly, it is fundamentally based on faith which intelligently and intelligibly recognizes the complete radical objective difference between the nature of God's supreme divinity and that of man's inferior humanity. The mystic is fully apprized by faith that the object of his own subjective affections is not merely another human person; it is a divine Person, notably Jesus Christ, who is simultaneously endowed with a human nature and, therefore, with a subjective superhumanized Personality of His own. Yet, the mystic's superhumanized supplemental affectionate subjective feeling for and regard for Jesus Christ embraces His fundamental objective divinity and divine Personhood not merely His subjective superhumanized Personality.

But, the mystic's subjective superhumanized (i.e., by supernatural grace) conative affection does not embrace Christ fundamentally and intelligibly, it does so supplementally, experientially, and unintelligibly. It is unintelligible to the mystic that he should be the object of Christ's total sacrificial affection and equally unintelligible that he (i.e., the mystic) should, in return, seek to reciprocate sacrificially the same affectionate bodily feeling and mental regard for Christ. In brief, this conative subjective experiential religious intersubjective affectivity is cognitively blind in the same sense that the proverbial adage "love is blind" characterizes the affectations which conatively bind people to each other and allow for interpersonal communication in which "sweet nothings" are exchanged in mere gestures, sighs, moans, and gibberish.

The mystic's purgative suffering is excruciatingly disturbing.

The mystic's purgative suffering in both the subjective body's somatic sensuous sensitivity and the psychic mind's impassive intimacy are particularly intense and excruciatingly disturbing precisely because the somatic will, on the one hand, is deprived of its sublime exquisite self-gratifying religious excitement which previously stimulated the somatic will to become zealously bodily active in the affairs of God and the Church. On the other hand, the psychic will, in its turn, is deprived of an imperturbable profound self-sustained religious serenity which previously pacified the psychic will enabling it to become mentally benignantly impassively religiously and prayerfully absorbed and entranced in God through extended periods of prayerful attention.

The upshot of the Holy Spirit's withdrawal from the mystic of every experiential trace of righteous self-gratifying somatic excitation (viz., exultation) and religious self-justifying psychic pacification (viz., inspiration) is that the selfhood's religious psychosomatic eager sensitive emotional inducements and docile emotionless intimate conduciveness to engage in the service and prayerful communion with God vanish. The mystic's somatic willful zealous eagerness becomes replaced with a listless diffidence and his psychic willful serene solicitude for God becomes replaced with a disorientating restlessness and pervasive brooding anxiousness.

Neither of these very serious disturbances is inherently clinical. They are not of themselves the offshoot of some latent pathological bipolar imbalance or morbid self-preoccupation. They are symptomatic of an intense struggle within the mystic's own charismatic psychosomatic personality and willfulness to either persistently continue or to abruptly discontinue to be interpersonally prayerfully consecrated and committed to, active in, and solicitous for Jesus Christ, God/Superman, His Sacramental Church, and his Messianic mission.

461

For, the previous religious stirring exultant bodily feelings and pro-found mental yearnings prompting this consecration and commit-ment to God have vanished. The mystic no longer experiences either proximate emotive sensitive righteous feelings or remote righteous intimate yearnings for God. The "dark night" begins with a loss of re-ligious sensitized feelings and concludes with a loss of religious in-timate longings for God, especially for Jesus Christ who is God In-carnate in humanity and supernaturally present to the mystic in the Church's sacramentality.

Now with the vanishing of these religious incentives prompting the mystic's willful prayerful personalized self-involvement with God, not only does the mystic have no longer a righteous sensitive enthusiastic zeal and pensive intimate prayerful ache and longing for God, but the more he persists in prayerfully attending to God the more acute becomes his awareness of his own bodily emotional right-eous sterility and concomitantly his own mental emotionless right-eous instability. Instead of God being the source of his own religious benignant sensuous emotional zest and intimate emotionless serenity, God seems to have become the occasion for his religious emotional lethargy and emotionless disorientated restlessness.

The mystic's former subjective self-assured righteous willful psychosomatic security issuing from his personalized experience of God's delicate sensuous sweetness and imperturbable intimate com-panionship is shattered. The very Godhead who had been his bul-wark against the temptations of the world's selfishness and the flesh's sensuality seems insouciant to his plight and predicament. This seem-ing divine insouciance and aloofness becomes even more acutely and painfully experienced in the periods in which the mystic attempts to prayerfully collect himself and give his whole-hearted attention to God. These periods of prayer are no longer periods of spiritual re-vitalization. They become trying and disturbing periods of excruciat-ingly painful religious bodily demoralizing unemotional aridity and mental alienating desolation.

At this point in his pilgrimage toward God, the mystic not only suffers acutely the intellectual darkness of faith, a darkness which is occasioned by the actual supernatural, sacramental Self-revealed presence of God's awesome Triune Godhead overshadowing his own natural soulful intelligence, he suffers the darkness of hope as well which includes a total memorial amnesia of his own past righteous experiences and future expectations increasing his sense of social helplessness to extricate himself from his religious crisis and predicament. In addition, he also suffers the darkness of charity which includes his own lackluster psychosomatic loss of affectionate attention to God's own infinitely amiable merciful benevolence and noble friendship. In brief, the mystic is subjectively wretched and suffers anything but the blissfulness of God's blessedness, holiness, and blessings. God's blessedness seems lost forever to the mystic's own personalized religious experience.

Caught up in the excruciating throes of this religious turmoil, the mystic learns that any relief from this inner excruciating travail and any hope of remaining faithful to his prayerful consecration to God is paradoxically unavailable apart from God Himself. There is no remedy for his unmitigated religious misery apart from God Himself. Knowing this does not prevent the mystic from seeking sustenance from his confessor, from his companions, friends, family, experienced religious authors, and even medical professionals. But, such recourse only serves to further convince the mystic that God alone can deliver him from the religious morass of his own misery.

Further, the failure of these other sources to relieve him from his tormenting religious suffering serves to further acerbate his inner strife and turmoil in prayerfully turning to God for relief. St. John himself clearly states that he is not writing about this "dark night" while he is caught up in its throes. He is writing this mystagogical treatise following his emergence from this harrowing religious experience. In other words, he is writing about it after he is well established at least within the second phase of the mystical life, the illuminative stage, in which he comes to appreciate the tremendous benefits which suffering through this purgation has yielded. Indeed, the closing part of his treatise, the *Dark Night*, enters into the second major phase of the mystic's pilgrimage to God, the illuminative phase.

There is a threefold cruciformity that pervades the mystic's life.

It is important to appreciate that the threefold cruciform elements repeatedly emphasized by St. John of the Cross are all simultaneously and concurrently operative throughout every phase of the mystic's pilgrimage to God. Faith, hope, and charity including the anthropological seat of each of these three theological virtues, the intellect, the memory, and the will, concur with each other in each of the three phases of the mystical life: the purgative, illuminative, and unitive. And, in keeping with the threefold height, width, and depth of the cruciformity of Christ's cross of crucifixion, the three distinct orders corresponding to this cruciformity, the fundamental, the supplemental, and the complementary, concur simultaneously with each other in every phase of the mystic's pilgrimage up Mount Carmel.

The orthodox foundation for this cruciformity is vertically the order of existence which is metaphysical, ontological, hierarchical, natural and supernatural (i.e., human and superhuman). This is the order of faith in which the soul's intellect enjoys a conscionable priority over the intellectual will's volition and freedom of choice. The paradoxical supplemental edifice proper to this cruciformity is horizontally the order of resistance which is itself, paraphysical (i.e., mathematical), catalogical (i.e., typological), and historical, cultural and cultic, humanistic and super-humanistic. This is the order of hope in which the personhood's egological selfhood self-consciously and memorially possessively orientates itself backward through the historistic past and forward through the futuristic future.

It must be further stipulated that within this supplemental order this egological self proper to the human person is memorially humanistically conscious of its own historical vulnerability both in regard to its historical origin and its historical destination. Its self-confidence is restricted to the horizon of its own historical life-span. The mystic, accordingly, prayerfully confides his security to Christ, God/Superman, who eschatologically in His invincible conviction not only enters and passes through history's ephemerality but also deathlessly passes transhistorically beyond its mortal fatality in His bodily resurrection and ascension into heaven. The mystic's superhumanistic hope of transcending the vicissitudes of his own historical vulnerability convincingly reside in surrendering himself to Christ's very own Gospel life-style in complete obedience to His Gospel commands. It is a hope that transcends the hopelessness of his body's own fateful historical demise.

The mystic's subjective freedom of self-control.

There is still another aspect of the supplemental order which is crucial to the mystic's spiritual journey to a perfect union with God in contemplative prayer. Within this subjective order of the personalized self's will and its freedom of somatic manipulative and psychic managerial self-control, the will's volition takes conscientious precedence over the mind's mental fabrications and suggestive thoughts and the body's fanciful and sensuous fantasies. This is not a moral freedom of what the will may or may not dutifully operatively do, but a contractual freedom of what the selfhood's will must or must not consequentially constructively make of and for itself to advance and promote its own self-serving autonomous attitudinal morale (i.e., self-humanizing triumphal spirit). This is a contractual freedom which entails an intrapersonal and interpersonal agreement within one's own selfhood and among selves other than one's own self.

This purely humanistic morale (i.e., have-attitude of possessively having a guaranteed autonomous social security) is one of forceful domination and enforced subjugation. Paradoxically, the Christian mystic's superhumanistic morale (i.e., be-attitude of possessively having less selfishly self-managed and self-manipulated control in the horizontal order of resistance in order to transcendently become more morally virtuous in the vertical order of existence) is that of Christ's very own Holy Spirit, the Selfless Spirit of Truth, an indomitable morale of humility and complete sacrificial submission to God-the-Father's providential Holy Will. This be-attitudinal mindset proper to Christ is nothing less than Christ's Self-surrender to His Messianic mission to liberate mankind from the prison of its own selfish self-centered self-controlled selfhood to enable mankind to serve God-the-Father with the same self-detachment and self-abandon made manifest in Christ's very own self-immolation on the cross of crucifixion.

This egological self-centered humanistic freedom of self-control is conscientiously a self-humanizing freedom that paradoxically must sacrificially willfully advance one of its dichotomous willful psycho-somatic selves at the expense of its polar opposite self. There are three prototypical willful polarized personalities and self-humanized selves delineated in the previous commentary on the *Ascent*. There is the psychic anesthetic and the somatic kinesthetic self at opposite poles to each other and in between the hybrid esthetic self that is a fusion of the other two. The self's willful mindset and self-humanizing have-at-titude must be one of hostility in promoting one of these personality's at the expense of the other. In paradoxical contrast to this mindset, the mindset of the Christian mystic must be that of Christ's own be-attitu-dinal mindset of unconditional hospitality requiring a complete sacri-ficial self-detachment and mortification of its own partisan domineer-ing self-serving selfish self-interest and domineering humanistic tri-umphant morale.

The full import of the preceding paragraph should not be lost on the reader of this commentary. Left to his own self-humanizing self-hood, the human person within his autonomous selfhood is a virtual prisoner of his own domineering selfish self-interests, self-humanized manipulative and/or managerial self-control, and domineering com-bative morale. Further, he is self-alienated within the very psychoso-matic constitution of his own egocentric willful selfhood. Whatever autonomous self-fulfillment he procures exclusively within his own subjective (worldly) order of resistance is merely a supplemental and not a fundamental self-fulfillment. Such self-fulfillment is as fleeting as is the course of history's own fateful ephemerality.

That is, a life-insurance and the social security afforded by a na-tional endowment of specific entitlements (viz., the entitlement to fin-ancial assistance in periods of extreme poverty, etc..) cannot guaran-tee a citizen's welfare beyond the threshold of the body's historical physical mortality. Christ's super-humanizing self-fulfillment liber-ates the selfhood from its own historical futility, mortality, and doom. Christ's liberation is a fundamental self-fulfillment in the transhistor-ical fundamental hierarchical order of existence and not merely in the historical supplemental transient order of resistance. That is, the self-humanized self that dies to its selfish self-serving self-interests in sac-rificially serving Christ's Selfless Selfhood rises through Christ's resurrection and ascension into the immortal and everlasting realm of God's own eternal and immutable existential security. This is the crux of the Christian's mystical life. Either to live humanistically in the style of the world's temporary selfish self-serving advantages or superhumanistically in the Gospel style of Christ's Selfless-serving immortal unending security.

Hence, there is a dying and rising which occur simultaneously. Yet, while the mystic continues to exist historically within the order of resistance, there is no personalized conscious experience of the ultimate rising. There is, rather, the protracted experience of the dying to self and one's very own personalized selfish social self-interests (viz., conveniences, social securities, and social contracts). When the mystic arrives beyond the threshold of physical death, there will be no further dying, but only a resurrectional ascension into God's Triune Godhead without further historical transition. Certainly, the mystic may experience fleetingly the thrall of Christ's own paradisiacal Selfless self-fulfillment in attaining the unitive stage of the mystical life. But, in the purgative stage described in the ordeal of the "dark night" the mystic experiences the dying to his selfish selfhood without the benefit of experiencing the rising anew in the pristine freshness and liberation of Christ's very own Selfless Selfhood.

The mystic's freedom of self-determination.

This brings us to the third heterological cruciform order in which the vertical and horizontal beams of the cross are reconciled with each other by Christ's very own crucifixion. This reconciliation is effectuated between the person's own objective soulful intellectual will and its own subjective selfhood's psychosomatic will. That is, it is effectuated between the impersonal dutiful moral will and the personalized mandatory conscientious sacrificial amoral self-serving will. The former will chooses appropriately when it chooses conscionably what it ought to choose "to do" commensurate with the practical truth of such conduct. The latter will appropriates decisively when it conscientiously "makes" or procures possessively for its own personalized self what it already has made and/or must "have" to supplement for its own neediness and deficiency. The former will is a purposeful drive that is end-directed while the latter will is a purposeless need which is entirely self-centered and self-serving. When the two wills coalesce conscionably and conscientiously the human person "makes do" what ought to be done and must be made to be done to both be naturally happy and to securely subjectively have the experience of such immortal transhistorical happiness. When this coalescence is effectuated at the supernatural level with the person's soulful will acting in view of God-the-Father's Holy Will and not merely its own natural happiness, a supernatural happiness of holiness ensues.

When this coalescence occurs supernaturally and superhumanistically it integrates the inalienable moral freedom of choice objectively inherent in the human person's intellectual will with his subjective alienable indomitable (i.e., heartened with the Holy Spirit's indomitable morale) freedom of selfless (i.e., self-detached) self-control proper to his selfhood's psychosomatic will. The former is the antecedent will while the latter is the consequential will. That is, the intellectual will's moral obedience can be reasonably and logically spelled out syllogistically in keeping with its ontological metaphysical foundation.

An inherently Supreme Good ought to be honored primarily.

God is an inherently Supreme Good. Therefore, honoring God primarily ought to be done. The selfhood's mental will's mandatory self-boosting and self-reinforcing morale is spelled out conditionally and consequentially in keeping with its deontological need to overcome its built-in impotency.

If X is posited then Y must follow. X is willfully (i.e., forcibly) posited. Therefore Y ineluctably follows. But, in reverse, when Y does not ineluctably follow. Therefore, X is not willfully (forcibly) and successfully linked to Y.

Syllogistic reasoning is categorical whereas conditional reasoning is hypothetical. Conscionable reasoning is based on what actually truthfully exists as being inherently good and appropriate for the will to voluntarily choose. Conscientious reasoning is based on overcoming whatever resists the self-humanizing will's own willful (i.e., forceful) self-humanization (i.e., self-idealization and self-realization) achieved only through a sacrificial volitional willfulness, effort, and productive endeavor. This is the social order of culture. The former is fundamental in the order of nature while the latter is supplemental in the order of culture. When the two concur, each complements the other by reason of its own proper priority. The fundamental complements the supplemental fundamentally while the supplemental complements the fundamental supplementally. When this complementarity prevails, the vertical order of nature dovetails with the horizontal order of culture. That is, the causal hierarchical order coalesces with the historical influential order.

Within this coalescence is transposed to the supernatural plane, the objective practical Truth of the intellect buttressed by the divine light of faith informs inerrantly the intellectual will's conscience under the aegis of the Church's Magisterium. And, correspondingly, the subjective heroic sacrificial conscientious commitment of the self's volitional will's willful humble steadfast submission to this objective Truth gives testimony to the influence of Christ's Holy Spirit within the depths of the person's own willful selfhood. For the person's willful self becomes bolstered by the Holy Spirit instilling in his will a divine indomitable steadfast hopeful triumphant morale and confidence in the trustworthiness of Christ's own resurrection and ascension as a super-conscientious authentication of the objective Truth of His divine Authority and Power over the vicissitudes of history and the body's mortality.

In this cruciform coalescence the human person acts both conscionably and conscientiously. That is, he acts both conscionably in a reflective awareness in that his supernaturally formed conscience intellectually governs the freedom of what he chooses to dutifully do and, on the other hand, he superhumanistically forces himself conscientiously in a reflexive self-awareness to volitionally undertake heroically and sacrificially whatever he needs must undertake to "make" happen what is required to facilitate what he ought to do.

In this coalescence there is a further freedom of self-determination that binds together the fundamental intellectual will's freedom of choice with the supplemental selfhood will's sacrificial freedom of self-control. Thus, in the matter of eating, a person ought to eat with moderation in order to act virtuously and healthily in keeping with the purpose of eating. Further, a person must forcibly curb his need for sensual gustatory self-indulgence to facilitate practicing the virtue of temperance in the matter of eating. Such a person, for example, ought not only conscionably choose to eat moderately but must earnestly and conscientiously make himself take smaller portions and even less delectable servings to facilitate the moral virtue of temperance. That is, he must practice fast and abstinence.

In this freedom of self-determination there coalesces both the person's intellectual will's dutiful conscionable observance of an objectively truthfully informed will together with the same person's willful self's sacrificial and conscientious authenticating transformational subservience to this objective conscionable truth. In this cruciform coalescence there ensues in the liberated freedom of a person's self-determination a simple freedom of service to a noble objective cause that transcends that subjective willful service itself. When these three forms of service are supernaturally sublimated in union with Christ's very own inimitable Selfless service both to God-the-Father's Holy Will and to mankind's redemption, sanctification, and beatification, there further ensues the integral sublime performance of a super-humane liberated freedom acting superheroically as the "servant of God." This liberated sublime freedom of self-determination is prophetically made manifest principally in our Blessed Mother, Mary, and the apostles and saints in communion with Christ's very own Selfless Selfhood. Christ declares that He comes to serve and not to be served.

Here in this liberated super-humane freedom sustained and integrated by the Holy Spirit of Giftedness, the human person's obligatory intellectual will and self-sacrificial selfhood's will complement each other. However, when a person's egocentric self-sacrificial will selfishly sacrifices his obligatory will to his own partisan selfish self-serving self-interest the two wills clash. Therefore, there is a further volitional element that is crucial in achieving this complementary cruciform coalescence. This is the element of a sacrificial self-surrender and self-commitment on the part of the human person's psychosomatic willful self. Unless the human person's willful self has sacrificially surrendered and selflessly committed itself to its transcendent fundamental self-fulfillment in the order of existence, it cannot "make" itself suffer and endure the excruciatingly painful rigor of its own total self-denial and self-detachment from its own selfishness. Its own persistent selfish demand for its own partisan self-reliant social security and selfish self-control are too formidable to be overcome by its own effort alone. On a purely humanistic plane the selfhood's psychosomatic will cannot sacrificially selflessly totally surrender its own partisan selfish self-interest without a superhumanizing influence stemming from the Holy Spirit.

Even the soldier who patriotically volunteers to put his life on the line for his country is trained and equipped to defend himself from his own death in combat. His military duty is neither an act of martyrdom nor a total sacrificial selfless self-surrendering of his life in behalf of his enemy as he enters military service. At best, it is humanistically an unselfish act of public service but not superhumanistically an entirely selfless act of self-surrender to this public service. When he parts with his friends and family he hopes for a safe-return from his military service.

It should be noted that the categorical logic inherent in the objective order the human person's intelligence is intelligibly reasonable and based on an intelligibility that is the cause for its reasonableness. In this reasonableness, it is the intellect's intelligible reasonableness that directs and informs the intellectual will's volition. In the syllogism formulated above, the will is obligated to honor God above every other being. The cause for this is God's absolute supremacy and primacy. At the same time, the will remains free to choose otherwise. It is morally obligated but not causally necessitated. The moral obligation is both intelligible and reasonably (i.e., causally) intelligible; because God is a Supreme Being and worthily deserving of the supreme honor and tribute of worshipful adoration. This divine worthiness is not caused by the will's volition to worship God; it is caused intelligibly and reasonably by God's inherently supreme worthiness and Goodness.

The consequential conditional (i.e., hypothetical) logic of the <if X then Y> elenchus format is neither a causal logic nor a reasonably

471

informed logic. It is a volitional logic. If one willfully posits X from which Y necessarily follows, Y is the forced offshoot of X. However, given that Y does not occur, it follows that it does not forcibly issue from X. In this elenchus, there is no inherent intelligible reason why Y ensues from X even when it does occur. It happens volitionally and willfully (i.e., forcibly; it is forced to happen) but not spontaneously and causally.

This logic is the basis for the experimental sciences which are willfully and skillfully cultivated by the human person's forcible intervention into the order of nature. In this logic, the human will's volition is not a reasonable and intelligible volition directed by the intellect's reasonable intelligence; it is a volitive and willful volition that forcibly imposes itself on the subjective mind's intuitive reasoning which is not based on the inherent intelligibility (viz., identity) of what is reasonable. Rather, it is based on the associative congruence of what is intuited. For example, $2 + 2 = 3 + 1$; the two additions are equivalent but not identical. They are forcibly (i.e., willfully) equated with each other. To willfully insist on this precise equivalence is tantamount to sacrificing other similar equivalences (viz., 5-1, 4+0, etc.).

The mystical life entails a superhuman heroic martyrdom.

The utter heroic sacrificial selflessness, self-commitment, and self-donation required of the mystic is possible only on a superhumanistic and superhumane level accomplished only and singularly by Jesus Christ, God/Superman, through His Holy Spirit whose advocacy and giftedness the mystic receives as the benevolent gift of Christ's infinite Selfless generosity. It is in this sense that it is said that Christ was born to die. He was born to heroically and sacrificially give of His infinite generosity to transform the moribund unfathomable selfishness, impotency, and deficiency inherent in the human person's willful psychosomatic selfhood.

Such superhuman heroic martyrdom is the mark of the saints and notably that of the martyrs whose own death purchased the conversion of their persecutors. It is made possible only through the divine subtle influence of the Holy Spirit sacramentally alive within the Christian Catholic mystic's innermost intimate selfhood supplying him with an indomitable buoyant heartening steadfast morale (viz., a super-self-humanized sacrificial spirit of benevolent self-donation which is Christ's very own Holy Spirit).

Of course, in Christian terms and in terms of the mystical life, this utter heroic selfless sacrificial total self-surrender issues from the theological virtue of charity. This is the charity which is the consummate love of God-the-Father which Christ demonstrated in his Self-immolation on the cross of crucifixion. In this Self-immolation His humanity both in its own natural constitution of body and soul and in its self-cultivated superhumanization of His personalized Selfhood became fully divinized and integrated into the Triune Godhead's supreme divinity. In this Self-immolation our own humanity has been superheroically elevated superhumanly to a superhumanistic and superhumane sacramental order of benevolent amicability and amity with God's own Triune Godhead.

Again, this is not effectuated without the Giftedness of the Holy Spirit indwelling within the pith and heart of the mystic's willful selfhood. This is the Holy Spirit of Truth buoying up the mystic with His indomitable courage of charitable divine love and fruitful gifts empowering the mystic to requite in kind the Father's providential merciful bountiful love incarnated in His Son, Jesus Christ. Christ's very own Holy Spirit of Selflessness becomes the mystic's steadfast and undaunted mainstay throughout his pilgrimage up Mount Carmel to the heavenly Jerusalem.

Hence, while it is the case that the experiential subjective personalized life of the mystic is one of intellectual darkness, memorial amnesiac mortification of his subjective bodily feelings and mental bearings, together with a total sacrificial benevolent self-surrender of his selfish willfulness and autonomous self-control to the Father's Holy Will, he experiences also, in return, a sublime religious exquisite sensitivity, delicate intimacy, and integrating peace which is Christ's very own gift to the mystic of His very own Holy Spirit of Selfless Self-Giving amiable Benevolence.

Thus, within the reconciliation on the cross of Christ's self-immolation in which the vertical and horizontal crossbeams are cruciformly reconciled with each other, the human person's soulful nature becomes completely reconciled with his selfhood's self-humanized culture. The two are no longer at enmity with each other. The moral order of the soul's inalienable sovereign freedom of choice and the self-fulfilling order of the selfhood's buoyant morale of autonomous freedom of selfless self-control become superhumanly, cruciformly, and sacramentally integrated and harmonized. Again, this can be accomplished only superhumanly through Christ's mediation and not otherwise. For, man is not created merely for an order of righteous natural happiness but for a supernatural order of merciful holiness, God's very own sublime divine righteous holiness.

The mystical life engages three distinct complementary loves.

Summarily, there are three distinct loves corresponding to the three distinct configurations of the cross of Christ's crucifixion: the vertical and horizontal beams together with their cruciform intersection. There is the soul's intellectual will's fundamental dutiful drive for happiness, the selfhood's mental will's supplemental sacrificial need for skillful self-mastered social security, and the combined needful drive and driving need for a masterfully secure communal immortal virtuous happiness together with a virtuous happiness socially secure. When this is sublimated to a supernatural order, there is a basic drive for holiness benevolently and providentially granted by the Father, a supplemental need for a be-attitudinal transhistorical imperishable bodily security sacrificially purchased by Christ, and an integrated reconciled driving need coupled with a needful drive for an amicable divine benevolent friendship amicably gratuitously granted by the Holy Spirit of Christ and His Father.

There are three complementary loves which the mystic has for God. There is a dutiful voluntary love, a mandatory sacrificial volitional self-controlled love, and a volunteer self-donated love. That is, there is the dutiful, the self-sacrificial, and the amicable love. The first is fundamental, the second is supplemental, and the third is their complementary integration. Our Lord addresses all three of these loves when he asks St. Peter in three successive questions, "do you love Me?" These three integrated loves are by the supernatural sublimation of the Godhead's own Trinitarian loving loveliness elevated to a heroic and superheroic loveliness made manifest in the martyrs and saints. What is impossible to man is possible to God. They correspond to Christ's three distinct offices of prince, priest, and prophet.

Vertically, Christ by reason of His divinity partakes of the Father's very own regal nature and majesty. He is a gift to mankind from God-the-Father. Horizontally by reason of His Self-immolation on the Cross Christ acts as the priest who sacrifices Himself to expiate for mankind's sins. And, cruciformly by reason of His Gospel and His Gospel life-style he prophetically testifies to and authenticates the sovereign primacy of His heavenly Father's paternal authority in the power of the Holy Spirit alive in the depths of the Selfless Selfhood of His own superb Self-humanized Humanity.

This threefold cruciform loveliness makes manifest first the human person's fundamental natural drive for meritorious excellence as the absolute standard of what constitutes normal conscionable upright noble conduct in the exercise of a person's inalienable intellectual freedom of choice. In this respect, the human person is a sovereign ruler of his own ultimate destiny, a regal ruler under the supreme regal authority of God-the-Father's Godhead. Secondly, it makes manifest the person's supplemental self-cultivated self-centered need to be placed sacrificially at the service of Christ, the consummate Master of the self's self-reliant autonomy, to securely guarantee the personalized bodily self its own masterful social self-control and security. This is a subjective need that the mystic himself cannot fully fundamentally supply nor procure for himself exclusively within the horizontal historical horizon of his own memorial ephemerality as the secular world mistakenly assumes to be the case. Indeed, by reason of this very subjective need the mystic humanistically experiences within himself and between himself and other selves a competitive self-alienated freedom of social self-control, self-reliance, and security.

Cruciformly and thirdly, this loveliness makes manifest a fundamental-supplemental complementarity and solidarity intrapersonally within a person's personal moral character, charismatic personality, and integral personage, on the one hand, and interpersonally in his rapport and support and regard for other persons, (viz., his neighbor) on the other. But, again, this is only integrated through the gift of the

Holy Spirit with His own sublime gratuitous gifts and fruits.

It goes without saying that this threefold loveliness cannot be culminated within the human, the self-humanizing, and humane order of mankind's creation apart from God's supernatural graciousness and the Church's supernatural sacramentality. The human person is not only created by God but destined by God to adoptively partake supernaturally of God's very own divinity. Hence, human righteous excellence is found only in the holiness of God-the-Father's own un-excelled excellence and merciful justice. A guaranteed self-humanized social self-fulfillment is found only in the God-the-Son's sacrificial Self-immolation on the cross of His crucifixion in which His personalized self-centered will is sacrificially Selflessly centered on His Father's providential Holy Will. His resurrection and ascension into heaven is the cornerstone of the human person's guaranteed self-fulfillment beyond the supplemental order of secular history's ephemeral horizon doomed to extinction.

Lastly, a peace-making solidified conscionable soulful self together with a conscientious selfless soul is found only through the fortitudinous and steadfast morale of God-the-Holy Spirit's Giftedness which is nothing other than the infinite eternal reciprocal friendship existing between the Father and Son sacramentally and unctuously alive within the very heart and pith of the mystic's own hospitable and humbled willful selfhood.

It cannot be sufficiently emphasized that all three of these loves rooted in the three theological virtues of faith, hope, and charity cooperate concurrently in the mystic's pilgrimage up Mount Carmel. The fulcrum on which they teeter is that of contemplative prayer. Contemplative prayer begins with meditative prayer rooted in religious sensory images and sensuous fantasies and emotional zealous religious fervor. This initial stage of prayer gives way to contemplative prayer which transcends the reach of the senses and the reach of the person's egocentric subjective selfhood. This contemplative prayer is not rooted in the selfhood's psychosomatic will. It is rooted in the soul's intellectual will. Nonetheless, it engages the selfhood's psychosomatic will precisely because it is the person's psychosomatic subjective conscientious selfhood's humanistic self-serving morale which must be sacrificially reconciled with the person's objective conscionable moral rectitude.

The mystical life engages both an intellectual and experiential encounter with God.

The human person may be reflectively conscious of the substantive body and soul's operative public activity of sensing, appetizing, thinking, and willing (and, similarly, of engaging in contemplative prayer). Further, this reflective awareness is not egocentrically self-absorbed; it is transsubjectively centered within the human person's inalienable and induplicable personhood's nature transcendent to and independent of the human person's subjective private selfhood and self-absorption. Reflexive self-awareness, on the other hand, is very much subjectively and privately egologically self-centered. The mystic is very much personalistically preoccupied with his own private experiential and personalized egocentric dimension of his sacramental prayer-life with the Trinity. Liturgical prayer is fundamentally communal (i.e., impersonal) and public whereas mental prayer is supplementally social (i.e., personalized) and private.

This egocentric subjective personality is the very crux of the human person's selfhood whose subjective personalized psychosomatic will is distinct from his objective impersonal (i.e., nonpartisan) intellectual will. The mystic attains to contemplative prayer in the measure that he successfully detaches himself from and transcends not only objectively the physical reach of the senses but also subjectively the vicissitudes of his own self-centered selfhood's willful selfish self-serving self-attachments, and partisan self-interests.

The mystical experience of God's supernatural sacramental presence in the soul is a reflective awareness which is impersonal (i.e., not personalized) and not to be confused with the reflexive religious awareness of experiencing psychosomatically that presence within the emotional feelings and emotionless bearings of the selfhood's psychosomatic will. An ecstatic religious bodily feeling of exultation or an enthralling religious mental bearing of sublime serenity are completely subjective personalized mystical experiences which are not essential to the mystical life itself. What is crucial to the mystical life is that the mystic become self-sacrificially and as a volunteer victim totally self-surrendered through faith, hope, and charity to the friendly benevolent familiarity of God's Triune Godhead that completely transcends his own personalized subjective experiences. It is only in this transcendence that he himself becomes fundamentally informatively divinely elevated, supplementally transformatively divinely assimilated, and complementarily integrally self-fulfilled in and through a divine reality that exceeds his own self-centered impotent subjective neediness.

The mystic is initiated into the life of the Blessed Trinity through the Church's sevenfold sacramentality. In this manner the mystic is born, nurtured, sustained, confirmed, cleansed, consecrated, blessed, graced, etc., directly by the Father, the Son, and the Holy Spirit. This sacramental entry into God's Triune Godhead is efficaciously personal but not personalized until the mystic himself prayerfully engages God within his own personalized experience of God's sacramental presence. The church's sacramentality is a communal public and not a social private entry into God. Hence, it seems impersonal because it is not yet experientially personalized. Yet, it is eminently personal because of God's Triune Personhood engaging the human being's self-subsistent unique inalienable personhood. These fundamental sacramental, ecclesial liturgical prayers must be supplementally consummated by mental and paraliturgical personalized prayer.

Mental prayer is pointedly personalized because it enters into a human personhood's self-humanized self-conscious self-subsistent social self-mastery. There will always remain a disparity between liturgical and mental prayer just as there is a disparity between a human person's communal human nature and self-humanized self-centered social culture. This disparity is overcome when the two are reconciled in a fundamental-supplemental complementarity achieved efficaciously by Christ Himself in His Paschal Mystery following His Incarnation.

Mystical mental prayer is moreso the Blessed Trinity praying in the mystic than it is the mystic praying to the Blessed Trinity. The Father initiates, the Son consummates, and the Holy Spirit integrates the mystic's prayer-life. This reaches its climax in contemplative prayer. The obstacles preventing the mystic from being totally surrendered to this Trinitarian prayerful embrace are the world, the flesh, and the devil. These three notable obstacles are rooted in the mystic's subjective egocentric willful selfhood: the proverbial threefold me, myself, and I. The mystic must overcome all three to be completely free to allow the Blessed Trinity to be the endless infinite life of his own finite mortal vitality. The mystic himself begins this behemoth task of conquering and skillfully mastering his own selfish selfhood but even this beginning is spurred on by the Holy Spirit's unctuous graciousness.

In the final analysis this task can only be fully accomplished by the Holy Spirit's own efficacy which reaches its climax with the total demise of the selfhood's own selfishness entailing a most painful humiliating suffering while he becomes transformed into Christ's own humility as a Servant to both the Father's Holy Will and to liberate mankind from the prison of its own willful selfishness.

Thus, the mystical life is largely preoccupied with one's own self-reflexive selfhood and the personalized religious experiences which are germane to this selfhood's own psychosomatic makeup. Certainly, this is paradoxical. Christ in His Gospel enunciates this paradox. Unless one dies to himself he cannot live beyond the supplemental dimensions of his own subjective selfhood. Implicit within this same paradox is the more radical paradox that mankind cannot be its own liberator from the confines of its own servile selfhood. This can only be achieved by a superhuman messianic liberator. The mystic knows this to be Jesus Christ, God/Superman.

The mystic's subjective self versus his objective soul.

The person's psychosomatic self is a fallen self-alienated selfhood, alienated within the dichotomous make-up of its very own selfhood itself (i.e., the human person's own subjective personality). The human person is not only self-alienated by Adam and Eve's original fall from grace, he is alienated from God and from selves other than his own self. In this alienation he is adrift in an alienated secular world of aliens and the prey to the devil's duplicity. His personality is susceptible to redemption only with, through, and in Christ's own divinized persona (i.e., Self-superhumanized Personality). It is only in the measure that the human person's own fallen and self-alienated personality is informed by, transformed into, and integrated into Christ's superhuman-humanized-humane Personality that he can become a full-fledged member of Christ's Mystical Body, the Sacramental Church, not only here on earth but moreso in the heavenly Jerusalem.

The mystical life is fundamentally the superhuman reality of God's Triune graciousness alive in the mystic's soul. Grace is not like the sun's luminosity quite lifeless in itself. It is a dynamic vitality that is God's very own intelligent and free Triune unique and universal family divine liveliness. This graciousness cannot be experienced since it exists in the human soul quite independently and transcendent to the human person's ego-conscious willful self-centered subjective awareness of it. In Adam and Eve's fall from grace, their own subjective self-centered willful selves became alienated from their spiritual soul's interior intellectual freedom. St. John of the Cross rightfully refers all mystical activity to the human soul. It has been the burden of this verbose commentary to emphasize that the person's subjective selfhood is distinct from the person's objective soul. Now that this distinction is laboriously recognized from the context of the thrust of this commentary, it is very important to also emphasize that the principal font of the mystic's mystical (i.e., religious) personalized experience of God (i.e., self-conscious pious prayerful awareness) is the supernatural activity of God's Triune divine graciousness dynamically alive in the mystic's soul.

The theological virtue of faith is the intellect's innate credulity brought to a superhuman perfection of docility and hospitality regarding the truth of what is inherently and obviously eminently credible. This credulity entails a spontaneous appetency on the part of the intellectual will's volition to love what is truly and truthfully inherently beneficial to its innate drive for natural happiness and supernatural holiness. God's infinite luminous vitality sacramentally floods the human soul and leaves it in darkness because the soul's spiritual intellect is unable to naturally absorb and comprehend this infinite splendor; not because the soul's intellect is seriously impaired but because the human intellect by the light of its own native intelligence is inadequate to become informatively illuminated by God's infinite effulgence. Yet, it is through the divine presence of this luminous graciousness that the mystic sagaciously through the supernatural gift of faith knows and fathoms God's testimonial Self-revelation in the sacraments and in Sacred Scripture and Tradition under the Church's vicarious magisterial authority. Through the theological virtue of faith the soul's intellectual will jubilates in this divine presence of God's supreme infinite Triune sublimity.

The intellectual will's joy is spiritually distinct from the sentient body's own enjoyment. In eating something delectable such as a wedge of apple pie, the human person's sentient body enjoys the pie's delicious taste. At the very same time, the intellectual will delights in the truth that this delicious taste is merely temporary and not enduring. The will's delight in the truth of the apple pie and its deliciousness is both enduring and intangible and for this very reason ethereally delicate and imperishable. By reason of this ethereality it seems almost negligible when compared to the sentient body's instantaneous tangible enjoyment of the pie's succulent affectivity however temporary this enjoyment may be.

The mystic is reflectively aware through faith of the truthful benevolent supernal joy and gladness which surpasses all understanding that God's sacramental presence affords it. Not only does this joy transcend and escape the sentient body's tangible detection but, moreover, the mystic is not here self-consciously (i.e., reflexively) and egocentrically aware of God's Triune sacramental presence in his soul but merely consciously (i.e., reflectively) and intellectually aware through the gift of faith that fortifies and sublimates the intellect to enable it to gaze directly in faith at God's august Triune glorious Personhood. The sublime joy available to the mystic remains intellectually within the soul's interiority but not necessarily concomitantly experientially within the subjectivity of the mystic's selfhood.

Since it is a supernatural joy the mystic is not subjectively and experientially (i.e., egocentrically) aware of it unless and until God wills this to be so. For, again, grace is not lifeless as is the sun but alive with God's infinite Trinitarian intelligent, free, and Personal universal Triune family loveliness. Further, this soulful sublime joy by way of effusion and resonance may, God willing, resonate within the very person's very own subjective psychosomatic egocentric willful selfhood whenever this selfhood is hospitably self-sacrificially disposed to be-attitudinally welcome this sublime joy within its own psychosomatic subjective willful selfhood. But, again, this be-attitudinal hospital disposition is entirely superhumanistic; it is not within the control of the person's own self-centered willfulness other than dispositively.

That is, the human person has an overriding need to experience for himself this sublime joy but, at the same time, has no inalienable right to it. It is gratuitously given through God's own providential volition. But, again, granted only when the mystic's self-serving self-centered will is sacrificially and be-attitudinally disposed (sufficiently self-detached from its own selfishness) to welcome and submissively entertain such a sublime religious experience without seeking to possessively clutch it. It is precisely at this point that the mystic begins in earnest to experientially crave God's sublimity that the account of St. John's *Dark Night* has its beginning. For the drama of the "dark night" is nothing other than the mystic becoming divested of his own intractable selfishness under the influence of the Holy Spirit who actively takes over the task of completing the mystic's willful purification of his remaining selfish attachments that impede his personalized experience of God's Triune benevolent supernatural graciousness.

Our Carmelite Holy Father with unerring insight lists the seven selfish religious (viz., selfish self-righteous) self-attachments which serve as cardinal obstacles to the mystic's total prayerful sacrificial self-surrender to the divine loving embrace of God's Triune Godhead. It is clear from his consummate account that the mystic's struggle to overcome these cardinal obstacles cannot be successfully achieved on his own initiative alone. He may manfully and ascetically strive to rid himself of these cardinal aspects of his own religious selfish self-attachments which hinder his advance in contemplative prayer. But, in the final analysis, the core resistance of his selfishly self-serving self-alienated will endemic to his fallen nature can only be overcome and become ultimately fully purified by God-the-Holy Spirit's own super-natural initiative. This purgative initiative is vividly described by St. John in the mystic's painful experience of the "dark night's" gripping travail similar to a woman's laborious suffering in giving birth to her offspring.

The cruciform structure of the mystical life.

Before launching out into this mystagogical masterpiece there are additional points that must be made regarding the integral dialo-gical logic inherent in this cruciform mysticism which we have in this commentary been extracting from St. John's writings. The cross's ver-tical order is orthodox, the horizontal order is paradoxical, and the cruciform reconciliation of these two disparate orders is heterological. That is, it integrates the orthodox with the paradox without sacrifi-cing one to promote the other. The logic proper to each remains intact in their mutual cruciform integration. The vertical order is an inform-ative order in which the soul's intellect informatively takes normative precedence over the intellectual will's volition.

The horizontal order is a transformative order in which the self's serviceable will forcibly transformatively takes volitional precedence over the mind's conceptual fabrications. That is, the mind's notions and thoughts are the product of the will's own willful fabrication. The cruciform order is a performative order in which the person's soulful dutiful meritorious will and the same person's serviceable sacrificial submissive will complement each other in a "make do" fundament-al-supplemental performative complementarity.

Accordingly, the cruciform dialogical order itself is in its logical-ity not an analogous logic peculiar to the ontological vertical logic of the hierarchical metaphysical order of existence. Neither is it simply a catalogical or typological logic proper to the horizontal historical mathematical order of resistance. It is a dialogical logic that embraces in a complementary manner both disparate forms of rational ortho-dox and irrational paradoxical logic. In other words, dialogue em-braces both a prosaic literal personal syllogistic logic of categorical statements that transcend history's ephemerality together with a his-torical poetic personalized figurative mathematical logic of metaphorical utterances proper to story-telling and dramatic narration.

Dialogue embraces both in a fundamental-supplemental complementarity. This dialogue is notably evident in Sacred Scripture itself in which Christ through His parables ingeniously and dialogically synthesizes together the human person's hierarchical sober personal public moral obligations as a responsible member of the community of mankind together with the historical dramatization of exemplary paragons of paradigmatic personalities acting as role models which the same human person must himself imitate and emulate with a spirited unselfish influential morale sufficient to socially serve, edify, and boost up his fellowman and neighbor.

This dialogical order does not consist of a dialogue between two persons who face each other with opposite views. It is conducted by and within one and the same person in dialogical discourse involving his conscionable soul (God's Truthful voice resonating in the soul's interior), on the one hand, and his conscientious self (authenticating this conscionable voice within his own subjectivity), on the other. This dialogue can be extended to an interpersonal context. It is not restricted to an intrapersonal engagement.

Yet, when it is extended to engage another person, it is imperative for the success of the dialogue that one of the two persons be able, first, to conduct a dialogue within his own personhood between his hierarchical and his historical, his natural inalienable operative identity and his cultural alienable functional social self. For, every human person is both a generalist and a specialist. He must engage both dialogically and reconcile one with the other in his own personhood in order to dialogue with another person who may be locked into one of these orders to the exclusion of the other. In brief, a dialogue can only ensue when two separate persons can respectively within his own personhood hospitably entertain the opposing position endorsed by his opponent.

Indeed, the mystic in his own prayer-life engages dialogically not only his own soul's trans-experiential sacramental elevation to God but also his own selfhood's experiential sacrificial mystical prayerful benevolent sublimation to God. But, this is not accomplished other than in Christ, with Christ, and through Christ in the subtle influence of the Holy Spirit. It is in this pacific prayerful dialogical accomplishment that the mystic himself becomes a peace-maker for selves other than his own self. This is the overriding missionary spirit of the mystic as he suffers through the "dark night" trials of prayerfully surmounting his own selfishness to mount the summit of Mount Carmel. It is in this pilgrimage that he prayerfully and ascetically strives to bring to others the peace of Christ mediated through his own Christocentric transformation, a peace which the world cannot give.

Culture and the cult of religion.

It must not be overlooked that the very nuclear core and heart of all culture is the cult of religion. A person's very selfhood is in its self-humanizing endeavor a religious self in its very pith, heart, and nuclear core. Certainly, the entire construct of culture derives from mankind's enterprising productively functional self-humanizing selfhood. God creates the universe of existence. Man, made in the image and likeness of God, culturally recreates the world's pluriverses of resistance. This selfhood is never one and the same entitative unitive selfhood for all mankind. One dabbles in artifictional myths if one mistakenly construes that the world of mankind's cultural employment and deployment enjoys any manner of entitative unity and universality.

The world of the human person's self-cultivation is not an existing reality apart from the unique individual inalienable subsistent person who is self-consciously aware of his own personalized self-cultivated and self-cultivating selfhood occupying an associative fallible role within the self-civilized worlds of culture. Culture is a serviceable resistant self-humanization that resists existing apart from the person's inalienable individuality. All of culture as a man-made enterprise is typically secular and not sacred. Nonetheless, the very pith, heart, and core of all culture is the cult of religion.

This resistancy which is peculiar to and which pervades the entire order of culture is encountered by the human person in all instances of his own self-humanized cultivated social self-development. Consider, for example, the pioneer who takes ownership of a remote

485

uninhabited land that remains primitively in its natural state overrun with trees. He picks out a spot to build his dwelling out of the trees of the forest. These trees are naturally wooden but their wood is not naturally the materials of the cabin he plans to build. The trees resist being cut down and having their wood converted into the wooden cabin. The pioneer must willfully and forcibly overcome the resistance inherent in the trees to be transformed into a wooden cabin. This resistancy can only be overcome by force which demands that the human person's willful self forcibly exert itself to, in turn, exert the body to exercise its own force to overcome the resistancy inherent in the trees. The trees themselves naturally and spontaneously develop from embryonic germs, such as the acorn in the case of the oak tree, to mature full-grown plants. The power to initiate this propagation and maturation is inherent in the tree itself and its seedlings. This propagated growth and maturation, then, is a possibility inherent in all natural living beings.

By contrast, there is no innate power for the trees to become transformed into a wooden cabin. This is inherently and naturally impossible. It becomes possible not naturally but culturally when the wood of the trees resisting such a transformation are forcibly transformed by man's forcefulness into a wooden cabin. This impossibility is the order of culture which has its forceful initiation in the human person's self-centered self-serving own willfulness. This forceful willfulness is not to be confused with the human person's soulful objective intellectual will. It is the willfulness of the same human person's subjective willful selfhood.

The very core and crux of this resistancy is rooted in the human person's own willful selfhood whose inherent neediness and self-serving and self-centered impotence forcibly resists willing (viz., viscerally liking or cerebrally caring for) whatever does not cater to its own selfish self-centeredness. This resistance is the concupiscent residue of Adam & Eve's fall from grace; it is the residue of original sin. As a result of original sin, the human person's subjective self-centered self-serving psychosomatic willfulness (i.e., selfhood and personality) is self-alienated from his objective soul's intellectual will's purposeful volitions. To completely overcome this alienation and his willful selfhood's own resistance to everything that is not selfishly self-serviceably self-centered and self-fulfilling, the human person must do violence to his own willfulness. That is, he must forcibly in a paradoxical manner counter this ingrained selfishness and concupiscence of his self-centered willfulness.

Humanistically on his own, he can never fully succeed in overcoming and subduing this selfish willful egocentric resistancy. This can only be accomplished superhumanistically and heroically in virtue of Christ's own superhumanistic volunteer dying to His own utterly Selfless Self-centeredness. Christ volunteered to sacrificially substitute His own volitional Self-centered Selfless willful Selfhood for the selfish willfulness of every created human person's selfhood. By this substitution He enables the human person to reciprocally volunteer, in turn, to exchange his own willful selfish self for the gratuitous gift of Christ's Selfless Selfhood (i.e, super-humanized Personality). However, this can be accomplished by the Christian disciple only forcibly, sacrificially, and even heroically by willfully giving up his own self-possessive secular cultivated have-attitude in favor of Christ's very own counter-culture be-attitudinal redemptive mentality. This demands that the Christian disciple not merely flee from the secular world's self-centered activity but that he fly to Christ to be liberated from the prison of his self-centered selfishness he inherited from Adam and Eve.

Religion is man's commitment to his own subjective self-humanization, his own integral civilization and self-fulfillment. This commitment is inexorably sacrificial whether it remains exclusively within the subjective horizontal reach of history or whether it objectively transcends this reach in its self-humanized commitment and addresses the transhistorical reach of the hierarchical order of reality. If it remains entirely within the horizontal reach of history, mankind religiously and deliberately sacrifices his fundamental self-fulfillment which can only be achieved in the hierarchical order of existence completely transcendent to the horizontal reach of the civilized worlds of culture. However, even by imprisoning himself within the supplemental historical horizontal order of resistance, the secular humanist must sacrifice one aspect of his dichotomous psychosomatic selfhood to advance its polar opposite.

The idealist opposes the realist, the romanticist the pragmatist, and vice versa. Every exclusively secular humanistic religion religiously, brutally, and mercilessly sacrifices some dimension of mankind's dichotomous selfhood to advance its own slanted polarized and polarizing self-serving commitments. If a cultic religion transhistorically transcends secular history's own boundary, it ceases to be purely secular and becomes somehow sacred. For, it addresses a reality that transcends religion's own egocentric self-serving cultic core. This sacral character is not perforce supernatural simply because it is transhistorical. However, in that it somehow addresses an overriding reality that transhistorically transcends mankind's own historical demise, it implicitly and inchoately addresses itself to God as St. Paul himself suggests in reference to the classical Greek temple on the Acropolis dedicated to the "unknown God."

Now, the sacred is itself in the hierarchical order of existence either absolutely or relatively sacred. Only the absolutely sacred can sanctify the relatively sacred. The relatively sacred could not sanctify the absolutely sacred other than relatively and negligibly. Further, there cannot be two separate absolutely supreme sacred realities. For, if one is absolutely supremely sacred it encompasses all that is perfectly sacrosanct within its own unique and induplicable absoluticity and supremacy. Were there two such supreme absolutes, both would existentially be only relatively absolute and supreme vis-à-vis the other. In such a relativity neither would be absolutely sacred nor supremely sacred. If there is no absolute sacred reality (viz., God), neither could there be found in reality any merely relative sacred reality including the human person himself.

For, the absolutely sacred reality (viz., God) is the safeguard and guarantee for the relative reality's (viz., the human person) own sacrosanct sacredness. That is, were there no objective absolute sacred primary reality (viz., God) neither could the human person himself be guaranteed his own sacredness and special inviolable sovereign dignity. Furthermore, the human person in his subjective imperative religious need to find his self-fulfillment in and through such an objective absolute sacred Being would be doomed to a hopeless futility.

Any religious cult, therefore, that is sacrificially committed to an objective absolute sacred reality transcending the cult's subjective impotent need itself partakes at least implicitly in a monotheistic religion which is itself relatively sanctified in the measure that it is sanctified by what is absolutely sacred beyond its own subjective self-centered sanctification.

Indeed there are recognizably at least three distinct monotheistic religious cults: Judaism, Islamism, and Christianity. But, of these three, only the third presents itself as the prototypical paradigmatic religious theistic cult of all cults. This is the religious cult of Roman Catholic Orthodox Christianity. For, in the Christian cult of all cults, the very cult of religion is not only itself sanctified by what is absolutely sacred and transcendent to the religious cult itself, it is itself in its cultic religiosity absolutely sacred. For, the cult of all cults is the cult of Jesus Christ, God/Superman. He Himself in His sacrificial Self-immolation consummated in His Paschal mystery instituted the superhumanistic religious cult of Christianity. This cult is both historical in context and transhistorical in its sacrificial religious commitment and culmination. By His own total kenotic sacrifice, Jesus Christ, God/Superman, transformed the very nuclear willful egocentric self-serving subjective willful core of the human person's heart and mind into a divinely, superhumanistically, religiously devout and reverent liberated cultic Selfless willful selfhood hospitable to the absolute Holiness of the Godhead that exists in the objective order of reality transcendent to the human person's own subjective selfhood.

In brief, the human person's own subjective willful self-centered selfhood's imperative need for its own authentic religious autonomous social self-fulfillment---i.e., authentic self-cultivated self-humanization and self-integration intrapersonally within its own selfhood and interpersonally with selves other than its own selfhood---can only be achieved fundamentally if it is to be achieved at all beyond the subjectivity of its own solipsistic selfhood and transhistorically beyond the secular historicity of its own subjectivity. Without Christ's Divine/superhuman mediation the human person's imperious personalized religious craving for the authentic social self-fulfillment of his own personality would remain hopelessly futile and frustrated.

This authentic self-fulfillment cannot be accomplished merely supplementally within the horizontal order of secular history. It can only be accomplished eschatologically when history's own culmination attains its transhistorical destiny in the fundamental heavenly domain of reality proper to the human person's immortal superhuman destiny. In other words, this is accomplished only through Christ's Paschal Mystery involving His death, resurrection, and ascension which makes possible for the human person his access to his own fully fundamental self-fulfillment which his subjective religious needful selfhood imperiously craves.

In the human person's willful selfhood's threefold prototypical personalities previously sketched out in the commentary on the *Ascent*, the psychic, the somatic, and their psychosomatic hybrid synthesized personality, there is a threefold secular humanism which these personalities personify. Hence, they are occasions for three antipodal humanistic agnostic (and/or atheistic) religious cults. All three are entirely immanently humanistic and do not transcend the reach of history's own anthropocentric self-absorbed subjective horizontality. The psychic personality is entirely introverted within its self-absorbed intimate cerebral inertial concentration while the somatic personality is entirely extroverted in its self-absorbed focus on the body's kinetic visceral sensitivity. The hybrid personality is simultaneously an intro and extro diverted attentiveness self-absorbed in its own esthetic creativity and productivity.

There are notable exemplars of each prototypical personality previously delineated. There is the exemplar of the music composer who like a phantom specter manages remotely not only his own psychic impresario musical self but also remotely (through his musical compositions) both the viscerally active orchestra instrumentalists and the instrumentally inactive cerebral musical conductor at the podium. The musical score is the autocratic centerpiece regulating and controlling the musicians' automatic and technocratic manipulation of their musical instruments under the conductor's autonomic managerial control. The conductor both semi-autocratically interprets the musical score and simultaneously semi-automatically oversees and

490

coordinates the musician's performance of it. The conductor is the intermediary between the composer and the musical instrumentalists. He must substitute (i.e., both by way of an empathic sympathy for the instrumentalists and an empathic telepathy with the composer) and exchange himself with the composer and concentrate telepathically on managerially interpreting the composer's own cerebral spectral (i.e., phantom) inspiration while simultaneously overseeing and sympathetically controlling the phenomenal (i.e., spectacular) manipulation of each diverse musical instrument expertly and viscerally played by the instrumentalists who are the members of the orchestra.

In sum, the composer's psychic impresario self is a comprehensively introverted self concentrating on the entire musical composition unlike the performer who is an extroverted focal self involved with only a segment of the composition. The conductor himself cannot be either totally introverted as is the case for the composer impresario or totally extroverted as is the case for each individual instrumentalist. He must be simultaneously both a comprehensive manager intensively concentrating on the entire musical score and extensively a focal manipulator controlling each segment of the score performed by each diverse instrumentalist. In sum, while the musical score is being actually performed, the three prototypical personalities remain both antipodally differentiated from each other and performatively in tension with each other. Indeed, any exclusively secular religious humanism finds its religious self-fulfillment and central core either introvertedly in a utopian romanticism typical of the musical composer's own cerebral introversion; extrovertedly in a cornucopian pragmatism typical of the musical performer's own extroverted focus on his body's skillful visceral manipulation; or divertedly in the neutralist accommodator hybrid personality typical of the conductor's simultaneous partial attentiveness to both his cerebral and visceral involvement. This middle position is a compromise between a complete utopian and complete cornucopian sociability.

These three antipodal personalities constitute three different central agnostic (and/or atheistic) religious idols which typologically are entirely self-humanistic instances of secular atheism that actively militate against a divine sacred reality transcendent to the sphere of

491

their own subjective self-humanized religious experience. For example, an atheistic socialistic government demands a religious sacrificial commitment of its citizens who forcibly are required to submit their self-serving will to a cultivated self-humanistic phantom authority that inhabits that government's bureaucratic comintern apparatchik. That anonymous dictatorial phantom authority may have a human face but the authority that is commanded by that face, such as the face of Hitler of the face of Stalin, is a merciless anonymous phantom authority that strikes fear in all of the citizens of that government.

This is a romantic-type cultic religion that is completely autocratically forcibly imposed and buttressed by mythical conjectures. Pragmatic and esthetic paradigmatic types of personalities have their own peculiar versions and variations of a humanistic atheistic secular religiosity. It is very much the case that any such purely secular agnostic religious humanism becomes inevitably belligerently atheistic precisely because it is a forcibly willfully self-imposed religious cult seeking its own domineering self-righteous subjective self-control. In so doing, it refuses to acknowledge any supreme moral authority transcendent to its own autonomous self-subsistency.

But, these three prototypical personalities which serve paradigmatically as the core for atheistic religious humanistic cults only come to the forefront in society's self-cultivation as deviant offshoots of Christianity itself. After all, atheism means literally a falling away from theism, a falling away from God who is a Supreme Intelligent Sovereign Being and a falling away from what is God-centered. Hence, even within Christianity itself a social group may romantically, deviantly, and cerebrally seek its own humanistic cult of Christianity. Such, for example, is the case for that sect of Christianity which proclaims a Christianity to be a religion that discards the disciple's shouldering for himself Christ's cross of crucifixion. In this sense, the Christian disciple is entirely saved by the merits of Christ and not by his own endeavors. Such a cult of divine predestination is very romantic and cerebrally promotes a religious outlook that authoritatively embraces and sanctions an anonymous phantom "god" and "spirit" that resides exclusively within the selfishly self-serving selfhood of the Christian disciple that imperiously demands for its own self a guaranteed personalized water-tight religious security from God. Such a "god" is an anonymous phantom specter precisely because such a personalized guarantee of mankind's liberation cannot be found in the venerable tradition and Bible of God's Self-revelation overseen and interpreted by the Catholic Church's Magisterium.

The Christian Catholic Orthodox disciple of Christ, on the other hand, is required to completely transcend the horizontal and subjective humanistic limitation of all three of these prototypical, paradigmatic, personalities in pursuing his cultic religious commitment and self-sacrificial be-attitudinal religious self-fulfillment in, with, and through Christ. He is required to be completely transhistorically and metanoetically converted to the sacred reality of God's own absolute supreme monotheistic sacredness in the immortal and eternal hierarchical order of reality transcendent to history's ephemeral horizontality. In so doing, he is required to sacrifice his managerial control of his own selfish self-centered self-contained introverted religious equilibrium and to sacrifice manipulative control of his self-contented extroverted religious feelings. Indeed, he is required to religiously sacrifice his very selfish partisan psychosomatic selfhood in all of its prototypical facets to the Master of all sacrificial cultic religious self-fulfillment: Jesus Christ, God/Superman.

For, in the religious cult of Christianity, the human self can only find his fundamental paramount self-fulfillment in God with God and through God in the Trinitarian Personhood of the Father who initiates, the Son who consummates, and the Holy Spirit who integrates this religious self-fulfillment.

Three distinctively different valuable goods.

There are three distinctively different valuable goods which engage the Catholic Christian mystic's attention. Two are valuable goods-as-such quite independent of the human person's appetency for them. The other third one is a serviceable non-such-good which is only valued as worthwhile in the measure that it productively fulfills a person's self-centered need. Of the first two valuable goods, one is relatively pleasurable good because its value is consumably perishable and temporary while the other is absolutely delightfully an invaluable good because its value is consummately imperishable and immortal. An apple is an example of a pleasurable valuable good. It is nutritional apart from its being eaten and it is appetized (i.e., sentiently loved) because it not only nourishes the corporeal body's drive for its own metabolic homeostasis, it is also pleasurably enjoyed by the body's appetent sentiency. The full truth of the apple's nutritional and pleasurable worth is found only in the second invaluable good. This invaluable good is wholesomely a noble, honest, honorable, consummate, and imperishable good quite independent of and transcendent to the person's sentient appetency to consume the apple to benefit from its nutritional and pleasurable value.

Truth itself is such an invaluable good above and beyond the truth of the apple's perishable worth. Truth-as-such harbors an imperishable transcendent worthiness (which is naturally appetized by the human person's soulful volition) precisely because such truth reveals the immortal transcendent dignity of the human person's overall holistic destiny and well-being beyond the body's own mortal well-being. Not only does such truth-as-such nourish the soul's drive for immortal and imperishable metaphysical happiness (i.e., personal well-being) which is the birth-right of every human person, the person's soulful will delights with a purely spiritual delight independent of all bodily sentiency in possessing such imperishable metaphysical truth-as-such.

The human person's corporeal body is both pleased and satisfied in consuming the ripe apple plucked from the apple tree. This sentient pleasure and satisfaction is itself good because the object of the body's instinctive appetency (viz., the apple) is itself inherently valuable and nutritionally good. The human person's incorporeal soul is both spiritually delighted and edified in honoring transcendental truth-as-such above and beyond grasping intellectually the truth of the perishable apple. For the imperishable entitative reality of truth-as-such transcendent to the apple itself is worthy of a consummate imperishable spiritual (i.e., immaterial and inorganic) soulful delight and edification. Certainly, this insight into truth-as-such is neither sentiently satisfying nor pleasing to the body's appetency because it transcends the body's sentiency. Truth-as-such as an imperishable transcendent reality grasped by the soul's intellectual intelligibility completely beyond the body's appetent sentiency. Even the apple's truth does not reside in its sentient trappings such as its flavor and nutritional value, shape, color, etc..

Its truth resides in the intellect understanding its apple-as-such entity over and above its perishability. The apple-as-such, the communal entitative apple that is common to every existing physical apple is not itself physical and tangible but metaphysical, and intangibly intelligible to the human person's inorganic soulful spiritual (i.e., immaterial) intelligence.

The intellect insightfully and intelligently grasps that the apple-as-such is essentially and categorically a fruit of a plant, the apple tree, that is itself fruitful in growing apples and regenerable from the seeds it generates within the apple's core. This truth is more delightfully enjoyable to the soul's purely spiritual volitional appetency than is the particular eaten apple pleasurable to the body's appetent sentiency. Why? Because with this truth the human person can soulfully, imperishably, volitionally, and fruitfully possess and enjoy the imperishable truth of apple-as-such over and above the perishable apple that it eats out-of-hand. Such truth-as-such is an immortal, imperishable, honest good benefiting not merely the body temporarily by consuming the apple-in-hand but by benefiting the soul everlastingly and delightfully through the consummate enduring imperishable enduring knowledge of the apple-as-such's fruitful nature and fructification.

Of course, again, there is a knowledge of not only the truth of the apple-as-such but, moreover, of transcendental truth-as-such itself and ultimately of what is existentially absolute Truthfulness (viz., God). The soul's intellectual will cannot naturally appetize (i.e., love) and appetently possess and spiritually enjoy such absolute transcendent imperishable Truthfulness in the way that the human body can sentiently appropriate the apple by possessively consuming and enjoying it as one's own private possession. Such absolute divine Truthfulness is imperishably, immutably, and immortally eternal and consummate; it cannot be possessively consumed as one's own but only appropriately honored, obeyed, respected, and revered as a reality that transcends one's own being as a human person.

This Truthfulness is not to be confused with the communal metaphysical truth-as-such which is naturally and loveably knowable to every human person's soulfully volitional intelligence. This theological Truthfulness is the very eminence of truth-as-such existing in God as the Supremely eminent reality in the domain of existence. The human person can naturally know the communal transcendental truth-as-such of all that exists in the cosmic material domain of reality but only virtually the very eminence of such truth existing theologically and supremely in God's absolute eternal Truthfulness.

It is important to appreciate that the recognition of the transcendental metaphysical truth-as-such is the soulful intellect's own innate perfection. And, this truth-as-such is not to be confused with knowing the truth-as-such of the apple-as-such. When the body's eye sees an apple in a tree, it does not behold every apple that exists but only this particular apple. It is the intellect that can behold every particular apple in terms of knowing generically the apple-as-such above and beyond every specific apple that the body's eye can see.

The human person's soulful intellect is not limited to knowing only the essence-as-such of material cosmic realities such as the apple. It recognizes the very essence-as-such of transcendental truth-as-such which is not reducible to any one nor to all of the cosmic essences in the physical universe of reality. In this manner it can by analogy recognize the supreme reality of God as the Supreme essence of truth-as-such transcendent to every creature. For, whereas every creature is an entitative essence having existence, God the Creator is essentially and entitatively existence itself.

Hence, the soul's intellectual will can appropriate (i.e., possess) and spiritually delight in the communal truth-as-such as its own innate valuable and worthwhile communal good-as-such (viz., well-being and happiness) which is common to every individual human person. This communal truth-as-such is not the possessive property of any one person. To emphasize this communal transcendent dimension of the truth-as-such which is the soulful will's good-as-such, a special sovereign authority is commonly recognized in every established community of human person's to rule and govern all members of that community in the light of such transcendental and communal truth-as-such. Furthermore, this sovereign authority is himself subject to the same governance as is every citizen of this community. The human person's inalienable dignity is his sovereign authority to be responsible for his own choices and volitional conduct obligated to honor and obey his intellect's conscionable truth-as-such. Each person is morally and conscionably responsible for his own voluntary choices and conduct.

Furthermore, by dutifully choosing to honor and conscionably respect the transcendental communal truth-as-such in all of his own freely elicited choices and conduct, the human person soulfully delights in achieving the very perfection not only of his own will but of his own personhood. Thus, it is conscionably inappropriate for the human person to willingly and freely honor and reverence the consumable delicious apple in the tree rather than to honor the transcendental truth-as-such of what constitutes the very essence and nature of the apple-as-such. Further, it is conscionably inappropriate for the human person to honor and reverence the truth of the apple-as-such instead of the communal transcendent truth-as-such which is neither reducible to nor limited by any specific material reality such as the apple. The inalienable dignity of the human person is his soulful ability to transcend and immortally outlive all the vicissitudes of his mortal body's material existence. Further, he is sovereignly able to govern his volitional conduct in view of this immortal communal transcendence.

Thus, the soul's intellectual willful choices dutifully and conscionably conducted are themselves delightfully honorable in the measure that they appropriately honestly honor what is truthfully and humanly good-as-such for every human person without exception. Such honorable good-as-such is worthy of the human person's dutiful obedience and respect. Yet, this communal transcendent good-as-such is not the very eminence and acme of what commands complete and total obedient voluntary respect and honor on the part of the human person. For, the transcendent communal good-as-such is not itself the eminent Absolute Goodness which is proper to God's own existence and infinite benevolence. The human person's natural happiness and perfection is not explicitly God's very own eminent divine blessedness, beatitude, and holiness.

However, it is virtually God's own Goodness inasmuch as it is this very Goodness which is the origin and source of the human person's own existence and immortal human happiness. This human happiness as the ultimate attainment of the human person's personal communal plenitude is found ultimately in God alone but not by the human person's own efficacy. It is only by God's supernatural and eminent benevolence. Left to himself the human person can attain to knowing, honoring, and worshipping God's absolute Truthfulness and Goodness only imperfectly with much difficulty.

Such a totally absolute and eminently honorable Goodness that is God can only be humanly honored communally inasmuch as God as a consummate eternal invaluable Goodness cannot be personally possessed by any one individual such as is the case with the edible apple that is personally possessed by the one who actually eats it. Indeed, a person's moral character is itself only inherently honorable and morally upright in the measure that he can conscionably and dutifully uphold, honor, and serve the truth, the whole truth, and nothing but the truth in his ordinary conduct as the very beneficial good and perfection of that conduct. In doing so he virtually honors God's own Truthfulness and Goodness. However, the human person is able to dutifully, conscionably, and honorably honor God in a manner which is befitting God's own eminent benevolent Goodness only superhumanly in the measure that God Himself supernaturally reveals Himself to the human person and supernaturally enables that same person to trustingly and dutifully render thanks and praise to God for this supernatural beneficence.

Such is the case with Jesus Christ, God/Superman. He is God's infinite Goodness incarnate as the Godhead's Second Person endowed with a divinized human nature and superhumanistic self-cultivated superhumane personality. Through, with, and in Christ in virtue of the human person's baptized entry into the Church's sacramentality, the human person may supernaturally, superhumanly, superhumanistically, and superhumanely adore, worship, thank, and dutifully honor God's absolute Goodness in a divine eminent manner worthy of God's infinite benevolence. In so doing, the human person may delightfully within the very personal interior of his own soul supernaturally rejoice, delight, and exult in God's very own beatitudinal blessedness.

But, again, this is not a supernal delight which is afforded the human person naturally. It is entirely a gratuitous gift on the part of God. Furthermore, it is not a supernal delight in which the body's sentiency can fully participate since this supernal delight is purely inorganic and wholly spiritual befitting God's own absolute immutable and eternally immaterial spirituality.

The third instance of a valuable good.

The third instance of a valuable good is the serviceable nonsuch-good which is not inherently worthwhile in the same way that goods in the hierarchical order of existence are inherently worthwhile. Rather, it is a quasi-good in the historical order of resistance. That is, it is a good only in the measure that it supplies and provides a useable self-centered service to the human person's personalized social self-subsistence. When it fails in this regard, it becomes unusably useless and no longer serviceably worthwhile. This is a good which is not actually good but only has the wherewithal to offset the human person's self-serving need and active usage of it. Indeed, it does not even exist independent of the human person's forcible cultural fabrication and usage of its serviceability. This serviceable good may be either serviceable to the corpuscular body's functional instrumentality as a tool or serviceable to the psychic mind's functional communication as a symbol. A simple shovel is an example of the former and any symbol whether merely graphic, phonetic, or otherwise is an example of the latter.

The shovel implementally facilitates the somatic body's own kinesthetic self-manipulated bodily work and functionality while the symbol implementally facilitates the working mind's own anesthetized self-management and communication with others. The tool can be culturally expanded into a machine and the symbol into a language whether merely spoken or written. Tools facilitate a person's working manipulation of his own bodily physiological mobilization and productive functionality and symbols facilitate a person's working management of his own mental psychological immobilization and communicable functionality. But both the tool and the symbol are only serviceably useable within the cultural historical and sociological context within which they are humanistically cultivated.

An American transplanted to the Chinese culture on China's mainland would have to be initiated into that culture to become familiar with its cultural instrumentation and language before he could make serviceable use of its facilities to advance his own personality. He would have to replace his knife and fork with chop sticks and substitute his English discourse with a Chinese dialect. In the process, he would be exchanging his American folklore, customs, and civility for those of the Chinese culture.

A successful proficient usage of a tool provides automatically a self-satisfying sensational sensuous gratification to the body's willful somatic toil and effort while a successful usage of language provides autocratically a self-justifying notional intimate vindication to the mind's willful psychic toil and effort. The human person's willful selfhood is more successfully self-fulfilled somatically (i.e., with a feeling of self-satisfaction) and psychically (with an equipoise bearing of self-justification) when the tool and the symbol in their more complex mechanical and linguistic configurations are successfully skillfully and proficiently mastered. Tools and symbols are suitably worthwhile only in view of their serviceable usage in facilitating the functional productivity and ease of the somatic body and psychic mind's willful enterprises. The somatic body functions proximately to mechanically skillfully manipulate its own comfortable satisfying self-control. The psychic mind functions remotely to bureaucratically skillfully manage its own comforting justifying self-control. The tools and symbols they deploy are entirely non-such-goods considered apart from their successful self-serving usage and deployment.

Where the apple is inherently nutritional independent of being eaten the safety pin is useless apart from its actual usage to pin something together; the word "the" is useless apart from its actual usage as a meaning communicable from one self to another self. A good-as-such is inherently worthwhile and valuable whereas a non-such-good is only worthwhile in view of the human person's fabrication and self-serving deployment of it.

The three valuable goods figure prominently in the mystic's life.

These three disparate goods, the consumable, consummate, and serviceable, figure prominently in the mystic's spiritual prayer-life. The principal and primary good which is the object of Christian prayer is the supernatural consummate, honest, and honorable good-as-such which is God's own Godhead miraculously Self-revealed in Sacred Scripture and sacramentally instantiated in Christ's Catholic Orthodox Church. This invaluable good may be enjoyed delightfully and dutifully for its own sake by the soul's intellectual will. The spiritual joy and gladness enjoyed by the intellectual will exists objectively within the human person's soulful interiority and is not as-such-experienced subjectively within the human person's subjective psychosomatic reflexive personality.

The human person as mystic is conscious of it in the same way that he is conscious of simply seeing, touching, and sensing and enjoying things sentiently through his bodily senses and appetency. This completely spiritual and supernatural divine joy transcends the substantive body's corporeality and sensate appetent organicity. Hence, it is not a delectable or delicious or pleasant joy peculiar to the corporeal body's sentiency.

The point being emphasized here is not different than that of the consideration of the virtue of justice. Justice as the moral obligation and habitual willingness to render to an authority what is dutifully the proper right of that authority is not residually reducible to a sentient sensibility. Brute animals enjoy instinctive sentient sensibility and appetency. Yet, there is no sensibility of authority, or of justice, or of obligation within such brute sentient sensibility transcendent to their instinct for self-preservation. Justice is strictly a matter of the human person's soulful spiritual inorganic intelligibility which transcends the body's sentient sensibility. In the case of the human person's own human sensibility, however, since this sensibility is per-

501

meated by the soul's intellectual life and volitional animation, the virtue of justice or its inverse, injustice, may be in an ancillary manner sensed within the human body's sentiency and appetency.

Thus, in witnessing someone actually stealing another person's private property, the eye can see an act of injustice and the body's instinctive appetency can become angry. Similarly, in witnessing someone genuflecting in front of the Blessed Sacrament, the eye can see an act of justice toward God's Supreme Authority and the body's instinctive appetency can become pleased.

However, the delightful joy which the human person entertains in regard to the actual soulful volitional choice and act of justice whether it be his own choice and deed or someone else's choice and deed, this spiritual delightful joy is entertained principally in the interiority of the person's soul. It transcends the person's self-centered selfhood and subjectivity. Nonetheless, this spiritual joy may in its effulgence resonate within the very body of the human person since the body's own life has the source of its animation from the soul. While this human body is material in the same sense that a stone is material, plant life is botanical, and animal life is zoological, thus human body's material, botanical, and zoological nature is animated with an intelligent and freely governed spiritual soul. By reason of this spiritual animation, the body's own objective corporeal sentiency and, especially, its subjective visceral sensitivity and mental intimacy may also residually partake of the soul's delightful spiritual joy which the human person entertains in the will's choice of acting justly and nobly befitting the will's own innate drive to act for its own immortal well-being in common with other human persons.

It is in this residual sense that the human person within his very own subjective personality may experience personalistically extrovertedly and/or introvertedly within his willful selfhood a residual sensitized emotional bodily satisfaction and/or intimate emotionless mental vindication concomitantly with the soul's spiritual delight in choosing to act justly and nobly. This is the characteristic of a God-fearing and law-abiding patriotic citizen in a Christian nation.

What is the case even in the matter of basic ethical and moral conduct in the human person becomes moreso the case in the matter of supernatural religious conduct. When the mystic obediently in faith honors Christ in the Eucharist, there is a supernatural spiritual delightful joy in the mystic's soul who freely chooses to recognize that in justice he owes his very existence and his own innocence entirely to Christ's redeeming freedom purchased by Christ's very Body and Blood which he receives in Holy Communion. This objective supernally spiritual joy (i.e., entirely inorganic, immaterial, and transcendent to all that is bodily sentient, sensational, and inspirational) may affluently, residually, and incidentally resonate subjectively within the human person's psychosomatic personality and willful selfhood.

This resonance occurs differently in the mystic's subjective psychosomatic personality than it does in the soul's spiritual supernaturalized interiority. Within his extroverted willful bodily self, the mystic may experience a pious and devout self-satisfying sensationally sensitive enjoyable exhilarating religious experience whereas in his introverted willful mental self, he may experience a pious and devout self-justifying inspirational intimate profound enjoyable righteous tranquility. Or, it may be the case that he experiences in a hybrid manner both extrovertedly and introvertedly a semi-sensitive and semi-intimate righteous experience of Christ's inexorable justice tempered by His infinite mercy. Now, when the mystic actually undergoes personalistically such righteous experiences, he becomes subject to the temptation of exploitatively using these subjective experiences from the soul's interior spiritual jubilation to automatically, on the one hand, facilitate his own somatic self-sufficient religious selfish gratification and/or to autocratically, on the other, facilitate his own psychic self-sufficient religious selfish justification. This is precisely what occurs when the mystic exploitatively makes serviceable use of such religious experiences to aggrandize his own autonomous self-contented and/or self-contained social security rather than to give glory and honor to God's transcendent Goodness.

The mystic ascends Mount Carmel by God's Triune Graciousness.

St. John of the Cross sagaciously indicates at the outset of his

Dark Night seven various capital selfishly self-serving attachments that impede the mystic from advancing into the very womb of contemplative prayer and perfect union with God's sacramental presence in his soul. He enumerates these as pride, greed, lust, anger, gluttony, envy and sloth. These are so sensitively and intimately rooted within the human person's willful selfhood's egoistic subjective selfish psychosomatic willfulness that the mystic by his own ascetic exertions cannot without the supernatural and superhuman help of God and recourse to the Church's sacraments divest himself of these selfish self-serving attachments. St. John begins the *Dark Night* by describing each of these capital selfish self-serving attachments and explains how they impede the mystic's advance to a perfect union with God in contemplative prayer.

The entire thrust of the *Dark Night* is to describe the anguish and excruciating misery the mystic himself subjectively and experientially suffers, first in his bodily somatic and then in his mental psychic willfulness, in the process of the Holy Spirit's direct influence to divest the mystic of these seven capital selfish attachments which impede the mystic's advancement to perfect prayerful union with God in contemplative prayer. The mystic who endures and suffers through the excruciating religious experiences of both phases of the "dark night" (viz., the senses and the spirit) eventually emerges purged of his selfish need to pridefully, greedily, lustfully, angrily, gluttonously, enviously, and slothfully exploit his personalized religious experiences of God for his own self-aggrandizement.

He gradually in suffering through the ordeal of the "dark night" becomes submissively disposed to forego any and every personalized selfishly self-appropriated religious experience in order to serve more selflessly his neighbor and God in His Sacramental Church. When he is eventually confirmed in this resolution after an extended period of religious bodily emotional aridity and religious mental emotionless anxiety he becomes so subserviently and humbly disposed toward serving God's glory rather than his own glorification that he may subsequently through God's own initiative (in the unitive stage of the mystical life) actually religiously experience within his own subjective psychosomatic willfulness the very somatic sublime emotional bodily exultations and psychic profound emotionless mental calming consolations which he had previously resolved to forego for the greater and honor of God.

In his pilgrimage up to the summit of Mount Carmel, the mystic who ardently seeks to prayerfully contemplate God's "face" in the very Godhead of God's Triune Personhood has no greater sponsor than Mary, our Lady of Mount Carmel. By commending and consecrating himself to the sacramental womb of Mary's Immaculate Heart, the mystic is assured of reaching the Triune summit under her maternal ecclesial care. She is not only the mother of Jesus Christ, God/Superman; she is the mother of His Sacramental Church, the Mystical Body. And not only is she the spiritual mother of all of the members of this Mystical Body but the mother of their spiritual Godliness, the mother of God's graciousness alive in the soul of each Christian.

Her spiritual maternity avails her of a special and unique prayerful intercourse with the Blessed Trinity. She is simultaneously of all of God's creatures the Father's very singular daughter which cannot be said of any other human being or created angel. Indeed, she is also the sister of every Christian precisely because of her singular status as the choicest daughter of the Father. In this singularity she is created immaculately to be susceptible to being the Son's mother. And this maternity is accomplished both through her Immaculate Conception as the Father's singular daughter and her espousal to the Holy Spirit through whom she conceives the Son. The mystic's pilgrimage to the summit of Mount Carmel is a Trinitarian pilgrimage. The Son's Incarnation is not for the purpose of Christ establishing His own will but for the purpose of testifying to the Father's Holy Will who, in turn, testifies to the Son's messianic mission to mediate the liberation of all of mankind from its own selfish self-alienating willfulness.

The mystic's task is to volunteer without reservation to accompany and participate in Christ's liberating messianic mission. This task exceeds the mystic's very own human resources. This task requires that the mystic superheroically undergo the same martyrdom that Christ endured on the cross of His crucifixion. Christ died to his own Self-humanized psychosomatic willfulness not because He was in any iota self-centeredly selfish and not because He Himself in His

505

humanity needed to undergo such a sacrificial self-immolation. He volunteered to suffer such a humiliating and indescribable agony precisely to empathically substitutively insert His own sufferings and immolation for the sufferings of every member of mankind and especially for each and every one of his disciples.

The mystic left to himself is unable on his own to superheroically join his own sufferings to those of Christ and, thereby, to accept Christ's sufferings as his own not only for his own salvation and sanctification but also for the salvation of others. This is too daunting. God-the-Father who exists infinitely above and beyond the mystic seems to the mystic to be of little avail to assist him in his own mystical sufferings and weakness and to, thereby, enable the mystic to transcend his own misery and selfishness. After all, the summit of the mystic's pilgrimage is to ascend to the Father who remains infinitely beyond the mystic's finite reach. God-the-Son Himself in His Incarnation exists below and beneath the mystic in a profound Self-abasement, Self-immolation, and volunteer humility which is also infinitely beyond the reach of the mystic's own ascetic efforts to become humbly self-detached and united with Christ in Christ's consummate sacrificial Selflessness. Who, then, is there to assist the mystic to divest himself of his own egocentric selfishness and to deliver him from his weakness and fearfulness?

The Holy Spirit of the Father and Son's personal loveliness is the mystic's own personal Gift of loveliness and indomitable courage to enable the mystic to accomplish superhumanly, superhumanistically, and superhumanely what no human can accomplish on his own. This Holy Spirit is secreted within the infinite depth of the mystic's innermost intimate psychosomatic willful selfhood.

And who within the Church's sacramentality apart from Christ Himself is more intimately wed to the Holy Spirit's Giftedness than Mary, Mother of the Son and daughter of the Father? Our Blessed Mother's Immaculate Heart is the Church's sacramental womb. The author of all the sacraments, her divine Son, Jesus, is conceived, born, and nurtured from her sacramental womb and maternal breasts under the auspices of the Holy Spirit. The mystic who patterning himself after Mary prays that she may mother in him the very divine life that she mothered in her divine Son, Jesus, is the mystic who is best disposed to respond to the unctuous influence of the Holy Spirit within the depths of his own willful selfhood.

Robed with the brown scapular of Carmel, the mystic enters into a threefold engagement with Jesus Christ, the Way, the Truth, and the Life. Vertically, the mystic following Mary's lead communes with the Father through the Son. This is effectuated by Christ's Incarnation in which He identifies Himself with every created human being. Christ is born into the very same nature of every human person. Further, He weds the Father's providential care and love to every one who partakes baptismally and eucharistically of the Blessed Sacrament. Horizontally, Christ further communicates with every human being through His Gospel which is both an oral and written tradition. His Gospel teachings and conduct educate the disciple regarding the Kingdom of God. Cruciformly, Christ's Holy Spirit, the Spirit of Truth, integrates the mystic with the Father and Son's own amicable integrity and infinite benevolence. In brief, the Father initiates, the Son consummates, and the Spirit integrates. Mystical prayer is less the mystic embracing God and more God embracing the mystic. The greatest obstacle to this is not God but the mystic himself in his own self-centered willful selfish selfhood.

The ascent to Mt. Carmel entails a descent into one's own selfhood.

To better appreciate the genius and holiness of St. John of the Cross made manifest in his *Dark Night*, consider the following scenario. A wayfarer with a large canteen full of a special delicious tonic to accompany him on his journey to find the fabled fountain of youth comes to a spring-fed stream of exquisitely pure water, the very well-source of the fable that guides his journey. He wishes to avail himself of this water by filling up his canteen with it in the place of the tonic already contained there. Before filling his canteen with the pure spring water he must empty his canteen and pour out the tonic. Further, he must rinse the canteen with the spring water to insure that it itself is completely devoid of all traces of the tonic it previously contained. This process of emptying the canteen and rinsing it out is precisely what occurs in the *Dark Night*. The canteen as a container mirrors the psychic selfhood's will which of itself is a container empty of all preconceived willful devotional notions and self-contained intimate self-serving self-justifying selfish religious vindications. The tonic in the canteen mirrors the somatic selfhood's will which of itself is full of its own devotional sensational sensitized self-serving selfish self-contented religious satisfaction.

Now, in the case of the mystic approaching the pure divine stream of God's very own baptismal water, he must first, before completely experiencing the purity of this miraculously blessed sublime water, empty his own psychic will of all of its self-serving selfish righteous experiences of self-contained intimate religious self-justification and expel from his own somatic will all self-serving selfish self-righteous experiences of self-contented sensitized religious self-satisfaction. After all, his mystical journey of perfect union with God is not explicitly to advance his own glory but to share in God's glory. No matter what decisive ascetic steps of mortifying his own selfishness he undertakes to achieve this he falls short. He cannot empty his somatic willfulness of its own feelings and need for religious self-exultation and selfish sensitized stirrings. And, even if he succeeds in some measure to accomplish this, there remains in his psychic willfulness its own bearing and need for religious self-sustained serenity and self-contained intimate impassivity (i.e., imperturbability).

Given the futility of the mystic's own active initiatives to successfully purge himself of his willful psychosomatic selfish selfhood's motivational need for religious somatic stimulating bodily gratification and psychic pacifying mental justification to prayerfully serve God, God Himself in the Person of the Holy Spirit abiding within the innermost recesses of the mystic's willful selfhood takes the initiative on His own to complete the ascetic purgation and purification already begun by the mystic. For, until this purgation and purification is complete, the mystic is impeded by his own selfhood's selfishness from experientially drinking of the pure sublime waters of God's very own Triune Godhead, and from experiencing the prayerful climax and acme of his pilgrimage to God.

This purgation occurs initially in the mystic's bodily visceral willfulness where he experiences urgent needs for devout stimulating feelings of self-satisfaction motivating him to actively serve God in serving His Church and his neighbor. With the cessation of these pious stimulating feelings of reassuring self-centered religious satisfaction, the mystic is prone to cease altogether from further engaging in this prayerful service to the Church and others. Why this cessation? He has no further incentive to continue this prayerful service. When this stimulating feeling of religious zeal vanishes and is completely withheld by the Holy Spirit's influence, the urgent need for this gratifying religious stimulation becomes increasingly more acute. In the absence of this religious stimulation the mystic experiences a very troubling boredom and religious despondency. To continue to prayerfully serve God during this prolonged religious emotional sterility seems to the mystic to be more like play-acting than engaging in a genuine sincere zealous service to God and his neighbor. To continue this willful prayerful service to God, Church, and neighbor in this religious emotional vacuum is tantamount to forcing one's own somatic will to act when it lacks the self-gratifying religious emotional stimulus motivating its action.

This, then, is the crux, the misery, and the perplexity of the purgatory which characterizes the "dark night of the senses." What was previously so easy to accomplish when the mystic was stimulated with his own personalized self-satisfying religious emotional feeling of exultation has become humanly impossible to continue when this feeling no longer stimulates the somatic will to prayerfully engage in these same religious exercises and services. Indeed, the mystic in this position is required to forcibly resist the very resistancy of his own willfulness to persistently continue in his prayerful serviceable activity. That is, he must forcibly resist his somatic will's overriding bodily need to have its own satisfactory religious self-fulfillment fulfilled merely supplementally and selfishly in the horizontal order of having rather than selflessly and fundamentally in the vertical order of being. The selfhood's willful need for self-fulfillment can only fully be satisfied in the fundamental vertical order of being beyond the supplemental order of having. In other words, to experience possessively having a selfish self-centered religious satisfaction of prayerfully serving Christ is tantamount to being less identified with Christ Himself transcendent to and objectively independent of that subjective experience itself of pious self-satisfaction.

A similar but retrospective mental religious purgative experience occurs again under the influence of the Holy Spirit in the mystic's psychic willfulness when the mystic is purged of his own mental assurance of religious self-vindication. His need for a stable mental bearing of profound and self-assured equilibrium (i.e., a calm mental deportment) to be emotionlessly and impassively disposed to prayerfully and devoutly adore God is shattered when this mental serenity deserts him. This religious enjoyment of mental serenity becomes abruptly disrupted by the Holy Spirit's influence to withdraw it. When this occurs, this demanding religious need itself ceases also, in its turn, to be experientially pacifically justified. What occurs henceforth in the intimacy of the mystic's psychic self-centered mental willfulness is not a religious emotional embolism which is the case for his sensitized somatic self-centered bodily willfulness. There occurs a religious emotionless mental agitation, consternation, and pervasive vague and foreboding anxiety which completely discombobulates the mystic's previous religious mental prayerful placidity and serenity. With the loss of this pious serenity, the mystic has neither further motivation nor incentive to willfully continue his former custom of cultivating mental prayer in the service of God, the sacramental Church, and his neighbors.

And where the emotional embolism occurs within the selfhood's superficial somatic body's kinesthetic sensitivity, this disturbing consternation and brooding anxiety occurs within the selfhood's innermost anesthetized innermost mental intimacy. It is all the more disturbing and disquieting for having in the psychic will's emotionless mental placidity a turbulence which is alien to the mind's previous imperturbability and tranquility.

To continue to prayerfully adore God in this religious mental perturbation is doubly difficult because a complete lack of religious mental composure and equipoise makes it impossible to pray with any sustained recollection and self-assured self-justified attention to God. When the will's needful demand for its own self-assured selfish self-serving religious justification, validation, and vindication is no longer experienced as self-fulfilling, the mystic has no motivation nor incentive to further prayerfully and piously attend to God transcendent to his own subjective need to supplementally experience his own pious justification. He experiences no further religious consolation in his prayerful attention to God and the Church. Again, in this position the mystic is required to forcibly resist the very resistancy of his own psychic willfulness to be prayerfully devoted to God's justice and justification rather than to have his own self-serving religious self-centered justification fulfilled.

In both of these cases the mystic's own psychosomatic willfulness is impotent to become completely selflessly self-detached from his own selfish need to possessively have and safeguard his own autonomously secure and self-assured religious somatic bodily self-satisfaction and religious psychic mental self-justification. The selfish residue of original sin is too dominant in the mystic's subjective willful personality to allow him on his own to overcome and surmount the tug of its captivity. Victory over his own willful selfishness and impotency can only be accomplished by the unctuous influence of the Holy Spirit that subtly, unobtrusively, and spiritedly influences the willful self to surmount and overcome its own resistancy to everything threatening its own religious selfish self-possessive self-secured self-interest and self-serving attitude of self-sufficiency. Through this unctuous Pneumatic influence the mystic faithfully surmounts his own selfishness and perseveres in mental prayer and charitable actions in spite of the persistent bodily religious emotional embolism and mental religious discombobulations that discourage his further continuation in his commitment to prayerfully surrender his life to the Father through Christ in the power of their Holy Spirit.

This perseverance is made possible by a superhuman and super-humanizing indomitable and steadfast morale which supplies in the very innermost intimate heart of the mystic's willful psychosomatic selfhood a super spirited courage, stamina, and hope to persevere in the face of what otherwise seems utterly hopeless. In remaining faithful to these religious exercises and prayerful devotion throughout the severe religious disturbances in both body and mind, the mystic gradually becomes metamorphically transformed into the Personality of Christ Himself embracing the very messianic selfless be-attitudinal mindset proper to Christ's very own redemptive and sanctifying Persona (i.e., divinized Personality) and superhumanized Selfhood.

In the process of this metamorphic transformation, the mystic undergoes a profound suffering and anguish. The reason for this is found in the context of his self-humanized personality itself. Nothing is more constitutive of one's own personality than one's familiarity with the body's kinesthetic emotional sensitivity, on the one hand, and the mind's anesthetized emotionless intimacy on the other, including one's own personalized attitudinal mindset (i.e., one's tacit personalized nonnegotiable motivational aspirations).

What happens when these familiar traits of one's own personality are completely loss to one's own self? One undergoes a radical experience of self-alienation. Of course, one is being liberated from one's own built-in dichotomous psychosomatic inherited self-alienation through original-sin. Yet, the experience of losing completely the personality with which one is most familiar is itself painfully disconcerting and unsettling. One's self-confidence and sense of self-reliance, self-sufficiency, and social autonomous security are severely disrupted and dissolved. Familiarity with and self-reliance on one's memorial past and familiarity with one's expectant future plans are not only partially interrupted in an annoying way. They are completely dissolved and disrupted in an alarming way.

Paralyzed by a complete lack of religious zeal and emotional feeling for God and things of God, on the one hand, and pervasively anxious and disturbed in one's emotionless religious equipoise at the very thought of God, on the other, the mystic is no longer either in touch with his own once familiar personality traits and feelings nor prayerfully in touch with God who formerly was the anchor and bulwark of his religious devotion, mental bearing, pious activity, and prayer-life. There is no human mortal that can comfort the mystic who finds himself in this miserable religious situation. This is not a technical or pathological problem which can be cured by an expert steeped in some technical, psychological, or medical field of endeavor. It is radically a religious dilemma that reaches to the very heartfelt and inmost intimate core of the human person's self-humanized personality. A person who is head and heels in love with another and who finds himself spurned and rejected by this other cannot find solace and healing from his family doctor or psychiatrist.

Only God objectively and fundamentally transcendent to the mystic's subjective self-centered personality can supply selflessly to the mystic what the mystic desperately wants to have supplied merely supplementally and selfishly. At this purgative period in the mystic's prayerful journey to the Father through Christ, it seems that he would be emotionally piously self-content and emotionlessly piously self-contained to merely self-assuredly have momentarily his religious self-serving selfish need experientially gratified and justified. And, the Holy Spirit may actually supply this experience of devout bodily religious gratification and mental religious justification intermittently to allow the mystic to be even selfishly self-assured that he is not completely forgotten and neglected or rejected by God. The greatest blessing for the Catholic mystic is to visit with the Eucharistic Blessed Sacrament. For, here the mystic is both in the actual presence of Christ existing sacramentally independent and transcendent to the mystic himself and the same Christ existing sacramentally and graciously within the interiority of his own soul.

St. John of the Cross entitled his mystagogical treatise the *Dark Night of the Soul.* It would have been better entitled the "dark night of the self." The subjective egocentric psychosomatic willful selfhood presented in this commentary was neither known nor expounded in the 16th century in which St. John lived. While St. John's mystagogical treatise enters into this personalized psychosomatic egological subjectivity and describes its mystical contour with remarkable nuance and clarity, he does so without explicitly speaking of such an egological psychosomatic personality. He does so exclusively within the context of the human soul. This soulful context is very fortuitous to the mystical life. For, while the mystical life of the Catholic Orthodox Christian occurs largely within the subjectivity of his own mortal and de/materialized personality and willful psychosomatic selfhood, it is actually rooted and based within the objectivity and interiority of his own personal spiritual and immortal soul. The soul is the seat and chair of the mystical life because it is the soul which harbors intellectually the supernatural gift of faith which is the cornerstone of the mystical life.

It is the soul that is immortal and immaterially spiritual. The human person's egocentric psychosomatic willful selfhood is merely experientially and de/materialistically spiritualistic. It is such by harboring mentally willfully manageable non-tactual phantom notions in its psychic dimensionality and by harboring bodily willfully manipulable tactual sensational imagery in its somatic counterpart. Both of these psychosomatic dichotomous parts are mortal and even self-alienable during the course of a person's lifetime prior to his physical death.

It is to be noted that the theological virtue and gift of faith is the anchor and mainstay of the mystical life both in its pilgrimage to surmount the purgative throes of the "dark night" and in its quest to gain the summit of Mount Carmel and repose in perfect unitive communion with the Blessed Trinity. Faith is incomplete without the theological virtues of hope and charity. Faith itself is a voluntary obedient intellectual belief (i.e., trust) in an indefectible authority worthy of such trust. It is entirely objective and transsubjective. Hope partakes subjectively and confidently in this faith. It is a volitional trust-bound convinced and confident sacrificial self-service to the indomitability and invincibility of this trustworthy authority (viz., God). Charity is a faith-filled and faithful volunteer amicable trusteeship testifying to the unfailing steadfast integrity of this trustworthy authority.

The basic difference between the *Ascent* and the *Dark Night* is the difference in the agent who oversees and conducts the mystic's program of kenotic self-abnegation and self-renunciation. In the *Ascent* the mystic is in charge of his own ascetic program of self-denial. In the *Dark Night* it is the Holy Spirit who takes over this charge. In the *Ascent* the mystic's activity is incipiently oriented toward God anticipating contemplative prayer whereas in the *Dark Night* this orientation becomes increasingly more intense with the increased intensification of the mystic's engagement in a thorough-going "dying to self" preliminary to "rising to God" as the climax of the Paschal Mystery. The mystic through contemplative prayer becomes not only supernaturally and sacramentally in the ontological order of existence

514

wedded to God because God has in His Trinitarian Personhood sacramentally first wedded Himself to the mystic's human nature, there also follows in the subjective phenomenological order of the human person's psychosomatic self-cultivated selfhood the culmination of this wedding with the mystic's own metamorphic mystical experience of this wedding. The major obstacle to this mystical metamorphic experience is the selfhood's very own self-centered resistant self that must become a self-surrendered selfless non-resistancy. This is precisely what the *Dark Night* addresses in examining the self's self-sustained resistancy to God's gracious gratuitous Personal embrace of the mystic in every crevice of the mystic's natural human constitution and cultivated self-humanized personality.

Without further to-do, the actual mystagogical text of our San Juanistic Carmelite spirituality will be addressed in the next segment of this commentary.

THE DARK NIGHT Book I, Chapters. 1-14. OVERVIEW: A TREATISE ON THE PASSIVE NIGHT OF THE SENSES.

It is typical of our Carmelite mystical doctor to provide both an esthetic poetic delineation of the mystic's religious experience and a subsequent prosaic account in non-poetic terms explaining the meaning of the mystical poem and its poetic metaphors. The advantage of this approach is formidable. The poetic rendition of the mystical experience provides the affective savor and subjective personalized experiential orientation of the mystic's religious encounter with God while the more prosaic account of this poetry supplies a more analytical sober objective explanation of the same mystical experience. This dialogue between the poetic and prosaic allows our SanJuanistic mystagogical treatises to capture both the personalized flavor of the mystical life's affective subjectivity simultaneously while understanding objectively and prosaically the very morphology of the mystic's dynamic objective human nature and subjective personality sublimated to a divine Trinitarian supernatural sacramental embrace. In this dialogical manner St. John encompasses both the ontological objectivity proper to dogmatic and moral theology and the phenomenological subjectivity proper to mystical theology itself.

In explaining the first verse of this poem beginning with the words, "One dark night," St. John tersely states what the entire ordeal of the "dark night" entails. It is a passage of painful, harsh, and agonizing prolonged psychosomatic mortifications beginning with the mystic's predominant religious selfish self-love and ending with his amorous religious selfless love of God that is both divine and sweet. This mystical passage from the mystic's preoccupation with his own selfish religiosity to his complete selfless absorption in God transpires within the womb of his prayer-centered life; namely, contemplative prayer which has its seat in the soul's supernatural intelligent freedom. Throughout this ordeal of dying to self and rising to God, the mystic prayerfully encounters and enters through contemplative prayer into the Triune family of God's own Godhead within the nebulosity and obscurity of supernatural faith.

Further, this contemplative prayer is entirely passive. For, it is not the mystic himself at this stage of his ascent to Mount Carmel who is taking the initiative to ascetically and sacrificially mortify his own sensuality and mentality. Rather, it is the Holy Spirit that is taking the initiative to withhold from the mystic special delightful and supernal mystical ingratiating experiences to which the mystic has become accustomed throughout his meditative prayer-life. When the mystic successfully passes through this mortifying ordeal, he will find that he has reached a mystical climax in which he has, through God's mortifying initiative in his life, vanquished to some degree the three enemies of every Christian who seeks to become conformed to Christ: the devil, the world, and the flesh. This first phase of the dark night, the senses, is more focused on the mystic's sensuality and flesh together with the mystic's considerable suffering and anguish in being deprived of and purified in regard to his own religious sensuality (i.e., religious sensitized emotional feelings of self-contented comfort or self-malcontented discomfiture).

Chapter1: The addictions of those who are prayerfully entering into contemplative prayer.

These spiritual addictions are found in mystics who are well along in the practice of meditative prayer. This is the prayer which is typical of the recitation of the rosary involving imagery and sensitized feelings. In this meditative prayer the mystic recites by rote the specific prayers attached to the rosary beads while actually focusing on the specified mysteries of Christ's life, death, and resurrection as they are pertinent to His own mother, Mary, and her maternal cooperative role in His messianic mission. The religious impact of such prayerful meditation is that the mystic incites and arouses within himself and his own religious emotional sensitized feelings and sensuality the very same intensive empathy toward Christ that His own Blessed Mother would herself have entertained. This sensuous empathic religious feeling is aroused by the mystic's entertainment of personalized imaginary sensational episodes of the major events in Christ's life. This religious prayerful meditative empathy encourages the mystic to substitute his own self in the place of Christ and His Blessed Mother throughout the major events of Christ's messianic mission. In this manner the mystic is spurred on to imitate and emulate Christ and Mary's own religious feelings in specific Gospel events which he sensationally and sensitively pictures to himself in his own imagination. Another important meditative prayer is the traditional 14 "stations of the cross."

During this initial stage of the mystic's meditative prayer life, the mystic enjoys many sensuously exultant and exuberant religious encounters with Christ and through Christ with Christ's Heavenly Father, on the one hand, and Christ's Holy Spirit, on the other. The mystic is prayerfully enveloped in the Blessed Trinity. God-the-Father remains infinitely above and beyond the mystic in heaven's timeless eternity; God-the-Son in His profound humility incarnated in the resurrected human flesh of His Eucharistic sacramental presence remains infinitely below and humbly beneath the mystic; and God-the-Holy-Spirit remains infinitely within the vicissitudes of the mystic's own objective soul and innermost inner intimacy and subjectivity. During the initial phase of the mystic's absorption with God through meditative prayer, he is religiously comforted, soothed, elated, and enamored with God's Trinitarian benediction and by God's own effusive sublime touches. This initial phase of the mystic's meditative prayer-life is that of the honeymoon in which God caresses the mystic with pious sensuous endearing stimulating feelings inciting, in turn, the mystic to affectionately love and adore God with deep intense emotional fervor and zeal.

During this period the mystic finds all the ascetic practices of self-abnegation, mortification, solitary prayer, dutiful obedience, etc., to be both easy and welcome. What the mystic cannot appreciate, however, is that he is still very much at the sophomoric level of divine love. For, he still is encumbered with a selfishly self-centered religiosity of which he is not aware. He will become painfully and severely aware of this religious selfish self-attachment to his pious sensual delights when he begins to experience being weaned from his own customary religious gratifying experiences. This occurs by the Holy Spirit's direct intervention in his prayer-life when the mystic is denied any further religious exuberant sensuous gratifications and satiations. This onset of experiencing no further stimulating emotional religious feelings is an unwelcome novelty in the mystic's prayer-life, especially when he has to continue meditatively to sensationally, dramatically, and prayerfully image to himself Gospel scenarios which previously evoked and elicited distinctive strong sensuous emotional religious resonances in himself. Without these pious emotional resonances, he is no longer stimulated and prompted to prolong his prayer periods and to become actively engaged in works of mercy.

St. John in a very masterful manner, befitting his life-long priestly office as a confessor to penitents, especially to cloistered Carmelite nuns and friars, expounds and examines the many selfishly self-centered addictions with which every mystic is beset at the outset of his pilgrimage to God up the summit of Mount Carmel. He masterfully capitulates all of these selfish self-centered faults under seven cardinal faults. These are the seven hinges on which all self-centered selfish religious motivations gravitate. It is very important to appreciate that these seven self-centered selfish life-style faults come to the mystic's attention explicitly when the mystic is prayerfully engaged

518

with God. They largely focus on the mystic's sensuous emotional bodily feelings of religious self-contentment or his impassive emotionless mental bearings of religious self-containment toward God which are elicited when the mystic is engaged in prayerful meditative amorous attention to God with whom he knows by faith that he is in sacramental communion. Hence, it is not just God his Creator infinitely above in heaven with whom he is prayerfully communing. It is with God's family Triune Godhead by whom he is intimately sacramentally enveloped that he is prayerfully communing in his meditative orisons.

In this initial stage of the Catholic mystic's meditative prayer-life, he is dutifully practicing moral virtues compatible with the ten commandments and the Church's teaching. He is also able to easily remember his prayerful mystic experiences and to recall them to mind not merely in order to verify that they really happened, but to relish them anew in the religious enjoyment which they afforded him in the first place and even to anticipate that they will recur again in further moments of prayerful communing with God. Indeed, the mystic at this initial meditative phase of his prayer-life is almost securely self-assured that these marvelous and comforting religious experiences will inevitably be forthcoming whenever he opens himself to prayer. In vernacular terms, the mystic is self-assured that he is hooked on God. To make it eminently clear that at this stage of the mystic's prayerful attachment to God, this attachment itself is more a selfish self-attachment to the mystic's own religious experiences of God, St. John proceeds in the following chapters to enumerate and to examine in some detail the seven religious faulty selfish self-attachments (i.e., addictions) to which the mystic is prone. These addictive self-attachments occur in the mystic who has become somewhat proficient in meditative prayer.

These are pride, covetousness, lust, anger, gluttony, envy, and sloth. This commentary will not explore in depth and detail St. John's own masterful examination and analysis of these capital religious selfish self-attachments. It is much better for the reader of this commentary to peruse for himself this masterful account of our Carmelite mystagogue. However, a few observations regarding these selfish faults are in place.

All of these capital selfish self-serving addictions are named vices in the English translation of our text. But, again, they are not strictly speaking immoral vices opposed to moral virtues. Virtues and vices are qualities of the soul's intellectual volition not of the self-hood's mindful self-serving willfulness. Virtues and vices are habits which fortify or weaken the intellectual will's own volition to will what is conscionably morally uprightly noble or unconscionably downright immorally ignoble. Both moral virtues and immoral vices engage what are conscionably purposefully reasonable or unreasonable activities to be intentionally willed and to be done or not to be willed and not to be done.

These capital addictions being propounded by St. John are rooted in the selfhood's volitional mindful have-more attitudinal mindset regarding its own self-control of its bodily and mental affections in the service of its own paramount willful selfish self-serving interest. They are more an issue of cultivating and controlling skills or the failure of cultivating and controlling skills rather than developing moral habits. Moral habits are developed by disciplined conduct based on intelligible reasons conscionably and objectively directing the person's soulful will and freedom of choice. Skills are cultivated through training in artful functions that facilitate the acquisition of what supplementally offsets a person's social ineptitude. Skills are dys/functional techniques of accomplishing what the selfhood's self-serving will needs to supplementally fulfill its own paramount autonomy to which it is decisively committed.

Such skills and training required here by the mystic to overcome these seven capital selfish addictions are those which facilitate the mystic's willful self-mortification and sacrificial self-abnegation of his own self-centered selfish willful self-attachments framed within a selfish humanistic have-more attitudinal mindset. They are counter-cultural skills inasmuch as they engage the mystic in deliberately, willfully, and sacrificially ignoring and even repressing everything which is not germane to his own overriding interest in pursuing Christ's messianic mission in achieving Gospel holiness to which he is self-committed and consecrated.

Quite apart from any supernatural and superhumanistic engagement, the person who is committed to becoming outstanding in any special career field of endeavor must selfishly mortify and repress his interest and engagement in actions and pursuits that are only tangential to his success in attaining the fulfillment of his overriding dominant career interest be this in the field of sports, education, politics, banking, acting, business, social service, etc.. The mystic's life pursuit is not a self-imposed career but objectively a supernatural calling to Gospel holiness and subjectively a superhumanistic mission (i.e., sending) by Christ to participate in the world's redemption as a member of Christ's Sacramental Church.

Such skills in the case of the mystic attaining to Gospel holiness and the messianic mission of evangelizing the world, address the seven capital spiritual addictions and pitfalls which involve the mystic's prayerful and merciful selfless self-service rendered to others in behalf of God. Do the mystic's willful actions render service to God and others moreso than to the mystic himself who engages in them? That is, are these actions with their underlying motivation such that they advance God's glory and sincerely render salvific service to both the mystic himself and his neighbor or are they such as to advance the personalized aggrandizement of the mystic's own selfish self-centered religious zeal and piety?

In the case of these capital willful addictions these skills are functional inasmuch as they successfully and sacrificially inculcate bodily and mental self-control in suppressing all selfish self-serving motivations that detract from the mystic processively fulfilling and achieving his overriding commitment to the Blessed Trinity in prayerfully living out the Gospel's life-style of holiness in the manner manifested by Jesus Christ Himself. These seven capital selfish addictions if left unchecked are culturally selfish self-serving functional impediments to the mystic's discipleship of Christ ingrained within the mystic's very own partisan have-more humanistic selfish attitude resulting from Adam & Eve's fall from grace.

These sevenfold capital addictions are rooted in the mystic's subjective self-serving willful overriding dominant have-more attitudinal humanistic mindset regarding what is of paramount interest to advancing and safeguarding his own personalized autonomous social security in the horizontal reach of his own body's deficiency and historical mortality. There are two humanistic antipodal attitudinal mindsets to be considered here: the have and the have-not attitudinal mindsets. The have attitude is a completely selfish self-centered partisan competitive attitudinal mindset. The have-not is a less selfish but still selfish self-centered partisan and competitive attitudinal mindset. Both the have and the have-not antipodal mindsets are entirely humanistic since they both have a selfish built-in partisan bias proper to each.

A country declares war on another country. The citizen who patriotically volunteers to fight militarily thereby sacrificially risking his life in defense of his country has a less selfish have-not attitude regarding his own mortal personalized social security. It is a have-not mindset regarding the value of his own life vis-à-vis his country's autonomous security. He does not esteem or value his own life above his country's social security and is willing to sacrifice is own life to defend his country's autonomy. The citizen who opposes the war and refuses to volunteer to serve militarily in its defense values his own life's mortal social security above that of his country. In this instance he exercises a selfish have attitude regarding his own autonomous livelihood and personalized social security vis-à-vis that of his country's autonomy.

Both of these have/have-not humanistic attitudes are ambiguously selfish. Whereas the patriotic volunteer does less selfishly place his own personalistic life in jeopardy in defense of his country, he does have hope and confidence that he will be able to sufficiently and selfishly protect his mortal self in battle from certain death. Even failing in this, he has hope of defending his country's autonomy and independence. That is, he is not totally selfish. The citizen who very selfishly balks at volunteering esteems his own personalistic autonomous self security as having more importance than the security of his country's social autonomy. The volunteer is less selfish but still selfish to some degree in seeking to safeguard his own life. Furthermore, his ambiguous selfishness is manifest in the partisan interest he has vested in the autonomy of his own country over and above the autonomy of countries threatening his own country.

The Catholic Christian attitude, on the other hand, is neither a humanistic have nor a have-not attitude. It is a be-attitudinal mindset. It is an overriding attitude that esteems and deems that the hierarchical immortal order of being takes fundamental precedence over the supplemental historical mortal order of having. In other words, the be-attitude Christian mindset is privatively and sacrificially an unbiased and noncompetitive selfless humanistic have-not attitude inasmuch as it is completely unselfishly opposed to the previous two antipodal humanistic attitudes which are both in some measure selfishly and self-centeredly still operative within the horizontal historical order of the body's mortality. It is a be-attitudinal mindset precisely because it selflessly sacrifices the horizontal order itself and the human person's personalized mortal subjectivity and selfhood in deference to the vertical hierarchical order's immortal primacy.

Certainly, this is a superhumanistic heroic attitude of utter willful self-centered selflessness. The difference between this be-attitudinal outlook and outreach and that of the have-not less selfish humanistic attitude of the patriot is that the latter still relies on his own self to achieve his self-fulfilled social security within the mortal historical reach of the horizontal order itself while the former relies only on God for his own immortal self-fulfillment within the hierarchical order transcendent to the historical order itself. Of course, it goes without saying that the be-attitudinal mindset can only be heroically self-fulfilled in the hierarchical order by God's initiative above and beyond the mystic's own puny resourcefulness. In other words, it is a heroic superhumanistic and superhumane attitude that transcends the mystic's willfulness and subjective personality.

Certainly, the volunteer patriot who places his own life at risk to defend his country militarily may be both patriotically selfish in a partisan humanistic sense and superhumanistically heroically selfless in a Christian non-partisan sense if he freely sacrifices his life in battle to defend and protect his country and his fellow soldiers and countrymen. What is being emphasized here is that such a total selfless self-sacrifice is not possible on a merely humanistic level; it is superhumanistically enacted only with the supernatural grace of God. Such a sacrifice is tantamount to the Gospel's declaration that there is no greater love than to give one's life for one's neighbor. Of course, in the case of Christ's very own sacrifice, His selflessness is animated by the Holy Spirit vibrantly alive in His redemptive messianic mission.

In sum, the seven capital addictions are serious impediments to the mystic's ascetic Gospel prayer-life and life-style of self-abnegation and holiness. This training program of self-abnegation and mortification is not directed objectively, reasonably, and conscionably in the same way that the moral virtues are reasonably governed. It is, indeed, an irrational program in the same sense that Christ's cross of crucifixion is unreasonable. Keeping the commandments entails no sacrifice objectively speaking. To eat sparingly rather than as a glutton requires no sacrifice objectively in the sense that eating healthily to be well nourished does not require that one stop eating permanently or even that one interrupt one's eating for an extended period of time.

On the other hand, arriving at a proper moral and virtuous diet (viz., eating temperately) and maintaining it does require and demand subjectively that a person deliberately, willfully, and sacrificially curtail and/or suppress his self-serving sensitized feelings and craving for sensuous gustatory self-contentments. Otherwise, his selfhood's willful self-serving self-attachment (i.e., sensuous addiction) to such satiating delectable gustatory pleasure will inhibit his eating temperately, reasonably, and virtuously.

While it is irrational for the ascetic mystic to deliberately deny himself what is gustatorially enjoyable regarding food, such an abstention is supplementally conditionally requisite to enable the same mystic to objectively practice eating temperately and virtuously. What is the case for eating is also the case for the other three moral virtues of courage, prudence, and justice. The seven capital addictions are remotely geared to supplementally facilitating subjectively the objective practice of the moral virtues. Proximately, they are geared to diminishing the human person's willful self-serving selfhood's proneness to selfishness and loss of self-control. The human person pursuant to original sin is willfully and subjectively prone to selfishness which is ingrained in his overall dominant attitudinal humanistic mindset which esteems and cherishes what is deemed to be of paramount partisan self-interest and value in advancing and securing his own mortal psychosomatic self-contentment and self-containment; that is, his self-fulfilled social security.

This self-centered selfishness becomes explicitly problematic to the Catholic Christian mystic who seeks to live the Gospel life-style explicitated and articulated publicly in a formal liturgy and privately in an informal paraliturgical prayer-life. It is this very psychosomatic willful addictive selfishness which is targeted by these seven capital faults. These addictions single out and magnify the different ways that the mystic's egocentric selfhood may both indulge and become willfully self-attached (i.e., addicted) to its own spiritual and self-righteous selfishness. The Gospel antidote to this selfish self-centered self-righteous addiction is for the mystic to become converted from a mere humanistic have-more attitudinal mindset to Christ's very own superhumanistic be-attitudinal messianic mindset. The rationale for this is that the fundamental order of being-more is fundamentally prior to the supplemental order of having-more. Being more in the immortal fundamental order of existence is ultimately more blessed than having more in the mortal supplemental order of resistance.

Accordingly, these seven capital addictions promoting one's willful partisan and self-alienating self-righteous selfishness are triggered by a humanistic have-more attitudinal mindset. This have-more attitude begets an egoistic "me-me-me" competitive syndrome. To countermand this partisan competitive humanistic mindset a complete conversion and total metanoetic superhumanistic surrender to Christ's own be-attitudinal messianic and self-kenotic mindset is necessary. Putting on the "mind of Christ" is nothing less than subjectively within one's egological selfhood's willfulness living an ascetic Gospel prayer life-style of self-denial and sacrificial self-abnegation. In doing so, the mystic will confront explicitly these seven deadly spiritual addictions typical of a worldly-minded mindset and will contend with them forcibly and willfully to overcome and suppress them.

In the final analysis, the mystic will discover that he cannot completely accomplish this on his own; he has not within his own human-

istic morale and fortitude the wherewithal and stamina to successfully and efficaciously heroically countermand his own have/more
attitudinal partisan selfishness and self-interest. This can only be
achieved superhumanistically, supernaturally, and miraculously
through God's own sacramental graciousness. What is impossible to
man is possible to God. While the mystic is totally committed and
sacrificially self-surrendered to remaining loyal to Christ's messianic
mission and mindset, he is fully aware that he must frequently have
recourse to the sacrament of reconciliation to overcome his failures
and shortcoming in living up to his consecrated commitment to follow Christ.

What is the heroic measure or standard of self-denial required by
this ascetic Christian program of sacrificial self-abnegation and mortification? It is unlimited. Why so? Because the protagonist of this program is God's very own infinite holiness which in the divine Person
of Jesus Christ's own self-humanized Personality is manifested to be
utterly and totally selfless in His sacrificial kenotic self-abnegation
made manifest in the humility of His passion, crucifixion, and martyrdom. St. John of the Cross recognizes this and emphasizes this by insisting that the mystic is to prefer nothing nada in the place of Christ'-
s total selflessness in advancing and serving God's own glory. This
excludes every vestige of selfishness in the service that the mystic
seeks to render to God in his own ascetic Gospel life-style and prayer-
life.

It must be further noted that in the vertical hierarchical order of
existence all of the person's natural and supernatural activities are operationally non-productive and, hence, non-industrious activities. The
cognitive act of seeing does not make or produce the object of its vision. Similarly with every other cognitive activity whether it is sentient
or intelligent. The appetitive activity of eating does not make or produce the object of its consumption (viz., the body's well-being). The
immediate intransitive beneficiary of the act of eating is the body's
sustenance and growth. Similarly with every other appetitive activity
whether sentient or intelligent (viz., the soul's intellectual will).

On the other hand, the selfhood's activities are all functionally
productive and at the service of the selfhood's self-centered usage

and self-fulfilled mental vindication and bodily satisfaction in over-coming the self's own social deficiencies. Thus, when the selfhood's psychic mental self has a notional ideation of a wheel, this notion remains vain and idle unless further successfully deployed, fabricated, and put to use. The same holds for the selfhood's somatic willfulness whenever it functionally wills its own self-serving self-fulfilling self-satisfactory bodily ease and self-contented mobility by means of a wheel, it must fabricate such a wheel and put it to successful usage. These mindful volitions are always dys/functionally, productively, and transitively usefully serviceable in carrying out the selfhood's own self-fulfillment. Otherwise, such self-serving volitions remain merely wishful, inefficacious, and futile.

The upshot of the preceding paragraph is that the human person's selfhood is paramountly selfishly self-centered in pursuing its own autonomy and social self-sufficient self-fulfillment. This selfishness is confined to the horizontal and historical order of the human person's subjective personality; it is not a trait of the human person's objective sovereign personhood. This selfishness is rooted in the rebellious fall of Adam and Eve from the original graciousness of God's Goodness in which they were created. As a result of this fall, every human person with the exception of Christ and His Blessed Mother is subjectively prone to seek its self-centered willful self-fulfillment by dint of its own prowess in conjunction with selves other than its own self. This selfishness is self-alienating in that it engages in a humanistic have/have-not attitudinal competitive contention.

The two prototypical antipodal have/have-not-attitudinal ideological mindsets are that of the idealist/pessimist and the realist/optimist. The former is a negative introverted rationalist mindset while the latter is an extroverted empirical positive one. In view of a container that is half empty and half full, the former's attitude is to evaluate the container in terms of its half-empty lack of content and the latter's attitude is to esteem the container in terms of its half-full content. The former attitude is negative in that emptiness is precisely and rationally the absence and lack of whatever is the container's content without even having have to specify what the contents may happen to be. The latter attitude is positive but imprecise in that the contents themselves are subject to empirical inspection and need not be precisely what one esteems them to be.

If the human person's selfhood is addressed merely subjectively, ideologically, and phenomenologically as though such a selfhood had its own autonomy apart from the human person's own personhood, the antipodal tension between the idealist and the realist remains a contentious self-alienating insoluble deadlock even if one adopts the have-attitude of the neutralist that combines the antipodal attitudes into one dichotomous attitude. The short-coming of these have/have-not paramount humanistic attitudes is that they of themselves preclude the human person's self-fulfillment in the ontological hierarchical immortal order of the human person's actual existence beyond the historical order of his personality's resistance and mortality in a world of his own cultural fabrication and self-humanization.

The solution and resolution of this ideological impasse and futility is the attitudinal mindset introduced by Christ and held open to His disciples. This is the be-attitudinal mindset that finds the human person's integral and total self-fulfillment in the objective hierarchical natural order of being beyond the subjective historical cultural order of having. Hence, the Church's documents and Gospel pronouncements of Vatican II sum up this difference by stating explicitly that being more is more than having more. Christ's messianic be-attitudinal mindset insists that the human person finds his immortal self-fulfillment in sacrificing his selfish selfhood and subjectivity by placing his self totally at the service of his immortal destiny in the hierarchical order of being and existence beyond his mortality and death in the historical order of having and resistance.

The upshot of the previous paragraph is that to live out the beatitudes which are enunciated in the Gospel, the mystic must not simply wishfully will to be "poor in spirit." The mystic must industriously, productively, and artificially cultivate (viz., train) himself in his subjective bodily and mental conduct to forcibly and restrictively curtail his own egological selfish self-serving willfulness regarding his own personalistic partisan mortal social security. The established Gospel way to insure that this is accomplished is for the mystic to commit himself to embracing the Gospel counsels of poverty, chastity, and obedience.

Here in the issue of these seven capital faults, the mystic encounters the paradox of all paradoxes. This is the prospect of becoming proud of one's very own religious humility (i.e., unselfishness). It is a paradox precisely because the conscientiously religious and pious person is one who is so not by his own personalized egological initiative but, moreso, by God's own divine gracious intervention. This paradoxical mystery requires that the mystic must repeatedly and never-endingly be attitudinally resigned, converted, and surrendered to praying for God's graciousness to arrive at his transhistorical immortal self-fulfillment beyond the pale of this life's historical mortality.

Hence, it is imperative and not merely dutifully commanded that the Christian ascetic mystic willfully, sacrificially, and kenotically repeatedly surrender himself metanoetically to the primacy and to the guidance of the Blessed Trinity under the tutelage of the Catholic Church's Magisterium. That is, it is imperative that the Christian mystic become daily repeatedly converted to Christ's own messianic Selfless mindset and to Christ's own messianic compassionate Selfless Sacred Heart. It is imperative that this conversion be not merely personal in the hierarchical order of obedience but personalistic in the historical order of sacrificial commitment. The mystic must forego his me-attitude and adopt Christ's be-attitude.

Chapter 2: How spiritual pride stunts and maims the mystic's prayer-life.

It investigates how pride maims and renders imperfect the mystic's best sincere religious endeavors and prayers. The stimulating sensuous emotional feelings of religious pious self-contentment and self-gratification are so vigorous in the mystic that his religious zeal and ardor for God is encouraged and he is prompted to actively engage in many religious activities which seemingly increase his dedication to and love of God and the Church. At the same time, he hasn't the slightest clue that his personalized religious motivations and eagerness to serve God and the Church are more selfishly self-centered and prompted than they are unselfishly edifying in God's sight. What the mystic overlooks is that his Gospel life-style and prayer-life afford him religious emotional sensuous religious emotional feelings fueling his prayer-life and religious service to others. It is not God that he is actually serving; rather, it is his own religious selfish self-contentment and aggrandizement that he is proudly advancing.

Chapter 3: How spiritual avarice and greed mar the mystic's prayer-life.

It investigates religious avarice or greed. The mystic can never have enough of religious contentment which is usually supplied by his greedy attachment to religious items, practices, and devotions. He is never fully religiously self-content and securely self-assured with the religious experiences that God gratuitously provides him. He is both infatuated and more secure in his attachment to the practices, the religious items, and the rituals themselves moreso than to God who is the very object of all such prayerful devotions and exercises.

Chapter 4: How lust detracts from the mystic's spiritual prayer-life and growth.

It investigates the experience of lust which becomes aroused in the novice during moments of his prayer-life. When the mystic is deeply engrossed in prayer he may find himself suddenly and unexpectedly visited with gross unsolicited sexual urgings. They may be induced simply by the mystic's unwitting sensuous proclivity to have his venereal needs satisfied along with the affluence of his religious sensuous stimulations. Or, again, they may be induced by the devil to bedevil the mystic during his prayerful moments of meditative recollection. Thirdly, they may be induced precisely because the mystic is fearful of having them occur. He may have such a very delicate and sensitive venereality that the simple prospect of having unwelcome and unexpected sexual urgings is itself sufficient provocation to have them happen. St. John also mentions other conditions which may prompt these unsolicited and unwelcome sensuous lustful urgings.

Chapter 5: How anger detracts from the mystic's prayer-life and growth.

Anger is another of these capital faults. Anger here is understood to be a peevishness and irritation centered precisely on the mystic's spiritual prayer-life. This peevishness more often occurs in the aftermath of the mystic's prayerful honeymoon with God. When it happens that the sweetness and delightfulness disappears and vanishes in his prayerful intercourse with God, he finds himself quite irritated with the loss of this religious stimulating enjoyment and self-contentment. With this disappearance he finds himself irritated with almost everything and everyone around him.

Chapter 6: Self-righteous gluttony is another debilitating fault.

The next capital fault examined is that of religious gluttony. Every mystical novice, St. John notes, falls prey to one or another of the different aspects of this imperfection. At the very outset of his prayer-life the mystic enjoys special experiences of divine exultation and jubilation. These are so infectiously delightful that the mystic becomes enamored with them. So much so is this the case that the mystic urgently has recourse to prayer to savor and revel in these ecstatically delightful religious encounters with God. He cultivates prayer more for a taste of these self-ingratiating prayerful experiences than for God who transcends these experiences themselves. Eventually the mystic will learn that he must sacrificially forego such delightful ecstatic prayerful experiences and remain steadfastly and prayerfully orientated toward God especially in the absence of such religious solace and comfort.

Chapter 7: Envy and sloth are two additional serious debilitating faults.

Here, St. John speaks of the sixth and seventh capital faults which are self-righteous envy and sloth. Religious envy occurs when the mystic feels diminished in observing a spiritual perfection or activity in his neighbor which he himself lacks. At some point when he finally cultivates the skill of sacrificial self-abnegation, he will with the cultivation of this skill have acquired through further conversion to Christ the proper beatitudinal mindset and empathic heart of Christ Himself and with this he will through charity have a selfless rather than a selfish regard and esteem toward his neighbor's spiritual perfection which may very well exceed his own.

The imperfection of sloth underscores, once again, the mystic's lack of ascetic self-control over his own somatic religious emotional feelings of discontentment. Rather than astutely and sacrificially pursuing his prayerful meditative communications with and commitment to God and his industrious activity in behalf of Holy Mother the Church and others, he becomes lax in these prayerful exercises and pursuits precisely because he no longer experiences any delightful and stimulating religious enjoyment of God in his mystical prayer--life.

Chapter 8: Rationale for the ordeal of the "dark night."

It is important to emphasize that the incentive which spurs on this mystical drama which St. John calls the "dark night" is nothing less than the mystic's advancement to contemplative prayer. Again, contemplative prayer is notably the prayer which transcends both the resources of the mystic's animal objective sentient nature and his self-cultivated self-humanized subjective somatic sensuality and sensitive emotional feelings. Indeed, the initial motive for this ordeal is to provide sufficient incentive for the mystic to put aside the meditative discursive prayer which elicits empathic feeling and sensuous religious zealous self-contentment. When the mystic's familiar religious zealous emotionally stimulated feelings cease and dry up, there is no further inducement for the mystic to persevere in his prayer-life.

The sweet and effusive dilation of his own religious sentiments no longer accompany his prayer life and ascetic practices. This is similar to the individual who has been eating and relishing a splendid fare for many weeks on end. When he is admitted to the hospital and is fed intravenously rather than orally, he experiences no gustatory delight in his nourishment. His desire to be further nourished in this manner is minimal. If this intravenous method of being nourished continues for some weeks or months without the benefit of eating any solid foods, the patient may eventually lose all appetite for food and even for life itself.

Now, the primary objective of prayer is to praise and give glory to God. Of course, there are ancillary objectives, especially to thank and petition God for his blessings as well as to intercede in behalf of the need of others other than one's own self. Hence, it behooves the mystic to pray to God not because he himself is emotionally infatuated with his own religious delight and effusive emotional elation and exulted feelings of self-contentment, but because he is obligated to render homage to the God to whom he owes his very existence, well-being, and ultimate happiness and holiness. This initial honeymoon phase of the mystic's prayerful "love affair" with God eventually dissipates and the mystic finds himself no longer able, even with his most strenuous self-solicited efforts of memory recalling past prayerful experiences and self-induced emotional religious feelings, recapture or sustain his prayerful fervor and zeal which have now subsided.

What has occurred here, as St. John explains, is a process of weaning in which the mystic is being deliberately denied by the explicit intervention of the Holy Spirit the religious emotional stimulations which he had been experiencing up to this time. With the disappearance of these effusively expansive religious sensuous delights, there vanishes the mystic's previous motivations and impetus to continue to be actively engaged in meditative prayer together with spiritual and corporeal works of mercy. Yet, the primary objective of meditative prayer to adore God and to undertake religious good works to serve God, linger in the mystic's commitment.

Hence, the only recourse for the mystic is to persevere in prayer and good works by a sheer deliberative willful decision to do so even though he finds no further religious motivational satisfaction and fervor in his prayerful meditations. This perseverance is nothing less than the mystic continuing his pilgrimage to God by beginning to traverse a religious terrain which is nothing less than an arid desert with no sapient provisions of water or food to sustain him nor any self-assured religious feelings that he is following the right direction to reach an upcoming oasis or, even more remotely, the desert's end. His will to continue now can only be one of sheer willfulness. There is no self-serving self-fulfilling motive to do so which can emotionally stir him or provide him with any religious sensuous solace or comfort. This characterizes the first ordeal through which the mystic must doggedly persevere. This is named the "dark night of the senses" by St. John of the Cross.

He states that it is a bitter and terrible ordeal. Yet, it is only the initial phase of this "dark night" and not the most harrowing and painful phase. This ordeal of the cessation of the mystic's sensitized sensual religious experiences is rather superficial compared with the ulterior ordeal which challenges the mystic's tranquilized cerebral intimate religious experiences. These are more penetrating and challenging because they reach to the very core and nucleus of the mystic's willful selfhood. St. John states that these more penetrating religious disturbances are "the dark night of the spirit." Of course, by "spirit" here St. John is not explicitly designating the soul's own inorganic spirituality. The soul's own objective intellectual and volitional operations transcend both the corporeal body's objective animal sentiency and the corpuscular body's self-humanized subjective sensuality (i.e., its physiology). The "spirit" here to which St. John addresses himself is the mystic's willful psychic mindfulness along with its inspirational notions and its intimate religious pious bearings of self-serving self-vindication.

More attention will be given to this second and more severely harrowing phase of the mystic's contemplative prayerful "dark night." For the moment, it suffices to indicate why this second phase is more frightfully harrowing and tormenting. This is because it enters into the innermost intimate intimacy of the selfhood's psychic religious devotional willfulness. The hallmark of this devout and consecrated religious willful mindfulness is its motivational impetus to attain and maintain an emotionless bearing (i.e., equanimity) of self-assured calm, tranquility, and serenity which typifies contemplative prayer. When this tranquility prevails, the mystic can spend extended periods in contemplative prayer without any willful inclination to engage in any other exercise. However, when this inner mental self-vindicated reverent religious calm is disturbed as is the case in the "dark night of the spirit" the mystic's very innermost inner willful self-assured religious serenity is not only assaulted but shattered. When this occurs, there is no further religious inducement or motivation to pursue and/or to persevere in contemplative prayer.

Here, in the "dark night of the spirit" the issue is no longer persevering in meditative prayer engaging the senses and the imagination. This has been transcended by the mystic when he has recourse to complete contemplative prayer when faced with the ordeal of the "dark night of the senses." The mystic forcibly retreats into his inner inmost intimate willful self to escape from the completely harrowing religious emotional aridity which he unwittingly endures and experiences from his previous habit of praying meditatively. This initial phase of the "dark night" is induced by the Holy Spirit, St. John explains, precisely to prompt the mystic to seek a higher form of inward intimate contemplative prayer beyond the ephemeral, phenomenal, sensational figures, forms, and the sensuality peculiar to the imagination, the focus of meditative prayer. Such prayer is less befitting and commensurate with the completely insensate spirituality of God's own absolute immutable, indivisible, spiritual nature. Hence, the mystic forcibly retreats into the inner unimaginative, emotionless, nonsensitized, and notional religious inspirations proper to the selfhood's psychic mindful willfulness.

This initial period of aridity is encountered by all mystic's who persevere in meditative prayer. Indeed, those novices who are most intensively engaged in meditative prayer will more quickly and more unexpectedly find themselves experiencing the cessation of all emotional feelings of religious self-satisfying elations. This is now not merely the result of the mystic's own self-induced ascetic practices of mortification and self-denial. This onset of religious aridity experienced during the mystic's periods of prayerful recollection unwittingly befalls the mystic in spite of his most resourceful attempts to overcome this emotional dryness. In other words, the active phase of the mystic's ascetic life where he deliberately strives to deny himself any selfish religious self-indulgence gives way to this passive phase in which the Holy Spirit takes the initiative to wean the mystic away from his accustomed comforting and comfortable stimulating emotional feelings of religious exhilaration and exultation.

There is an inescapable paradox which is endemic to this entirely subjective, phenomenological, and epistemological religious encounter with God. The more acutely the mystic religiously feels the presence of God, the less it is God that he actually encounters and the more it is his own self's subjective humanistic affective impressions of God that he is entertaining. Feelings awaken a person to the body's subjective somatic sensitivity and affectivity. They alert a person to the body's own subjective affective homeostasis not cognitively but conatively. In terms of the mystic's religious feelings regarding God, these feelings are apophatic in that they do not provide the mystic with knowledge of God directly but only indirectly in terms of what God is not rather than in terms of what God is.

Thus, the mystic relying on these religious feelings may apophatically declare that God is sweet and sweetness itself which is sweeter than honey. However, God is eminently spiritual and immaterial. It is otiose to compare Him to honey which is material and endowed with physical qualities such as sweetness. God is metaphysical and not endowed with physical qualities. It would be similarly the case were the mystic to declare that God based on these religious feelings is deemed to be a loving God. God's benevolent love is in no way an affective, sensuous, and sensitizing love. God's love and loveliness exceeds and transcends what is physical and tangible and material.

Such feelings are entirely deceptive and misleading. Paradoxically, they are not signs of God's presence to the mystic but, moreso, of God's absence. The more the mystic becomes willfully preoccupied with and self-attached to these motivational stimulating religious subjective somatic feelings of exhilaration and elation, the less attached he is to God that objectively transcends these feelings. The entire thrust of the "dark night of the senses" is to purify the mystic's self-attachment to these motivational religious feelings in order to allow the mystic to become attached to God objectively transcendent to and independent of these feelings themselves.

St. John of the Cross is emphatic in insisting that the cornerstone of the mystical life is the supernatural and theological gift of faith which is objectively seated in the soul's intelligence. The mystic's intellectual soulful entirely spiritual metaphysical approach to God is cognitive and entirely removed from the body's affectivity. Such intellectual cognitive knowledge is itself in no way susceptible to the sentient physical body's subjective self-humanized somatic affectivity. Such objective intellectual knowledge is not susceptible to the doubts and the incertitude that is peculiar to the human person's subjective psychosomatic personality's sensitized somatic perceptions and/or de-sensitized psychic conceptions.

The reader should readily appreciate that the transition from meditative to contemplative prayer is neither a smooth nor a simple one. It involves a complex process of advancing into contemplative prayer only to retreat back to meditative prayer. The difference between these two stages of prayer is a historical difference rather than one of stature. It is the difference between an acorn and an oak tree; the former is immature and the latter is mature. The process of maturing involves the acorn becoming a sprout, and a sapling before arriving at being a full-blown tree burgeoning with its own acorns. The case is similar for the mystic's prayer-life which is his life-line in communing with God's Triune Godhead.

It can never be sufficiently emphasized that contemplative prayer has its seat within the mystic's objective soul rather than within the mystic's subjective selfhood. Nonetheless, contemplative prayer engages the mystic's selfhood inasmuch as the mystic seeks to not merely to encounter God intellectually, metaphysically, objectively and personally as befits his dignity as a sovereign immortal person but also subjectively, personalistically, and religiously within the mortal subjective selfhood of his own psychosomatic personality and affectivity in companionship with selves other than his own self.

Chapter 9: Signs that the mystic is engaged in this ordeal of being purged of his self-serving religious pious emotional feelings and sensitivity.

The first evidence of this is the complete loss of every self-serving sensitized satisfaction, whether religiously devotional centered on God or profanely worldly centered on the things and functions of everyday life. This does not mean that the mystic is bereft of all emotional feelings. It means that he no longer finds any contentment and motivational emotional stimulation to be or to continue to be actively engaged in his accustomed daily functions and religious activities within which he usually finds considerable religious pious self-satisfaction and contentment and motivational enjoyment. Hence, his prayer-life at this point is more a matter of routine than a recharging of his religious resolve and intimate interpersonal association with God in whom and with whom he has been confiding his most precious feelings, aspirations, and enjoyments. The same holds true for his regular daily activities, functions, and duties. His lack of emotional motivation and zeal to be busy with these affairs, both religious and secular, leave the mystic listless and bereft of any spur to urge him on. This lackluster disposition persists and becomes prolonged quickly developing into a somber mood that engulfs the mystic as does the dreary overcast sky of winter engulf the landscape with a grey pall.

Yet, this prolonged listlessness alone is insufficient to establish that the mystic is genuinely in the throes of a religious glumness. For, St. John explains, the mystic may be suffering from a melancholy rooted in some deficiency of his physiological make-up. Hence, this symptom of prolonged moodiness must be accompanied by a second prevalent symptom. While the mystic is entrenched in this somber despondent dyspeptic mood he is mindful of his coolness and lack of religious fervor toward God and is most solicitous and concerned by this absence of devotion. He is convinced that he is no longer serving God diligently and astutely as he was before this lack of religious zeal and emotional fervor enveloped him. He finds it inexplicable that he no longer feels any sensitized sensuous motivationally exhilarating exultations in praying to and serving God in his busy religious and secular engagements. This second symptom confirms that it is not due to laxity or backsliding, nor to a melancholic propensity that he no longer has a religious zest for serving God and feeling tremendous pleasure in so doing.

St. John explains the reason for this religious emotionless gloom. It is because God, the Holy Spirit, is shifting the mystic's egocentric subjective awareness from his own bodily fanciful sensitized righteous feelings to his more mental intimate non-sensitized notional righteous bearings. In Gospel terms, the Holy Spirit is converting the mystic's prayer-life from focusing on external sensational religious activities to concentrating on internal mental inspirational religious prayerful musings. He is converting the mystic from a Martha busy actively engaged personality to a Mary idle contemplatively engaged personality. In terms of our present commentary, the Holy Spirit is shifting the mystic's egocentric righteous consciousness from focusing on his own subjective somatic righteous sensationally stimulating (i.e., stirring to action) sensitized emotional bodily excitations to concentrating on his own subjective psychic righteous sedating (i.e., calming to facilitate inactive musing) intimate emotionless mental prayerful inspirations.

When we recall that infused contemplation is first channeled objectively through the mystic's immortal spiritual soul which is naturally susceptible to intellectually and volitionally receive God's infinitely supernaturally spiritual gratuitous gift of His own supernal divine graciousness, it is the selfhood's subjective psychic willfulness which is more proportionately suitable (by reason of its desensitized non-tactile dematerialization) to experience emotionlessly within the hidden internal intimacy of its own psychicity the divine effulgent spill-over from the soul's reception of God's divine supernatural effusion. The mystic's prayerful inward mental emotionless calm inspirational devotional aspirations become increasingly more accentuated and prominent the more his outward sensational emotional religious exciting feelings subside and diminish. Of course, this means that the mystic becomes less consciously absorbed in his outward prayerful busy practices and imaginatively sensational focus of prayer. In the place of this conscious focus, he becomes more subconsciously (i.e., absent-mindedly) absorbed in his inward prayerful non-busy imperturbable practice of concentrating unimaginatively and conceptually on the very crux and nub (i.e., the gist) of the Gospel message Christ communicates to Holy Mother, the Church, and to her faithful members.

This transition from meditative prayer to contemplative prayer may be somewhat conveyed by attending to any one of the many parables which Christ preached. These parables are very imaginative and readily conjure up scenarios which are both fanciful and engaging to the point that the person who delves into them quickly inserts himself as a protagonist into the parable. Recreating imaginatively the scenario of the parable is the easy part. Interpreting the parable in terms of the paradigmatic Christian role-model which the parable depicts is more difficult.

This requires intuiting notionally the very gist of the parable which most people fail to grasp. Thus, the parable of the Good Samaritan depicts the disciple of Christ as a role-model neighbor to everyone he encounters. In this parable, the disciple of Christ is a stranger to no one. This intuitively grasped paradigm is not reducible to an imaginative figure in the tableau which Christ's parable conjures up. Rather, it engages the disciple not merely personally but, moreover, personalistically within the inner most intimate awareness of his own self-centered mindful willfulness as a self vis-à-vis every other self.

The difference between meditative and contemplative prayer in respect to this parable is rather stunning. In meditative prayer the mystic engages this parable as a scenic spectacle involving individuals that are extraneous to himself. He imagines this scenario and strives to recreate in his own imaginative fascination empathic feelings typical of the different actors alive in this scenario. In contemplative prayer the mystic no longer focuses on his visceral self and his endeavors to relive empathically the feelings and temperament of the principals delineated in the parable. He intuitively discerns himself intimately and mentally as the very role-model depicted in the parable. In this mental intuition the scenario is not longer made up of actors who are engaged in a spectacle which remains extrinsic to himself, the scenario engages his very own self as though he were a spook and a phantom living out each role-model represented in the parable. In this contemplative musing the parable becomes intrinsic to his own personality revealing the very core and pith of his own ethos.

St. John further explains that it is only when the mystic's religious sensationally (i.e., imaginatively) induced prayerful temperamntal empathic feelings are no longer excitingly engaging and favor-

ably influencing the mystic's life and activity that he will search elsewhere to be nurtured and religiously sustained by God in his devotional practices. In this search, the mystic within his subjective intimate psychic willfulness continues to experience an inner inward mental calm attentiveness and solicitude for God in spite of the utter
symptomatic disappearance of his former outward emotional zeal
and fervor. While the mental religious motivational inward inspirations no longer prompt the mystic to be busily engaged with his habitual outward religious functions, he may continue his prayer-life
and charitable services in a rather robotic manner sustained by his inner inward mental calm and continued commitment and resolution to
faithfully and loyally serve God. The mystic now is more inclined to
retreat quietly apart from everyone and become more mentally prayerfully self-composed and emotionlessly absorbed with God. What is
symptomatic of this prayerful seclusion is that the mystic is no longer
prone to focus on what is sensationally stimulating but to concentrate
on what is imperturbably and notionally devoid of all imaginary con-
fections.

The counsel that St. John has for the mystic when he finds himself in this relaxed, idle, quiet, prayerful composure bereft of all specialized and habitual imaginative Gospel scenarios and sensationally
stimulating empathic feelings...he counsels the mystic to sustain as
long as possible this disengaged mental prayerful absorption in God.
For, in the measure that the mystic is able to prolong and sustain
these periods of prayerful quietude in which his outward activity is
suspended and his very subjective inclination itself (i.e., his somatic
busy-willfulness) is inert, he will soon experience inwardly, intimately, and emotionlessly a profound imperturbable repose and
serenity smacking of God's very own eternal immutability. The mystic in this suspended stage is inwardly absorbed with prayerfully
musing, pondering, and concentrating on God intimately rather than
being focused on anything in Sacred Scripture which is specifically
delineated, pictured, visualized or sensitively imaged.

In this prayerfully concentrated trance the mystic is more mentally, mindfully, and willfully susceptible to inspirational suggestions.
The reason for this is that in this prayerful trance the mystic is not

preoccupied with anything configurationally (i.e., audiovisually and tactilely). Indeed, this is the very key to this prayerful contemplation. It is completely bereft of any special tactile sensational preoccupation peculiar to the self's imaginative configuration. Indeed, it is only when the mystic is able to successfully and mindfully retreat into this non-tactile, insensate, impassive mental framework that he is really able to attain to this prayerful contemplative quietude which St. John is describing.

Of course, the mystic's subjective psychic mindful willfulness is not itself completely impassive as is the case with the soul's intellect vis-à-vis its objects of knowledge which transcend it. The mystic' psychic willfulness is re-creatively active. This is the selfhood's mental genius to be inventively creative. Yet, in this superhumanistic prayerful trance of contemplative concentration the mystic is neither inventively preoccupied nor interested in any special metaphorical exemplification of God. The mystic is completely disposed to be amenable and quietly prayerfully and idly attentively concerned with God's metaphorical architectonic exemplarity. And in this inward mental trance-like attentiveness and caring composure the mystic is absorbed with God without any special imaginative focus of absorption. Indeed, it is the very hallmark of this contemplative prayer that it is obtuse and vague and devoid of any special mental notional or sublime conception. The mystic is more intent on mentally caressing and fondling God in a care-free absorption than in analyzing and becoming more learned regarding God's divine metaphorical characteristics.

At this phase of contemplative prayer, the mystic is more intent on his own self-centered immanent intimate care and concern for God than he is for God's characteristic metaphorical attributes imaginatively configured. Not only is the mystic no longer perplexed by his body's lackluster devotional aridity, this very lack of emotional bodily fervor facilitates the mystic's attentiveness to a mental prayerful intimate self-absorption with God. The mystic is comforted in his ability to sustain prolonged periods of inner mental calm, quietude, and serenity while intimately absorbed with God whom he willfully enfolds within the innermost intimacy and subjectivity of his own selfhood.

St. John emphasizes that the mystic's own inventive genius here is itself inactive and at rest. So much so is this the case that the mystic is unable on his own initiative to busy himself mentally with inventing different notional conceptions of God. None of these would be suitable nor befitting to God's own grandeur and ineffability. Hence, the mystic is quite stupidly and dumbly left helpless in this initial stage of contemplative prayer. If he tries to take charge of his own contemplative prayerful inactive subconscious caring attentiveness, it eludes him as would a balloon filled with air elude one's grasp the moment one would seek to collapse the balloon within his fist. However, if the mystic perseveres in this contemplative mode of idle caring care-free intimate absorption in God, he will eventually experience a very intimate, delicate, calm, solitary, justifying, impalpable impassive righteous vindicated mental serenity which is antipodal to his previous palpable sensitized emotionally stirring elated bodily righteous feelings.

It is absolutely vital and important here in properly grasping this initial onset of contemplative prayer as described by St. John to differentiate it from the "centering prayer" which is so commonplace today. Centering prayer as it is widely accepted today is a prayer that is trumpeted as being preliminary to contemplative prayer itself and, more often, confused with contemplative prayer itself. It is proposed as a preparation for the mystic to enter fully into contemplative prayer proper. This occurs when the mystic self-consciously (i.e., egocentrically self-consciously) empties his mind of all thoughts such that his mind becomes a mindless mind. Of course, this ascetic exercise does not free the mystic from a preoccupation with his own willfully mindful inventiveness to empty the mind of all notionality. Rather, it accentuates and activates the mystic's own willful inventiveness to accomplish this self-emptying task for himself and by himself. Such a willful mental posture is the exact opposite of what St. John is describing and urging. St. John insists that it is only when the mystic's mindset is completely idly and uninventively inert that it is conducive to engage in infused contemplative prayer.

Furthermore, the infused contemplative prayer which St. John is propounding (even in its initial phase) is not restricted to the mystic's subjective self-conscious egocentric private selfhood. Genuine contemplative prayer immanently experienced subjectively within the mystic's own private psychic willfulness occurs when the mystic is completely transcendently (i.e., transcendent to his own psychosomatic willful subjectivity) soulfully and intellectually and volitionally engaged publicly and sacramentally with God's infinite supremely superlative Graciousness. Indeed, paradoxically enough, when the mystic does actually subjectively experience within the imponderable depth of his own psychic willful intimacy the imperturbable religious tranquility afforded to him by infused contemplative prayer, he will not experience God as absolutely present to him. Rather, he will experience God as absolutely absent. This very profound religious intimate experience of God's immutable eternality motivationally awakens in the mystic a profound yearning, aching, and pining for God that becomes more intensively acute the more the mystic prayerfully experiences a religiously infused contemplative tranquility that defies every description which the mystic tries to apply to it.

There is still another consideration that differentiates the San-Juanistic presentation of contemplative prayer from the centering prayer that is currently in vogue. The person entering into centering prayer does so with much willful effort. On the other hand, the onset of contemplative prayer as expounded by St. John is not the offshoot of the mystic's effort but, rather, the offshoot of the loss of meditative prayer along with the emotional religious fervor and zeal it afforded the mystic. The seat of contemplative prayer proper to the Christian disciple is the person's intelligent soul and not the same person's subjective mental selfhood. Contemplative prayer includes the person's subjective selfhood supplementally by way of completion but not fundamentally by way of inception.

There is yet a third sign, offered by St. John, to authenticate the mystic's settlement and immersion in the throes of the "dark night of the senses." At this point in the mystic's pilgrimage to God, he can no longer successfully manage to resume his customary meditative prayer-style in which he empathically substitutes his putative empathic feelings of and for Christ, our Blessed mother, Mary, and other saints, for his own personalized feelings which he sensationally and imaginatively self-induces in his meditative style of praying the rosary, for example, the stations of the cross while empathically visualizing and imaginatively recreating fancifully Gospel scenes. No matter how diligently he tries to return to his former customary way of praying he cannot do so nor can he extract from such prayer anything of the beneficial religious fervent motivational feelings which he previously experienced. When this third sign is in place, it provides additional evidence that the mystic's inducement to advance to a more intimate style of contemplative prayer is in the offing and that his emotional malaise and vagrant moodiness is not due simply to some physiological malady and protracted emotional depression.

Chapter 10: Guidance for the mystic in the way he is to conduct himself while suffering through this complete loss of religious emotional feeling and self-contentment.

The most urgent difficulty for the mystic who finds himself bereft of all religious emotional feeling and self-contentment toward God (viz., Jesus' Sacred Heart) is that he becomes convinced that God has abandoned him and left him to his own devices. To overcome this, the mystic is most often resolved to renew with greater determination his commitment to meditative prayer in which he no longer finds any religiously sensitizing succor or contentment. Of course, at this point such prayer becomes merely a matter of rote and no longer remains a matter of devotion and zeal. What the uninformed mystic does not appreciate is that his loss of sensuous religious savor is a preliminary stage to his advancement to a higher form of contemplative prayer. St. John explains that the mystic's near frantic efforts to feverishly and steadfastly continue in this meditative prayer actually impedes his transition to contemplative prayer which leaves behind religious imaginative visualizations and other tactile religious stimulating impressions. As long as these mystics remain uninformed about the real purpose of this emotional aridity, he will continue doggedly with this rote prayer and experience something of a stalemate in his prayerful pilgrimage toward ultimate union with God.

The mystic who becomes properly informed of what is actually occurring---a needed transition from discursive meditation with its succession of religious sensational (i.e., imaginatively inventive) impressions to a more stable non-sensational inspirational intimate mode of prayer---is to be comforted and reassured that God has not abandoned him and that he is actually advancing in his prayer-life. This mystic is to persevere in his prayer-life by remaining patient and confident that God has not abandoned him and that he in due time will discover for himself a more prayerfully intimate access to God. In conjunction with this patient persevering resignation, the mystic must have the attitude that leaving aside his customary rote meditative prayer-style is the thing to do. He is to remain quietly resigned to his lack of religious fervor and to continue to pray by simply remaining idle and bereft of all thoughts, images, special prayer requests, and even oblivious to annoying distractions. "They must be content simply with a loving and peaceful attentiveness to God, and live without the concern, without the effort, and without the desire to taste or to feel Him."

Now, one might immediately construe that this is a SanJuanistic approval and promotion of what has been previously mentioned in this commentary as "centering prayer." This recommendation and counsel by St. John is not to be confused with "centering prayer." For, again, this method of prayer as described by the proponents who have fostered and advanced this mode of prayer involves an active willful effort to become detached from the body's influence on the part of the one who is praying. This is in direct contradiction to what St. John is advocating. To remain simply, attentively, and lovingly in the presence of God does not entail a willfully deliberative self-annihilation of all bodily activity. Neither does it entail the cessation of all mental activity. For, again, to engage in such a self-centered mental engagement is to strive to advance one's own willful self-centered self-control. On the other hand, St. John's mystagogical counsel to the mystic is to surrender to Christ and to surrender the will's self-control to Christ and not to strive more willfully and skillfully to retain a self-centered prayerful mind-control over one's own selfhood.

Since the very seat of contemplative prayer is the person's objective soulful intellectual absorption in the actual sacramental presence of the Blessed Trinity within the soul's interiority, this counsel of St. John toward the mystic to remain quietly and attentively in loving concern for God does not entail at this initial phase of contemplative prayer the mystic's total kenotic self-empting of the mind of all mental notions and distractions. Rather, it is a counsel urging the mystic to be insouciant toward the morbidity of the imagination and the body's lack of religious sensitized stimulation and feeling toward God.

It is almost inevitable that the mystic who strives to remain quietly, patiently, and lovingly in the presence of God will find himself afflicted with many distractions, concerns, and preoccupations with his daily affairs. St. John's counsel is not to be interpreted to mean that the mystic is to forcibly and deliberatively oust these from his field of conscious attentiveness. Were he to do this, he would allow his distractions to further distract him from lovingly attending to the reality of God's sacramental presence in his soul. This loving attentiveness is not without its distractions at this initial stage of the mystic's contemplative prayer-life. Hence, he very much must rely on the theological gift of faith (i.e., trusting in God-the-Father) and his theological gift of hope (i.e., prayerfully confiding in God-the-Son) and prayerfullyappealing to the Holy Spirit. By skillfully ignoring and patiently suffering all distractions, nagging concerns, towering unwelcome scruples, an overriding aura of wasting time, and his prolonged painful lack of religious fervor and zeal---by faithfully (i.e., in prayerful trust) and confidently (i.e., in prayerful hope) persistently and prayerfully attending to God's sacramental presence---the mystic will be "doing a great deal without activity on his part." That is, the mystic will be allowing himself to transit from discursive to contemplative prayer under God's (i.e. God-the-Holy-Spirit) divine influence precisely because he is relinquishing his own willful self-control and surrendering it to God.

Certainly, this initial contemplative phase of the mystic's prayer--life demands a self-abnegation and a willful self-denial of the mystic's own self-serving and selfish self-vested self-sustained righteous willfulness. Certainly, this self-abnegation is not entirely a passive engagement. It is extremely painful. It demands exertion and sustained willful skillful effort which cuts against the very grain of the mystic's willful resistant selfish selfhood and humanistic me-attitudinal mind-set which is inherited from original sin. But, here the mystic is not counseled by St. John to ascetically concentrate on his own training skills of self-denial which he has been habitually embracing. Further increased fasting from food and from mental activity is not what St. John is counseling here. Rather, he is encouraging the mystic to be resigned to the body's loss of sensitivity, religious emotional exhilaration, lack of devout feelings, and the near-total absence of reverent sensuous righteous self-contentment.

The mystic is now entering into the impassive mental phase of his advancement to intimate prayerful union with God. This does not mean that he has abandoned the ascetic training which he has been habitually practicing. What it means, is that now he is experiencing the unexpected and unwelcome rigors of being without the bodily motivational religious incentives which previously stirred him to prayer and to engage in the corporeal and spiritual works of mercy. The mystic is now entering into the mental phase of the purification "of the spirit" in which God (viz., the Holy Spirit) is assuming the initiative in the mystic's ascetic religious training. "If the mystic should desire to do something himself with his interior faculties, he would hinder and lose the goods which God engraves on his soul (i.e., his soul's subjective selfhood) through that peace and idleness."

It is the case that the mystic's prayer-life and Gospel life-style is maturing. His subjective conscious attentiveness is shifting from his sensuous bodily sensations, excitement, and sensitivity to the intimacy and placidity of his mental insensate and non-tactile notions and volitions. He would not be inclined to shift from the somaticity of the body's feelings and excitement to the intimacy of the mind's somnolent bearings if he did not suffer the complete loss and "drying up" of his body's religious sensitivity.

Chapter 11: God's fire of love is the mystic's prayerful reward after suffering through his purgative ordeal involving the loss of his religious sensuous zeal and fervor.

Here St. John explains in a very adroit and masterful way the onset of contemplative prayer replacing the prolonged loss and emptiness of being without meditative prayer. The mystic has been at this stage suffering for a long time the loss of any religious zeal and fervor for God. His prayer-life has been sustained by his objective trust in Christ's resurrection and his confident hope in Christ's crucifixion that he himself is indeed in his prayerful exercises and ascetic Gospel life-style really and truly united with Christ's very own Paschal Mystery celebrated at Mass. He has been experiencing the dullness of his own intelligence, the hopelessness of his own efforts and initiative, and the stupor of his own affectionate feelings for God. But, now, in his prayerful sustained quiet, idle, trustful, confident, and mentally attentive commitment to God he begins to experience a most dire religious yearning, longing, and aching for God which is the more intensively intimate because it is in no wise sensitively sensuous. In other words, it is not a superficial longing and pining which emanates from the body's own somaticity external to his inner mental selfhood. Rather, it is a most profound and deep-seated ache emanating from the very depth, pith, core, and marrow of his willful innermost intimate psychic selfhood.

Initially, this yearning is so slight and delicate that it seems hardly noticeable to the mystic. This may be because the sensuous religious somatic part of the mystic is not yet completely purged of its own craving for feeling and having its own bodily religious self-contentment. Progressively, this religious mental longing and aching for God becomes increasingly more acute until the mystic experiences such a prayerful righteous intimate home-sickness for God that he seems unable to attend to anything else even outside the periods of his prayerful mental musings.

However, before the mystic actually becomes ensconced in this contemplative prayer he finds himself in a no-man's land in which he is not yet settled into contemplative prayer and is no longer enjoying the vigor of religious zeal stimulated by his previous exercises of meditative prayer with its sensational Gospel scenarios accompanied by sensuous religious feelings of self-contentment and an eagerness to be actively bodily engaged in the corporeal works of mercy. The mystic has been patiently and steadfastly persevering in idle prayer in spite of this prolonged and seemingly interminable loss of all religious affectionate interest for God and devotion to him accompanied by all of the complications which arise from such a loss. Our Carmelite Holy Father explains that this prolonged trial patiently endured by the mystic has procured for him more blessings than he could possibly have anticipated. Not the least of these is the mystic's arrival and secure settlement into the exercise of contemplative prayer.

Chapter 12: The benefits brought about to the mystic through enduring this ordeal of the loss of sensuous zeal for God and for meditative prayer.

Characteristic of all of these benefits is the maturing of the mystic from a stage of religious adolescence to that of religious adulthood. In the first place the mystic is made aware of a more profound and intimate dimension in his own subjective selfhood as well as his genuine abject misery in the bowels of his body's somaticity. When the mystic was sensuously stimulated and eagerly religiously energized to become actively engaged in every kind of activity in serving the Church and others and fully prayerfully self-contented with the religious sensuous pious affection that he felt toward God, the mystic was completely ignorant of the utter insufficiency of his own religious bodily contentment. His prolonged prayerful suffering of the loss of this somatic religious self-gratification had made him realistically aware of the poverty and impotent insufficiency and unreliability of his own bodily selfhood.

This newly acquired self-awareness of his body's own unreliability and religious dejection is more precious to God than all of the mystic's active devout endeavors of the past. This is the case because these previous religious engagements were undertaken less for the selfless service of God's glory than for the mystic's own righteous selfish bodily self-gratification and self-contentment. The mystic was previously unaware of this. The purification and purging of his body's religious self-indulgence in its own selfish pious feelings and emotional glorifications has made the mystic aware of his craving for this emotionally self-righteous self-indulgence.

Another benefit is that the mystic is now prepared to prayerfully communicate with God more respectfully and courteously recognizing and reverencing God's august majesty. God is no longer a "buddy" to the mystic; someone who is there to grant his requests, to accommodate him, and to render him his prayerful favors. Hence, the mystic now becomes more conscious of the tremendous infinite chasm that separates his own self from the grandeur of Christ's own regal majestic omnipotent Selfless Selfhood. With the complete uprooting of the mystic's sensuous religious self-focused self-gratifications finally accomplished, the mystic's own soulful intelligence becomes increasingly more clairvoyant in beholding truth's intelligibility about God-the-Father's absolute transcendence and immeasurable infinitude above and beyond the mystic's own presumptuous false subjective prejudices and self-centered blinding assumptions.

The mystic becomes intellectually more acutely cognizant of his creaturely finite contingent existence compared with God's eternal eminent existence. Further, the mystic grows in spiritual humility toward God and towards his neighbor. That is, his self-righteous criticism of the faults and failings of his neighbor become less pronounced and less incessantly prominent in his own mind and way of thinking. Additionally, he becomes more submissive and obedient to God and the prudent counsel of others in his prayerful pilgrimage to perfect union with God.

Chapter 13: Other benefits of this "dark night of the senses."

Here St. John reviews the other seven deadly capital imperfections to which the mystical novice is susceptible in his own religious prayer-life. Suffering steadfastly through the numbing rigors of praying dutifully and respectfully to God in spite of a total and complete emotional apathy toward God and his prayerful exercise and lifestyle, the mystic is weaned from his own religious avarice consisting in his coveting special religious objects and his own personalized enjoyable prayer exercises and rituals. He becomes inured to engage in prayer in spite of his feeling of apathy and even antipathy toward prayer itself. He no longer experiences spiritual lust as a result of this loss of religious zeal. Further, he no longer experiences a ravenous need for religious sensuous exultations and an additional need to indulge himself in them. The mystic's somatic willful selfhood becomes purified from its concupiscent need for all sensuously stimulating bodily engagements whether secular and earthbound or sacred and heaven sent.

Quite apart from curing these capital deadly imperfections, the mystic's own memory entertains a memorial awareness of God triggered by a foreboding fear of departing from Him and backsliding in his prayer-life. Furthermore, he is now enabled to engage God in prayer humbly with a chastened spirit devoid of all the faults to which he was previously prone with his me-attitudinal mindset. He is now more securely converted to Christ's be-attitudinal messianic mindset. His prayer-life is now directed principally and primarily toward God and no longer motivated to advance his own religious-self-gratification and self-aggrandizement.

He now also lives his Gospel life fortified by the Holy Spirit's own indefatigable stamina rather than relying on his own failing and puny self-self-righteous determination. Inclusively, the mystic is now practicing the three supernatural theological virtues of faith, hope, and charity, as well as the supernatural cardinal moral virtues of prudence, religious justice, temperance, and courage. St. John sums up these benefits by citing Sacred Scripture, as he most frequently does throughout his writings. These benefits bring on the delight of peace, an habitual mindfulness of God, a solicitude for Him, a purity of heart, and the practice of virtue.

Returning to the remaining three cardinal faults of anger, envy, and sloth, St. John indicates that the mystic acquires through this strenuous religious bodily purgation the exact opposite emotional counterparts of these three faults. Spiritual anger gives way to meekness, spiritual envy to generosity, and spiritual sloth to tolerance. In addition to these previous benefits the mystic also at God's good pleasure receives at times unexpectedly and gratuitously spurts of religious sweetness, a refined love for God, and an awakened and enlightened intellectual acuity regarding God's august supreme divinity and attributes. Further the mystic acquires a liberty of spirit in which the twelve fruits of the Holy Spirit are experienced and enjoyed. He is also liberated from the grasp and influence of his enemies, the world, the flesh, and the devil.

Chapter 14: With the mortification of the mystic's sensuous religious willful needs, he is now able to advance to a full-blown infused contemplative prayer-life.

With the ordeal of the "dark night of the senses" behind him, the mystic is prepared to enter fully into the second and more advanced stage of the mystical life, that of contemplative infused prayer. Of course, this stage has its own harrowing and excruciatingly painful ordeal through which the mystic must navigate. The suffering endured by the mystic in undergoing the mortification of his religious sensuality will seem tame compared to the ordeal of the mystic's subsequent suffering through experiencing the complete tribulation and discombobulation of his religious self-maintained and self-contained mental equilibrium and equipoise.

Prior, however, to attaining to this consummate stage of contemplative prayer, the mystic in the process of enduring his religious sensuous bodily mortification must be prepared to endure terrible temptations and harrowing mental experiences. These are allowed by God because the mystic's advancement toward perfect union with God entails such further purifications. Sometimes Satan's evil spirit of fornication buffets the mystic with foul and lurid imagery which are a torment to the mystic. Another time an evil vertiginous spirit of scrupulosity assails the mystic. The terrible havoc and consternation that this evokes in the mystic defies description. These severe trials which rattle and strain the mystic's religious sensitivity are allowed because they serve as an inoculation. By introducing a virus into the body, the body itself reactively resists the virus to such an extent that it becomes immune to its baneful effects. Similarly, by introducing into the body these spiritually disheartening viruses, the body's religious sensitivity and emotivity become immune to the baneful effects of these viruses.

St. John concludes this treatise on the "dark night of the senses" by noting that no specific time-limit can be assigned to this period and phase of religious mortification. Nor are the different temptations, trials, and terrors uniformly experienced by every mystic. Mystics who have a considerable tolerance for suffering are severely and quickly chastised while others who do not have such an endurance experience a much longer period of chastisement. These latter mystics arrive at the contemplative stage of prayer much later in life. Further, these latter mystics do not experience this chastisement as one unremitting ordeal. Their very lack of resignation to this ordeal prolongs the ordeal itself. In the final analysis, St. John concludes, whether it is the case of the durable or the tentative mystic, each must suffer the ordeal of mortifying his religious sensitivity for an extended period of time to insure that its mortification is complete and sufficient to allow him to conclusively pass on to contemplative prayer.

THE DARK NIGHT. Book II Chapters 1-8 TREATISE ON THE PASSIVE NIGHT OF THE SPIRIT.

Chapter 1: The beginning and rationale for this purgation over and above the purgation of the mystic's righteous contented sensitivities.

It would be a serious mistake for the reader of this extended commentary to bypass our Carmelite Holy Father's treatise and to substitute this reflection in its place. This reflection is to be treated simply as a footnote to the original treatise. This segment of the *Dark Night* constitutes the very crux and pith and nub of the integral purgation of the mystic's own subjective egocentric willful selfish selfhood in his pursuit of becoming supernaturally transformed into Christ's very own superhumanized divinized Personality (which is not to be confused with His divine Person). His account of this is so masterful and rich in specific detail that it presents a rare insight into this hidden and very private personalized haven of the mystic's inmost intimate selfhood and avails the committed mystic to be thoroughly conversant with the underlying rationale of the severe and tormenting trials to which he will be subjected as he continues steadfastly to advance in contemplative prayer toward a perfect supernatural union and spiritual familiarity with God in God's Triune Godhead.

It is eminently clear from the text of our Carmelite Holy Father that any progressive advance toward perfect union with God is entirely at the behest and pleasure of the Holy Spirit's agency and not the mystic's own devices or initiative. The previous extended purgative episode involving the mortification of the mystic's somatic religious sensitivities is only a preliminary prelude to this "dark night of the spirit." Indeed, St. John points out that the mortification of the mystic's religious somatic sensitized selfish self-righteous self-gratification and self-contentment remains incomplete until and unless this further radical purification of his inmost inner psychic willful selfhood's own proper religious self-justification and self-vindication is itself, in turn, purified of its own selfish righteousness.

Indeed, after the initial mortification of the mystic's religious sensitivities is consummated the mystic is freed from his addiction to the religious stimulations to which he was previously a prisoner. He is now able to engage in contemplative prayer's psychic serene and tranquil amorous attentiveness to God above and beyond the interference of religious exuberant stirrings or lack of such stirrings in his somatic body's prolonged moods of forlorn feelings of despondency. This entirely ethereal contemplative intimate love for God is no longer suffused with the body's sensitivity and visceral affectivity. This sensuous emotional mode of amorous feeling has by now vanished and is replaced with a more subtle and intimate emotionless, and cerebral amorous placidity. Bodily emotional feelings of stirring sensitive religious exultation have given way to a reverent mental bearing (viz., composure) of emotionless intimate serenity.

Nonetheless, our Carmelite Holy Father is quick to add, the mystic is still not completely rid of the somatic body's sensuous religious needs and tension. Furthermore, it happens that the mystic suffers in brief spurts even more intense and acutely terrible trials of aridity and ennui within his body's somatic religious sensitivities before he becomes securely and skillfully advanced in the practice of contemplative prayer. When these periods of despondency occur they are presentiments of a prolonged purgation of the mystic's psychic inner inmost intimate willful selfish selfhood. Nevertheless, the severity and intensity of these trials and temptations affecting the mystic's emotional bodily feelings are no where near as terrible and tortuous as are the impending trials of his selfhood's selfish emotionless mental bearing.

Prior to the onset of this "dark night of the spirit" the mystic becomes somewhat secure in his habitual practice of contemplative prayer and during this period enjoys a copious and resplendent intimate interior sedate mental assurance of profound pious self-righteous justification. So resonant is this pious mental bearing of self-assurance that it sometimes redounds to the mystic's somatic counterpart to feel exuberant devout emotional exultations which are even more keenly felt in the aftermath of the body's prolonged religious aridity and lack of emotional stirring.

The upshot of these somatic exuberant religious delights is surprisingly enough the experience of severe stress within the body's physiology even to receiving fractures of the body's bones, infirmities, stomach disturbances, other debilities as well as a mental fatigue and weariness. Because of the somatic body's infirmity the mystic, St. John explains, cannot sustain for any prolonged length of time in his psychic religious willfulness the spiritual placid amorosity with which he has become familiar; at least, not the intensive placid amorosity proper to the ultimate stage of perfect communion with God to which the mystic aspires. Thus, it is not surprising that the mystic in this initial stage of contemplative prayer, prior to undergoing a complete mortification of his psychic religious self-centered selfish willfulness, finds himself susceptible to experiencing spurts of ecstatic emotional sensitized feelings along with the physiological disturbances that these incur. When the subsequent mortification of the selfhood's psychic religious willfulness is complete, these rapturous emotional offshoots of contemplative prayer will no longer occur. For, the mystic's mental willful selfhood will be liberated from the constraints and tensions peculiar to his body's somatic sensitivity.

In the psychosomatic make-up of the human person's willful selfhood there is a polar have/have-not tension between the mind's intimate inner bearing (i.e., composed and concentrated self-containment) and the body's sensitive outer feeling (i.e., sensuous self-contentment). When the human person is consciously absorbed with the body's outward sensitive feelings (i.e., likes and dislikes regarding what is bodily pleasant or unpleasant, comfortable or uncomfortable), he remains oblivious to the mind's inward intimate bearing (i.e., cares and concerns regarding what is of paramount important to its self-interest). And, vice versa, when the human person is consciously preoccupied with the mind's own inward intimate bearing (i.e., overriding cares and concerns), he in turn remains insouciant to the body's outward feelings and sensitivities. In the one case the visceral takes precedence over the cerebral whereas it is simply the reverse in the other case. Of course, in the profile of anyone's personality, it may be ascertained that a person is predominantly cerebrally introspective or viscerally extrospective. But even in such distinctive personality profiles there still exists a polar tension between the cerebral and the visceral.

This polar tension is due to the magnetic force that characterizes the functional impotency proper to the selfhood's psychosomatic willfulness. The selfhood's somatic will's built-in impotent need is to be motivationally stirred to bodily action whereas the selfhood's psychic will's built-in impotent need is to be motivationally sedated to mental inaction. Each is impotent to function without a motivational inducement and prompting which is proper to each's peculiar mode of productivity. The body produces its effect (viz. making hand-crafted instruments) outwardly with the technical use of the body's members whereas the mind produces its effect (viz., making mind-crafted notions) inwardly within the mind's phantom womb. Accordingly, when the human person is actively and consciously idly absorbed in thought, he is oblivious to the body's emotional (i.e., motivating) stirring sensitivity and feeling. Contrariwise, when the human person is actively and consciously engaged with his body's emotional feelings and movement, he is oblivious to the mind's emotionless (i.e., motivating) musing and impassive insensate bearing (viz., composure).

Given this polar tension within the human person's psychosomatic willful selfhood, the mystic cannot prayerfully attend completely to the psychic mind's willful idle intimate emotionless inward notional impassive musing until he becomes completely willfully self-detached from the body's busy sensitive outward sensational fantasies. Similarly, the same human person cannot prayerfully attend completely to the somatic body's willful sensitive sensational fantasies until he becomes completely willfully self-detached from the mind's reclusive idleness (viz., day-dreaming). It is a matter of record that a person who submits to hypnosis (either self-induced or technically induced by another person) enters into a static subconscious mode of awareness in which the body's kinesthetic sensitivity is completely neutralized.

Indeed, when a person is in a full-blown state of hypnotic trance, the somatic body is so numb that any person completely hypnotically imbued does not respond to the somatic body's stimulation. The hypnotized person is in a trance in which he is subconsciously impervious to the somatic body's sensitivity. The whole impetus of the transcendental meditation practiced by the adepts of Far Eastern religions is to become so securely entrenched subconsciously in the psychic reach of one's personality that he becomes immune to the somatic body's sensitivities.

Of course, the reverse is also the case. An athlete that is completely immersed in a competitive sport involving the body's active coordinative skillful engagement remains oblivious to the mind's own proper self-detached impassive immobilized functioning apart from the body's own movement. Were any athlete in the process of his sportive competition remove his attention from the body's focal skillful movement to attend to mentally solving a mathematical problem, his mental attention diverted from his body's athletic feat would seriously impair his body's athletic prowess.

St. John's account of the Catholic Christian mystic's transition from prayerfully attending to the somatic body's subjective sensitivity (viz., meditative prayer centered in the body's sensational fanciful imagery) to attending to the psychic mind's subjective intimacy (viz., contemplative prayer engaging the mind's impassive notionality beyond the reach of the body's sensational imagery) is not a transfer that is willfully, technically, and forcibly self-induced and self-controlled. Rather, it is the offshoot of the mystic's loss of religious self-contented feelings in the body's outward sensitivity when the mystic experiences a prolonged lack of fervent self-contented righteous emotional stirrings. It is precisely this prolonged impious forlornness and unemotional despondency that prompts and precipitates the mystic to become more acutely self-conscious of his own religious self-contained detached devout mental bearing (viz., caring and concern) proper to his selfhood's inward emotionless psychic willful intimacy.

This transition from meditation to contemplation is effectuated by the Holy Spirit who withholds from the mystic the devout emotional feelings that contribute to the mystic's religious emotional zeal and fervor characteristic of his religious self-contentment. When these feelings vanish the mystic becomes at a loss to continue his meditative prayer-life. In this loss accompanied by a lack of religious stimulation that is conducive to meditative prayer and religious service, the mystic slowly and tentatively discovers a more intimate and less busy mode of impassive emotionless contemplative prayer bereft of all reverent bodily feelings and emotional stimulations.

The advantage of this form of contemplative prayer is that it introduces the mystic to a more placid intensive and comprehensive and appreciative amorous attentiveness to God. This is the case precisely because the mind's subjective conceptual grasp of notions is comprehensively more intense whereas the body's subjective imaginative perception of such notions through its fanciful imagery is precisely more extensive but less intensively comprehensive. Evidence of this is the mind's mathematical notion of a point (viz., an inextended linear extension) which defies all imagery. When such a notion is depicted fancifully (viz., ".....") in a succession of imaginary points, for example, these points miss completely the mind's comprehension of what crucially and critically constitutes a point. A point may be imagined apart from an extended line but it cannot discard linearity's extensiveness in spite of its own inextension. In other words, a point is notionally the termination of a line's extension.

Another instance of this radical differentiation between the mind's notional non-tactile intensive grasp and the body's sensational tactile imagery extensive perception is that of the triangle. Notionally a triangle is simultaneously, comprehensively, and implicitly every and any three-sided figure with three angles. One cannot perceptually imagine this impassive and inert geometric tri-angularity. For, in imagining an isosceles triangle one is not imagining an equilateral triangle; the two do not coincide. To fully grasp the comprehensive notion of triangle imaginatively, one would have to imagine simultaneously the three distinctive triangles: the right-angle, equilateral, and isosceles. But, in doing so, one does not perceptually grasp the notion of a triangle notionally in which the three different triangles are prototypically one and the same triangle.

The second subjective advantage that contemplative prayer has over meditative prayer is that it provides the mystic with a more subjectively intimate pivotal encounter with God than that afforded by meditative prayer. Meditative prayer due to the imagination's fanciful superficial depictions provides the mystic with more of a peripheral and extraneous encounter with God. When the mystic prayerfully and fancifully images Christ suffering in the Garden of Gethsemane, he is acting in the role of a spectator extraneous to the Gospel scenario.

On the other hand, when the mystic prayerfully grasps the notion of Christ's suffering as the mental anguish and suffering of all Christians, including the mystic's very own mental anguish, he is acting in the role not merely of a spectator onlooker but of a phantom specter that is indistinguishable from Christ Himself in the Gospel scenario. In other words, the mystic intuitively and notionally grasps Christ and himself as intimately one and the same selfhood.

Chapter 2: Faults of mystics proficient in contemplative prayer.

These faults are of two kinds: habitual and intermittent. Of course, the intermittent faults are those which still linger in the mystic's religious somatic personality in which he still entertains within his outward body prominent highly sensitive paranormal experiences, temptations, and trials. The habitual faults, on the other hand, are those rooted in the mystic's religious psychic inward personality. These faults are rooted in the inmost intimate core and pith of the mystic's psychic willful self-serving selfhood. These are more inwardly, intimately, and radically deep-seated than are the outward sensitive faults proper to the mystic's physiological somatic emotional religious make-up.

The mystics who are now proficient in sedate contemplative prayer continue to harbor, unbeknown to them, a mental have me-attitude attachment that is still possessively very selfish. They have not as yet cultivated a be-attitudinal have/not sacrificial selfless mindset which is Christ's very own messianic salvific be-attitude. To come by this evangelical missionary messianic be-attitude mindset proper to Christ's own superhumanized and super-self-cultivated Personality (totally docile to the Holy Spirit), the mystic himself must undergo severe, terrible, and tormenting trials within his religious psychic willfulness' selfishly self-centered consciousness. The mystic's own selfish self-righteous devout mental willful sedate self-containment must be uprooted in the very pith of its innermost inward selfhood's intimacy. This uprooting and purgation is effectuated in the mystic's ordeal of suffering through "the dark night of the spirit."

St. John's description of the typically intermittent trials point to the mystic's somatic personality which continues to experience sensational visions and similar paranormal religious encounters. The prolonged experience of such paranormal encounters render the mystic susceptible to misconstruing that he is experiencing a special personalized communication and friendship with God and the angels. These paranormal experiences may also include the diabolical blandishments and deceits which mislead and enchant the mystic into misconstruing that he has an exaggerated importance which, indeed, he has not. Thus, he may become more arrogantly infatuated with these paranormal experiences than with his pursuit of a perfect prayerful mystical union with God. These mystical distractions from his pilgrimage to the summit of Mount Carmel are further evidence of the mystic's need for a complete mortification of his religious psychic willful selfhood.

Chapter 3: A rationale for the additional mortification of the mystic's religious psychic willful self-centered mindful personality.

First, note that St. John emphasizes the integral unity of the human personality when he points out that despite the antipodal dichotomy within the human person's psychosomatic subjective willful personality, both polar counterparts of this personality are still sustained by one and the same induplicable and nonsubstitutable personal substratum (i.e., the mystic's sovereign personhood). That is, it is one and the same person that both viscerally willfully imagines sensational tactile fanciful imagery and cerebrally conjures up nontactile insensate prototypical notions in spite of the fact that these functions are mutually polarized. Of course, St. John himself does not explicitly equate this willful polar psychosomatic dichotomy with the mystic's self-centered egological personality. This commentary's entire thrust is to introduce to the reader this subjective horizontal historical dimension inherent and implicit in our SanJuanistic mystagogy. There was no egological exposition of the human personality in St. John's day. Yet, the mystagogical description provided by St. John squares perfectly with the egological account supplied in this commentary. This is the major contention and rationale for preparing and offering this commentary.

Secondly, also note that the real and culminating mortification of the mystic's somatic religious superficial kinesthetic sensitivity begins with the mortification of his sedate static psychic religious radical intimate selfhood. In phenomenological terms, the mystic's outer personalized somatic willful religious sensitivity is merely symptomatic of God's divinizing activity while the mystic's inner personalized psychic willful religious intimacy is the very core and nucleus of God's transformatively divinizing activity. Until the nuclear core of the mystic's religious personality is radically mortified (i.e., purged of its intimate self-centered selfishness), the mortification of the mystic's somatic self remains as yet unfinished. Consequently, with the final mortification of the mystic's religious psychic inner intimate willful selfhood, his outer somatic willful self will have completed its own consummate and perfect mortification.

Lest the reader misconstrue this final statement, let it be understood that the very polar have/have-not opposition prevailing between the human person's visceral and cerebral subjectivity and willful selfhood is the reason that the complete mortification of the mystic's selfish self-centered religious bodily feelings depends on the ultimate mortification of the mystic's selfish self-centered religious (viz., self-righteous) mental bearings. When the human person is consciously immersed in and attached to the body's concrete mechanical movement and sensitivity, he is virtually oblivious to the mind's impassive subconscious idle thoughts and intimacy. The reverse is the case when the human person is absorbed in his thoughts.

Hence, the mystic only becomes completely and ascetically self-detached from his religious prayerful meditative fantasizing fueling his emotional feelings and fervor when he becomes completely self-absorbed in his cerebral mental cogitations. The stereotypical absent-minded professor is an example of a person who is completely mentally self-absorbed. It is only when the mystic becomes habitually skilled and adept in praying contemplatively with full recollection that is not interrupted and interspersed with meditative prayer that the somatic body's urgent need for its own religious sensuous satisfying stimulation and self-contentment completely subsides and becomes completely quelled.

Thirdly, the mystic who has attained to this preliminary stage of sedate and pacific contemplative prayer prior to this ulterior mortification is ignorant of his own religious mental selfish self-serving self-centeredness. He is still like a child who goes to the dentist and is more interested in the lollipop he will receive as a reward for submitting to the dentist's skillful repair of his teeth than he is of the benefit itself this repair will provide him. This severe and radical mortification of the mystic's religious willful psychic self will without any mitigation severely compromise the normal exercise of the mystic's intellect, will, and memory. The mystic's natural intelligence becomes stunted when confronted through faith with the luminosity of God's stupendous infinitude available in the sacraments; his subjective selfhood's religious psychosomatic volition undergoes a vertiginous vertigo when confronted with the vicissitudes of its own impotency and ineptitude; his memory suffers a well-nigh complete amnesia by becoming engulfed and engaged with eternity's transhistorical timelessness.

The mystic who encounters Christ in Christ's very own supernatural Self-revelation encounters He who is the same, yesterday, today, tomorrow, and forever. This Jesus Christ, God/Superman, overwhelms the mystic's intellect, will, and memory. He is both God and man, timelessly eternal, yet historically timely. He is supremely majestic and infinitely powerful, yet humanly finite and humbly impotent. He is the great transcendent and incomprehensible unapproachable "I AM" of the Old Testament, yet the little infant babe cradled in Mary's maternal arms and the mangled bloody body nailed to the cross' cruciformity in the New Testament. The human intellect is stunted by the splendor of this august mystery; the self-humanized psychosomatic will impotently clutches at this potent mystery; the memory's memorialization becomes eschatologically transhistorical in remembering this most historical mystery.

Chapter 4: A description of the mystic's divinized transformation through the "dark night of the spirit."

The full impact of the onset of the dark night of contemplative prayer is that the mystic can no longer live in terms of his familiar life-long personality depending on the normal operation of his intellect with its innate intelligibility and developed reasoning; or the immediate availability of his memory to readily furnish him with a memorial record of his past life and its larger historical events including his customary outlook toward the future; and his willful self-reliance on his own skillful self-control to manage his life and his affairs both secular and religious. He now lives at the mercy of God in all of these vital sectors of his life. He is now a complete stranger to himself and especially to others who either do not discern this remarkable change his personality is undergoing or, even if they do, no longer have the same sociability toward him as before.

The mystic afflicted with the throes of this contemplative dark night has no other recourse if he is determined to steadfastly prayerfully remain loyal to his commitment to seek a more perfect communion with God in God's Triune Godhead through the Church's sacramentality…he has no other recourse than to live trustingly in the theological virtue of faith, confidently in the theological virtue of hope, and faithfully in the theological virtue of charity. Of course, this trust is more an issue of voluntary obedience than it is one of intellectual enlightenment. This prayerful confidence, again, is more an issue of hoping in a transcendent eternal outcome beyond the historical hopelessness of his present misery, affliction, grief, and helplessness. And, his steadfast faithful charity toward God is moreso his own resignation to sacrificially suffer his inescapable misery in union with Christ's very own Paschal Mystery than it is one of experiencing the joy of Christ's resurrection and ascension into heaven.

For, in the throes of this oppressive, protracted, and tormenting trial of the "dark night" of his psychosomatic selfhood's self-righteous willful justification, the mystic experiences no intellectual insight, no overriding anticipation of imminent release from his intractable impotency, and no affectionate zeal, but only an intimate aching and longing for God who remains ever absent and elusively beyond the mystic's reach and grasp. In sum, the mystic experiences no consolation and no relief either within his somatic body's loss of sensitive feelings which offer no religious self-righteous self-satisfying self-contentment or within his psychic mind's loss of its equipoise intimate bearing which, in turn, offers no religious self-righteous self-justifying self-containment.

St. John emphatically stresses that all of this compounded and vexing misery is a great grace and a great blessing for the mystic. For, the mystic's mundane, natural, and merely self-humanistic personality is being transformed not by any self-starting or self-motivating initiative on the part of the mystic himself. It is not a metamorphosis undertaken by the mystic's own skillful ingenuity; something of a successful self-fulfilled self-cultivated humanism. Quite to the contrary, it is a metamorphosis in which the mystic's own personality, his own willful self-centered selfhood, is being supernaturally, sacramentally, superhumanistically, and superhumanely transformed into nothing short of Christ's very own divinized merciful Personality (again, not to be confused with Christ's divine Personhood). Not only is he sacramentally becoming more fully integrated into Christ's mystical body, the Sacramental Church, but he is becoming more and more metamorphically assimilated in terms of his own Christian personality and his selfhood, into the very resurrected glorified Eucharistic Body of Christ. This metamorphic transformation is hastened by his reception of Holy Communion. In this reception, it is not Christ that is being physically consumed by the communicant; rather, it is the communicant that is being assimilated and consummated into the divinity of Christ's own glorified and divinized body.

Chapter 5: The mystic's religious intimacy with God undergoes affliction and torment.

This protracted trial of the mystic's own psychosomatic willful selfhood becoming transformed into Christ's very own superhumane Personality is no longer confined to the strictures suffered within his body's religious insensitivity; it now assaults and assails the inner sanctuary of his innermost religious mental intimacy with God. This is the inner sanctum to which the mystic had become accustomed to prayerfully repair to find solace from his body's jejune and desolate religious morbidity. This is the "closet" and cloister to which the Gospel invites the mystic to repair in praying to God. His customary quiet, serene religious mental equilibrium is now shattered. His religious self-confidence is sundered. His previous periods of pacific and pacifying prayerful trysts with God whose embrace he subconsciously was certain of experiencing vanishes completely and utterly. It is replaced with a terrible, tormenting, and terrifyingly dogged mental discombobulation, disorientation, and foreboding tribulation.

His prayerful consecrated and reverent attitude to embrace Christ's own be-attitudinal messianic mindset and Gospel ascetic lifestyle is no longer requited with a religious intimate experience of secure blessedness. It is now, in the throes of this terrible assault on the very mettle, spirited courage, and nuclear core of his innermost intimate Christian commitment to Christ...it is now undergoing a wretchedness and most miserable anguish and anxiousness beyond anyone's power to evaluate, eliminate, or to relieve.

Yet, St. John states unequivocally that this entirely subjective religious mental turmoil and innermost intimate distress is inherently and systemically endemic to contemplative prayer. It is an inescapable purgative process which the mystic must undergo in order to personally and personalistically enter into and experience within his own innermost intimate personality Christ's infinite merciful selfless love and loveliness. It must be borne in mind that this transforming mystical experience which the Christian mystic suffers is taking place within his self-cultivated personality that is nothing other than his self-humanized self-cultivated psychosomatic subjective body. This body with its mystical suffering is not to be confused with his objective substantive sentient animal body. This mystical suffering occurs within his subjective insubstantive corpuscular body with its somatic self-humanized kinesthetic sensitized tactility, on the one hand, and with its psychic self-humanized static intimate lack of tactility, on the other.

And, again, it cannot be overemphasized that it is one and the same person as an inalienable, induplicable, subsistent, immortal substratum that both is objectively a substantive sentient animal body and subjectively a non-substantive quasi-body. The human person's objective substantive body remains substantively one and the same subject that undergoes all of the changes which materially occur to the human person throughout his lifetime. It is one and the same substantive body that is young or old, well or ill, here or there, embrionically growing and developing and/or fully mature, etc.. It is this substantive body which is substantively animated by the human person's immortal, spiritual soul.

The human person's self-cultivated and subjectively self-humanized insubstantive corpuscular psychosomatic body is a mere quasi-body precisely because it lacks any substantivity of its own. The same human person's objective substantive body is a holistic whole which cannot be reduced to any of its component parts be these mineral, plant, or animal. The subjective psychosomatic body, on the other hand, is reducible to the sum total of its component parts; it is in this sense that it is corpuscular rather than corporeal. Given this distinction, it is not at all surprising that the anatomical heart cannot continue to naturally exist as a vital organ outside of a person's bodily homeostasis. It has no substantive existence of its own as is the case for the human body considered metaphysically as a substantive holistic whole that is not reducible to any of its component parts.

St. John raises and answers a doubt which confounds every mystic that is afflicted with this assault on his religious psychosomatic willful selfhood. Why does God (i.e., the Holy Spirit) who is so subtle, gentle, dove-like, and unctuous inflict and bring about such unspeakable torment and misery to the mystic? The answer provided by St. John in no way tarnishes nor compromises the Holy Spirit's own delicacy. Rather, it addresses the mystic's own religious crudity. Indeed, this abrasive and disruptive effect which the Holy Spirit's unction has on the mystic's psychosomatic religious bodily kinesthetic sensitivity and mental static intimacy is due to the mystic's own egocentric self-centered rebellious selfishness. This selfishness cannot sustain nor entertain this effusive Pneumatic unctuousness. It is not that the mystic's religious motor is lacking in oil to grease its mechanical parts or lacking in gas to fuel its engine. It is the case that the mystic's religious motor itself needs a radical overhaul of its parts which do not mesh together and of its fuel system which cannot function with the Holy Spirit's refined unctuousness.

Since the mystic in his psychosomatic selfhood is not merely a conscious sensitive anatomical mechanism but, moreso, an intimate self-conscious personality, this major overhaul incurs a terrible and terrifying suffering and anguish in the innermost core and pith of this personality's inwardness and subjectivity. It is not a matter of fine-tuning but rather of replacing the mystic's familiar personality with a completely different unfamiliar superhumanized and superhumane personality (viz., that of Christ's own Personality). In this overhaul the mystic is not rewarded with a self-awareness of blessedness for his striving to live out the Gospel life. Rather, he seems to be cursed with the misery and wretchedness of suffering his own total self-alienation.

It seems that God is no longer his safeguard and imperturbable security. God has become alienated from the mystic along with the mystic's suffering his own self-alienation. Worse, God is now not merely a stranger to the mystic but one who deliberately withholds from the mystic stirring sensitizing comforting affection and pacifying intimate reassuring serenity of the love and loveliness which He promises in His Gospel message to provide to those who follow Him. And even worse still, it seems to the mystic that he has been altogether rejected by God.

This overwhelming conviction of divine rejection is not the least of the debilitating doubts which haunt and daunt the mystic's religious loss of mental equilibrium. He cannot find any comfort or solace either in God or in any other individual regardless of that individual's professional or ministerial competence. The mystic remains disconsolate and mired in his own misery and nebulous disquietude. What is most confounding to the mystic at this point is that it seems he has abandoned everything in search of God and now finds himself without succor or support since he has burned his bridges which he has crossed to reach God.

Furthermore, St. John points out, the mystic's own lack of an impeccable moral character, his own lack of grit and a self-sustaining indomitable morale in his personality are additional occasions for suffering and undergoing his terrible and terrifying religious ordeal of self-purifying self-alienation. This is comparable to a nugget of gold which becomes more perfectly and thoroughly its own element when it is subjected to the flames of an intense fire. Under the infinite fire of the Holy Spirit's purifying love and loveliness, the mystic's objective moral character proper to his human nature and subjective morale proper to his self-humanized personality are transformed into the moral holiness proper to the Father and into the indomitable righteous morale proper to the incarnate Son, Jesus Christ.

While the mystic is undergoing this metamorphic transformation, he suffers a self-alienation which is much more radical and excruciatingly painful than that of any immigrant who is forcibly evicted from his own homeland and forced to live in a foreign culture devoid of any personal material resources or friends to assist him in adjusting to this strange and seemingly inhospitable environment. His lack of familiarity with the foreign language he is now required to use is only symptomatic of his inmost impotency to cope with his new surroundings.

Chapter 6: A more vivid and personalized description of this religious psychosomatic purgative ordeal.

Note, again, that St. John in his treatise describes this ordeal as occurring within the mystic's soul. Of course, the mystic's spiritual soul itself is entirely beyond the psychosomatic suffering which occurs within the mystic's subjective bodily self-awareness. The soul is not the mystic's egocentric selfhood. The soul is utterly simple and inorganically spiritual. St. John had no explicitly developed egology in which to explicitly couch his descriptive account of the mystic's subjective experiences. Accordingly, he attributes everything to the soul. Today in more contemporary terms we speak of the human person as suffering such subjective rigors. Certainly, the human person is endowed with an animating soul which is the substantive dynamic principle of his sovereign intelligent and free activity by which he morally governs his own immortal destiny.

Hence, St. John's addressing the soul as the principle subject which undergoes such religious suffering is completely compatible with our present-day understanding of the human person as the ultimate substrate of all of the individual human being's endeavors. In the final analysis, the sacramental spiritual Christian life is channeled principally and radically through the human soul which is the spiritual substantive vitalizing principle of all of the human person's activity.

Under the intense fire of the Holy Spirit's unctuous amorosity which was previously so welcome and spiritually energizing, the mystic now experiences with the loss of this unctuous amorosity his body's devout and zealous sensitivity hardening into a crusted earth devoid of water's fluidity and his mind's reverent intimacy quaking and reeling with doubts erupting into clouds of nebulous nagging anxiety. St. John assures us that this religious devastation is necessary in order that the mystic may be resurrected from this muddle to the eschatological resurrection for which he supernaturally hopes and to which he prayerfully aspires.

The tormenting crux of this suffering is the mystic's loss of his own self-assurance and conviction that he is safely cuddled under the almighty power and indomitable protection of God's love. He is convinced that God has abandoned him and left himself to his own devices. This overriding dispiriting conviction robs him of his customary confidence of praying to the Father in Jesus Christ with an interpersonalized confidentiality and trust that he was formally actually exercising. Besieged with these overwhelming unwelcome and unsolicited haunting troubling doubts, the mystic is no longer comforted by either emotional sensitive religious feelings or a remotional intimate religious inner reassuring bearing of God's almighty presence. His prayer-life itself becomes an additional torment and aggravation. For, it only serves to continually accentuate and emphasize the terrible religious misgivings which he experiences penetrating to the innermost intimate sanctuary of his personality.

All of this is compounded by his growing awareness of his own self-alienation from all of his companions and fellow humans. He is acutely aware of how different he is from them in their daily activities, enjoyments, and self-assurances. They seem to him to be so very normal and typical while he himself regards himself as entirely untypical and abnormal. He is unable to adequately describe his plight even to his own confessor. It seems too incredible for anyone to readily believe or to understand. How can one who is diligently seeking an intimate friendship and association with God's Triune Godhead explain to someone else the very intimacy he experiences with this Godhead? Such an explanation or narration to someone else would seem to be the epitome of personal arrogance and presumption. Furthermore, the mystic's acute awareness now of the august majesty and infinite grandeur of God increases his own self-awareness of his own miserable poverty. How, possibly can he imagine that he himself has anything of an intimate and a genuine rapport with this infinitely transcendent Deity?

So thoroughly religiously sterilizing and mortifying is this spiritual ordeal that the mystic's every familiar religious emotional fervent bodily self-righteous feeling and remotional reverent self-righteous mental bearing previously cultivated and enjoyed is virtually effaced and snuffed out. What remains is a terrible excruciatingly painful mental anguish and relentless foreboding. This religious mental anguish and bodily despondency cannot be alleviated with any known medical remedy that would either anesthetize the body's sensitivity or hypnotize the mind's intimacy. The mystic's pain and suffering of the mortification of his own religious selfish self-centered psychosomatic attachment must be endured without the benefit of any medicinal reprieve. In this manner, he suffers as Christ suffered in His Passion without the benefit of any reprieve from the brutality of His captors.

In brief, St. John states, God reduces the mystic to the dust of the earth in order to subsequently resurrect the mystic to the immaculate vault of heaven's ethereal, eternal, limpid delights. The mystic who manages do endure such a tremendously excruciating ordeal in this present life is not detained by any detour to purgatory when he finally physically dies. He is spirited away directly to heaven and bypasses the rigors of purgatory. He has already meritoriously passed through purgatory in his steadfast endurance of this psychosomatic religious purification.

Chapter 7: Still further afflictions suffered by the mystic caught up in this religious strait.

Prior to the onset of this religious ordeal penetrating into the innermost intimate recesses of the mystic's psychosomatic subjective religious willfulness, the mystic was enjoying throughout the day a lingering and comforting recollected awareness of the "presence of God" sacramentally alive in the very depth of his mental consciousness. With the arrival of the binding strictures of this second more intense "dark night" the mystic's awareness of God's presence is completely eclipsed. His prayerful periods of recollection become intensively more difficult and more turbulent.

The very anticipation of trying to become prayerfully recollected becomes itself an additional torment precisely because it further places the mystic in the very pith and crux of his frightful affliction. It is precisely because he had completely and prayerfully abandoned himself to God that he is in such a frightful situation. The more he has recourse to God the more intense does his mental anguish, anxiety, and disorientation become.

Here, St. John emphasizes that it is the mystic's willful selfhood that bears the brunt of this protracted trial. This is so because previous to this trial it is precisely the mystic's unsuspected willful self-serving selfish religious autonomous self-righteous bodily self-contentment and mental self-containment which implicitly motivated his prayerful commitment and devotion to God. This prayerful commitment afforded the mystic many superb and exquisitely sensuously exuberant gloriously exultant religious feelings. There is no earthly or mundane engagement which could compare with the exuberant affectivity of these stimulating religious feelings. Similarly, this prayerful commitment afforded the mystic protracted and periodically lengthier self-sustained profoundly intimate serenely secure religious mental assurances of God's precious and treasured love. With the arrival of the second stage of this "dark night" there is no further affectionate or intimate trace of God's subjective "presence" for the mystic's self-assurance and self-confirmation that God is attentive to his prayers.

So forlorn and stricken in the stricture of this complete disappearance of all righteous experiences of God's "touches" in his life, the mystic is further distressed when he recalls his past religious experiences and deems that they are lost and gone forever, never to be restored to him. He has no doubt about their loss forever since he is completely aware of his own forlornness and complete lack of resourcefulness to recuperate and to revive them. Further, he has no expectation that they will ever return in the future because he cannot even prayerfully recollect himself sufficiently to regain God's attention. God, to every intent and purpose, has abandoned the mystic to his own resources who, left without God's touches, has melted into a muddle of bodily unemotional desolation and mental emotionless agitation and disquietude.

To give the reader something of the deep-seated consternation and misery of the mystic imprisoned within the maws of this ordeal,

St. John cites a special passage of Sacred Scripture which is found on the lips of the prophet, Jeremiah. This to be found in Lamentations 3:1-10. It is a harrowing and fearfully frightening description of the prophet's abject misery in not only being abandoned by God but moreso of being the object of God's indignation. And, this is the very nub of this "dark night." God is no longer the precious fountainhead of the mystic's autonomous security and religious confident self-assurance. The mystic is convinced as he is sinking and wallowing in his own sea of emotional feelings of religious destitution and emotionless disoriented bearings of foreboding religious anxieties that God's almighty strength and succor is now no longer his ally but allied against him. Where God was previously a tower of his completely self-assured religious safeguard and commitment, God now wells up as an insurmountable tower undermining his own lack of religious self-control and self-determination.

The ordeal of the "dark night" is precisely an ordeal because it is a complete counter-cultural program which undertakes to overturn and uproot the very motivational route which individuals follow in becoming humanistically assimilated and conditioned to becoming successful personalities in their competitive social environment. Motivations are subjectively self-centered and selfishly self-serving. They are fostered by the overriding and paramount self-interest to which a person is willfully and attitudinally committed. This self-interest is humanistically always social and bonds socially with others allied with it. If it is idealistic and romantic, it is committed to a worldview that is dominantly mentally conceived and rationalized. If it is realistic and pragmatic, it is committed to a worldview that is dominantly bodily perceived and empirically investigated.

These worldviews are entirely social and humanistically self-centered and serviceably self-fulfilling. These worldviews are antithetical to each other. One is utopian and other cornucopian. That is, the one seeks social self-fulfillment in what a person mentally dreams to be fictionally possible whereas the other one seeks social self-fulfillment in what he imaginatively schemes to be factually possible. The former is at the service of a person's mental self-fulfillment whereas the latter is at the service of a person's bodily self-fulfillment.

Motivationally a pragmatic utilitarian person's humanistic social self-fulfillment (i.e., personalization and personification) is prompted and induced by his emotional visceral feelings which stimulate him to pursue his own bodily self-centered selfish self-righteous self-satisfaction and automatic self-contentment. The overriding issue with him is his body's comfort and contented self-satisfaction. A romantic unitarian person's social self-fulfillment (i.e., personalization and personification) is motivationally prompted by his emotionless cerebral bearings which sedately seduce him to remain inactively mentally musing (i.e., day-dreaming) in the pursuit of his own selfish self-righteous self-vindication and autocratic self-containment. The overriding issue with him is his mind's complacency and self-contained self-vindication. The mystic, accordingly, on the supernatural plane of the religious self-cultivated development of his personality initially follows the path of his own selfish self-serving automatic outward autonomous religious self-contentment and/or selfish self-serving autocratic autonomous inward religious self-containment.

But, in following this typically humanistic route the mystic is not fully serving God selflessly in this initial stage of his own religious self-cultivation. Rather, he is inadvertently serving his own religious selfish self-righteous self-aggrandizement and social security. This egocentric selfishness inherent in his willful psychosomatic selfhood is a rebellious legacy which he has inherited from Adam & Eve. It is precisely this self-centered autonomous religious selfishness which is the upshot of the suffering and throes which the mystic must undergo in the "dark night" in order to become purged of the constraints this selfishness entails.

The mystic's subjective painful experiences of the superhumanistic transformations of his own selfhood's willfulness is the very reversal of his own selfish self-centered motivational religious sensitized bodily stimulations, on the one hand, and the very reversal of his own motivational religious intimate mental sedations, on the other. In the onset of this complete psychosomatic "dark night" the mystic's willful somatic religious automatic autonomous emotional stimulations become emotional deflations while their counterpart, the mystic's willful psychic religious autocratic autonomous emotionless sedations, become overanxious agitations. The upshot of this, of course, is that the mystic now no longer experiences (i.e., is conscious of) within his own psychosomatic autonomous (i.e., self-controlled) selfish willful personality evidence of God's own strength boosting and reinforcing his own religious zealous feelings, on the one hand, nor evidence of God's strength bolstering and reinforcing as well his religious self-confident bearings (mental equilibrium), on the other.

With an increasing growing alarm the mystic becomes increasingly aware that his total reliance and confidence in God to sustain and fortify him in everyone of his religious endeavors is fading away. In brief, his selfish self-centered egocentric certitude of his own autonomous religious self-control and self-mastery become seriously stricken. His religious selfishly self-sustained self-cultivated psychosomatic personality is sundered much to the dismay and consternation of the mystic himself when his religious emotional bodily feeling of righteous self-contentment, on the one hand, and religious emotionless mental bearing of righteous self-containment not only diminish and wane but utterly vanish and fail.

St. John insists that while this traumatic ordeal is a great grace for the mystic who is being liberated from the prison of his own religious selfishness, the mystic is to truly be pitied who is suffering this harrowing anguishing agony of the aridity of his religious emotional bodily feelings coupled with the agitation of his religious emotionless mental bearing. The mystic is engulfed in his own mountainous religious doubts and turbulence from which he cannot foresee even the slightest glimmer of hope of ever escaping. Furthermore, the mystic can no longer through recourse to prayer be assured of feeling and entertaining God's support and sustenance for his religious welfare and security. He becomes persuaded to expect that he is doomed to die in this lamentable stage of religious disarray. In the meantime, he is counseled to live by faith which objectively transcends his subjective misgivings.

The mystic's vacant religious feelings compounded by his religious discombobulating anxiety become more acutely disturbing when he fails to find any remedy or relief from either his spiritual counselor/confessor or from secular professional medical experts.

576

Consulting with these persons only reinforces his own sense of complete helplessness and abandoned forlornness. St. John here describes this state as one who "is imprisoned in a dark dungeon, bound hands and feet, and able neither to move, nor see, nor feel any favor from heaven or earth." (Is not St. John here describing his own protracted imprisonment and shoddy treatment by his fellow-Carmelites?) Indeed, the mystic himself who is caught up in this inner conflict is prone to esteeming himself as an abject misfit.

St. John concludes this description of the mystic's misery by insisting that God allows this prolonged religious malaise to run its course until the mystic is sufficiently chastened and purified within the innermost intimate bowels of his willful selfhood. That is, God allows the mystic to suffer in this religious strait as long as it take for the mystic to be delivered from his insidious attachment to his own autonomous religious selfishness and relentless need for his own social security and self-sufficiency. In the final analysis, this selfishness and self-attachment must give way to and be replaced by Christ's very own total Selfless Self-detachment which is underwritten by His messianic be-attitudinal mindset. The mystic must put on the heart and mind of Christ.

St. John indicates that this radical purgation to be completely efficacious must, in some cases, continue over the span of several years. This observation itself makes more than evident how tenaciously and resistantly deep-seated is the rebellious legacy which we all inherit from our original parents, Adam & Eve. It provides a further insight into the tremendous ordeal that Christ suffered in His cruel passion and death to overcome this willful selfish resistance in mankind in order to liberate the human person from the prison of his own egocentric selfish self-centeredness.

Nonetheless, over the span of this years-long purgation the mystic does experience periodic reprieves in which he enters the illuminative stage of his mystical pilgrimage up the religious slopes of Mount Carmel. In the periods of these illuminative reprieves the mystic gains further insight into the underlying rationale for his undergoing the unrelenting stress of this "dark night." That is, he begins to acknowledge his own religious failings and religious selfishness to the extent that he begins to recognize his need for such purification and how this ordeal actually brings him more associatively one with Christ's own messianic suffering and mission.

But, again, St. John notes that the mystic's full recognition and acknowledgement of his own religious shortcomings when these periods of reprieve are granted to him fall short of a complete efficacious self-abnegation. He mistakenly misconstrues that he has sufficiently overcome his religious selfishness in order to be spared any further tormenting religious purification. But, suddenly, without warning he finds himself thrust back into the very same religious wretchedness from which he had deemed himself to have been rescued. This renewal of his religious morass becomes even more severe and strenuous than any previous siege. He now moreso than before is stricken with the misery of his complete helplessness. Where he had shortly before experienced the relief of being rescued from his religious plight, he now is thoroughly convinced that even if he is again rescued it will be only to be plunged back again into this religious miasma.

At this point St. John reflects on the condition of the souls in purgatory. They too suffer "great doubts about whether they will ever leave their afflictions (or whether they) will end." And, note that in purgatory the suffering soul is beyond the duration of historical time. He experiences a transhistorical duration which is protractively timeless and endlessly timeless. Such souls know conclusively that they do love God albeit imperfectly but this assurance is also accompanied by their suffering the terrible fate that God does not fully requite this love because they are unworthy of Him. They cannot shake off the effects of their expectation of this terrible fate.

Chapter 8: Further afflictions that beset the mystic in this religious ordeal.

The mystic is not merely chagrined but entirely dispirited in his inability to efficaciously pray to God and to assuredly either bodily sensitively feel or mentally enjoy any intimate souci that God is attentive and responsive to his prayer. Indeed, all subjective religious savor and self-assurance of God's sacramental presence in the mystic is completely missing and absent. In lieu of "God's providential presence" the mystic experiences only "God's relentless absence." It is very much paradoxically the case that the very touchstone of subjective mystical experience is not to know God as He objectively exists but to experience Him within the subjective anthropocentric epistemic awareness of the mystic's own psychosomatic affectivity. Hence, when the mystic in the throes of this "dark night" does no longer experience even the slightest trace of a religious bodily affectivity or mental serenity redolent of God, he has no further experiential evidence of God's favor resting on him personally and personalistically.

St. John here counsels the mystic in the manner that he is to conduct himself and his prayer-life during this protracted ordeal. He states that in this religious situation the mystic must not attend to prayerful reflection but content himself with keeping "his mouth in the dust." He is to accept his lot and allow God to have his way by suffering through the torment of this prolonged purgation. At this point as a fitting conclusion to his account of this "dark night" St. John reiterates the threefold purgation of the intellect, memory, and will which is affected by this ordeal. This is nothing less than the intellect's loss of its own native intelligibility, the memory's amnesiac loss of its own historical memoriality and remembrances, as well as the selfhood's will's own loss of its own self-sustained self-controlled autonomy and social security.

THE DARK NIGHT. Book II Chapters 9-25 TREATISE ON THE PASSIVE NIGHT OF THE SPIRIT.

Other delightful effects of this dark night of contemplation.

Within the context of this "spirit and truth" symbiosis engaging the soul's objective intellect and intellectual will, on the one hand, and the selfhood's subjective mindful will, on the other, there is according to St. John both a differentiation and an intercourse. In contemplative prayer the mystic may receive by infused enlightenment an understanding from God that is principally intellectual and not accompanied by a subjective concomitant amorous affectionate sublime visceral exultation and/or profound cerebral enthrallment. On the other hand, the actual reverse may occur in which case the infused excited religious visceral elation and/or sedated cerebral serenity have no accompanying inspirational intellectual insight. St. John explains that this is quite the case because this prayerful infused dark contemplation is simultaneously one of divine luminosity and divine amorosity.

When this divine illumination enlightens the soul's intellect it leaves the selfhood's will in limbo and, correspondingly, when this same divine illumination heats up the selfhood's psychosomatic will with its love, it leaves the intellect in the darkness of its ignorance. St. John points out that this very difference occurs even within the natural order of fire when one can, on the one hand, discern the fire's light at a distance without feeling its heat and on another occasion experience its heat more than its light when very close to its flame. This intercourse between the soul's intellect and the selfhood's will is one that engages the fundamental priority of knowledge, on the one hand, and the supplemental priority of love, on the other.

In the vertical objective order of existence knowledge, fundamentally, takes precedence over love precisely because knowledge is informative and in this guise conscionably directs and governs the love inherent in the soul's intellectual will. The intellect has direct access to the truth of reality. Thus, there is an adage which the Scholastic philosophers and theologians never cease repeating: "one cannot love what one does not first know." On the other hand, in the horizontal subjective order of resistance, love, supplementally, takes precedence over knowledge and truth precisely because such love while transformative brings knowledge to a perfection and conclusion which is beyond knowledge's power to do so.

In this respect this amorous and affectionate love issuing from the selfhood's self-serving willfulness has a direct influence and bearing on the selfhood's willful attachment to and interest in the object of its affectionate love. Whatever the selfhood's psychosomatic will affectionately loves it sacrificially cherishes and treasures for its own self-serving self-interest and self-fulfillment. The object of its love becomes transformed through this love; it becomes increasingly important and valuable precisely because it is cherished, appreciated, and treasured as fulfilling the selfhood's willful deficiency. Hence, unless the selfhood's will willfully, conscientiously, and selflessly cherishes the conscionable truth enunciated by the soul's intellect, this truth, albeit its transcendence and independence and fundamental inherent importance apart from the selfhood's subjective interest, exercises little directive and regulative efficacy on the personhood's conscientious cultural self-humanized and self-civilized self-fulfillment.

Indeed, when the mystic's psychosomatic will is still a prisoner of its own selfishly self-centered humanistic partisan me-attitude, its selfish self-interest dominates what it cherishes and treasures in terms of its own self-fulfillment. While this is the case, the mystic's subjective willful psychosomatic conscientious wants and imperative needs are at loggerheads with his objective conscionable obligations vis-à-vis God. As long as this selfish self-centered me-attitude lingers and persists, the mystic remains both blind and impotent to submissively, meekly, humbly, and promptly selflessly and sacrificially embrace the primacy of God-the-Father's Holy Will which he is in conscience obliged to honor and adore.

Motivationally he is still seeking to be conscientiously exploitatively bodily emotionally stirred and mentally emotionlessly enchanted by this conscionable moral obligation. In the absence of sensitive bodily self-righteous stimulation and/or intimate self-righteous mental entrancement which is the case during his prolonged "dark night" trial and tribulation, he bemoans his own lack of bodily righteous verve and/or mental righteous nerve in the service of God. He remains selfishly and exploitatively prayerfully engaged with God. He has not, as yet, become completely sacrificially converted to Christ's Selfless compassionate heart and be-attitudinal mindset.

In view of the preceding, it is most interesting to listen to St. John's differentiation between light and heat in the sapiential infusion which God grants to the mystic through the choir of angels during and in the aftermath of his prolonged prayerful contemplative darkness. This intercourse between the personhood's objective soul and subjective selfhood is a dialogical intercourse between what is completely transcendently objective and completely immanently subjective within the personhood of the mystic's prayerful life and communion with God, the Blessed Trinity.

The objective transcendent order is that of one's conscionable intellectual will and moral obligation while the subjective immanent order is that of one's psychosomatic conscientious will and careful solicitous self-centered concern. The one is fundamental and the other supplemental. When each takes precedence over the other within its own proper priority, there is a reconciliation and harmony between what is conscionably and morally (i.e., truthfully) objectively rightfully appropriate and what is conscientiously and caringly (i.e., conscientiously) subjectively self-righteously appropriated. The infused loving wisdom imparted to the mystic through the choir of angels arrives in the soul as a wisdom of supernatural intellectual clarity and arrives in the mystic's selfhood as a fire of love.

This infused loving wisdom does not always bring about immediately a harmony and reconciliation between the mystic's objective transcendent conscionable soul and his subjective immanent conscientious selfhood. For, St. John notes that at one time there may be intellectual clarity in the mystic's soul through this infused loving wisdom and no concomitant willful ardor for God in the mystic's self-hood's heartfelt sensitivity and no willful profound deep-seated entrancement and fondness for God in the mystic's selfhood's mindful intimacy. Other times, it may be just the other way round. When this lack of harmony occurs, we have the situation which St. Paul himself describes when he declares what a miserable person is the Christian who does not willfully want what he ought to will, on the one hand, and dutifully wills what he does not really want, on the other.

However, when both the soul and the self are in harmony through the infusing of this loving wisdom, there does occur a reconciliation reconciling what is inherently and objectively conscionably rightfully appropriate to God---truly good and inherently worthwhile; namely God's infinite Goodness dutifully and respectfully loved---with what is subjectively conscientiously possessively righteously appropriated in regard to God; namely, God's infinite Goodness appreciatively and sacrificially selflessly loved. In other words, God's truly objective appropriate valuable Goodness which ought to be loved for His own sake now becomes, additionally, loved affectionately, cherished, valued, and treasured appreciatively as the self's total selfless (and not selfish) self-fulfillment. It is very clear, however, that this reconciliation and harmony cannot be brought about without the "dark night's" purgative program of self-abnegation requiring the mystic to sacrificially divest himself of his selfhood's willful self-righteous self-attachments and humanistic partisan me-attitudinal selfish self-interests.

It should also be noted how influential the angels are in mediating the infused wisdom which God imparts to the mystic both in terms of the soul's intellectual knowledge and in terms of the psycho-somatic selfhood's conative affectivity. Of course, the intellect is simultaneously undergoing its own purgation since its own natural insightful knowledge is not entirely eclipsed but severely adumbrated under the shadow of the eminent knowledge through faith of God's very own Triune divinity fully supernaturally present to the intellect's contemplative prayerful gaze. Just as the angel, Gabriel, mediated God's message to her regarding her call to her unique maternity, so also the mystic's own guardian angel in conjunction with the hierarchy of angelic choirs communicates God's wisdom to the mystic in the infused enlightenment which occurs in the process and aftermath of the mystic's prayerful contemplative purification.

This infused wisdom may come as a cognitive informative directive to the soul's intellectual will or as a conative transformative inspiration to the selfhood's psychosomatic willfulness. In any event, this role reserved to the angels reveals also the tremendous influence which the devil and his demonic minions also can exercise in the life of the mystic. This explains, in large measure, why discernment left to the Church's Magisterium is so crucial in protecting the faithful from bogus mystical experiences and visions.

There is still one further point which should be emphasized issuing from this commentary on the text of St. John. Where the immediate impact on the selfhood's somatic will is the extensive ardor, zeal, and fervent bodily affection for God which the mystic experiences throughout the body's religious emotional feeling and sensitivity, it is a profound and deep-seated ache, pining, and longing for God which the mystic experiences within the abysmal pith of the mind's religious emotionless bearing and intimacy. The more the trial of the mystic's willful mental self persists and progresses, the more the mystic experiences both the absence of God and intensively his increasing mindful concern and need for God in spite of the complete absence of any and every religious feeling of devotion for God within his body's sensitivity.

This dark night of the mystic's spirit impacts intensively and painfully his psychic mindful willfulness by acutely intensifying his mindful awareness and concern for God's absence as well as an increasing awareness of his more urgent need for God to provide for his own total self-fulfillment. Not the least of the mystic's misery and mental anguish is his growing conviction in suffering through the "dark night" that God has completely abandoned him. This conviction is borne out by the complete loss of all emotional affectionate bodily devotional feeling for God, on the one hand, and a loss of God's soothing, consoling, and calming mental reassuring entrancing quietude and bearing, on the other.

Sometimes, this dark contemplation is, as previously noted an infused wisdom to the soul's intellect without touching and affecting the selfhood's willfulness. Other times, it is simply the reverse. Sometimes, it engages both together. However, when the mystic is suffering through the ordeal of the "dark night" it seems that it is the selfhood's will that experiences more God's infused affectionate touch moreso than it is the soul's intellect which cognitively profits from this infusion. And, before a complete reconciliation is brought about between the personhood's innate soulful intellectual cognitivity and his self-cultivated selfhood's affectivity, a reconciliation in which the two are symbiotically and peaceably joined "as one," it is more likely that it is the personhood's self that first experiences an infused volitional affection from God moreso than it is the intellect which concomitantly or cognitively receives this divine touch. Why is this so, St. John asks?

This is an intriguing and subtle question because St. John's response to it casts even more light on the interplay that occurs between the personhood's objective spontaneous innate soul and his subjective self-cultivated prompted selfhood. Of course, there is no mention of a selfhood in the text itself of St. John's treatise. Yet, from our ongoing commentary it should be increasingly obvious to the reader that in contrasting the selfhood's will in terms of a compassionate affectionate love to the intellectual will's activity completely aloof from such affectivity, this compassionate love itself does not really occur in the substantive body's animal appetitive sensibility. It actually occurs as a sensuous empathic love within the corpuscular body's kinesthetic sensitivity as an emotional feeling; that is, within the selfhood's subjective self-conscious somatic willfulness rather than in the corporeal body's objective appetency. The vehemence of the mystic's experience of religious exultation is such that whenever this infused effusion is supernaturally visited upon the mystic, as St. John explains, he feels carried away against his own willfulness.

As further indication that this infused experience of divine compassion occurs subjectively within the personhood's selfhood rather than objectively in the soul, the soul's intellectual will's own volitions are such that they themselves are inorganically and spiritually independent of the body's sentiency and sensuality and, hence, of the corporeal body's animal passions and the selfhood's subjective sensuous compassions. Furthermore, the mystic can subjectively experience (i.e., feel) these vehement religious sensitive exultations, when they do occur, within his own somatic selfhood's willfulness because this willfulness need not be perfectly purified of its own selfishness to allow for this. On the other hand, the intellect's own purification brought about by its own cognitive nebulosity when overshadowed by the brilliance of God's Triune Godhead sacramentally present and evidently so through the theological gift of faith, must be completely nebulized in order for the intellect to efficaciously receive the infused wisdom which is given by God during the mystic's absorption in dark contemplative prayer.

However, this observation by St. John should be considered only in the context of the infused touches which accrue to the mystic in the dark night of contemplative prayer. For, indeed, all mystical experiences within the subjectivity of the selfhood's psychosomatic willfulness are received through the sacramental presence of God's own supernatural graciousness abiding in the soul. It is important to take note of this. Both the mystic's infused subjective mystical emotional sensitized body stimulations and emotionless intimate mental sedations are the offshoot of God's sacramental supernatural presence within the substantive soul's inorganic spiritual nature.

The mystic's self-cultivated selfhood has not the eminent spirituality proper to the soul itself. Hence, the mystic's subjective experiences of God have not the actual objective spirituality proper to the soul's own inorganic spirituality and certainly not proper to God's own divine spirituality. Yet, for all of this, they are genuine experiences of God's transcendence when these experiences themselves have their origin in God and not merely in the mystic's own illusions or the devil's machinations.

It is a singular feature of the mystical life for the Catholic Christian mystic that God is simultaneously fully objectively present and fully subjectively absent to the mystic. God is objectively through faith contemplated as fully present in the very Triune Personhood of God's own Godhead. Gazing on the Holy Eucharist with the gift of faith, the mystic beholds and is in the actual dynamic living presence

586

of God's Triune Godhead. Further, the mystic's very own body is it-self the temple of this same Godhead.

Yet, within the subjective phenomenological constitution of the mystic's psychosomatic selfhood, God is experienced as absent rather than as present. The mystic's religious subjective bodily feeling and mental bearing toward God's Godhead is a pining and aching need for God which becomes intensively more needful the more acutely the mystic experiences and entertains God's impact within his intimate mental bearing over and above his sensitive bodily feeling.

The fire of love which is infused into the mystic even before his purgation reaches its completion is experienced by the mystic as an aching for God. This aching is a homesickness which anyone who has been unwittingly away from his native home for any extended period of time would fully appreciate. The "home" for the mystic, of course, is the very bosom of the Blessed Trinity. This ache differs considerably between the selfhood's somatic willful self and its psychic willful counterpart. In the former it is more like a sensitized tactile stirring pleasantness while in the latter it is rather an intimate non-tactile serene care-freeness. Thus, this ache in the former case is more extensive permeating the body's sensitivity yet superficial even though it is still within the subjectivity of the selfhood's personalized bodily sensationalism.

In the latter case, it is more intensive and more radical since it touches the inmost intimate recesses of the mystic's volitional non-tactile intimacy. The reason for this difference is that the somatic body responds to religious stimuli directly commensurate with its own kinesthetic tactility (i.e., as proximate feelings) while the psychic mind responds to religious sedations indirectly commensurate with its own anesthetic lack of tactility (i.e., as remote and impassive bearing).

This, of course, is very paradoxical. For, while the emotional feeling of God is sensitively superficial it seems to the mystic that God is very near at hand experienced through this visceral feeling of divine exultation. On the other hand, while the emotionless longing for God is radically intimate it seems to the mystic that God is far off in this mystical bearing of inmost intimate cerebral serenity. What these mystical experiences evoke in the mystic is, on the one hand, a greater aching need for God's self-satisfying bodily righteous contentment and, on the other, a greater aching pining for God's self-justifying mental righteous self-containment. Both of these aches evoke profound sighs and suffering for the mystic who finds no consolation and no solace apart from fully possessing and cherishing God in God's own Trinitarian Godhead.

So much so is the complete loss and absence of these mystical experiences of God a grievous suffering for the mystic that in the complete absence of such mystical experiences of God, he becomes convinced in the ordeal and excruciating suffering of the "dark night" that God has completely abandoned and forsaken him. If he could be convinced otherwise, he would readily and willingly suffer the absence of these mystical encounters with God. But, no one can convince him of this precisely because his very own self-confidence and social security is strengthened and invigorated by these mystical experiences. In their absence, his self-assured sense of righteous security is shattered both in terms of his bodily righteous self-gratification and mental righteous self-vindication.

It remains that objectively the mystic is fully apprised through the supernatural gift of faith that God in God's Triune Godhead remains fully sacramentally present. This simultaneous objective real presence and experienced subjective absence of God would obtain between husband and wife when the husband is in jail behind bars and the wife is separated from him by the jail bars. He is fully present to her but still remains absent from her tender caress. Correspondingly, the mystic's subjective bodily religious zeal has no stimulus to motivate the body to become busy in the service of God and His sacramental Church and members; further his subjective mental religious piety has no corresponding serenity to motivate the mystic to become more intimately absorbed and surrendered to God in prayerful recollection. The mystic is like an émigré exiled from his homeland and too forlorn and longing to return home to be able to busy himself with adjusting to his new situation.

How is it, then, that the mystic caught up in the throes of this "dark night" and left only with a pining and aching for God can still find within himself the wherewithal to still keep prayerfully searching for Him? St. John explains this by pointing out that the delicate intimate and exhilarating mystical sensitive touches of God which first enamored the mystic remain to haunt him and to keep alive this unquenchable desire he continues to have to further experience God's infusive splendor and peaceful serenity. Eventually, in the mystic's persistence to relentlessly pursue this prayerful quest, there dawns on him by infused wisdom that the miseries and trials he is experiencing are not due to God's withdrawal and insouciance but moreso to his own sinfulness and resistance to God's infinite graciousness.

In the light of this infused wisdom the mystic begins to appreciate and to measure the immense benefit he is receiving and has received throughout this "dark night's" ordeal. He becomes aware that he has been and is continuing to be purged of his own self-centered selfishness and his imprisonment within his own selfhood. Thus, his soulful intellect becomes enlightened to the marvelous transformation occurring in him which he could never have accomplished on his own. This infused illumination allows the intellect to become more perfectly integrated into the sublime divine wisdom of Christ's cross of crucifixion revealed only through the theological virtue of faith.

The upshot of this is that the mystic's psychosomatic willful self will become be-attitudinally more divinized than me-attitudinally humanized and more alive to God-the-Father's Holy Will than to the secular world's alluring self-centered selfish fleeting and ephemeral social security. The mystic's supernatural gift of faith will become more credulously trusting. This fidelity to faith's trustworthiness will increase in the mystic. And, in turn, the supernatural gift of hope will become convincingly more hopeful precisely because its very subjective confidence and prayerful confidentiality rests on the objective credibility of the infallible authority of Christ's own Godliness.

An explanation of why this mystical transformation is a sheer grace.

God is not encountered by the mystic other than in solitude and alone. This should not be surprising. When two espoused individuals are in their honeymoon, they seek to be apart from others and alone to enable each to become more intimately familiar with the other.

Similarly, the mystic must part company with his own self-humanized personality in order to commingle with and become transformatively integrated into Christ's very own superhumanized Personality. This can only take place by the sacrificial self-annulment of the mystic's own self-humanized personality. For, the love with which the mystic is enamored of God here is not principally and fundamentally a love which is the mystic's innate drive to possess God appropriately as is the case with the soul's intellectual will which is conscionably and morally obligated to love God as the supreme adorable objective goal and purpose of this love. Rather, the love here is one of a self-fulfilling need. It is a love in which the mystic is fond of, cares for, and appreciates for his own selfless self-fulfilling need the object of his love.

This love is as paradoxical as it is elusive to the mystic. It is a love for God which surpasses the soul's objective intellectual willful dutiful love. This latter love is fundamental and principally fundamental. The mystic must be conscionably obedient to God-the-Father's Holy Will; worshipfully, nobly, rightfully and, morally obedient. This noble love of itself is not sacrificial; it is meritorious. The immediate beneficiary of eating is the person's body and its metabolic well-being. The immediate beneficiary of worship directed principally to God is the person's is the person's everlasting happy holiness (viz., Godliness).

But, just as the moral meritorious virtue of temperance cannot flourish unless the human person subjectively practices sacrificially unselfish self-restraint and self-denial in his subjective need for bodily gustatory delectable self-satisfaction and self-satiation, so also is it the case that moral meritorious virtue of general justice cannot flourish unless the same human person subjectively practices sacrificially unselfish self-restraint and self-denial in his subjective need for mental equitable non-tactile self-justification and self-vindication. And, additionally in the supernatural order the meritorious virtue of general justice cannot flourish unless the same human person subjectively practices heroically and selflessly the self-restraint and self-denial of his subjective need for mental self-righteous self-justification.

Indeed, what explicitly the "dark night of the spirit" accomplishes in the mystic's willful mindful awareness is the very loss of this emotionless self-centered selfish non-tactile self-justified mental deeply intimate serenity socially self-possessed and convincingly secured. This is nothing other than the false maxim fully embraced by some non-Catholic Christians: "once saved, always saved." This false security is also tantamount to the mental security that many Catholics entertain when they construe that simply as a practicing member of the Catholic Church their social autonomy is everlastingly safe and secure. Oh! Yes! There may be a delay in purgatory; but, heaven itself is a sure bet.

When this self-fulfilling need is selfishly satisfied or justified merely supplementally, this needful appreciative affectionate love itself fails to achieve a full self-fulfillment. This love remains selfishly and affectionately partisanly but not fully self-serving. It is only when this self-humanizing amorously affectionate love is entirely selflessly self-serving that it is fully self-serving and fully self-fulfilling. This, of course, entails a paradox. The selfhood will's supplemental need for something to fulfill its craving for complete somatic self-satisfaction, on the one hand, and for complete psychic self-justification, on the other, cannot be fully achieved or attained merely supplementally, partisanly, and selfishly.

It can only be achieved and attained fundamentally when the selfhood's will actually appreciates and cares sacrificially selflessly for the object of its own self-fulfillment with an enamored affectionate love that transcends its own partisan selfish self-interest. This love is entirely sacrificial. The selfhood's psychosomatic will must completely and sacrificially forego its own partisan self-serving selfish self-interest in order to find its selfhood fulfilled fundamentally, conscientiously, and authentically beyond its supplemental neediness. That is, it must volunteer itself sacrificially to the object of its affection and careful concern to find its authentic total self-fulfillment.

If the selfhood's willful need for supplemental self-fulfillment is fulfilled merely supplementally, this supplemental self-fulfillment only serves to further expansively intensify this need, not to fulfill it. This is borne out in experience. The alcoholic who seeks added somatic self-confidence and security in the emotional comfort afforded

591

by alcohol succeeds in becoming further addicted to this spiritual concoction. Not only does his own self-humanized spirit and personality not become more securely somatically autonomously independent and self-satisfied, the alcoholic becomes increasingly more insecure, dissatisfied, and dependent on alcohol. Similarly with every other addiction whether it be on the part of the selfhood's somatic will attached to its own autonomous emotional visceral satisfied self-contentment or the selfhood's psychic will attached to its own autonomous emotionless cerebral justified self-containment.

Ultimately, what the human person in the selfhood of his own personhood humanistically seeks is his own autonomous self-righteousness consisting in the confluence of his psychosomatic need for autonomous self-contentment and self-containment simultaneously fully and totally satisfied and justified. But, this is impossible if the selfhood's will remains merely within the confines of its own supplemental self-humanizing partisan selfish social self-interest.

The individual that risks and possibly even ultimately loses its life by plunging into a burning building to rescue someone else's pet cat or dog finds a self-fulfillment beyond the confines of his own supplemental craving even if the pet is not itself deserving of this sacrificial act of heroism. For, at the very least the individual that dares to sacrificially love and care for whatever transports himself beyond the confines of his own selfishness has gained some measure of his own dignity as a member of a community of individuals with credentials and values that are not limited and restricted to their own partisan selfish self-serving isolated self-interests. Of course, such an act of heroism is not fully authentically and conscientiously heroic because it does not measure up to the objective fundamental conscionable truth of the real worth of the pet animal for which the individual sacrifices his own life to save.

In the final analysis, the selfhood's psychosomatic will must sacrificially transcend its own self-serving selfishness to conscientiously and authentically fully fulfill its self-serving need for its own justified and vindicated self-righteous autonomy. That is, it must paradoxically die to its own selfish selfhood in order to find its selfhood's authentic self-fulfillment. This death, of course, is not fundamentally physical. It does not aim at the corporeal body's substantive demise. It is a quasi-spiritual death inasmuch as the psychosomatic selfhood's willfulness (i.e., personality) is itself not fully spiritual as is the case with the person's spiritual soul. This selfhood is constituted of the psychosomatic corpuscular insubstantive materialized somatic body together with its counterpart, the insubstantive dematerialized psychic mind. The one is physiological while the other is psychological. That is, both are only accessible through the personhood's own self-conscious awareness of his own selfhood and ego-centered subjectivity.

This psychosomatic selfhood must die to its partisan selfishness as the very condition for its transformation into a selfless self-giving servant self rather than a selfish self-serving self. Such a death entails the radical transformation of a personhood's personality. This cannot be accomplished merely unctuously and persuasively. It can only be accomplished forcibly by doing violence to one's own humanistic personality. Such violence, however, is not a moral violation. Rather, it is a forceful sacrificial self-abnegation. It is not a violence wrecked on a person other than by one's own selfhood. It is a violence directed to one's very own self, one's very own personality.

This violence for the mystic entails a suffering that is more intense and painful than the mere loss of one's homeland and welfare which an immigrant experiences when forcibly driven from his homeland and forced to live in an alien country without normal means of self-sustenance. This sufferance for the mystic entails a loss of all that is familiar to his own personality including his own autonomy, his own satisfactions, justifications, and self-righteous indignation. This sufferance cuts to the very core and nub of the mystic's self-humanized and self-cultivated personality. Nothing, nada, nothing is spared.

This suffering is not only described as a prolonged "dark night." It is described by St. John of the Cross as a pit of darkness whose nebulosity exercised in faith leaves the intellect deprived of its native intelligence's acuity, the memory sustained by hope in a status of amnesia regarding everything with which it would be normally familiar in its past recollection and future anticipations; and the will (i.e., the selfhood's psychosomatic willfulness) suffused with charity (i.e., an amicable friendship with Christ) stymied in all that it would have and would want to be socially secure of its own autonomous self-reliance. This purification of the mystic's selfish self-attachments cannot be achieved nor attained by the efforts of the mystic alone.

The mystic through his own self-humanizing efforts cannot successfully and sacrificially forego his own personality with all its familiar proclivities and self-attachments. Even those who sacrificially volunteer to commit suicide, such as those who make a pyre of themselves or a bomb of themselves to protest against their opponents and to prove to others the merit of the cause they espouse as well as their own self-justification; such suicidal victims do not succeed in transcending themselves and their own self-centered selfishness. They merely confirm that their self-serving partisan self-interest remains very much selfish and selfishly self-centered.

Another individual could only emulate such mistaken heroism by seeking himself to be self-detonated and self-burned to death to join the cause of the suicide victim. For, the cause itself is suicidal and non-liberating beyond the pale of the suicide's testimonial to his own selfish commitment. Similarly for those who espouse euthanasia as a liberation from suffering itself.

In brief, for the Catholic Christian mystic, it is only God's divine supernatural influence in the mystic's life that can accomplish such a complete personality transformation. Furthermore, God does not accomplish this by remaining aloof and alien to the mystic's own self-centered personality and selfish selfhood. Quite to the contrary. Christ through the Holy Will of His Heavenly Father bequeaths and endows the mystic with His very own Holy Spirit, the Spirit of Truth, the Third Person of the Blessed Trinity, the Spirit of Christ's own divinized Personality. This Advocate and Paraclete superhumanistically enables the mystic to sacrificially do violence to himself and to his own personality and self-humanizing spirit (i.e., self-serving domineering pluck).

For, this Holy Spirit not only supernaturally viscerally stimulates and cerebrally inspires the mystic to become transformed into Christ's Personality, the object of his superhumanistic careful concern, admiration, and devotion, this same Spirit supports, sustains, and supplies the indomitable stamina required for the mystic to persevere throughout the excruciatingly painful and arduous ordeal undergoing this transformative self-immolation and self-mortification.

The mystic is a prisoner of his own slavishly and selfishly self-serving personality and becomes liberated and freed from his own selfish self-attachments through suffering and undergoing this ordeal of the "dark night." In sum, it is God who accomplishes this in the mystic. The mystic's role is simply to submissively and humbly submit to trusting in the Father's Gospel revelation, hoping in Christ's resurrection, and loving in the selfless charitable ingratiating persevering sacrificial love that is the hallmark of the Holy Spirit's divine vitality and giftedness.

The divine security afforded the mystic throughout this purgative darkness of contemplative prayer.

Note must be made of the radical difference between the vertical order of existence and the horizontal order of resistance. This difference has been previously indicated earlier in this commentary. It is well to recall this here as we ponder the mystagogical wisdom pointed out by St. John regarding the beneficent divine security afforded the mystic while he staunchly and steadfastly remains faithful to his prayerful vigil while suffering through the darkness of this prolonged period of purgation.

The mystic's personalized subjective experience of God proper to the horizontal order of the mystic's religious self-centered self-cultivation and self-humanization is that of being reflexively conscious of God's absence. This is in direct opposition to the objective personal theological belief in God proper to the vertical order of the mystic's sacramental life of divine grace in which the mystic is reflectively conscious of God's Trinitarian presence. Awareness of this absence is spoken of frequently by St. John as a wound.

By emotionally stimulating the mystic's subjective bodily sensitivity with delicate divine elations and sublime ardor, the mystic feels proximately the presence of God. This stimulation, however, does not completely satiate nor satisfy the mystic's needful deficiency for such stirring divine touches; it only awakens and intensifies the mystic's need to be fully sublimely satiated and satisfied by these touches. This the mystic cannot self-induce nor self-control these touches on his own initiative. Similarly in respect to the mind's intimacy which is sedated emotionlessly to enable the mystic to experience inwardly God's presence remotely in a profoundly serene and calmly secure composure. Yet, again, this divine touch only awakens and deepens the mystic's need to be fully divinely justified and self-contained by these touches. And, again, the mystic cannot self-educe nor self-control these touches on his own initiative.

There is a basis for this disparity between God's presence and His absence simultaneously impinging on the mystic's prayer-life as he suffers through this prolonged period of purification. Knowledge in the objective vertical order of existence is truthfully informative of the reality that transcends the mystic himself. Such knowledge is inherently re-presentative of the reality that is cognized. This is the case whether it is sentient or intelligent knowledge. There is an informative medium to such knowledge which in the case of the senses is an image and in the case of the intellect is an idea. The senses do not sense images any more than does the intellect understand ideas. These informative media are precisely and literally media and not intermediaries between the cognitive faculties and the object cognized.

In the case of the mystic's supernatural knowledge of God, it is unequivocally clearly stated by St. John that no medium (viz., idea) is adequate to enable the mystic to truthfully and intellectually cognize God in God's Triune Godhead unless this informative re-presentative medium is actually the divine reality itself of God's own supreme divinity. Thus, by the theological gift of faith the mystic is cognitively eminently in the actual presence of the transcendent supreme reality of God's Trinitarian Godhead. This is unerringly, authoritatively, and infallibly trustworthy and reliable.

On the other hand, knowledge in the subjective horizontal order of resistance is falsely transformative of the reality that transcends the mystic himself. Such knowledge is inherently mis-representative of the reality of which the mystic is reflexively aware within his reflexive consciousness. This is the case whether it is an issue of the tactile knowledge peculiar to the somatic imagination's fabricated phantasies or the non-tactile knowledge peculiar to the psychic mind's notional conceptions. The somatic imagination's imagery and the psychic mind's notional conceptions serve as intermediaries between the mystic's self-conscious awareness and the reality itself that transcends this awareness. That is, the mystic is not aware of any transcendent reality, God included, in terms of his own subjective personalized imaginative perceptual feeling or notional conceptual bearing which he entertains toward that reality.

In view of this transformative aspect of the mystic's subjective personalized "knowledge" of any reality which transcends his own consciousness of it, the mystic is actually in the very absence of the reality itself of which he is self-consciously aware. Such knowledge is entirely paradoxical and not in the least orthodox. Indeed, it is not literally knowledge at all inasmuch as knowledge is cognitive. Rather, it is knowledge only in a metaphorical sense; an as-if knowing rather than an as-is knowing.

It is clearly stated by St. John in other places of his writings that the mystic is not to place any probative trust in his own subjective conscious mystical experiences as having anything more than a symptomatic knowledge of God. God's divine reality is not revealed to the mystic through these religious experiences which are entirely subjective and personalized. What such subjective religious experiences reveal to the mystic is moreso his own subjective religious affections and attitude toward God. That is, such religious awareness is more a transformatively conative knowledge which is a religious affectionate (or, disaffectionate) emotional bodily feeling and/or emotionless mental bearing toward God moreso than an informatively cognitive knowledge of God's divinity.

It reveals more about the mystic's attitude toward God than it does about the divine reality of God Himself. Yet, such quasi-knowledge is critical to the rounded and complete integrity of the mystic's integration into God's divine Trinitarian life as a member of the Church's sacramentality which incorporates the mystery of Christ's own incarnation and paschal passage from earth to heaven. While the mystical life of the Christian who is objectively by God's graciousness alive in the life of the Blessed Trinity through the mediation of the sacraments, this same supernaturally divinized life has its completion subjectively in the mystic's own self-cultivated, self-centered, and self-civilized personality.

Such transformative quasi-knowledge considered supernaturally and superhumanistically in the mystic's subjective religious horizontal experience of God is more a hopeful possession of the reality of God who transcends this religious experience whereas in the vertical order of knowledge, informative knowledge itself places the mystic in the actual cognitive presence of the reality of God through the supernatural gift of faith which is unerringly trustworthy. Thus, on the one hand, the mystic by the supernatural virtue of faith is infallibly in the actual presence of the Supreme reality of God that transcends this knowledge. With his soulful intellectual will, the mystic is supernaturally and sacramentally enabled to actually dutifully love, adore, and delight in God in God's actual transcendent presence and Godhead. On the other hand, the mystic by the supernatural virtue of hope is invincibly, subjectively, and paradoxically convinced and confident with Christ's very own resurrectional confidence of fully possessing God in the hereafter beyond his present subjective religious awareness of God's absence..

Given this radical disparity between these two irreducible orders of the cross's cruciformity, it may be more appreciated why the mystic's subjective religious experience of God's complete absence during his prolonged process of purification and darkness affords him a divine protection and security even while he miserably suffers the loss and dissolution of his own self-reliable, self-possessed, and self-controlled autonomous social security and familiar personality. During this prolonged period of religious anguish in which he suffers his familiar personality's own dissolution and self-alienation, he is constrained to live cloaked in the theological virtues of faith and hope; that is in the complete trust and confidence available to him through the Heavenly Father's divine providentiality and the Son's memoriality. It is in the intellectual umbrage of faith's luminosity and the me-

morial assurances of hope's hopefulness that the mystic will efficaciously reach his goal of achieving his objective of religiously experiencing even in this present life a friendly communion in love with the
Blessed Trinity.

St. John of the Cross points out that the only religious experiences which can misguide and mislead the mystic astray are those
which are entirely self-centered, subjective, and selfishly self-serving.
When these religious experiences are neutralized, even to the point
that they no longer present to the mystic suggestive temptations, the
mystic has become freed from his slavery to his own selfish self-
centeredness. In this freedom he is free to live with the selfless freedom of the Holy Spirit, the very spirit of Christ and the Heavenly
Father's divine freedom. Certainly, the price of this freedom taxes the
mystic to the utmost limit of his own self-reliant resourcefulness. Indeed, it ultimately strips the mystic of his own self-cultivated, self-
civilized, and self-humanized personality with its partisan me-attitude of hostility toward all that threatens his own personalized self-
reliant social autonomy.

When this metamorphical transformation is finalized, the mystic's superhumanized personality will be modeled on Christ's very
own paradigmatic divinized Selfless Servant Personality. In the inter-
im during the anguishing ordeal of the "dark night" the mystic undergoes an austere training of self-deprivation and mortification in
which he progressively acquires the superhumanistic skills of Christ's
very own self-control and self-mastery under the tutelage and stamina of Christ's very own Holy Spirit.

Stricken with the misery of his own helpless predicament which
the prolonged "dark night" brings to him, the mystic loses all proneness to vaunt himself and his own religious righteousness. He is too
much aware of his own lack of religious exuberance and fervor, his
own lack of self-confidence, his own uneasiness and anxious foreboding, his own helplessness, his own forlornness and social isolation
from others. This misery which pervades and permeates his emotional feelings and moods, on the one hand, and his emotionless bearings
and trances, on the other, are too overpowering and too pervasive to
allow him to boast about himself either to his colleagues or to God.

St. John raises the following question. How can it be that God who is Goodness and Graciousness itself could have such a deleterious and devastating effect on the mystic's piety and devotion? Why wouldn't it be only normal for the mystic to piously and devoutly delight and profitably relax and rest in the serenity of God's eternal immobility and bliss? The response to this question is readily forthcoming from St. John. It is because of the mystic's own depravity that this is not possible. Even if God were to infuse into the mystic sublime experiences of God's own bliss, the mystic could not profit from this bliss because while suffering through the ordeal of the "dark night" he is still bent on his own me-attitude selfishly self-serving self-interest and exploiting everything to supply this need including God's own bliss.

It is only when the mystic becomes sufficiently divested of his own selfish heartfelt and selfish me-attitude mindset steeped in its partisan hostility that he will be able to profitably partake of God's very own benevolence and bliss. At this point, he will have acquired Christ's very own selfless empathic heartfelt compassionate sensitivity and Christ's very own beatitudinal messianic mindset. Until this stage of purification is reached, the mystic remains prone to exploititatively "make use" of God's gratuitously infused sublime touches for his own personalized possession and consolation rather than for God's own glory and with a superhumane selfless love divested of all selfish self-interest.

St. John additionally explains that in the throes of the "dark night" the mystic advances to God through suffering. Such suffering, he insists, is a blessing precisely because it more quickly transforms the mystic into the volunteer victim exhibited by Christ in His passion and crucifixion in which He substitutes Himself as a volunteer ransom to atone for our sins and transgressions. By joining his own sufferings with those of Christ, the mystic more readily and more quickly becomes conformed to Christ even to the point of offering his own sufferings as prayerful intercession for the benefit of the salvation and sanctification of others. In this manner, the mystic enters into the very charity of Christ in which Christ makes manifest a measure of His infinite mercy and love which prompts Him to give His life not merely for a friend but even for enemies who sinfully are still at enmity with Him.

St. John adds still another reason why the emotional religious aridity and the emotionless religious anxiety which assail the mystic during his long ordeal of purification provide him a divine security without which he would not profitably advance to his perfect union with God. The stress and anguish which this "dark night" brings on intensifies the mystic's interest and attentiveness to God from whom he seems to be so estranged. He becomes more eager to address and salute God in the grandeur of His divine majesty. He becomes more solicitous about his feelings and bearing toward God and his neighbor and taking to heart and adopting more assiduously Christ's be-attitudinal mindset. In brief, he becomes more intensely intent and single-mindedly determined to serve God in his neighbor and of ignoring all issues which detract from this single-mindedness.

COMMENTARY ON
THE SPIRITUAL CANTICLE

The Cross cruciformity.

The paradigmatic and programmatic outline of this commentary is the configuration of Christ's cross of crucifixion. This cross contains three different, disparate beams. The upright and vertical beam points to heaven's immutable eternity beyond earth's time and temporality; the horizontal cross beam spans the entire history of mankind living on earth in its pilgrimage to heaven; the intersection of the two beams forms the cross' cruciformity. In this cruciformity there is the march of a Christian's eschatological salvation history toward heaven alongside the march of secular history toward its doomsday. These three beams with each's special orientation engage three separate and disparate orders inherent in the Christian's life. The vertical order is ontological-metaphysical; the horizontal order is phenomenological-paraphysical; the cruciform intersection of these two orders integrates and reconciles together the two previous orders. The vertical order entails a logic that is orthodox; the horizontal entails an order that is one of paradox; and the cruciform order entails a logic that is heterodox engaging both previous orders simultaneously. The logic proper to the vertical order is the logic of analogy; that of the horizontal involves the logic of typology and catalogy; the cruciform order inculcates both of the two previous logical formats by way of dialogue.

Thus, the vertical order has a terminology peculiar to its own logic. It employs such general metaphysical terms as intellectual, intelligibility, orthodox, fundamental, truth, obvious, transcendent, existing and existence, literal, categorical, objectivity, essence and essential, etc.. The horizontal order has a disparate paraphysical more specialized terminology such as experiential, unintelligible, paradox, prototypical, supplemental, provable, devious, immanent, resisting, metaphorical, story-telling, subjectivity. The knowledge peculiar to the vertical order is that of insightful knowing by essence, intelligence, presence such that when a person bites into an apple and tastes its sweetness, the intellect discerns and discriminates that sweetness is an incidental quality of the apple but not the apple in its very essence. The knowledge peculiar to the horizontal order is that of knowing by appearance not essence; by intuiting, congruent, compatible and incongruent, incompatible associations while remaining ignorant of their nature; by absence rather than by presence when one observes the TV screen's electronic depiction of an apple rather than the apple itself.

When these two disparate orders of knowing are dialogically reconciled there results a knowledge which engages both disparate orders heterodoxically. In this case, the same human person is privy to both the apple's essence objectively and to its mere appearance subjectively. The very same person simultaneously objectively understands this essence and remains subjectively ignorant of it; he fundamentally knows the apple in its essence and supplementally remains ignorant of this essence and is conversant merely with its appearance. In the one case, it is the real apple that is really present to the knower and in the other case, this real apple is absent and only its appearance is known. When the apple in its physical substance is knowingly present, it is obviously present; when the apple's non-substantive corpuscular characteristics are the object of knowledge, it is deviously present. The orthodox knowledge transcends the knower and attains to the reality itself of the apple while the paradoxical knowledge remains immanent within the knower and fails to attain to the reality itself of the apple. The orthodox knowledge attains to the very existence of the apple where the paradoxical subjective knowledge resists such an attainment. The terminology of the orthodox is to be taken literally (as is) while that of the paradoxical knowing is to be taken metaphorically (as if). Finally, the orthodox knowing is dogmatically immutable and definitive whereas the paradoxical knowing is mutably (viz., historically) transient, transitional, and only captured descriptively; not definitively.

There is a remarkable difference between the mystic's objective and his subjective encounters with God. Objectively, it is the very reality of God that is personally encountered. In this encounter God remains unambiguously distinct from the mystic himself in God's majestic and eternal grandeur. This God remains objectively the very same reality that others personally encounter and speak of. Subjectively, it is the mystic's own divine transformation that is personably experienced. In this superhumanizing and superhumane transformation, the mystic experiences himself infused and transfused with God's very own divinity. This experience of God differs remarkably from one stage of experience to another and from one person to the other.

There is in this threefold cruciform dialogical engagement a Trinitarian anthropology. The vertical order is directed toward God-the-Father. The horizontal order is orientated toward God-the-Son. The cruciform order itself is enveloped with the Father and Son's Holy Spirit. That is, the Father initiates, the Son consummates, and the Holy Spirit integrates. That is, the vertical order is that of the Father's creative initiation and paternal providence over the human person. The horizontal order is that of the Son's sacrificial re-creation and re-demption of the human person's fall from the Father's graciousness. The cruciform order itself is that of the Holy Spirit's integrity and integration reconciling the vertical and horizontal orders with each other. Objectively to the mystic God is always present while subjectively God is always absent.

Vertically and hierarchically this order is based on the underlying holistic metaphysical principle that the holistic whole exceeds its constitutive parts. Thus, the human person, as an existing entity within the universe of reality, is naturally constituted of the substantive principles of matter (viz., body) and spirit (viz., the soul). This is enunciated by stating that "man is a body; man is a soul." In this statement, man is holistically both a body and soul; but not reducibly so. That is, the human person as a man is not partially a body and partially a soul. The whole of man-as-such is body and the whole of man-as-such is soul. Considered holistically, the constitutive principles constitute one and the same integral whole. Considered constitutively, they remain distinct within the same integral holistic whole.

Within this hierarchical order of the cross's vertical beam, the human person is a *homo sapiens* that is a creature of God and is ordered to God as causally issuing from God and predestined in his finality to be directed toward God. In this order, the human person is fundamentally a unique, intelligent, free, sovereign unsubstitutable responsible being whose destiny is immortal and whose intelligible horizon and freedom penetrates into the realm of eternity, the realm of the immutable and the ideal; the realm of God's divine existence.

Within the historical order of the cross's horizontal beam, this order is based on the underlying epistemological and phenomenological principle that the piecemeal whole is reducible to its component parts. This quasi whole is perforce always a mathematical whole. Thus, if we again consider the reality, the human person, as constituted microscopically, his bio-chemical constitution comes to the forefront. In this dimensional framework, his biological make-up consists of his major physiological systemic organisms (viz., heart, lungs, kidneys, intestines, brain, etc.) These organisms themselves are each, in turn, reducible to their sub component parts.

Thus, there is no more to the heart's organism than its physiological organic parts and to its blood's make-up its reductive chemical components which, in turn, may be further reduced to molecular particles and, still further, to atomic and sub-atomic components. Briefly, there is no enduring holistic heart-as-such entity as there is an ontological enduring entity, man-as-such. Rather, there is only a functional heart enterprise facilitating the blood's circulation. There is no heart-as-such remaining identically one and the same organism throughout its lifetime. It continues to processively undergo its own re or degeneration through its lifetime. One cannot declare that every physiological part of the heart organism is the heart itself as can be stated that every substantive component of man-as-such is holistically man itself. Every part of the heart organism is only a segmented part of the heart. The human person's organic heart may technically be replaced with an alternative heart. But, man-as-such, constituting the very objective nature of each human person cannot be in any way substituted; it is essential to the human person's constitution.

Here in the horizontal order we deal with mathematical-paraphysical piecemeal enterprising functional wholes and not any metaphysical entitative holistic wholes. It is the same entity man-as-such that constitutes the human person ontologically throughout a person's entire existence. The same human person phenomenologically considered is an enterprise which continues to processively mutate throughout a person's historical life-time on earth. Similarly, with the human person's every other bio-chemical and socio-political organistic make-up in the subjective order of the human person's epistemological and phenomenological constitution.

Within this historical order of the cross's horizontal beam, the human person is a *homo laborens*. In this respect, the human person takes the initiative in advancing his own self-humanization and self-cultivation. Here the human person is not objectively theocentrically ordered but subjectively anthropocentrically self-orientated. There is no causality in this order; there is only a push-pull influence of the human person's self-humanizing willful self-control that is devoid of purpose and finality. In this self-orientation the human person is entirely self-serving in pursuit of his own overriding self-centered self-interest. In this order the human person is supplementally an anonymous, autonomous (viz., self-sufficient), mindful substitutable self-controllable self-centered dichotomous social personality processively evolving through a temporary mutating span of space-time that is doomed to extinction.

The cross's cruciformity includes the joining of the vertical and horizontal beams together to form a cross. Within this juncture of the cross's cruciformity, the two separate and disparate hierarchical and horizontal orders are integrated and reconciled with each other within the Paschal Mystery of Christ's crucifixion. Within this cruciform order itself, the human person through Christ's mediation as God/Superman becomes an integral and integrated *homo sapiens* and a *homo laborens*. On the one hand the human person can ponder wisely, unerringly, and effortlessly the fundamental truths of all reality without toil and labor. On the other hand, he must toil laboriously and productively with much effort to civilize his sociability with selves other than his own self and to safeguard himself by cultivating his environment to serve his basic needs. Paradoxically, he is unable here to ponder wisely on the ultimate purpose and meaning of the product of his effort and toil. In this cruciform order integrating and reconciling the former two orders (viz., heaven's immutable eternity with earth's historical transitoriness, the human person becomes *homo oecumenicus*, the ecumenical human person.

The human person's task here is to engage both beams simultaneously without confusing the two together nor forfeiting what is peculiar and proper to each while integrating each with the other in a complementary fashion. This integration and reconciliation demands that the human person, on the one hand, recognize his own personhood in its essence as that of an immortal enduring unsubstitutable sovereign dynamic entity; this is an objective approach. On the other hand, the same human person must recognize his own personhood in its appearance as a mortal transitional substitutable enterprising synergetic dichotomous personality, subjectively speaking. In this same objective, subjective opposition, the human person understands intelligently and objectively the universe of God's creation within which he is a creature while simultaneously remaining subjectively ignorant of the world of his own self-cultivation and self-humanization in which he resides within a provincial civilized culture. God's creation is known as a stable and an enduring presence whereas the world of man's own involvement lacks such stability and presence. It is the same tree that one might visit 50 years later but never the same city which one would visit within the same span of time. The original city is absent 50 years later. It is objectively the very same person that one visits 50 years later but subjectively a considerably different personality; the earlier personality is absent.

The fundamental hierarchical order is orthodox; the same person remains identical within his own personhood. The supplemental historical order is one of paradox; the personality continues to evolve within the same personhood. The personhood's natural perduring identity is intelligibly recognizable, objectively speaking; whereas the same personhood's subjective evolving sociable personality is not recognizable, subjectively speaking. How can one recognize in a person's mature personality his earlier youthful personality? This objective-subjective differentiation cannot be said of the tree or the brute animal which have no subjective self-conscious awareness. This can only be said of the human person. Thus, the very same person in his very personhood is both objectively present and subjectively absent to himself. Objectively, I am always the same person throughout all of my historical development but subjectively I am never quite the same personality. Objectively, I enjoy an ontological immortal status while subjectively I am always phenomenologically in process. Fundamentally I remain identical with my own being whereas supplementally I continue to evolve re/de/generatively from one processive stage to another.

Objectively speaking, the truth of the human person considered as a man-as-such is invariable. No human person throughout all of creation is other by nature than a man-as-such constituted of body/soul substantive principles. Subjectively speaking, there is no such invariable truth regarding the human person's self-cultivated personality. There is only a theoretical mental conjecture and corresponding empirical proof regarding the human person's self-cultivated enterprising personality and make-up. The make-up of the human person considered objectively is obvious inasmuch as he is what he is naturally and cannot be otherwise according to the principle of identity. The same human person's make-up considered subjectively is devious inasmuch as culturally and processively he is not what he purports to be and purports what he is not. For example, within his subjective personality the human person considered in terms of the mind's intimacy he is psychic but not somatic; conversely, considered in terms of the body's sensitivity he is somatic but not psychic.

Further, considered objectively, the human person is continuous with the universe of creation as an entity within it. In this manner the human person is known transcendentally as a reality among realities. Considered subjectively, the human person is self-enclosed within the immanence of his own selfhood. Situated within this immanence he learns of everything from the perspective of his own dichotomous ego as that which radiates from and remains immanent within this egological hub.

The objective order is one of existence in which the human person's very existence depends on a universal reality, God, transcendent to him. The subjective horizontal order is one of resistance in which the human person's self-serving will is the nuclear core and bastion of all resistance in the world of man's own self-humanization and self-cultivation. There is no cultivation and civilization without forceful and self-centered willful intervention. Where existence is the hall-mark of the vertical order, resistance is the horizontal order's hall-mark. A tree resists being reduced to lumber; it must be forcibly and willfully cut down, hewn, and fashioned into lumber. In the final analysis, the human person's self-centered will must paradoxically be forcibly overcome regarding its own selfish resistance to becoming civilized and artfully cultivated to become productively proficient in conjunction with selves other than its own self.

The cruciform integral order is one of consistency. Within this order the human person is engaged in reconciling his objective moral responsible personhood with his subjective amoral (i.e., technical) accountable personality. Objectively, the human person operates intentionally (i.e., purposefully), energetically and spontaneously through the sentient and soulful faculties with which he is naturally endowed. These operations are directed toward an immortal transhistorical communal destiny which is identical for every individual human person. Subjectively, the same human person in virtue of his transcendent personhood functions synergetically, autonomously (i.e., self-servingly and socially), and motivationally through psychosomatic facilities which are productively and socially self-cultivated. These functions are orientated toward the human person's temporary social welfare and safeguard throughout his mortal duration.

This integral cruciform order of reconciliation must both uphold the fundamental order of existence fundamentally and the supplemental order of resistance supplementally. When this fundamental/supplemental ordering is sustained, the two disparate orders complement each other. That is, the vertical communal immortal moral order of family existence that transcends transhistorically all phases, stages, and spans of the human person's historical resistance holds a *fundamental* primary priority. On the other hand, the horizontal social transitional and mortal technical order of resistant sociability historically unfolding and evolving periodically and chronologically holds its own *supplemental* subsidiary priority. When these two orders remain thus mutually and reciprocally ordered they complement each other and become consistent with each other.

It is of utmost importance to recognize that these two disparate orders cannot be completely reconciled with each other simply naturally and humanistically. This can only be brought about supernaturally in the objective order and superhumanistically in the subjective order. Without the order of grace, the human person cannot attain to his universal destiny: union with the Trinitarian family and Godhead. Further, without Christ's cross of crucifixion, the human person cannot attain to his authentic eschatological (i.e., transhistorical) self-fulfillment. This self-fulfillment entails a violent sacrificial submission of the person's willful resistant selfhood converted to a willful self-donation and surrender to Christ's very own volunteer Self-surrender of His own crucified Selfless Selfhood graciously and benevolently offered to substitute for the human person's reluctant self.

Vertical: intellectual – intelligible – orthodox – fundamental – truthful – obvious – transcendent – existing – literal – categorical - objective

Horizontal: experiential – unintelligible – paradox – supple mental – provable – devious – immanent – resisting – metaphor ical - story – subjectivity

Vertical: knowing by essence… intelligence… presence…. biting into the apple… tasting its very essence… it is sweet

Horizontal: knowing only by appearance… ignorance… absence… watching the TV apple… only its appearance… it is not an apple.

Cruciform intersection of the two: essence & appearance --- intelligence & ignorance --- heterodox --- fundamental & supplemental --- presence & absence --- truthful & provable --- obvious & devious --- transcendent & immanent --- existence & resistance --- literal & metaphorical --- dogmatic & historical

The truth will set you free.

Here we will conduct a dialogue engaging the vertical with the horizontal order of the cross' cruciformity. This dialogue will recognize that the analogical logic inherent in the ontological order is to be retained ontologically whereas the typological logic pertinent to the phenomenological order will remain phenomenologically. This is the most vital part of this dialogue. The logic inherent in each order must be respected and not diminished in finding a dialogical reconciliation between the two. The same terminology at times may be deployed in both orders. The meanings of these terms so employed are not univocal; they become equivocal. The equivocal terms are not reducible to each other nor educible from each other; they remain equivocal. The meaning of these terms is to be ascertained within the logic of the order within which they are deployed.

The vertical cross beam is fundamental, natural, and theocentric in the universal order of creation issuing from God. The horizontal cross beam is supplemental, cultural, and anthropocentric in the order of the human person's worldly self-cultivation and self-humanization. The disparity between these two orders will be indicated throughout this dialogue. In the personalism advocated and propounded by Pope John Paul II, the human person is the key to understanding the reconciliation between these two orders. It is the same human person as an incommunicable (i.e., inalienable), induplicable, subsistent   sovereign free and intelligent substrate that is by nature objectively, dynamically, and spontaneously cognizant and free. At the same time, this very same person subjectively within the subjectivity of this same personhood cultivates and develops a self-serving autonomous (i.e., social) alienable selfhood with its own distinctive self-motivated knowing and freedom. By nature the human person is one in the immortal transhistorical community of individual human persons. By culture the human person is interpersonally an associate with other selves within the subjectivity of his selfhood in dys/functional worlds subject to historical transition.

One can only love what one first knows. This is fundamental. The intellect's knowledge of the Truth fundamentally precedes the Will's freedom to love. However, the intellect cannot fully know the Truth if the will does not love and treasure it beyond every other love. The will's Freedom supplementally precedes Truth supplementally.

The Truth of the intellect precedes the will's Freedom fundamentally while the will's Freedom to love freely precedes supplementally the intellect's knowledge of the Truth. The intellect's Truth is intelligible but not experiential while the will's Freedom is experiential but unintelligible.

It is reasonable for the intellect to truthfully govern the will's freedom to choose what truthfully exists and is worthy of the will's love.

It is unreasonable for the will to necessarily love the Truth lovingly, honorably, and preciously since the will is willfully free to love whatever it wills to love and to treasure.

When the fundamental Truth precedes the will's Freedom fundamentally and directs and governs it conscionably...

When the supplemental Freedom of the will precedes the Truth supplementally and freely embraces it whole-heartedly...

The two complement each other integrally; each in solidarity and accord with each other.

The intellect's reasonable Truthfulness regarding what really exists honorably prevails while the will's unreasonable Freedom regarding its willful freedom to resist what actually exists also freely prevails.

St. Augustine in his typical masterful style sums this up as follows: Love the Truth and do whatever you will. The implication is that the will who freely treasures the Truth above every other choice honors both the Truth itself (viz. God) as well as its own Freedom.

THE SPIRITUAL CANTICLE: Stanzas 1-8

Stanza 1:

Objectively: God in His very divine essence is present (by grace) but hidden by transcendence. Intellectual faith

Subjectively: God is felt experientially as absent. Memorial hope.

Objectively: God is not reducible to one's subjective experience of Him,

Subjectively: A devotional experience of God is not an intellectual beatifying vision of Him as He really exists.

Objectively: God in His Trinitarian Godhead abides in the soul through sanctifying and actual grace

Subjectively: One's experience must also be hidden in God and not manifest within one's feelings & musings

Objectively: God will be known perfectly only in the next life

Subjectively: One cannot in this life experience God perfectly present but only in the next life.

Objectively: God is to be sought through faith which transcends human understanding

Subjectively: God is to be sought prayerfully in a sacrificial love that sacrifices one's pious sensitive feelings and one's pious intimate musings of Him (i.e., religious consolations, exultations, and delights of Him).

Objectively: God is ineffable and beyond the reach of one's natural intelligence; faith is darkness.

Subjectively: One must live in hope humbly suffering the lack of any experiential enjoyable feeling or inspirational musing of God and from God.

Objectively: God cannot be totally possessed as is the case with an apple that can be totally consumed.

Subjectively: God can only be possessed by a love that sacrifices self-love; for God is more precious than one's self

Objectively: God is truly sacramentally present in the soul...the body is the Holy Spirit's tabernacle.

Subjectively: The mystic remains restless and moans in his awareness that he aches for God who continues to remain absent and beyond his grasp. God is the most precious object of the mystic's reverent attention; his Beloved.

Objectively: The mystic believes through faith in God's divine personal sacramental presence.

Subjectively: by self-mortification and self-denial the mystic is attached to God alone in poverty of spirit. So intensive is this divine attachment that the mystic moans and groans in feeling and gauging his own bleak emptiness. At the same time this prayerful sighing, moaning, and groaning occurs because he continues to hope to enjoy God blissfully.

Objectively: God is like a deer who lives alone apart from and beyond the universe of creation.

Subjectively: God touches the mystic's pious feelings and arouses his affection only to depart and vanish and leave the mystic smitten with his love but completely unable to find the God of his pious and reverent affection.

Objectively: God seems to be like the fleet and graceful deer that refuses to be captured

Subjectively: the mystic is severely wounded by the intense sensitized glorious feeling of God's splendor and the profound intimate serenity of God's eternal immutability. But, these wonderful experiences of God leave the mystic's heart teasingly inflamed and the mystic's mind helplessly inspired with God's grandeur. This love is a gaping and incurable wound whose cure is God alone who seemingly refuses to cure this wound He has inflicted on the mystic.

Objectively: God is like the fleeting deer that refuses to be captured.

Subjectively: the mystic is so helplessly wounded by the exalted experience of God's divine loveliness that he is severely and intensively tortured by this love itself which leaves him helplessly pining and aching for his Beloved whom he is completely unable to reach out and embrace.

Objectively: God is ineffably transcendent to all of creation.

Subjectively: the exquisite religious pious divine and sublime touches (i.e., sensitized emotional feelings and intimate serene devotional musings) which the mystic experiences of God's sublimity and loveliness only serve to painfully awaken the mystic to his own abject misery in failing to perfectly embrace God without any further delay.

The upshot of this is the mystic's realization that he has through this experience of divine love detached himself completely from the secular world's securities and friendships as well as from his own self-centered satisfactions and justifications only to be denied the very Beloved to whom he has become completely attached. He now recognizes himself to be in a "no man's land;" he is neither in heaven's divine delights nor on earth with its secular diversions.

The mystic endures excruciating suffering in his helplessness to fully embrace his Beloved to whom he is so vehemently attached that he has become completely self-detached from everything that is not God, including detached from his own selfhood. – *The Dark Night of the Soul.*

Stanza 2:

The bride is sick, suffers, and dies in the intellect, memory, and will.

The intellect: because lacking in the beatific vision

The memory: because of the prospect of not merely living but also dying without God

The will: because she does not possess God

Stanza 3:

Seek God through her own efforts of moral discipline and ascetic self-denial and penance

Strive to contend vigorously against the world's lures & mockery; the flesh's weakness , and the devil by prayer & mortification

Stanza 4:

The bride seeks God in His creation of the heavens and of earth. They cannot substitute for God Himself.

Stanza 5:

The many natural beautiful wonders of creation are merely traces of His greatness and beauty. God is more directly discovered in the mystery of Christ's Incarnation and Paschal Mystery.

Stanza 6:

All these marvelous and wonderful traces of God's Beauty only increase the bride's love for God and her restlessness and sorrow in not fully possessing God above and beyond His creation.

Stanza 7:

The bride is dying of love and languishing because this love remains unfulfilled and cannot be satisfied with mere messengers of God. These messengers only intensify this love and increase the bride's longing and aching.

Stanza 8:

While the mystic remains alive in the body, he is dead in his spirit since the most precious object in his life, his love for God, remains beyond his possession. Where your treasure is, there also is your heart.

One can only love what one first knows. This is fundamental. The intellect's knowledge of the Truth fundamentally precedes the Will's freedom to love.

However, the intellect cannot fully know the Truth if the will does not love and treasure it beyond every other love. The will's Freedom supplementally precedes Truth supplementally.

The Truth of the intellect precedes the will's Freedom fundamentally while the will's Freedom to love freely precedes supplementally the intellect's knowledge the Truth.

The intellect's Truth is intelligible but not experiential while the will's Freedom is experiential but unintelligible.

It is reasonable for the intellect to truthfully govern the will's freedom to choose what truthfully exists and is worthy of the will's love.

It is unreasonable for the will to necessarily love the Truth lovingly, honorably, and preciously since the will is willfully free to love whatever it wills to love and to treasure.

When the fundamental Truth precedes the will's Freedom fundamentally and directs and governs it conscionably...

When the supplemental Freedom of the will precedes the Truth supplementally and freely embraces it whole-heartedly...

The two complement each other integrally; each in solidarity and accord with each other.

The intellect's reasonable Truthfulness regarding what really exists honorably prevails while the will's unreasonable Freedom regarding its willful freedom to resist to what actually exists also freely prevails.

St. Augustine in his typical masterful style sums this up as follows: Love the Truth and do whatever you will. The implication is that the will who freely treasures the Truth above every other choice honors both the Truth itself (viz. God) as well as its own volitional Freedom.

THE SPIRITUAL CANTICLE: Stanzas 9-16

Preliminary

In the previous segment of this commentary it was noted that this entire commentary would be modeled on the cruciformity of the cross of Christ's crucifixion. This cross has two separate beams and three configurations: the vertical, horizontal, and the intersection of the two to form the cross itself. We indicated the peculiarities proper to each of these three configurations. We can now add several other considerations to the previous listing.

Each of these three configurations has its own built-in logic. The logic proper to the vertical order is the logic of excellence; that of the horizontal is the logic of equivalence; and, that of the cruciform order is the logic of compatibility and reconciliation. The logic of excellence is a metaphysical logic in that this logic is based on a holistic indivisible whole that cannot be reduced to its constitutive parts wherever such a whole involves such parts. The logic of excellence is a mathematical logic in that this logic is based on a piecemeal divisible whole that can be subdivided into its component parts. The logic of compatibility is a logic of integrity which is based on the compatibility of the two previous logics. This logic both sustains the irreducibility and non-educibility of metaphysical and mathematical reasoning. At the same time, this logic advances the compatibility of each vis-à-vis the other when each remains within its proper fundamental-supplemental prioritization.

In the metaphysical logic of excellence, every human being is naturally constituted of a holistic indivisible whole human nature which is not reducible to its body-soul constitutive parts. Inasmuch as Peter is human, he is substantively constituted of body and soul. Peter's one and the same human substance is both a bodily (i.e., material) and soulful (i.e., spiritual) substance. There are not two substances that make up Peter's human nature. There is only one holistic substance with two constitutive parts. One and the same Peter is indivisibly both material and spiritual even though his material body is not his spiritual soul. That is, Peter's body is wholly human and Peter's soul is wholly human even though the body is not the soul and vice versa.

In the mathematical logic of equivalence, every mathematical whole is culturally reducible to its piecemeal divisible components. The arithmetic integer, 1, is reducible to any combination of multiple fractions such as ½ + ½ or 1/3 + 1/3 + 1/3, etc.. The same is the case for any segment of the geometric unilinear dimension, the line. Any segment line, x---y, is divisible into its smaller sub-segments. In view of both of these mathematical factors, one and the same number "1" and one and the same segment line, x-y, are reducible to their sub--segments. In view of this, one cannot reasonably identify any component part with its original mathematical whole. One cannot state reasonably that 1/3 of a line *is* wholly the whole line or that ½ of 1 *is* wholly 1. In a logic of equivalence, the part is not equivalent to the piecemeal whole. Yet, one can state in a metaphysical logic of excellence that the soul is wholly human and the body is wholly human because Peter's human nature is holistically and indivisibly a whole of excellence which is not reducible to its constitutive parts.

Now, Peter is metaphysically constituted of a holistic whole of excellence, his human nature; and he is also mathematically composed of many different piecemeal wholes of equivalence, such as his body members. In view of his human nature, every constitutive of Peter (whether material or spiritual, essential or incidental) is wholly holistically and indivisibly one and the same human nature. In view of his fragmentary components (viz., his bodily members), each fragmentary component of Peter (regardless of its importance or function) is a non-holistic piecemeal whole reducible to its component parts. Thus, Peter's arm and legs are made up of physiological and anatomical parts (viz., bones, muscles, cells, etc.) to which they are reducible. In other words, the individual, Peter, is both reasonably a metaphysical whole of excellence and irrationally a mathematical whole of equivalence; but, not for the same reason. One is reasonably so by a logic of excellence while the other is irrationally such by a logic of equivalence. In other words, "reason" and "reasoning" differs completely in meaning when applied objectively or subjectively within a metaphysical or mathematical context.

These two logics are compatible with each other providing the one is *fundamentally* prior wile the other is *supplementally* prior. If

Peter *is* fundamentally a mathematical compound divisible piecemeal whole, he cannot be supplementally a metaphysical indivisible holistic whole. On the other hand, where Peter *is* fundamentally a metaphysical holistic whole, he can *have* supplementally and additionally many mathematical complex piecemeal wholes. Thus, there is a logic of integrity, *complementarity*, and reconciliation in which each antithetical logical reasoning can be compatible with the other. This occurs when metaphysical logic *is* fundamentally prior to (i.e. independent of) mathematical logic while the latter *has* supplementally a priority of its own vis-à-vis the former. This integral prioritization is one of completion. For example, when the human person is conceived, he is lacking many body members which have not yet grown and developed. He has not as yet arms and legs. Yet, every constitutive of this newly-conceived embryo is fundamentally holistically and metaphysically human albeit not yet fully developed and full grown. When the human person later grows and develops his body members, such as his arms and legs, he is supplementally, piece by piece, and mathematically more fully human in his full-grown anatomical physiology.

Now, Peter who lacks arms or legs (or both) is still fundamentally holistically human. However, supplementally he is less than fully human in his anatomy and physiology. Peter does not subjectively experience his fundamental metaphysical holistic objective human nature and identity. But, he does subjectively experience his supplemental mathematical piecemeal physiological and anatomical humanism, at least in part; especially in the use or in the loss and the absence of his body's anatomical components such as his arms and legs when he is deprived of these. Here, without the use of these bodily members, he is severely handicapped in his functioning as a human being even though such a terrible loss does not detract from his fundamental holistic identity as a human being.

Another example of this fundamental-supplemental complementarity is any sensory faculty such as the nose. Metaphysically there is but one faculty of smelling but there are anatomically two separate nostrils; there is but one metaphysical faculty of sight but anatomically and mathematically there are two separate organs. Similarly with the heterosexual faculty of procreation; there is but one heterosexual faculty but two separate organs: the male and the female. If we insist on making the piecemeal anatomical supplemental whole as fundamental which it is not, this precludes and eliminates altogether the underlying metaphysical holistic unit-identity of these faculties. This, indeed, is the case today with the current claim that the human embryo is not yet human. This claim is based on approaching the embryo's supplemental physiological and chemical make-up as though it were the fundamental make-up of the embryo. The more fundamental metaphysical reality is that each and every part of the human embryo is wholly and holistically human with one and the same metaphysical holistic unit-identity nature.

Catholic Christian mysticism takes into account both the fundamental metaphysical vertical holistic order of existence and the supplemental mathematical horizontal piecemeal order of resistance. The former is the order of *being* while the latter is the order of *having*. *Being-more* is fundamentally more than *having-more* is supplementally more. Yet, *having-more* supplementally brings to completion what *being-more* cannot of itself complete. Being-more is objectively in the order of nature while having-more is subjectively in the order of culture. It is possible to cultivate artificial arms and legs to supplementally complete the human body's proper anatomical functioning when such members are missing. It is possible to have crutches and canes to supplementally assist one in walking when one's legs are lame and no longer agile.

The Spiritual Canticle is a dialogical logic between the objective order of being and the subjective order of having. This dialogue engages in the reconciliation, integration, and solidification of the two orders within the cruciformity of Christ's cross of crucifixion. It is framed within the mystery of the Catholic Church's supernatural foundation that includes a cruciform marital union between a bride and groom. The groom is God, a divinity of three Persons, and the bride is the creature, the human person. It is a dialogue between Christ, God/Superman, as the groom in the vertical order and man as the bride in the horizontal order. Christ refers to Himself in the Gospel as the Bridegroom. Considering the Church vertically, she is a sacramental institution in which the mystery of the Trinity *is* really, existentially, liturgically, supernaturally, and holistically God *being* present to mankind. Considering the Church horizontally, she is Christ's Mystical Body which is made up of the "people of God," the individual human persons who are Christian disciples. These Christian disciples *have or have-not* within themselves subjectively, prayerfully, and experientially an awareness of God's objective holistic fundamental sacramental presence and supplementally of that same presence in themselves and other Christian disciples.

When the two orders of the Church are wed together cruciformly, there is established an objective sacramental marriage between God, Jesus Christ, sacramentally incarnate in His Church and sacramentally incarnate in the members baptized into this Church. In addition, there ensues an interpersonal subjective prayerful marriage between the Church's Christian disciples and the one divine Groom, Jesus Christ, in the vertical order and an intrapersonal prayerful discourse within the Mystical Body between the "people of God" bonded socially together as children of one and the same God-the-Father. All of this is conducted under the auspices and unctuous sanctifying influence of the Holy Spirit.

Subjectively, the Christian disciple is experientially addressing Christ, the Groom, as a bride that has been graciously and mercifully embraced and espoused by God. Objectively, Christ the Groom, is responding to the bride in terms that are proper to God's own divinity and supremacy. The two irreducible and non-educible vertical and horizontal orders are in dialogue with each other within the framework of a bride and groom conversing with each other. The divine Groom speaks from the vertical order's transhistorical eternity while the bride speaks from the horizontal order of history's ephemerality. In the vertical order, Christ as God is not merely the summit of creation; He is the very *Beingness* infinitely beyond the contingency of all creatures. In the horizontal order, the disciple of Christ is aware of his own *Nothingness* as the very abysmal core of his own selfhood infinitely removed from God's *Beingness*. The marital dialogue between Christ as the Groom and Christ's disciple as the bride within the mystery of the Church's sacramental constitution awakens the mystic's acute awareness of the abyss of his own *nothingness* separating himself from the infinite transcendence of God's *Everythingness*.

The mystic becomes experientially aware that his own bottomless *nothingness* desperately needs God's inexhaustible *Everythingness.* In this awakened awareness he experiences in his bodily sensitivity and in his mental intimacy something of this infinite *Everythingness.* He falls in love. He cannot fail to fall in love with God's infinite loveliness. God's irresistibility overcomes the built-in resistance of his own willful *nothingness.* Yet, when God seemingly withdraws from the mystic's own subjective religious bodily sensitive experience the tenderness of His delicate touch and from the mystic's own subjective religious mental intimate experience the serenity of His consolation, the mystic is left to wrestle to overcome his built-in self-centered abysmal selfishness which persistently resists surrendering its own willfulness to God's providential Holy Will. When the mystic persistently and prayerfully continues to heroically contend with his own willful resistancy through the unctuous influence of the Holy Spirit, he eventually rediscovers experientially something of the fullness of God's infinite sublime loveliness both superficially in his body's sensitivity and deeply in his mind's intimacy. This is the drama of the *Spiritual Canticle.*

Stanza 9:

The mystic is smitten with love and wounded by this love. He is wounded because he is love-sick and unable to cure himself of this sickness nor to find someone who can heal him. He is sick because this love itself cannot be brought to consummation. It remains unfulfilled. Only God Himself can consummate this love. Why doesn't God bring this love to its proper consummation? This lack of fulfillment on the part of God who is Goodness itself leaves the mystic stricken and greatly distressed.

Stanza 10:

The mystic is sick with love and with longing for God. He is listless, restless, forlorn, lost in vagrant day-dreaming; he is home-sick and cannot focus on anything specific. This home-sickness is characterized by 3 symptoms: 1) longing and aching for God; 2) no interest in anything else; 3) annoyed and vexed with having to deal with others and being involved in mundane things. The mystic realizes that God alone can cure his malady. Indeed, it is very much the case that when the mystic can and does eventually turn to God "with his whole heart," he becomes susceptible to receiving from God a perfect cure for his love-sickness. What actually holds him back from completely surrendering to God is his own entrenchment within his selfish self-centeredness. By experiencing this absence of God, his "heart" becomes purified of its own self-attachment to himself. "Heart" here must be understood to be the very nuclear core of the mystic's willful bodily self (i.e., self-centered self-interest and self-importance).

It must be noted that the terrible trial of the mystic's experience of the complete loss of all emotional religious fervor and zeal for God in the body's sensitivity must not be confused with simple depression. Simple depression whether chronicle or not is occasioned by a specific trauma. A young man or woman who loves another and finds that this love is not requited does not seek assistance from a psychiatrist to relieve his emotional distress; he seeks relief from the person whom he admires and loves.

Stanza 11:

The mystic begs God to reveal Himself completely even if this entails the soul's flight from the body (i.e., inevitable physical death). It is a matter of record that in the Old Testament were God to completely reveal Himself to anyone, Moses included, this would have brought about immediate death.

At this point, St. John of the Cross differentiates between three separate and distinct Self-revelations of God to mankind in which He makes Himself present: 1) by God's essence and power as the Creator of the universe; 2) by supernatural sacramental grace in the soul; 3) and, by experiential divine touches within the mystic's own selfhood. The first two cases are entirely objective and independent of the mystic's own willfulness. As the Creator of the universe, God in the Trinity of His Godhead makes this one Godhead's divine nature manifest to mankind. As the Author of sacramental grace, God in the Trinity makes manifest His Triune Personhood to mankind. The third is entirely subjective and very much dependent on the mystic's own self-centered willfulness to correspond with God's Personal Self-manifestation.

This Self-manifestation makes itself felt in the mystic's willful bodily sensitivity as a tender devotional feeling and affectionate liking for God. It also makes itself borne in the mystic's willful mental intimacy as a serene pious bearing and amorous caring for God. When the mystic prays that God reveal Himself he has all three of these ways of God become more vividly present and manifest. Of course, the death that the mystic would udergo and suffer would differ with each manifestation. If God's almighty power were made manifest in something of a physical disaster, this could be the untimely physical death of the mystic. If God's stupendous holiness and merciful moral power were made manifest miraculously in the Sacrament of the Eucharist, for example, this would mean the death of the mystic's subjective personalized bodily sensitive and mental intimate experience of God. After all, to observe such a miracle objectively demonstrated would awaken and fortify the mystic's belief and faith in God above and beyond any need for a private bodily emotional feeling or mentally emotionless caring for God. Finally, if God were made manifest to the mystic subjectively in the mystic's private stimulated religious feeling and intimate religious caring for God, the latter's intimate caring would eclipse and bring completely to naught (i.e., death) the mystic's bodily feeling for God.

St. John further points out that any form of death does not pose a threat for the one who is totally in love with his beloved. Suffering even death itself is no deterrent to the lover who is madly in love. Love is stronger than death; it is immortal and outlives death itself. Such love is a testimony to the human person's immortality. And, indeed, such love is memorialized by others throughout the ages of time. But, it must be emphasized that this love is not merely a dutiful love; it is a sacrificial love. It is a love that emerges sacrificially from the mystic's willful selfhood and not merely from the mystic's soulful intellectual will.

This love is a sickness because it weakens the mystic's willful selfhood. At this stage of the mystic's love-affair with God, it is very much an imperfect love. It is not yet a completely charitable selfless love for God. It remains in the very heart of the mystic's willful bodily selfhood a love that is both self-attached to the mystic's own bodily religious experiences of God as well as to Christ Himself. When this love becomes later a love that is purified of the mystic's selfish attachment to his body's own religious sensitivity and feelings, it will be a strong charitable selfless love for God above and beyond all selfish considerations.

Stanza 12:

Here the mystic is levitating toward God more urgently than is a stone plummeting toward earth. The mystic turns toward God in faith. Through faith the mystic is inerrantly, objectively, personally, and infallibly united with God who is sacramentally through sanctifying grace present in the mystic's soul. At the same time, by reason of hope the mystic is subjectively, personalistically, experientially, and fallibly united with Christ in hope because Christ has freely and sacrificially substituted His own subjective Personality in the place of the mystic's subjective personality when Christ suffered His death on the Cross and made Himself the mystic's scapegoat.

Paradox: Sacramentally and objectively by faith the mystic is more infallibly in the presence of God than he is subjectively and experientially by hope in which he experiences God as absent and not fully and securely in his own possession as his Beloved. In this subjective fallible personalized experience of God through his own sensitive bodily feelings and/or through his own intimate mental bearings, the mystic suffers excruciating anguish in not fully possessing God and in not having absolute assurance of such a possession.

Here, a distinction must be made between the objective intellectual will which is the human soul's appetitive faculty and the subjective willful selfhood which is the human person's self-serving facilitator. The difference between these two wills is crucial in appreciating the significant difference between dogmatic and moral theology, on the one hand, and mystical theology on the other. The soul's intellectual will is an obedient will that is subject to the intellect's recognition of the truth-as-such of whatever is practically and conscionably worthy of willing and choosing. An obedient willing Love of the Truth is objectively and fundamentally a LOVE OF WISDOM (literally, philosophy). This is the foundation for Dogmatic and Moral Theology. This obedient "love of God" is a wise love when it loves God appropriately in regard to God's infinite worthiness deserving of such love. When a person willingly loves God wisely and appropriately, the person's obedient love is meritorious.

The reverse is very much the case in the instance of the human person's subjective self-centered willful selfhood. Where the person's intellectual will is directed to love appropriately and fittingly, the same person's willful selfhood services and serves the person's self-interest by appropriating possessively (i.e., selfishly) whatever it is that the person loves. Hence, this will does not love its object of love because it is inherently worthwhile and worthy of such love. It is simply the reverse. This self-centered will bestows an importance on the object of its love simply because it needs it for its own self-centered service. Thus, whatever this will possessively loves is that which the person treasures as of paramount importance for his own self and his own selfhood's self-fulfillment. Now, when the mystic lovingly and possessively treasures God (i.e., the God of faith) above every other treasure, this love itself becomes wise with a subjective, supplemental, sacrificial wisdom metaphorically described as a *Wisdom of Love*.

Here, the priority is not on intellectual truth but on amorous love. This is the priority that belongs supplementally to Mystical Theology. This sacrificial "Godly love" is a wise love when it heroically and superhumanistically transcends and overcomes its own selfish self-centered possessiveness. When this is accomplished through an ascetic program of self-denial, the Catholic Christian mystic finds himself able to heroically possessively treasure God primarily and his neighbor charitably, he enters into the very *Wisdom of Love* which is not merely a wise love but wisdom's very amorous loveliness. In experiencing subjectively such wisdom, the mystic's sacrificial love of God and neighbor becomes intimately united with Christ's very own Paschal Mystery.

The reason why the mystic at this stage of his pilgrimage toward God finds himself in such straits and suffering so much anguish and travail is that his possessive love and longing for God remains unfulfilled without any self-assurance and security that it will ever be fulfilled. That is, he lives in hope but not yet with that love which is perfectly the supernatural love of charity.

Stanza 13:

This verse marks the end of the Purgative phase of the mystic's union with God and the beginning of the Illuminative stage. Up to this point the dialogue between the mystic as bride and Christ as groom has been conducted by the mystic himself from within the mystic's own horizontal subjective religious experience of being experientially deprived of God's transcendent presence. In this present verse, the dialogue shifts to the vertical objective order inasmuch as the mystic commences to have religious experiences of being experientially alive in God's transcendent presence.

It must be noted again what has caused the severe suffering and anguish which has characterized the Purgative stage of the mystic's pilgrimage to God. This suffering was occasioned by the mystic's loss of his religious (i.e., zealous) bodily sensitive feeling and affectionate liking for God, on the one hand, and his loss of his religious (i.e., pious) mental intimate bearing and amorous caring for God. With the loss of these religious devotional feelings and bearings, the mystic no longer experiences any self-satisfying religious bodily stimulating righteous self-contentment as well as no self-vindicating religious mental pacifying righteous self-containment. His zeal for God has dried up and his mental serenity has given way to a restless disturbing anxiety. In other words, his love of God was not characterized as loving God with a pure heart and with an unstinted single-mindedness. His love was still mired in his own self-centered selfishness and religious self-attachment.

But, still the mystic has persevered in prayerful devotion to God throughout his mystical torments rooted in his supernatural faith and hope that God continues to be faithful to His promise to dwell in the mystic as in His own tabernacle. The long and seemingly interminable siege of the mystic's "dark night" unexpectedly gives way to such bodily feelings and mental bearings of ecstatic piety and devotion that he finds himself in a new predicament. His inner intimate mental religious experiences are at odds with his outer bodily religious experiences. His bodily religious experiences expansively dilate and stimulate his body's sensitivity and resonance while his mental religious experiences contractively concentrate and soothingly permeate the mind's intimacy.

The body's religious dilation inhibits the mind's own religious contraction. Hence, the mystic cries out to have the body cease hampering the mystic's mental selfhood from becoming intimately swallowed up and vanishing within Christ's very own intimacy. So ecstatically entrancing is this intimate experience of Christ that the mystic becomes oblivious to the body's sensational sensitivity. That is, the body seems to have become numb.

This rapturous love awakens the mystic to love God unselfishly under the unctuous influence of the Holy Spirit. That is, this love is fanned into a burning flame of love by the breath of the Holy Spirit. This burning love is experienced deeply within the innermost intimate recesses of the mystic's willful mental selfhood as a combustible fire which burns up and purifies the mystic of the residue of any lingering selfishness. It is a flame that seeks to become increasingly more flammable. This love transforms the mystic's self-centered love into the superhumanistic and superhumane generous selfless love of charity bearing the fruits of the Holy Spirit listed by St. Paul in the 1 Corinthians 13:4-7.

Stanzas 14 & 15:

The bride here experiences and praises the groom's sublime magnificence and grandeur. Here the mystic enters into a formal espousal (i.e., engagement) to God as a prelude to becoming completely and consummately wed to God in the final Unitive stage of his mystical journey. The mystic's religious sufferings cease and are replaced with a sensitively sweet and intimately serene love.

These two verses are prototypical of the mystic's experiential love for God. But, not every mystic will experience this love in the same manner. In these transports of love in which the mystic is himself embraced within the Trinitarian womb of God's own Godhead, he experiences many supernal blessings with the following characteristics: an infinite abundance, inestimable riches, rest and recreation (i.e., refreshment & revitalization), secrets, hidden knowledge of God, God's awesome power and strength, splendid spiritual (i.e., reverential) sweetness, gratification (i.e., exultation), intimate quietude and divine light (i.e., inspiration), God's august wisdom manifest in His creation, the fullness of blessings, and a removal of all dehumanizing evils.

The bride experiences God as the eminence and infinitude of all that is attributable to God without reservation. That is, the mystic experiences that God is not merely good but Goodness itself; not merely wise but Wisdom itself; not merely lovely but Loveliness itself, etc.. Further, the mystic experiences that what is in God His very Goodness is identical with His very Wisdom, Loveliness, etc.. That is, the mystic experiences God as "my God and my All."

It cannot be sufficiently emphasized or overstated that the mystic's experience of these divine grandeurs is distinctively different from an intellectual grasp of these same grandeurs. Intellectually in terms of dogmatic theology the mystic's understanding grasps God apart from and transcendent to the mystic himself. But, experientially in terms of mystical theology, the mystic's experience of these same divine grandeurs is "as though" (i.e., in a metaphorical sense) the mystic himself were experientially full of these sublime divine grandeurs which transcendently are proper to God alone.

These marvelous and stupendous religious experiences of God are still not evidence of the actual marriage of the mystic with God which is the final Unitive stage in the mystic's journey. The reason for this is that in this present Illuminative stage the mystic is still not completely yet purified and purged of his self-centered selfish religious attachments. Further, these ecstatic transports are only sporadic and not long lasting. And the mystic remains prone to experiencing the devil's temptations and enticements luring him away from God.

Stanza 16:

The mystic is habitually at peace and mentally recollected and serene. The mystic's greatest joy is to offer to God in one compound offering a spiritual bouquet of the many blessings, virtues, gifts, and spiritual enhancements he has experienced and received from God's infinite and merciful generosity. It is for the mystic an exquisite joy to be able to return to God "love for love."

To blunt and to interfere with this the devil still has access to the mystic's sensuality and bodily sensitivity and emotional feelings through his manipulation of the mystic's imagination. He afflicts the mystic with all manner of improper suggestive sensuous images. To ward off the devil's assaults, the mystic has recourse to his guardian angel including all the host of angels beseeching them to be protected from the devil's blandishments.

THE SPIRITUAL CANTICLE: Stanzas 17-24

Preliminary

Prior to commenting on the verses, 17-24, we will again reiterate that this commentary is based on the cruciformity of the cross of Jesus Christ which encompasses a Triune Trinitarian threefold order. This order itself is a transcendental order which is the disjunctive property of being-as-such; the metaphysical touchstone for the human soulful intellect's intelligibility for all that exists within the domain of created and uncreated reality.

For, whatever exists in reality, God included, is a being-as-such. But transcendental being-as-such (i.e. the formative object of the human person's intelligence) is itself neither prior nor posterior. And, because it is neither it may be either disjunctively. Hence, every exiting reality within the universe of existence is itself either a prior or posterior being-as-such. God, for instance, is a prior-being-as-such in reference to every reality that is not itself God (i.e., all of creation). And every creature in existence is a posterior-being-as-such in reference to the reality of God who is paramount within the universe of reality.

This transcendental order and ordering is itself threefold: initial, additional, and complementary. Another way of stating this is that there is a threefold order within the universe of reality among all the various beings that exist, God included. There is the order of the originator and the originated; the culminater and the culminated; the integrator and the integrated. This is not an issue of causation *per se* but simply of a prior-posterior referral of one reality to another reality. God-the-Father precedes God-the-Son originatively while the latter precedes the former consummately. God-the-Holy-Spirit precedes both integrally as their integral integration.

Cruciformly the cross of Jesus Christ embraces these three orders. Vertically it is the hierarchical order of initiation which originates with the Father's Holy Will. Horizontally, it is the historical order of culmination and consummation which culminates with the Son's crucifixion and death on the cross as the historical climax of the Old Testament and the historical onset of the New Testament (i.e., the BC and AD). And, cruciformly, it is the integral order of integration that eschatologically integrates the historical and eternal orders together under the influence of the Holy Spirit who is the integral integration of the Father and Son's separate wills incarnated and triunely integrated into humanity's redeemed, sanctified, and glorified human will through Christ's own humanity and Paschal Mystery.

Congruent with this there is a triune cruciform liberating, redeeming, and sanctifying freedom which mankind inherits from, through, and with Christ as a baptized adopted child of the Father in the power of their Holy Spirit. St. John of the Cross identifies this threefold liberation and redemption with the intellect, the memory, and the will. The intellect is liberated and sanctified through faith, the memory through hope, and the will through charity. What the Sanjuanistic texts do not explicitly state but what they implicitly and unerringly indicate is that these three pillars of the spirituality of the mystical life are cruciform in their mutual ordering.

Faith is fundamental to hope and charity. The mystical life is rooted and anchored in faith and the soul's intellect through which the human person can reasonably and vertically reach even to the gate of heaven and God's domain of eternal existence. The mystical life also embraces in the same human person's hopeful historical experiences of his own dreams, expectations, and self-fulfillment which is centered in a hope that is supplemental to faith. The mystical life of faith is principally a dutiful and voluntary obedient willing intellectual embrace of that authority (viz., God) which is truthfully objectively inherently trustworthy and honorably (i.e., conscionably) deserving of trust and the will's respectful obedience. A person of faith is obediently and voluntarily trusting.

The mystical life of hope is the confident and even convinced sacrificial willful self-surrender of the human person to what he trustingly believes. The person of hope becomes a trust-bound confidant of his own trusting belief and is self-convinced of the need to tenaciously serve and cling to this belief. The mystical life of charity is the person's sacrificial volunteer self-determination to conscientiously and faithfully be a steadfast trustee and witness to the moral authority (God) in whom he places his confident expectation.

A person of charity is integrally intellectually rooted in faith and sacrificially surrendered to serving this faith in hope. That is, he is simultaneously willingly obediently conscionably *trusting* in what is obviously truthful (i.e., worthy of such trust) and willfully conscientiously *trust-bound* in sacrificing himself to serve the Author of this objective conscionable truth. Finally, in the integral integration of his conscionable obedient will and his conscientious self-sacrificial will he becomes a sacrificial and *faithful volunteer trustee* that lives and bears witness and testimony to both what he believes in and hopes for. That is, he objectively willingly honors what is worthy of all honor above and beyond everything else (viz., God). Subjectively, he willfully sacrifices his own selfish self-interest to hopefully find his fulsome self-fulfillment in serving what he believes is supremely honorable above every other worthwhile value.

In view of this, there are two separate will's in the human person's anthropological make-up: the objective soul's intellectual goal-directed will and the subjective self's self-serving mindful and heartfelt dichotomous will. The objective will is the human person's intellect's own appetitive drive to appropriately love and to respectfully honor whatever the intellect grasps as truly good. The subjective will is the same human person's self-centered and self-serving mindful and heartfelt dichotomous will. The objective will is liberated through supernatural faith which enables the will to willingly love and obey the truth of God's Self-Revelation. The subjective will is liberated through supernatural hope which enables the will to willfully sacrificially serve the Truth of Revelation by memorially forgetting and foregoing its own hopeless historical self-attachment and incompetent self-control by confidently surrendering itself to the hope of Christ's Mastery of life made manifest in His resurrection to eternal life. When these two wills complement each other they charitably, superhumanly, superhumanistically, and superhumanely (i.e., cruciformly) witness and testify to the very masterful supernatural Life of Christ's Selfless service both to His Heavenly Father and to mankind's liberation, sanctification, and glorification.

Commensurate with this cruciformity there are three separate Christian emancipations and freedoms inherent in the human person's anthropological make-up. There is objectively and vertically the inalienable freedom of choice in which the human person exercises his own sovereign moral authority and responsibility. There is subjectively and horizontally the alienable freedom of self-control in which the human person personalizes and takes charge and is accountable to himself and others for his own social functions, motivations, and social autonomy (i.e., social self-reliance). And, congruently, there is the reconciliation of these two freedoms when the same human person both personally and personalistically, conscionably and conscientiously is steadfastly self-determined to live a lifestyle which integrates and reconciles these two freedoms with each other.

The Christian Catholic mystic's "dark night" of purgative and ascetic suffering is, in keeping with this cruciformity's threefold orders. It involves these three different cruciform freedoms. The freedom of obediential trust is won when the mystic in faith chooses to obey not his own sovereign authority but a higher moral authority (viz., God) whom he cannot fully understand. The freedom of sacrificial self-control is won when the mystic in hope decides to sacrificially forego his own personalized social autonomy and security (i.e., his social self-reliance) and submit his life's service to Christ's own messianic mission of liberating all of mankind from the prison of mankind's enslavement to its own selfishness. The freedom of self-determination is won when the mystic volunteers to both obedientially and sacrificially together become a volunteer selfless servant and disciple of Christ's Gospel of love. Why is this "dark night" of purgative suffering threefold? Because the mystic must walk by a trusting faith in God's moral authority and not his own; by hoping in God's indefectible security and not his own defectible social security; and by God's merciful forgiving love and not by his own sense of justice and self-righteousness.

When the mystic endures this excruciatingly arduous and long-lasting painful purification in which he becomes simultaneously super-humanly personally *informed* by faith, superhumanistically personalistically *transformed* by hope, and super-humanely able to *performatively* behave charitably as a disciple of Jesus Christ, he advances to the subsequent mystical illuminative stage in which he becomes increasingly aware of being completely engaged to Jesus Christ in a mutual act of self-giving which anticipates the total self-giving proper to spiritual marriage itself. In this illuminative stage and increasingly in the subsequent stage of espousal, the mystic recognizes and experiences his own threefold liberation through the auspices of the Blessed Trinity mediated by Jesus Christ, God/Superman.

The mystic becomes *superhumanly* not merely obediently subordinated to God-the-Father's moral authority but the Father's very royal son and daughter. In addition, the mystic becomes *superhumanistically* not merely a spectator in the drama of Christ liberating mankind from its own self-centered selfishness but a sacrificial companion cooperatively conjoined with Christ's own crucified oblation. And, cruciformly, the mystic becomes *superhumanely* through the indwelling of the Holy Spirit simultaneously alive with the very benevolent love and loveliness that bonds the Father and the Son together for all eternity.

The Spiritual Canticle records the mystic's subjective experience of his historical transition from his initial very painful stage of experiencing and suffering through the loss and the disappearance of God intellectually, self-consciously, and as the most important treasure in his life. Intellectually the mystic loses personal sight of God when God becomes personally less important than merely adhering to doctrinal and moral tenets of faith. Self-consciously the mystic loses a personalized interest in God because he becomes deprived of the religious bodily feelings and mental bearing pertaining to his own social security and peace of mind. With the loss of this personalized self-assurance of God's guaranteed protection, he seems to have also loss any and every personalized enjoyment and commitment to God. Finally, and most importantly, the mystic seems to have lost God altogether as the most important reality in his life with the integral disappearance of God combined in the two previous losses.

The mystic subsequently and much later discovers providing he perseveres in prayer and in trust, hope, and love of God in spite of God's apparent triple disappearance from his own pious and reverent prayerful experiences and prolonged wretchedness and forlornness in being abandoned by God...he discovers that he has through his own tenacity and through God's own graciousness advanced and prospered in his own sacrificial willful attachment to and love of God. So much so that he no longer finds faith to be a wall separating himself from God but a translucent "face-to-face" encounter with the Blessed Trinity. He further finds that there is no lingering selfish sensuous or hyped-up self-centered concern within his own transformed selfhood and personality to detract from his total sacrificial self-surrender to Christ and through Christ to the Father's Holy Will. He further finds that he is able superhumanely able to respond and to requite Christ's infinitely merciful love and loveliness with a selfless charitable love (viz., the Holy Spirit's love and loveliness) of his own commensurate with the Father and Son's own mutual love and benevolent graciousness.

In sum there are three divine loves. Vertically there is a dutiful meritorious sacramental love of God beyond all other loves because God is supremely worthy of such love. This is the foundation for the vertical transcendent immortal dignity of the human person's inalienable moral right to life, liberty, and respect from others for the sacredness of his life. This is the foundation for religious love which horizontally is a fervent and devoted love that treasures and sacrificially cherishes God above and beyond any and every selfish self-centered interest and security. Thirdly and cruciformly there is a selfless volunteer heroic love that conscientiously and most generously amicably treasures God's merciful loveliness and friendship in conjunction with a dutiful obedient love that conscionably honors and worships God's majestic Benevolent Goodness and Bounty.

Initially as a novice the mystic loves God but imperfectly with a self-centered interest which gradually becomes purged of its own selfishness. Additionally, the experienced mystic has learned through his long-suffering purgation to love God unselfishly and through this unselfish love to affectionately regard all other selves with the very same forgiving merciful love which is lavished on him by God. Finally and conclusively the expert mystic has learned through God's merciful graciousness and benignity to love God with God's own unstinted generosity that requites God's infinite Love with a love that is itself divinized by God's own gracious Loveliness.

In sum, there are two separate distinct wills in the human person's anthropological constitution: the vertical antecedent and the horizontal consequential will. The former is the person's objective soulful conscionable freedom to choose *to do* or *not do* what the person conscionably *ought or ought not do* commensurate with the human person's ultimate immortal transcendent well-being. The latter is the person's subjective self-centered conscientious freedom of self-control *to make or not make* what it *may or may not* conscientiously *functionally* make to advance the person's own personality's authentic self-fulfillment.

Stanza 17:

In this stage of being formally engaged to Christ as a couple is engaged in a promissory way prior to actual marriage, the mystic experiences a sensuous reverent sensitized delicate bodily elation toward Christ together with an intimate exquisite mental serenity. The mystic is no longer in the seemingly never-ending barren desert of experiencing bodily God's absence and mentally God's remoteness including a complete absence of religious feelings accompanied by mental religious disquietude and anxiousness.

Now the mystic yearns and hungers for a greater personalized mental intimacy with Christ, an intimacy within the very pith and innermost intimacy of his own self-centered psychic willfulness. Having become purified of his intimate willful selfish self-interest in Christ, and now experiencing something of a calm and serene intimate selfless self-interested willful concern and solicitude for Christ, he seeks to further deepen and to refine this selfless intimacy by wishing to have all bodily sensitive reverent feelings to cease altogether and to cease detracting from his complete preoccupation and attention to his innermost intimate willful psychic cerebral self rather than to his sensitive somatic visceral self.

Of course, it should be understood that this increased intensified yearning on the part of the mystic for a more intensive intimacy with Christ is subtly and delicately influenced by Christ and His Heavenly Father's *Holy Spirit* abiding superhumanistically within the abysmal depths of the mystic's willful selfhood. The "breathing out" of the Holy Spirit serves as an expiration to expel and quell the mystic's willful self-contented bodily emotionally stirring pious sensitivity and "breathing in" as an inspiration to deepen and dilate the mystic's willful self-contained mental innermost calm emotionless pious intimacy.

Now, it is easy to fathom that a ship on the ocean is much more desirous of calm rather than turbulent waters. It is very much the same with the mystic's subjective experiential reverent endearing experience of Christ in this stage of his spiritual journey to the summit of Mount Carmel. He has succeeded somewhat through his long-suffering purgation in which he has divested himself of his stubborn selfishness and now he has a more urgent yearning and pining for an utmost intimate calm willful self-contained prayerful communication. Even on a purely humanistic plane, the more the human person becomes accustomed through calm introspective training to become "at home" and familiar with his inner cerebral intimate self, the less he seeks to be disturbed by his body's visceral stirrings and sensitivity.

Stanza 18:

This is a continuation of verse 17. It is a plea on the part of the mystic to be removed from the body's religious stimulations. It is notable that young couples who fall in love usually seek to flee from others who may become spectators to their personalized intimacy. Further, they seek to become familiar with each other's most intimate secret thoughts, wishes, and willful ambitions over and above each other's sensitive feelings and temperamental moods. The very same is the case with the mystic as a bride encountering Christ, the Bridegroom.

Stanza 19:

This overriding thirst for a more intensive spiritual and willful reverent psychic intimacy on the part of the mystic continues to increase ever more solicitously. St. John speaks of this increasingly more intensive solicitude as pertaining to the mystic's soul. Actually, it pertains to the mystic's subjective willful self rather than to the mystic's objective soulful will. The soulful will does not have any sensationally sensitized (i.e., stirring) feelings or insensate intimate (i.e., calm sedating) caring concerns for what it willingly loves. Its love is purely intellectual and spiritual beyond all bodily affectivity or disaffectivity. The mystic's soulful intellectual willing love is not susceptible to the deception and self-centered selfishness as is the case with the mystic's self-centered willful love.

And, again, the mystic's self-centered willfulness is itself dichotomous in that it is either/or *both focused centrifugally on* the body's
outer visceral sensitivity and sensuous emotional self-contentment *as
well as centered centripetally on* the mind's inner cerebral intimacy
and non-sensuous emotionless self-containment. The mystic-bride
seeks to retreat with Christ the Groom within the innermost calm and
serene utterly hidden introspective intimacy of the will's psychic selfhood. Here the mystic will be fortified with the gifts and fruits of the
Holy Spirit and will communicate with Christ beyond feelings and
beyond imagery and beyond spoken words and bodily gestures. The
mystic will be hidden occultly from the gaze and curiosity of all idle
spectators and all who are alien to this utmost intimate prayerful
communications of the mystic's humanity with Christ's divinity.

Stanza 20-21:

In these two verses St. John of the Cross describes the finalizing
marital transformation of the mystic's self-centered willful psychosomatic selfhood under the subtle and delicate influence of the Holy
Spirit. In this transformation, the mystic's lower outer willful devout
sensitive sensuous bodily emotional self along with its sensational
stirring imagery is numbed into insensibility. By this bodily numbing
the mystic is protected from all the vagrant distractions that idle imagery occasion and all diabolical interference which the devil initiates
through his paranormal sensuous temptations he introduces into the
imagination.

Further, the mystic's intimate prayerful communication with
Christ is further strengthened by the supernatural gifts of faith, hope,
and charity which cleanse the mystic's soulful intellect, memorial
egocentric selfhood, and self-centered willfulness from their weakness inherited from the original sin of Adam & Eve. Additionally, the
mystic's sensitized sensational emotional bodily feelings which grip
the mystic and make him an addictive prisoner of their seductive sensuality; these sensualities are completely subjugated to the mystic's
magnetic love and passionate overriding affection for Christ.

Through faith the mystic's soulful intellectual will is enlightened to be supernaturally enabled to obediently adore and worship God-the-Father's Holy Will. Through hope the mystic's own egocentric selfhood's memory of its own historical vulnerability and inevitable death is super-humanly fortified with a confidence in its own life-long immortal resurrection through Christ's own bodily resurrection. Through charity the mystic's selfish self-centered willfulness is transformed into Christ's very own merciful generous self-giving and self-surrendering super-humane and heroic Selfless Selfhood.

The crux of this advanced stage of prayerful religious devout communication between the mystic as-bride and Christ as-Bridegroom is that the mystic now experiences Christ's merciful infinite divine magnanimity within the very nuclear core, pith, and marrow of his own innermost intimate willful psychic prayerful stilled selfhood as a calm and stilled ocean's fathomless depth. All reverent and reverential awesome sensitive feelings and/or intimate carings and solicitous concerns for Christ are no more than ripples on the surface of this profound and peaceful immersion in God's immutable eternal serenity.

Stanza 22:

All that is transformatively accomplished in the mystic's own objective soulful personhood and subjective self-centered personality is accomplished through Christ-the-Bridegroom's agency under the subtle undetectable influence of the Holy Spirit who is more delicately intimate to the mystic's willful innermost intimacy than the mystic is intimate to his own selfhood. This transformation is further brought to perfection by the merciful graciousness of Christ's magnanimity.

In other words, this transformation culminates in the mystic's reverential awesome experience of Christ's very own Selfless amorosity serenely and profoundly flooding the mystic's own innermost intimacy. The mystic becomes aware of reaching the very bridal chamber of Christ's Sacred Heart and Messianic Mindset. The mystic is experientially aware that his own ecstatic experience of Christ is commensurate with Christ's very own divine merciful magnanimity. The mystic experiences Christ's divine infinite justice not as a punitive presence but as the very unction of the Father's infinitely immeasurable and inexhaustible mercy. Like an ocean-liner that has come into port, the mystic rests delightfully within the bosom of Christ's own divinity and loving embrace.

Stanza 23:

Here the mystic becomes more intimately conversant with Christ's Incarnation and Paschal Mystery. Not catechetically but experientially as though the mystic were personalistically experiencing *in persona Christi* his own personal salvation history including the incalculable price that Christ paid to ransom His bride of predilection from the prison of the seven capital sins and the devil's tentacles.

Stanza 24:

The bride-mystic becomes reflectively and prayerfully in contemplative prayer more fully ensconced in the spiritual marriage that Christ has prepared from all eternity for His own bride of predilection. Furthermore, the bride-mystic becomes reflectively and prayerfully able to reverently revel in the awesome mantle of her very own bridal divine bounty adorned with superlative gems and precious gifts and fruits of God's unbounded generosity.

THE SPIRITUAL CANTICLE: Stanzas 25-32

Preliminary.

We continue our cruciform commentary on our Carmelite Holy Father's mystagogical writing, *The Spiritual Canticle*. In this preliminary outline we will contrast the vertical order of knowing with the horizontal order of knowing. Again, *knowing and knowledge* are equivocal when employed separately in each of these two orders. In the vertical order, knowing is always a cognitive assmilative activity whereas in the horizontal order it is a conative non-cognitive productive enterprise. This is the case whether in the vertical order one is considering sentient knowledge or intellectual knowledge. And, again, this is the case whether in the horizontal order one is considering somatic sensuous sensitive bodily knowing (i.e., feeling) or psychic non-sensuous intimate mental knowing (i.e., bearing).

All knowledge is that of the human person. It is the human person that sees sentiently with the body's organic eyesight and ponders intelligently with the soul's inorganic intellectual insight. Certainly, the human person could not visibly see without the medium of light nor see without the healthy organs of sight. Nonetheless, it is neither the optical organs themselves that "see" what is sensible nor the intellect itself that fundamentally "sees" what is intelligible; it is the human person that sees through these faculties. Hence, all the many differentiated acts of sensing and understanding in the vertical order are undertaken by one and the same person. Furthermore, the human person not only knows sentiently and intelligently but is also *aware* and *conscious* of such knowledge. Such awareness is not egocentric nor self-serving. It is simply an awareness of the reality that is sensed and understood.

Now, such knowing and knowledge in the vertical order is always transsubjectively objective. The human person does not "see" the eye's act of "seeing;" it sees the *seeable* reality independent of the eye's eyesight. In visibly seeing the *green grass* the human person is consciously aware of knowing and seeing the reality itself, *green grass*, and not merely some image or mirage. Similarly in intelligibly pondering the grass' green-as-such color, the human person is not intellectually consciously aware of knowing an idea or concept of green-as-such but the actual entitative reality (i.e., essential nature) of the grass' color existing independently and transcendently to the intellect itself.

While the body's *eyesight* cannot visibly see the color, green-as-such, apart from the grass that is green, the soul's intellectual *insight* can intelligibly "see" the color, green-as-such, apart from the grass itself. Nonetheless, while such intellectual knowledge and knowing is immaterially metaphysical (i.e., beyond the grass' physical and material existence), it is still a knowledge of the reality, green, existing independent and transcendent to the intellect itself. The color, green-as-such, is not green simply because the human person through the intellect knows it to be green. Rather, the intellect knows this color, green-as-such, to be actually green because it is ontologically green independent of the intellect's knowledge of it. When the human person states that "the grass is green," he is acknowledging intelligently that he knows the truth of the grass' real color, green-as-such.

The situation is completely reversed in the horizontal order of knowing and knowledge. Here, again, it is the same human person that engages such knowledge and knowing. Yet, it is not the same person who engages his personal public and objective *dynamic* and *energetic* intelligent and sentient nature. Rather, it is the same person who engages his own personalized private and subjective self-serving, self-conscious, ego-centric *impotent* and *synergetic* self-cultivated selfhood. In the vertical order the object of knowing and knowledge is not productively created by the human person but merely assimilated by his senses and the intellect. In the horizontal order, it is simply the reverse. The human person himself self-consciously cannot *know* the "green grass" without productively fashioning some imaginary figment or some mental notion of it. In such cases, such *knowing* is not being knowledgeable concerning the "green grass" but, rather, having knowledge about it. Further, the human person subjectively within his own self-conscious self-centered awareness of the "green grass" is not in touch with the reality itself but merely with its sensational image or inspirational notion which he has imaginatively and/or mindfully fabricated for himself and his own usage.

This occurs, for example, when one has taken a photograph of the "green grass" and is able even when the reality itself ceases to exist to continue to gaze at this green turf by examining the photo. The photo is more an imaginary factual epistemological visualization of the "green grass" than it is an actual "seeing" of the ontological reality itself. Indeed, the photo reveals more about a human person's epistemic self-conscious attentiveness and appreciation of the "green grass" than it is does about the reality itself of the "green grass." Another example of this self-conscious awareness is the same human person's memory of his mental notion of such "green grass" which he cherishes from his encounter with it in a long ago past moment of historical time.

In this horizontal order of the human person's *having knowledge*, such *knowledge* is not principally *informative* of reality transcendent to and independent of the human person. Rather, it is *mis--informative* inasmuch as it is not the reality itself which is directly known or cognized. Rather, it is the human person's transformative fabrication of the original reality that is self-consciously fashioned and attended to. Indeed, it is precisely this self-serving and egocentric attentiveness which is most distinctive of such subjective *knowledge* and *knowing*. For, such *knowledge* is most assuredly not informatively cognitive regarding the objective reality itself. On the other hand, it is unquestionably transformatively revealing regarding the human person's personalized bodily feeling for and/or mental regard for the object which it has taken such pains to fabricate as a memento for itself and its own safe-keeping.

Consider a photograph that one keeps of his parents who are deceased. The photo informatively misrepresents them inasmuch as they objectively no longer actually exist as seen in the photo. Yet, the photo does subjectively and transformatively reveal the bodily sensitive feeling and mental intimate caring that the person who preserves this photo has toward the persons pictured. It is in this sense that such consciously self-serving and self-centered *knowing* on the part of the human person's selfhood and subjectivity is more properly transformatively *conative* than it is informatively *cognitive*. The photo reveals the transformative subjective temperamental and sentimental *conative* selfhood of the person who cherishes and treasures the photo moreso than it does the informative objective reality of the parents in the photo.

When it comes to *trust*, one can trust one's objective cognitive knowledge in the vertical order but one cannot trust one's subjective conative knowledge in the horizontal order. In the objective order it is the reality itself which is known in its actual existence while in the subjective order it is a fabrication substituting for reality itself which is known. In the objective order, the reality known exists independent of a human person's conative sensitive feelings and intimate caring for it (viz., liking or not liking it; caring or not caring for it). On the other hand, this conative infusion is precisely the hallmark of the subjective order of *knowing*. Objectively, knowing and knowledge is orthodox; that is, it is knowledge of what informatively exists. Subjectively, knowing and knowledge is paradoxical; that is, it is more an issue of ignorance than cognizance. That is, the photo of one's parents on one's dresser reveals not the truth about one's parents but reveals the proof of one's subjective personalized regard and interest in these persons. On the one hand, objective knowledge is truthful concerning which one would be lying if one deliberately misrepresented it. On the other hand, subjective knowledge is only (ap)provable regarding one's self-serving bodly temperamental feelings or mental sentimental interests. Here there is not truth but merely proof. The photo of a person's parents in the house *proves* the person's affection and care for, interest in, and importance of his parents in his own subjectivity and personalized affectionate selfhood.

Objective knowledge is personally more valuable and worthwhile for the human person's immortal community well-being while subjective knowledge is more personalistically valued and esteemed for the human person's own historical social security and welfare. Objective knowledge is inherently *conscionable* in that the truth of such knowledge binds and obligates the human person to willingly exercise his soulful freedom of choice in deference to such truth. Subjective knowledge is, in turn, *conscientious* in that the proof of such knowledge demands that the same human person solicitously exercise his selfhood's willful self-centered self-controlled self-interest in view of fulfilling himself beyond the subjectivity of his own selfish self-centeredness and in view sacrificially serving a cause transcending his own subjectivity.

Note well the radical difference between these two orders of *knowing* as they impact on the mystical life of the Catholic Christian. In the objective vertical order the mystic *by supernatural faith knows* intellectually the very reality of God's own Triune Godhead. That is, he is in the very sacramental and supernatural *presence* of this divine and sublime reality as gratuitously Self-revealed by God. On the other hand, this public presence is not personalized nor internalized. It remains distinct and transcendent to the human person's own personalized possession. This is the case even when by supernatural grace this divine Trinitarian Personhood abides sacramentally in the person's human soul. On the other hand, in the subjective horizontal order the mystic *by supernatural hope knows* his own personalized superhumanistic and self-cultivated *experience* of God which is also gratuitously granted on the part of God. This experience is felt outwardly in the somatic body's sensitivity and/or entertained inwardly in the psychic mind's intimacy. But, paradoxically enough, this personalized experience is not of God's actual presence; it is an experience of God's *absence*.

When these two non-educible and irreducible orders of knowledge and knowing are cruciformally integrated and reconciled with each other there ensues a heterodox knowing in which the same person acts both conscionably and conscientiously; that is, he acts truthfully and approvingly. In this manner the *informative* and *transformative* orders become integrally the cruciform *performative* order. In such an integral integration the human person acts on a plane that is supernatural buttressed by sacramental grace and the sacramental Church's ministry. Such performative activity engages simultaneously a tripartite cruciform order proper to the Blessed Trinity. Vertically, by the sacrament of baptism, the human person is informed with grace as a child of God-the-Father who initiates the human person's redemption from all eternity. Horizontally, it is God-the-Son who consummately transforms this same human person to sacrificially facilitate his historical redemption in view of the sacrament of the Eucharist. And, cruciformly, it is God-the-Holy-Spirit that joins into one indissoluble integrity both the eternal and historical orders of the human person's redemption, sanctification, and ultimate glorification by integrating the same human person into the sublime amicability of the Blessed Trinity.

In sum, there are three different compatible and complementary dimensions to the human person. In the vertical order the human person is a *homo sapiens* who in virtue of knowing the Truth is able to conscionably and personally govern his own conduct accordingly. In the horizontal order the same human person is a *homo faber* who in virtue of his own personalized industry can conscientiously and interpersonally cultivate his own personality and social autonomy. In the cruciformity of the first two orders the same human person is a *homo oecumenicus* who in virtue of his supernatural assimilation into Christ's Eucharistic Sacramental Church is able to reconcile his objective conscionable conduct with his subjective conscientious enterprises.

The Catholic Christian mystic and, notably the Carmelite, is simultaneously prayerfully engaged in all three of these cruciform orders. Objectively, he prays publicly through the Catholic Church's orthodox sacramental rites in the light of faith. Subjectively, he prays privately through the Catholic Church's paraliturgical practices and saintly sanctioned pieties and traditional devotions in the conviction of hope. Cruciformatively, he integrates within his same personhood his public and private prayer such that he engages in one fundamentally and the other supplementally to bring to perfection in himself the very sacramental supernatural charitable mercy of Christ, God/Superman, reigning overall from within the bosom of the Blessed Trinity.

The mystic accomplishes this more perfectly by freely surrendering himself to Christ's Blessed Mother, Mary, in the same Holy Spirit of self-surrender that Christ Himself undertook when He as God-the-Son became her first begotten Son-of-Man. By freely entering into Mary's spiritual motherhood as mother of both the Head of the Sacramental Church, Jesus Christ, and the Church's bodily members, the mystic enters completely into the Blessed Trinity's very bosom. Mary's Immaculate Heart is the maternal womb of the Church's sacramental life alive in all her members.

Stanza 25:

We must not overlook that at this point in *The Spiritual Canticle* the mystic has reached the pinnacle of his spiritual pilgrimage up the Mount of Carmel to become espoused to God in the very same espousal that God has personally in the Personhood of the Blessed Trinity espoused himself to the human person. In the OT God-the-Father espouses Himself personally to His chosen family, the Israelites. In the NT God-the-Son espouses Himself incarnationally to his renewed family assembly, the Sacramental Church. And, in this Church, God-the-Holy-Spirit espouses Himself to the Mother of this Church, the Blessed Virgin, Mary and to her children.

In the vertical order of this espousal there is a clear-cut stature and status. Either one is in the state of grace or not; either baptized or not; either morally virtuous, honest and upright, or not. There is no middle ground nor process of becoming espoused to God. In the horizontal order of this espousal, on the other hand, there is a process and no status. Either the prayerful mystic is progressively advancing or regressively retreating from Christ. And, this advance and/or retreat are each respectively processively progressing or regressing. Hence, even when the mystic reaches the stage of sublime union with the Blessed Trinity, there continues to be a process of sanctification. This espousal, of course, is a covenant in which the contractual partners surrender to each other without reservation the totality of each's own existence. Only the sacramentally immersed human person who with the grace of the Holy Spirit has made such a total self-commitment to Christ can progressively enter into Christ's own total Self-commitment and espousal to Him as a member of His own Mystical Body, the Sacramental Church.

What our Carmelite mystagogue is expounding here in this verse and the subsequent ones is a progressive refinement of this espousal to the Blessed Trinity. St. John repeatedly ascribes this refinement to the human person's soul. The soul is fundamentally the root source of all mystical experiences which are anchored in the objective supernatural gift of faith illuminating the soul's intellectual intelligence with the graciousness of God's own Trinitarian presence. Yet, the mystical experiences themselves occur within the human person's subjective egocentric selfhood which is dichotomously a somatic willful bodily sensationally sensitized sensuous self or a psychic mindful inspirationally intimate non-sensuous cerebral self. In other words, the mystic either experientially encounters God through his body's subjective bodily sensitivity or mental intimacy under the influence of the Holy Spirit abiding within the innermost inner recesses of the human person's willful selfhood. The Holy Spirit is the very breath and breathing of this mystical experience.

In breathing there is an expiration and an inspiration; that is, a breathing out and a breathing in. Breathing in expands the lungs while breathing out contracts and constricts them. Breathing in God's Godliness expands and dilates the body with a somatic pious sensitivity experienced as exultation and jubilation. This prompts the human person to sing and dance and to become bodily active with gestures resonating and manifesting this sublime excitation. Indeed, the very vitality and resonance of this sublime mystical experience is not confined to some special erotic physiological part of the human body's sensitivity such as is the case with the pleasure of eating or taking some drug. It is ethereally diffused throughout the entire body's sensitivity. Such a somatic mystical experience motivates the mystic to zealous action which, most likely, will take the form of the corporeal works of mercy such as feeding the hungry, sheltering the homeless, clothing the naked, etc..

It is absolutely important, at this point of the mystic's union with God, to emphasize that the mystic himself is not in charge nor in control of these sublime mystical bodily sensitized experiences of prayerful exuberance and exultation. It is not the case that he recollects himself in prayer to experientially feel more enthusiastically and sensationally God's sublimity coursing through his body as one climbs aboard a roller-coaster to feel the thrill of being bodily suspended in air at one moment and plunging to earth at another. These bodily exquisite and delicate sensuous exultations are not under the mystic's willful self-control and manipulation. They occur and dissipate at God's good pleasure and not the mystic's bidding. This lack of willful self-control is precisely one of the indications of the truly divine and sublime origins of these experiences. At this stage of the mystic's progressive prayerful union with the Blessed Trinity, it is God's glory which the mystic faithfully seeks and not his own self-secure bodily gratification, contentment, and satisfaction. He has already become completely detached from his own religious self-gratification in the preliminary purgative stage.

The stage of breathing which is opposite to breathing in is that of breathing out in which the lungs contract. Breathing out does not engage the human person's willful bodily sensitive sensuous self but his willful mental intimate non-sensuous sedate self. In this breathing out the mystic expels completely from his willful selfhood all outward exciting bodily superficial, sensational, sensuous, sensitive experiences of God leaving his egocentric attention to be willfully concentrated exclusively inwardly on his mind's calm, profound, inspirational, non-sensuous, intimate innermost experience of God. Understandably, this inner mental intimate experience of God does not engage the body's sensational, sensuous, sensitivity; it is not exciting. Rather, it is a calming and quiescent sublime experience of God that is intimately cerebral and non-sensuous and beyond the body's reach. Indeed, such non-mystical and non-pious experiences occur in a familiar way when a person is completely absorbed in some day-dreaming reverie and becomes oblivious to everything engaging his senses and bodily sensitivity.

The mystic's subjective experiential espousal and union with the Blessed Trinity becomes progressively more prayerfully fused and bonded with God when his religious experience becomes concentrated on his inner intimate willful mental emotionless awareness of God's eternal immobility and immutability which excludes all pious bodily feelings and excitement. Contemplative prayer is more perfectly contemplative the more the mystic is absorbed in the mind's serene devout soothing inspirations and willful inner self-contained reverent bearing rather than focused on the body's exciting expansive feelings of divine exhilaration.

Stanza 26:

St. John continues in this verse to describe the mystic's ongoing progressive refined prayerful experience of the Blessed Trinity's infinite Godliness. He speaks of the mystic's experience of being immersed and saturated with God to the point of becoming inebriated with the Holy Spirit and oblivious to everything happening around him which is of such notable importance to worldly-minded persons. So completely immersed in God is this refined mystical experience that the mystic himself becomes impervious to his bodily needs and sensitivities. Indeed, the mystic finds himself in the very wine cellar itself of God's divine distillation. In other words, he has at his disposal the choicest divine wines with which to regale himself.

What St. John is emphasizing here is that the mystic is no longer advancing progressively in an increasingly more refined experiential union with God through the medium of his selfhood's bodily superficial outer sensuous sensitivity but, now, exclusively through the medium of his selfhood's noumenal inner mental non-sensuous intimacy. This remarkable differentiation between the human person's subjective inner mental and outer bodily willful selfhood may be better appreciated if we differentiate between the mental notion of a triangle and its corresponding bodily image. One and the same notion of a triangle is intensively, inclusively, and comprehensively the paragon for any and every triangle that could be imaginatively and sensationally imaged by the body's imagination. The notion of a triangle as a "three-sided figure" includes simultaneously, occultly, and intimately the isosceles, equilateral, and right-angle triangles. On the other hand, a special image of one of these three triangles in the body's imagination excludes the other three. In other words, a mental notion is more intensively and intimately a fusion of what is conceived than is any bodily imaginary image of the same notion.

This differentiation between the mystic's reverent superficial prayerful outer bodily experience of God and his inner mental more profound experience underscores the progress the mystic undergoes in arriving at a more perfectly refined union with God. St. John proceeds to indicate that this refinement and ever-increasing intensive union with God involves all 7 gifts of the Holy Spirit which are wisdom, understanding, knowledge, counsel, fortitude, piety, and awe of God. Further, these 7 gifts of the Holy Spirit engage the three theological virtues of faith, hope, and charity supernaturally enlivening the three pivotal points of intelligence, memory, and will involved in the mystic's encounter with God. He gives an instance of this refinement when he singles out the mystic's willful love of God-the-Father's awesome majesty and splendor. The mystic's mystical love of the Father's august awesomeness becomes more perfectly refined when it progresses from being outwardly manifest in the mystic's bodily exalted and expansive reverent feelings for the Father's infinite grandeur to being more quietly manifest in the mystic's inward mentally concentrated appreciation of the Father's inexhaustible merciful providential paternal care and tenderness.

Our Carmelite doctor offers another telling point in differentiating between an objective theological knowledge of God which is lacking in devotion and piety, on the one hand, and a theological piety and devout love of God which, in turn, is lacking in understanding and intelligibility. This differentiation marks out, again, the radical difference between the horizontal and vertical orders of the cross' cruciformity. In the vertical order, knowledge precedes the will's dutiful volitions. Knowledge is informative. One cannot love well what one does not antecedently truthfully know. In the horizontal order, it is entirely the reverse which is the case. Love is transformative. Love takes precedence over the mind's mindful awareness. Unless a human person sacrificially takes a greater willful self-interest in one thing rather than in another or, again, in one person rather than another, this same person will not be mindfully prompted to become more familiar with and more attentive to one thing or person to the exclusion of other things and persons.

Given this subtle distinction St. John notes, a person with a firm faith but little understanding may be endowed with a more intensive pious and devout love of God than one who is very learned in the discipline of theology. Similarly, one who is well informed in dogmatic theology may be exceedingly more learned than he is devout in his love for God. Of course, the optimum is to have one who is both learned in dogmatic theology and one who is also steeped in a mystical love of God. For, such a one would be more spurred on to explore more probatively and cogently the infinite depths of God's divine intelligibility. Finally, it is important for every beginning mystic to appreciate that advancing in love of God does not demand that one first become proficiently learned in mystical theology. The important point to emphasize is that becoming madly in love with God is the only way to come to grips with God's miraculous merciful love for mankind.

Stanza 27:

Such is the seeming madness of God's love for mankind that God-the-Father through His gift of His only Son to mankind has made Himself a prisoner of the human person's own willfulness. God-the-Father in His august majesty cannot cease to be infinitely removed from His creature, the human person. Yet, He providentially sends His only Son, Jesus Christ, God/Superman, to become infinitely below the human person through His filial humility to His Father's Holy Will. The Father allows His only Son to become a sacrificially immolated volunteer victim of the Father's love for the human person to restore the human person to the Father's paternal divine embrace. The only return that the mystic can make for such divine folly is to return to God the very favor with which he has been favored. The only response that is commensurate with such reckless sublime love is a kindred love.

Stanza 28:

The only activity that remains for the mystic is that of a sacrificial love in which the mystic willfully prefers to selflessly serve God's glory and merciful love rather than his own self-centered and self-serving worldly selfishness. This, of course, is only possible because the mystic is now living in virtue of the Father's providential and paternal care, the Son's Selfless victimhood, and the Holy Spirit's unctuous influence. What is vitally important to appreciate here is that this elevated and advanced stage of spousal union with Christ and through, with, and in Christ with the Father's Holy Will in the power of their Holy Spirit…this advanced union does not attract the attention of those with whom the mystic daily lives and has commerce.

The mystic's total absorption in God does not demand that he cease visiting the store to purchase whatever commodities and food he needs for his daily fare. It does not demand that he abandon his given state in life be it lay, religious, or clerical. The tremendous change which has been effectuated in the mystic's life is more within the inner occult recesses of his innermost inner intimate willful selfhood than in his outer bodily physiology and conduct. He will be walking the same way he has always walked and speaking the same vernacular language as previously. The mystical life is a hidden life precisely because the mystic's psychic inner willful self is not directly available to empirical inspection and observation.

Stanza 29:

At the same time, the mystic who has advanced to this most intimate union with the Blessed Trinity is less and less disposed to be engaged with others whose cares and concerns are focused on their worldly enterprises and adventures. Such a mystic is not apt to be interested in the stock market's daily fluctuations or the prospect of one political party being voted in and another being voted out. This does not mean that such a mystic must be physically removed from the world's commerce and worldly enterprises. Oh no! What it means is that the mystic's own cares and concerns are not a prisoner to such worldly affairs. Hence, the mystic may be fully engaged in having stock and attending to political matters without becoming so attached to these affairs as to be in the least anxious about them. But, what is more probably the course of conduct followed by the mystic is to entrust these affairs to someone else while he busies himself more with conducting himself as living a Gospel prayerful lifestyle of Mary rather than one typical of Martha.

Stanza 30:

What is proper to the vertical objective order is the unit-entity identity and identification of all that exists in the universe of reality. God-as-God in God's own independent divinity cannot be metaphysically identified with any creature's own dependent creaturelyness. Similarly, no individual existing creature can be metaphysically identified with any other regarding its individual existence. Each individual is unique and not repeatable. By contrast, what is proper to the horizontal order is the enterprising exchange and exchangeability between opposites. All such enterprising exchanges are rooted in the proportionality peculiar to mathematical notation. Thus $\frac{1}{2}$ is similar and equivalent to $2/4$ but not identical with it. The human person's mindful self can intuitively discern the similarity between these opposite fractions. Similarly, the Ark of the Covenant in the OT is intuitively comparable to the Blessed Virgin, Mary, Mother of Jesus Christ in the NT carrying God in her sacramental womb. Of course, some exchanges are commutative and some are not.

In this specific verse St. John is marveling at the exchangeability of Christ's Divine/superhuman incarnate divinized Personality with all of His magnificent superhumanized Selflessly Self-giving gratuitous gifts and talents abounding in the Holy Spirit's own Gifted Selflessness being exchanged for the mystic's own self-humanized personality. This exchange, of course, is not commutative (i.e., reversible) and takes place within the mystic's deepest innermost intimate serene inspirational psychic willful selfhood beyond his body's superficial excitable sensuous sensational sensitivity. What the mystic experiences is virtually Christ's very own Selfhood as his own because Christ in His Paschal Mystery has already as a volunteer scapegoat sacrificially substituted Himself for every human person in His crucified act of oblation to God-the-Father's Holy Will. Just as the priest in the Mass offering up the bread and wine makes possible by the Holy Spirit's intercession the actual miraculous transformation of these creaturely species into the Uncreated glorified reality of Christ's Body & Blood, so also there is exchanged in this mystical espousal the mystic's own subjective personality and selfhood for that of Christ's own subjective Personality (i.e., Persona not to be confused with His divine Personhood). St. Paul describes this when he exclaims that he no longer experiences his own self but the very Selfhood of Christ alive in himself.

The mystic totally obediently and sacrificially surrenders himself and all that he is and has to Christ's own total obedient and sacrificial Self-surrender. In this mutual self-surrender all the mystic's moral virtues and charismatic gifts are transposed into supernatural moral virtues and superhumanistic charisms commensurate with Christ's superlative divinized objective human nature and Self-cultivated subjective glorified Personality. This exchange is effectuated by the Holy Spirit's intercession. It is a miraculous mystical exchange precisely because it simultaneously involves both God's miraculous efficacy in conjunction and in communion with the mystic's full-fledged willful cooperation. So unctuously delicate and appropriate is this communion of the human and divine wills that it seems to the mystic that his own subjective willful will is that of the Holy Spirit while it, indeed, remains his own personalized willfulness. This mutual intimacy between the mystic and the Blessed Trinity is spoken poetically (i.e., intuitively) as a garland.

Here St. John differentiates three different types of garlands. It is notable that these three types, those of virgins, doctors, and martyrs, encapsulate again the cross' cruciformity. What is singularly characteristic of these ringlets of flowers is that they all three together form a larger ringlet and crown adorning the Sacramental Church's saints who are members of Christ's Bride. Recall that the vertical order is fundamentally that of the hierarchical Church; the horizontal is that of the charismatic Church; and, their cruciform intersection is that of the domestic Church. Doctors notably uphold and advance the Church's teaching in matters of faith and morals. Virgins witness to the Church's charismatic selflessness and giftedness most frequently made manifest in the manifold religious communities committed to living to the full the Gospel councils of poverty, chastity, and obedience. And martyrs witness to the Church's cruciform divine hierarchical authority integrated as one with her volunteer giftedness frequently repeated throughout her redemptive history. Of course, again, the bond that binds together all these garlands is the bond of Christ's very own superhumane amiable merciful love (viz., charity) of friendship.

Stanza 31:

This verse continues the same theme as the previous one. The bond that weaves together all of these garlands and flowering ringlets is the bond of charity. What is so marvelously amazing here in this mystical love is that Christ's infinite merciful immeasurable love for the mystic seems to be the very same love with which the mystic, in turn, selflessly and gratuitously loves Christ as his own Beloved treasure. Of course, we know from Christ's passion and crucifixion that this Selfless love which He bestows on the mystic is won only through excruciating suffering. The mystic experiences this very same totally Self-giving Love as his very own only in conjunction with considerable excruciating sacrificial suffering entailing the loss of his own self-centered personality attachments for Christ's Selfless Personality and universal unbounded Giftedness.

This charitable friendly amiable love and loveliness is characterized by three traits. It is a strong superhuman heroic enduring tenacious love. It is a singular love that is completely divine and by reason of its divinity completely selflessly self-giving. For this reason it is a love which both captivates God and makes God its prisoner. Thirdly, it is a love which is totally anchored and grounded in an unshakable faith. In brief, it is a charitable friendship love which is the coalescence of the supernatural gifts of faith and hope. Again, the cross' cruciformity is highlighted here. It is objectively faithfully grounded inerrantly in its vertical unbounded everlasting trust of God and subjectively trust-bound unflinchingly in the hopeful conviction that historically and horizontally this hope is not in vain and will be fulfilled in Christ's transhistorical resurrection and ascension.

Again, St. John is striving to emphasize and highlight God's own simplicity that the mystic experiences in the very intimate pith of this divine merciful amicable amorosity. It is clear that the cross' cruciformity is not entirely simple since it encloses three different dimensions. Yet, in the crucible of Christ's divine and sublime charitable merciful Love and Loveliness the vertical and horizontal beams of the cross (viz., faith and hope) achieve an integrity and integrality in which each is perfectly reconciled and intertwined with the other to dissolve in a divine superlative amiable divine Love that embraces both in a friendship that is both trusting, trustful, confident and convincing.

Stanza 32:

Mystical love is captivating; it is gripping and riveting. The mystic's love for God as his own Beloved is divinely captivating. This love is threefold in keeping with the cross's cruciformity. It is vertically, virtuously, and objectively spontaneously dutifully obedient; it is horizontally, attitudinally, subjectively, and affectionately sacrificially that of a devoted servant; it is integrally, cruciformly, and unitively, a totally amicable self-giving reciprocal divine friendship. This *agape*

658

love is the mystic's amorous abandonment to and basking in Christ's unfathomable gratuitous mercifulness. It is captivating in the sense that Christ Himself has volunteered to become graciously captive to the mystic's own amorous embrace. The very presence of Christ in the Eucharist is evidence of this divine captivity.

Christ's merciful love for mankind prompts Him to remain as a prisoner in the tabernacle at the beck and call of the mystic who chooses to visit Him there. St. John notes that God does not love the mystic because the mystic himself is lovable; the mystic becomes lovable and loving with an *agape* love because He is loved by Christ in virtue of the Father's infinite merciful Goodness. This very *agape* divine love & loveliness abides in the innermost inner intimate recesses of the mystic's heartfelt and mindful selfhood in the Person of the Holy Spirit.

THE SPIRITUAL CANTICLE: Stanzas 33-40

Preliminary.

In these final verses we reach the pinnacle and culmination of the mystic's union with the Blessed Trinity's own divine simplicity which is so simple that God's divine Godhead is totally identical with the Father, the Son, and their Holy Spirit. So sacramentally, interiorly, and intimately is the Catholic Christian mystic wed through Christ's mediation to the Trinity that the mystic's very own divinized personality transformed into the *Persona* of Christ's own superhumanized heroic Selfless Personality experiences within itself something of the total simplicity proper to God's own Triune Godhead.

The very core and crux of this wedding between God and the mystic is the cruciformity of love. The love that comes alive in the Paschal Mystery of Christ's culminating act of divine and sublime Self-donation is a cruciform love; it is threefold encompassing the threefold theological gifts of faith, hope, and charity. And, as previously emphasized these threefold gifts themselves are centered in the person's soulful intellect, his mindful memory, and his self-centered will. The human person by reason of his intellect has objectively a natural access to the heavenly realm of eternity and a supernatural access by grace to voluntarily respond to God's Self-manifestation of His infinite Paternal Goodness revealed in the Old and New Testaments and the Church's sacramentality.

In this voluntary response the Catholic Christian mystic is enabled through the gift of faith in the sacrament of Baptism to address God as his own Father and as a member of God's Triune family. This is the vertical order of the cross in which the mystic voluntarily (i.e., freely) worships, adores, thanks, and beseeches His own Father with a dutiful love which he rightfully owes to the Father. This "divine right" is the root of the mystic's very own inalienable dignity and inalienable right to be himself universally respected albeit his own shortcomings and failings in life. In this dutiful faith-anchored love the mystic, like Christ Himself, is totally obedient to the Father's Holy Will and is loved by the Father with a divine love that is the same love reserved for His only-begotten Son, Jesus Christ.

The same human person by reason of his mindful memory is subjectively afforded as a member of the Church's Mystical Body a self-cultivated access to the very historical Self-manifestation of God-the-Son especially in the Sacraments of Reconciliation and the Eucharist. Further, he comes to be subjectively conscious of Jesus Christ within the consciousness of his own historical existence in the measure that he himself becomes willfully super-culturally and super-civilly self-humanized by advancing little-by-little from his infancy to his adulthood through an ascetic life of self-denial more and more Christ-like both in his attitudinal mindset and in the very heart of his deepest aspirations. Within the innermost sanctuary of this very personalized mindful (i.e., willful) memory the mystic becomes transformed in his own personality by willfully (i.e., forcibly) converting his own mental attitude and heartfelt feelings to those of Christ's own be-attitudinal redemptive mindset and heartfelt empathy toward his neighbors.

Indeed, by a heroic mindful self-purification of his very

memory---his past eventuation and future aspirations---he has super-humanistically through Christ's very own sacrificial heroism little-by-little willfully divested himself of his own selfish-self-centered mind-set and become more masterfully confirmed in Christ's very own masterful Selfless service both to the Father, Holy Mother, the Sacramental Church, and to his neighbor. In this spiritual maturation, the mystic has become increasingly masterful with the mastery of Christ's very own heroic Self-denial and Self-control of His own motivations, emotional impulses, and serene inspirations. Here the mystic is not excelling in an eminently dutifully virtuous love but in a serviceable selfless sacrificial love. This sacrificial love is in the horizontal order and progresses through successive stages of purification in which the mystic becomes increasingly less selfishly self-centered and more self-lessly self-centered. Unlike the dutiful virtuous love---proper to the vertical order---in which the mystic ought to love God because God is infinitely loveable and worthy of such love, this sacrificial love is such that the mystic needs *to* and must willfully love God (i.e., cherish God) to enable his own mindful self to become lovely with a loveli-ness that is Christ's very own superheroic superhumanistic selfless loveliness.

In the matter of God-the-Father's love for the mystic, the mystic himself is loved with an infinite divine love. For God-the-Father does not love the mystic because the mystic himself is loveable; rather, He loves the mystic because He (i.e., the Father) Himself is eminently loving. Hence, He loves the mystic paternally with a divine benevol-ence that wills the mystic to be infinitely benevolent as He Himself is such in His very existence and divine nature. In the matter of God-the-Son become incarnate in the very flesh of everyman including the mystic, He makes possible in His Paschal Mystery for every human person to be willfully and sacrificially transformed within the histor-ical subjectivity of the mystic's own personalized self-cultivated will-fully self-centered personhood into the *selfless loveliness* of His (i.e., Christ's) own superhumanized and superdivinized Self-cultivated sacrificial servant Persona (i.e., Personality).

These two irreducible and non-educible orders of the cross, the vertical and horizontal---i.e., the communal in which the human person is ontologically "at one" with every other human person in the family of humanity and the social in which the human person finds that he is phenomenologically an intrapersonal and interpersonal associate with other persons in society---engaging the mystic's natural objective inalienable soulful freedom of choice and conscionable responsibility, on the one hand, and his self-cultivated subjective self-centered alienable freedom of conscientious mindful and heartfelt self-control and social accountability, on the other, …these two orders become reconciled cruciformly by the God-the-Holy-Spirit abiding superhumanely within Christ's own subjective Persona enabling His superhumanized Selfless Personality to become as submissively lovingly wed to God-the-Father as was His own divinized objective human nature and soulful will dutifully lovingly obedient. In bestowing His very own Holy Spirit, the Spirit of Truth on the Apostles and the Sacramental Church's Mystical Body, each member of this Church, including the Catholic Christian mystic is supernaturally and superhumanistically and superhumanely gifted with the Holy Spirit's Giftedness.

By reason of God-the-Holy Spirit's divine Giftedness the mystic is able to reconcile his objective willing dutiful love for the Father with his subjective sacrificial willful love for the Son. That is, the mystic as a superhuman sacramentally graced person is able to reconcile within his own personhood his conscionable soulful dutiful love for the Father's infinite lovability with his conscientious self-centered sacrificial love for the Son's superhuman heroic loveliness. In this regard the mystic himself becomes infinitely loveable by reason of the Father's infinite paternal love for him and superhumanistically (i.e., selflessly) lovely by reason of the Son's Selfless brotherly love for him. In this reconciliation the mystic's love for God becomes integrally a sacrificially virtuous love together with a duty-bound sacrificial love. That is, this love is not merely faith-based fundamentally, objectively, and trustingly; it is faith-bound supplementally, confidently, subjectively, and hopefully; furthermore, it is faithfully subjectively objective and objectively subjective in its integrality. That is, it is conscionably conscientious and conscientiously conscionable.

What this brings about in the mystic is a consummate wedding

with the Blessed Trinity in which his very own personhood's objective soulful nature and subjective self-cultivated selfhood become integrally reconciled with each other. The mystic experiences the peace
of Christ which the world cannot give. At the same time, he experiences even on this side of heaven something of the beatitude of the
beatific vision reserved for the saint in the heaven of the Church's
New Jerusalem. Objectively by reason of his intellectual intelligibility
he fully recognizes God's existential eminence as God and his own
creaturely existence which is infinitely inferior to God's divine existence. Subjectively by reason of his mindful historical memory eschatologically subsumed into the very eternity of the Blessed Trinity's immutable Godhead by Christ's redemptive Paschal Mystery, he experiences himself transported into the very bosom of this Triune family
Godhead. While he remains fully cognizant of the disparity between
God's divine immortal infinity and his own historical mortal finitude,
he experiences by reason of the Holy Spirit's Giftedness a volunteer
gift of himself to the Triune Supreme love that is both not possessively his own and yet enjoyed and religiously experienced as his very
own.

This is the divine love which St. John of the Cross is describing in
these final verses of the *Spiritual Canticle*. The mystic who plumbs
this love and deciphers for himself the depth of these verses will most
assuredly be plumbing the depths of our Blessed Mother's own sublime Trinitarian love and lovable loveliness. Such consummate mystical love is peculiar to all Christian espousal love. It is a love which is
reserved for the spouses themselves. Those who would intrude on it
venture into a sanctuary which is reserved for the spouses alone. Yet,
such is this divine espousal love that it is simultaneously communal
and sociable. It integrates and reconciles a person's objective personal
voluntary dutiful obligations to God with his subjective personalized
affections and self-detached voluntaristic attachments to God. In doing so it enables the human person to become a personage in the company of the saints who themselves have become the integral integrated Personal, Personalized Personage that is Jesus Christ, God/Su-
perman.

This integral cruciformly integrated love is freely mediated by

Jesus Christ, God/Superman. At the same time, it is freely embraced by the Catholic Christian mystic himself. In this embrace the mystic freely (i.e., voluntarily) dutifully obeys his divine Father's Holy Will providentially made objectively manifest in the moral obligations of the 10 commandments. He, additionally, freely (i.e., voluntaristically & forcibly) sacrificially becomes be-attitudinally self-detached from the subjective prison of his own selfish servile selfhood liberated by Christ's Gospel life-style and very own Self-oblation on the cross of His crucifixion. The mystic is liberated from the prison of his own self-centered selfishness and from the guilt of his own disobedience to God made supernaturally possible by Christ's precious Blood, the sacramental currency of the Church's redemptive economy. In this twofold vertical and horizontal liberation, the Catholic Christian mystic is enabled to enter into a volunteer self-giving freedom of the Holy Spirit's own Giftedness. This is the freedom of self-determination. This freedom is the integral freedom of both being virtuously (i.e., vigorously voluntarily) noble in choosing God above and beyond all other choices together with having Christ's very own sacrificial sufficient masterful forcible self-control over his own bodily feelings and mental bearings to transcend his own self-centered selfishness.

This integral cruciform freedom of self-determination is such that the Catholic Christian mystic is simultaneously (vertically) objectively fully trusting in the Father's providential Holy Will, and (horizontally) subjectively hopefully convinced and confidently trust-bound to being resurrected to immortal life with Christ following the oblation of his own selfhood in union with Christ's oblation. This integral (cruciform) freedom of self-determination integrates his objective dutiful love with his subjective sacrificial love into a superhumane *agape* love of friendship allowing and enabling the mystic to be a fellow companion with Christ and freely (i.e., as a volunteer offering) joining Christ's mission of redeeming, sanctifying, and glorifying mankind. Here the Catholic Christian mystic under the unctuous influence of the Holy Spirit becomes a faithful unwavering indomitable trustee (i.e., witness & prophet) of God's very own freedom and gracious loving loveliness. Here the mystic without ceasing to be a creature of God, his Creator, experiences religiously through God's magnificent and gracious benevolent largesse, his own ability to requite the Father's infinite providential and paternal benevolence with the Son's own filial exuberant volunteer love under the auspices of the Holy Spirit's influential benediction abiding within the innermost intimacy of his own selfhood.

Stanza 33:

Here the mystic recognizes that through the grace of Christ's own redemptive Paschal Mystery including the gift of the Holy Spirit's own Giftedness, he now is endowed with a divine graciousness and beauty of his own commensurate with God's own loveliness and goodness. In view of this, he not only merits being loved by God not merely condescendingly but even as a full-fledged member of the family of the Blessed Trinity.

Stanza 34:

Here the mystic recognizes that his peaceful accord between his objective conscionable nature and his subjective conscientious self-cultivated self enables him to find his restful abode in God's Triune bosom above and beyond all of the vicissitudes of his own inner and outer conflicts.

Stanza 35:

Here the mystic recognizes that the epitome of his religious communion with God's Trinitarian Godhead is nothing less than the awesome and stupendous immutable and eternal solitude of God's own solitary Godhead. The more perfectly the mystic communes with God the more patently he becomes aware that the only one with whom he can fully personally share this communion is God alone. This is typical of all spousal love that it is the mutual espousal love of the spouses alone. Anyone who attempts to insert himself in this love seems to be an intruder unless it is one actually born of this love such as is the case with children born of wedded love.

Stanza 36:

Here the mystic is so inebriated with the very divine love that is proper to God's own divinity that he is emboldened to revel joyfully in a joy that is beatitudinal precisely because it is redolent of the Trinitarian family Love which is crystallized in the Person of the Holy Spirit. In this crystallization it is impossible to differentiate between the lover and the Beloved.

Stanza 37:

Here the mystic recognizes along with St. Paul that "he himself no longer lives; it is Christ that is his very own life." Here, then, the mystic becomes aware that in himself he is experiencing something of the very mystery of Christ's incarnation as the God/Superman, Christ's Self-oblation on the cross, Christ's indwelling in the Sacred Eucharist, as well as Christ's bodily resurrection and ascension into heaven. In other words, the mystic recognizes that it is only in, through, and with Christ that he has reached his own fulsome authentic identity, personality, and self-fulfillment.

Stanza 38:

Here the mystic recognizes that his own life will reach its total consummation when he becomes divinely enabled by reason of God's infinite benevolence and benediction to return God's love measure-for-measure.

Stanza 39:

Here the mystic anticipates becoming so perfectly transformed into Christ as to become indistinguishable from the very divine beloved vitality which is characteristic of the Holy Spirit personifying the munificent love that enfolds the Father and Son's mutual divine embrace.

Stanza 40:

Here the mystic reflects on himself and recognizes that by reason of God's Trinitarian grace and loving graciousness he himself in his natural faculties and self-cultivated self-centered propensities is completely at peace with himself, an indomitable peace that only Christ,

God/Superman can grant to his own disciple in bestowing on him the gift of His own Holy Spirit.

It seems to me only fitting to point out that this consummated communion between the mystic and the Blessed Trinity mediated through Christ reaches its apex and summit (of Mount Carmel) only in the measure that it approaches somewhat the august mystical communion that exists between our Blessed Mother, Mary, and her first begotten Son, Jesus Christ. She as Mother of the Sacramental Church is also Mother of the Church's Mystical Body which is constituted of all the bodily members of that same Church. Having recourse to our Blessed Mother is tantamount to becoming the child of the same mother who has herself given birth, nursed, and nurtured and become herself the most eminent mystical disciple of the very one, Jesus Christ, who is the very summit of Mount Carmel. We can pray to Mary accordingly: "Mary, Mother of Christ and Mother of the Church, Mother in me the life which you mothered in your Son, Jesus Christ, God/Superman."

COMMENTARY ON
THE LIVING FLAME OF LOVE

THE LIVING FLAME OF LOVE. Stanza 1:

O living flame of love

That tenderly wounds my soul

In its deepest center! Since

Now You are not oppressive,

Now Consummate! If it be Your will:

Tear through the veil of this sweet encounter!

The "Living Flame" is the Holy Spirit. The wound that it inflicts within the "soul's very center" is a description which more befits the mystic's egocentric selfhood than it does the mystic's spiritual soul. The soul in its utter spirituality is incapable of having a "center." The very term, center, entails a mathematical and graphic orientation; it entails a spatial reference to vortices or a periphery which is circumstantial to the center but off-center vis-à-vis the center's spatial centrality. The soul being entirely spiritual can abide nothing of materiality, physicality, sensibility, spatiality, etc.. In view of its spirituality the human soul cannot be directly experienced. However, it can be directly understood in its dynamic intelligibility. Dynamically it imbues the substantive body with a dynamic holistic organicity and vitality such that one may declare that the human body is "alive." That is, it spontaneously initiates the body's botanical vital operations which are holistically beneficial such as the growth and nourishment of the body's own organic bodily members as well as procreating new bodily life to perpetuate its own species.

Above and beyond the body's botanical vitality it dynamically vitalizes the human body's zoological activity involving the senses and the body's mobilization spurred on by the body's sentient instinctive appetitive drives. And, even above and beyond the body's own botanical and zoological organic extended organization, the human soul is endowed with vital activities proper to its own spiritual inorganic incorporeality. These are the activities of thinking and willing which transcend completely the reach and compass of the body's complex organs and tangible corporeality itself.

In no strict sense is the soul the "center" of any of these human vital activities. While the soul in terms of its own substantive incorporeal spirituality remains really distinct from the body's corporeality, it dynamically and holistically vitalizes the substantive body in such a manner that the soul itself does not become extended while dynamically vitalizing the body's extended extensive organs and organicity. The human soul by dint of its spirituality is holistically wholly in every separate organ of the body's physiological organicity. In other words, the body's foot, hand, heart, eye, and instinctive sentient drive, etc., are "alive" with one and the same soulful vitalization and human life. The one indivisible spiritual soul is not the center of any of these vital activities; the soul is spiritually diffused throughout all of these vital activities without being itself constrained or reducible to any one operation considered separately or to all of them considered conjointly.

The human soul is immortal by reason of its innate dynamic indivisible inorganic spirituality. That is, it cannot perish with the substantive body's perishable corruption because, unlike the body's physiological complexity, it itself is utterly indivisible and devoid of all complexity. The human soul is not susceptible to dissolution because of its innate inorganic simplicity; hence, it is immortal and does not perish with the body's corruption and degeneration when it can no longer sustain the soul's dynamic vitality. Further, the corporeal material substantive body itself within its complex corporeality harbors no centrality or center-point peculiar to mathematical geometric spatiality.

However, there is such a centrality in the insubstantive corpuscular body which is susceptible to the human person's subjective sensational sensitized pleasurable and/or painful conscious sensations. The very core and nucleus of such conscious sensitized sensations is metaphorically referred to as the human "heart." It is this human heart of the mystic that is contentedly satisfied (i.e., pleased) or discontentedly dissatisfied and displeased with such emotionally religiously charged sensitizing sensations. This "heart" is not itself a special organ or organism such as is the case with the heart that pumps the blood to be circulated throughout the body's vessels. This centrifugal "heart" is presented in poetic and metaphorical terms since it is likened to the point in a circle which is tangent to every point on the circle's circumference without itself being reducible to any part of the circumference itself. It is a centrifugal center because it "stretches itself" outward to be "in touch" with all the segments of the circle to itself. A person with this "heart" is usually emotionally compassionate and sympathetic toward his own somatic self as well as towards hearts other than the person's own self. Such a "heart" is endowed with a pathos imbued with feelings, moods, and empathies.

This center point is the very gist and nuclear core of the circle's circumference. The circumference and every segment of the circumference is constituted of a geometric line. In addition, every radius or spoke connecting the circumference (i.e., circle rim) with its center is also an extended line. The center-point, on the other hand, is in no way itself a linear extension; it is a linear inextension in simultaneous contact with every extended circle segment. It is itself devoid of all extended linearity while it is the very nuclear core which is coextensive with every extended part of the circle. Similarly, while the corpuscular body's sensitized pleasures and pains are consciously subjectively experienced differently and coextensively by the mystic within his corpuscular body's complex physiological extension, they all converge within the person's nuclear heart-felt satisfied and/or dissatisfied subjective egocentric selfhood which is not reducible to any one of these bodily complexities.

The other center point in the human person's subjective self-conscious bodily awareness is that of the *mind*. This alternative central point within the mystic's subjective experience of the body's corpuscularity is not centered on the sensitized body's religious emotional sensations but on the body's non-sensitized emotionless religious inspirations of self-contained justification (validation) and/or non-self-contained vindication (i.e., self-invalidation). Unlike the heart this mental center is a centrifugal center. It seeks to "gather" every separate divisible segment of the circle within its own indivisibility to become entirely validly religiously self-contained and entirely self-vindicated and self-sufficient (viz., socially autocratic in its autonomy) within its own mental framework and setup. The typical compassion of such a person's mind is not of an emotional bodily *feeling* (viz., like or dislike) but, rather, that of an emotionless mental inspirational *bearing* (viz., caring or not caring) toward one's own psychic selfhood, on the one hand, and toward psychic selves other than one's own self, on the other.

This mental empathy is not one of *pathos* but rather one of *ethos*. Like-minded persons do not communicate empathically by bodily feelings or emotions (viz., hugs, hand shakes, etc). They communicate telepathically with other minds empathically not by emotional sensitized feelings and bodily gestures but telepathically by symbolic language susceptible only to notional conceptualization and cerebral interpretation. Two spiritual persons are of "one mind" and "like-minded" when they both entertain the same emotionless inspirational religious bearing, self-vindication, and self-justification, concerning issues of fundamental importance. Persons who participate in the same religious denomination share telepathically the same sympathetic ethos peculiar to that denomination's fundamental adherence. At the same time, they experience telepathically an antipathy toward the ethos of religious denominations other than their own. The same holds for participants in the political process who are partisanly and prejudicially like-minded in opposition to opponents who are not so partisanly like-minded.

This pathological ethos is not to be confused with morality and ethics. The moral/ethic order is rooted in the hierarchical order of nature. The ethos indicated here is endemic to the historical order of culture. It consists of what is most paramountly important to a person's self-serving social security and autonomy. Somewhat superficially but still significantly the ethos of any team in a competitive sport is the over-all mindset to skillfully prevail over one's opponent. Within this mindset all the members of the team are "at one" in the ethos of their camaraderie. Christianity's over-all ethos is that of Christ's very own redemptive messianic mindset: to save souls by sacrificially offering up one's own life in union with Christ's own redeeming crucifixion. The Catholic Christian ethos is unquestionably counter-cultural inasmuch as the worldly secular humanistic cultural outlook is inherently self-centeredly selfish rather than self-centeredly unselfishly selfless. The human person inherits Adam and Eve's legacy of original sin and is prone to cultivating a prejudicial and partisan ethos of self-alienating selfishness. The Catholic Christian ethos is prejudicially a non-partisan ethos of non-alienating selflessness. This entails that one love benignantly the enemy of one's own Catholic Christian ethos. It most frequently happens that one's enemy is precisely the person who claims to adhere to one's own Catholic Christian ethos but fails to practice this ethos to the full.

The principal motivating prayerful activity peculiar to the mystic's human heart is one of religious stimulation while the activity proper to his human mind is one of religious sedation. Religious stimulation spurs the mystic to bodily action whereas sedation induces quietude and bodily inaction. Religious stimulation is predominantly provoked by sensational imagery while religious sedation is evoked by inspirational non-tactile notions devoid of all tactile imagery. Such mental religious notions are susceptible to being exemplified in striking sensational tactile imagery but are not themselves clothed with such spectacular tactile trappings. Rather, they themselves are more spectral, spooky, and elusive in very much the same way that the geometrical point is itself mentally elusive. It is grasped more by what it is not rather than what it actually is. It is an inextended quantum.

Similarly with the mystic's mental religious experience of his notional inspiration of his own religious "union" with God as a "point" in which he and God are indivisibly one in the manner of a geometric point is "at one" with every linear circular part of the circle. This "at oneness" affords the mystic a considerable mental peace in which the mind enjoys an equipoise bearing of complete self-contained and self-justified religious serenity vis-à-vis a self other than its own self. It is a fellowship of sociability, camaraderie, and substitutable partnership in which one is "at home" with one's "alter ego." This mental bearing of religious fellowship is more intimately intensive than is the somatic sensitive feeling of such fellowship. The intimate mental bearing of religious fellowship is centripetal and convergent while the sensitive bodily feeling of fellowship is centrifugal and divergent. Paradoxically, the former culminates in a sociability that statically confuses and confounds the associates together in an inner intimate speechless bodiless togetherness while the latter diffuses and binds the associates together in an outer sensitive bodily demonstration (viz., dancing, hugging, etc.) of togetherness.

In the case of the *heart* the mystic enjoys a religious central feeling of having sensitively an indivisible "oneness" with God in all his extended body complexity; the body is gloriously dilated and expanded. In the case of the *mind* the mystic experiences a religious bearing of having intimately an indivisible "oneness" with God in his own inextended bodiless mind. The mind left to its own ministration seeks to be self-hypnotically sedated. Under the unctuous influence of the Holy Spirit it is a plenitudinous sedation which floods the mystic's mindfulness. Of these two centers one is more indivisibly inextended and experientially "centered" than is the other. When the mystic is sensitively emotionally centrifugally self-contented, this religious self-contentment is diffused throughout the body's physiological complexity. The mystic experiences a sublime radiant "glory" and exultation which radiates throughout the body's somatic sensitivity. When the mystic is intimately mindfully self-contained, this religious self-containment is centripetally concentrated within the mind's physiological incomplexity which is not empirically observable as is the case with the body's sensational sensitivity. This religious self-containment is experienced as a sublime placidity in which everything converges in one undifferentiated egocentric selfhood that is completely open to all other selves that transcends this person's own selfhood. Here there is no lingering intrapersonal or interpersonal self-alienation.

Now, for the Catholic Christian mystic, such religious experiences can only be authentically and sincerely divine and derivative from God if they in no way are subject to the mystic's willful self-control and exploitation. This can only be the case when these are entirely gratuitously afforded the mystic without the benefit of the interference or meddling of his own self-centered and entirely self-serving egocentric heartfelt and mindful willfulness. Every human person has a self-humanized "spirit" attending to his own selfish self-serving cultivation. This humanistic spirit is entirely selfishly self-serving. Within this humanistic spirit there are "religious" peak experiences induced by a person's own autonomous self-serving efforts. These are willfully obtained and sustained by the person himself and are not superhumanistically endowed by God but by the mystic's own willful exertions. Such is the case with a sport figure who relishes his victory over his opponents or a guru who relishes his victory over his own bodily and/or mental waywardness.

In the case of the Living Flame this "Spirit" which stirs the mystic's outer heart and quiets the mystic's inner mind is the very Holy Spirit of the Blessed Trinity. To fully appreciate the depth of St. John's grasp of the presence of the Holy Spirit within the Catholic Christian's subjective willful selfhood, it is appropriate to liken this Holy Spirit to the tongues of fire which alighted on the heads of the apostles at Pentecost. Of course, the Holy Spirit fundamentally abides in the mystic's soul in the sacramentality of grace. In this fundamental residency the Holy Spirit is simultaneously one with the Father and the Son. This fundamental sacramental residency is one of status; it is permanent as long as the mystic remains in the state of grace by reason of his obediential soulful will dutifully subordinated to the Father's Holy Will made manifest in the Son's incarnation and ecclesial sacramentality. This sacramental presence cannot be directly experienced anymore than can the human soul itself be directly experienced. That is, the human person cannot have a self-centered and self-conscious awareness of his own soul and God's sacramental indwelling there. Indirectly he can have such an experience when he experiences for himself the peace of Christ's Paschal Mystery which is radically the reconciliation of his subjective self-centered self-fulfilled selfhood reconciled with his objective grace-filled soul destined to abide everlastingly in the bosom of God's Triune family and familiarity.

The Catholic Christian mystic experiences the Holy Spirit as a Living Flame. He is a burning flame that does not totally combust what He renders flammable. Physical fire combusts what it burns and it becomes more of a flame the more its combustible material is thoroughly combusted. Not so with the Holy Spirit's flammability. Where a fire becomes extinguished when a forest is finally completely reduced to ashes, this is not the case with the fire of the Holy Spirit inflaming the mystic's heart and mind. Initially this fire is very oppressive because it must combust the heart's selfish need for its own self-serving religious sensuous pleasurable bodily sensitized self-contentment. It is not before and not until this visceral religious selfishness has been completely combusted within the fire of the Holy Spirit's flame that the mystic's own heart can become inflamed with a divine fire that no longer painfully assails its own religious self-contentment but blissfully delights and dilates its entire complex bodily sensitivity with a glorious selfless exuberance and zeal.

When this religious purgation "by fire" of the mystic's selfish heart has been sufficiently accomplished, the Holy Spirit proceeds to subsequently inflame the mystic's mind with a comparable purgation "by fire" suitable to the mind's own selfish self-orientation. Initially this fire is, again, exceedingly oppressive because it must combust the mind's selfish need for its own self-serving religious autonomous (i.e., self-sustained) vindicated mental self-containment. It is not before and not until this cerebral religious selfishness has been completely combusted within the fire of the Holy Spirit's flame that the mystic's own mind and mind-set (i.e., have-attitude) can become inflamed with a divine fire that no longer painfully assaults its own religious selfish self-vindication but, rather, consummates this same mind with a selfless mental serenity and sublime (be-attitudinal mindset) placidity that penetrates to the innermost inner intimacy of the mystic's abysmal selfhood.

The Holy Spirit's flaming charitable Love and Loveliness which penetrates the very nuclear center of the mystic's somatic sensitive selfhood does not penetrate the mystic's heart with the same divine flaming saturation that it brings to the mystic's psychic selfhood. For, in the case of the mystic's heart this flame does not penetrate to the innermost intimate center of the mystic's selfhood. It remains in the outer surface periphery of the mystic's sensuous somatic selfhood. That is, the mystic feels the Holy Spirit's flame as his very own flaming zeal and bodily religious glory. But this religious mystical somatic supersensitized religious "feeling" is not as completely "at one" with the Holy Spirit's very own flaming fire as is the case with the mystic's psychic superintimate religious "bearing" in which there is a consummate "at one" interpenetration in which the mystic can no longer differentiate between his own innermost intimate selfhood's imperturbable religious composure and the Holy Spirit's flammable impassive consummation. In the one case, the Holy Spirit extensively inflames the mystic's heartfelt bodily sensitized feeling while in the other case the Holy Spirit intensively inflames the mystic's mental intimate equipoise.

Again, this difference of divine saturation may be explained in terms of different forms of fire. A wood-burning fire differs from that of coal, oil, and even gas. The wood must be dried out before it can burn thoroughly and it burns unevenly and with considerable shooting flames as it becomes more fully inflamed and combusted. Coal burns less spectacularly but with a still more intense fire penetrating its substance. Crude oil, such as kerosene, burns more readily and offers less resistance and refined oil even moreso. But, gas burns with such a quiet intensity that it seems well-nigh impossible to differentiate between the gas fumes and the flame itself. Gas offers no resistance at all to the fire that burns it. Indeed, it seems not to be combusted but to be fire itself.

In the final analysis, St. John pleads with God to simply "tear" the veil that now separates the mystic from being completely swallowed up in God's Triune divinity as will be the case after death in the beatific vision. For, it seems that by reason of these sublime mystical experiences that the mystic remains so sensitively and intimately replete and saturated with the very divinity of the Holy Spirit's infinite gratuity, benignity, and graciousness that he actually savors and experiences within his own selfhood the very familiarity of the Blessed Trinity's Trinitarian Godhead. Of course, these religious experiences are entirely subjective in their experientiality but for all of that they are for the mystic by reason of the theological gifts of faith, hope, and charity a veritable experience of God's own eternal transcendency immanently permeating and sublimating his own selfhood. Again, one must be reminded that such experiences are not as permanent as the sacramental presence of the Holy Spirit's graciousness in the mystic's soul. These experiences are transitory. But albeit their transiency they leave an indelible memorial residue and imprint within the mystic's memory.

THE LIVING FLAME OF LOVE. Stanza 2:

O sweet cautery,

O delightful wound!

O gentle hand! O delicate touch

That tastes of eternal life

And pays every debt!

In killing You changed death to life.

In this verse we learn that the "living flame" is both "one" and "three." It is one because God in His Godhead is one while this one divinity harbors three distinct divine Persons: the Father, Son, & Holy Spirit. This "living flame" imparts to the mystic's selfhood three distinctive traits proper to the three divine Persons. The Holy Spirit is likened to a *cautery*, the Son to a *gentle touch*, and the Father to a *gentle hand*. Of course, these are metaphorical descriptions of the Blessed Trinity's influential impact on the mystic's psychosomatic selfhood. It must be noted that in the vertical order of the mystic's sacramental encounter with the Blessed Trinity, the human soul's sacramental reception of the very graciousness of the Blessed Trinity is not one of ontological identity but sacramental elevation from the natural state of creation to the supernatural state of adoption into the Trinity through the redeeming mediation of Jesus Christ. The mystic is not rendered sacramentally identical in his own ontological being with God's the very own Beingness. Nonetheless, the mystic receives a new identification by participation and not by nature as a "child of God" in the family of the Blessed Trinity.

In the horizontal order pertaining to the mystic's own psychosomatic selfhood there is a comparable impact on the mystic's subjective selfhood by becoming sacramentally introduced into the Blessed Trinity. This impact is not one of elevated participation, it is one of association. This horizontal order is not one of information as is the case with the vertical order; it is one of transformation. Here the mystic becomes sacramentally and superhumanistically transformed into Christ's very own superhumanistic Selfhood. This transformation entails a paradox of dying to one's selfish self-centeredness and rising anew to the Selfless Selfhood that is Christ's very own Self with His super-self-centered Selfless Self-humanized Personality engaging the empathic sensitivity of His Sacred Heart and the telepathic intimacy of His Messianic Beatitudinal Mindset. This dying and rising engages the mystic's own willful self-involvement and self-cooperative partnership and engagement.

This personality transformation is processive; it is a journey, a life-long pilgrimage which passes through three distinctive stages peculiar to the mystical life. Before the mystic becomes completely transformed into Christ's very own super-humanized Personality, he must be first completely purged of his own self-centered selfishness. This stage has itself two phases, an active and a passive phase. In the active phase the mystic engages in a rigorous ascetic life of self-denial and mortification in which he deliberately detaches himself from his own selfishly self-serving sensuous attachments and worldly me-centered possessive have-attitudinal self-serving mindful interests. The second phase comes into its own when the Holy Spirit influentially at the level of the mystic's experiential religious encounter with God in his bodily exultation and/or mental serenity suffers the complete loss of these religious sensitizing and intimate motivational consolations. The Holy Spirit withholds these religious motivational consolations from the mystic. In this loss the mystic comes to experientially suffer a seemingly endless bleak awareness of his own misery and turpitude deprived as he is of God's enhancing sensitive and intimate caresses. This suffering is excruciatingly painful and difficult to endure. Without these singularly comforting exquisitely exciting religious emotional exultations and self-justifying consoling sublime sedate intimate periods of prolonged divine serenity previously enjoyed, he has no further motivation to push ahead in his prayerful endeavor of becoming more unselfishly conformed to the mind and heart of Christ.

When this period of purgation has sufficiently advanced to the point that the mystic is submissively resolved to endure his own mortification and suffering in his quest to become more completely conformed to Christ's own sacrificial suffering, he emerges into the second phase of his Christocentric personality transformation. This is the illuminative stage in which he begins to discern how profitable and beneficial has been his prayerful perseverance in following Christ by "taking up" his own cross of humiliation and deprivation throughout the seemingly never-ending ascetic program of self-denial and mortification totally bereft of comforting motivational experiences of God. This enlightened discernment subtly introduces him to the third terminal phase which is the marital union with the Blessed Trinity. The distinctive hallmark of this third phase being described here in the *Living Flame* with remarkable clarity and detail is the volunteer transformative empathic assumption of the mystic's own self into Christ's own super-empathic Selfhood. The preliminary stages of the mystic's trying metanoetic conversion and volitional sacrificial surrender to Christ's own Lordship and Mastery entailing that he forcibly overcome his own selfish resistancy give way to an uncontrollable periodic rush of religious Christ-centered exultation and consolation which he blissfully welcomes and embraces.

The most apt metaphor chosen by St. John of the Cross to describe the complete fusion of the mystic's own personality into that of Christ is that of a "living flame" of love. Of course, this is an associative exchange in the same way that one person may substitute for another person in any athletic competitive sport or work force involving team-work. Christ Himself has as a sinless scapegoat substituted His own impeccably self-centered Selfless Selfhood in the place of every human being's peccably sinful selfish self-centered selfhood. In the final stage of this mystical marital union the mystic has finally succeeded in becoming heroically completely transformed into Christ. He has overcome all resistancy to Christ's very own sacrificial be-attitudinal disinterested Selflessness. The mystic's own selfishly ingrained self-serving selfish have-attitude of self-interest has been finally combusted within the fire of the Holy Spirit's consummate flame of Christ's merciful Love and Loveliness. The mystic now has put on Christ's be-attitudinal mindset of being more devoted to serving the vertical order of existence rather than having and sustaining a have-attitude within the horizontal order of his own selfish self-serving resistance. What endures is the Holy Spirit's Flaming Love in which the mystic's own selfish merciless love has been combusted and transformed into Christ's own Selfless Merciful Love. His selfish combative have-attitude has become sublimated into Christ's selfless pacific be-attitude.

St John metaphorically likens this final phase of the mystic's selfhood becoming swallowed up in the merciful flaming fire of the Holy Spirit to God's hand wielding a cautery which touches the mystic's egocentric self ever so gently to wound it and in this wounding to, thereby, heal it. One must keep in mind that in the 16th century a cautery was a standard medical practice. This is similar to a branding iron which cattlemen use to brand their cattle and, thereby, to mark them as their own property. Cattle, of course, have no sensitized feeling. They are brute animals. They do sense pain and have no self-awareness of any sensitized feeling of pain entailing their suffering (i.e., self-conscious endurance) of such pain. The 16th century physician wielded a hot iron heated in a flaming fire and used it to burn away a person's bodily infection and to, thereby, enable the diseased part of the body to begin to heal. Such a cautery inflicted a painful wound which served to bring about a healing and cure of a serious infection. Today in modern medicine this same procedure is effectuated less painfully in laser, chemical, and radiation treatments.

In St. John's metaphor the *cautery* itself inflicting a wound is likened to the Holy Spirit's impact on the mystic's self. The very *gentle hand* wielding the cautery is God, the Father, and the *delicate touch* that the cautery imparts to the mystic's egocentric selfhood is that of God, the Son. One and the same Godhead is engaged in this transformation of the mystic's selfish concentricity into Christ's Self-less eccentricity. Yet, there are three distinctively different divine and sublime subtle religious experiences which the mystic suffers. He experiences an exquisite *reverential delight* from the cautery's wound inflicted by the Holy Spirit, *a taste of eternal life* from the Son's delicate touch, and *a divine self-vindication* and justification from the Father's gentle hand.

Cautery: The burning cautery inflicts a wound not to harm the mystic but to heal the mystic of his seemingly hopeless needful suffering for God. The mystic pines and yearns to be perfectly wed to God in such an intimacy that he can no longer differentiate between himself and God. This needful suffering seems hopeless because the mystic is fully aware that of himself and by his own resourcefulness he is completely unable to ever fulfill on his own initiative this deep needful yearning for God. Certainly, the mystic has lived through and suffered perseveringly a very prolonged arduous and very strenuous period of being painfully wounded by the Holy Spirit's flaming love without experiencing the curative ardor of that love. He has suffered through the purgative stage of this cautery and experienced his self's egocentric willful selfishness reduced to cinders.

What now remains are burning embers that offer no further resistance to the flaming fire that consumes them. Accordingly, what remains for the mystic is a chastised selfhood which offers no further resistance to the Holy Spirit's flaming merciful love proper to Christ's own Selfless Selfhood. Accordingly, the mystic now becomes himself inflamed with a burning reverential benignant delight that seems to be God's very own infinitely consummate blissful flame of delight. It is so overwhelmingly awesome that the mystic cannot express it with any word that is adequate to convey its sublimity. He is reduced to sighing inexpressible sighs.

O Delightful Wound: The cautery's wound is most paradoxical. It is inflicted only to heal and not to cause pain. Yet, its very process of healing involves itself an element of pain. In other words, the cautery must wound in order to heal. The paradox here is that in the mystical life the more the mystic experiences God's very own loving flame of merciful benignity and graciousness as his very own, the more intensively does the mystic yearn and pine to be totally completely engulfed in this exquisitely sublime and delightful loveliness. Paradoxically, the more the mystic is healed with an increasingly healthy religious experience of God's boundless magnanimity and benignity, the more intensely and intensively the mystic yearns to be utterly dissolved in this ocean of love.

St. John describes a most rare transverberation of divine love which occurs only in those individuals who have special roles as founders of new religious orders. This is explained by comparison with a log of wood which is completely engulfed in fire. When someone takes a poker and pokes at it there darts out from the log spurting flames of fire and sparks. Similarly, the mystic whose self is completely on fire with God's own benevolent benignity experiences special spurting flames of love when it seems that a special pointed dart afflicts and penetrates its own furnace of divine love.

This "living flame" is such that the mystic experiences himself at the center of the universe which is aflame with God's burning love. So awesome and all-consuming is this experience that the mystic cannot fathom any limit or boundary to the expansiveness and compass of this love. The mystic seems to be full of God's own infinite fulsomeness. The upshot of this sublime experience is that the mystic himself is no longer confined to the subjective personalized subjectivity of his own egocentric selfhood. He is no longer alienated from the reality of God which transcends his own egocentric selfhood. He is no longer self-alienated within his own selfhood nor self-alienated from other selves and from God's own Godhead in the vertical ontological order of existence transcendent to his subjective horizontal phenomenological order of resistance. Furthermore, this mystical experience of God's flaming loveliness may be experienced completely intimately inward within the self's innermost mental intimacy or sensitively outward within the self's outmost bodily sensitivity. In the latter case, it may appear in the body in the form of the stigmata with which several saints have been blessed such as St. Paul, St. Francis, and Padre Pio.

Gentle Hand: God-the-Father most mercifully causes death in the mystic's willfully self-centered selfish selfhood only to bring about a life of the self which is an enduring and benevolent immortal life transcending the fateful transiency of history's horizontal horizon. The Father permits the death of the "old man" to allow and make room for the "new man" which is Jesus Christ, God/Superman. This "new man" will rise gloriously from the strictures of the historical man to live forever in the Father's heavenly kingdom.

Delicate Touch: The Son-of-God penetrates subtly into the inner-most intimate recesses of the mystic's selfhood touching it delicately and absorbing it into His own Selfless Selfhood. At this point the fire of God's love no longer combusts the mystic's selfish selfhood. Its selfishness has already been combusted. Hence, at this point it is no longer oppressive because the self no longer offers any resistance. The mystic's selfhood is itself engulfed in this fire of love. And so delicate does this divine fire "touch" the mystic's own selfhood that it is a marvel that Christ who is omnipotently powerful can be so gentle. This "touch" is so delicately sensitized in the mystic's body and intimately refined in the mystic's mental experience that every other touch other than Christ seems course, crude, and rough by comparison.

That Tastes Eternal Life: This divine touch of Christ that penetrates into the mystic's innermost intimate selfhood imparts an experience of eternity. To fully appreciate the magnitude of this mystical experience consider that the intellect which is a faculty of the spiritual soul is itself intellectually open to the reality of eternity which surpasses and transcends its own immortal status. Yet, it grasps eternity intellectually as the very absence of temporality's cosmic movement and the absence of every change which occurs instantaneously beyond the boundary of cosmic time within the intellect's own utterly spiritual activity of thinking and understanding. Eternity is synonymous with immutability. Not even the purely spiritual reality of the angels is entirely immutable. Their knowledge does develop and change throughout their angelic existence. Granted that such mutability is beyond the limitation of cosmic movement and temporality, it is still not eternal. It has been called aeviternal and quasi-eternal by Scholastic philosophers and theologians because the changes which occur in their intellectual understanding occur instantaneously and not through any process of logical reasoning as is the case with the human intellect.

The mystic's subjective mind which is constitutive of his subjective egocentric selfhood and intimate personality has no immortality of its own proper to the person's human soul. It is entirely mortal in keeping with the substantive human body's mortality. This human mind which is the psychic center of the human person's subjective subconscious egocentric self-awareness is found in the subjective horizontal order of the human person's self-humanized and self-cultivated psychosomatic personality. This mind is not to be confused with the human intellect. It is not substantively spiritual and immortal as is the case with the human soul's innate spirituality. It is quasi-spiritual by comparison with its subjective egocentric sensitized somatic bodily counterpart also found in the subjective horizontal order of the human person's self-humanized psychosomatic personality. Unlike the brute animal's sentient corporeal body which has no egocentric subjective self-conscious bodily sensitivity and mindful intimacy over and above its own brute sentiency, the human person by dint of his personhood has such a refined egocentric somatic (i.e., bodily) sensitized and/or intimate psychic (i.e., mental) self-awareness of his own mortal corpuscular selfhood.

Thus, the mystic as a human person can subjectively egocentrically experience (i.e., sensitively feel) his sentient substantive body's objective sentiency and subjectively experience (i.e., intimately care about and be concerned for) this same substantive body's animation emanating from the dynamism of the substantive soul's spiritual immortality. It is all the more the case that the human person can subjectively egocentrically experience by bodily feeling and mental caring the supernatural ordering of the sentient substantive body's objective sentiency and its vitalizing spiritual life emanating from the substantive soul's spiritual vitality. Nonetheless, these subjective mystical (i.e., religious supernatural) sensitized emotional religious bodily feelings and intimate emotionless mental religious concerns occur within the order of the human person's subjective horizontal historicity. In other words, they are themselves removed from the vertical ontological domain of eternity's immutability and the human soul's own transhistorical immortality.

How, then, could the mystic possibly experience within his innermost intimate selfhood---immersed in history's doomed evanescent and processive transiency---the inexorable immutability of God's eternity? Certainly, it can be only an "as-if" experience of God's eternal immutability. This would be experienced as a profound immeasurable innermost intimate mental calm serenity and placidity that is remarkably superhumanistically possible because the mystic becomes "touched" by Christ's very own superhumanistic incarnate Selfhood incarnate within the Church's sacramentality. That is, the mystic in reaching that processive ascetic self-purification from a radical selfishness proceeding to an unselfishness becomes completely transformed at this historical point into Christ's very own Selflessness which he (i.e., the mystic) encounters in the Sacrament of the Holy Eucharist. In this encounter the mystic under the auspices of the Holy Spirit becomes enabled in a volunteer self-giving to sacrificially exchange his own personality for that of Christ's overriding merciful redeeming sacrificial Personality through the Giftedness of Christ's own Holy Spirit already imparted to the mystic.

What the mystic experiences in experiencing the immeasurable and imponderable immutability of God's eternal existence is Christ's unique and priceless gift of His own peace, a peace that passes and surpasses all understanding. This profound mystical experience of utter peaceful serenity includes a harmony and perfect reconciliation between the mystic's subjective mental be-attitudinal submissive willful sacrificial mental surrender to Christ together with his objective conscionable subordinate willing obedience to the Father's Holy Will. This profound impassive mystical experience of God's eternity within the mystic's own personhood issues from the coalescence of an obedient conscionable dutiful love of the Father's Holy Will in the vertical order of existence, a submissive conscientious kenotic love of the Son's willful sacrifice in the horizontal order of resistance, combining to yield a self-giving volunteer reciprocal agape friendship charitable love in the cruciform order of subsistence steeped in the Holy Spirit's own gratuitous Givingness.

This imperturbable and impassive serenity is not the result of a complete cessation and voiding of all willful needs and wants attained by a technical hypnotic trance induced by transcendental meditation in which the mystic would be mentally impervious to the body's sensitivity and even oblivious to his own private thoughts and mental musings and cravings. This nirvana typical of the Orient is the epitome of the human person completely and inescapably self-enveloped and absorbed in the horizontal order of his own egocentric mental self-centeredness. Whether this transcendental hypnotic trance is skillfully attained entirely alone or with the assistance of some "cryptic spirit" appealed to by a special mantra, this nirvana is the very antithesis of the Catholic Christian mystic's experience of Christ's peace transporting the mystic to experiencing an imperturbable impassivity that is the Godhead's very own divinity existing eternally transcendent to the mystic's own historical, temporal, durational mortality. The mystic experiences subjectively a self-fulfillment of God's own deity which completely transcends the self's own self-centered selfhood in the horizontal order of its willful resistancy. So fulfilling is this experience of Christ's peace that the mystic's own selfhood experiences a fulsome self-fulfillment that not only eclipses but consummates every self-alienation within its own selfhood.

In this consummation in which the mystic experiences himself to be well-nigh in perfect communion with the Blessed Trinity, he experiences the living flame of the Holy Spirit's radiant benevolence no longer as combusting his own self's selfishness. Rather, there is no selfish resistancy left to be combusted. His very selfhood is alive with the Holy Spirit's flaming love. Just as a purely refined natural gas burns with such intensity that not even a trace of its burning (viz., smoke) is detectable, so also the mystic's very selfhood is aflame with the Holy Spirit's benevolent fire of the Father and Son's mutual love. There is not even left an irregular flicker in this consummate love so profound is the mystic's experience of its own imperturbable impassivity similar to God's very own eternal immutability.

This flame includes all of God's divine and sublime distinctive attributes such as an indomitable strength (viz., a heartened courage and stalwart mindset) to endure every trial; a wisdom to fathom even

God's own fathomless divinity; a love steeped in God's own loveliness that conquers all by its alluring attractiveness; a transcendental beauty that not only discerns but also partakes of the harmony of the universe; a benignity toward everyone imbued with God's own graciousness.

Pays Every Debt. Here St. John reveals the very mystery of suffering. There is nothing which seems as abhorrent to everyone as suffering. There are some sufferings which are more painful and seemingly insufferable than others. Suffering a tooth ache, for example, seems like a lesser suffering than suffering a broken heart. If one lives in a technically advanced culture, one can readily visit a dentist and become relieved of a tooth ache. On the other hand, there is no remedy for a broken heart. A heartfelt suffering is more insufferable than a physical injury in that one may more quickly find relief from the one than from the other. And still more insufferable suffering is a reversal or dissolution of one's have-attitude and overriding mindset. One's have-attitude reveals that which is of paramount importance and interest to a person's personality, social security, and self-confidence. Any reversal or comeuppance which upends or compromises one's overriding attitudinal mindset threatens that which is most intimate and important to the autonomous security of one's very personality, selfhood, and self-esteem.

Yet, what is demanded of the Catholic Christian mystic is a radical conversion and rejection of his very own have-attitudinal self-serving mindset by adopting Christ's be-attitudinal messianic mindset. This conversion is not a one-time affair. Rather, it is a daily battle which undermines the mystic's own innermost intimate homeostatic mental bearing of social self-security. This battle entails a suffering which shatters the mystic's very own personality and selfhood's most intimate mental serenity and bodily sensitivity penetrating even to the very marrow of the mystic's bones. This suffering is excruciatingly painful precisely because there is no technical reprieve or cure. It leaves the mystic in a bodily feeling of helplessness and a mental quandary of utter loneliness and abandonment.

Yet, the upside of every suffering and especially this excruciatingly painful suffering brought on by a resolute metanoia undertaken

687

in union with Christ's own Paschal Mystery is its eventual transformation into Christ's very own divine peace and joy in enduring suffering's misery by redeeming suffering itself from its dehumanizing degradation and meaninglessness. Suffering without Christ is insufferable; suffering with Christ is not merely sufferable but efficaciously redeeming not only for one's own self-dehumanization but also for others who have yet to learn that Christ has saved mankind not from suffering itself but from suffering's dehumanizing ignominy. Christ's disciple has received the gift of His Holy Spirit to buoy up his personality's feeble heart and irresolute mind. No person left to his own self-humanized personality has a heart-felt feeling (i.e., courage) to welcome or endure the distress of the body's sensitized throbbing pains nor a resolute careful self-determination to welcome or endure the loss of the mind's own inner inmost intimate self-assurance and social security. Yet, surrendering one's self unconditionally to Jesus Christ, the Way, the Truth, and the Life, entails just such sufferings which are unbearable without the Holy Spirit's divine forbearance indomitably bolstering the mystic's feeble courage to heroically suffer the insufferable in response to Christ's Selfless Love which conquered such suffering by transcending its degradation and meaninglessness.

In Killing You Changed Death to Life: St. John differentiates two types of life: that which is a beatified life available only in the hereafter and a perfect spiritual life available to the mystic in this present life. This perfect spiritual life on earth is a union in love with Christ, through Christ, and with Christ. This means a union in obediential, sacrificial, and amicable love. It is a Trinitarian love which is complete obediential subordination to the Father's Holy Will, a complete sacrificial submissive self-emptying with Christ's very own kenotic Filial Holy Will, and a complete giving self-surrender of the mystic's very selfhood bolstered by the Holy Spirit's unbounded Givingness.

This means that the "old self," the selfishly self-centered personality, with its overriding self-serving have-attitude gives way to the "new self." This is nothing less than Christ's very own Selflessly self-centered Personality that is endowed with a messianic be-attitude of being more self-full-filled with God's benignant serving Graciousness than having a servile have-attitude of being solicitous exclusively for one's own self-centered selfishness. This transformation from death into life is procured through a suffering to which the mystic must be irrevocably committed. But, again, this suffering demands a super-heroic active resolution and endurance beyond the mystic's own re-sourcefulness. It is only under the bolstered auspices of the Holy Spir-it that the mystic can acquire the messianic be-attitudinal mindset proper to Christ Himself.

St. John emphasizes that one should not be surprised in seeing the mystic suffering great joy in the very pith of excruciating suffer-ing. It is the Paschal Mystery of rising beyond death in the very throes of suffering death itself. It is the mystery which confounds everyone including the mystic himself who can only be more perfectly united with Christ's divine joy and jubilation in the measure that he is also completely wed to Christ's redeeming passion and suffering. Integral to this divine joy for the mystic is the complete confidence and assur-ance that this commitment to suffering in union with Christ is not meaningless and merely selfishly self-centered. It is suffering in which the mystic transcends the servility of his own isolation and self-alienated insularity. Not only does this suffering join the mystic more perfectly to Christ but increasingly more perfectly with all of mankind which has become his innermost intimate neighbor. It is no wonder then that the Little Flower, St. Therese of Lisieux, had such a profound and imponderable desire to suffer Christ's suffering as her very life's ambition. Neither is it any wonder that those who are gif-ted with the stigmata consider it such a choice gift.

THE LIVING FLAME OF LOVE. Stanza 3

O lamps of fire!

In whose splendors

The deep caverns of feeling,

Once obscure and blind,

Now give forth, so rarely, so exquisitely,

Both warmth and light in their Beloved.

Lamps of fire! St. John immediately indicates that lamps give off both light and heat. What are these lamps? They are God's divine attributes which give off light to the soul's objective intellect by giving intelligible and conscionable direction to the intellectual will's drive for its own immortal happiness. These same divine attributes give off heat in the self's subjective mindful awareness motivating the selfhood's willful need for its own historical security and self-fulfillment. The intellectual will's own volition is spontaneously (i.e., instinctively) moved to love (i.e., to possess) what is appropriately (i.e., truthfully) good-as-such. The selfhood's willful volition is forcibly (i.e., urgently) moved to love (i.e., to appropriate) possessively what is (i.e., usefully) a self-serving self-fulfilling good. Hence, the intellectual will instinctively seeks to possess only what it should appropriately possess based on the inherent intelligible truthful value and worth of what it chooses to love. In this sense, it is "moved" (i.e., directed and attracted) to love God appropriately for His own sake since God is consummately the very unexcelled eminence and consummation of all Goodness.

On the other hand, the selfhood's mindful will seeks to appropriate possessively what is self-servingly useful to fulfill its own subjective deficient needs and lacking needfulness to assure its own masterful social self-sufficient (i.e., autonomy) self-fulfilment. Hence it does not seek to possess what is conscionably (i.e., appropriately) good-as-such but, rather what is conscientiously and possessively fulfillingly self-serving. In this sense, it is "moved" (i.e., motivated) to love God not appropriately for God's own sake but, rather, to possessively appropriate God for its own self-centered self-fulfillment. The human person's intellectual will "loves" intelligently as directed by the intellect; in this way it is enlightened to choose what it morally (i.e., appropriately) and truthfully ought to choose. Or, in exercising its innate and inalienable freedom, it chooses (inappropriately) what it ought not to choose. The human person's self-centered mindful will, on the other hand, "loves" urgently (i.e., conscientiously, selfishly, and forcibly) what it must choose to satisfy its self-serving need for sensuous bodily social self-contentment or to pacify its self-serving need for intimate mental social self-containment (i.e., self-justifiable self-fulfillment).

The human person's intellectual will loves impartially and nonpartisanly. In loving God, it is not "my" or "our" God that it loves. The intellectual will cannot possess God possessively but only appropriately and personally in what is appropriate to God's own divine Godhead. On the other hand, the human person's mindful will loves partially and partisanly (i.e., self-servingly, possessively, appropriatively, and personalistically). In loving God, it is "my" or "our" God that it loves. In this love it "cherishes" God because this love is prompted (i.e., motivated) by the selfhood's sensitive bodily feelings of self-contentment (i.e., feeling religiously secure and contentedly self-fulfilled) and/or by the selfhood's intimate mindful bearings of self-containment (i.e., a self-confident religious self-justified self-fulfilled equipoise). Further, its love for God is not prompted by God's own objective infinite Goodness but by its own subjective selfish self-centered neediness (i.e., lack of masterfully secure bodily social sensitized self-contentment or social mental intimate self-containment). The intellectual (i.e., soulful) will is a purposeful drive to personally (i.e., non-partisanly) possess what perfects its communal authentic happiness. This human person's intellectual will is joyfully ennobled and edified in loving God honorably befitting God's supreme and sovereign majesty. God is worthy of such adorable love and the person's intellectual will is sublimely delighted in truthfully adoring God, the eminent unexcelled consummate perfection and goal of its innate inalienable drive for immortal happiness.

The human person's mindful will is a self-serving need to personalistically and partisanly (i.e., socially) possess (i.e., and even demand) what fulfills its own self-serving psychosomatic (i.e., intimate mental and/or sensitive bodily) social autonomy (i.e., masterful self-sufficiency). This subjective mindful will is personalistically authentically and conscientiously self-fulfilled in cherishing and appreciating and prizing God not usably for the person's own subjective religious selfish self-satisfaction and self-justification but selflessly and self-sacrificially befitting God's objective primacy and supremacy transcendent to and independent of the human person's own subjectivity and needfulness. This person's selfhood is transformed from a selfish to a selfless religious service through active and passive stages of purgation and self-purification in which the human person (i.e., mystic) becomes religiously self-detached from his own ego-centric selfishness. When this is eventually achieved through much suffering, the human person (i.e., mystic) does not cherish and appreciate and prize God because God is usably selfishly self-satisfying (i.e., providing a pleasurably socially secure temperamental religious sensitive stirring bodily feeling of self-contentment) and/or selfishly self-justifying (i.e., providing a profoundly socially secure sentimental religious intimate reassuring mental bearing of self-containment).

In other words, when this self-purification is sufficiently completed and the human person is transformed into Christ's very own Selfless Sacred Heart and Messianic Mind-set proper to the third stage of the mystic's religious wedding to the Blessed Trinity through Christ's redemptive sacramental mediation, this mystical human person "loves" God not only objectively obediently and adoringly with his intellectual will as befits God's own sovereignty, but, moreso, subjectively, amorously, sacrificially, and worshipfully with his mindful will by a total dying to and foregoing of all selfish self-centered love. This kenotic sacrificial self-emptying further enables the same person (i.e., the mystic) to "love" God with his mindful will not only sacrificially but to further lovingly cherish God self-determinatively, appreciatively, and authentically above and beyond his own social selfish self-interest.

In this appreciative love the mystic cherishes God precisely because his own totally selfless sublime sensitive bodily pious feeling for God and/or profound steadfast intimate mental reverent caring for God is no longer under his own selfish willful control but prompted by an exultant bodily emotional feeling and a soothing mental quiescent imponderable caring for God issuing from the Holy Spirit's own affluent ebullience. This superhumane sublime affluence of spirited sensitized bodily feeling and overwhelming profoundly soothing mental solicitude for God transcends the mystic's own subjective socially selfish self-centeredness providing him with an authentic divine ecstatic self-fulfillment as he is transported beyond the subjective alienating strictures of his own selfishness. He can now volitionally surrender and give himself totally as a volunteer gift and service to God under the Gifted impetus of the Holy Spirit's own exuberant totally free uninhibited Self-Givingness.

In sum, in the final third stage of the mystic's journey to the summit of Mount Carmel and a perfect union with God, the mystic loves God (vertically) suitably, (horizontally) sacrificially, and (cruciformly) most affectionately, conatively, and effusively with an exquisite affection that is not possessively his very own but, rather, God's very own which he merely experiences as a gift from God's (i.e., the Holy Spirit's) own infinite Triune Family Giftedness (i.e., Divine Friendship). In that he loves God suitably, he loves God by the conscionable enlightenment provided by the intellect. In that he loves God affectionately and appreciatively, he loves God by the conscientious sublime affection (i.e., heat) which he feels in his body's sublime pious sensitive stirrings and/or bears in his mind's sublime tranquil and serene reverent intimate equipoise. Accordingly, this third cruciform stage of the mystic's union with the Blessed Trinity's Godhead through Christ involves a love that is sublimely and supernaturally enlightened through the intellect's supernatural gift of faith (trust in what is supremely trustworthy) and simultaneously a love that is sublimely and supernaturally liberated through the mind's (i.e., the memory's) supernatural sacrificial gift of invincible convinced hope in overcoming secular history's hopelessness in the face of his own bodily mortality.

These two obediential (vertical) and sacrificial (horizontal) loves give way to a love of God that is self-determinatively both a sacrificial self-surrender and a fully self-detached volunteer self-donation in which the mystic affectionately and appreciatively and amorously cherishes God precisely because he is able supernaturally and super-humanely to both religiously bodily feel and mentally care for God self-fulfillingly and serviceably (i.e., socially) with an immense bodily religious feeling and mental reverential concern that corresponds to the infinitely immutable Goodness and Merciful Graciousness of Christ's own Holy Spirit. In this manner, the mystic is not only conscionably and conscientiously religiously a devout obedient child and servant of God-the-Father but, moreso, a sublime friend of this Father having become enabled by the Holy Spirit's Giftedness to socially requite the Father's own infinite Graciousness and Love with Christ's very own Selfless bodily affectionate superhumane charitable compassion and superhumane mental concern to Selflessly serve, honor, and glorify the Father's Holy Will.

When God supernaturally and sacramentally through the supernatural gifts of faith, hope, and charity is personally in the Blessed Trinity revealed to the mystic, the mystic himself is supernaturally informatively, transformatively, and performatively (i.e., cruciformly) enabled to become himself lovingly enveloped in God's Triune Godhead with a love that is sacrificially divinely befitting and enlightened, on the one hand, and appreciatively inflamed, on the other. It is God in God's own Trinitarian Godhead that simultaneously enables the mystic to cruciformally love God intelligently, intelligibly, conscionably, and suitably, on the one hand, and sacrificially, empathically, appreciatively, conscientiously, and ardently, on the other.

God is the lamp that supernaturally enlightens the intellectual soul through faith, the mindful self through hope, and the willful self through charity. Knowing God intellectually through faith the human person's soulful will is super-enlightened intelligibly while the same human person's selfhood knowing God through charity is ardently and empathically super-inflamed with God's own benignant loving loveliness. The mystic's soulful love is an enlightened love while the mystic's selfhood love is an inflamed selfless love. Enlightened divine love is the mystic's personal wise objective obdiential "love of Truth" which is immutably eternally centered on the Father while his corresponding inflamed appreciative amorous subjective "True Love" is the mystic's historical experience within his own personalized subjective selfhood of Christ's own Selfless Holy self-fulfilling Spirit of Love culminating in an eschatological eternal heavenly Triune Blessedness.

These two aspects of divine love engage an objective personal intellectual theocentric contemplation, on the one hand, and an experiential subjective personalized anthropocentric contemplation, on the other. St. John emphasizes that God may supernaturally infuse a "love of wisdom" which is theologically more lucid than it is amatory. On the other hand, God may supernaturally infuse a "wisdom of love" which is mystically more ardent than it is theologically lucid. Or, again, God may simultaneously infuse both wisdoms which complement each other in one and the same individual. In the latter case, the infusion which penetrates the mystic's soul affords the mystic a personal (i.e., impartial) theological enlightenment regarding God's objective eternal majesty and grandeur whereas the same infusion which redounds to the mystic's subjective selfhood affords the mystic a personalized (i.e., partisan) subjective mystical experience of his own anthropological divinized and sublimated amorosity.

"The city had no need of sun or moon, for the glory of God gave it light, and its lamp was the Lanb." (Revelation). Just as in the Heavenly Jerusalem the glory of God is the light of the saints and angels so also is God's glory the very "lamp" that lights up the mystic's mystical encounter with the Father through the Son in the power of their Holy Spirit. The mystic's knowledge of God is both humanly natural and superhumanly supernatural. Humanly and naturally the mystic's intellect can intellectually, philosophically, and remotely contemplate God and His divine attributes in the absolute generality of God's own supreme infinite eternal divinity (i.e., Godhead). In this theocentric contemplation God remains infinitely and impersonally beyond the personal volitional grasp of the mystic's own immortal happiness. Superhumanly and supernaturally through the gift of faith, however, the mystic is enabled to personally contemplate God's PERSONAL Self-revelation present to the point that the mystic is able to voluntarily choose God-the-Father's own eternal infinite Paternal Blessedness as his very own personal supernatural immortal happiness. Indeed, through sacramental baptism the mystic is supernaturally adopted into the Father's Godhead and enlightened by the infinite glory of the Father's paternal effulgent luminosity.

Quite remarkably and supernaturally the Father who exists onto-logically infinitely beyond the creaturely existence of the mystic be-comes personally present to the mystic's spiritual soul through the sacramental presence of His infinite graciousness effulgently illumin-ating the mystic's soul with His paternal glory. It is in the very pellu-cidity of this paternal glory that the mystic beholds through faith in contemplating God's Godhead not merely abstractly in general terms but concretely in the very Person of the Father. The Father no longer is infinitely removed from the mystic's personal grasp. He supernat-urally places Himself within the mystic's personal grasp. In doing so, the mystic through faith is illuminated pellucidly with an enlighten-ment that is infinitely powerful, divine, dynamic, eternal, blessed, holy, intelligent, perfect, absolute, free, etc.. Each of these supremely divine attributes of God's Paternity enlightens the mystic with its own luminous scintillation by reason of God's sacramental gracious-ness abiding within the spiritual interior of the mystic's soul.

No creature is actually infinite; this is a prerogative of God alone. By reason of God's infinity, whatever is identified with God as a di-vine attribute is identical with God's own Godhead. It is the case that Peter is a man and enjoys this attribute in common with every other individual human being. Yet, Peter is not humanity; he is not the to-tality of what it is to be human. God, on the other hand, is the infinite totality of whatever is identical with His Godhead. Thus, God is not only divine; God is divinity. God is not only intelligent; God is intelli-gence. Similarly with every other divine attribute. Moreover, God is not only entitatively one; God is simply one and the very simplicity of oneness. To wit, there cannot be two separately existing Gods. God is supremely and uniquely one to the point that God is uniqueness itself (i.e., incapable of being duplicated). God is not only grand and im-mensely grand and great, God is grandiosity itself, magnificence, ex-cellence, majesty, immeasurable splendor, etc.. All of these attributes are attributable to God not relatively inasmuch as He creates a creaturely universe but absolutely as such without reference to His omnipotent creativity.

St. John of the Cross is emphasizing that while all of these multiple supremely divine attributes exist in the Paternity of God's Godhead without distinction and discrimination, they sacramentally resonate pellucidly in the mystic's soul with a distinctive divine scintillation that enlightens the mystic with a plethora of scintillating luminosity revealing the stupendous magnificence of the Person of the Father in an infinite majestic splendor. Such is the divinely Paternal presence of this divine splendor that the mystic is aware that this eternal immeasurable divine infinity is not merely remotely infinitely beyond the mystic's own personal grasp but personally supernaturally illuminating, expanding, and divinizing the interior intelligible volition (i.e., love) of his own soul's spiritual personhood. Each one of these divine theophanic splendors, in turn, induce the mystic to love God's Paternity not merely obediently as infinitely remote but, moreso, filially as a child regards and esteems his/her own father who is the source of his/her very being, life, livelihood, and advancement.

This very same supernatural and sacramental Paternal divine luminosity and graciousness present interiority within the mystic's soul vertically also penetrates to the mystic's selfhood horizontally and subjectively. First it penetrates to the mystic's mindful and memorial selfhood through the supernatural gift of hope. Of course, in the vertical order God's grace is present ontologically as "being" God's very divine presence to the mystic through faith. In the horizontal order, God's grace is present phenomenologically to the mystic as "having" God's divine presence and graciousness personalistically (i.e., possessively) in the Person of God-the-Son. That is, the mystic within his own mindful self's self-humanized personality "has" Christ's very own super-humanized personality as his very own in the measure that he "has" sacrificially and kinetically died to his own historically "past and future" self-centered mindful selfishness and become converted to Christ's own beatitudinal messianic mindset and Selfless Sacred Heart (i.e., Christ's superhumanized Personality; not to be confused with His divine Personhood).

In Christ's Paschal Mystery He who is utterly sinless becomes sin in order to transform the mystic's own subjective self-centered selfish sinfulness into Christ's Selfless Sinless Selfhood. This Paschal Mystery has its culmination in Calvary when Christ Himself sacrifices His own Sinless memorial mindful Self for the sinner's sinful human memorial mindful self. He substitutes Himself as a sinless scapegoat in the place of the mystic to ransom, redeem, and to atone for the mystic's selfish sinfulness. What is required of the mystic, in turn, is to allow his own self (i.e., subjective personality) to be sacrificially substituted and replaced by Christ's own sacrificial Sinless Self. This means living the Gospel life of the be-attitudes in which he becomes superhumanistically transformed from a "have-more" competitive humanistic attitude centered on the selfishness of his own social security to a "have-less-be-more" superhumanistic social be-attitude emulating Christ's very own Father-centered total commitment, Gospel life-style of self-abnegation, and unconditional devotion to the Father's Sovereign Holy Will transcendent to his own (i.e., the mystic's) subjectivity beset with the vicissitudes of secular history's mortality.

In this horizontal phenomenological encounter with Christ, God/Superman, the mystic encounters the Lamb who takes away the sins of the world which means the mystic's very own sinfulness. But, this is not without the mystic's own cooperation. Unlike the Father's personal divinity present in the mystic's soul through His infinite divine graciousness which is efficaciously accomplished through the supernatural auspices of the Church's sacramentality, the Son's personal divinity is absent to the mystic's mindful selfhood until and unless the mystic himself becomes be-attitudinally disposed to fully embrace Christ's very own be-attitudinality. This does not happen instantly unless it be by the grace of martyrdom; it happens processively and chronologically in stages. Paradoxically, the mystic in this horizontal encounter with God through the Son-of-God who is the Son-of-Man prophesied in the Old Testament again encounters God's Godhead personally sensitively and intimately and not merely remotely as a deity infinitely beyond his grasp. Indeed, so personally is this subjective encounter that the mystic becomes enabled to personalistically possess God as his very own personalized possession.

And, it must be emphasized that Christ who is both the Son-of-God and the Son-of-Man, is resplendent with the same divine infinite splendor as is the case with God-the-Father. But, there is this difference. God's majesty, magnificence, almighty omnipotence is made manifest to the mystic's subjective mindful selfhood epiphanically through Christ's manhood especially His super-self-cultivated-humanistic Personality (i.e., Christ's own superhumanistic Selfless Selfhood). This epiphanic revelation of God through Christ's humanity harbors a paradox that is peculiar to the subjective order of the human person's subjective mindful self-centeredness. This is the paradox that while Christ is the "light of the world" any person with a worldly-minded "have-more" selfish attitude remains blind to Christ's divine luminosity. This includes even those Christians who are endowed with the supernatural gift of faith and are baptized into the Church's sacramentality. Why this paradox?

In the subjective horizontal order of the self-cultivated and self-humanized human personality, it is not reality itself transcendent to the human self that is immediately and directly encountered. Rather, it is the human person's very own self-centered selfhood that is the intermediary to all that he experiences. It is an ego-centric matrix which is not inherently cognitive but, moreso, conative. In other words, the mystic's subjective encounter with Christ, the God/Superman, is through his own subjective self-centered emotional feelings and emotionless mental yearnings and concerns rooted in his own have-attitudinal selfish social self-interests. The mystic's predominant bent (because of his inherited concupiscence of original sin) is to possess Christ possessively for his own selfish social security. Thus, he seeks to secure his own sensuous bodily religious (i.e., divinized) gratified self-contented self-fulfillment and his own intimate mental religious (i.e., divinized) vindicated self-contained self-fulfillment (i.e., integral religious self-righteousness) by possessing Christ possessively (i.e., selfishly and self-attachedly) rather than dis-possessively (i.e., selflessly and self-detachedly).

In his subjective religious mystical experiences of God's Godhead in the Person of Christ who is God incarnate in human flesh, he experiences God's infinite Godhead more as absent rather than as present. The reason for this is that he experiences Christ's divinity within his own subjective conative bodily sensitivity and mental intimacy. Here within this self-centered psychosomatic subjectivity Christ's divinity is made manifest anthropocentrically, and theandrically, but not theocentrically. That is, God is mystically experienced as immanent within the mystic's own subjective humanity but not experienced transcendently as God-the-Father exists immutably and eternally in His own infinite supreme sovereign majestic glory. Paradoxically enough, the mystic experiences God's glory as absent rather than as present within his own mystical experiences.

Yet, after a prolonged period of both an abstemiously active Gospel kenotic program of ascetic self-abnegation followed by an excruciatingly painful passive purging and renouncing of his selfishness, the mystic little by little becomes completely metanoetically converted to Christ's own Gospel lifestyle and be-attitudinal messianic mindset including Christ's selfless empathic sacred heart. At this point, he no longer has the selfish have-attitudinal mindset of prayerfully beseeching Christ to spare him his own sacrificial suffering but the selfless be-attitudinal mindset of beseeching Christ to be allowed to share more generously in Christ's very own messianic redemptive suffering. When the mystic arrives at this state of awareness and conversion, he has attained to the illuminative stage of his approach to a perfect union with the Blessed Trinity.

When this total conversion is accomplished following years of painstaking and painfully excruciating suffering while he endures a radical transformation from his humanistic have-more attitudinal personality to Christ's superhumanistic have-less be-more be-attitudinal Personality, the mystic experiences within the conative resonance of his own subjective psychosomatic selfhood and personality Christ's very own empathically super-sensitive emotional devout feelings (viz., His Sacred Heart) and Christ's very own empathically super-intimate emotionless reverent carings and concerns (viz., His messianic beatitudinal mindset). At this stage of the mystic's complete conversion to Christ he experiences Christ as the "light of the world" with all of the omnipotent power and glory that belongs to the Father's infinite Godhead. But, here the mystic no longer experiences Christ as possessively "his very own" but dispossessively as "our very own." In other words, his Christian sociability is no longer sectarian; it is universal. It transcends the self-limiting boundaries of his own subjective egocentric solipsism.

In this total conversion which is the termination and culmination of the sacrificial love which Jesus makes manifest to the mystic, the mystic himself in keeping with Christ's very own Paschal Mystery "passes" from the sacrificial stage of suffering the death and dying of his own self-alienated selfishness to the charitable friendship stage of befriending Christ's own passion and death as his very own messianic mission in life. Here the mystic recognizes that Mary, Christ's very own mother, is the perfect model of Christ's disciple who embraces this redemptive messianic mission as her very own. This stage of total self-surrender to Christ affords the mystic a prolonged period of untrammeled illumination in which he recognizes the enormous benefits which have accrued to him while he was living through the excruciatingly painful purgative throes of experiencing and enduring his own bodily religious churlishness and mental religious disorientation and discombobulation symptomatic of his total loss of selfish self-control and self-centered social incompetence.

This illuminative stage of mystical advancement enables the mystic to experience both in his subjective bodily sensitized emotional feelings as well as in his inmost intimate emotionless serene concern and solicitude religious empathy and social zeal for the redemptive welfare of others through his total conversion to Christ's Selfless sacrificial empathic feeling and concern for humankind's redemptive welfare. Here at this stage of his mystical advancement the mystic experiences within himself Christ as the "light of the world" and Christ's divine multi-faceted luminosity in temperamental nuanced zealous empathic sensitized bodily feelings which are redolent of Christ's own Sacred Heart. In addition, the mystic experiences within himself Christ's same multi-faceted luminosity in sentimental nuanced profoundly pious empathic intimate mental bearings and yearnings redolent of Christ's own be-attitudinal redemptive mindset. These illuminative experiences are preliminary to the mystic entering into the third and final stage of his perfect union with Christ and with the Blessed Trinity in a love that is not merely a sacrificial love of self-denial and dying to one's selfish selfhood, but an *agape* love of friendship in which the mystic renders to God the benevolent and benignant love which he receives from God.

This third and final stage of becoming perfectly wed and united to the Father through the Son in the power of the Holy Spirit finds the mystic loving God simultaneously obediently and objectively with an enlightened intellectual will and subjectively and sacrificially with a mindful selfhood shorn of its memorial past (i.e., forsaken) and future (anticipated) selfish self-attachments. This third stage is mediated by the Holy Spirit of both the Father and the Son abiding within the innermost inner subjective recesses of the mystic's self-serving psychosomatic willful selfhood. Now that this will is mindfully divested of its self-centered selfishness it is enabled to willfully will what is divinely beneficial to its own social wellbeing and security without becoming alienated from selves other than its own self, on the one hand, nor become self-alienated from God, on the other. In this regard, the mystic's willful selfhood through the supernatural gift of charity is able to totally surrender its own volition to the service of Christ and Holy Mother, the Church, without any reservation or hesitation. In this total self-surrender the mystic experiences the very Giftedness of the Holy Spirit's infinite generosity and benignity which is nothing less than the Father and Son's mutual infinite love for each other.

Here the mystic is not only superhumanely fortified with the very gifts and Giftedness of the Holy Spirit's own totally uninhibited divine freedom and boundless goodness but also the fruits which flow from these gifts. Further, he experiences these not merely within the objective transhistorical interiority of his spiritual soul bereft of all partisan sentiency, sensitivity, and intimacy proper to its total angelic immateriality, he also experiences these within the subjectivity of his sensuous bodily sensitivity and non-sensuous mental intimacy. That is, he experiences the Holy Spirit's infinite divinity and divine attributes as both objectively as divine luminosity and subjectively as divinized amorosity. Thus, it is within the reconciliation and integration of the superhumane cruciformity of Christ's cross of redemption that the Holy Spirit integrates the vertical and horizontal beams of the cross and reconciles the ontological order of existence with the phenomenological order of mankind's fallen (through original sin) resistancy to this fundamental order of existence. Further, this Christocentric cruciform agape love infused with the Holy Spirit's own supreme charity is eschatologically for the mystic an experience that is simultaneously transcendentally of the heavenly hereafter and immanently of the historical transiency of the here and now.

Delightful love! There is a threefold divine cruciform delightful love imparted by the Father, the Son, and the Holy Spirit to the mystic who has attained to a perfect contemplative prayerful union with God. Vertically, nobly, obediently, and soulfully, it is a supremely delightful exquisite angelic joyful *informative* love that is redolent of the Father's infinite eternal immutability. This joy is proper to the soul's utter spirituality which is able supernaturally to entertain God's infinity informatively and virtually; that is, able to contemplate and, therefore, to volitionally, passively, and objectively appetize God's infinity holistically albeit not totally in the very mode of the Father's eternity. It is reserved to God to contemplate totally God's eminent infinity in its actual immeasurable totality.

Horizontally and sacrificially, it is a superbly redemptive and salutary ingratiating love experienced subjectively within the mystic's innermost inward intimacy, selfhood, and personality. It is a *transformative* love that converts the mystic from a self-alienated selfish egotist to a befriended, liberated, selfless utterly committed disciple of Christ. There is no greater love than to lay down one's life for a friend. That is, Christ's sacrificial redemptive love educes from the mystic both a heartfelt exuberant zealous and a profound imperturbable grateful gracious be-attitudinal mindset toward his (i.e., the mystic's) own selfhood, the selves of others, and toward Christ's totally amiable Self-giving amicability. Christ's redemptive love begets both a benevolent amorosity and a renewed and reformed life within the mystic's selfhood and personality.

Cruciformly, there is a fulsome *performative* love of God's own superb, unexcelled, infinite charitable gracious benevolence which integrates the vertical & horizontal orders with each other. This friend-begetting love emanating from the Holy Sprit is simultaneously experienced subjectively, ecstatically, and immanently within the mystic's own willful psychosomatic selfhood as a sublime and benignant familiar amorosity of both exhilarating sensitive emotional bodily feeling and profound intimate mental emotionless sighing-yearning that are dilated and inflated with the Holy Spirit of Christ's own immeasurable charitable benignity. At the same time, it is experienced objectively and transcendently within the mystic's soulful volition as a transhistorical levitating otherworldly never-ending rapturous delight symptomatic of the Father's all-encompassing vast ever-perduring blissful paternal providentiality oblivious to earth's historical transiency.

Again, it is very important to emphasize that these three cruciform theophanic and epiphanic divinizations experienced by the mystic occur integrationally but not at the same pace. The objective vertical order of the mystic's human growth in the discipline of moral virtue and an upright noble moral character cannot advance without there being simultaneously in the subjective horizontal order of the mystic's humanistic self-development a comparable ascetic training in a rigorous program of self-abnegation. The two orders need not proceed at the same pace; but they must both be advancing in conjunction with each other. The fundamental moral order cannot advance without being supported by the supplemental kenotic order of self-denial. Each of these orders complements the other. When they both reach their cruciform integrated climax there ensues a humane fusion of the two such that the human person is no longer merely acting personally/personalistically (i.e., humanly and humanistically) but personably and humanely.

However, this Christocentric cruciform climax cannot come to fruition merely on the natural and human level. It can only come to fruition on the superhuman, the superhumanistic, and superhumane level. For, this maturation and fruition of the human person's own personhood is due less to this human personhood's own initiative and moreso to God's Triune initiative. The Father initiates, the Son consummates, and the Holy Spirit integrates. The superhuman super-informative supernatural; the superhumanistic super-transformative supercultural; the superhumane super-performative and super-natrual-cultural are the outcome of the mystic's becoming cruciformally enveloped in a Trinitarian Life and Loveliness. In this respect, the mystic becomes more the very offspring of the Blessed Virgin Mary, the Mystical Rose, who has been herself super-eminently enveloped in a Trinitarian Life and Loveliness. In this regard, she is the mother of the Sacramental Church and all of the members baptized into the holiness of this Church.

The description of the mystic's divinization in this commentary may seem exaggerated but St. John of the Cross would not seem to think so: "The (mystic) becomes God from God through participation in Him and in His attributes, which (he) terms the 'lamps of fire.'" In the cruciform transport of God's loveliness the mystic attains to a cruciform freedom that is more divine than human albeit that it is a humanly divine freedom. It is vertically an obedient adoring freedom to choose the Father's primacy above every other good or person (the mystic's own self included) in the universe of creation; it is horizontally a liberated freedom from his own self-attachment to the flesh, the world, and the devil arrived at by sacrificially succumbing to Christ's own befriending redemptive sacrifice; it is cruciformally a freedom for totally embracing in a volunteer embrace the friendship of the Blessed Trinity through the Holy Spirit's effusiveness in prompting the mystic to socially and messianically embrace the mystic's neighbors with God's own salvific and befriending benignity.

In whose splendors. St. John emphasizes that this divinization and glorification of the mystic is such that the mystic experiences God's own divine attributes as his very own. He provides the simile of the flame in a candle living off the air that fans the flame. The fire's flame is such that it is indistinguishable from the air which fans it. The fire's flame breaths the air which oxygenates its flaming. God's splendor of truth, beauty, love, goodness, freedom, joy, holiness, eternal immutability, etc., enlightens and inflames the mystic with divine luminosity and flaming fire. Whatever be the movement of these splendors that the mystic experiences, this movement is peculiar to the mystic and not to God Himself who is eternally immutable.

St. John proceeds to explain that these sublime splendors are divinizing "overshadowings." Note that the candle's flame could cast a shadow of the candle itself at the very base of the candle. This is, also, inevitable for the mystic. After all, God is infinite and the mystic is finite. It is not the case that God's infinite luminosity cannot render the mystic's soul transparently luminous. Rather, it is the case that the mystic's soulful spirituality cannot itself as a crystal reflecting the sun's light completely absorb God's infinite pelucidity. Hence, a shadow results from this infinite luminosity penetrating into the mystic's soul with the glory of God's immeasurable majestic Personal presence. Nonetheless, the shadow of this splendid presence will itself be delicately diaphanous because of the soul's own spirituality.

Each separate divine attribute of God imparts to the mystic a distinctive shadow peculiar to that attribute. This also holds for the gifts and fruits which the Holy Spirit gratuitously and graciously imparts to the mystic. Thus, it is in the very "shadow" of God's very own sublime wisdom, understanding, knowledge, counsel, piety, fortitude and reverence that the mystic will be protectively and providentially filled and ingratiated. Further, it is with the fruits of the Holy Spirit that the mystic will be glorified and divinized: charity, joy, peace, patience, kindness, goodness, generosity, gentleness, faithfulness, modesty, self-control, and chastity. St. John exclaims: "O abyss of delights!"

The deep caverns of feeling. These caverns are the mystic's three disparate faculties: the intellect, the memory, and the will. As previously explained in earlier parts of this commentary, these are not all three faculties of the soul. They are, nonetheless, three cruciform centers of the mystic's anthropological personhood. The intellect, in the vertical order is a faculty of the soul and inherently spiritual with the soul's own innate spirituality. What is crucial here in this stanza's explanation is not the intellect's cognition (i.e., knowledge of God) but its volitional appetite (i.e., driving thirst to possess God). The memory is not so much a faculty as it is a facilitating memorial facilitator in the horizontal order of the person's egocentric willful psychosomatic mindful selfhood. Further, the will described here in this stanza is not exclusively the soul's volitional intellectual will, but the selfhood's self-centered self-serving will in cruciform synchronization with the former.

St. John insists that these three anthropological volitional centers of the mystic have an unbounded divine capacity. They are boundless caverns whose very boundlessness remains unknown and unexperienced by the mystic until and unless the mystic becomes aware virtually of how completely barren he is as long as he is not totally replete with God's merciful love and loveliness. Indeed, it is only when the mystic is fully purged of every scintilla of his own willing voluntary desire, willful sacrificial self-volitive attachment, and total volunteer self-surrender to nothing (*nada*) but God's very Triune Godhead is he made aware of his own utter nullity and abject misery in failing to be filled with God's own immeasurable merciful loveliness. In other words, the mystic cannot return God's infinite Trinitarian love in a manner commensurate with God's own sovereign august majesty, inexhaustible mercy, and infinite benignity until and unless he has finally succeeded to love God with his whole heart, mind, and strength.

Certainly, the soul's intellectual will's capacity for God is not that of a subjective self-serving self-centered need but one of an objective purposeful drive. The human person is endowed with an innate drive for immortal perfection and excellence. Naturally, this excellence is common to every human person; it is the common immortal transcendental good-as-such toward which each person is naturally directed. While this common good embraces every creaturely good in the universe of creation, it is not itself reducible to any one creaturely good nor to all them considered together. It is an immortal ontological good-as-such peculiar to the human person and to the sovereign dignity of his personhood innately able to responsibly govern his own conduct. While the human person naturally wills and loves an immortal communal good-as-such (viz., happiness) common to every human person as his ultimate goal, he is free with an inalienable freedom to choose whatever exists in the universe of creation as well as the Creator as a fulfillment of this natural goal.

But, only God who is absolute ontological infinite Goodness can absolutely fulfill the human person's innate volitional drive for happiness and immortal everlasting well-being. Accordingly, while the soul's will is not an eminently infinite loving drive (viz., appetite); it is a virtually infinite loving drive that cannot fully attain to an immortal everlasting happiness and well-being unless and until it loves appropriately (i.e., obediently, voluntarily, and worshipfully) God's own supreme infinite merciful Goodness primarily in preference to every other love. This can only be accomplished supernaturally by God's own graciousness. On a purely natural plane, the human person can know God only remotely as infinitely beyond the grasp of his creaturely existence. It is only supernaturally that God manifests Himself to the human person personally with a family familiarity proper to God's very own Triune Personhood. Through this divine and divinizing Triune supernatural manifestation inherent in the Catholic Church's sacramentality and Magisterium the human person through the supernatural gifts of faith, hope, and love is rendered capable of embracing God's majestic infinite grandeur, glory, and omnipotent power both worshipfully as a creature and interpersonally with a divinized blessed love that partakes of God very own Triune Family Blessedness.

Certainly, the mystic's soulful love is not one of an affectionate bodily "feeling" nor of a concerned mental "bearing or caring." It cannot be since the soul is entirely spiritual and immaterial; it is not in any sense bodily, corporeal, or tactile. How then does the mystic subjectively, personalistically, and experientially "feel" and "care" for God's Triune divinity and Godhead whom he loves objectively from within the interiority of his soulful volitional worshipful desire and divine delight? He feels and cares for God's Supreme Family Primacy when he thirsts for God's merciful Justice and Peace which he experiences as rampantly missing in the world of mankind's self-cultivation and even among the members of the Sacramental Church including himself. It is when he thirsts for Truth above and beyond the myths and deceptions that abound around him. It is when he thirsts for Holiness which is God's own merciful unbounded Goodness. It is when he craves to behold a Beauty whose very shadow in creation hides more than it reveals. Indeed, it is when he through faith recognizes to the full the fulsome miraculous presence of God in the Church's sacramentality and his own paltry prayerful worshipful adoration and embrace of the divine friendship extended to him by God's benignant graciousness.

The mystic's historical memory and self-centered self-serving subjective willfulness, on the other hand, are subjective needs. These are not purposeful drives for immortality. Indeed, they are historically mortal as the human body itself is mortal. Nonetheless, they are unbounded and insatiable needs. For, they are the needs of the human person whose very personhood is sovereignly immortal. These are not personal but personalized needs peculiar to the human person's sociability with selves other than his own subjective self-cultivated selfhood, subjectivity and personality. They are rooted in the human person's need to attain to his own self-assured social welfare and fulsome self-fulfillment befitting his sovereign dignity. As needs they are deficiencies. Indeed, they are impotent deficiencies that are unable to supply for their own deficiencies other than supplementally. The human person is not only innately endowed with drives for food, sex, drugs, and shelter. He has a self-centered need to supplementally socially provide himself (and other selves) with the self-fulfilling sufficiency of these goods.

Thus, the human person may supplementally fashion and cultivate a shovel to artificially cultivate a garden to provide himself with food. A shovel is a makeshift tool that serves to supplementally secure his social need for food's sufficiency. But, if he becomes possessively attached to his shovel, he will paradoxically become unable to fulfill his supplemental need for a completely transhistorical self-fulfilled sociability. By this possessive attachment he becomes alienated both from his own self's sociability and the sociability of others. Indeed, it is only at the point that the human person experiences his own utterly indigent hopeless and helpless transhistorical social insecurity and bodily mortality that he experiences something of the imponderable depth of his own subjective empty neediness and nothingness.

Yet, this helpless sensitized bodily feeling and intimate mindful concern has a depth of indigent needfulness which is unfathomable. When the human person finds himself in dire straits and finds himself bereft of ready resources to provide for his own social neediness to supplementally secure for himself alone or with the help of other selves his own transhistorical immortal welfare he becomes acutely aware that he cannot fathom the depths of his own subjective social neediness and lack of security. The unfathomable depth of this indigent neediness only truly dawns on the human person when he comes to recognize and to acknowledge the depth of degradation to which Christ descended when He mercifully and sacrificially befriended mankind by saving the human person from the bottomless pit of his own selfhood. Jesus Christ alone can provide the human person's selfhood with a transhistorical immortal undying security; this is the security of His own Bodily Resurrection from the dead. Christ has made death deathless.

It is when the mystic is superhumanistically awakened to this merciful love through faith and faith's empowering subjective superhuman hopeful Christian conviction and confidential prayerful hope in Christ that the mystic becomes aware of his own heartfelt cavernous bodily feeling and mindful yearning need for Christ. He experiences his wounded love whose imponderable woundfulness (i.e., needfulness) can only be cured by Christ's own immeasurable merciful redemption. The mystic experiences his own profound heartfelt mindful emptiness and needfulness only when he has memorially become purged of both his sinful rueful past and his foreboding anxious future. This purgation is undertaken actively when the mystic embraces the ascetic life of self-denial advocated by Christ in the Gospel. Here the mystic embraces the Gospel counsels of poverty, chastity, and obedience to the Church's authority. It is brought to completion when the Holy Spirit in the mystic's prayerful "dark night" becomes purged of all selfish attachments obstructing his total surrender to God's supreme primacy.

Similarly with the mystic's willful selfish psychosomatic self-centeredness that supplementally both needs and is unable to become socially transhistorically self-secure beyond its own subjective self-alienation, its alienation from other selves, and its alienation from God. It is only when the mystic finally succeeds in becoming completely purged of his own selfishly self-centered competitive have-attitude mindset that he, according to St. John, experiences something of the imponderable profundity of his own subjective social neediness, emptiness, and nothingness (viz., *nada*). The mystic, again, experiences something of the unfathomable depth of his own subjective needful nothingness when he encounters Christ's merciful friendship within the bowels of this very woundedness. In this religious encounter, the mystic is no longer under any illusion regarding his own impotency and futility. Because he no longer harbors any further illusion, he not merely recognizes Christ's merciful redemptive gratuitous friendship from within the bowels of his own nothingness, he has become enabled to surrender his purged and self-detached selfhood to this amicable ingratiating divine and sublime friendship. At this spousal point he becomes superhumanistically enabled by the power of Christ's own Holy Spirit unctuously alive in his own puny selfhood to become self-detachedly self-surrendered to Christ's own prior sacrificial Selfless Self-surrender to the mystic. That is, he becomes through the Holy Spirit's unction self-detachedly able to become attached to Christ as Christ Himself seeks to selflessly possess the mystic.

In this spousal union of the two wills (i.e., Christ's and the mystic's), the mystic becomes fully aware of his own unquenchable need to totally volunteer to surrender himself to Christ's prior volunteer surrender of Himself to the mystic. At the same time, the mystic becomes fully aware that in his profound emptiness and nothingness (viz., *nada*) he cannot of himself alone, apart from the Holy Spirit, requite Christ's loveliness with a commensurate volunteer sacrificial self-giving amicably befriending loving loveliness. Yet, the mystic comes to experience Christ's very own benignant merciful befriending loveliness when through the Holy Spirit's infinite unctuous benignity and Giftedness he begins to experience his own heartfelt and be-attitudinal mindset's solicitude not only for his own redemption and sanctification but, moreso, for the salvation and sanctification of his neighbors and even those who persecute him. In brief, he comes to recognize in himself Christ's very own messianic be-attitudinal solicitous mindset and heartfelt commiseration for the salvation and sanctification of all of humanity.

Once obscure and blind. There are two sources of a bodily eye's loss of sight: obscurity and blindness. In the dark of night the faculty of sight can see but cannot succeed in seeing because the lack of light. On the other hand, even when it is daylight this faculty cannot see if it is impeded by a cataract; it is blind. If this is the case for the body's eyesight, it is moreso the case for the soul's intellectual insight. The mystic's soul is in obscurity if it is not illuminated by the supernatural light of God's own infinite glory. That is, it cannot prayerfully contemplate God in God's Triune Godhead; God remains obscure to the mystic in such a case.

On the other hand, if the mystic's soulful intellectual will remains voluntarily allured by the body's sentient pleasure and in this manner not completely obediently and subordinately bound to God supernaturally revealed in the tenets of faith and the Church's sacraments, the mystic remains blind to God's supernal Self-manifestation. Accordingly, the mystic may be in the obscurity of darkness if he becomes voluntarily more preoccupied with the natural light of his intelligence rather than with the supernatural light of God's own glory illuminating his intellect to the marvels revealed by faith. Or, the mystic may be in the blindness of darkness if he becomes voluntarily preoccupied with the pleasures of the senses rather than utterly voluntarily absorbed with the divine spiritual delights rooted in his supernatural prayerful contemplation and possession of God.

There is another blindness which is only implicitly alluded to here in these paragraphs. It is the blindness which comes when the mystic through his self-centered willful selfhood becomes subjectively more attached to his own selfish self-interest rather than to God's glory objectively supernaturally manifest within the interior of his soul as God's very own merciful graciousness. In this case, the mystic remains in the state of grace objectively, soulfully, and supernaturally but subjectively is still attached to the social security of his own selfish possession even, for example, of his own mystical enjoyment of God. Such a self-attachment and lack of mortification need not be a grave but, rather, a venial sin. Yet, this is sufficient to render the mystic blind regarding the light of God's glory which is supernaturally flooding his soul's interiority.

The final observation of St. John is very penetrating. Whether this supernatural darkness has its origin objectively in a lack of God's glory supernaturally flooding the soul, as is the case in mortal sin, or subjectively in the mystic's lack of a completely pure heart and be-attitudinal mindset, this darkness is insurmountable without God's supernatural initiative. For, the mystic's familiarity with this darkness is a barrier to becoming familiar with God's supernatural glory and divine merciful blessed bliss. St. Therese, the Little Flower, recognizes and acknowledges this to be the case when she exclaims that in the mystical life "all is grace." In other words, it is not what the mystic can do for God that counts; rather, he must count on what God can do for him. And, this is not surprising since St. John notes previously in his mystagogical text that God's unrelenting love for the mystic is infinitely greater than the mystic's love for God.

Now give forth so rarely, so exquisitely, both warmth and light to their Beloved.

"These lamps...give forth to God in God with loving glory... these very splendors they have received.,,,they render the Beloved the same light and heat they receive...in an excellent way because of the active intervention of its (i.e., the mystic's) will."

When there is a genuine love of friendship between two friends, a love that is as reciprocal as it is spontaneously dutifully forthcoming because it is mutually contracted; a love that is sacrificially reciprocally pledged for life; and a love that is ardently a total self-surrender of each friend's innermost inner intimacy; such a spousal love withholds nothing of what each friend *is and has* in the measure that such friends will to each other that which is most excellent in each's own *being and having*. This friendship is something of the very love which the mystic and God exchange with each other. Certainly, this love is initiated, consummated, and integrated by God in God's family Triune Godhead. Yet, it is still a reciprocal love. God seeks to be loved by the mystic in the divine family friendliness of God's own sublime Triune Personhood.

The mystic is enabled to engage in such a love because God bestows on the mystic through the mediation of Jesus Christ, God/Superman, God's own Godliness in the many Godly attributes that are God's very own divinity. Thus, the mystic returns God's beneficent, benignant, benevolent, inexhaustible gratuitous Loveliness beneficently, benignantly, benevolently, inexhaustibly, gratuitously; that is, in a lovely and generous manner befitting God's own merciful Graciousness. The mystic returns to God in his own triune cruciform anthropological constitution the very divine and sublime Loveliness which God has deigned to superhumanly, superhumanistically, and superhumanely bestow on the mystic. The mystic is able to love God with God's very own Loveliness precisely because God has bestowed this Loveliness on the mystic. St. John points out that a king who in his regal authority rules over several nations is able in view of this authoritative rule to deed such nations to someone else even though these nations don't exist in virtue of the king's own individual existence. In other words, while the mystic is not himself existentially God, he is endowed by God to bestow on God and whomever else God's very own Loveliness and unexcelled Blessing and Benediction.

Why so? Because the mystic now willably (dutifully), willfully (i.e., sacrificially by commitment), and willingly (i.e., by a gratuitous self-donation and self-surrender) possesses God in a completely detached manner of self-possession without actually owning God as his very own personalized property and possession. That is, he does not love God other than in a manner befitting God's very own Godliness. Yet, it is with his very own mystical love that he dutifully, serviceably, and befriendedly loves God. In this he revels more fully in God's divinely befriending loving graciousness precisely because he can, in turn, requite this very infinite Loveliness with a comparable befriending love of his very own.

The mystic is informatively, transformatively, and performatively on a supernatural order enabled to love God with an infinite love that is everlastingly enduring, empowered with God's own bounty, beauty, strength, wisdom, goodness, holiness, justice, friendliness, graciousness, benediction, benevolence, freedom, etc.. These divine attributes of God each awaken as divine lamps in the mystic a supernal luminosity and intensity to both be *levitationally* lifted up to the eternal heaven of God's Triune Godhead and *ecstatically* experiencing immanently within his own flesh the very fire of God's burning Love that now burns without combusting the mystic's flesh. Note well that this reciprocal befriended union of God with the mystic and he with God is one of wills. The mystic is not assumed into God's ontological divinity and Godhead so as to cease to exist in his creaturely existence. The mystic enjoys the very power of God's Holy Will because God has endowed the mystic with this power inasmuch as the mystic's own will is completely supernaturally surrendered, subsumed, and sublimated into God's Holy Will.

This sublime love exchanged between God and the mystic is the very same which the mystic will have in heaven following his bodily death and his assumption into God through the beatific vision. The difference between heaven and this present life is that in heaven the mystic will intellectually and supernaturally behold God's infinite glory and splendor without the veil of faith whereas in this life this splendor is shrouded in faith. This does not mean that this very divine glory is not available and really present to the mystic in this life. It rather means that the unveiled splendor of this divine supernal glory remains veiled in this life and will become a "face to face" encounter in heaven.

St. John continues to elucidate and refine the stupendous refulgence of the mystic's supernatural and supernal wedding with God's Triune Godhead. The mystic's very objective solitary supernaturally enlightened happiness and subjective self-centered inflamed social security are both refulgent with God's own Godliness in that the mystic is simultaneously objectively conscionably aware and subjectively conscientiously experiencing his own ability to render to God God's own divine Holiness which infinitely exceeds his own creaturely finite worth. Furthermore, this total self-gifted superhumanly enlightened and superhumanistically inflamed selfless self-surrender gift of the mystic to God is mediated by the superhumane supernal Giftedness of the Holy Spirit. By reason of this supernal pneumatic mediation this selfless (i.e., totally self-detached) self-donation on the part of the mystic integrates and harbors the very divine love with which the Father and Son mutually embrace each other in an eternal divine friendship. In other words, the refulgence of this divine amicable love engulfing the mystic is a cruciform refulgence in which there coalesces in one integral integrality the mystic's vertical objective enlightened superhuman intellectual *personal* love and horizontal subjective inflamed superhumanistic selfless self-centered *personalistic* love. The cruciform integration of these two disparate loves through the Holy Spirit's superhumane supernal mediation yields a *personable* amiable divine love that is simultaneously engulfed within the Father and Son's mutual eternal amicable embrace.

St. John does not stop here in presenting his nuanced and subtle clarification of the sublime tonality and resonance peculiar to this total pneumatically Gifted self- abandonment and self-giving of the mystic to God. He further proceeds to explain that this total self-donation is a love of superb unexcelled excellence, fruition, praise, and gratitude. In regard to *love* there are three aspects to the unexcelled excellence. 1) The mystic requites God's own supreme merciful and gracious loveliness not with the mystic's own love but with God's very own Triune loveliness (i.e., unctuously mediated by the Holy Spirit). Further, the mystic loves God in God and not simply within the interior of his soul's graciousness nor his self-centered subjectivity. That is, the mystic is ecstatically transported objectively to heaven and subjectively beyond his own subjectivity (i.e., he is "beside himself"). 3) This singular mystical love enables the mystic to love God objectively blissfully with God's own eternal Blessedness and subject-ively utterly selflessly with a social security (i.e., interpersonal solid-arity, charity, righteousness) that is God's very own merciful infinite holiness and amorosity alive in Jesus Christ incarnate, God/Super-man.

In regard to the *fruition* (i.e., the enjoyment and relishing) of this love, there is, again, a threefold superb unexcelled excellence. 1) The mystic enjoys God delightfully by reason of God's own blissful super-nal joyfulness. This occurs when the mystic through faith beholds in-tellectually in the very Personhood of God's Godhead God's divine attributes not merely remotely but interiorly and personally within the soul's spiritual interiority. This sublime and supernatural pres-ence of God's infinite attributes evokes in the soul's intellectual will an angelic jubilation that is refulgent with God's eternal immensity. 2) Through this celestial jubilance the mystic delights in God alone without further mediation or interference on the part of any creature. 3) This supernal enjoyment is noteworthy because it neither includes nor entails any scintilla of a subjective self-centered self-serving reli-gious self-attachment of selfish self-satisfaction or justification on the part of the mystic's own willful selfhood.

In regard to the *praise* which the mystic renders to God through this love, there is, again, a threefold excellence. 1) First, the mystic ob-jectively within the interiority of his soul praises God dutifully thereby acknowledging God's own supreme authority and primacy. 2) The mystic praises God for the immeasurable benefits and bless-ings it receives from God including the very supernal delight itself which enables the mystic to praise God jubilantly. 3) The mystic praises God not because the mystic himself is good but because God in God's Goodness is worthy and deserving of all worshipful praise and adoration.

In regard to the *gratitude* which the mystic renders to God through this superb love there are, again, three excellent qualities. 1) There is a gratefulness for the natural and spiritual benefices the mys-tic receives from God through the benevolence of this merciful love. 2) There is a further gratitude for the very cruciform integrity and in-tensity of levitational spiritual weightlessness and burning heartfelt intimate amorosity proper to the quality of praise available to the mystic through this love. 3) Finally, there is further gratitude precisely because the divine purity of this love enables the mystic to praise God befitting God's very own Godliness.

It is most fitting in concluding this commentary on the third stanza to reflect on St. John's remarkable and enlightening account of the nuances and reverberations which mark the mystic's nuptial union with the Blessed Trinity. The more we are able to assimilate and to penetrate into the sublimity of this union that culminates only fully in heaven, the more we become able to fathom in some appreciable measure the sublimity of the special union that our Blessed Mother, Mary, enjoyed with the Blessed Trinity. To ponder somewhat this imponderable assimilation of Mary as the singular daughter of the Father, the singular mother of the Son, and the singular bride of the Holy Spirit, let us transpose somewhat the awesome Canticle sung by St. Paul in Ephesians 1:3-10:

Praised be the God and Father of our Lord Jesus Christ,

Who bestowed on *Mary* in Christ every spiritual blessing in the heavens.

God chose *Mary* in him before the world began, to be holy and blameless (i.e., immaculate) in his sight.

He predestined *Mary* to be his *singular daughter* through Jesus Christ, such was his will and pleasure that all might praise *her* for this glorious favor he has bestowed on us in bestowing Christ to us through *Mary.*

In him and through his blood Mary has been redeemed, And she remained Immaculate so immeasurably generous is God's favor to her.

God has given *her* the wisdom to understand fully the mystery, the plan he was pleased to decree in Christ.

A plan to be carried out in Christ, in the fullness of time, to bring all into one in him, in the heavens and on the earth.

THE LIVING FLAME OF LOVE. *Stanza 3:*

Addendum: contemplative prayer and blindness.

When during the time of this espousal... St. John notes that the mystic is afforded by the Holy Spirit immediately before the marital union itself and not only during the union itself ingratiating divine caresses including troubling anxieties. These are granted to further whet the appetite of the mystic to increase his love and affection for God in anticipation of more intense and intimate ingratiating amorous delights to come. St. John reminds the mystic that the agency and principal author of this marital union is the Holy Spirit. In the mystic's ardor and eagerness to enter into the very bosom of God's amicable love and loveliness the mystic is to bear in mind that God (i.e., the Blessed Trinity) is even more intensively seeking to enter into the very heart and mind of the mystic's own amicable love.

At this level of the mystic's union with God the mystic's prayer-life is entirely one of contemplative prayer. The very key and gist of this contemplative prayer is not that the mystic is actively praying to God but, rather, that God is praying within the mystic. The task of the mystic is to allow the Holy Spirit this initiative in his prayer-life. His failure to do so will obstruct the advancement and culmination of this marital union. This obstruction can occur in three principal ways which St. John identifies as three different sources of blindness. He specifies the three sources of such blindness. The spiritual director of the mystic who lacks experience and interferes with the inspirations, intimations, and Breath of the Holy Spirit is the first occasion for this blindness. The devil is the second, while the mystic himself is the third.

Prior to examining these three stipulated obstacles to contemplative prayer, it is appropriate to clarify still one more time the very activity of contemplative prayer as put forth by St. John himself. It is an activity that transcends the reach of the senses. The soul itself of the human person enjoys an intellectual and volitional activity that inherently transcends the reach of the senses. The soul itself is fundamentally the very seat of contemplative prayer inasmuch as through the supernatural gift of faith the mystic is enabled by the light of God's very own Triune Godhead's infinitely lucid glory to gaze directly at God's supernal Triune gracious Personhood mediated by Jesus Christ's incarnation as God/Superman. It is very important that it be understood that the Catholic Christian mystic is enabled supernaturally to gaze in faith directly on God's Triune Godhead Self-manifested sacramentally through the Church's Magisterial apostolic ministry. Of all of the sacraments, the Blessed Eucharist is the very source and summit of God's Self-manifestation of the Godhead's Triune Personhood to mankind.

In beholding Christ's humanity the mystic beholds Christ's divinity. The very same divine Person that is Jesus is both Son of the Father and Son of Mary. In gazing on Jesus incarnate the mystic also gazes on God the Father who remains infinitely removed from Christ's incarnation inasmuch as the Father remains existentially in heaven transcendent to the cosmos and to earth as a planet within the cosmos. Yet, through Christ's mediation, the Father is present to the mystic in the very merciful Graciousness proper to the Godhead's unique and monotheistic Divinity as the Supreme and sovereign Being transcending the created universe. To know Jesus Christ is to know the Father. Further, this supernal divine merciful Graciousness which inhabits the human soul's interiority received at Baptism also includes the Holy Spirit, the Third Person of the Blessed Trinity. For, the Holy Spirit is gratuitously given in baptism to the member of the Catholic Church's sacramentality founded by the apostles who received the Holy Spirit at Pentecost. Indeed, this very same Holy Spirit enters more influentially within the Church's mystical members at the reception of the sacrament of Confirmation.

By reason of this divine merciful Graciousness supernaturally inhabiting the spiritual soul of the mystic, the mystic may consciously in faith prayerfully directly gaze on this supernal indwelling and contemplate the very source and summit of this indwelling in the sacrament of the Holy Eucharist celebrated daily by the priest who officiates at the Mass. Jesus Christ, God/Superman, sacramentally incarnate in Holy Mother, the Roman Catholic Church and her members, through His Paschal Mystery of Crucifixion, Resurrection, and Ascension into heaven is the efficacious and sufficient medium of the supernal presence of God's Triune family Godhead to the Church's bodily mystical members.

This divine and supernal ultra Personal Triune indwelling penetrates into the very subjective bodily psychosomatic constitution of the mystic in the Person of the Holy Spirit. Sacred Scripture declares that the very body of Christ's disciple is the temple of the Holy Spirit. Hence, the very phenomenological, self-humanized, subjective selfhood, personality, and psychosomatic (viz., mind and heart) subjectivity of the human person issuing from the human person's non-substantive mortal synergetic corpuscularity harbors the indwelling of the Holy Spirit as a candle's flame brings the candle to its consummation. The same one and only Holy Spirit that guides and sustains the Church's Papal Head and Magisterium subtly influences and sustains the mystic's wayward pilgrimage to perfect union (viz., holiness) with the Blessed Trinity in this life and everlastingly in the next life of heaven.

The mystical prayer-life which is advocated and delineated by St. John of the Cross is the prayer-life which develops under the advocacy of this same Holy Spirit within the nuclear confines of the human person's psychosomatic social selfhood issuing from his mortal body's corpuscularity to which each human has access through the psychosomatic reflexive awareness of each human person's own unique and inalienable personhood. This reflexive awareness of his own bodily psychosomatic constitution affords the human person a conscious experience of his own willful subjective self-control (viz., management and manipulation) of his own selfhood's historical psychosomatic evolvement in social interpersonal conjunction with selves other than his own self.

The human person by reason of the energetic dynamism of his own spiritual inorganic nature exists within the community of persons destined for an immortal transhistorical and enduring communal spiritual existence transcendent to the mortal physical cosmos of which the earth is a planetary member. By reason of God's infinite merciful supernatural graciousness and Self-revelation, this immortal metaphysical supernatural everlasting destiny is known to be God's very own Triune divine family friendship and Godhead which is providentially and paternally made supernaturally amendable to Christ's disciple by the sacramental ministry and authority of Holy Mother, the Roman Catholic Church. The mystical bodily members of this Sacramental Church are baptismally and sacramentally supernaturally and integrally molded into Christ's very own cruciform Eucharistic sacramental Body.

This cruciform molding engages the disciple's very own cooperation. Vertically and objectively, it engages supernaturally the mystic's own intellectual and volitional faithful obedience to the Father's Holy Will made manifest in the Church's moral and dogmatic authority vested in the Magisterium. Horizontally and subjectively it engages superhumanistically the mystic's own self-centered heart and mind self-sacrificially committed to hopefully serving Jesus Christ as companions in His own total Selfless commitment to the Father made manifest in His crucifixion. In this companionship, the mystic is also committed to serving his neighbors with the same sacrificial selflessness made manifest by Jesus Himself. The integrality of this cruciform cooperation entails that the mystical disciple of Christ under the infinitely unctuous influence of the Holy Spirit surrender himself and his own psychosomatic selfhood spousefully to Christ's very own Selfless Masterful Self surrender of Himself to all the members of His Sacramental Church, His own Mystical Body.

This total self-surrender of his own psychosomatic selfhood on the part of the mystic engages prayerfully the selfless commitment to Christ of his heartfelt body's sensitivity and feelings, on the one hand, and his mindful body's intimacy and mental yearnings and bearings, on the other. When the mystic is prayerfully immersed in his own bodily feelings and sensitivity he is formally engaged in meditative prayer which focuses on the imagination's sensational stimulations and vibrancy together with the body's empathic and sympathetic feelings whereby the mystic strives to sacrificially substitute his heartfelt bodily selfish self (viz., self-satisfaction and self-contentment) and bodily functions for Christ's very own compassionate Selfless Sacred Heart.

When the mystic is prayerfully immersed in his own mental

cares, bearing, and yearning enclosed within the sanctuary of his own mind's inaccessible sanctuary, the selfhood's innermost inner nuclear intimacy, the mystic is formally engaged in contemplative prayer which concentrates on the mind's non-sensational and not-tactile sedations (viz., the mind's own quiescent notions) and attitudinal mindset. Within this mental sanctuary the mystic no longer feels the body's sensitivity and stimulations. The mystic experiences his body as having entered into its nuclear core devoid of all the sensitive motions and stimulations engaging its functional toil and empathic involvement with others. The mystic finds himself "at one" with his own selfhood's own inner isolated intimacy. Within the void of his own intimacy the mystic concentrates on his mind's very own self-centered attitudinal mindset and self-orientation (i.e., self-justification). Here the mystic entertains no bodily empathic sensitive feelings but only bodiless telepathic empathic selfish carings and concerns. Here the mystic struggles with his own selfishly self-serving have-attitude mindset and strives under the unctuous influence of the Holy Spirit to sacrificially substitute his own have-more attitude selfish self-justification (viz., autonomous self-containment) mindset for Christ's have-less be-more be-attitudinal Messianic mindset of selfless self-justification.

To appreciate to the full the difference between meditative and contemplative prayer, consider any of the many parables Christ offers for his disciples' prayerful reflection. Consider the parable of the Good Samaritan. When the mystic prays this parable meditatively, he remains a spectator imaginatively conjuring up the scenario of the parable. He may perceive himself as the victim of robbers or as the one who befriends the victim. In every case, he remains in his mental prayerful posture of empathizing sympathetically with the different members of this Gospel scenario and substituting himself compassionately with each of them as individuals other than his own self. That is, he remains somewhat alien to the Gospel parable as someone attending to it as a spectacle involving selves other than his own self.

This changes dramatically when the mystic attends to the same parable through contemplative prayer rather than meditative prayer. When the mystic prays this parable contemplatively, he becomes a phantom specter mentally conjuring up the scenario of the parable. He now is more totally himself involved not merely as a spectator but as the very self (viz., ghostly phantom) that is in his very own innermost selfhood the very victim or Good Samaritan in his own life-style and attitudinal mindset. Here he weighs and evaluates himself not merely as one who is an example of the victim or befriender of the victim; he here engages himself as the role-model victim or befriender. The parable now speaks to him with a telepathic mental empathic bearing and not merely associatively as a bodily example of such empathy. The issue here is no longer one of someone else's self-contented social bodily righteousness but moreso of one's own self-contained righteous sociability and neighborly mindset redolent of Christ's very own Be-attitudinal Selfless Messianic mindset.

In this contemplative prayer the mystic no longer is merely a spectator in the Gospel scenario occurring to selves other than his own self, but the very specter phantom self of the victimized person robbed and left for dead as well as the Good Samaritan who happens upon the victim and befriends him. Furthermore, the mystic in contemplative prayer more intimately and intuitively discerns that the real protagonist of this parable is the victim who is viciously deprived of his righteous dignity and left for dead. For, the victim resembles more Christ Himself nailed to the wood of the cross and dying from neglect even by most of His very own disciples who have abandoned Him in His dereliction. Immersed in this mental contemplative prayer devoid of the tactile trappings of the imagination's sensational tactility and bodily sensitivity, the mystic within the naked self of his own self-centered inner sanctuary and selfhood encounters the Selfless Self of Christ as his own "alter ego" or as an alien to his own sociability and selfhood.

If the mystic from within the very womb and pristine intimacy and sociability of his own selfhood finds himself "at one" with Christ's own Selfless Selfhood's catholic sociability proper to the benignant uninhibited fellowship of the Father & Son's own Holy Spirit's fellowship, the mystic finds Christ of the parable in both the role of the victim and that of the Good Samaritan. For, Christ in His priesthood not only offers himself as victim on the cross but also officiates over his own victimhood thereby serving as a scapegoat substitute for mankind's victimhood inherited in original sin from Adam and Eve. Christ liberates mankind from the degradation and enslavement to his own selfish selfhood by offering Himself to the Father as a scapegoat and ransom for mankind's dereliction. It but remains for the mystic to embrace, in turn, Christ's heroic and gratuitous sociability and to substitute his own servile selfish selfhood for Christ's liberal Selfless Selfhood.

In contemplative prayer the mystic is more under the unctuous intimate influence of Christ's own Holy Spirit and less under the influence of his own imagination and bodily sensitivity. The mystic is more internally engaged within the very intimacy and sanctuary of his own selfhood's mental self-awareness and autocratic self-containment. This self-awareness is still a corpuscular body awareness. Indeed, if the brain which is contiguous with the body's overall corpuscular physiology becomes injured, this impacts severely on a person's ability to reflectively and reflexively engage his own mental self-awareness (viz., his ability to think). Further, the mystic is only able to become transformed from clinging to his own selfishly self-centered have-attitude humanistic competitive mindset to embracing Christ's Selfless be-attitudinal reconciling superhumanistic mindset under the unctuous influence of Christ and the Father's Holy Spirit abiding within the pit and pith of his nuclear mental selfhood.

It is here within the very bosom of contemplative prayer that the mystic encounters the cruciform conjunction between the commandment to love God primatially and to love one's neighbor sacrificially within the same primacy of loving God. Christ in loving His Father's Holy Will primarily served that Holy Will by sacrificially and Selflessly loving (i.e., befriending) mankind's selfishness thereby enabling mankind with the unctuous divine influence of the Holy Spirit to selflessly requite God's own loving Loveliness. In this total response to Christ's own love, the mystic finds himself cruciformatively and Christocentrically hierarchically and vertically obedient to the Father's Holy Will and historically and horizontally "at one" not only with those who befriend him but also with those who are still selfishly at enmity with him. In brief, the mystic is crucified to

Christ's own cross of crucifixion. The mystic's self and soul are reconciled within the peace of Christ that the world itself cannot give.

We now return to the three major obstacles to contemplative prayer. The spiritual director who lacks experience in contemplative prayer may ignorantly restrict, discourage, and impede the mystic's advancement in contemplative payer and, thereby, abandon contemplative prayer itself. Meditative prayer is the initial form of contemplative prayer centered on sensory imagery and imaginary scenarios. This is very beneficial in actively arousing amorous sensitized emotional feelings and empathy toward God. However, these feelings themselves keep the mystic focused on himself and on his own self-serving subjectivity rather than on God who objectively transcends not only the mystic's own subjectivity but the entire objective order of creation.

At some point in the mystic's prayer-life there occurs a transition from meditative to contemplative prayer. This is accomplished, again by the initiative of the Holy Spirit, when the mystic grows weary of meditative prayer precisely because of the "dark night of the senses" there is no further religious satisfaction and gratification available in such prayer. St. John observes that this cessation of emotional religious feeling occurs more quickly in those committed to living the evangelical counsels of obedience, poverty, and chastity. He further instructs the mystic as to how he must conduct his prayer-life when he finds himself in this predicament of being unable to further pursue his habitual mode of meditative prayer. The mystic should no longer seek to pray meditatively by actively focusing on religious sensational imagery designed to evoke satisfying religious emotional empathic feelings and religious contentment. Rather, the mystic should simply seek to become recollected and to remain passively in "loving attention" to God.

This "loving attention" is the key to contemplative prayer. It is unerringly clear from St. John's ensuing description that this prayer is beyond the reach of the senses, all of the senses, and notably the sense of sight and hearing. These two senses are together the focus of audio-visual sensational experiences arousing sensitized emotional feelings of religious contentment. The mystic is to enter into solitude and silence. In other words, the mystic is to exercise his soulful intelligence and intellect above and beyond the compass of sensory knowing and feeling. How does this come about? It is innate to the soul's intellect and intelligence to transcend the sensibility and sensuality of the senses. When the eye, for example, sees sightfully the green of the grass, the intellect sees insightfully green-as-such. When the ear hears harkenly the sound of the bell, the intellect hears intelligently ringing-as-such. Now, green-as-such and ringing-as-such are entirely intelligible and not at all sensible. In other words, the intellect need not consider nor attend to any specific shade of green nor any specific tone of sound in attending to green-as-such and ringing-as-such. For, green-as-such and ringing-as-such are both intelligibly qualities of the grass and the bell's metal but not confined to either the grass' specific shade of green or to the bell's specific metallic sound.

The mystic may intellectually ponder both green-as-such and sound-as-such without even conjuring up the grass or the bell. Assuredly, green-as-such is a color and sound-as-such is a tonality. But, the intellect ponders these physical, tangible, sensible colors and tonalities metaphysically, intangibly, and immaterially; that is, intellectually and intelligibly in the solitude and in the silence proper to the human soul's own interior spirituality and immateriality. In so doing, the intellect has a superior knowledge of the green of the grass and the tone of the bell than do the senses that sensibly see and hear these physical and tangible colors and sounds. Why so? Because the senses are limited to seeing and hearing grass' special shade of color and the bell's special tonality whereas the intellect is able to understand the very entitative "as-such" of color itself apart from the grass and of sound itself apart from the bell. While the eye can see that the grass is a special shade of green and the ear hear that the bell peals a special sound, these senses cannot "see" nor "hear" that green and pealing are themselves qualities of the grass and the bell and distinguishable "as such" from the grass and bell themselves.

Briefly, whereas the senses, such as the sense of sight and hearing, can discern physical and tangible colors and sounds within the physical bodies that are colorful and tonal, the senses cannot differentiate these sounds and tones from the specific material bodies themselves. That is, they cannot discern the very truth and intelligible communal entity of these colors and sounds. The intellect, on the other hand, is able to insightfully and intelligibly discern the "as-such" of color and sound above and beyond the physical bodies themselves which are endowed with specific tangible colors and sounds. In other words, the intellect intelligibly and immaterially grasps the "as-such" entity of color and sound above and beyond the material, tangible, and palpable specific shades of color and tones of sound existing materially in physical bodies.

When this context is transferred to knowing intellectually the reality of God transcendent to all of creation and not only to the physical cosmos, the senses are hindrances to knowing God since God is utterly immaterial, metaphysical, and intangible. God in God's own divinity is only accessible intelligibly to the soul's intellectual knowledge. Thus, the intellect discerns the reality of God only in terms of its own formal transcendental object of intelligibility and understanding, being-as-such. For, the intellect can discern not only the being-as-such of color and sound independent of colorful and tonal physical bodies, it can discern being-as-such metaphysically and independently of all physical bodies. In so doing, it is able in view of its own inherent intellectual intelligibility discern God as a Supreme Being transcendent to not only to the intellect of the one who is contemplating God but transcendent to all of creation. For, a Supreme Being is the very Beingness of being-as-such outside of which nothing exists.

Miraculously, God becomes physically visible and tangible in the incarnation of Jesus Christ. But, even here, neither the body's eye nor ear can detect or discern Christ's divinity. This remains discernible only to the soul's intellectual intelligence that can insightfully grasp that divinity is completely in its intelligibility entirely beyond all physical sensibility. But, even in this intellectual discernment, the human intellect cannot comprehend the infinite intelligibility of Christ's divinity. This remains incomprehensible to the human intellect's own native intelligence. Assuredly the human intellect grasps that inasmuch as God is infinite God is totally the very totality of whatever is formally and literally attributable to Him. Thus, God is not only divine (i.e., unexcelled); God is divinity itself (i.e., excellence). Hence, whatever is inherently and formally not only excellent but excellence itself, is attributable to God's divinity. Thus, for example, greenness cannot be said of God inasmuch as greenness, while infinitely green, is incompatible with redness. On the other hand, goodness which is infinitely good may be attributable to God. For, it is not incompatible with God's infinitude. God is infinite good and infinite truth without any incompatibility.

The supernatural gift of faith is additionally required for the soul's intellectual intelligence to discern that Christ is metaphysically divinity over and above His physical humanity. Pondering the Blessed Sacrament of the Eucharist, what is obvious to our bodily sight is the physical sensibility of bread and wine and to our intellectual insight is the metaphysical intelligibility of Christ's divinity above and beyond the bread and wine. While this intellectual insight of the Eucharist's divinity is rigorously intellectual and not inherently sentient or physical or tangible, it is supernaturally and not naturally intellectual. That is, it is only "in the supernatural light of faith" that the mystic's soulful intelligence can insightfully discern the metaphysical reality of God's divinity in the consecrated host. Therefore, it is only within the utter solitude and silence of the mystic's soulful spiritual and metaphysical interiority that the mystic can ponder and contemplate God sacramentally incarnate in the Eucharist. That is, the mystic need not be actually viewing the Eucharist with his body's eyesight or tasting the Eucharist on his tongue to discern the supernatural reality of God's divinity. This discernment is principally intellectual and not sensorial. It occurs principally and contemplatively within the soul's interior spiritual solitude and silence.

Both before, while, and after receiving the Holy Eucharist, the mystic is to contemplatively and prayerfully ponder intellectually and interiorly within the soul's silence and solitude the supernatural and august reality of God's Triune divine presence through Christ's ecclesial sacramental incarnation. This is principally a passive intellectual activity inasmuch as the intellect does not "create" its own knowledge but passively receives it. It is one thing to "know" through supernatural belief that God is present in the Eucharist; it is another to adore and to love Him obediently. This love and obediential adoration engages the soul's intellectual will over and above the soul's intellect. Furthermore, it also engages the mystic's willful subjective selfhood that can either willfully oblige and submissively accede to this prayerful obedient contemplative soulful adoration and love or willfully impede it. What prayerful contemplation adds to this intellectual knowledge is a "loving attentiveness." What the mystic's willful subjective selfhood adds to the soul's obediential worshipful love is an affectionate "loving attentiveness" and solicitous concern and caring for God Self-revealed in the Eucharist as the Person of Jesus Christ, God/Superman.

Now, this "loving attentiveness" may be one of meditative prayer or contemplative prayer. If it is of meditative prayer it is a subjective self-centered affectionate attentiveness that engages the body's sensational imaginative sensitivity and the mystic's self-centered heartfelt conscious willful empathic temperamentality. Here the mystic is engaged prayerfully and subjectively and actively with God not eplicitly objectively and intellectually but sensorially in terms of the corpuscular body's sensitized emotional religious feelings culminating in righteous self-centered self-contentment and self-gratification. In meditative prayer the focus is not God theocentrically transcendent to the mystic's subjectivity. Rather, the focus is God anthropocentrically impacting on the mystic's own heartfelt subjective bodily sensitivity. This meditative encounter with God is always with Jesus Christ, God/Superman, precisely because in Christ's incarnation He makes Himself manifest anthropocentrically to mankind. Yet, paradoxically enough, this meditative prayerful subjective encounter with Christ and through Christ with the Blessed Trinity, is not an encounter with God "as present" but, rather, with God "as absent." This is so because this self-centered anthropocentric subjective bodily prayerful "awareness" of God is not "per se" a cognitive (viz., informative knowing) but rather a conative feeling (viz., self-transformative knowing) for God. It is not an encounter with God as God "is" but rather inasmuch as the mystic "has" or "has not" an affectionate sensitized bodily feeling for God.

At some point in the mystic's assiduous and persistent engagement in meditative prayer, there ensues a self-righteous religious discontentment precisely because such prayer in itself is not principally an objective theocentric encounter with God as God exists transcendent to the mystic's own subjective pious and devout anthropocentric religious sensitized bodily experiences of God. The mystic loses "touch" with God inasmuch as his own bodily religious sensitivity ceases to be affectively emotionally influenced through self-induced and self-controlled meditative attentiveness to the body's sensational imagery however centered and focused on Gospel themes this attentiveness may be. In this prolonged period of experiencing no further customary religious enthusiasm, fervor, and gusto for God, Holy Mother, the Sacramental Church, devout activities and charitable engagement, the mystic finds himself in the "dark night of the senses" in which there is no further aroused religious bodily sensitivity in direct proportion to the singular effort which he meditatively exerts to self-induce such pious emotional feelings.

During this prolonged period of religious ennui and boredom typical of the "dark night of the senses," the mystic finds no pious satisfaction in meditative prayer regardless of the effort which he doggedly and persistently invests in his periods of special prayerful reflection. Without his being explicitly aware of it, he is being weaned away from meditative prayer and gradually prepared to shift his prayerful attention away from the focus of the body's sensational imagery to the mind's notional intimacy devoid of all sensations and sensitive stimulations of emotional feelings. This shift remains completely anthropocentric. The mystic is not shifting his prayerfully subjective attentiveness from his own self-centered awareness of God immanent within his own selfhood. He is shifting his prayerful subjective attentiveness from the outer bodily sensitive perimeter of his own self-centered selfhood to the inner mental insensitive innermost intimate sanctuary sedately devoid of all bodily sensitivity and tactility. Contemplative mystical prayer as propounded by St. John finds its culmination from within the innermost nuclear intimacy of the mystic's mental self-centered selfhood.

How is the mystic to conduct his prayer-life when he no longer is actively engaged in meditative prayer and not yet fully ensconced in contemplative prayer? St. John counsels the mystic to remain simply in a passive "loving attentiveness" which may be translated into a serene mental composure not concentrated on thinking notionally but, rather, concentrated on maintaining as much as possible an attentive affectionate "caring" and "concern" and solicitude" for the Blessed Trinity whom by faith and hope he knows resides in the Person of the Holy Spirit within the innermost inner rececesses of his own selfhood. Sacred Scripture declares that the human body is the temple of the Holy Spirit. The reader can now appreciate by reason of this commentary that this "body" is not merely the objective corporeal animal body which is animated by the human person's spiritual and intelligent free incorporeal soul. This "body" also includes the subjective corpuscular body which psychosomatically is the human person's self-cultivated subjectivity, selfhood, and personality that has in its peripheral bodily sensitivity a heartfelt self-centered outer empathic willful self and in its nuclear mental intimacy a mindful self-centered innermost inward telepathic willful self.

At this point of entry into and pursuance of contemplative prayer, the mystic is not to revert to meditative prayer engaging in self-induced sensitized emotional religious feelings of bodily contentment and emotional enthusiasm. He should, rather, conduct himself passively and more introvertedly and introspectively rather than extrovertedly and extrospectively focusing on his bodily sensitive self rather than his inner mental intimate non-sensitive and non-sensational self. This "attentiveness" should not be one of active self-conscious notional thinking (viz., day-dreaming) but one of simply caring, concern, and solicitude for God, Holy Mother, the Sacramental Church, and for the members of this Church.

It is important here to differentiate between the contemplative activity proper to the soul's own faculty of intelligence and the contemplative function proper to the selfhood's own facility of mental adroitness. Further, it is important to differentiate between the soul's soulful totally spiritual and incorporeal human interiority and the self's utterly self-centered psychic (i.e., mental) spiritualized and humanized de-sensitized corpuscular intimacy. The human soul's spiritual interiority is not isolated from the universe of reality (both created and Creator) to which it is informatively open and truthfully theocentrically identified. On the other hand, the selfhood's self-centered mental de-sensitized intimacy is anthropocentrically isolated from the universe of reality transcendent to its own psychic corpuscular spiritualized subjectivity.

What binds together this soulful transcendence and metaphysical theocentric continuity with the universe of reality, on the one hand, and the self-centered mental immanance and phenomenological anthropocentric discontinuity with the same universe of reality, on the other, is that both of these disparate orders subsist and are sustained within one and the same personhood of each human person. The same human person who by nature is objectively and ontologically in his personhood a sovereign immortal intelligent and freely subsistent incommunicable (i.e., inalienable) and induplicable individual is simultaneously by the self-cultivation of this very same personhood has subjectively and epistemologically (i.e., phenomenologically) an autonomous mortal psychosomatic communicable (i.e., alienable) and duplicable sociable willful self-centered dichotomous outward heartfelt bodily personality together with an inward attitudinal caring mindset personality.

The very same person may alternately contemplate intellectually and intelligently the universe of reality transcendent to and independent of his own personal sovereign immortal existence, on the one hand, and contemplate the cultural world of mankind's own self-cultivation, on the other hand, which is immanent to his own personhood's interpersonal social welfare and personalized mortal sociable security, on the other. Contemplation in the former case is cognitively informative whereas the contemplation that is proper to the latter within the innermost inward intimacy of the same person's self-centered awareness is conatively transformative. In the former case, the person's intellectual soulful will wills to possess reality appropriately commensurate with reality's inherent worth whereas in the case of the latter, the person's self-centered (i.e., self-serving) psychosomatic will wills to appropriate whatever it appropriates possessively commensurate with the self's self-centered neediness to fully secure and guarantee its own mortal social self-suffiiciency.

The difference between these two cruciform orders, the hierarchical, and the historical, is the difference between *being* which is fundamental and *having* which is supplemental. The human person objectively and fundamentally *is* an independent sovereign immortal being in the community of other immortal human persons within the universe of God's creation whereas subjectively the same human person *has* an interpersonal and interdependent mortal sociability in conjunction with the selves of other human persons within an autonomous world of the human person's own making. In the fundamental order the human person becomes sovereignly personable by the disciplined reasonable and responsible practice of forming an upright moral character. In the supplemental order the same human person becomes autonomously personable by the skillful development of a personality that is socially charismatic (i.e., influential).

God exists both naturally and supernaturally in the hierarchical objective order supremely and sovereignly transcendent to and independent of the human person's own relative sovereign immortal existence. God has no cultural claim of autonomous (i.e., self-sufficient) sociability within the interdependent sociability of human selves. In other words, in the ontological order, God's sovereign supremacy is of primary importance. In the phenomenological order, God's sovereign supremacy becomes transformatively of autonomous (i.e., sociable) importance not by way of upholding God's supreme sovereignty but by way of transposing this supremacy into a Self-centered utterly Selfless and Self-effacing oblative serviceability upholding and advancing the autocratic selfless sociability of every human person's mortal personality.

In other words, Jesus Christ, God/Superman, objectively, ontologically, and contemplatively defers theocratically to the sovereign primacy of His Father's Holy Will. Subjectively, phenomenologically, and contemplatively He defers autocratically to the autonomous primacy of His own psychosomatic will's Selfless Self-oblation in behalf of liberating every self-humanized selfhood from its slavish servility to its own mortal craven selfish sociability. In volunteering to die, rise from the dead and ascend into heaven, Christ subjectively and contemplatively renews and rekindles the hope of the self-humanized person's mortal social personality to successfully, supplementally, and self-fulfillingly suffer its own historical social dissolution in the expectation of rising to a new and renewed life of transhistorical selfless sociability in the Self-fulfilling promise of Christ's own bodily Selfless resurrection and glorification in the heaven of the Blessed Trinity.

Contemplative prayer is twofold. It is objectively the mystical person's faith-filled intellectual beholding and voluntary soulful embrace of and delight in the Father's Holy Will supergraciously and benignantly inundating the human soul. It is subjectively the same mystical person's hopeful faithful beatitudinal mindset willfully superheroically and superhumanistically in a kenotic self-oblation and commitment selflessly submitted to participating in Christ's very own Paschal Mystery. Contemplative prayer is objectively fundamental inasmuch as the mystic is aware of the God-the-Father's paternal providential merciful gracious presence sacramentally mediated by God-the-Son. This awareness is not anthropocentrically self-centered; it is theocentric. Contemplative prayer is subjectively supplemental inasmuch as the mystic is self-aware of God-the-Son's filial merciful graciousness superhumanistically liberating his own (i.e., the mystic's) psychic contentious selfhood from its servile selfishness to the total self-fulfillment of Christ's own super heroic kenotic Selfless Selfhood and Charismatic Personality. This awareness is anthropocentrically and reflexively self-centered. Yet, this reflexive awareness is in no way self-enclosed or self-restricted. It is a self-fulfilled selfhood that is only supplementally self-consciously self-centered. In that it is self-fulfilled it is fully open, amenable to, and hospitable to the ontological order that fundamentally transcends its own phenomenological subjectivity.

This twofold contemplative prayer is superherorically, superhumanistically, and Christocentrically embraced by the mystic by the efficacy of God-the-Holy-Spirit who is the Father and the Son's joint love and benignant Loveliness alive in the mystic. In that this twofold contemplative prayer is simultaneously objectively a super-obediential act of the soul's voluntary willfulness and subjectively a sacrificial utterly selfless action of the self's self-controlled willfulness, it is jointly a total integral self-determined self-surrender and a volunteer self-donation of the mystic's own freedom to the Blessed Trinity's sovereign supreme Freedom.

This contemplative prayerful faith-filled loving attentiveness towards God's supernatural presence could not take place if the mystic were self-consciously (i.e., self-centeredly) focused on his own subjective emotional religious feelings be they one of religious contentment or discontentment (i.e., aridity). The mystic in passively and credulously receiving and lovingly entertaining and delighting in God's presence within the soul's spiritual solitary and stilled interiority. Indeed, the mystic receives God in a manner that is commensurate with God's very own serene eternal immutability and sovereign monotheistic divine sovereignty.

Furthermore, so important and vital is this objective fundamental intellectual contemplative credulous and voluntary awesome obediential gazing on the actual supernatural presence of God's gracious divinity within the soul's solitary and stilled interiority that St. John emphatically states that the mystic is to even forego his subjective contemplative supplemental "loving attentiveness" itself in the measure that it may hinder and detract from the soul's utter passivity of its contemplative intellectual willing gaze. Such subjective self-centered selfish affectionate "attentiveness" would most assuredly be a distraction and a hindrance to the mystic's objective contemplation of God. Were this the case, this attentiveness would not be directed toward God's presence within the soul's interiority but, rather, actively focused and concentrated on the mystic's subjective willful self-centered self-control and self-possessive hold on God.

The mystic finds himself to be more conducively prone and disposed to contemplative prayer when he no longer finds any religious savor, feeling, or subjective bodily contentment in meditative prayer. The principal characteristic of this intellectual contemplative attentive gazing on the supernatural presence of God within the soul's spiritual interiority is its idleness, stillness, and insularity from all sentiency, and from the movement peculiar to physical bodies and to the imagination's own subjective sensational imagery. The mystic cannot attain to this refinement of intellectual contemplative attentiveness toward God's supernatural divine presence if he is preoccupied with

and attached to in any way with the senses and their subjective sensational tactility or with the sensitivity and motility of his own body's
subjective religious feelings. St. John declares that God calls the soul
to the desert to be fed with the manna of His own divinity. St. John
refers to this contemplative gazing as a divine and sublime wisdom
which is attained only passively without any special initiative or exertion on the part of the mystic's own busy self-centeredness. In this
sense, it is no different from the mystic's bodily eye gazing on the
apple tree other than to point out that it is the mystic's intellect gazing on heaven's divine sacramental Graciousness within the spiritual
intangible and stilled interiority of his own soul.

St. John insists that the benefit that accrues to the mystic who attains to this idle prayerful intellectual supernatural contemplation is
inestimable. Remaining within the intellectual and spiritual insularity
of this prayerful contemplative gazing and pondering the mystic is
passively disposed to receive the most refined, pure, and delicate
blessings and anointings from the Holy Spirit which are congruent
with the Holy Spirit's own imperturbable and serene, immutable, immaterial, supernal divinity. St. John also cautions that this soulful intellectual insularity may be very easily disturbed and even impeded
by unnecessary intellectual cogitation, incessant subjective mental reminiscing, and a willful busy self-conscious attempt to manage and
self-control this contemplation. Furthermore, he decries any and
every such disturbance and interference regardless of its source or occasion as a most grievous impediment and interference to God's initiative of fashioning within the mystic His own divine masterpiece
while the mystic is prayerfully and contemplatively docile to God's
direct influence.

St. John continues to point out that spiritual directors are more
often than not the very one's who interfere with this mode of contemplative prayer as it is unfolding and developing in mystics. St. John
repeats that meditative prayer is merely a means to contemplative
prayer. When one reaches the end of a journey, one does not continue
to retrace one's steps; one ceases to journey; one comes to a point of
rest and relaxation. What occurs in contemplative prayer is accomplished by God's own incomparable initiative and mastery and not

by any spiritual expert's own direction. The very hallmark of intellectual contemplative prayer is its generality and refusal to be reduced, focused, or concentrated on anything specific which detracts from the generality of God's divine nature and attributes. This very hallmark stringently requires that the mystic be completely detached from having and seeking to entertain any special subjective religious sentimental feeling and contentment.

So vehemently insistent is St. John on the mystic's complete detachment from every specificity whether it be sensible, intellectual, memorial, or self-consciously the mystic's own willfully self-controlled attentiveness to his own subjective religious bodily feelings and mental bearings that he declares that God will unfailingly respond to the mystic's total self-detachment from all specificity by bathing the mystic in His own benignity in the same way that the sun unfailingly radiates its own solarity. In other words, God will not fail to impart to the mystic divine caresses, blessings, and anointings commensurate with God's own infinite delicacy, purity, immensity, immateriality, immutability, and benignity. It is imperative for the mystic to prayerfully advance intellectually toward God and to contemplate God in a manner commensurate with God's own infinite and incomprehensible indivisible divinity and Godhead.

This requires that the mystic's own intellect not be embroiled in specific musings that are not befitting God's own incomprehensible generality and transcendence to all of creation. For example, God is not merely good; God is Goodness; God is not merely light, God is Lucidity. These incomprehensible Goodness and Lucidity cannot be misconstrued for any one special good or luminous object, thing, or person be this person merely human or angelic. It is imperative that the mystic intellectually contemplate God's Goodness and Lucidity in their utmost uncircumscribed transcendent universality and generality. Why? The mystic in supernatural faith is intellectually contemplating the actual supreme personal sacramental presence of God's infinite Triune Godhead within the interiority of his own soul.

There is no creaturely being or intellectual concept that is adequate to intellectually represent God's Godhead in this Godhead's own supernatural glorious infinite supernatural presentedness. It is vital and imperative that the mystic be intellectually and contemplat-ively absorbed in universal generalities commensurate with God's own infinitude and utter simplicity. The divine supernatural love which this prayerful contemplative knowledge evokes in the mystic's soul is itself as inchoate as is the mystic's knowledge of God impenet-rable by reason of its generality. After all, divine Goodness can only be understood in terms of the infinite generality of God's own divine "ness."

But there is a singular difference between the mystic's soulful prayerful intellectual contemplation of God and his soulful volitional love. For, whereas the mystic's soulful intellectual knowledge has its culmination in the intellect; his soulful volitional love has its culmina-tion in the actual possession of the reality which is the finalizing ob-ject of this love. Thus, while the human intellect is actually finite in its knowledge and understanding of God and only virtually infinite, its comprehensible understanding of God will always remain simply fi-nite even in heaven when the mystic contemplates God through the Beatific Vision. On the other hand, the human soulful will in spite of the finitude of its own volition is able in supernaturally loving God to actually possess God's infinitude proper to God's own infinity. This does not mean that the mystic's love of God is itself infinite. But, it does mean that the mystic is in his volitional love appropriately in love with God who is infinitely loveable. On a mere natural plane, the mystic's soul cannot love what it first does not intellectually know. But, on the supernatural plane God may impart a greater love to the mystic's soulful will than He does knowledge to the mystic's soulful intellect.

St. John reassures the mystic who enters in faith into this sublime contemplative intellectual attentiveness to the reality of the Blessed Trinity sacramentally present within the solitude and stillness of his soul's interiority that his complete lack of concomitant religious (i.e., devout and pious) sensitized bodily feelings and intimate mental bearings toward God are not essential to this prayerful contemplative gazing. Why not? God Himself (i.e., the Holy Spirit) will provide the mystic sublime emotional bodily exultations and emotionless mental serenity commensurate with His divine presence. Indeed, any deliberate volitional exertion on the part of the mystic to provoke or evoke within himself religious emotional feelings or emotionless bearings would only detract from and interfere with the intellectual insularity and immutability of this contemplative prayer.

Contemplative prayer achieves and attains to its perfection when the mystic's objective natural ontological order is integrated with his subjective cultural phenomenological order. This occurs when his objective soulful activity is integrated with his self-centered psychic selfhood. However, this cannot be effectuated naturally or culturally apart from Christ's superhuman, superhumanistic, and superhumane mediation. God creates the human person without the human person's own cooperation. Even though this creation involves the parent's cooperation, this cooperation does not extend to the parent's offspring. Indeed, Adam and Eve's creation involved no parents other than God's own parenting.

Contemplative prayer in its twofold soulful and self-centered contemplation can only reach its integral perfection when the mystic's psychosomatic self is not only psychically mentally detached from the body's religious somatic sensitivity but moreso psychically mentally self-detached from its attachment to its own inner intimate selfhood's mental selfishness. That is, the mystic must undergo a complete metanoetic attitudinal transformation. The mystic must forego his own selfish have-attitudinal mindset and adopt Christ's selfless be-attitudinal messianic mindset. In other words, the mystic must die to his own selfish have-more attitudinal self and come to life with Christ's have-less be-more be-attitudinal mindset. Contemplative prayer can only be exercised fully and integrally after the mystic has first of all suffered through the kenotic self-emptying and purging of his psychic self's own selfish attitudinal mindset.

St. John severely castigates spiritual directors who advertently or inadvertently interfere with the mystic's seemingly idle and insular activity of remaining simply in the posture of prayerful contemplative prayer over and beyond the sensationally stimulating engagement of meditative prayer steeped in the body's somatic subjective religious feelings. Such directors who through their own lack of experience misconstrue this prayerful contemplative "idleness" as "wasting time" instruct the mystic to return to meditative prayer engaging the senses and sensational imagery. In so doing they interfere with God's own initiative in transforming the mystic into Christ's own messianic beatitudinal mindset and superhuman Personality. The singular advantage of contemplative prayer is that the mystic has attained to such a total self-detachment that he is now properly disposed without any further resistance to correspond to the Holy Spirit's own utter subtle and delicate bodily sensational and/or mental inspirational influence of divine amorosity.

In the mystical life everything is accomplished by God. The Father initiates, the Son consummates, and the Holy Spirit integrates. Now that the mystic has suffered through a complete self-detachment from the selfishness of his own psychosomatic egocentric selfhood and is no longer---thanks to both the "night of the senses and spirit"---a prisoner of his own subjective selfish self-centered religious bodily feelings and mental bearings, why would he revert to these religious sensitive selfish feelings and intimate selfish bearings while he is engaged in contemplative prayer? Now that he has succeeded in transcending the confinement and self-controlling clutch of his own subjective temperamental self-centered needs and sentimental wants, his subjective have-attitudinal selfish self-interest and mindset has yielded to Christ's own beatitudinal disinterested messianic mindset. Having arrived at this intellectual objective transcendence proper to contemplative intellectual prayer, the mystic is now disposed to passively receive within his own subjectivity sensitive exultations of exquisite religious bodily self-contentment and intimate consolations of profound mental serenity which no longer remain under his own willful subjective selfish self-control but entirely under the influence of the Holy Spirit's own Selfless benevolent initiative.

Even and especially in the absence of all subjective sensitive emotional religious divine bodily somatic stimulation and intimate emotionless religious divine mental sedation the mystic while remaining in the insularity and essentially spiritual intransitive intellectual activity of simply attending reverently to God's sacramental Personal merciful gracious presence within the soul's interiority enjoys Christ's peace and tranquility that passes all understanding. This peace and tranquility derives from the perfect reconciliation within the mystic of his objective personal nature with his subjective self-cultivated personality. While remaining in this state of suspended intellectual devout and reverential attentiveness to God rooted in faith the mystic's subjective self-centered self-serving volitional imperious demands and chastened needs no longer interfere with nor impede his objective soulful volitional drive to attentively honor, praise, worship, adore, thank and reverence God appropriate to God's own Triune Personal Godliness supernaturally and sacramentally present within the soul's interiority.

The second source of the mystic's blindness to attaining and remaining within the sanctuary of this contemplative prayer is the devil. Recall that St. John insists that the very hallmark of this contemplative prayer is its utter generality which is commensurate with the ideal intangible utterly spiritual nature and attributes of God's own divinity. God is Goodness, Beauty (i.e., beautifulness), Joy (i.e., joyfulness), Light (i.e., lucidity), Truth (i.e., truthfulness), etc.. Whatever be the spontaneous supernatural sublime enjoyment, delight, jubilation, bliss, etc. that the mystic may spontaneously entertain objectively within the interiority of the soul's intellectual will commensurate with contemplating in faith God's Triune supernatural presence, this bliss need not overflow into the psychosomatic subjectivity of his bodily sensitivity and mental intimacy. Indeed, it may be that this contemplative prayer is not accompanied by any soulful blissful sublime volitional enjoyment at all within the soul's interiority. St. John does point out that God may enlighten the mystic without inflaming him with supernal love or, inflame the mystic without enlightening him.

In gazing at the apple in the tree a person may reach up and pluck the apple to take a bite of it. He may spontaneously in tasting the apple taste its proper flavor and be aware of this taste as being pleasing or displeasing. Such awareness is not principally subjectively self-centered. Indeed, the person may suddenly become aware of his own selfhood engaging in this activity if he is startled to learn that someone else is watching him. But, in the absence of such an intrusion his entire attention may be focused exclusively on the apple and its pleasant or unpleasant flavor whichever be the case.

On the other hand, if the person plucks the apple and does not bite into it but rather entertains subjectively the sensational image of himself eating the apple in a pie spiced with all the delicate spices proper to an apple pie, he is now focused on his somatic sensitive subjective bodily feelings rather than on the apple itself. This attentiveness to the apple is similar to the mystic's intellectual attentiveness to God in contemplative prayer. In contemplative prayer the mystic is oblivious to his own subjective psychosomatic self-centeredness and remains completely absorbed in God's supernatural presence transcendent to his own self-centered subjectivity. If, on the other hand, the mystic deliberately adverts to his own self-centered bodily religious feelings or mental religious bearings he interrupts the intellectual insularity of this contemplative prayer and, thereby, interferes with it.

It is precisely in this manner that the devil, the second source of the mystic's blindness regarding contemplative prayer, succeeds in interrupting and interfering with contemplative prayer. The devil preternaturally infuses subjective religious feelings that stimulate the mystic's somatic body's sensitivity. Such feelings are more immediately satisfying to the mystic's subjective bodily needs and demands. Such sensuous religious satisfactions and contentment are more palpable than are the ethereal and entirely spiritual and intangible supernal delights present in the mystic's intellectual volitional soul. These very tactile and sensuous sensitized feelings distract the mystic from his attentiveness to contemplative prayer. In this manner, the devil succeeds in foiling the mystic's advancement to a more perfect and sublimely spiritual encounter and union with God at the level of God's own supernatural Trinitarian Personhood.

The third source of this blindness which impedes the mystic from engaging fully and without impediment in contemplative prayer is the mystic himself. The mystic in his own rank ignorance may foolishly consider such contemplative prayer an idle pastime since he himself is not busily active in exerting his own initiative. He is not exerting himself productively. Indeed, the quintessence of contemplative prayer is that it is intransitively non-productive; it is entirely an informative activity which immediately benefits and redounds to the enlightenment of the mystic himself. The very benefit of the eye's seeing is that it is informed regarding what is seeable. The eye does not make its visible object seeable; it simply engages in a sight of the object by actually gazing on it. It is the same case with the mystic's soulful intellect and intelligence which gazes on God in faith sacramentally and Personally present within the soul's spiritual and stilled interiority.

Of course, as long as the mystic remains objectively in the intellectual insularity of contemplative prayer, his subjective psychosomatic selfhood need not in any way be actively engaged in this prayerful activity. If the mystic's bodily and mental self-centered volitional needs and demands have not been completely purged and purified in advance, the mystic will be unable to engage in contemplative prayer. For, he would be too volitionally attached to securing the subjective needs of his own body's sensitive self-contented satisfaction and his mind's intimate self-contained justification to be able to attend objectively and intellectually to God's sacramental and supernatural present Graciousness within his soul's interiority. The mystic's soulful awareness of God is in no wise a self-centered self-conscious subjective awareness. It is an objective awareness that transcends the mystic's psychosomatic egocentric subjectivity.

Accordingly, the very unction of contemplative prayer is completely bereft of any and every sensuous gut sensitized feeling proper to the mystic's subjective somatic body and every nonsensuous cerebral intimate bearing proper to the mystic's subjective psychic mind. Contemplative prayer's very womb is the mystic's soulful entirely immaterial, intangible, metaphysical, spiritual interiority. Unless and until the mystic is completely self-detached from his own subjective psychosomatic needs and wants, he remains unable to transcend the craving demands of his own selfhood's needful subjectivity. Hence, if the mystic himself is still prone to sensuously experience God within the sensitivity of his own somatic body and/or to experience God within the intimacy of his own psychic mind, this proneness (i.e., selfishly self-centered have-attitude as opposed to Christ's selflessly self-centered be-attitude) will impede his entry into and sustained engagement in contemplative prayer.

The key to contemplative prayer is that it is the supernatural prayerful medium in which the mystic is completely disposed to be docile and responsive to the initiative of the Holy Spirit abiding within him. In the vertical order of existence, the mystic is assimilated supernaturally to God's own Triune subsistent Personhood. In the horizontal order of resistance, the mystic offers no further subjective resistance to this objective supernatural assimilation. In the cruciform order reconciling the two previous orders and cross beams of the cross, the order of existence and the order of resistance are reconciled with each other in an order of subsistent integrity, solidarity, peace, harmony, and consistency. That is, the mystic's very own self-centered selfhood is now both fulfillingly and securely satiated sensuously with God's exultant consolation and sedated intimately with God's inspiration above and beyond all of the mystic's selfish self-centered demands and selfish self-control. In this manner the mystic acquires a social autonomy that is no longer in competition with selves other than his own self. For, his own selfhood no longer makes any selfishly self-serving demands on other selves.

THE LIVING FLAME OF LOVE. Stanza 4:

How gently and lovingly

You wake in my heart.

Where in secret You dwell alone;

And in Your sweet breathing,

Filled with good and glory,

How tenderly You swell my heart with love!

At the outset of his commentary as it is St. John's wont to do, he states "the soul here addresses its Bridegroom...". Throughout our own commentary we have taken the liberty to insert "mystic" in the place of the soul. It is notable that St. John always speaks of the mystic personally in terms of the soul rather than in terms of his

745

"person." In our commentary we have repeatedly construed that all of the activity imputed to the soul by St. John is not restricted to the soul's own vitality as the substantive principle of life in the mystic's body. Again, it is St. John's wont to refer all human activity to the soul in the same way that it is understood that it is the human person in his own personhood that is the subject of all that occurs within, through, and by his own agency.

Bearing this in mind, let us substitute "mystic" for "soul" in the following two paragraphs which introduce St. John's commentary on this fourth verse of the *Living Flame*. "The mystic here addresses her Bridegroom with deep love, esteeming Him and thanking Him for two admirable effects sometimes produced by Him through this union, noting also the manner in which each is wrought, as well as another effect which overflows in the mystic from this union.

The first effect is an awakening of God in the mystic, effectuated in gentleness and love. The second is the breathing of God within the mystic, and this is effected through the good and glory communicated to the mystic in this breathing. And that which overflows in the mystic is being tenderly and delicately inspired with love."

In substituting "mystic" in the place of the "soul" it becomes more immediately patent that this activity of God's "awakening" and "breathing" in the mystic need not occur explicitly and exclusively within the soul's own spiritual interiority as is the case with contemplative prayer which has its residency within the mystic's soulful intellectual and volitional engagement. Indeed, this "awakening" and "breathing" occur within the mystic's very psychosomatic subjectivity which is his self-humanized and self-cultivated egocentric selfhood.

It is clear that the essential activity proper to the human soul's own spirituality admits of no such "awakening" or "breathing." This "awakening" occurs as a subjective egocentric self-awareness and this "breathing" engages the mystic's interplay between and within his own somatic and psychic volitional subjective dichotomous selfhood. Since this very subjective psychosomatic selfhood is rootedly the self-humanization and self-cultivation of the mystic's own corpuscularity, this "love" which the Holy Spirit breaths into the mystic is entirely

746

and subjectively anthropocentric. Whereas in verse three the mystic is spiritually, theocentrically, and superhumanly lifted to heaven in contemplative prayer, in this fourth verse the mystic within the very humanism of his own subjective psychosomatic bodiliness is superhumanistically filled with the very vitality of the Holy Spirit of Christ's incarnation.

This "awakening" is succinctly the mystic's self-awareness of his own selfhood from within the very nuclear core and pith of his most inward and intimate psychosomatic self-conscious volitional subjectivity becomes aware that his imponderable neediness, helplessness, and emptiness (i.e., *nada*) is now replete and imbued with the very fullness of the "*breath*" and "*breathing*" of Christ and the Father's eternal and immutable infinite Holy Spirit of an amorous fellowship devoid of all selfish self-attachment and self-service.

It must be borne in mind that at this point in the mystic's mystical union with God the mystic's own psychosomatic volitional self is no longer committed to the social security of his own selfishly self-serving humanistic have-attitudinal mindset. After a prolonged period of grueling and agonizing suffering (viz., the mystic's "dark nights") his self-alienating self-serving entirely selfish humanistic have-attitudinal mindset has become exchanged for Christ's very own superhumanistic Selfless messianic be-attitudinal mindset. The mystic's clinging selfish self-attachment even to his own mystical experiences of God have now given way to Christ's very own Selfless self-centeredness.

Accordingly, the mystic's purely humanistic and entirely futile quest and imperious need to compensate for his own profound subjective social insecurity rooted in the immeasurably profound neediness and emptiness of his own corpuscular psychosomatic selfhood becomes transformed into the mystical wisdom of St. Paul. This apostle revels in his own weakness which is his very spur and motivational incentive to turn to Christ who alone can compensate for this weakness by supplementally providing His own superhuman, superhumanistic, and superhumane divine strength (viz., the Holy Spirit) to not only fill this social neediness and emptiness but, moreover, to fulfill it with the infinitude of the Blessed Trinity's own infinite loveliness and merciful graciousness and benevolent fellowship.

At this point in the mystic's entry and advancement to the very culmination of his pilgrimage to God, he is endowed with the very personality proper to Christ delineated in the Beatitudes. He is totally impoverished within the hubris of his own purely humanistic spirit of selfish self-domination and completely submissive to the mastery of Christ's own Selfless superhumanistic Holy Spirit of Gifted Givingness. He is meek, pure of heart in having no selfishly self-serving motivation; a peace-maker precisely because he is himself "at peace" within the subjective and objective orders of his own personhood humiliated by having undergone sacrificially for Christ and the Gospel the abasement of his own egoism; and fully self-fulfillingly vindicated in his insatiable thirst and hunger for a self-righteousness that is not of his own making but born of Christ's merciful Selfless Self-giving love.

God's very own supreme Goodness and Glory proper to Christ's own divinity and incarnated in His own humanity are here transmitted to the mystic through the agency of the Father and the Son's own Holy Spirit. The mystic becomes aware of God's own Goodness and Glory alive within the very marrow of his own bones, the heartfelt pulsations of his own subjective willfulness, and the utmost inward inner fathomless intimacy of his own mindfulness.

St. John states that there are many variations of this "awakening" in the mystic's self-awareness of God's superhumanistic affluence and unction within the innermost center of his own psychosomatic willful selfhood. This one peculiar to the mystic's culminating marital union with Christ is most elevated and beneficial. It is characterized by the mystic experiencing within his own subjective egocentric psychicsomatic selfhood the grandiose convergence of all the powers of heaven and earth within his own personhood. This grandiosity does not emanate from the mystic's own egocentricity. No! Rather, it emanates from his subjective anthropocentric experience of being filled with the eminence of God's own divinity. That is, the mystic is filled with very Holy Spirit of Christ's own humanity since all of creation has been created by and for Jesus Christ.

St. John further describes this "awakening" as the mystic experiencing within his own subjectivity God's own divine movement as the supreme agency underlying the entire universe of creation. He quickly qualifies this "mystical experience" of "divine movement" as not belonging God who is eternally immutable but, rather, as peculiar to the human person's experience of God's own power, substance, and grace anthropocentrically within his own personhood. Indeed, this is not unlike experiencing the sun's "rising" in the morning through the horizon of one's own bodily vision. What is occurring in the mystic's subjective experiential awareness of this "divine vortex" is the mystic's personalized experience of Christ's primacy and supremacy throughout the entire universe of creation.

St. John further explains the anthropocentric aura of the mystic's experience of himself being the very center and "divine vortex" of the universe. It comes from the very subjective epistemic illusion that every self other than one's own self seems to be similar to one's own self. When the mystic experiences himself as becoming increasingly more conscious of God's causal, providential, paternal, and influential vortical centrality in himself, he experiences this as though it were God Himself undergoing this vortical change within the entire universe.

The upshot of this "awakening" is that the mystic becomes increasingly more self-conscious of God's substance, power, and grace providentially and paternally permeating every scintilla of creation. This "awakening" comes as an ever increasingly acute self-awareness that God in the Person of the Holy Spirit sacramentally and secretly dwells within the innermost inner recesses of the mystic's own egocentric volitional selfhood. This "awakening" cannot be conveyed in words, our Carmelite mystic declares. Possibly, it is similar to Christ's own bodily transfiguration on Mount Tabor. So splendid and translucently divine did His body become that the apostles could not directly gaze on Him. Similarly, the mystic's own egocentric willful selfhood becomes so fully self-aware of God's infinite excellence permeating his own psychosomatic personality that he, thereby, is made "gentle and charming" with all the grace and allure proper to Christ's own supernal Personality (again, not to be confused with His Personhood).

This singular awakening and dawning of the Blessed Trinity within the innermost inward and outward volitional selfhood of the mystic's egocentric subjectivity and self-awareness is marvelously the mystic's awareness of his own self shorn of its previous self-centered constrictive selfishness and now adorned with Christ's very own hospitable Deified Selfless Selfhood (i.e., supernal Personality). There is no further hint, residue, or even shadow of any alienation either within the mystic's own subjective psychosomatic selfhood, between the mystic's subjective willful self and his objective soulful obediential will, nor between his own self and Christ's Selfhood suffused through and through with the Holy Spirit's infinite amorosity, vigor, vitality, benignity and uninhibited freedom.

What is more, there is now effectuated within the very core and nucleus of the mystic's psychosomatic subjectivity and willful selfhood a reconciliation between his psychic (i.e., mental) and somatic (i.e., bodily) bipolarity. This means that the mystic's somatic self-serving need and demand for a socially secure (i.e., autonomous) sensitive righteous self-contentment (i.e., satisfying and gratifying bodily feeling) and/or socially secure intimate righteous self-containment (i.e., vindicating and justifying mental bearing) are no longer at logger-heads with each other. Rather, they are fused together in a bodily feeling/mental bearing of self-righteousness that is no longer a grasping selfishly self-centered self-alienating righteousness but an entirely radiantly dispensing and diffusing ingratiating charming and supernal saintly personality redolent of Christ's very own messianic beatitudinal Personality.

It is important to recall that in any musical composition and rendition, there is the composer who willfully composes the musical piece within the intimate inward non-tactile cerebral secrecy of his own mind and there is the orchestra instrumentalists who willfully perform the piece and give it a musical tactility discernible and enjoyable to the body's own outward empirical sensitivity. Composing the piece is a mental cerebral endeavor while performing and enjoying the piece is a bodily emotional endeavor. The composer willfully experiences his own cerebral self-justification and vindication in endowing the musical piece with its own compositional autonomy while the orchestra members willfully experience their own emotional self-satisfaction and gratification in endowing the same musical piece with its proper orchestral harmony and sonority.

The composer qua composer is not the performer and vice versa. Similarly the mystic's willful non-tactile cerebral bearings and visceral tactile feelings are in polar opposition to each other. The composer's social autonomy (i.e., self-resourceful sufficiency) is not that of the instrumentalist and, vice versa, the latter is not that of the composer. The composer's social autocratic autonomy and self-justification is entirely socially solitary; there is but one composer and one musical composition. The instrumentalist's social automatic autonomy and self-satisfaction is socially multiple; there are many instrumentalists who coordinate together their instrumentality.

It is the conductor of the musical piece that brings together in one fused rendition the composer's composition with the orchestra's instrumental rendition. It is the conductor who self-righteously fuses together the composer's musical self-vindication and the instrumentalist's musical self-satisfaction. Certainly, one and the same person may alternatively act and serve subjectively in the role of the composer, the instrumentalist, and the director of the orchestra. The person that does so, however, will be assuming three distinctly different psychosomatic personalities and roles. Of the three disparate personalities, it is the conductor who fuses the other two together.

This special singular "dawning" of espoused divine love which emerges in the mystic merges the mystic's own disparate polarized willful psychic cerebral intimate righteous self-vindication and somatic visceral sensitive righteous self-satisfaction in one and the same psychosomatic fused self-righteousness. There is no longer any lingering self-alienation and polarization within the mystic's own psychosomatic personality and subjectivity. There is only a Trinitarian symphony, harmony, and epiphany between his inward cerebral and outward visceral self. The one initiates as does the Father and the other consummates, as does the Son heaven's eternal and ethereal harmony of reciprocal love and amorous friendship and amity. These two psychosomatic willful poles are integrated into one and the same infinite love and loveliness which is that of the Holy Spirit.

751

St. John concludes that there is in the mystic's most intimate inward and sensitive outward subjectivity and personality a breathing and breath of the Holy Spirit that is so exquisitely inwardly intimate and exquisitely outwardly sensitive that words are inadequate to describe and circumscribe this mystical experience of God's Trinitarian presence. In fact, St. John adds that attempting to describe this in words runs the risk of minimizing and betraying the loftiness, magnanimity, magnitude, and delicacy of this singular experience. He further explains that such a singular experience is not typical of the mystic's usual encounter with God.

St. John poses the question as to how God's omnipotence and grandeur can be experienced by the mystic as such a gentle and hospitable presence. It is very much the case that the Holy Spirit is depicted in the Gospel as a dove. The explanation given is that God's glory dilates and diffuses through the mystic's visceral bodily sensitivity with the purity and subtlety of God's own ethereal spirituality and not that of the body's usual sensuality. At the same time, this same glory penetrates into the mystic's cerebral mental intimacy with the impassability and immutability of God's own eternity and not with the mind's typical abysmal emptiness and desolation.

In this exulted and sublime experience of God the mystic becomes enabled to requite God's unbounded love and loveliness as one friend befriends another friend. In requiting God's love the mystic is regaled in experiencing that his own enjoyment and rejoicing in God's sublime love bestows on God, in return, a joy to God commensurate with the glorious love he himself receives. Love between amicable friends who love each other virtuously and selflessly is a love whose joy is experienced in bestowing delight on the beloved. Integral to the exquisite love and joy experienced by the mystic is the delightful joy of returning to God, love for love. This is possible because God lavishes on the mystic the immensity of His own infinite riches and Gifted gifts, benevolence, holiness, and benignity.

Made in the USA
Lexington, KY
21 January 2011